Numerical Analysis and
Scientific Computation

Numerical Analysis and Scientific Computation

Jeffery J. Leader

Rose-Hulman Institute of Technology

PEARSON

Addison
Wesley

Boston   San Francisco   New York
London   Toronto   Sydney   Tokyo   Singapore   Madrid
Mexico City   Munich   Paris   Cape Town   Hong Kong   Montreal

Publisher: Greg Tobin
Acquisitions Editor: William Hoffman
Editorial Assistant: Mary Reynolds
Managing Editor: Karen Guardino
Production Supervisor: Cindy Cody
Marketing Manager: Yolanda Cossio
Marketing Coordinator: Heather Peck
Media Producer: Sharon Smith
Prepress Supervisor: Caroline Fell
Manufacturing Buyer: Evelyn Beaton
Cover Designer: Barbara T. Atkinson
Cover photograph: © Special Photographers/Photonica
Compositor: TechBooks

0-201-73499-0

1 2 3 4 5 6 7 8 9 10 PBT 07 06 05 04

To my parents,
Dennis and Jeanne Leader

Preface

Numerical analysis is the study of algorithms for the problems of continuous mathematics. Lloyd Trefethen (1992)

Elementary numerical analysis is a marvelously exciting subject. With a little energy and algebra you can derive significant algorithms, code them up, and watch them perform. G. W. Stewart (1998)

THIS BOOK REPRESENTS the numerical analysis course I have taught for the past nine years, first as a required course for sophomore engineering majors and currently as an elective course for juniors and seniors in mathematics, computer science, physics, and engineering. It has been strongly influenced by my summertime computational consulting work at the U.S. Army Research Laboratory (Adelphi, MD), Naval Surface Warfare Center (Dahlgren, VA), and Air Force Research Laboratory (Dayton, OH), and other consulting and research experience; it has also been influenced by conversations with my colleagues and of course by other texts I have turned to over the years.

I hope that what sets my text apart from other introductory numerical analysis texts are the following features:

- Quick introduction to numerical methods, with roundoff error and computer arithmetic deferred until students have gained some experience with real algorithms
- Modern approach to numerical linear algebra
- Explanation of the numerical techniques used by the major computational programs students are likely to use in practice (especially MATLAB, but also Maple and the Netlib library)
- Appropriate mix of numerical analysis theory and practical scientific computation principles
- Greater than usual emphasis on optimization

- Numerical experiments so students can gain experience
- Efficient and unobtrusive introduction to MATLAB

The MATLAB material is introduced in optional subsections at the end of each section. If you'd like your students to learn MATLAB as part of this course, these subsections provide a way to slowly introduce them to it and a chance for them to engage in actual numerical experimentation to build their intuition about scientific computing. If you're not using MATLAB in your course, you may encourage your students to skim these subsections for the extra material and foreshadowing they sometimes contain, but you may use the text without using MATLAB. I have used this approach to teach MATLAB in my classes and have had success with it.

My experience in scientific computing has been that almost every problem reduces, at some level, to a problem in root-finding, nonlinear optimization, or numerical linear algebra, and that the first two cases frequently involve the solution of a linear system. The text starts with root-finding (chapter 1), principally in one dimension, because students will be familiar with it from the calculus. It then moves straight into numerical linear algebra (chapters 2 and 3) because of its crucial importance and so that this material will be available as needed in later chapters. Chapter 4 introduces polynomial interpolation as a tool for deriving other methods and splines as a tool for representing curves given in terms of data. Chapter 5 introduces the basic techniques of numerical quadrature, emphasizing those algorithms employed by MATLAB and Maple. Quadrature of ODEs is given a similar treatment in chapter 6. Nonlinear optimization is covered in chapter 7, and some basic ideas and methods of approximation theory are discussed in chapter 8.

I try to avoid falling into the trap of first introducing a completely new mathematical idea and then teaching computational techniques for it. If students don't already know the mathematical problems—root-finding, finding maxima and minima, differentiation, and integration from the calculus, and first-order ODEs from the calculus or an ODEs course—it will be hard for them to appreciate why they need to know numerical methods for them. Hence I have avoided teaching the Fourier transform, *then* its discrete version the DFT, and then the computational method known as the FFT, for example. However, I have strayed from this principle to introduce the QR and singular value decompositions, as these are not yet standard in a matrix or linear algebra course.

In class, I ask students for ideas about approaching a problem like root finding or about improving a method we have already seen. To mimic that approach in the text, in several sections I briefly discuss alternate methods to the main one I introduce and develop in that section. These brief discussions offer students alternatives I want them to know about, even if we do not discuss them in detail in class or in the text. By the end of the course, these are the kinds of ideas I want them to start suggesting, such as replacing linear approximations with quadratic ones, for example. If you prefer to skip these brief discussions, of course you may.

In emphasizing the ideas behind methods and the mixing of methods I hope to encourage students to feel that they "own" these methods. Too often students feel that they cannot tweak existing algorithms or software, when in fact, adding heuristics is often necessary. In my experience students need to be told that it's OK to fiddle with the methods. That's actually one of the big reasons that people who are only going to *use*, not *write*, numerical software need a course like this; they need to know enough of the ideas to be able to pick good initial guesses, to approximate needed derivatives, to select the right method or the right parameters.

Over the past decade or so the practice and teaching of numerical analysis have undergone a number of changes. Fewer people write significant amounts of code; they rely more on packages like MATLAB, the similar Octave, GAUSS, and more specialized packages. Also, people are solving bigger and bigger problems, thanks to advances in computer hardware and the availability of powerful software from Netlib, NAG, and so on. This leads to a need for a greater understanding of the ideas behind algorithms and how to tweak them to get them to converge in a timely fashion—choosing proper initial guesses, mixing methods intelligently, adjusting algorithmic parameters—but less need for understanding the algorithms in sufficient detail to write professional level code. (In fact, I believe that writing code should be left to *teams* of experts.) There is greater emphasis on *scientific computation* as opposed to *numerical analysis*.

On the pedagogical side, at many institutions, the theoretical content of calculus courses has been reduced and computer algebra systems have been introduced. This creates a two-fold challenge: First, instructors must work around the students' lesser analytical background, and second, students used to seeing a computer algebra system spit out the answers to all their problems must be convinced of the need for *numerical*, as opposed to *symbolic*, techniques. Students today come to a numerical analysis course with less numerical computing experience than before, thanks to computer algebra systems. This book aims to respond to these pedagogical changes by emphasizing ideas in a way that appeals to geometric thinking (linear and quadratic approximations, for example) and by providing examples of the types of things that cannot be done by computer algebra systems and hence the need for numerical methods.

I mention the possibility of parallelization for several methods but do not develop parallel algorithms in detail. I do not believe a first course in numerical analysis is the place for emphasizing parallel computing, although students should be made aware of its existence. Even if students have access to such a machine, programming it is likely beyond their ability.

This text is *not* intended to be a reference. It is meant to be worked through by students so they learn the subject. I try to avoid dry statements of theorems in favor of rigorous derivations that show the ideas behind the methods. I do not believe that students can appreciate many of the theoretical aspects of the material until they have some experience with numerical computing—all the more because of their experience with computer algebra systems. This text aims to produce students who can competently use standard computational software, including choosing the right method for the job and advising others on the major benefits and pitfalls of various methods. I have had success with this in my current position and hope it works for you in yours.

Each section is meant to be one lecture, although you may find that you need more or less time. The Problems sections contain basic problems that can be used to ensure understanding and do not require new computational resources beyond those required in the preceding sections. The MATLAB subsections introduce MATLAB commands and explore the material through numerical experimentation. Students can use these subsections as self-teaching MATLAB tutorials. I ask students to hand in their output from the `diary` command and to annotate it with brief comments on the results. Some of the Additional Problems may require new computing tools equivalent to those covered in the MATLAB subsections. Additional Problems numbered 10 and above may be more challenging; the last two or three Additional Problems usually are relatively difficult.

The text contains more material than can be covered in a single quarter or semester. In a ten-week quarter I typically cover the following sections: 1.1–1.9; 2.1–2.9; 3.1–3.6; 4.1–4.4; 5.1–5.3, plus ideas from 5.6 and 5.7; 6.1–6.3, plus ideas from 6.5 and 6.6; and 7.1–7.3 (plus 7.4 and 7.5 if time permits). The course I teach is oriented somewhat toward numerical linear algebra because I believe so many other problems, such as the numerical solution of PDEs, rely on a knowledge of this material, and that many of the problems in those other areas involve getting a linear system solver to work well. More material from chapters 5 and 6 could be included at the expense of material from the latter half of chapter 2. Because of dependencies it will probably be necessary to cover 1.1–1.4, 1.7, 2.1–2.3, and 4.1 in any event.

Prerequisites are a year-long course in the calculus, the basics of matrix algebra, and for chapter 6 the basics of first-order ODEs. Some of the material in chapter 8 is at a more advanced level and requires additional mathematical maturity. Programming experience is not required (if MATLAB is to be used).

My father-in-law wrote in the preface to one of his books that 'The making of a book is the work of many hands.' I have found this to be true. I want to thank Addison-Wesley for publishing this book and to acknowledge in particular Cindy Cody, Joe Vetere, and RoseAnne Johnson at Addison-Wesley; Chris Miller and her group at TechBooks; Louise Gache, the copyeditor; Michael Brown, who wrote the solutions, and the several accuracy checkers; and the many other individuals who have helped make this book.

I also want to acknowledge the helpful comments I have received from a number of anonymous reviewers who suggested changes to the order of presentation, commented on the clarity of various passages, and pointed out errors and omissions. Four years' worth of numerical analysis students at Rose-Hulman Institute of Technology have used the manuscript and were of great help in refining the material, and I gratefully acknowledge their assistance. I wish I could name them all here. Any errors that remain are of course my own.

My colleagues at Rose-Hulman Institute of Technology were very supportive during the time I wrote this book; I want to thank in particular S. Allen Broughton, Ralph P. Grimaldi, and Robert Lopez (now at Maplesoft) for their encouragement and advice.

Over the years I've benefitted from the chance to study and work with a number of numerical analysts who have helped me grow in my understanding of the field. I especially want to acknowledge my advisor, Philip J. Davis, of Brown University; David Gottlieb, also of Brown University; and Bill Gragg, of the Naval Postgraduate School.

I also gratefully thank two people who have been very helpful to me in a great many ways over the course of my career: Robert L. Borrelli and Courtney S. Coleman, both of Harvey Mudd College.

Last but not least I thank my wife, Meg, for her help on this project, and I also thank her and our children Derek and Corrinne for their patience while their father worked long hours on this book.

Jeffery J. Leader
Terre Haute, IN

Contents

3 Iterative Methods 196

4 Polynomial Interpolation 247

5 Numerical Integration 298

6 Differential Equations 381

7 Nonlinear Optimization 446

8 Approximation Methods   508

1 Nonlinear Equations

1.1 Bisection and Inverse Linear Interpolation

TIME AND TIME AGAIN the solution or simulation of a scientific or engineering problem results in the need to solve either a root-finding problem or an optimization problem. In the former case we seek the solution of an equation or set of equations; in the latter case we seek the point(s) where a function takes on its maximum or minimum value. Even when our goal is to fit a curve to some experimental data or numerically solve a differential equation, for example, we almost always reduce the problem to one of the two types listed above. In this chapter we look at the problem of finding a root of a nonlinear equation; in Chapters 2 and 3 we will look at linear systems of equations, and optimization problems in Chapter 7.

Root-Finding   The root-finding problem is to find a solution x^* of $f(x) = 0$. (There may be many solutions, but we are only seeking any one of them.) The solution is called a **root** of the equation or a **zero** of the function f. For special cases there are often special approaches: The quadratic formula applies if f is a quadratic, and the zeroes of $\sin(x)$ are common knowledge. Sooner or later, however, it becomes necessary to solve a problem that does not fit into a known special case. The simplest examples are equations like

$$\cos(x) - x = 0$$

and polynomials of degree 5 or higher. (There is a cubic formula for degree 3 polynomials and a quartic formula for degree 4 polynomials, but it has been shown that there can be no similar formula for polynomials of degree 5 or higher. Unless a factorization is obvious, numerical methods must be employed.) A more complicated but quite common case is that of finding where the solution of a differential equation passes through zero, when the differential equation itself must be solved numerically.

1

Using trial and error is one possibility. There is nothing inherently wrong with this approach, but it lacks a theory that predicts how rapidly it will find a solution (to within a given tolerance), and it is difficult to automate. In practice, different root-finding problems may need to be solved tens or hundreds of times within a single run of a program. (For example, this might be true of a computer-aided design package that must determine where various curves intersect.) Because of this we will need to find methods that are *fast, reliable,* and *easily implemented,* ideally without the need for a human to make a judgment at any stage of the process.

*Exhaustive
Search*

The first method we will consider is the method of **exhaustive search** (also called **direct, graphical,** or **incremental search**). Suppose that f is continuous on some (not necessarily finite) interval. By the Intermediate Value Theorem, if we can find two points a, b such that $f(a)$ and $f(b)$ have opposite signs, then a zero of f must lie in (a, b). One way to find such a pair of points is to pick some x_0, an initial guess as to the location of a root, and successively evaluate the function at

$$x_0, \quad x_1 = x_0 + h, \quad x_2 = x_0 + 2h, \quad x_3 = x_0 + 3h, \dots,$$

where $h > 0$ is called the **step size** (or **grid size**). When a change of sign is detected, we say that we have **bracketed** a root in this interval of width h. (The interval $[x_i, x_{i+1}]$ over which the change of sign occurs is called a **bracket;** see Fig. 1.1.) At this point we may repeat the process over the smaller interval $[x_i, x_{i+1}]$ with a smaller h to bracket the root more precisely.

The exhaustive search method is equivalent to plotting the function and looking for an interval in which it crosses the x-axis. This is very inefficient, so let's look for a better approach.

Suppose that we have found, by any means, a bracket $[a, b]$ for a zero of a continuous function. Rather than searching the entire interval with a finer step size, we might reason that the midpoint

$$m = \frac{a + b}{2}$$

is a better estimate of the location of the true zero x^* of f than either a or b. After all,

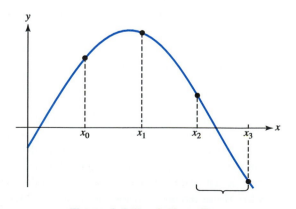

Figure 1.1 Bracketing a Zero.

$|a - x^*|$ could be as large as the width $w = (b - a)$ of the interval if x^* is near b, and similarly for $|b - x^*|$, but

$$|m - x^*| \leq \frac{1}{2}w$$

Bisection

since x^* lies either in the interval to the right or to the left of m (except in the extremely unlikely case that $x^* = m$). This is the idea behind the **bisection method** (or **binary search**): If f is continuous in the region of interest and $[x_0, x_1]$ is a bracket, that is, $f(x_0)f(x_1) < 0$, then we set

$$x_2 = \frac{x_0 + x_1}{2}$$

and compute $f(x_2)$. If $f(x_2) = 0$, we are done; otherwise either $f(x_2)$ and $f(x_0)$ have opposite signs, in which case $[x_0, x_2]$ is a new bracket half the size of the previous one, or $f(x_2)$ and $f(x_1)$ have opposite signs, in which case $[x_2, x_1]$ is a new bracket half the size of the previous one. In either case we have reduced our uncertainty as to the location of the true zero x^* by 50% at the cost of a single new function evaluation (namely the computation of $f(x_2)$). We may now repeat this process on the new interval, finding its midpoint x_3 and then a smaller bracket with x_3 as an endpoint, and so on, until a sufficiently narrow bracket is obtained.

Example 1.1.1

Consider the function $f(x) = \cos(x)$, which has a zero at $\pi/2 \doteq 1.5708$. (The symbol $\doteq$ means that the indicated value is correctly rounded to the number of significant figures given.) Since $f(1) \doteq 0.5403$, $f(2) \doteq -0.4161$, and f is continuous, the interval $[1, 2]$ is a bracket. Its midpoint is $x_2 = 1.5$. Since

$$f(1.5) \doteq 0.0707,$$

we have $f(1.5)f(2) < 0$ and so we replace $x_0 = 1$ with $x_2 = 1.5$, meaning that $[1.5, 2]$ is our improved bracket. The next midpoint is $x_3 = 1.75$, giving

$$f(1.75) \doteq -0.1782$$

so that $[1.5, 1.75]$ is the new bracket. If we had to stop now, our estimate of the location of the true zero could be any value in $[1.5, 1.75]$; choosing its midpoint $x_4 = 1.625$ minimizes the worst-case error. ∎

Unless we have the misfortune to choose the wrong interval at some step because a rounding error makes a positive value negative, or vice versa, this method must converge to some zero of f in the initial bracket. That is, as the iteration count k increases, we must have

$$\lim_{k \to \infty} x_k = x^*$$

for some x^* that lies in the initial bracket and for which $f(x^*) = 0$. Furthermore, since the width of the bracket is halved at each step, we can predict how long it will take to achieve any desired precision. If the width of the initial interval is w, then after the first bisection step the width of the new bracket is $w/2$, and after the second step it is $w/4$.

In general, after n steps the width of the resulting interval is equal to $w/2^n$. So to reduce an interval of initial width 1 to an interval of width 10^{-4}, we would need n to be large enough that

$$\frac{1}{2^n} \le 10^{-4}$$

$$10^4 \le 2^n$$

$$n \ge \log_2(10^4)$$

$$\doteq 13.2877.$$

So, $n = 14$ iterations would suffice. Since the error is at most 10^{-4}, the answer should have four correct figures after the decimal place (possibly off by one unit in the fourth decimal place). Of course, although this guarantees that the width of the final interval is 2^{-14} (note that $2^{-14} \le 10^{-4} \le 2^{-13}$) and that its midpoint will be an estimate good to within 2^{-15}, the actual error may be much smaller. In fact, performing 14 iterations of the method on $f(x) = \cos(x)$ with the initial bracket $[1, 2]$ and using the midpoint $x_{16} \doteq 1.57077$ of the final interval as our estimate of the true zero $\pi/2 = 1.57079\ldots$ gives an actual error of 2.6×10^{-5} as compared to the bound of 3.1×10^{-5}. The error bound represents a worst-case scenario. Often our results will be considerably better.

The sequence generated by the bisection method is guaranteed to converge to a root; exhaustive search is not (after all, it could step right over a pair of closely spaced roots if h is not sufficiently small; see Fig. 1.2). Bisection will also be much faster in general. However, we have paid a price for these advantages: Bisection requires us to find an initial bracket, whereas exhaustive search requires only a single initial guess lying to the left of the presumed root. Finding that initial bracket may well require an initial graphical search (or trial and error).

Consider again the function $f(x) = \cos(x)$, but now suppose that we have found the initial bracket $[0, 1.6]$ instead, for which we have $f(0) = 1.0000$ and $f(1.6) \doteq -0.0292$. Bisection will work, but noting that $|f(1.6)|$ is very much smaller than $|f(0)|$ might

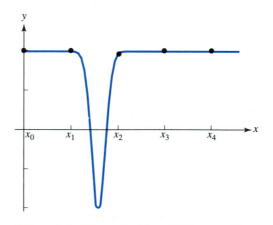

Figure 1.2 Exhaustive Search Misses a Blip.

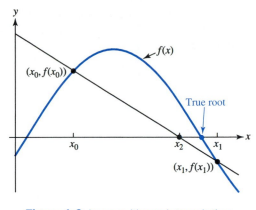

Figure 1.3 Inverse Linear Interpolation.

Inverse Linear Interpolation

incline us to choose a new point much nearer $x_1 = 1.6$ than $x_0 = 0$. If we choose, say, $x_2 = 1.4$, then $f(x_2) \doteq 0.1700$ and so $[1.4, 1.6]$ is a new, smaller bracket; the bisection bracket would have been $[0.8, 1.6]$ which is four times as wide. This suggests another method, which is known as **(inverse) linear interpolation** (also called **false position** or ***regula falsi***): Given a continuous function f and a bracket $[x_0, x_1]$ for a zero of f, fit a straight line to the points $(x_0, f(x_0))$ and $(x_1, f(x_1))$ (see Fig. 1.3). This line is said to interpolate f at these points, and if f is approximately linear over the interval, then the zero of the line should be a good estimate of the zero of the function. (The method is called *inverse* interpolation because we are using the interpolated line to find an x value, not a y value as usual; we write x as a linear function of y.) Since the y-values are of opposite sign, $f(x_0)$ is not equal to $f(x_1)$ and so the equation of the line may be written in slope-intercept form as

$$x = \frac{x_1 - x_0}{f(x_1) - f(x_0)} y + \left(x_1 - \frac{x_1 - x_0}{f(x_1) - f(x_0)} f(x_1) \right) \qquad (1.1)$$

and may be solved for the x-intercept x_2 simply by setting $y = 0$:

$$x_2 = x_1 - f(x_1) \frac{x_1 - x_0}{f(x_1) - f(x_0)}. \qquad (1.2)$$

As before, either $[x_0, x_2]$ or $[x_2, x_1]$ is a new, smaller bracket. We now iterate until some **convergence criterion** is achieved, that is, until we meet some specified criterion for deciding that we are sufficiently close to the true answer. The width of the interval may not go to zero (if the approach to the root of the equation is one-sided; see Problem 1), so we cannot use that as the only convergence criterion. For the same reason, unless the width of the bracket is very small, the last computed endpoint is generally the best estimate of the location of the root, not the midpoint as before.

Inverse linear interpolation will converge to some zero of the function in the bracket; however, the rate at which it converges will depend on how nearly linear $f(x)$ is near its zero. We know from the calculus that if $f(x)$ is sufficiently differentiable then it is well approximated by a straight line over small intervals. For the type of functions usually

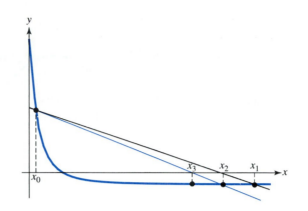

Figure 1.4 Tough Function for Inverse Linear Interpolation.

encountered in practice this means that inverse linear interpolation will usually be faster than bisection. (A function and bracket as in Fig. 1.4 will result in excruciatingly slow convergence until the bracket is very small.) We have given up the guaranteed, slow-but-steady-wins-the-race speed of bisection for a likely but neither guaranteed nor easily predictable improvement.

In the next section we consider a much faster algorithm known as Newton's method. Once again we pay a price for using the method: We require that the function be differentiable as well. Faster methods require more assumptions and offer fewer guarantees.

PROBLEMS 1.1

1. Use four iterations of bisection with the initial bracket [0.5, 1] to approximate the sole positive root of $\cos(x) - x = 0$. Repeat with inverse linear interpolation, using the same initial bracket; note the one-sided approach to the solution.

2. Show that there is a unique real solution of $5x^7 = 1 - 2x$. Use bisection to approximate it to four decimal places. Repeat with inverse linear interpolation.

3. The function $f(x) = \cos(5x)$ has seven zeroes in the interval [0, 4.5]. Use bisection and then inverse linear interpolation with that initial bracket (verify that it is

in fact a bracket) to find a zero to at least three decimal places. Find the actual error in your estimates using the known locations of the zeroes of the cosine function. Comment on your results.

4. Use bisection on $f(x) = x^2 - 5$ to approximate $\sqrt{5}$ to at least four decimal places. Compare your error estimate to the actual error.

5. Use inverse linear interpolation with the initial bracket [0.25, 2] to approximate a zero of $f(x) = 1/x^3 - 10$ to three decimal places. Repeat with bisection. Comment.

MATLAB 1.1

Numerical analysis is the study and design of methods that may be used to solve the mathematical problems of engineering and the sciences by iterative algorithms in a reasonable time and with desirable error properties.[1] This can be done without access to a computer, as is clear from the names attached to some of these methods—such as

---

[1] Lloyd Trefethen writes: "Numerical analysis is the study of algorithms for the problems of continuous mathematics."

Newton (1642–1727), Euler (1707–1783), and Gauss (1777–1855). These individuals had much more primitive computational tools at their disposal than we do today.

For all the obvious reasons, however, it is best to gain experience with these methods by running them on a calculator or computer. These subsections will focus on the MATLAB environment; however, you may use C++, Fortran, Maple, Mathematica, or any other computational tool. Even if you are not using MATLAB in your course, it is important that you read these sections and attempt the computations in the environment you are using.

The MATLAB package is an interactive computing environment and programming language (from The MathWorks, Inc.). You should read this section at the computer and enter the commands as you read them; afterwards you should experiment, varying the functions used, etc. Run MATLAB by double-clicking on the MATLAB icon (in Windows) or typing `matlab` or possibly `matlab6`[2] at the prompt (in Unix, which is case-sensitive). You should see a shield with an image of a surface followed by something like the following:

```
Commands to get started: intro, demo, help help
Commands for more information: help, whatsnew, info,
subscribe
```
»

The » symbol (called the *guillemotright*) is the MATLAB prompt. We are now using MATLAB in what might be called immediate mode—essentially, as a calculator.

Let's try a few simple calculations. At the » prompt, type 3+4 followed by the Enter key. That is, enter:

```
» 3+4
ans =
    7
```

Let's keep playing. Enter:

```
» 3-4
ans =
    -1
» 3*4
ans =
    12
» 3/4
ans =
    0.7500
» ans^2
ans =
    0.5625
»
```

---

[2] If you prefer the simpler interface of previous versions of MATLAB, try entering `matlab -nojvm` instead.

The variable `ans` is automatically assigned a value by MATLAB. Other variables may be assigned values in the obvious manner. Enter:

```
» x=5,y=2
x =
    5
y =
    2
» x+y,x^y
ans =
    7
ans =
    25
»
```

(Notice that more than one command may be entered on a single line.) Let's try bisection on the function $f(x) = \sin(e^x)$. First we'll get a plot of the function. Enter:

```
» x=0:.1:3
```

to make a row vector x (that is, a list of values) with entries ranging from 0 to 3 in steps of .1. Enter:

```
» y=sin(exp(x));
```

to compute $\sin(e^x)$ for every x in the vector and assign those values to y. The semicolon at the end suppresses printing of the results. The arguments of `sin` are assumed to be in radians. Enter:

```
» y
```

(without a semicolon) to see the y-values. Now enter:

```
» plot(x,y)
```

to see a plot of the function. (The `plot` command automatically connects the dots to draw a continuous piecewise linear curve.) Enter:

```
» grid
```

to overlay a grid on your plot. Look at the figure again; there are six zeroes evident in this interval. We are effectively performing an exhaustive search.

This graph is too choppy. Let's try again with a finer grid. In MATLAB 6 or later you should see the command that defined x in the Command History window. You can click on it to retrieve it. You may also press the up arrow (cursor up $\boxed{\uparrow}$) key.[3] The last command you entered should reappear. Keep pressing the key until you find the line in which you defined x. Once you have it, use the left cursor key $\boxed{\longleftarrow}$ to edit it to read x=0:.01:3 and then press enter; that is, enter:

```
» x=0:.01:3;
```

---

[3] There will be slight variations in how MATLAB responds on various systems (e.g., Unix or Windows).

(note the semicolon at the end). This makes x a vector of values ranging from 0 to 3 in steps of .01. Now find in the lower left hand window or cursor up to the line defining y, re-enter it unchanged (it automatically uses the new x), and do the same for the plot and grid commands. The graph appears much smoother now, although if we zoomed in, we'd see that it is as choppy as before.

Let's use bisection to try to find the first zero of $f(x)$ in [0, 3]. It appears to be near 1.2. We'll take [1.1, 1.4] as our initial bracket. Enter:

```
» x0=1.1,x1=1.4
x0 =
    1.1000
x1 =
    1.4000
» m=(x0+x1)/2
m =
    1.2500
» sin(exp(m))
ans =
   -0.3417
```

From the graph, it's clear that $f(x_0) > 0$ and $f(x_1) < 0$, so our new bracket should be $[x_0, m] = [1.1, 1.25]$. Enter:

```
» x1=m;
```

and re-enter the command for computing m and $f(m)$ using the up cursor key. That is, enter:

```
» m=(x0+x1)/2
m =
    1.1750
» sin(exp(m))
ans =
   -0.0964
```

The new bracket is [1.1, 1.1750]. On the next iteration you should find that $m = 1.1375$ and $f(m) \doteq 0.0226$ so that [1.1375, 1.1750] is the current bracket; its midpoint is our best estimate yet of the location of the zero.

You should repeat this using inverse linear interpolation. Enter:

```
» clear
```

to clear the values of all variables. (Ask for the value of, say, x1 after entering the clear command.) Then redefine x0 and x1 using the cursor up key, and define their corresponding function values. That is, enter:

```
» x0=1.1,x1=1.4
» y0=sin(exp(x0));y1=sin(exp(x1));
```

Now use iteration on x2=x1-y1*(x1-x0)/(y1-y0) to get the x-intercept. Remember to update your y0 or y1 value when you change x0 or x1 to equal x2. You can check the current width of your interval. Enter:

» x1-x0

(If this is about 10^{-k}, then we know the answer to about k decimal places; e.g., if $a = 0.1234$ and $b = 0.1233$, then $|a - b| = 1E - 4$, and so we conclude that these two values agree to nearly four decimal places.) Perform a total of ten iterations of inverse linear interpolation. When you are done, use the command quit or exit to exit MATLAB.

If you are used to using Maple or Mathematica, you may wonder if there is a command to save a worksheet. Earlier versions of MATLAB did not have this capability, but the MATLAB command diary stores a record of your subsequent work as the text file diary.txt. You enter diary when you first start up MATLAB and then read the file later. If you are using MATLAB6 or later, however, the next time you start up, all your previous commands will be available using the Command History window or the cursor up ↑ key. (You may need to enter the desktop command to see them.) You may also use the drop-down menu under *File* to find the *Save Workspace As* option and save all your work, including defined variables, in a file that can be reloaded later using *File, Import Data* or the Current Directory window. You don't need to do this now, but in the future you may wish to do so.

There is much more to MATLAB, including a programming language, as we'll see in later sections. By the end of the course you should feel very comfortable using MATLAB, which is widely used in industry and research because of the ease and rapidity with which programs for scientific computation may be written in it.

ADDITIONAL PROBLEMS 1.1

6. Use the bisection method on $\sin(x) = 0$ to approximate π to four decimal places.

7. Using bisection starting from the initial bracket [0, 2], estimate the number of iterations that would be required to find a root of $e^x - 4x = 0$ to four decimal place accuracy. How many iterations are needed until the midpoint of the interval is actually correct to four decimal places?

8. Using bisection starting from the initial bracket [0, 2], estimate the number of iterations that would be required to find a solution of $\cos(\sin(x)) = 0.75$ to four decimal place accuracy. How many iterations are needed until the midpoint of the interval is actually correct to four decimal places? How many iterations are needed for inverse linear interpolation to produce a value that is correct to four decimal places?

9. a. Justify Equations (1.1) and (1.2) by finding the equation of the line $x = my + b$ between the two points $(x_0, f(x_0))$ and $(x_1, f(x_1))$ and then finding its x-intercept.

b. What happens if inverse linear interpolation is applied to a linear function $f(x) = ax + b$? Is the same true for bisection?

10. By the method of exhaustive search, use MATLAB to find the zeroes of $\sin(\ln(x))$ that lie in (0, 30] to three decimal place accuracy. Include plots of the function near the zeroes.

11. a. A version of the cubic formula for finding the real roots of the cubic equation $x^3 + ax^2 + bx + c = 0$ is as follows: Find

$$A = \frac{a^2 - 3b}{9} \quad \text{and} \quad B = \frac{2a^3 - 9ab + 27c}{54}.$$

If $B^2 - A^3 > 0$, there is a single real root given by

$$x_1 = -\operatorname{sgn}(B)\left(\alpha + \frac{A}{\alpha}\right) - \frac{a}{3},$$

where $\alpha = \left(\sqrt{B^2 - A^3} + |B|\right)^{1/3}$, and $\operatorname{sgn}(\mu) = \mu/|\mu|$ if $\mu \neq 0$ and $\operatorname{sgn}(0) = 0$ is the **signum** (i.e., sign) function. If instead $B^2 - A^3 \leq 0$, then there are three real roots given by

$$x_1 = 2\sqrt{A}\cos\left(\frac{\theta}{3}\right) - \frac{a}{3},$$

$$x_2 = 2\sqrt{A}\cos\left(\frac{\theta + 2\pi}{3}\right) - \frac{a}{3},$$

$$x_3 = 2\sqrt{A}\cos\left(\frac{\theta + 4\pi}{3}\right) - \frac{a}{3},$$

where $\theta = \arccos(-B/A^{3/2})$. (There is a version of the cubic formula that can find complex roots also; after all, you could always use synthetic division to obtain a quadratic equation after finding the single real root.) Use the cubic formula to find the real roots of the equation $x^3 - 2x^2 - 5x + 1 = 0$.

b. Use the method of inverse linear interpolation to find any root of the equation $x^3 - 2x^2 - 5x + 1 = 0$.

c. Use the cubic formula to find the real roots of the equations

$$x^3 - 8x^2 + 20.75x - 17.5 = 0 \quad \text{and}$$

$$x^3 - 3x^2 + 3x - 1 = 0.$$

d. In the case $B^2 - A^3 \leq 0$ (three real roots), verify that the product of the roots is equal to $-c$.

12. Use the MATLAB commands `x=0:.1:1` and `y=sin(x)` to get a vector `y` of values of the sine function. Use standard linear interpolation of these values to estimate $\sin(0.15)$, $\sin(0.55)$, and $\sin(0.95)$; that is, fit a straight line between adjacent points, and use the values from the line to approximate the sine function. Compare your approximate values to the true values.

13. A zero of a function f is said to be **isolated** if there is an open interval that contains that zero but no other zeroes of the function. (That the zeroes are isolated is an implicit assumption in the derivation of most root-finding methods.) How many zeroes does the function $\sin(1/x^2)$ have in the interval $(0, 1)$? Is each one isolated? If we define $g(x) = \sin(1/x^2)$ if $x \neq 0$ and $g(0) = 0$, is every zero of g isolated?

14. Consider a projectile that moves horizontally through the atmosphere at a high speed. In this case the air resistance is typically modeled by $F_R = -kmv^2$, where m is the mass of the body and k is a positive constant that depends on the geometry of the body as well as other factors, and that must be determined experimentally.

a. Show that Newton's law $F = ma$ leads to the ODE IVP $dv/dt = -kv^2$, $v(0) = v_0$, and solve it for $v(t)$. Assume $v_0 > 0$.

b. Solve the ODE IVP $\sim(t) = dx/dt$, $x(0) = x_0$ for $x(t)$.

c. Suppose that the projectile is fired from $x_0 = 10$ meters with an initial velocity of $v_0 = 10$ meters/second. At $t = 3$ seconds the projectile has reached $x = 37$ meters. Use a root-finding technique from this section to estimate k. Be sure to give the correct units for k.

15. Find a simultaneous solution of the linear system of equations $x^2 + y^2 = 1$, $1/x + 2y = 1$ by solving for y, substituting into the equation for x, and using bisection to find a solution to this equation in one unknown. Interpret your solution geometrically.

1.2 Newton's Method

The bisection and inverse linear interpolation methods are too slow for many applications. Typically these methods gain one additional correct significant figure for every several iterations. For example, if the error at step n of the bisection method is ε, then to reduce it to $\varepsilon/10$, which corresponds to gaining one more correct significant figure in the answer, requires m additional bisections, where

$$\frac{\varepsilon}{2^m} = \frac{\varepsilon}{10}$$

$$2^m = 10$$

$$m = \log_2(10)$$

$$\doteq 3.3219.$$

Every correct significant figure costs us about three iterations. The inverse linear interpolation method exhibits similar behavior.

Bisection and inverse linear interpolation are sometimes used where program length is a consideration. For example, bisection is often used in calculators because the code for it takes so little memory to store. Its guaranteed convergence is also attractive. However, the slow convergence is a problem when function evaluations are expensive, and in many problems of interest the function evaluations are very expensive. Another difficulty is that these methods require an initial bracket. What do we do if we cannot find one?

Suppose that f is a continuous function. If we pick two initial points x_0, x_1 that do not necessarily form a bracket, we can still interpolate a linear function to f,

$$y = \frac{f(x_1) - f(x_0)}{x_1 - x_0} x + \left(f(x_1) - \frac{f(x_1) - f(x_0)}{x_1 - x_0} x_1 \right)$$

and use its x-intercept

$$x_2 = x_1 - f(x_1) \frac{x_1 - x_0}{f(x_1) - f(x_0)}$$

as an improved estimate of the location of a zero of f. (Note that this is the same formula as for inverse linear interpolation.) If x_0 and x_1 do in fact form a bracket, this will be precisely an inverse linear interpolation step. If they do not form a bracket, this is an extrapolation to a point outside the interval $[x_0, x_1]$ (or $[x_1, x_0]$ if $x_1 < x_0$). In either case

Secant Method   we take x_1 and x_2 as our new pair of bracketing points. This is the **secant method:** Pick any two distinct points, draw the secant through them, and use the x-intercept of that secant line as the new estimate of the zero of the function, discarding the oldest point (see Fig. 1.5). We don't check whether or not the two current points form a bracket. Hence the secant method may take an inverse linear interpolation step (bracket) or an extrapolation step (non-bracket) on any given iteration.

Example 1.2.1   Consider again the very simple function $f(x) = \cos(x)$ and the initial points $x_0 = 0, x_1 = 1$. Since $f(0) = 1.0000$, $f(1) \doteq 0.5403$, this is not a bracket, and so the

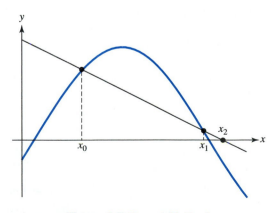

Figure 1.5 Secant Method.

Step	Bisection Method	Inverse Linear Interpolation	Secant Method
1	1.5	1.33333333333333	1.33333333333333
2	1.25	1.40000000000000	1.40000000000000
3	1.375	1.41176470588235	1.41463414634146
4	1.4375	1.41379310344828	1.41421143847487
5	1.40625	1.41414141414141	1.41421356205732
6	1.421875	1.41420118343195	1.41421356237310
7	1.4140625	1.41421143847487	1.41421356237310

Table 1.1 Comparison of Methods for $f(x) = x^2 - 2$; $x_0 = 1$, $x_1 = 2$; Solution: $\sqrt{2} \doteq 1.41421356237310$.

bisection and inverse linear interpolation methods are not applicable. The secant method gives

$$x_2 = x_1 - f(x_1)\frac{x_1 - x_0}{f(x_1) - f(x_0)}$$

$$= 1 - 0.5403\frac{1 - 0}{0.5403 - 1.0000}$$

$$\doteq 2.1753,$$

and so the new pair of points is $x_1 = 1.0000$, $x_2 \doteq 2.1753$. Since $\cos(x_2) \doteq -0.5684$, $[x_1, x_2]$ is actually a bracket, and the next step will be an inverse linear interpolation step, giving $x_3 \doteq 1.5728$. The true solution is $x^* \doteq 1.5708$. ∎

As is evident from Table 1.1, which compares the bisection, inverse linear interpolation, and secant methods for the function $f(x) = x^2 - 2$, the secant method can be considerably faster than the previous methods. (Notice from the table that a new correct decimal place is gained every one to three iterations for the bracketing methods, but that the secant method can pick up several correct decimal places each iteration. In the table, decimal places that agree with the answer are <u>underlined</u>.) We will soon quantify how much faster the secant method is.

In addition to its speed advantage, the secant method does not require an initial bracket. The price paid is that it may fail to converge: If $f(x_0) = f(x_1)$, for example, then the interpolated line is horizontal and there is no x-intercept. For a function that is asymptotic to the x-axis, the sequence of iterates may diverge (see Fig. 1.6).

What happens if we fix one of the two initial points and slide the other one towards it? As $x_1 \to x_0$ with x_0 fixed, the slope of the interpolated line will tend to $f'(x_0)$ (assuming that f is in fact differentiable at x_0). It appears that, if f is differentiable, we might be able to choose a single initial point x_0, form the tangent line to f at that point

$$y = f'(x_0)x + (f(x_0) - f'(x_0)x_0),$$

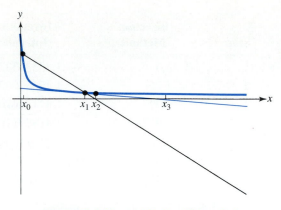

Figure 1.6 Secant Method Diverging.

and then set $y = 0$ to find the x-intercept of the tangent line

$$0 = f'(x_0)x + (f(x_0) - f'(x_0)x_0)$$

$$x = x_0 - \frac{f(x_0)}{f'(x_0)} \tag{1.3}$$

Newton's method

(assuming $f'(x_0) \neq 0$). This value of x should be an improved estimate of the location of a zero of f, if the tangent line approximation is a good approximation near x_0 (see Fig. 1.7). This is a new method called **Newton's method** (or **Newton-Raphson iteration**): Pick a point x_0 on a differentiable function f. Compute

$$x_1 = x_0 - \frac{f(x_0)}{f'(x_0)}$$

$$x_2 = x_1 - \frac{f(x_1)}{f'(x_1)}$$

$$x_3 = x_2 - \frac{f(x_2)}{f'(x_2)}$$

$$\vdots$$

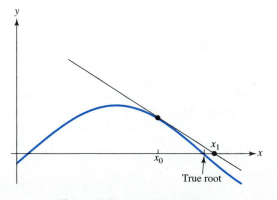

Figure 1.7 Newton's Method.

until some stopping criterion is met. The final value x_k is an estimate of the location of a zero of f.

Example 1.2.2   Let $f(x) = \cos(x)$. We'll apply Newton's method with $x_0 = 1$ to attempt to find a zero of f. We have

$$x_1 = x_0 - \frac{f(x_0)}{f'(x_0)}$$

$$= 1 - \frac{\cos(1)}{(-\sin(1))}$$

$$= 1 + \cot(1)$$

$$\doteq 1.6421$$

$$x_2 = x_1 - \frac{f(x_1)}{f'(x_1)}$$

$$= 1.6421 + \cot(1.6421)$$

$$\doteq 1.5707$$

$$x_3 = x_2 - \frac{f(x_2)}{f'(x_2)}$$

$$= 1.5707 + \cot(1.5707)$$

$$\doteq 1.5708,$$

which is already correct to the number of digits displayed. This is much faster than the other methods we have considered so far. Of course, had we chosen $x_0 = 0$ instead, then x_1 would have been undefined since the derivative of f is zero at the origin. In practice this problem is easily addressed by perturbing the given x_0 slightly. ■

Newton's method can diverge (similar to the case for the secant method indicated in Fig. 1.6), and in principle it can cycle (see Fig. 1.8), though the latter is unlikely to occur in practice. Newton's method is a robust and powerful tool that is used in many areas of scientific computation.

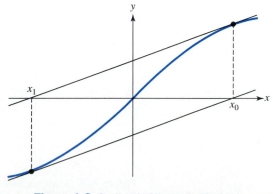

Figure 1.8 Cycling in Newton's Method.

If we assume that f is twice continuously differentiable, then we can derive Newton's method (Eq. (1.3)) in a different manner. (This derivation will be useful later.) For such an f we have the Taylor polynomial with remainder representation:

$$f(x) = f(x_0) + (x - x_0)f'(x_0) + \frac{1}{2}(x - x_0)^2 f''(\delta_x)$$

(for some δ_x between x_0 and x). We are looking for a point where $f(x)$ is zero; setting $f(x) = 0$ in the above equation gives

$$0 = f(x_0) + (x - x_0)f'(x_0) + \frac{1}{2}(x - x_0)^2 f''(\delta_x)$$

$$x = x_0 - \frac{f(x_0)}{f'(x_0)} - \frac{1}{2}(x - x_0)^2 \frac{f''(\delta_x)}{f'(x_0)}$$

$$x \approx x_0 - \frac{f(x_0)}{f'(x_0)}$$

upon neglecting the term in $(x - x_0)^2$ (which will be small when the initial guess x_0 is near x). We have arrived at Newton's method again.

Difficulties in Root finding   Notice that Newton's method will have difficulty if $f'(x^*) = 0$. We say that a zero of a differentiable function is **simple** if $f'(x^*) \neq 0$. If x^* is not a simple zero of f, then the graph of f flattens out near the root because the derivative of the function is zero there. Many different root-finding algorithms will have problems with a function like $f(x) = x^2$, which has a zero that is not simple and cannot be bracketed; Newton's method will converge, but very slowly (see Fig. 1.9).

You may have noticed that we have contented ourselves with finding any zero of a function, not all zeroes of the function. The latter problem is simply too difficult to solve for a general function. For one thing, we rarely know how many zeroes the function has, so we do not know when to stop looking for them. Also, experience shows that methods like the secant method and Newton's method tend to have zeroes that they like and return to for most initial guesses; we may have to get very close to the other zeroes if we hope to converge to them. (This phenomenon can be quite exasperating in practice.) If we have some way of bracketing each zero, or if the function is of a very special form, such as a polynomial, then we will generally be able to find all zeroes of the function. But for a

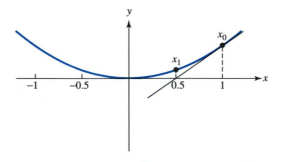

Figure 1.9 Newton's Method for $f(x) = x^2$.

Method	Advantages	Disadvantages
Exhaustive search	Few assumptions	Slow Inefficient
Bisection method	Guaranteed convergence Guaranteed rate	Slow Needs bracket
Inverse linear interpolation	Guaranteed convergence Usually faster than bisection	Variable rate (can be slow) Needs bracket
Secant method	Fast	Needs two initial guesses May diverge
Newton's method	Very fast One initial guess	Requires derivative May diverge

Table 1.2 Comparison of Methods Root-finding.

general function, which may have zeroes that are nonsimple, or which are closely spaced and hence hard to resolve, or which may just barely cross the x-axis and then come up again so the function appears to be of one sign near the zeroes, this is an extremely challenging problem.

We need new language to describe how much faster the secant method and Newton's method are than the other methods considered thus far. In the next two sections we will develop such language and give a convergence theorem for Newton's method. We end this section with a summary of the advantages and disadvantages of the methods we have discussed (see Table 1.2). For Newton's method, the most noticeable disadvantages are the need to find the formula for $f'(x)$ and the extra computational effort required to evaluate $f'(x)$ at each iteration in addition to $f(x)$. Recall that, as evidenced by the product rule, if $f(x)$ is complicated and hence expensive to compute, $f'(x)$ may be much more so.

PROBLEMS 1.2

In each case, compare your answer to the corresponding problem in the previous section and comment.

1. Use Newton's method to approximate the sole positive root of $\cos(x) - x = 0$. Repeat with the secant method.

2. Use Newton's method to approximate the sole real root of $5x^7 + 2x - 1 = 0$.

3. Use Newton's method to find a root of $f(x) = \cos(5x)$ in the interval $[0, 5]$ to at least three decimal places. Find

the actual error in your estimate using the known locations of the zeroes of the cosine function. Then use a different initial guess and find a different root.

4. Use Newton's method on $f(x) = x^2 - 5$ to approximate $\sqrt{5}$ to at least four decimal places. What is the actual error? What happens if you apply Newton's method to $f(x) = x^2$?

5. Use Newton's method to approximate a zero of $f(x) = 1/x^3 - 10$ to three decimal places.

MATLAB 1.2

Your version of MATLAB may or may not have symbolic differentiation capabilities. Enter:

```
» diff('x^2')
```

If you receive the expected result, you will be able to perform some symbolic manipulations in MATLAB (which uses the Maple kernel for this purpose; the mhelp command may be of use). For the types of large problems commonly encountered in practice this is of less practical use than it may seem at first. Symbolic differentiation is rarely a practical tool for real-world problems.

Let's try Newton's method on the function $f(x) = \frac{1}{2}xe^x - 2x^2$. As before, let's start by plotting it to get a feel for the function. Enter:

```
» x=0:.05:3;
```

and then enter:

```
» y=.5*x.*exp(x)-2*x.^2;
```

(note the extra periods). The periods before the asterisk (multiplication) and caret (exponentiation) in the line defining y instruct MATLAB to perform the indicated operations entry by entry; otherwise, multiplication of the vector x by the vector exp(x) of values of e^{x_i} would be an undefined vector–vector product. The default operations of MATLAB mimic matrix algebra operations in a very natural way, so a special symbol is needed for this elementwise procedure. As another example, $f(x) = 1/x^3 - 10$ should be entered as 1./x.^3-10 if x is a vector. Now, enter:

```
» plot(x,y),grid
```

The rapid growth of the exponential function makes it hard to see what's happening. Change x to go from 0 to 2.5, recompute y, and then plot the graph again. There is a zero at the origin, another near 0.4, and another near 2.2. Let's try to find the latter two zeroes to better precision using Newton's method.

It will be easiest to use what is called an *inline function,* that is, a function entered at the keyboard. Enter:

```
» f=inline('.5*x.*exp(x)-2*x.^2');
```

(be sure to use the single quote character '). We may not need the ability to evaluate f at a vector x, but leaving in the periods allows that as an option. The optional MATLAB Symbolic Toolbox, if available, can be used to evaluate symbolic derivatives. If you do not have access to it, you must take the derivative $(xe^x/2 - 2x^2)' = e^x/2 + xe^x/2 - 4x$ by hand. Enter:

```
» fp=inline('.5*exp(x)+.5*x.*exp(x)-4*x');
```

The symbols f and fp now represent functions. The command feval may be used to evaluate an inline function. Enter:

```
» feval(f,3)
```

to find the value of $f(x) = \frac{1}{2}xe^x - 2x^2$ evaluated at $x = 3$. That is, `feval(f,3)` gives $f(3)$. (From here on we'll omit most of the output of commands in the MATLAB discussions.) This also works if `f` is the name of a standard MATLAB function, in quotes, e.g., `f='sin'`. However, for an inline function we can use the even simpler `f(3)` to get a value. Enter:

```
» f(3)
```

The use of `feval` is optional for an inline function. Now we're ready to use Newton's method. Let's start with the root near $x_0 = 0.4$. Enter:

```
» x0=.4;
» x0=x0-f(x0)/fp(x0)
```

This gives $x_1 = 0.3611$. Cursor up and re-enter the last line to find $x_2 = 0.3574$. Cursor up and re-enter it again; the value does not change. To the precision displayed, the root is at 0.3574. To have more digits displayed, enter:

```
» format long
» x0=.4;
» x0=x0-f(x0)/fp(x0)
```

This gives $x_1 = 0.36106860486687$. Iterating the last line by repeatedly entering it gives, successively,

$$x_2 = 0.35743611821915,$$

$$x_3 = 0.35740295895202,$$

$$x_4 = 0.35740295618139,$$

$$x_5 = 0.35740295618139.$$

From this point on the values no longer change. The correct digits are (rounded as indicated) 0.36, 0.357, 0.35740296, and 0.35740295618139 (if we assume that the last value is correct). As a check, enter:

```
» f(x0)
```

(Note, is actually the most recent value now.) This is roughly $5E-17$, which is quite small. As another check, enter:

```
» xleft=x0-1E-4;xright=x0+1E-4;
```

and evaluate `f(xleft)` and `f(xright)` to see that a zero is bracketed between `xleft` and `xright`. (You may enter `format` to return to the default display of numeric values if desired; calculations are still done with about sixteen digits, but only four decimal places will be displayed.) Conceivably roundoff error is deceiving us by making one of these values appear to have a sign opposite to its actual sign, but this is very unlikely.

As mentioned above, the `feval` command can also be used with MATLAB-supplied functions and M-files (MATLAB programs). For example, enter:

```
» feval('sin',x0)
» feval('sin',pi/2)
```

to evaluate the sine function at $x = x_0$ and then at the point $x = \pi/2$. The command `feval('myfun',x0)` or `name='myfun';feval(name,x0)` runs the MATLAB program `myfun.m` with the input argument `x0` and returns its value at that argument. (See Section 1.4 for more about MATLAB programs.) In most situations in which we use an inline function, an M-file would work just as well, and in practical applications it is highly likely that we would be calling an M-file instead. However, inline functions are convenient for our demonstrations.

Now use a different initial guess to find the root of $f(x) = \frac{1}{2}xe^x - 2x^2$ that lies near 2.2. Check your answer by computing the value of $f(x)$ at that point and by showing that it lies in a bracket.

ADDITIONAL PROBLEMS 1.2

6. Solve for the third smallest positive root of $x - \tan(x) = 0$ by bisection, inverse linear interpolation, the secant method, and Newton's method. Create a table with successive iterates of each method in separate columns. Comment on the speed of the methods.

7. Use Newton's method to approximate all real zeroes of
$$p(x) = 2x^5 - 7x^4 - 3x^3 + 25x^2 - 23x + 6.$$

   (*Hint:* Graph $p(x)$ first.) Does Newton's method perform equally well for all zeroes? Repeat with the secant method.

8. Use Newton's method to approximate all real zeroes of
$$p(x) = x^7 - 6.65x^6 - 3.475x^5 + 112.3x^4 - 194.88x^3$$
$$-361.02x^2 + 1306.4x - 999.02.$$

   (*Hint:* Graph $p(x)$ first.) Does Newton's method perform equally well for all zeroes?

9. Give an explicit formula and initial points for a function for which the secant method and Newton's method will diverge in the manner indicated in Figure 1.6.

10. Apply Newton's method to $f(x) = (x - 1)^2 + 0.1$ with initial condition $x_0 = 1.1$. Explain the results in terms of the graph of f.

11. **a.** What happens if the secant method is applied to a linear function? What happens if Newton's method is applied to a linear function?
    b. Sketch the graph of a function for which you could choose x_0 very close to one root of an equation but

for which Newton's method would converge to a root far from it.

12. **a.** Bracket the roots of $x^4 - 6.7302x^3 - 15.608x^2 + 44.46x + 74.487 = 0$.
    b. Use the secant method to find all real roots of this equation.
    c. Use Newton's method to find all real roots of this equation.

13. Use the secant method to approximate a zero of $f(x) = 1/x^3 - 10$ to six decimal places.

14. The **logistic model** for the size of a population is the solution of the **logistic equation**
$$dP/dt = kP(M - P).$$

   Here $M > 0$ is the maximum number of individuals that the region can support, and $k > 0$ is a constant such that, when the population is small,
$$dP/dt \approx (kM)P$$

   (the population size initially grows exponentially).
   a. Show that the logistic model is
$$P(t) = \frac{M P_0}{P_0 + (M - P_0)\exp(-kMt)}$$

   in the range
$$0 < P_0 < M$$

   by separating variables and using partial fractions.

b. Suppose a lake has 100 trout in it. A year later it has 347 trout in it. If the net birth rate $\beta = kM$ of the trout is believed to be 2.1 per year, what is the maximum population M of trout the lake can support under the logistic model? Use Newton's method to determine M.

15. Apply Newton's method to $f(x) = x^2 + 1$ using the complex initial condition $x_0 = 1 + i$. (This may be entered in MATLAB as x0=1+i; MATLAB will handle the complex arithmetic automatically.) Use another choice of x_0 to find the other root.

1.3 The Fixed Point Theorem

It has been said that "a good proof is one that makes us wiser." We are going to study Newton's method in some detail and establish sufficient conditions for it to converge to a zero of the function in which we are interested. In doing so we will gain a better understanding of how and why the method works and just how rapidly it converges.

In using Newton's method we choose an initial guess x_0 and then iterate it in what is in essence a feedback loop. We always set

$$x_k = x_{k-1} - \frac{f(x_{k-1})}{f'(x_{k-1})}$$
$$= N_f(x_{k-1})$$

$(k = 1, 2, \ldots)$, where the function

$$N_f(x) = x - \frac{f(x)}{f'(x)}$$

is sometimes called the **Newton transform** of f. An iteration of the form

$$x_k = g(x_{k-1}) \qquad (1.4)$$

Fixed Point Iteration

is called a **fixed point iteration** (or **functional iteration**), and any x^* such that

$$x^* = g(x^*)$$

is called a **fixed point** of g. A fixed point is a point where the graph of $y = g(x)$ crosses the line $y = x$. Newton's method is of this form; note that every simple zero of f corresponds to a fixed point of N_f. When Newton's method converges, it means that the fixed point iteration

$$x_k = N_f(x_{k-1})$$

is converging to a fixed point of N_f. That fixed point is a root of the underlying equation.

We first consider fixed point iterations generally and then specialize them to Newton's method. This is useful because iterations in the form of Eq. (1.4) appear frequently in numerical analysis.

If g is continuous, then a fixed point iteration based on g, if it converges, must converge to a fixed point of g. For if $x_k = g(x_{k-1})$ is used to generate a sequence $\{x_n\}_{n=0}^{\infty}$ and

$$\lim_{n \to \infty} x_n = x^*,$$

then

$$\lim_{n\to\infty} x_n = \lim_{n\to\infty} g(x_{n-1})$$

$$x^* = g(\lim_{n\to\infty} x_{n-1})$$

$$= g(x^*)$$

by continuity. However, a fixed point iteration does not always generate a convergent sequence.

There are many versions of the Fixed Point Theorem, which establishes conditions under which a function has a fixed point that may be found by fixed point iteration. The following version is appropriate for our work.

Theorem 1 (Fixed Point Theorem)

If g is continuous on $[a, b]$ and $g : [a, b] \to [a, b]$, then g has a fixed point in $[a, b]$. If in addition g is differentiable on (a, b) and there is a λ, $0 < \lambda < 1$, such that $|g'(x)| \leq \lambda$ on (a, b), then this fixed point is unique and the fixed point iteration $x_k = g(x_{k-1})$ converges to it for any $x_0 \in [a, b]$.

Proof.

Suppose g is continuous on $[a, b]$ and $g : [a, b] \to [a, b]$. We need to show it has a fixed point. If $g(a) = a$ or $g(b) = b$, then there is indeed a fixed point; hence let us assume that $g(a) \neq a$ and $g(b) \neq b$. Define $h(x) = g(x) - x$. Then $h(x)$ is continuous, and $h(x)$ has a zero in $[a, b]$ if and only if $g(x)$ has a fixed point in $[a, b]$. But

$$h(a) = g(a) - a$$

$$> 0$$

since $g(a)$ is in $[a, b]$ and hence cannot be smaller than a, and we have assumed that $g(a)$ is not equal to a. Similarly,

$$h(b) = g(b) - b$$

$$< 0,$$

and so by the Intermediate Value Theorem there is a $c \in (a, b)$ such that $h(c) = 0$, that is, such that $g(c) = c$, as claimed.

Now suppose in addition that g is differentiable on (a, b) and that there is a $0 < \lambda < 1$ such that $|g'(x)| \leq \lambda$ on (a, b). If p and q are two distinct fixed points of g, then by the Mean Value Theorem

$$\frac{g(p) - g(q)}{p - q} = g'(\theta)$$

for some θ between p and q. But $g(p) = p$ and $g(q) = q$ since p and q are fixed points, so

$$g'(\theta) = \frac{g(p) - g(q)}{p - q}$$

$$= \frac{p - q}{p - q}$$

$$= 1,$$

which is a contradiction. Hence there are not two distinct fixed points of g on $[a, b]$. The fixed point is unique.

It remains to show that we can find the fixed point x^* by fixed point iteration. Pick an x_0 in $[a, b]$. The sequence $x_k = g(x_{k-1})$ is well-defined since $g: [a, b] \rightarrow [a, b]$. Now

$$|x_n - x^*| = |g(x_{n-1}) - g(x^*)|$$

$$= |g'(\theta_n)||x_{n-1} - x^*|$$

$$\leq \lambda |x_{n-1} - x^*| \tag{1.5}$$

for some θ_n between x_{n-1} and x^*, by the Mean Value Theorem and the bound on $|g'(x)|$. Inductively, $|x_n - x^*| \leq \lambda^n |x_0 - x^*|$ and since $\lambda < 1$, $|x_n - x^*| \rightarrow 0$ as $n \rightarrow \infty$. So, $x_n \rightarrow x^*$. ∎

Example 1.3.1   On early computers, the fixed point iteration based on $g(x) = \frac{1}{2}(x + \frac{2}{x})$ was sometimes used to find $\sqrt{2}$ (or more generally $g_\alpha(x) = \frac{1}{2}(x + \frac{\alpha}{x})$ to find $\sqrt{\alpha}, \alpha > 0$). Does $g(x)$ have a fixed point? Note that $g(x)$ is continuous for $x > 0$ and that $g(1) = 1.5$, $g(2) = 1.5$, and $g'(x) = \frac{1}{2}(1 - 2/x^2)$. Since $g'(x) = 0$ at $x = \pm\sqrt{2}$, g takes on its extreme values at these points, and in particular $g(\sqrt{2}) = \sqrt{2} \doteq 1.4142$. Hence $g: [1, 2] \rightarrow [\sqrt{2}, 1.5]$ and so $g: [1, 2] \rightarrow [1, 2]$. Hence g has a fixed point on $[1, 2]$ (see Fig. 1.10). Since $|g'(x)| \leq 1/2$ over $[1, 2]$ (verify this), the fixed point in $[1, 2]$ is unique. To find it we could solve

$$x = g(x)$$

$$x = \frac{1}{2}\left(x + \frac{2}{x}\right)$$

$$0 = \frac{1}{2}\left(x + \frac{2}{x}\right) - x$$

$$0 = x^2 - 2,$$

or use fixed point iteration by choosing, say, $x_0 = 1$, and forming the sequence

$$x_1 = \frac{1}{2}\left(x_0 + \frac{2}{x_0}\right) = 1.5$$

$$x_2 = \frac{1}{2}\left(x_1 + \frac{2}{x_1}\right) \doteq 1.41666666666667$$

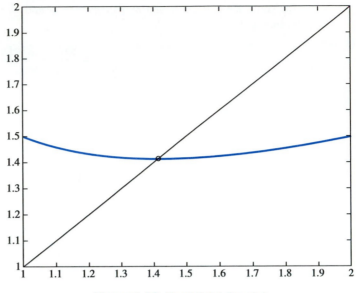

Figure 1.10 Fixed Point For $g(x)$.

$$x_3 = \frac{1}{2}\left(x_2 + \frac{2}{x_2}\right) \doteq 1.41421568627451$$

$$x_4 = \frac{1}{2}\left(x_3 + \frac{2}{x_3}\right) \doteq 1.41421356237469$$

(note that $\sqrt{2} \doteq 1.41421356237310$). Notice the rapid convergence:

1

1.41

1.41421

1.41421356237

(where only those digits which agree with $\sqrt{2}$ are listed). This method for computing square roots was used on early computers when only the four arithmetic operations were available, as it quickly finds the root using only those operations. ∎

Example 1.3.2   Consider the function $f(x) = e^x + x^2 - 5x$. It has two zeroes located at approximately $x = 1/3$ and $x = 7/4$ (see Fig. 1.11). One way to rewrite $f(x) = 0$ is as $x = g(x)$, where

$$e^x + x^2 - 5x = 0$$
$$5x = e^x + x^2$$
$$x = \frac{1}{5}(e^x + x^2)$$

so that $g(x) = \frac{1}{5}(e^x + x^2)$ is the iteration function (see Fig. 1.12). Taking $x_0 = 1/3$ gives

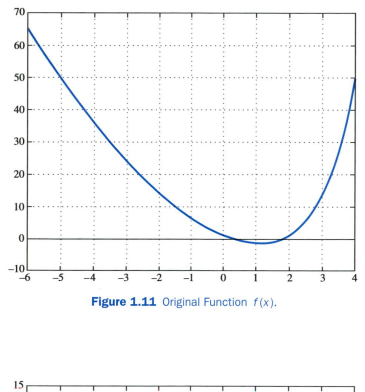

Figure 1.11 Original Function $f(x)$.

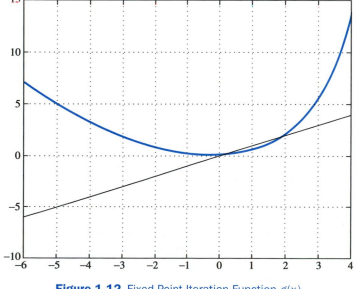

Figure 1.12 Fixed Point Iteration Function $g(x)$.

$$x_0 = \frac{1}{3}$$

$$x_1 \doteq 0.3013$$

$$x_2 \doteq 0.2885$$

$$x_3 \doteq 0.2835$$

$$x_4 \doteq 0.2816$$

$$x_5 \doteq 0.2809$$

$$x_6 \doteq 0.2807$$

$$x_7 \doteq 0.2806$$

$$x_8 \doteq 0.2805,$$

and in fact the method converges to 0.2805 (to four decimal places). Note, $g'(x) = \frac{1}{5}(e^x + 2x)$ and $g'(0.2805) \doteq 0.3770$, which is less than 1 in absolute value.

We have succeeded in finding one root of $f(x)$ by this method. Now let's take $x_0 = 7/4$ in hopes of finding the other root. We have

$$x_0 = \frac{7}{4}$$

$$x_1 \doteq 1.7634$$

$$x_2 \doteq 1.7884$$

$$x_3 \doteq 1.8357$$

$$x_4 \doteq 1.9278$$

$$x_5 \doteq 2.1181$$

$$x_6 \doteq 2.5603$$

$$x_7 \doteq 3.8990$$

$$x_8 \doteq 12.9109$$

$$x_9 \doteq 8.0972E4,$$

and clearly the method is diverging. The actual root is at 1.7340 so our initial guess $x_0 = 1.75$ was pretty good, but $g'(1.7340) \doteq 1.8263$ and so we could not have hoped that the method would converge.

Look again at Figure 1.11 and especially at Figure 1.12. It's hard to predict this behavior from the graphs, though you might notice in Figure 1.12 a steeper slope of the function near the second root than near the first. Using the derivative tells us right away when we can expect convergence near a given fixed point and when there's no hope (barring incredibly good luck). ∎

Newton's Method as a Fixed Point Iteration

From the Fixed Point Theorem we know that under appropriate conditions a numerical method of the form $x_k = g(x_{k-1})$ will converge to a common value (the solution) for all sufficiently close initial guesses. The rate of convergence is controlled by $|g'(x)|$ near the fixed point. (We say that the fixed point is **attracting** when $|g'(x)| < 1$.) The smaller the derivative (in absolute value), the more rapid the convergence. For Newton's method,

$$g'(x) = N'_f(x)$$

$$= \left(x - \frac{f(x)}{f'(x)} \right)'$$

$$= 1 - \left[\frac{f(x)}{f'(x)} \right]'$$

$$= \frac{f(x)f''(x)}{[f'(x)]^2}$$

(if f is twice differentiable). If x^* is a simple zero of f (so that $f'(x^*)$ is nonzero), then

$$g'(x^*) = \frac{f(x^*)f''(x^*)}{[f'(x^*)]^2}$$

$$= \frac{0 \cdot f''(x^*)}{[f'(x^*)]^2}$$

$$= 0,$$

and by continuity $|g'(x)| < 1$ in some neighborhood of the zero. This is the best possible case; sufficiently near x^*, the value of λ in the proof of the Fixed Point Theorem may be taken as small as desired. In this sense Newton's method may be viewed as a way of getting a best possible fixed point iteration for a given problem. Fixed point iterations that are not generated by Newton's method may also be used for root-finding.

Let's finish applying the Fixed Point Theorem to Newton's method. By continuity of $g'(x)$ (that is, $\frac{d}{dx}N_f(x)$), which requires that $f''(x)$ be continuous, that is, that f be twice continuously differentiable, there is a $\delta > 0$ such that $|g'(x)| \leq \lambda < 1$ for $x \in [x^* - \delta, x^* + \delta]$. (That is, if $g'(x)$ is zero at x^*, then $|g'(x)|$ is small near x^*.) But since the derivative of g is less than 1, in absolute value, it is growing less rapidly than the line $y = x$, and so if $x \in [x^* - \delta, x^* + \delta]$, then $g(x) \in [x^* - \delta, x^* + \delta]$. Taking $[a, b] = [x^* - \delta, x^* + \delta]$, $g(x) = N_f(x)$ meets all requirements of the Fixed Point Theorem. Hence:

Theorem 2 (Newton's Method Convergence Theorem)

Suppose $f(x)$ has a simple zero x^* in $[a, b]$, and that f is twice continuously differentiable on $[a, b]$. Then there is an interval about x^* such that Newton's method converges to x^* for any x_0 in that interval.

Note carefully that the theorem only guarantees convergence to a *simple* zero if we are *sufficiently* close, and that it requires that f be *twice* continuously differentiable near the zero.

PROBLEMS 1.3

1. a. Show that the fixed point iteration of Example 1.3.1 is the result of applying Newton's method to $f(x) = x^2 - 2$.

   b. Use the method to approximate $\sqrt{2}$ to at least eight decimal places using the initial guesses $x_0 = 1, 1.4, 2, 10$.

2. Solve the equation $x = 2^{-x}$ for x by performing fixed point iteration on it as given. (You may wish to plot $y = x$ and $y = 2^{-x}$ first to generate a good x_0.) Compare your results to using Newton's method on $f(x) = x - 2^{-x}$. Comment.

3. Attempt to use fixed point iteration to solve $x^2 = 3$ by rewriting it as $x = x^2 + x - 3$. What happens? Why? Now rewrite it as $x = \frac{1}{2}(x + \frac{3}{x})$ (show that this is equivalent to $x^2 = 3$) and try again. Why does this version work better?

4. a. An early method for performing division b/a on computers was to apply Newton's method to $f(x) = 1/x - a$ to find $1/a$ and then multiply it by b. Show that Newton's method for $f(x)$ requires only multiplication and subtraction, and that it converges for all $x_0 \in (0, 1/a]$. (*Hint:* Plot $N_f(x)$ and sketch a few iterates.) What happens if $x_0 \gg 1/a$?

   b. Use this method with $a = 3$ to approximate $1/3$. Use the initial guesses $x_0 = 0.5, 1, 2, 4$. In each case make a table showing only those leading digits in your answer that agree with the solution. What can you say about the rapidity of convergence of Newton's method in this case? (This method is still commonly used on high-performance machines to implement quadruple precision division.)

5. Let $g(x)$ be a continuously differentiable function with a fixed point x^* for which $|g'(x^*)| < 1$. Show that fixed point iteration of g will converge to x^* for any x_0 in some interval $[x^* - \delta, x^* + \delta]$ (with $\delta > 0$). What limits how large δ can be?

MATLAB 1.3

When working with fixed points, it's convenient to be able to overlay plots. For example, let's look for the fixed points of $3\cos(x)$. Enter:

```
» x=-5:.1:5;
» plot(x,3*cos(x))
» hold on
» plot(x,x)
```

(Use the `grid` command in addition if you like.) The `hold on` command tells MATLAB to hold the current plot so that subsequent plots will be overlaid on the held plot. The command `hold off` releases the hold.

   The command `help hold` will give more information on the `hold` command. In general, typing `help <command>` will give some basic information about that command. The built-in help is excellent and you should refer to it frequently as you learn MATLAB; it makes learning the language relatively easy. Use `help` frequently.

   You may also use the help from the drop-down *Help* menu. Selecting *MATLAB Help* gives you access to demos, an introduction to MATLAB, and other "getting started" material, as well as search capabilities.

   Type `help plot` and read about the `plot` command, including the color options for your plots. For example, enter:

```
» plot(x,x,'c')
```

to overlay a new $y = x$ line on your previous one, but now in cyan. Close the previous plot. Enter:

```
» plot(x,3*cos(x),'b+'),hold,plot(x,x,'yo')
```

You should get the cosine curve as blue pluses and the line as yellow circles. These options do not connect the dots. This is sometimes useful.

Let's do a fixed point iteration on $g(x) = 3\cos(x)$. The plot showed a fixed point near 1 and either one or two fixed points near -3 (we need better resolution to decide if it is one point of intersection or two). Enter:

```
» x0=1;
```

We could simply enter x0=3*cos(x0) repeatedly (using the $\boxed{\uparrow}$ key), but MATLAB has looping structures. Enter:

```
» for k=1:10,x0=3*cos(x0),end
```

(If the numbers go by too quickly, type `help more` for a useful option.)

The method seems to have converged to a fixed point near -2.94. Cursor up and re-enter the line with the `for-end` loop; it will start over with the most recent x_0, x0=-2.9388. Do another ten iterations.[4]

It appears that -2.9381 is a fixed point. Although we started with an initial guess near 1, we found another fixed point entirely. Enter:

```
» -3*sin(1)
```

The reason we found a different fixed point is that near $x = 1$, the derivative of $g(x) = 3\cos(x)$ is about -2.5244. The derivative is too large (in absolute value). Enter:

```
» -3*sin(-3)
```

Near $x = -3$ the derivative is 0.4234, which is small enough that if x_0 (or some later iterate) is sufficiently near it, we will see convergence.

Close the open figures, if you haven't already (see `help close` for a way to do this using a MATLAB command). Enter:

```
» x=-4:.01:-2;
» plot(x,3*cos(x)),hold on,plot(x,x),grid
» title('Fixed point of 3*cos(x)')
```

There's another fixed point near $x = -2.6$. But enter:

```
» -3*sin(-2.6)
```

The derivative is 1.5465. We won't be able to find this fixed point by simple fixed point iteration on $g(x)$. However, we can find any of the fixed points by Newton's method. Use Newton's method on $g(x) = 3\cos(x)$ to find the two remaining fixed points.

---

[4] In fact, MATLAB has stored x_0 to about fourteen places after the decimal point and will use *that* value in its calculations.

ADDITIONAL PROBLEMS 1.3

6. a. Estimate how many iterations it would take to find the sole fixed point of $\cos(x)$ to six decimal places by fixed point iteration of $x_k = \cos(x_{k-1})$ starting from $x_0 = 0.8$. Do this by estimating λ from the proof of the Fixed Point Theorem and then applying Eq. (1.5).

b. Use fixed point iteration on $g(x) = \cos(x)$ to find the fixed point to six decimal places. Compare your actual number of iterations to your estimate from part a.

c. Use Newton's method on $f(x) = x - \cos(x)$ to find the fixed point to six decimal places. Compare the number of iterations for Newton's method to the number of iterations from part b.

7. a. Show that the functions

$$g_1(x) = x^3 - 9x^2 + 27x - 24,$$

$$g_2(x) = 9 - \frac{26}{x} + \frac{24}{x^2},$$

$$g_3(x) = \sqrt{\frac{(9x^2 - 26x + 24)}{x}},$$

$$g_4(x) = \frac{(-x^3 + 9x^2 + 24)}{26}, \text{ and}$$

$$g_5(x) = \frac{2x^3 - 9x^2 + 24}{3x^2 - 18x + 26}$$

have the same fixed points, and that these fixed points are exactly the zeroes of $f(x) = x^3 - 9x^2 + 26x - 24$.

b. The zeroes of $f(x)$ are 2, 3, and 4. For each zero of f, determine which functions $g_1, \ldots, g_5$ will converge to that zero under fixed point iteration.

c. Do any of $g_1, \ldots, g_5$ correspond to Newton's method for $f(x) = 0$?

8. Consider again the function $f(x) = 1/x - a$ from Problem 4. Using $x_0 = 10^{-10}$, how many iterations are needed to get six decimal place accuracy if $a = 0.5$? Does this contradict the claimed rapid convergence?

9. a. Show that if $\mu \in (1, 3)$, then there is an interval on which fixed point iteration must converge to a unique fixed point for $g(x) = \mu x(1 - x)$. What happens if $\mu = 1$ or $\mu = 3$?

b. Find a formula for the fixed point as a function of μ.

c. Show that if $\mu > 3$, then this fixed point is not attracting. (If $|g'(x^*)| > 1$ we say that the fixed point is **repelling**.)

10. a. If $g(x) = \mu x(1 - x)$ with $\mu = 3.5$, find all four fixed points of $g(g(x))$. (If you have access to a computer algebra system such as Maple, assume $\mu > 3$ and find a formula for these points.) Show that two of them are fixed points of g and that the other pair forms a cycle $x_b = g(x_a), x_a = g(x_b)$.

b. For $\mu = 3.5$, iterate $g(x) = \mu x(1 - x)$ starting with $x_0 = 0.5$. Is the sequence converging? (This is called a period two cycle; it is interesting in the study of mathematical chaos but represents a form of failure to converge in numerical analysis.)

11. a. The Fixed Point Theorem is a special case of a more general result known as the Contraction Mapping Theorem. If D is a closed subset of $\mathbb{R}^n$ and $T : D \to D$, then T is said to be a **contraction** (or to be **contractive**) on D if there is an $s, 0 < s < 1$, such that $|T(x) - T(y)| \le s|x - y|$ for all $x, y \in D$. (We interpret $|\cdot|$ as a vector norm if necessary.) The constant s is called the **contractivity factor.** Show that if a function meets the hypotheses of the Fixed Point Theorem then it is a contraction on some $D \subseteq \mathbb{R}$. What is the contractivity factor s?

b. Prove that a contraction T must be a continuous function.

c. The **Contraction Mapping Theorem** states that every contraction mapping has a unique fixed point on its domain D, often called an **invariant set** or **attractor** in this context. Prove the Contraction Mapping Theorem.

d. Show that the function on $\mathbb{R}^2$ defined by $T(x, y) \to (\frac{1}{2}x + 1, \frac{1}{2}y)$ is a contraction. What is its contractivity factor? Find its invariant set analytically, and then verify that fixed point iteration converges to that fixed point.

12. a. Solve $x^3 - 7.8x^2 + 16.4x - 9.6 = 0$ for the largest root using Newton's method. Use MATLAB to plot the function to generate an initial guess. Would fixed point iteration in the form $x_{k+1} = x_k^3 - 7.8x_k^2 + 17.4x_k - 9.6$ be successful for any of these roots?

b. Create a convergent fixed point iteration for finding the positive root of $x^3 + 3.85x^2 - 4.9x - 17.2 = 0$, which is not Newton's method, by algebraically rearranging the equation $x = x^3 + 3.85x^2 - 3.9x - 17.2$. Plot your $g(x)$ together with the line $y = x$, and indicate the location of the fixed point and the slope of g at the point of intercept.

13. **a.** Use the method of Example 1.3.1 to find an approximation to $\sqrt{10}$ that is correct to as many decimal places as you can display on your machine (use `format long` if working in MATLAB).

   b. Suppose the method of Example 1.3.1 is to be implemented as an automated square root finder, that is, as a program that accepts $\alpha > 0$ and returns $\sqrt{\alpha}$. Suggest a good choice of initial condition x_0; x_0 must be a simple arithmetic (addition, subtraction, multiplication, division) function of α, and the closer it is to $\sqrt{\alpha}$ the quicker the program will run.

14. In an article in the journal *Chemical Engineering Science,* William W. Farr and Rutherford Aris consider the number of steady states that can be achieved for two sequential reactions in a well-mixed (tank) reactor. One condition under which a change in the number of such states can occur is when v and γ are such that

$$v^2 = \frac{[(\gamma - 3)^2 + 6]}{[3(\gamma - 2)^2]}$$

where $\gamma = E_1/R\bar{T}$ and $v = E_2/E_1$ are dimensionless parameters depending on the respective activation energies E_1 and E_2, the gas constant R, and the mean temperature $\bar{T}$.

   a. What is the form of Newton's method for finding a γ for a given value of v?

   b. Use Newton's method to find γ if $v^2 = 1, 2$, and 3, if possible.

   c. Can γ be found algebraically?

15. **a.** The proof of the Fixed Point Theorem requires that $|g'(x)| \leq \lambda < 1$, that is, that the absolute value of the derivative be not just less than 1 but bounded below 1. What might fail if this condition were replaced by $|g'(x)| < 1$? What if it were replaced by $|g'(x)| \leq 1$?

   b. In using the Fixed Point Theorem to establish the Newton's Method Convergence Theorem we made the claim that since the derivative of g is less than 1 in absolute value, it is growing less rapidly than the line $y = x$, and so if $x \in [x^* - \delta, x^* + \delta]$ then $g(x) \in [x^* - \delta, x^* + \delta]$. Give a rigorous proof of this claim.

1.4 Quadratic Convergence of Newton's Method

Convergence Criteria and Errors

Under appropriate conditions, Newton's method generates a sequence $\{x_n\}_{n=0}^{\infty}$ with the property that x_n tends to a zero x^* of the function f as $n \to \infty$. But this is a theoretical result; will it still hold true on a computer, with finite precision arithmetic and a finite amount of time? The finite precision arithmetic is not so much an issue with Newton's method, since if we are in the interval in which convergence is guaranteed, a small roundoff error will likely leave us in that interval, and from that point convergence is still assured. What we need is a **convergence criterion** (or **stopping criterion**) for the method, so that we know how to choose an n sufficiently large that x_n is approximately equal to the limit x^* of the sequence.

For bisection this was easily handled, since the width of the current bracket was a measure of the uncertainty in our knowledge of the root. More generally, we define the **absolute error** in an approximation x_n to a (typically unknown) true value x^* to be the quantity

$$\alpha = |x^* - x_n|,$$

and we define the **relative error** in x_n as an approximation to x^* to be the quantity

$$\rho = \frac{|x^* - x_n|}{|x^*|}$$

if x^* is nonzero. This may be a more useful measure of the error when $|x^*|$ is far from unity, since it's generally unreasonable to ask for an absolute error of 10^{-8} when the

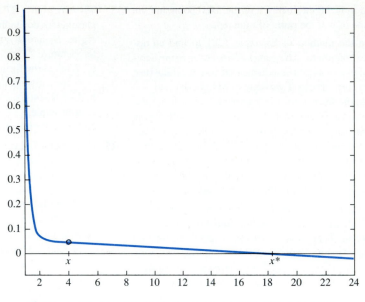

Figure 1.13 Small Residual Error but Large Absolute Error.

answer is on the order of millions, for example. If ρ is about 10^{-k}, then the computed value x_n is correct to about k decimal places.

For the secant method and Newton's method we do not have a bracket, and so we cannot estimate α or ρ with certainty. Ideally we would like to terminate the algorithm when α (or ρ) is less than some tolerance τ (say, relative error of no more than 1%, that is, $\rho = .01$). It is tempting to use

$$|f(x)| < \tau,$$

but it is possible for the **residual error** $|f(x)|$ to be small even though x is far from x^* (see Fig. 1.13). Because of this the criterion $|f(x)| < \tau$ should be used only in conjunction with at least one other criterion, or when there is sufficient knowledge of the f in question to be sure that this is a safe convergence criterion.

If the method is working, x_{n+1} should be a better estimate of x^* than x_n, so it might be reasonable to use

$$\alpha_{n+1} \approx |x_{n+1} - x_n|$$

$$\rho_{n+1} \approx \frac{|x_{n+1} - x_n|}{|x_{n+1}|} \tag{1.6}$$

to estimate the absolute and relative errors, respectively. This is especially so if x_{n+1} is generally a *much* better estimate of x^* than x_n is. Then we could choose to terminate the iteration if α_{n+1} (or ρ_{n+1}) is less than the tolerance. To have confidence in such a criterion, we would like to know just how much better x_{n+1} is than x_n as an estimate of the true solution x^*.

Rate and Order   Let's try to quantify how rapidly Newton's method converges to its limit. In calculus
of Convergence   we focus mostly on whether or not a limit exists; in numerical analysis we also consider

how rapidly that limit is approached. There are two key ideas: the **rate of convergence** and the **order of convergence** to the limit. When considering the rate of convergence, to the limit we take a sequence $\{x_n\}_{n=0}^{\infty}$ generated by a numerical method (or any other means) and a reference sequence $\{c_n\}_{n=0}^{\infty}$ to which we compare it. Suppose $x_n \to x^*$ and the reference sequence $\{c_n\}_{n=0}^{\infty}$ satisfies $c_n \to 0$. We say that $\{x_n\}_{n=0}^{\infty}$ converges to x^* with rate of convergence $\{c_n\}_{n=0}^{\infty}$ if there is a constant $K > 0$ such that

$$|x_n - x^*| \le K|c_n|$$

for all n sufficiently large. We write

$$x_n = O(c_n)$$

(or say that $\{x_n\}_{n=0}^{\infty}$ converges to x^* as $O(c_n)$), called the "big oh" notation. The reference sequence $\{c_n\}_{n=0}^{\infty}$ is commonly taken to be $c_n = a^n$ for some $0 < a < 1$, or $c_n = 1/n^p$ for some $p > 0$.

For example, the bisection method clearly converges at least as $O\left(\left(\frac{1}{2}\right)^n\right)$, because the error bound decreases by $1/2$ at each step ($K = 1$). From the proof of the Fixed Point Theorem, we see that for a fixed point iteration $x_{n+1} = g(x_n)$,

$$|x_n - x^*| \le K\lambda^n$$

where λ is the bound on the derivative of g, and K may be taken to be the distance $|x_0 - x^*|$ from the initial guess to the actual root. Hence the rate of convergence is $O(\lambda^n)$ for a convergent fixed point iteration that meets the conditions of the theorem.

Example 1.4.1 What is the rate of convergence of the sequence $\sin(1/n)/(1/n)$ to 1 as $n \to \infty$? From the Taylor series for the sine function we have

$$\frac{\sin(1/n)}{(1/n)} - 1 = n \sin\left(\frac{1}{n}\right) - 1$$

$$= n\left[\left(\frac{1}{n}\right) - \left(\frac{1}{3!}\right)\left(\frac{1}{n^3}\right) + \left(\frac{1}{5!}\right)\left(\frac{1}{n^5}\right) - \cdots\right] - 1$$

$$= \left[1 - \left(\frac{1}{3!}\right)\left(\frac{1}{n^2}\right) + \left(\frac{1}{5!}\right)\left(\frac{1}{n^4}\right) - \cdots\right] - 1$$

$$= -\left(\frac{1}{3!}\right)\left(\frac{1}{n^2}\right) + \left(\frac{1}{5!}\right)\left(\frac{1}{n^4}\right) - \cdots,$$

and for n sufficiently large the terms in $1/n^4$, $1/n^6$, and so on, are negligible. Taking $c_n = 1/n^2$ and $K = 1/3!$ (which, since it is an alternating series, suffices despite the neglected terms) shows that the rate of convergence is $O(1/n^2)$. ∎

The rate of convergence is a useful way to compare two methods when the two reference series are well known and easily comparable; for example, a $O(1/n^2)$ method certainly converges more rapidly than a $O(1/n)$ method. But Newton's method is $O(\lambda^n)$, where $\lambda > 0$ may be taken arbitrarily small if we are sufficiently near the zero. While this is obviously a desirable quality, we will need another notion of convergence speed to better quantify this and to compare it to other methods with this property.

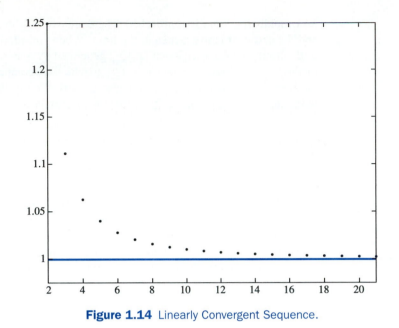

Figure 1.14 Linearly Convergent Sequence.

We say that a sequence $\{x_n\}_{n=0}^{\infty}$ with limit x^* has order of convergence 1 if there is a constant $0 < M < 1$ such that the limit

$$\lim_{n \to \infty} \frac{|x_{n+1} - x^*|}{|x_n - x^*|} = M \qquad (1.7)$$

exists. The constant M is called the **asymptotic error constant.** We say that the sequence or the method that generates it exhibits **linear convergence** (see Fig. 1.14.) Evidently a general fixed point iteration has order of convergence 1 with rate $M = \lambda$, since the absolute error $e_n = |x_n - x^*|$ satisfies

$$e_{n+1} \approx \lambda e_n$$

for large n. For Newton's method, however, λ may be taken arbitrarily small in the limit, and so we may take M as small as desired. Whenever

$$\lim_{n \to \infty} \frac{|x_{n+1} - x^*|}{|x_n - x^*|} = 0 \qquad (1.8)$$

(corresponding to $M = 0$ in Eq. (1.7)), we say that the method or sequence is **superlinearly convergent** (or simply **superlinear**). Newton's method is superlinear for a simple zero.

For some superlinear methods it may happen that there is some $p > 1$ such that

$$\lim_{n \to \infty} \frac{|x_{n+1} - x^*|}{|x_n - x^*|^p} = M \qquad (1.9)$$

for some $M > 0$. (Note that since $p > 1$, we do not need to require $M < 1$.) If e_n is the absolute error after step n, then this is the same as

$$\lim_{n \to \infty} \frac{e_{n+1}}{e_n^p} = M.$$

We say that the sequence has order of convergence p and that M is the asymptotic error constant (or **rate** or **ratio**). In the special case $p = 2$ we say that the sequence or the method that generates it exhibits **quadratic convergence.** For any p, if the method is convergent of order p, then

$$e_{n+1} \approx M e_n^p \tag{1.10}$$

in the limit of large n. Note that if $e_n < 1$ and $p > 1$, then e_n^p will be much smaller than e_n.

Order of Convergence of Newton's Method

Might Newton's method be convergent of some order $p > 1$? Yes. Newton's method exhibits quadratic convergence, as we now show. Consider a fixed point iteration $x_{n+1} = g(x_n)$ with the assumptions of the Fixed Point Theorem. Then

$$x_{n+1} - x^* = g(x_n) - g(x^*)$$
$$= g'(\theta_n)(x_n - x^*)$$

(for some θ_n between x_n and x^*) by the Mean Value Theorem. Hence

$$\frac{x_{n+1} - x^*}{x_n - x^*} = g'(\theta_n)$$

and so

$$\lim_{n \to \infty} \frac{|x_{n+1} - x^*|}{|x_n - x^*|} = \lim_{n \to \infty} |g'(\theta_n)|$$
$$= |g'(x^*)|,$$

justifying the previous claim that a fixed point iteration has order of convergence $p = 1$ if $0 < |g'(x^*)| \leq \lambda < 1$. What if $g'(x^*) = 0$ (as is the case for Newton's method)? The above argument shows that the fixed point iteration is then superlinear. Suppose that (in addition to the other hypotheses of the Fixed Point Theorem) g is twice continuously differentiable on some interval containing x^*. By Taylor's series with remainder,

$$g(x_n) = g(x^*) + g'(x^*)(x_n - x^*) + g''(\xi_n)\frac{(x_n - x^*)^2}{2}$$
$$= g(x^*) + g''(\xi_n)\frac{(x_n - x^*)^2}{2}$$
$$= x^* + g''(\xi_n)\frac{(x_n - x^*)^2}{2}$$

if $g'(x^*)$ is zero, for some ξ_n between x_n and x^*. Hence

$$g(x_n) - x^* = g''(\xi_n)\frac{(x_n - x^*)^2}{2}$$

$$x_{n+1} - x^* = \frac{1}{2}g''(\xi_n)(x_n - x^*)^2$$

$$\frac{x_{n+1} - x^*}{(x_n - x^*)^2} = \frac{1}{2}g''(\xi_n),$$

and so

$$\lim_{n\to\infty}\frac{|x_{n+1} - x^*|}{|x_n - x^*|^2} = \lim_{n\to\infty}\left|\frac{1}{2}g''(\xi_n)\right|$$

$$= \frac{1}{2}g''(x^*)$$

by continuity of g and convergence of the method. So if $g''(x^*) \neq 0$ then the method is quadratically convergent, with asymptotic error constant $\frac{1}{2}g''(x^*)$. (If $g''(x^*) = 0$, the order of convergence is even higher.) Note the key idea here: The order will be p if $g'(x^*)$ through $g^{(p-1)}(x^*)$ are all zero, but $g^{(p)}(x^*)$ is nonzero.

To apply this to Newton's method for a root-finding problem $f(x) = 0$, we already know that $N_f'(x^*)$ is zero, so we must check $N_f''(x^*)$. We have

$$g''(x) = N_f''(x)$$

$$= \left(x - \frac{f(x)}{f'(x)}\right)''$$

$$= \left(\frac{f(x)f''(x)}{[f'(x)]^2}\right)'$$

$$= \frac{f'(x)f''(x) + f(x)f'''(x)}{[f'(x)]^2} - 2\frac{f(x)[f''(x)]^2}{[f'(x)]^3}$$

if f is thrice continuously differentiable. Evaluating this at $x = x^*$ gives

$$g''(x^*) = \frac{f'(x^*)f''(x^*) + f(x^*)f'''(x^*)}{[f'(x^*)]^2} - 2\frac{f(x^*)[f''(x^*)]^2}{[f'(x^*)]^3}$$

$$= \frac{f''(x^*)}{f'(x^*)}$$

after using the fact that $f(x^*) = 0$ (and assuming that the root is simple so that $f'(x^*) \neq 0$).

Summarizing, if f is thrice continuously differentiable in some neighborhood of a simple zero x^* of f, then Newton's method converges quadratically to x^* (or faster in the uncommon event that $f''(x^*) = 0$) for all x_0 sufficiently close to x^*. It can be shown that if the zero is nonsimple, then Newton's method still converges, but only linearly.

Quadratic convergence is the kind of convergence that we would usually like to have in a method. How good is quadratic convergence? Typically for Newton's method, the asymptotic error constant is not greatly larger than 1. Take $M = 1$. If the error at step n is 10^{-4}, then

$$e_{n+1} \approx e_n^2$$

$$= (10^{-4})^2$$

$$= 10^{-8}$$

$$e_{n+2} \approx e_{n+1}^2$$

$$= (10^{-8})^2$$

$$= 10^{-16}$$

Newton's Method and Significant Figures

and so on. Looked at another way, if x_n is accurate to four decimal places, then x_{n+1} will be accurate to eight decimal places, and x_{n+2} will be accurate to sixteen decimal places; Newton's method roughly doubles the number of correct significant figures in the approximate solution at every iteration (once this limiting behavior begins). If we can get just a little bit of accuracy in our solution, the degree of accuracy will grow quite rapidly. This is worth repeating: Once it reaches the region where the quadratic convergence behavior begins, *Newton's method doubles the number of correct significant figures in the approximation at every iteration.*

This certainly justifies using $\alpha_n \approx |x_n - x_{n-1}|$ (from Eq. (1.6)) to approximate the absolute error in the solution, and using $\alpha_n \leq \tau$ or $\rho_n \leq \tau$ (for some small tolerance $\tau > 0$) as a convergence criterion for Newton's method. Unlike the case of bisection, a small α_n is not a guarantee that we are near a root, since Newton's method can remain near some point for several iterations, even though it is not converging to it. To guard against such a possibility, we may wish to check that $|x_{n+1} - x_n|$ is less than the tolerance for at least two successive iterations.

Example 1.4.2 Consider applying Newton's method to find the sole real root of $x^3 - 1.4x^2 + x - 1.4 = 0$ (see Fig. 1.15).

The iteration is

$$x_{k+1} = x_k - \frac{(x_k^3 - 1.4x_k^2 + x_k - 1.4)}{(3x_k^2 - 2.8x_k + 1)},$$

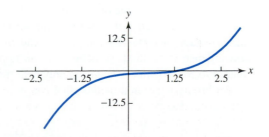

Figure 1.15 The Function $y = x^3 - 1.4x^2 + x - 1.4$.

and as the root appears to be near $x_0 = 1.5$ we will use that as our initial guess. We have:

$$x_1 = x_0 - \frac{x_0^3 - 1.4x_0 + x_0 - 1.4}{3x_0^2 - 2.8x_0 + 1}$$

$$\doteq 1.40845070422535$$

$$x_2 \doteq 1.40006688770576$$

$$x_3 \doteq 1.40000000423180$$

$$x_4 \doteq 1.40000000000000,$$

and 1.4 is indeed the root. The estimated and actual absolute errors are:

$$\alpha_2 = |x_2 - x_1|$$

$$\doteq 0.00838381651959 \qquad \text{(actual: } 0.00845070422535)$$

$$\alpha_3 = |x_3 - x_2|$$

$$\doteq 6.688347396521799E - 5 \text{ (actual: } 6.688770576102065E - 5)$$

$$\alpha_4 = |x_4 - x_3|$$

$$\doteq 4.231795580622588E - 9 \text{ (actual: } 4.231795802667193E - 9)$$

and as expected, Eq. (1.6) gives an excellent estimate of the absolute error. Had we set a tolerance of $\tau = 10^{-4}$, then we could have stopped with x_3 since α_3 is already less than this τ. Note that

$$\frac{\alpha_3}{\alpha_2^2} \doteq 0.9366$$

$$\frac{\alpha_4}{\alpha_3^2} \doteq 0.9459,$$

which suggests that the asymptotic error constant is roughly $M = .94$. For a method with order of convergence 1, this would have meant very slow convergence, but since Newton's method is quadratic we still have excellent convergence; $\alpha_2 \doteq 8E - 3$, $\alpha_3 \doteq 7E - 5$, and $\alpha_4 \doteq 4E - 9$, showing the roughly doubling number of correct significant figures at each iteration. ∎

Although convergence of Newton's method is guaranteed only if we are sufficiently near a zero, in practice it is not uncommon for it to recover from a poor initial guess and converge anyway (by finding its way into the neighborhood of the zero where convergence is ensured, sometimes in an apparently haphazard way). In any event, quadratic convergence is achieved only near the root.

Acceleration of Convergence   We briefly mention a method that can improve the speed of convergence of certain sequences. If $x_k \to x^*$ *linearly,* then it is a fact that the associated sequence

$$a_k = x_{k-2} - \frac{(x_{k-1} - x_{k-2})^2}{x_k - 2x_{k-1} + x_{k-2}}$$

converges more rapidly to x^*. This is known as **Aitken's Δ^2 process** for accelerating convergence. This technique is often built directly into a method or program.

Example 1.4.3 The sequence $x_k = 1/k$ converges linearly to zero. The Aitken's Δ^2 process gives

$$a_k = \frac{1}{k-2} - \frac{\left(\frac{1}{k-1} - \frac{1}{k-2}\right)^2}{\frac{1}{k} - \frac{2}{k-1} + \frac{1}{k-2}}$$

$$= \frac{1}{2(k-1)}$$

$(k \geq 3)$, and indeed

$$\frac{1}{2(k-1)} < \frac{1}{k}$$

for all $k \geq 3$. Of course it will not always be possible to achieve such simplification of the formula for a_k. ■

Note that on a machine with multiple processors we could have one processor(s) computing the numerical method x_k and another processor(s) computing the accelerated sequence a_k simultaneously. We repeat that this method is applicable only when the convergence of x_k is *linear*.

PROBLEMS 1.4

1. Show that any sequence that satisfies Eq. (1.9) with $p > 1$ for some $M > 0$ also satisfies Eq. (1.8).

2. Create a table that compares the errors for methods that are convergent of orders $p = 1, 2$, and 3. Assume $M = .5$ and $e_0 = .5$ in each case, and use Eq. (1.10). How much better is an order 3 method than an order 2 method?

3. Verify that Aitken's Δ^2 process accelerates the convergence of the sequence $x_k = 1/k^2$. Note, you must first verify that x_k converges linearly to zero.

4. Verify experimentally that the secant method has order of

convergence $(1 + \sqrt{5})/2 \doteq 1.618$ (that is, that roughly 60% more accurate significant figures are gained at each iteration in the limit).

5. **a.** Show that if $x^* = g(x^*)$ and $g'(x^*) = g''(x^*) = 0$, then the corresponding fixed point iteration is convergent of order at least 3.

   b. A function $f(x)$ is said to have a zero of multiplicity m at x^* if $f(x^*) = f'(x^*) = \cdots = f^{(m-1)}(x^*) = 0$ but $f^{(m)}(x^*) \neq 0$. Show that if $m > 1$, then Newton's method converges linearly, and give the asymptotic error constant.

MATLAB 1.4

The time has come to learn how to write programs in MATLAB. You may use any text editor or MATLAB's edit command (which launches the MATLAB editor). Using the MATLAB editor is certainly easiest unless you have a strong preference for some other editor. If you are using Windows, be sure that the editor you use saves your program as a plain text file.

Let's start with a very simple program that performs one step from the inverse linear interpolation method: Finding the x-intercept. Our program will input two pairs of points

(x_0, y_0), (x_1, y_1) and return the x-intercept of the interpolated line. Type the following program in your editor:

```
function x=intercept(x0,y0,x1,y1)
%INTERCEPT   Return x-intercept of line
x=x1-y1*(x1-x0)/(y1-y0);
```

Save this as `intercept.m`. Now enter:

```
» intercept(-1,2,3,1)
```

The x-intercept of the line connecting $(-1, 2)$ and $(3, 1)$ is produced. If you receive the error message:

```
??? Undefined function or variable intercept.
```

type `path` and make sure that you stored your file in one of the listed directories and that the file extension is `.m`.

Let's look at this simple program. The use of `function` in the first line lets MATLAB know that this is a function. The syntax is `function <output argument(s)>=<function_name>(<input argument(s)>)`. User-defined MATLAB functions are text files with the `.m` extension.

Anything following the percentage sign `%` is considered to be a comment. Type `help intercept`; MATLAB displays the first comment block of this program. Your program has been assimilated by the `help` command. Following the comment line are the MATLAB commands that compute the output argument. Notice that no end-of-program command is needed.

Let's add an error check. We need `x0` and `x1` to be distinct, `y0` and `y1` to be distinct, and `y0*y1` to be negative. Edit your program to read:

```
function x=intercept(x0,y0,x1,y1)
%INTERCEPT   Return x-intercept of line
if (x1==x0), error('Invalid x data'),end
if (y1==y0), error('No intercept'),end
if (y1*y0>=0), error('Not a bracket'),end
x=x1-y1*(x1-x0)/(y1-y0);
```

The first `if-end` pair (see `help if` for more details) prints an error message if the x-values are equal; MATLAB uses a double equals sign (`==`) to test for equality. The second `if-end` pair prints an error message if the y-values are equal. (In both of these cases it would be better to test for near equality, not just exact equality.) The third `if-end` pair prints an error message if the y-values are not of opposite sign; the pair of symbols `>=` tests if $y_1 y_0 \geq 0$. (See `help relop` for more information on the relational operators.) The `error` command prints the indicated error message and terminates execution of the program. (To simply print a message or variable, use the `disp` command, e.g., `disp('hello world')` or `disp(x)`.) Choose data to make each message appear, and check that your program behaves as intended.

This program may now be used like any other MATLAB function, which is an important aspect of MATLAB programming. For example,

```
» z=cos(intercept(-1,log(1/2),3,log(5)))^2
```

is perfectly valid. This is a big deal; MATLAB does not distinguish between your programs and its own. In fact, many MATLAB-provided functions are just MATLAB programs themselves. Enter:

```
» type fzero
```

to see the code for the MATLAB root-finding command. (Some functions are built in and can't be typed.) Looking at the code of such functions is a good way to learn MATLAB programming techniques and tricks.

If you edit a program (M-file) after you have run it, you may need to enter the command `clear functions` to see your changes take effect. Although MATLAB programs are interpreted, not compiled, when you first run a program, it pre-compiles that program for future use in that session. The command `clear functions` clears all pre-compiled functions so that the next time a program is run it will be checked (and pre-compiled) again. If you are editing a program and your changes don't seem to be having any effect, try clearing all functions.

The `if-end` pairs can be spread out over several lines, as can a `for-end` loop. (There is also a `while` command for use in a `while-end` loop.) That is, we may rewrite our function as:

```
function x=intercept(x0,y0,x1,y1)
%INTERCEPT    Return x-intercept of line
if (x1==x0)
    error('Invalid x data')
end
if (y1==y0)
    error('No intercept')
end
if (y1*y0>=0)
    error('Not a bracket')
end
x=x1-y1*(x1-x0)/(y1-y0);
```

Make the changes above and retest your program. In many cases formatting the constructs like this makes the program more readable. The MATLAB editor will suggest such formatting automatically.

Here's another sample MATLAB program:

```
function x=secant(f,x0,x1,N)
%SECANT    Perform N iterations of the secant method on
%          the inline function f, starting from x0, x1.
if (N<1), error('N must be at least 1'),end
```

```
for i=1:N,
  y0=feval(f,x0);y1=feval(f,x1);
  xnew=intercept(x0,y0,x1,y1);
  x0=x1;x1=xnew;
end
x=xnew;
```

Most of the error checking is performed in `intercept.m` (in fact, the bracket check could be removed from it). See `help colon` for information on what will happen if N is not an integer; see `help punct` for information on other punctuation symbols. Enter the program, save it, and test it.

For a cautionary note on testing for exact equality on finite precision machines, enter:

```
» 1-.8
» 1-.8==.2
» .2-(1-.8)
```

The test for equality fails due to the effects of finite precision arithmetic. One reason is that, although the rational number .2 has a terminating expansion in base 10, it has a nonterminating expansion in base 2. We'll discuss these issues in more depth throughout the text, but for now we note that a test for equality of quantities x_1, x_2 that are not known to be integers should usually be implemented in the form $|x_1 - x_2| < \tau$ for some small positive tolerance τ (possibly dependent on the size of x_1 or x_2).

The MATLAB package has some very sophisticated capabilities, although we don't get to all of them in this text. Learning MATLAB is important and useful for scientific computing, but it is still secondary to the goal of learning numerical analysis.

To explore some of MATLAB's other capabilities, enter:

```
» intro
```

Use the `help` command to learn more about these capabilities.

ADDITIONAL PROBLEMS 1.4

6. Justify the statement that if the relative error ρ in an approximation is about 10^{-k} then the approximation is correct to about k decimal places.

7. Show that the sequence $x_k = 2^{-2^k}$ converges to zero with order of convergence 2.

8. Householder's method

$$x_{k+1} = x_k - \frac{f(x_k)}{f'(x_k)}\left(1 + \frac{f(x_k)f''(x_k)}{2[f'(x_k)]^2}\right)$$

for $f(x) = 0$ has order of convergence 3 (**cubic convergence**) under appropriate assumptions on $f(x)$. Apply it to the functions $f(x) = 5x^7 + 2x - 1$ and $g(x) = 1/x^3 - 10$; compare it to Newton's method for these functions.

9. a. Show that if $f(x)$ has a zero x^* of multiplicity m, then $f(x) = (x - x^*)^m g(x)$ for $x \neq x^*$, where $g(x^*)$ is nonzero.

  b. Show that if $m > 1$, then the method

$$x_{k+1} = x_k - \frac{mf(x_k)}{f'(x_k)}$$

converges quadratically. (This is one of many methods known as **Schroder's method.**)

  c. Show that $f(x)/f'(x)$ has only simple roots. Write the Newton's method iteration for $f(x)/f'(x)$. What additional assumptions on f are needed?

10. If $x_k \to x^*$ and

$$\lim_{k\to\infty} \frac{|x_{k+1} - x^*|}{|x_k - x^*|} = 1,$$

then we say that the convergence is **sublinear.** Show that $x_k = 1/k$ converges sublinearly to zero.

11. a. Use Newton's method to find all real roots of

$$x^3 - 5.06x^2 - 10.392x + 46.2 = 0$$

to within an absolute error of no more than 10^{-6}, as estimated by Eq. (1.6).

b. Use Newton's method to find all real roots of

$$x^3 - 5.06x^2 - 10.392x + 46.2 = 0$$

to within a relative error of no more than 10^{-6}, as estimated by Eq. (1.6).

c. Use Newton's method to find all real roots of

$$x^3 - 1100x^2 + 100220x - 20000 = 0$$

to within an absolute error of no more than 10^{-6}, as estimated by Eq. (1.6).

d. Use Newton's method to find all real roots of

$$x^3 - 1100x^2 + 100220x - 20000 = 0$$

to within a relative error of no more than 10^{-6}, as estimated by Eq. (1.6).

12. a. What is the rate (not order) of convergence of $(\cos(1/n) - 1)/(1/n)$ to zero as $n \to \infty$?

b. What is the rate of convergence of $2/n^3$ to zero as $n \to \infty$? What is its order of convergence?

c. Show by example that a sequence can be superlinear but still not converge of order p for any $p > 1$.

13. Assume that the secant method has a well-defined order of convergence and that there is an M such that $|x_{k+1} - x^*| \approx M|x_k - x^*||x_{k-1} - x^*|$ for large k. Reason that the secant method has order of convergence $(1 + \sqrt{5})/2$. (The secant method is an example of a two-point iteration, dependent on two previous values, and so is more difficult to analyze than the one-point iterations we have been considering.)

14. The **Lanchester (combat) model** for two opposing military forces is, in its simplest form, given by $x' = -ay$, $y' = -bx$, where $x(t)$ and $y(t)$ are the sizes of the forces involved (e.g., numbers of combatants, tanks, or planes). The constants a and b measure the fighting effectiveness of the forces. The Lanchester model and variations of it are used by the military for wargaming simulations.

a. Use the chain rule to find a formula for dy/dx, and then solve it to show that $a(y^2 - y_0^2) = b(x^2 - x_0^2)$ for all $t \geq 0$. This is the **Lanchester square-law model.**

b. Show that $d^2y/dt^2 - aby = 0$, and use it to solve for $y(t) = y_0 \cosh(\sqrt{abt}) - x_0\sqrt{b/a} \sinh(\sqrt{abt})$. Do the same for $x(t)$.

c. Take $a = 0.15$, $b = 0.1$. For the initial conditions $(x_0, y_0) = (10000, 9000)$, $(x_0, y_0) = (10000, 8166)$, and $(x_0, y_0) = (10000, 5000)$, use Newton's method to determine the time, if any, at which the opposing forces are of equal strengths. What are those strengths? How long does each battle last, and who wins?

d. Take $a = 0.144$, $b = 0.1$. For the initial conditions $(x_0, y_0) = (12000, 10000)$, use Newton's method to determine the time, if any, at which the opposing forces are of equal strengths. How long does the battle last, and who wins?

15. a. Halley's method is

$$x_{k+1} = H_f(x_k) = x_k - \frac{2f(x_k)f'(x_k)}{2(f'(x_k))^2 - f(x_k)f''(x_k)}.$$

Show that Halley's method has order of convergence 3 for simple zeroes by showing that $H'_f(x_k)$ and $H''_f(x_k)$ vanish at the zero.

b. Apply Halley's method to $f(x) = 5x^7 + 2x - 1$ and $g(x) = 1/x^3 - 10$.

1.5 Variants of Newton's Method

Advantages of Newton's Method

Although we could construct a method with order of convergence higher than that of Newton's method, it's usually pointless to do so. Once Newton's method gets a few decimal places accuracy, it takes only a small number of additional iterations to get all the accuracy one might need. Of course, it could take a long time for the method to get this close to the solution. Even if the asymptotic error constant M is large, Newton's method is still as fast as one is likely to need a method to be to solve nonlinear equations in one variable in a practical situation.

However, note that bisection, inverse linear interpolation, and the secant method require us to compute a single new value of $f(x)$ at each iteration, whereas Newton's method requires both a new value of $f(x)$ and a new value of $f'(x)$. Typically the computation of $f(x)$ (and $f'(x)$) is by far the most time-consuming step of any of these methods, and the time required for the other arithmetic operations performed in combining those values is negligible. If this is not the case—if $f(x)$ is cheap (in terms of computation time) to evaluate—then virtually any method will be acceptable. But it is not uncommon for values of $f(x)$ to be computed by *another* program, which may take as much as several minutes to solve an ODE or PDE numerically or to perform a simulation to produce a single value of $f(x)$. When $f(x)$ is expensive to compute, Newton's method might be less attractive than a method that uses more iterations but for which the total number of function evaluations required to achieve a desired tolerance is smaller. Focusing only on the number of iterations, as we have thus far, can be misleading! A method that converges of order 3 or higher typically requires higher-order derivatives and uses more function evaluations per iteration. This means that such a method often is not actually an improvement over Newton's method in terms of run-time, even though it uses fewer iterations. Additionally such methods are usually more difficult to code.

Newton's method has other advantages. For example, if x_0 is complex then Newton's method can converge to complex roots of $f(x) = 0$, which is useful when such roots are desired. One of the biggest advantages of Newton's method, however, is that it generalizes in a natural way to nonlinear *systems* of equations. If we must solve a nonlinear system such as

$$f(x, y) = 0$$

$$g(x, y) = 0$$

for a simultaneous root (x^*, y^*) of f and g, then attempting to bracket it is going to be quite difficult. But Newton's method (using partial derivatives with respect to x and y) works fine. While there are many choices for a one-dimensional (that is, single-variable) zero-finding algorithm, in several dimensions a nonlinear root-finding problem is typically solved by some variant of Newton's method. For this reason we now discuss several such variants. You should bear in mind that the real need for and advantages of these variants are most apparent in the several variables case (discussed in Section. 1.8).

Difficulties with Newton's Method   In this section we address three types of difficulties with Newton's method:

■ It may not be possible to find a formula for $f'(x)$.

■ We may be able to find a formula for $f'(x)$, but it may be too expensive to compute.

■ Newton's method may fail to converge.

Let's start with the case where finding a formula for $f'(x)$ is not feasible. This may be due to the complicated nature of the formula; it may be due to the formula being supplied by the user as input in a computing environment where symbolic differentiation is not available; or it may be because $f(x)$ is measured data or is computed by another program that does not supply derivatives. The last case is very common; for example, when we ask where the solution of a certain differential equation passes through the origin. Then every value of $f(x)$ required by our root-finding algorithm involves a call to a numerical differential equations routine. This routine may supply only the solution, not the derivatives.

The obvious recourse in such a case is to use the secant method. The convergence order of the secant method is $p \doteq 1.6$, so convergence will still be quite rapid. We can request only a single initial guess x_0 from the user and use $x_1 = (1 + \delta)x_0$ (with some small δ) for the second guess.

If we dont't want to use the secant method, we could instead approximate the derivative $f'(x_k)$ by some means. One possibility is to use the approximation

$$f'(x_k) \approx \frac{f(x_k + h) - f(x_k)}{h} \tag{1.11}$$

Finite Differences

for some small $h > 0$. This is said to be a **finite difference** approximation to $f'(x_k)$, and if we use it in Newton's method the resulting scheme is sometimes called the **finite difference Newton's method** (or **Newton's method with finite differences**[5]). Note that instead of computing $f(x)$ and $f'(x)$ at each iteration, we compute $f(x)$ for two different values of x, which is usually comparable in computational cost to computing $f(x)$ and $f'(x)$.

More generally, we can replace the term $f'(x_k)$ in Newton's method by any approximate slope s_k, giving the method

$$x_{k+1} = x_k - \frac{f(x_k)}{s_k}$$

which is called a **quasi-Newton method.** The secant method approximates the slope using

$$s_k = \frac{f(x_k) - f(x_{k-1})}{x_k - x_{k-1}},$$

and the finite difference Newton's method uses

$$s_k = \frac{f(x_k + h) - f(x_k)}{h}.$$

(More generally we could let $h = h_k$ in the finite difference Newton's method, ideally choosing h_k so that $s_k \to f'(x^*)$ as $k \to \infty$. Note how the secant method achieves this automatically when it is convergent.) The finite difference approach is widely used.

Constant-slope Newton's Method

Another way to handle the lack of a formula for $f'(x)$ is to use the **constant-slope Newton's method,** which takes

$$s_k = c$$

for some constant c. In Problem 4 you will be asked to show that, for appropriate choices of c, this gives linear convergence; the closer c is to $f'(x^*)$, the more rapid the convergence near the zero.

In cases where it is possible to find a formula for (or otherwise compute values of) $f'(x)$ but the computations are so time consuming that it isn't practical to compute it at every iteration, once again we can use a quasi-Newton method such as the secant method, the finite difference Newton's method, or the constant-slope Newton's method. However,

---

[5] Finite differences are considered in more detail in Section 6.1.

in these cases it may be reasonable to compute values of $f'(x)$ every several iterations. A common approach is to use the constant-slope Newton's method with c initially taken to be $f'(x_0)$, and then after two to five iterations to recompute $c = f'(x_k)$ and use this value for the next two to five iterations, and so on. This approach attempts to strike a compromise between the benefits of having an accurate slope and the cost of computing it.

There are much more sophisticated quasi-Newton methods for root-finding in several dimensions, but let us look at the final difficulty mentioned previously: Failure of Newton's method to converge. One reason this can happen is because Newton's method is taking steps that are too large and so overshoots the root. For example, in using Newton's method on

$$f(x) = \frac{1}{x - 7}$$

to approximate $1/7$, we find

$$N_f(x) = x - \frac{(1/x - 7)}{(-1/x^2)}$$

$$= x + x - 7x^2$$

$$= 2x - 7x^2$$

and choosing $x_0 = 1$ gives

$$x_1 = -5$$

$$x_2 = -185$$

$$x_3 = -239945$$

and the method is clearly failing (see Fig. 1.16). We know that if we start sufficiently close to the answer we'll get the answer, but as we generally don't know the answer, this fact may not be helpful. (The difficulty of generating a good initial guess so as to get convergence is a common complaint in practice; most strategies for addressing it are heuristic, often developed case-by-case. A more soundly based approach is discussed in Section 7.2.) The **damped Newton's method** tries to "slow down" Newton's method by using a damping factor μ_k to reduce the size of the step taken from the current point. That is, we use

Damping

$$x_{k+1} = x_k - \mu_k \frac{f(x_k)}{f'(x_k)} \tag{1.12}$$

where $0 < \mu_k \le 1$ is a constant (for each k), and $\mu_k \to 1$ as $k \to \infty$ (so that the method is simply Newton's method near the root). In the case shown in Figure 1.16, we have $x_0 = 1$ and

$$N_f(x_k) = x_k - \mu_k \frac{1/x_k - 7}{-1/x_k^2}$$

$$= x_k + \mu_k(x_k - 7x_k^2)$$

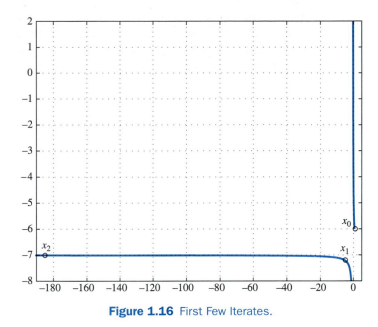

Figure 1.16 First Few Iterates.

for some choice of damping sequence μ_k. How do we choose the damping sequence? We generally want $|f(x_{k+1})| < |f(x_k)|$. If the method is converging, then eventually the usual Newton's method behavior should kick in and we will be able to take $\mu_k = 1$ for k sufficiently large.

In practice we often must experiment until a suitable choice of damping sequence is found. (In rare circumstances theory guides us.) If we have to solve this problem only once, then experimenting to find a damping sequence is probably wasteful; but if this technique is to be used to implement division on a high-performance computer, then this is a design problem, and time spent on it may be time well-invested. (Actually, for the division problem, there is a rule that always generates a suitable initial guess.) It is common in practice to know that we will frequently be solving problems from a narrowly defined class of very similar problems. A heuristic such as a damping rule that we find for one such problem often works well for the others in that class. In such a case, time spent experimenting is well invested. For example, this might be a small part of a numerical wind tunnel package for aircraft design, and every small proposed change in the design of the aircraft results in a similar but different problem. In such a case a heuristically determined damping rule is often good for a wide range of inputs. In such circumstances, we essentially have to solve the problem to figure out how to solve the problem—and other problems very close to it.

Example 1.5.1   Let's reconsider the problem of using Newton's method on $f(x) = 1/x - 7$ to approximate $1/7$. We'll use the same $x_0 = 1$, but we'll use the damping sequence (found by trial and error) $\mu_0 = 0.1$, $\mu_1 = 0.2$, $\mu_2 = 0.3$, $\ldots$ with $\mu_k = 1$ for $k \geq 9$.

This gives:

$$x_1 = x_0 + \mu_0(x_0 - 7x_0^2)$$
$$= 1 + 0.1(1 - 7(1^2))$$
$$= 0.4000$$
$$x_2 = 0.2560$$
$$x_3 = 0.1952$$
$$x_4 = 0.1666$$
$$x_5 = 0.1528.$$

The method certainly appears to be converging to $1/7 \doteq 0.1429$; in fact, after the first few iterations the damping is no longer helping us but rather is slowing us down (see Fig. 1.17.) Nonetheless damping the size of the step taken by Newton's method has had a beneficial effect: It turns a divergent sequence into a convergent sequence. ∎

Damping is an important strategy in a number of numerical methods, though the damped Newton's method is of much greater interest when dealing with problems in several variables. In the multivariable case a parameter such as μ_k in Eq. (1.12) is very commonly used in Newton's method, either to provide damping or to ensure that steps are not too small.

Mixing Methods   Another way to address the possibility that Newton's method may diverge is to use a *mixed method* that combines Newton's method with a bracketing method. Suppose we

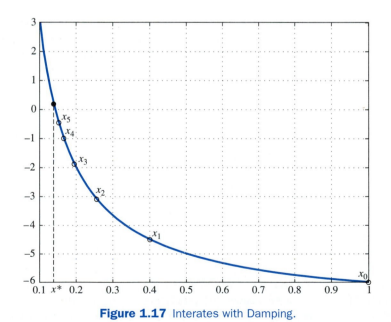

Figure 1.17 Interates with Damping.

are using the bisection method to solve a problem because of its guaranteed convergence. After we find the zero to the desired tolerance, it would be sensible to do several Newton's method iterations on it. If the bracket is small enough, then we are almost certainly in the range where Newton's method must converge and will double the number of correct figures at each iteration; since any number in the bracket is an estimate good to within the tolerance, we could use Newton's method and take its result as our best estimate if it stays within the bracket, and simply use the midpoint of the bracket if Newton's method fails.

Example 1.5.2 Consider finding the positive root of $x^6 - 10 = 0$. A plot suggests that the root is at roughly 1.5, and that $[1.4, 1.5]$ is a bracket. Indeed, if $f(x) = x^6 - 10$, then $f(1.4) = 1.4^6 - 10 = -2.4705$, $f(1.5) = 1.5^6 - 10 = 1.3906$. Two iterations of bisection gives $f(1.45) = 1.45^6 - 10 = -.7059$ (new bracket is $[1.45, 1.5]$), $f(1.475) = 1.475^6 - 10 = .2980$ (new bracket is $[1.45, 1.475]$). Now, Newton's method for this function is

$$x_{k+1} = x_k - \frac{x_k^6 - 10}{6x_k^5} = \frac{5}{6}x_k + \frac{5}{3}x_k^{-5}.$$

Taking $x_0 = 1.4625$ gives

$$x_1 = \frac{5}{6}x_0 + \frac{5}{3}x_0^{-5}$$
$$= 1.4678$$
$$x_2 = 1.4678,$$

and further iterates do not change this value. (This is the fixed point property.) Since it is in the bracket, we take it as the best estimate of the location of the root; the midpoint 1.4625 has a smaller worst-case error, but the value from Newton's method is almost certainly a better estimate. ∎

Safeguarded Newton's Method

We can do better than simply improving an estimate made by the slow but steady bisection method. We can combine Newton's method with bisection from the start. There are many ways to do this, sometimes called **modified, safeguarded,** or **globalized Newton's methods,** but we describe only one such approach. Suppose we have an initial bracket $[x_0, x_1]$ of a zero of a differentiable function f. Rather than use bisection or inverse linear interpolation, we might compute the Newton's method approximation of the zero

$$x_{new} = x_1 - \frac{f(x_1)}{f'(x_1)}$$

using either x_0 or x_1 as the initial point. If x_{new} is in the bracket, we use either $[x_0, x_{new}]$ or $[x_{new}, x_1]$, whichever is a bracket, as the new bracket. If x_{new} does not lie in $[x_0, x_1]$, we take a bisection step. Hence at each iteration we take either a Newton step—which should give excellent results in the limit—or a bisection step, which gives at least a

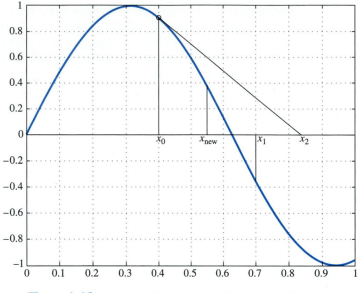

Figure 1.18 Newton's Method Goes Outside the Bracket.

50% reduction in the bracket size (see Fig. 1.18). Typically most steps are Newton steps after the first few iterations. Notice that if the approach to the zero is one-sided, the bracket width may not go to zero, so we must use additional convergence criteria (say, that successive values of x_{new} are very close together).

Example 1.5.3 Consider again the problem of finding the positive root of $x^6 - 10 = 0$, for which [1.4, 1.5] is a bracket. We'll use the globalized Newton's method. From Example 1.5.2, Newton's method for this function is

$$x_{k+1} = \frac{5}{6}x_k + \frac{5}{3}x_k^{-5}.$$

Taking $x_0 = 1.5$, the first Newton's step is

$$x_1 = \frac{5}{6}x_0 + \frac{5}{3}x_0^{-5} = 1.4695,$$

which is in the bracket; since $f(1.4695) \doteq 0.0697$, the new bracket is [1.4, 1.4695]. The next step is

$$x_2 = \frac{5}{6}x_1 + \frac{5}{3}x_1^{-5} = 1.4678.$$

(We could have used 1.4 as the starting point, but 1.4695 is almost certainly a better estimate as it was found by Newton's method.) This is in the bracket, and $f(1.4678) \doteq 2.9938E - 5$, so the new bracket is [1.4, 1.4678]. We are converging rapidly to the root, but our bracket is not shrinking swiftly because our approach is one-sided. This is not a problem as long as width of the bracket is not our only convergence criterion. ∎

In the worst possible case, this globalized method repeatedly wastes time computing x_{new} by Newton's method only to take a bisection step, but even in that case we will be slowly converging to a zero of the function. In the best possible case it is essentially the same as Newton's method with the added guarantee of a bracket. This is certainly superior to damping,[6] but unlike damping it requires an initial bracket.

In this section, we've looked at a number of variants of Newton's method: the quasi-Newton methods (finite differences, secant, constant-slope) for handling the derivative; the damped Newton's method for preventing divergence; and the globalized Newton's method for insuring convergence. They highlight the difficulties that are encountered in working with the function f and the difficulty of finding a sufficiently good initial guess. Each has its place in practice, and each represents an idea that can be applied to other numerical methods as well.

PROBLEMS 1.5

1. Perform three iterations of the finite difference Newton's method with $h = 0.1$ to approximate the sole real root of $5x^7 + 2x - 1 = 0$. Repeat with $h = 0.01$ and the same initial guess.

2. The secant method has order of convergence $p \doteq 1.6$ if it is working well; the finite difference Newton's method has order of convergence $p \approx 2$. If function evaluations are expensive, which is preferable for one-dimensional root-finding? What about the globalized Newton's method?

3. **a.** Use the globalized Newton's method to approximate a zero of $f(x) = 1/x^3 - 10$ to three decimal places.

   b. Draw the graphs of several functions for which Newton's method would fail to converge. Does the globalized Newton's method handle all of these cases adequately?

4. Prove that the constant-slope Newton's method converges linearly by treating it as a fixed point iteration. What are the restrictions, if any, on the slope c? What value of c gives superlinear convergence?

5. Write a MATLAB program that performs the constant-slope Newton's method. Input the function, slope, and initial guess and return the estimate of the root. Test it on several functions.

MATLAB 1.5

All of our results assume infinite-precision arithmetic, but the methods will be implemented on finite-precision machines. There are analytical methods for studying the effects of this, which we must discuss,[7] but for now we'll only investigate a danger lurking in the secant method and the finite difference Newton's method. Consider the latter algorithm, written as a quasi-Newton method $x_{k+1} = x_k - f(x_k)/s_k$, where $s_k = (f(x_k + h) - f(x_k))/h$ for some small $h > 0$ (from Eq.(1.11)). Let's try

---

[6] In practice damping is used for certain types of multivariable problems, as needed, while the safeguarded method described here is used to make robust single-variable root-finding routines.

[7] Some authors *define* numerical analysis as the study of roundoff errors; it's certainly a crucial part of the subject.

approximating the derivative of $f(x) = \ln(x)$ at $x = 1$ in this way; of course, $f'(x) = 1/x$ so $f'(1) = 1$. Enter:

```
» x=1;h=.1;
» (log(x+h)-log(x))/h
```

We get 0.9531, which is not unreasonable for this size h. Enter:

```
» h=10.^(-(1:20))
```

to create a vector of the values $10^{-1}, 10^{-2}, \ldots, 10^{-20}$. (Note that in forming the vector $1{:}1{:}20$, the step size may be omitted if it is 1.) Enter:

```
» (log(x+h)-log(x))./h
```

where the period ensures that the division is done entry by entry. The MATLAB response is:

```
ans =
 Columns 1 through 7
 0.9531 0.9950 0.9995 1.0000 1.0000 1.0000 1.0000
 Columns 8 through 14
 1.0000 1.0000 1.0000 1.0000 1.0001 0.9992 0.9992
 Columns 15 through 20
 1.1102 0 0 0 0 0
```

These are the estimates of the derivative for the corresponding values of h.

Let's plot the errors. Enter:

```
» plot(h,abs(ans-1)),grid
```

The plot is a bit rough, but from the plot and from inspection of the result `ans` of the experiment we see that the error decreases for a while, as expected, but starting from about $h = 10^{-12}$ it begins growing again.

We discuss finite differences further in Section. 6.1. For now we point out that there are two things going wrong in the above calculation when h is small: subtraction of nearly equal numbers in the numerator and division by a small number. These cause problems because a computer represents numbers with only finitely many bits,[8] which in the case of MATLAB corresponds to fifteen or sixteen decimal digits. Enter:

```
» format long
» pi
ans =
 3.14159265358979
```

By default, MATLAB works in double precision, meaning that about sixteen digits accuracy is available. (The exponent is handled separately, so the same number of digits is available over many orders of magnitude; see Section 1.7.) In particular, there is a

---

[8] In the widely used IEEE standard arithmetic, 32 bits are used in single precision (1 sign bit, 8 exponent, 23 mantissa), and 64 bits are used in double precision (1 sign bit, 11 exponent, 52 mantissa).

largest and a smallest positive real number on the machine. Enter:

```
» realmax
» realmin
```

to see them.[9] Anything larger than the result of `realmax` is set to `Inf`, a special variable for "machine infinity" (we say the operation **overflows**), and anything smaller than the smallest positive floating point number is set to zero (we say it **underflows** to zero). The `Inf` variable behaves as expected; enter:

```
» 1/0
» exp(1000)
» inf*2
» inf-inf
```

The result of the last operation is `NaN` ("not a number") and is another special variable produced under certain circumstances. See `help NaN` for further information.

There are necessarily only finitely many machine numbers, which we must use to model the entire real line. Enter:

```
» eps
» 1+eps
» ans==1              %Does this equal 1?
» 1+eps/2
» ans==1
» (1+eps/2)+eps/2
» ans==1
» 1+(eps/2+eps/2)     %Computer addition is not associative.
» ans==1
```

The value `eps` is the distance from 1 to the next largest machine number and may vary from machine to machine. The distance between machine numbers is not constant; the gap between numbers is larger when the numbers are larger.

The value of `eps` is important as it determines what a small error is on the particular machine. The effects of `eps` can be seen; enter:

```
» x=1;for i=1:100;x=x+eps;end;x
» x=1;for i=1:100;x=x+eps/2;end;x
```

Since the spacing between adjacent machine numbers is smaller when the numbers are smaller and larger when the numbers are larger, you will get different results if you try the above experiment with a different initial x; try it!

Even evaluating a function can be subject to error. Given a function $f(x)$, we may wish to evaluate it at some point x_0. On the machine it may well be that x_0 cannot be represented exactly, however, and so we actually will evaluate $f(x_0 + \epsilon)$ for some small ϵ (not necessarily the machine epsilon ϵ_M). Assuming that f is a differentiable function that can be evaluated exactly, we expect to make an error $|f(x_0 + \epsilon) - f(x_0)| = \epsilon |f'(\zeta)|$

---

[9] Actually `realmin` is the smallest *normalized* floating point number; it is not the smallest number representable. See Section 1.7.

for some ζ lying between x_0 and $x_0 + \epsilon$ (by the Mean Value Theorem). Note that the larger the derivative (rate of change) of f, the larger the expected error. For example, we expect that evaluating $\sin(x)$ gives more accurate results for x near $\pi/2$ (where the derivative is zero) than for x near 0, where the derivative is 1. Enter:

```
» err=1E-10;
» x1=.1;x2=pi/2;
» abs(sin(x1+err)-sin(x1))
» abs(sin(x2+err)-sin(x2))
```

As expected, the error is smaller near the point where the derivative of the function is smaller. Since the function's values are changing less rapidly at such a point, an error in the argument has less effect at such a point. (We sidestep for now the question of how the computer finds values of the sine function and whether that affects our reasoning.) Enter:

```
» err=1E-6;
» abs(sin(x1+err)-sin(x1))
» abs(sin(x2+err)-sin(x2))
```

to see this effect more clearly. (Recall that $\sin(x) \approx x$ for x near zero and $\sin(x) \approx 1 - (x - \pi/2)^2 \approx 1$ for x near $\pi/2$.) Compare the relative errors in this case also.

We'll discuss the effects of finite-precision arithmetic and roundoff error in greater detail in Section 1.7. For now we note once again that computer arithmetic differs from standard arithmetic in several important respects.

ADDITIONAL PROBLEMS 1.5

6. a. Show that Newton's method for $f(x) = 1/x - 10$ fails to converge if $x_0 = 10$. Give a sketch that demonstrates why this happens.

    b. Find a damping sequence that forces the damped Newton's method to converge for this function and initial guess.

    c. Does your damping sequence work if $x_0 = 100$?

7. Write a complete algorithm (pseudocode) for a safeguarded secant method.

8. Approximate the derivatives of $\sin(x)$, $\cos(x)$, and $\exp(x)$ at $x = 1.5$ by finite differences with $h = 10^{-k}$, $k = 1, 2, \ldots, 20$. What value of h gives the smallest error?

9. Approximate the derivatives of $\ln(x)$, $\cosh(x)$, and x^3 at $x = 1.5$ by finite differences with $h = 10^{-k}$, $k = 1, 2, \ldots, 20$. What value of h gives the smallest error?

10. a. Consider the convergence theorem for Newton's method, which guarantees convergence in some interval about a simple root (in effect, a bracket), and the safeguarded Newton's method, which requires a bracket. We have stated that Newton's method and the secant method may be used when a bracket cannot be found, but the convergence theorem and the safeguarded methods seem to indicate that in some sense a bracket is still needed. Comment on the importance of brackets in root-finding.

    b. Why is it preferable to use bisection rather than inverse linear interpolation in the globalized Newton's method?

11. Write a MATLAB program that inputs a function and its derivative (both as inline functions), a bracket of a zero of the function, and a positive integer N, and that performs N iterations of the globalized Newton's method. Demonstrate your program on at least three root-finding problems.

12. Use the constant-slope Newton's method to approximate a solution of $x^3 - 10 = 0$. Justify your choice of slope.

13. a. Use the constant-slope Newton's method to approximate a zero of $f(x) = e^{2x} - 2x^3 - 12$ to six decimal places. Use $f'(x_0)$ as the constant slope.

b. Use the constant-slope Newton's method to approximate a zero of $f(x) = 1/x^3 - 10$ to six decimal places, but update your slope every five iterations; that is, use $f'(x_0)$ as the initial constant slope, then $f'(x_5)$ when it becomes available, then $f'(x_{10})$ (if needed), and so on.

c. Repeat part c, but update every three iterations.

d. Compare your results to the standard Newton's method for this problem.

e. (Refer to Problem 4.) One way to improve the efficiency of this mixed Newton's method/constant-slope Newton's method strategy is to switch to a pure constant-slope Newton's method when the method is sufficiently near the root. The motivation is that at that point the constant slope is very close to the true slope at the root x^*. One way to implement this approach is to consider the method as a fixed point iteration $x_{k+1} = g(x_k) = x_k - f(x_k)/c$ and monitor the size of $g'(x_k)$; when it is (and stays) sufficiently small, the convergence is linear with ratio $|g'(x_k)|$. If $|g'(x_k)|$ is very small, then it may not be worthwhile to evaluate $f'(x)$ to gain quadratic convergence. Discuss this method and suggest a specific strategy for switching to the pure constant-slope Newton's method.

14. The Schrödinger wave equation, as used in the Kronig-Penney model of the movement of electrons in the band theory of solids, has solutions only when $f(\alpha a) = P \operatorname{sinc}(\alpha a) + \cos(\alpha a)$ lies in $[-1, 1]$, where $\alpha = \sqrt{2mE/\hbar^2}$, $P = mV_0 ba/\hbar^2$, $b > 0$ is the width of potential wells in the solid (assumed to be in the form of a square wave), $V_0 > 0$ is their height, and $a > 0$ is the period of the potential of the crystal lattice of the solid. (The sinc function is defined by $\operatorname{sinc}(x) = \sin(x)/x$, with $\operatorname{sinc}(0) = 1$.) Here m is the mass of an electron and $E > 0$ is the energy of the electron; $\hbar = h/2\pi$ where h is Planck's constant.

a. Plot $f(x)$ vs. x for $P = 100$.

b. What value of αa gives a solution if $P = 100$ and we require that $f(\alpha a) = 0.5$? Use the finite difference Newton's method.

c. If $a = 1 \text{ Å} = 10^{-10} m$, what is the energy of the electron in this case?

15. a. Let $f(x) = x^8$. If $x_k = 1/k$, how large must k be to ensure that $f(x_k) < 10^{-6}$? How large must k be to ensure that $x_k < 10^{-6}$? What does this imply for a test for convergence based on $f(x_k) \approx 0$?

b. What happens if you apply Newton's method to $f(x) = e^{-2x}$ and test for convergence based on $|f(x_k)| < \tau$ for some tolerance $\tau > 0$?

c. Show by example that $|f(x_k)|$ being small does not imply that $|x_k - x^*|$ will be small. Give an explicit function and values of x_k, $|f(x_k)|$, and x^*.

1.6   Brent's Method

All of the Newton's method variants require either that the derivative of f be known or that it be approximated. This is not always convenient. Let us return to the idea of (inverse) linear interpolation, where we started with a bracket $[a, b]$ of a zero of f and estimated the location of that zero as the x-intercept of the line determined by those two points. If we choose a third point c somewhere in the bracket, we can interpolate a quadratic to the function and use the zero of the quadratic as an estimate of the zero of the function. This idea is known as **quadratic interpolation** (see Fig. 1.19).

Quadratic
Interpolation
More specifically, suppose that f is continuous on the interval $[x_0, x_2]$ and that $[x_0, x_2]$ brackets a zero of f. Pick some point x_1 in (x_0, x_2), giving a triplet of points $[x_0, x_1, x_2]$. We seek a quadratic polynomial that interpolates $f(x)$ at these three points. Write the quadratic as $Q(x) = \alpha(x - x_2)^2 + \beta(x - x_2) + \gamma$; then we want

$$f(x_0) = \alpha(x_0 - x_2)^2 + \beta(x_0 - x_2) + \gamma$$
$$f(x_1) = \alpha(x_1 - x_2)^2 + \beta(x_1 - x_2) + \gamma$$
$$f(x_2) = \alpha(x_2 - x_2)^2 + \beta(x_2 - x_2) + \gamma$$
$$= \gamma$$

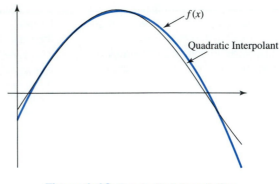

Figure 1.19 Quadratic Interpolation.

so $\gamma = f(x_2)$. (This is one advantage of writing the quadratic in the form we chose; another is discussed in Section 4.1.) Since the remaining unknowns are α and β, we may write this as the linear system

$$\begin{pmatrix} (x_0 - x_2)^2 & (x_0 - x_2) \\ (x_1 - x_2)^2 & (x_1 - x_2) \end{pmatrix} \begin{pmatrix} \alpha \\ \beta \end{pmatrix} = \begin{pmatrix} f(x_0) - f(x_2) \\ f(x_1) - f(x_2) \end{pmatrix}.$$

There is a unique solution of this system, given by

$$\alpha = \frac{(x_1 - x_2)(f(x_0) - f(x_2)) - (x_0 - x_2)(f(x_1) - f(x_2))}{(x_0 - x_1)(x_1 - x_2)(x_0 - x_2)}$$

$$\beta = \frac{(x_0 - x_2)^2(f(x_1) - f(x_2)) - (x_1 - x_2)^2(f(x_0) - f(x_2))}{(x_0 - x_1)(x_1 - x_2)(x_0 - x_2)}$$

(1.13)

and clearly the quadratic must have a root in $[x_0, x_2]$ since $Q(x_0)Q(x_2) = f(x_0)f(x_2)$ < 0. The roots r_1, r_2 of $Q(x)$ may be found by the quadratic formula. Let x_3 be the root that lies in the bracket. Unless $f(x_3)$ is actually zero—which is extremely unlikely in practice—we now have a new, smaller bracket of the zero of f, $[x_0, x_3]$ or $[x_3, x_2]$, and a new triplet of points for the next iteration. This is the method of quadratic interpolation.

Example 1.6.1   Suppose that $f(x) = \sin(x)$. Take $x_0 = -1, x_2 = 2$; then $f(x_0) = -0.8415$ and $f(x_2) = 0.9093$. Hence $[x_0, x_2]$ is a bracket. Choose an x_1, say, $x_1 = 0.5$. The quadratic is

$$Q(x) = \alpha(x - x_2)^2 + \beta(x - x_2) + \gamma$$
$$= \alpha(x - 2)^2 + \beta(x - 2) + 0.9093$$

and

$$\alpha = \frac{(x_1 - x_2)(f(x_0) - f(x_2)) - (x_0 - x_2)(f(x_1) - f(x_2))}{(x_0 - x_1)(x_1 - x_2)(x_0 - x_2)}$$

$$\doteq -.1980$$

$$\beta = \frac{(x_0 - x_2)^2(f(x_1) - f(x_2)) - (x_1 - x_2)^2(f(x_0) - f(x_2))}{(x_0 - x_1)(x_1 - x_2)(x_0 - x_2)}$$

$$\doteq -0.0104$$

so that $Q(x) = -0.1980(x - 2)^2 + -0.0104(x - 2) + 0.9093$. Write this as $Q(z) = -0.1980z^2 + -0.0104z + 0.9093$; by the quadratic formula, the roots are z_1, $z_2 \doteq -2.1694, 2.1169$, so (from $x = 2 + z$) $r_1, r_2 \doteq -0.1694, 4.1169$. The root $r_1 = -0.1694$ is in the bracket, so $x_3 = -0.1694$. Since $f(-0.1694) = \sin(-0.1694) \doteq -0.1686$, the new bracket is $[x_3, x_2]$, and the current triplet of points is $[x_3, x_1, x_2] = [-0.1694, 0.5, 2]$. This reduces the bracket width to

$$2 - (-0.1694) = 2.1694,$$

which is not as good as what we would have had from bisection (which would have reduced the width to 1.5), but is comparable.

Let's do another step. Since x_2 hasn't changed, the form of the quadratic will once again be $Q(x) = \alpha(x - 2)^2 + \beta(x - 2) + 0.9093$, but now x_3 replaces x_0, giving

$$\alpha = \frac{(x_1 - x_2)(f(x_3) - f(x_2)) - (x_3 - x_2)(f(x_1) - f(x_2))}{(x_3 - x_1)(x_1 - x_2)(x_3 - x_2)}$$

$$\doteq -0.3141$$

$$\beta = \frac{(x_3 - x_2)^2(f(x_1) - f(x_2)) - (x_1 - x_2)^2(f(x_3) - f(x_2))}{(x_3 - x_1)(x_1 - x_2)(x_3 - x_2)}$$

$$\doteq -0.1846$$

so that $Q(x) = -0.3141(x - 2)^2 + -0.1846(x - 2) + 0.9093$. Once again, write this as $Q(z) = -0.3141z^2 + -0.1846z + 0.9093$; by the quadratic formula, the roots are $z_1, z_2 \doteq -2.0205, 1.4328$, so (from $x = 2 + z$) $r_1, r_2 \doteq -0.0205, 3.4328$. The root $r_1 = -0.0205$ is in the bracket, and so $x_4 = -0.0205$. Since $f(-0.0205) = \sin(-0.0205) \doteq -0.0205$ (recall that $\sin(x) \approx x$ for x near 0), the new bracket is $[x_4, x_2]$ and the current triplet of points is $[x_4, x_1, x_2] = [-0.0205, 0.5, 2]$. The new width is

$$2 - (-0.0205) = 2.021$$

which is very little improved over the previous bracket. The method is working, but not rapidly. ∎

Müller's Method

If we do not necessarily start with and maintain a bracket, and we allow extrapolation (as was done in the secant method), using the root of the quadratic that lies closest to x_2, we have a method known as Müller's method. Müller's method is convergent of order approximately 1.84 and can find complex roots from real initial guesses (if the interpolated quadratic has no real roots). This can be advantageous—we can start with a real initial guess, and if the method needs to use complex values to find a solution, it will simply generate them.

Example 1.6.2 Consider again $f(x) = \sin(x)$ with $x_0 = -1, x_1 = 0.5$, and $x_2 = 2$. From Example 1.6.1, the roots of the interpolated quadratic are $r_1, r_2 \doteq -0.1694, 4.1169$. The one closer to x_2 is $r_2 \doteq 4.1169$, so we continue with $x_1 = 0.5$, $x_2 = 2$, and $x_3 = 4.1169$. Since $\sin(x_1) < 0, \sin(x_2) > 0$, and $\sin(x_3) < 0$, the outermost points $[x_1, x_3]$ no longer form a bracket. The quadratic through these points is

$$Q(x) = -0.3061x^2 + 1.0519x + 0.0300$$

(in practice we would expand this polynomial around x_2). The roots are $r_1, r_2 \doteq -0.0283, 3.4645$, and the root nearest the most recent point x_3 is $x_4 = 3.4645$. We now repeat with x_2, x_3, and x_4. In the limit the most recent point x_n should tend to a root, even if the width of the bracket does not go to zero. In this case we seem to be approaching the root π. Indeed, the next quadratic is $Q(x) = 0.0260x^2 + -0.9795x + 2.7645$ (note that the concavity has switched) with roots $r_1, r_2 \doteq 3.0726, 34.6294$ giving $x_5 = 3.0726$, followed by $r_1, r_2 \doteq 3.1383, 8.4680$ giving $x_6 = 3.1383$, followed by $r_1, r_2 \doteq 3.14160, 27.12094$ giving $x_7 \doteq 3.14160$ in good agreement with $\pi \doteq 3.14159$ ($\alpha \doteq 1.2E - 5$). The next iteration gives $x_8 \doteq 3.14159265386786$ with absolute error $2.8E - 10$. The order of convergence of 1.84 is nearly as good as the quadratic convergence of Newton's method. ■

Quadratic interpolation converges superlinearly, as does inverse linear interpolation, though quadratic interpolation is generally faster. When we compare quadratic interpolation to Müller's method and inverse linear interpolation to the secant method, we see that for quadratic interpolation vs. Müller's method and for inverse linear interpolation vs. the secant method, the bracketing method provides guaranteed convergence but giving up that guarantee gives greater speed and makes for easier analysis. For example, we can say exactly what the order of convergence is for Müller's method and the secant method. Quadratic interpolation will generally give rapid convergence to the root nonetheless.

Quadratic interpolation is usally quite fast. After all, if a function is sufficiently differentiable, then a quadratic should be a good fit for it even before we reach a scale so small that the function is approximately linear (by Taylor series reasoning). However, quadratic interpolation can provide poor estimates of the location of the zero if the function is not nearly quadratic on the current bracketing interval.

How can we improve the performance of quadratic interpolation? Once again we look to a mixed method. Suppose that f is continuous on the interval $[x_0, x_2]$ and that $[x_0, x_2]$ brackets a zero of f. We might try a quadratic interpolation step and see if the new bracket is much smaller than the original one. If it is smaller, we believe the quadratic interpolation method is working as expected. If it is not, we might reason that we are in a region where a quadratic model is a poor approximation. Hence on the next step we might try, say, an inverse linear interpolation step instead. If this gives little reduction in the width of the bracket, we might drop down once more and try bisection, which guarantees a 50% reduction in the width of the bracket. That may be enough to force the method into a range where the quadratic *will* be a good fit. We continue to try to use the quadratic interpolant when it seems to be working well, and use various heuristics to decide when to drop down to a simpler method.

In practice little is gained by using the inverse linear interpolation step, so in using a strategy of this sort one generally mixes just quadratic interpolation and bisection: If

Brent's Method   quadratic interpolation gives poor results, then we switch to bisection for a guaranteed improvement. This is **Brent's method** (also called the **Brent-Dekker method**), and there are many ways to implement it. Experience shows that it generally does not pay to switch from quadratic interpolation simply because a single iteration gives poor results; the method may recover. We usually switch only if at least two consecutive iterations give poor reductions in the interval width (or if the average reduction over two or more iterations is poor). Similarly, one might reason that if things are bad enough that the method switched to bisection then it makes sense to do at least two bisection steps in order to move the method away from the uncooperative region. Many of these decisions are a matter of programmer's choice; the programmer tests various heuristics to see which ones seem to work well on the types of problems that will be solved by the program. The key points are that (*i*) dropping the bracketing requirements of inverse linear interpolation and quadratic interpolation, giving the secant and Müller's methods respectively, gives greatly improved speed at the cost of possible failure to converge, and (*ii*) the superlinear methods may be made more robust by adding in a safeguarding strategy based on the (linear) bracketing method of bisection, as in the globalized Newton's method and Brent's method.

Inverse Quadratic Interpolation

We are actually using the term *Brent's method* generically to indicate a class of mixing strategies that maintain a bracket and do not use derivative information. In fact, what might be called the "classical" Brent's method uses **inverse quadratic interpolation;** that is, a quadratic $x = Q(y)$ is used as the interpolant (not $y = Q(x)$ as in quadratic interpolation). The desired x-intercept is then easily found as $x = Q(0)$. The computational benefit of using inverse interpolation in the form $x = P_n(y)$ with some polynomial P_n of degree n is that no matter what degree polynomial is used, finding the x-intercept $x = P_n(0)$ does not require that we solve a polynomial equation for x, as we would have to do if we fit $y = P_n(x)$ and needed to solve $P_n(x) = 0$ for x. The resulting methods are generally referred to as **inverse interpolation methods.** A slight complication is that the x-intercept need not lie in the bracket (see Fig. 1.20), but that is easily handled by simply taking a bisection step.

Brent's method with an appropriate switching strategy provides guaranteed convergence (given an initial bracket, and guarding against the possibility of pernicious round-off error destroying the bracket) and good speed, with bisection slowly but steadily moving the method to a region where the quadratic fit will be effective. It is this author's preferred method for one-dimensional root-finding problems. There are heuristics for

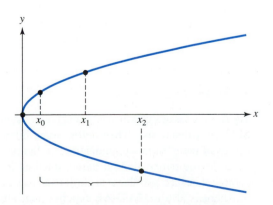

Figure 1.20 Inverse Quadratic Interpolation.

finding an initial bracket from a single initial guess; the guess itself establishes the scale on which the program should look for a solution. For problems in several variables, a variant of Newton's method is generally the best approach.

PROBLEMS 1.6

1. Perform three iterations of quadratic interpolation to approximate the sole positive root of $\cos(x) - x = 0$.

2. Perform three iterations of quadratic interpolation to approximate the sole real root of $5x^7 + 2x - 1 = 0$.

3. **a.** Write a detailed algorithm (pseudocode) for performing Müller's method. (Note that you must select a convergence criterion.) Terminate the algorithm if there is no real root of the quadratic.
   b. The order of convergence of Müller's method is (at least) the real root of $x^3 - x^2 - x - 1 = 0$. Find this value using Müller's method.

4. Write a detailed algorithm (pseudocode) for performing a simple version of Brent's method using quadratic interpolation (as in Eq. (1.13)). Assume that the method will switch to bisection if the last two quadratic interpolation steps have not reduced the function by at least as much as two bisection steps would have reduced it, and that when the method switches to bisection it always does two bisection steps before returning to quadratic interpolation.

5. Use quadratic interpolation to approximate a zero of $f(x) = 1/x^3 - 10$ to three decimal places.

MATLAB 1.6

The MATLAB zero-finding program `fzero` is based on Brent's method (using inverse quadratic interpolation). Enter `type fzero` to see the program listing. Look at it and find where the program is looking for a change of sign to find the initial bracket. You may wish to enter the `more on` command and re-enter the `type fzero` command to page through the program listing. By entering `help fzero` you will see that the calling sequence is `fzero(f,x0)` for some function f and initial guess x0. For example, enter:

```
» fzero('sin',3)
```

You may use an inline function or the name of an M-file (MATLAB program), in quotes, in place of the sine function. You may also use what is called a function handle

```
» fzero(@sin,3)
```

To force `fzero` to find a zero within a certain bracket, say [6, 8], enter:

```
» fzero(@sin,[6 8])
```

Try finding zeroes of cosine, tangent, etc. (Type `help elfun` for a list of elementary MATLAB functions.) Then define some inline functions (e.g., polynomials) and find zeroes of them. In most applications of interest, the function would actually be defined by an M-file rather than an inline function. Finding zeroes of polynomials is difficult enough that such problems are still used as test problems for root-finding programs.

There is also a MATLAB function that attempts to find all roots of a polynomial equation. The polynomial is entered as a vector. In MATLAB a row vector may be entered directly; enter:

```
» p=[1 2 1]
```

The roots of the polynomial $a_n x^n + a_{n-1} x^{n-1} + \cdots + a_1 x + a_0$ can be found by entering the coefficients in a vector such as p and using the roots command. Enter:

```
» roots(p)
```

This returns a double root at -1 as expected. Enter:

```
» roots([1 2 2])
```

This returns $-1 \pm i$ (the roots of $x^2 + 2x + 2 = 0$) as expected. The inverse of roots is poly; if r is a vector of roots of a polynomial, poly(r) is a vector of the coefficients of that polynomial. Hence poly(roots(x)) and roots(poly(x)) should both equal x (in infinite precision arithmetic).

As explained in help poly, the special case poly(1:20) is known as **Wilkinson's polynomial.** This is the polynomial of degree 20 with zeroes at $1, 2, 3, \ldots, 20$. Enter:

```
» roots(poly(1:20))
```

This should return the vector 1:20. As you can see, it does not, even though these roots are all simple and well-separated.

Looking ahead to Additional Problem 8, note that we can plot $f(x) = (x-1)^8$ by defining an x vector (see help linspace) and using plot. Enter:

```
» x=linspace(.8,1.2,200);
» plot(x,(x-1).^8),grid
```

To plot its expanded form, use c=poly([1 1 1 1 1 1 1 1]) to find the coefficients of the polynomial with roots at $x = 1$ with multiplicity 8, then enter:

```
» y=polyval(c,x);
```

to evaluate this polynomial at all points in the x vector. Enter:

```
» plot(x,y),grid
```

There is no visible difference at this scale, but as Additional Problem 8 demonstrates, there is a visible difference at smaller scales.

To see the effects of roundoff error and poor scaling in another form, enter:

```
» roots(poly([1 1 1 1 1 1 1 1]))
```

The numerical method, when applied to this entirely real problem with entirely real roots, generates answers with complex-valued roundoff error. As distressing as this may seem at first, roundoff error is roundoff error, and the fact that it happens to be complex-valued shouldn't concern us overly much. (However, the fact that the relative error is so large should concern us; type abs(ans-1) to see the size of the errors.) This is not a failing of MATLAB. These problems are simply difficult.

ADDITIONAL PROBLEMS 1.6

6. Use your version of Brent's method from Problem 4 to approximate a root of $\cos(12x) - x/2 = 0$ with the initial bracket $[0, 4]$.

7. Use your version of Brent's method from Problem 4 to approximate a root of $\cos(e^x) = 0$ with the initial bracket $[0, 4]$.

8. Plot $f(x) = (x - 1)^8$ for $x \in [0.9, 1.1]$ using a fine spacing. Repeat for $x \in [0.995, 1.005]$. Then plot $g(x) = x^8 - 8x^7 + 28x^6 - 56x^5 + 70x^4 - 56x^3 + 28x^2 - 8x + 1$ over the same two ranges. (Type `help axis` for help on adjusting the display of the plot.) Given that $f(x) = g(x)$ for all x, can you explain what's going on? How many roots does $g(x)$ have in principle, and in practice?

9. a. Verify that if all three data points lie on a straight line then the quadratic interpolant (Eq. (1.13)) is indeed a line ($\alpha = 0$).

   b. Verify that Eq. (1.13) is correct (including that the solution is unique).

10. Use Müller's method to find the zeroes of $f(x) = 8x^3 - 12x^2 - 50x + 75$. Check your answers with the MATLAB command `roots([8 -12 -50 75])`.

11. a. Write a detailed algorithm (pseudocode) for performing a simple version of Brent's method using inverse quadratic interpolation. You will need to derive a formula for the quadratic interpolant $x = Q(y)$. Recall that the x-intercept $x = Q(0)$ may fall outside of your bracket.

   b. Write a MATLAB program that implements your version of Brent's method. Assume that $f(x)$ will be given as an inline function. Type `help while` if you would like to use a while loop in your

program. Demonstrate your program on at least three root-finding problems.

12. a. What are the relative advantages and disadvantages of the following root-finding methods: bisection, inverse linear interpolation, secant method, Newton's method, quadratic interpolation, and Müller's method?

   b. What are the relative advantages and disadvantages of Brent's method and the globalized Newton's method?

13. a. Use the MATLAB command `roots([1 -6.04 13.68 -13.76 5.196])` to find all roots of

$$x^4 - 6.04x^3 + 13.68x^2 - 13.76x + 5.196$$
$$\doteq (x - 1.52)(x - 1.48)(x - 1.5)(x - 1.54).$$

Comment on your results.

   b. Find all real roots of $x^7 - 7x^6 + 21x^5 - 35x^4 + 35x^3 - 21x^2 + 7x - 1$.

14. The electric field $E_a(\theta)$ of a transmitting linear phased-array radar system can be approximated for small angles by $E_a(\theta) = \sqrt{N} \, \text{sinc}(\pi(D/\lambda) \sin(\theta))$, where $\text{sinc}(x) = \sin(x)/x$ and $\text{sinc}(0) = 1$. Here N is the number of elements in the array, D is the length of the array, and λ is the wavelength at which the system is operating. (Recall that $f\lambda = c$, where f is frequency and c is the speed of light.) If $N = 10$, $D = N \cdot 2\lambda$, and the frequency is 46 MHz, use Brent's method to determine what angle θ corresponds to a field strength of 0.5 V/m.

15. Use Müller's method to find all roots of $x^3 - x^2 - x - 1 = 0$. (Refer to Problem 3.) Note that you do not need to begin with complex values; they are generated by the method.

1.7 Effects of Finite Precision Arithmetic

In developing a numerical method for a given problem, we begin with physical or mathematical intuition about the particular problem and use that intuition to devise a scheme that we hope will converge to a solution of the problem. Since most methods do not converge in a finite number of iterations, we include convergence criteria that indicate when we have achieved practical convergence, that is, when we have found values sufficiently accurate for our purposes (or as accurate as we can reasonably hope to find).

In the process to devise a scheme that will converge to a solution, we must first determine wheather a method converges in the usual mathematical sense, as a limit.

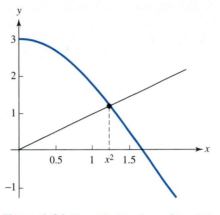

Figure 1.21 Fixed Point of $y = 3\cos(x)$.

Stability

Next, we must consider *stability,* by which we mean the sensitivity of the method to small errors such as roundoff errors. If a method converges only when infinite precision arithmetic is used, but not on a computer, then it will not be of much interest to us.

Here's an example of a method that is not convergent. Consider the problem of finding a fixed point of $f(x) = 3\cos(x)$ near $x = 1$ (see MATLAB 1.3). The direct application of fixed point iteration gives

$$x_{k+1} = 3\cos(x_k)$$

(see Fig. 1.21). There is a solution at $x^* \doteq 1.17$; however, since $f'(x^*) = -3\sin(x^*) \approx -2.76$, the fixed point is not attracting (we say that it is **repelling**) and the method cannot converge for any x_0 in a deleted neighborhood of x^*, *even using infinite-precision arithmetic.* The method is not convergent; Newton's method, of course, would be convergent for this problem.

Lack of stability is a different issue, however. To explore it, let's consider the two-step recurrence relation

$$x_{k+1} = x_k + x_{k-1} \tag{1.14}$$

with the initial conditions $x_0 = 1$, $x_1 = (1 - \sqrt{5})/2 \doteq -0.6180$. Then

$$x_2 = x_1 + x_0$$
$$= \frac{(1 - \sqrt{5})}{2} + 1$$
$$= \frac{(3 - \sqrt{5})}{2}$$
$$= \left[\frac{(1 - \sqrt{5})}{2}\right]^2 \doteq 0.3820$$

(the last step is not obvious, but it is correct). Similarly

$$x_3 = x_2 + x_1$$
$$= \frac{(3 - \sqrt{5})}{2} + \frac{(1 - \sqrt{5})}{2}$$
$$= \frac{(4 - 2\sqrt{5})}{2}$$
$$= \left[\frac{(1 - \sqrt{5})}{2}\right]^3 \doteq -0.2361$$

and in general

$$x_k = \left[\frac{(1 - \sqrt{5})}{2}\right]^k \tag{1.15}$$

($k = 0, 1, 2, \ldots$). The obvious numerical method for computing a value of x_k is just Eq. (1.14). For example, with the given initial conditions $x_0 = 1$, $x_1 = (1 - \sqrt{5})/2$, we have, using 16 digit arithmetic,

$$x_2 = x_1 + x_0$$
$$\doteq -0.61803398874989 + 1$$
$$\doteq 0.38196601125011$$
$$x_3 = x_2 + x_1$$
$$\doteq 0.38196601125011 + -0.61803398874989$$
$$\doteq -0.23606797749979$$
$$x_4 = x_3 + x_2$$
$$\doteq -0.23606797749979 + 0.38196601125011$$
$$\doteq 0.14589803375032,$$

and clearly this sequence should decrease to zero in agreement with Eq. (1.15). But this is not what happens! In Figure 1.22 there is a plot of x_k versus k.

As k increases, x_k initially decreases, as expected, but then begins increasing rapidly. By $k = 50$, x_k is on the order of 10^9; by $k = 100$, x_k is on the order of 10^{20}. Why? Look again at Eq. (1.14), which is called a *difference equation,* in analogy with differential equations. This particular difference equation is the **Fibonacci recurrence relation.** The general solution is

$$x_k = c_1 \left[\frac{(1 - \sqrt{5})}{2}\right]^k + c_2 \left[\frac{(1 + \sqrt{5})}{2}\right]^k, \tag{1.16}$$

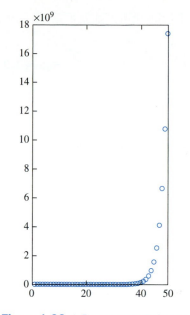

Figure 1.22 A Recurrence Relation.

where the values of c_1 and c_2 are determined by the initial conditions x_0 and x_1. In particular, the initial conditions $x_0 = 1$, $x_1 = (1 - \sqrt{5})/2$ give $c_1 = 1$ and $c_2 = 0$, leading to the stable formula Eq. (1.15). But if the values of x_0 and x_1 are not *precisely* equal to 1 and $(1 - \sqrt{5})/2$, respectively, then we will get different values of c_1 and c_2 that will almost certainly be nonzero. The graph in Figure 1.22 corresponds to $c_1 \approx 1$ and $c_2 \approx 0$ but $c_2 \neq 0$ due to the error in the approximation

$$x_1 = \frac{1 - \sqrt{5}}{2} \doteq -0.61803398874989,$$

which has an absolute error of about $5E - 15$ and a relative error of the same magnitude. This is the phenomenon of instability: A scheme that would give the correct value in exact arithmetic gives very wrong answers when implemented on a computer because small errors are exaggerated. (Look at the huge effect of errors on the order of 10^{-15} in Figure 1.22.) Throughout this book we shall have to modify many methods to change an unstable scheme (which would converge in exact arithmetic but not on a computer) to a stable scheme (which converges even on a computer). To do so it will be helpful to understand a bit more about computer arithmetic and how it differs from real arithmetic.

Computer Arithmetic   Computers store numbers in base 2 using the binary digits 0 and 1, called **bits** in this context. (Calculators and some special-purpose computers may use other bases.) Eight bits make a **byte.** One of the bits is used to represent the sign of the number; others are used for the mantissa (fractional part) and the exponent: $N = \pm m \cdot b^e$, where the number N has mantissa m (a number between 0 and 1 in a typical implementation), b is a fixed base (typically 2 or 16), and e is the exponent of the number.

Figure 1.23 Single Precision.

In the popular IEEE standard for computer arithmetic, a single precision number is stored using 32 bits (4 **bytes,** called a **word**) and a double precision number is stored using 64 bits (a **double word**). In single precision, 1 bit is devoted to the sign of the number, 8 bits are used for the exponent, and the remaining 23 bits are used to represent the mantissa, which contains the actual significant figures of the number. This is indicated in Figure 1.23. The number represented by these bits has the form $(mantissa)s \times (base)^{exponent}$ with appropriately chosen sign, and can have magnitude as small as about 10^{-38} and as large as about 10^{38}. These are the **machine numbers.**

The situation is actually rather more complicated than this. There is a normalization criterion and a hidden bit for the mantissa, and an offset is subtracted from the exponent. The machine numbers from about $\pm 10^{-38}$ to $\pm 10^{38}$ (and 0) are called the **normal** machine numbers; by relaxing the normalization criterion, some numbers smaller than 10^{-38} in absolute value can be represented. These are called **subnormal** machine numbers.

In double precision, 1 bit is devoted to the sign of the number, 11 bits are used for the exponent, and the remaining 52 bits are used to represent the mantissa. Note that double precision actually has *more* than double the significant bits of single precision— 52 as opposed to 23—because it does not double the number of bits in the exponent (8 in single precision as opposed to 11 in double precision, giving numbers that have magnitude as small as about 10^{-308} and as large as about 10^{308}). Double-precision arithmetic operations may take up to slightly more than twice as long to compute as corresponding single-precision operations, depending on the machine architecture, but on most current machines the principal advantage of using single precision is in storage space, not speed. Single precision gives about seven significant (decimal) figures and double precision gives about sixteen significant (decimal) figures. Once again there are subnormal numbers with magnitudes less than 10^{-308}.

Note that single precision and double precision are defined by the machine, not the programming language. This means, for example, that the same computation performed on two different machines may give two different answers due to differences in how numbers are represented and in how arithmetic operations are implemented. This issue of software portability has been a continual source of frustration for those who write and test numerical programs. Fortunately most computers you are likely to encounter use the same arithmetic system, known as the IEEE standard for floating point arithmetic. While there can still be slight variations even between implementations of IEEE standard arithmetic, you are much less likely to encounter such variations nowadays.

Floating Point   The representation system that we have been discussing is said to use **floating point**
Arithmetic   **numbers** because the variable exponent allows the decimal (or binary) point to move

within the significant figures. The machine arithmetic is then called **floating point arithmetic.** In controls engineering it is not uncommon to work with **fixed point numbers** and **fixed point arithmetic,** in which the decimal point has a fixed location, as was done on early computers.

For authors of high-quality numerical software, knowledge of the details of how computer numbers are stored and represented and related hardware issues are very important. For our purposes, however, we need to know the following: Computers represent numbers with a fixed number of significant bits (precision) and a limited exponent; programs using double-precision arithmetic will take longer to run than ones using single-precision arithmetic and will also require more memory; and floating point arithmetic differs from real arithmetic because the results must be computed and stored in finite precision.

Let's look at some differences between floating point arithmetic and real arithmetic. For a given implementation of floating point numbers, define $\mathrm{fl}(x)$ to be the floating point number nearest the real number x (breaking ties by rounding in the usual way). Then it is usual to model the result of adding x and y on the computer as

$$x \oplus y = \mathrm{fl}(\mathrm{fl}(x) + \mathrm{fl}(y)),$$

where $\oplus$ represents computer addition. In other words, our model for floating point addition is that the floating point sum of x and y is found by converting x to floating point form, converting y to floating point form, adding these floating point numbers correctly, and then converting the result to floating point form. Similarly for subtraction, multiplication, and division. We shall simply assert that this is a reasonable model for most machines.

For example, on a machine that follows this model, the result of adding $x = \pi$ to $y = \pi$ would be $\mathrm{fl}(\mathrm{fl}(\pi) + \mathrm{fl}(\pi))$; if $\mathrm{fl}(\pi) = 3.14159$ on the machine in question, then $x \oplus y = \mathrm{fl}(6.28318) = 6.28318$. Note that this is the correct value of $x \oplus y$ and an approximate value of $x + y$. If instead $x = \pi$ and $y = \pi/100$, then

$$x \oplus y = \mathrm{fl}(\mathrm{fl}(\pi) + \mathrm{fl}(z)),$$

where $z = \pi \oslash 100 = \mathrm{fl}(\mathrm{fl}(\pi)/\mathrm{fl}(100)) = \mathrm{fl}(3.14159/100) = 0.0314159$. Then

$$x \oplus y = \mathrm{fl}(\mathrm{fl}(\pi) + \mathrm{fl}(z))$$
$$= \mathrm{fl}(3.14159 + 0.0314159)$$
$$= \mathrm{fl}(3.1730059),$$

and if on our machine $\mathrm{fl}(\pi) = 3.14159$, then in all likelihood $\mathrm{fl}(3.1730059) = 3.17301$ is the result. The exact value of $\mathrm{fl}(3.1730059)$ depends on the machine.

Although these effects will occur on any machine, it is easiest to see them if we imagine a hypothetical machine working in base 10 that stores numbers in the form $.d_1 d_2 \cdots d_n \times 10^p$ where d_i is a digit, n is a positive integer, and p is any integer. In this idealized system,[10] called *n-digit floating point arithmetic,* all numbers are rounded to their n-digit form after any operation. (In Maple the `Digits` command may be used to simulate

---

[10] In fact, most calculators work in base 10, not base 2.

this system, which itself models floating point arithmetic on a real machine. Use `help digits` in MATLAB to see more about this command, if it is available on your system.) Hence to compute $\pi - 3.1415$ in five-digit floating point arithmetic ($n = 5$), we imagine entering π, which will be rounded to 3.1416 (or 0.31416×10^1 if the mantissa must be between 0 and 1), and then forming $3.1416 - 3.1415 = 0.0001 = 0.10000 \times 10^{-3}$. Note that if you try this in MATLAB you get:

```
» 3.1416-3.1415
ans =
   9.999999999976694e-005
```

Subtraction of Nearly Equal Numbers
because numbers are stored in base 2. This is an example of a common problem in numerical analysis: The loss of significant figures caused by the subtraction of nearly equal numbers. When we subtract two numbers that are nearly equal, we effectively cancel out the leading significant figures, leaving a much less precise number. On the hypothetical machine, the result $3.1416 - 3.1415 = 0.0001$ indicates that we have lost four significant figures from our data; any further calculations can have no more than one significant figure of accuracy, and any additional digits in the result, as in the MATLAB result `9.999999999976694e-005`, are just noise.

Example 1.7.1   Suppose we wish to multiply e by π on a machine that uses 5 digit floating point arithmetic. The result is $w = \mathrm{fl}(\mathrm{fl}(e) \cdot \mathrm{fl}(\pi))$, where $\mathrm{fl}(e) = \mathrm{fl}(2.7182818284590\dots) = 2.7183$ and $\mathrm{fl}(\pi) = \mathrm{fl}(3.1415926535897\dots) = 3.1416$ (note the rounding in each case). Hence

$$w = \mathrm{fl}(2.7183 \cdot 3.1416)$$

$$= \mathrm{fl}(8.53981128)$$

$$= 8.5398$$

with an absolute error of $|e\pi - 8.5398| \doteq 6.6E - 05$ and a relative error of $|e\pi - 8.5398| \,/\, |e\pi| \doteq 7.7E - 06$.   ∎

In MATLAB 1.7 we look at several other numerical issues. Common sources of numerical error include the subtraction of nearly equal numbers and division by small numbers. We need to check algorithms that must converge in infinite-precision arithmetic for stability with respect to the effects of roundoff errors, and make appropriate changes to the algorithms when we find them to be unstable. In fact, roundoff error is in many cases indistinguishable from error in the values of the given data (say, errors in the initial guess or in the initial conditions of an ODE initial value problem), so stability of a solution method with respect to small errors is desirable for many reasons. There are several mathematical concepts that attempt to capture these ideas—well-posedness, forward error, backward error—and we'll introduce and investigate them as needed.

MATLAB 1.7 is relatively long, but it makes many important points. As you work through it, consider the differences between what you see, what you expected to see, and what would be true of arithmetic on the real numbers $\mathbb{R}$.

PROBLEMS 1.7

1. a. Show that Eq. (1.15) is also valid for $k = 5$ and $k = 6$.
   b. Show that Eq. (1.14) with initial conditions $x_0 = 2$, $x_1 = 1$ gives the same values as Eq.(1.16) with $c_1 = 1$, $c_2 = 1$ for $k = 0, 1, 2, 3, 4$, and 5.

2. a. Using six-digit floating point arithmetic, compute e/π and π/e. Give the relative errors as well.
   b. Using six-digit floating point arithmetic, compute $\sin(1) + \cos(1)$. Give the relative error as well.

3. Using five-digit floating point arithmetic, compute $6/9 - 2 \cdot (1/3)$ using the usual order of operations. Comment.

4. Using three-digit floating point arithmetic, perform the following sum from left to right: $801 + 150 + 72 +$ $14 + 4 + 3 + 2 + 1$. Repeat but perform the sum from right to left. Comment.

5. a. Floating point numbers represent values of the form $(mantissa) \times (base)^{exponent}$. What trade-offs were made in deciding that double-precision numbers would have 52-bit mantissas with 11-bit exponents, as opposed to the 46-bit mantissas and 16-bit exponents that would have resulted from a straight-forward doubling of single precision? Could a 46-bit mantissa and 16-bit exponent have been used for double precision?
   b. How many bits would be used for a quadruple precision value? How would you suggest that the bits be distributed (sign, exponent, mantissa)?

MATLAB 1.7

Recall that MATLAB uses double precision. Let's plot the values found from Eq. (1.14) with initial conditions $x_0 = 2$, $x_1 = 1$ and the values found from Eq.(1.16) with $c_1 = 1$, $c_2 = 1$ (Problem 1). Enter:

```
» x0=2,x1=1
» x=[x0,x1]
```

(x is a row vector of two values, 2 and 1, in that order). Then enter:

```
» for i=1:10;xnew=x1+x0;x=[x,xnew];x0=x1;x1=xnew;end
```

to compute ten more values of x_k and append them to x. (This is not the most efficient way to do this.) Enter:

```
» plot(x,'y'),grid
» hold on
```

to plot them in yellow and hold the plot. Now enter:

```
» s1=(1-sqrt(5))/2;s2=(1+sqrt(5))/2;
» z=s1.^(0:11)+s2.^(0:11)
» plot(z,'r')
```

to evaluate $x_0, \ldots, x_{11}$ using Eq. (1.16), and plot the resulting values. Enter:

```
» hold off
» plot(z-x),grid
```

to plot the difference between these two vectors. The error is barely noticeable (note the scale). Repeat with more than ten additional points; what happens?

Let's look at some idiosyncrasies of floating point arithmetic. First, recall that there is a largest machine number and a smallest (positive) normal machine number. Enter:

```
» realmax,realmin
```

to see them. The value of `realmax` corresponds to the extreme case in Figure 1.23, that is, `realmax` corresponds to all 1s in the mantissa and exponent. The value of `realmin` corresponds to the smallest normal number but is not the smallest number. Values larger than `realmax` are said to overflow, and values smaller than `realmin` are said to underflow (and are set to subnormal numbers or zero). Since there are only finitely many choices of bits in Figure 1.22, there are only finitely many machine numbers. Enter:

```
» eps
» 2^(-52)
```

to see the distance between 1 and the next nearest floating point number (called the **machine epsilon**). The distance between two normal floating point numbers varies with scale; the distance between 2 and the next nearest floating point number is twice the machine epsilon, the distance between 4 and the next nearest floating point number is four times the machine epsilon, and so on. (This gives the same *relative* accuracy at all scales but growing *absolute* inaccuracy as the scale increases.) We see the significance of the machine epsilon later in the text.

Suppose we want to compute $2436.7 - 2.3751 - 2438.2$ using our five-digit floating point arithmetic. (Note that all of these numbers are perfectly represented in our system.) Enter:

```
» format long
» 2436.7-2.3751

ans =
   2.434324900000000e+003
```

which becomes 2.4343×10^3 or 2434.3 in our system. To find the error, enter:

```
» abs(2434.3-ans)
```

or about 0.025. Now let's finish the computation. We need to compute $2434.3 - 2438.2$; enter:

```
» 2434.3-2438.2

ans =
   -3.89999999999964
```

or -3.9000 to 5 digits. Let's get the correct value. Enter:

```
» 2436.7-2.3751-2438.2
```

to see that it is -3.8751. Our answer matches to only two significant figures (-3.8751 is -3.9 to two significant figures), despite the fact that each of the original three numbers is represented perfectly on our hypothetical machine. The subtraction $2434.3 - 2438.2$ has canceled the other three significant figures, though the real problem is the initial subtraction $2436.7 - 2.3751$, which results in an error of .02. This is a small error on the scale of some of the numbers in the calculation, but it is not an insignificant error on the scale of the desired answer -3.8751. Any future calculations with this result can be no more accurate than this weakest link, which has only two significant figures. Try this again on $2436.7 - .23751 - 2438.2$. Before you start, attempt to predict what will happen.

We'll see other cases where subtraction of nearly equal numbers causes unacceptably large errors, but for now note that performing the computation as $(2436.7 - 2438.2) - 2.3751$ gives the exact result. (Computer arithmetic is commutative but not associative.[11]) Although the problem is poorly scaled, rewriting it in this form addresses that problem.

Now suppose that we were to divide -3.9000, the result of our calculation, by a small number δ. Since the true answer is $x = -3.8751$, we have $-3.9000/\delta = x/\delta + E/\delta$, where:

```
» E=-3.9000-(-3.8751)
```

is the error -0.0249 in our computed answer. Hence any attempt to divide the result by δ will result in an additive error of $-0.0249/\delta$ in our solution. If δ is large this may not be a problem, but if δ is small this error could swamp the calculation, giving meaningless results. (Look again at the attempts to approximate $f'(1) = 1$ for $f(x) = \ln(x)$ with a very small h in MATLAB 1.5.) For example, enter:

```
» -3.9000/1E-10-(-3.8751/1E-10)
```

giving -249000000. This is a fairly large error on the scale of the true answer. Enter:

```
» -3.8751/1E-10    %Percentage of true value.
```

This problem was seen previously in the computation of the derivative of $\ln(x)$, and it can occur any time we divide by a small number (or multiply by a large number), especially when we are dividing the result of a previous calculation, which has its own error, by a small number. This is important: Subtraction of nearly equal numbers and division by small numbers are to be avoided when possible.

Since we cannot expect to evaluate functions with more relative accuracy than the machine epsilon, it would not be sensible to choose a convergence criterion of the form $\rho_n \leq \tau$ for τ about as large as ϵ (or smaller). But even if a tolerance on the order of ϵ were viable, it would usually be wasteful to ask for sixteen-digit accuracy in our answers, given the amount of error likely to be included in the initial data and/or modeling assumptions in a physically motivated problem.

Another area where floating point arithmetic raises a concern is the quadratic formula. If $y = ax^2 + bx + c$, then the roots of $y(x) = 0$ are $r_1, r_2 = (-b \pm \sqrt{b^2 - 4ac})/2a$. If a is small, then we may encounter the problem of dividing by a small number; but whenever $b^2 \gg 4ac$, $r_1 = (-b + \sqrt{b^2 - 4ac})/2a$ will involve the subtraction of the nearly equal numbers b and $\sqrt{b^2 - 4ac} \approx b$ in the numerator if $b > 0$. (This is not the case for r_2, which involves the addition of nearly equal numbers and so is not a concern; if $b < 0$, then r_2 is the tricky case and r_1 is fine.) For example, enter:

```
» a=1,b=10000,c=1;
» x=(-b+sqrt(b^2-4*a*c))/(2*a)
```

---

[11] Actually this is a statement about our *model* of floating point arithmetic. Computer arithmetic actually fails to be commutative in general because the numbers temporarily stored in the CPU during computation can have slightly more bits than the numbers brought in from memory. This is rarely of practical interest, however, whereas the nonassociativity *does* have deleterious effects.

giving $-1.0000e-004$ for the root. But, enter:

```
» a*x^2+b*x+c
```

This gives $-1.1177e-009$, which seems large for something that should be zero. The standard trick for this situation is called rationalizing the numerator, using the conjugate: Multiply $r_1 = (-b + \sqrt{b^2 - 4ac})/2a$ by $(-b - \sqrt{b^2 - 4ac})/(-b - \sqrt{b^2 - 4ac})$ to get the equivalent form $r_1 = -2c/(b + \sqrt{b^2 - 4ac})$ after some simplification. Like the formula for r_2, this involves only the addition of nearly equal numbers. Now enter:

```
» x=-2*c/(b+sqrt(b^2-4*a*c))
```

giving $-1.0000e-004$, which is the same as before *to the precision displayed,* but:

```
» a*x^2+b*x+c
ans =
     0
```

so that this is a better estimate of the root. A similar trick works for r_2 when b is negative. This form of the quadratic formula should always be used in computation.

ADDITIONAL PROBLEMS 1.7

6. In the notation of the MATLAB subsection, what formula would you use for r_2 to avoid the subtraction of nearly equal numbers when $b < 0$?

7. Using the Mean Value Theorem, where would you expect evaluations of $\sin(\ln(x))$ to be relatively inaccurate for $x \in (0, 6)$, and where would they be relatively accurate?

8. a. Set `format long` in MATLAB and enter the line:
`x=0;d=.1;for i=1:1000,x=x+d;end;x.`
Comment on your results, which are due to the fact that .1 does not have a terminating base 2 expansion. (This phenomenon caused the failure of a number of Patriot air defense missiles, which counted time in tenths of a second, to destroy incoming Scud missiles during the 1991 Gulf War.) Repeat for $d = .24, .25$, and $.26$. Why is the error smallest for $d = .25$?

b. Enter `realmax+1` and `realmax*2`. Explain why the former gives `realmax` again yet the latter gives `Inf`. Experiment to find how large `x0` must be to make `realmax+x0` overflow to `Inf`. Does this match the claim that MATLAB gives about sixteen-digit precision?

9. a. Compute `Inf-Inf, Inf/Inf, 3*Inf, 1/Inf`, and several similar quantities. Recalling that `Inf`

represents machine infinity and `NaN` represents not a number, do the results match your expectations?

b. Does your computer conform to the IEEE standard? (See **help isieee** in MATLAB. If you're using MATLAB6, the answer is yes.)

10. Create an example (in MATLAB or on a calculator) where the quadratic formula in the standard form gives a noticeably less accurate answer than the quadratic formula with rationalized numerator.

11. Floating point arithmetic rounds numbers in the usual way. For example, in three-digit arithmetic, 1046.1 becomes 1050 (i.e., $0.105E4$). Rather than rounding, one could also use chopping, which simply chops off extra digits or bits: In this case 1046.1 becomes 1040. Perform several numerical experiments to determine the effects of chopping versus rounding, and report your results. Is rounding clearly superior to chopping?

12. a. In MATLAB, let $x = 3E200$ and $y = 4E200$ and compute $z = \sqrt{x^2 + y^2}$. Since x, y, and z are each less than `realmax`, what went wrong?

b. The problem of computing z is poorly scaled. Let $\rho = 1E200$, and compute z in the mathematically equivalent form $z = \rho\sqrt{(x/\rho)^2 + (y/\rho)^2}$.

c. Repeat parts a and b with $x = 3E200$ and $y = 4$. Note that $(y/\rho)^2$ is less than `realmin`. Is this a problem?

d. How would you use this idea in the case $x = 3E - 200$ and $y = 4E - 200$?

e. What is a reasonable rule for selecting a value of ρ?

f. If w, x, y, and z are numbers greater than one and on the same scale, suggest an appropriate formula for computing $(x - y) + (w + z)$.

g. Repeat for $(x - y)^2 + (w - z)^2$.

13. For almost every $x_0 \in (0, 1)$, the iteration $x_{k+1} = 2x_k \bmod 1$ never reaches the fixed point at $x = 0$ for any k. What happens if you iterate this map on the computer? Experiment first, then give an explanation for your results.

14. Most calculators (e.g., the TI-89 and TI-92) work in base 10, often using a system called **BCD** (**binary coded decimal**). The calculations are done in base 10 although the digits are coded using bits via BCD. Which of the effects that we have discussed would be changed by working in base 10, and in what ways?

15. a. Consider a 32-bit word and an integer x. As it is an integer we might store it as its bitstring, preceded by a 1 if negative or a 0 if positive. (This is called the **sign-and-modulus** form. No exponent is used so that the representation is exact.) What are the largest and smallest integers that may be represented in this form? How many different integers may be represented in this way? In how many ways may 0 be represented?

b. If x is a negative number, then it may be stored in the **twos complement** form in which $2^{32} - x$ is stored rather than x; if x is positive, then it is stored as its bitstring in this scheme. Show that if $-2^{31} \leq x \leq 2^{31} - 1$, then the leftmost bit is 1 if x is negative and 0 if x is positive when x is stored in twos complement form. What are the largest and smallest integers that may be represented in this form? How many different integers may be represented in this way? In how many ways may 0 be represented?

c. Show that the representation for x, when added to the representation for $-x$, gives 0 in the twos complement form if the overflow bit is neglected.

d. Discuss the relative advantages and disadvantages of these two representation schemes.

1.8 Newton's Method for Systems

We've been looking at methods for solving a single nonlinear equation in a single variable. Systems of several nonlinear equations in several unknowns occur frequently in practice. An example from the calculus is finding the location of a minimizer of a differentiable function of two variables $w = F(x, y)$, requiring the solution of the system of equations

$$\frac{\partial}{\partial x} F(x, y) = 0$$

$$\frac{\partial}{\partial y} F(x, y) = 0$$

and in general each equation in this system will be nonlinear in x and y. If F depends on three variables x, y, and z, we would have a system of three nonlinear equations in three unknowns.

It's hard to overestimate the importance of Newton's method for systems in scientific computing. As stated in Section 1.1, time and time again a more complicated problem reduces to the problem of solving $F(x) = 0$, where x and 0 are now to be considered vectors in $\mathbb{R}^n$. If $F(x) = Ax - b$ for some matrix A, we may use the methods of Chapters 2 and 3; otherwise we most commonly use some variant of Newton's method for systems.

Newton's Method for Systems

Newton's method for systems is, like the one-dimensional Newton's method, a fixed point iteration based on a linearization of $F(x)$. If $F : \mathbb{R}^n \to \mathbb{R}^n$, then the Taylor series for $F(x)$ has the form

$$F(x) = F(x_0) + J(x_0)(x - x_0) + R(x)$$

(assuming sufficient differentiability) for some remainder term $R(x)$. Here

$$J(x) = \begin{bmatrix} \dfrac{\partial f_1}{\partial x_1} & \dfrac{\partial f_1}{\partial x_2} & \cdots & \dfrac{\partial f_1}{\partial x_n} \\[2mm] \dfrac{\partial f_2}{\partial x_1} & \dfrac{\partial f_2}{\partial x_2} & \cdots & \dfrac{\partial f_2}{\partial x_n} \\[2mm] \vdots & \vdots & \ddots & \vdots \\[2mm] \dfrac{\partial f_n}{\partial x_1} & \dfrac{\partial f_n}{\partial x_2} & \cdots & \dfrac{\partial f_n}{\partial x_n} \end{bmatrix}$$

is called the **Jacobian** (or **Jacobian matrix**) of

$$F(x) = \begin{pmatrix} f_1(x_1, \ldots, x_n) \\ f_2(x_1, \ldots, x_n) \\ \vdots \\ f_n(x_1, \ldots, x_n) \end{pmatrix}$$

and it plays the role of the first derivative of F. Newton's method is derived just as it was for the one-dimensional case: Neglecting the remainder term, we have

$$F(x) \approx F(x_0) + J(x_0)(x - x_0),$$

and setting $F(x) = 0$ gives what we hope is an improved estimate

$$0 \approx F(x_0) + J(x_0)(x - x_0)$$

$$J(x_0)x \approx J(x_0)x_0 - F(x_0)$$

$$x \approx x_0 - [J(x_0)]^{-1}F(x_0)$$

where $[J(x_0)]^{-1}$ is the inverse of $J(x)$. The iteration

$$x_{k+1} = x_k - [J(x_k)]^{-1}F(x_k)$$

is **Newton's method for systems.** For reasons that are discussed in Chapter 2, in practice it is preferable to solve

$$J(x_k)(x_{k+1} - x_k) = -F(x_k) \tag{1.17}$$

for $(x_{k+1} - x_k)$ and then add this quantity to x_k rather than attempt to compute $[J(x_k)]^{-1}$. If $J(x_k)$ is singular (noninvertible) for any k then the method fails, and if $J(x^*)$ is singular, then we should expect poor performance of the method. We can terminate when the approximate relative error

$$\rho_{k+1} \approx \frac{\|x_{k+1} - x_k\|}{\|x_{k+1}\|}$$

is sufficiently small, where

$$\|x\| = \left(\sum_{i=1}^{n} x_i^2 \right)^{1/2}$$

is the **norm** of the vector x with components $x_1, \ldots, x_n$. In essence this says to terminate when the step taken by Newton's method from x_k to x_{k+1} is small as compared to $\|x_{k+1}\|$. If iterations are not too expensive, then it is preferable to stop when ρ_k and ρ_{k+1} are both small, that is, when two successive steps are small, in case the method has simply taken an unusually short step for some iteration.

Example 1.8.1   To find the point of intersection of the circle $x^2 + y^2 = 1$ and the ellipse $\frac{1}{3}x^2 + \frac{1}{2}y^2 = 1$, we might write the nonlinear system

$$x^2 + y^2 - 1 = 0$$

$$\frac{1}{3}x^2 + \frac{1}{2}y^2 - 1 = 0$$

and seek a pair (x, y) that makes these two equations simultaneously vanish. We have

$$f_1(x, y) = x^2 + y^2 - 1$$

$$f_2(x, y) = \frac{1}{3}x^2 + \frac{1}{2}y^2 - 1$$

so

$$J(x) = \begin{bmatrix} 2x & 2y \\ 2x/3 & y \end{bmatrix}$$

is the Jacobian. If we use

$$\begin{pmatrix} x_0 \\ y_0 \end{pmatrix} = \begin{pmatrix} 1 \\ 1 \end{pmatrix}$$

for our initial guess, then

$$\begin{pmatrix} x_1 \\ y_1 \end{pmatrix} = \begin{pmatrix} x_0 \\ y_0 \end{pmatrix} - \begin{bmatrix} 2x_0 & 2y_0 \\ 2x_0/3 & y_0 \end{bmatrix}^{-1} F\begin{pmatrix} x_0 \\ y_0 \end{pmatrix}$$

$$= \begin{pmatrix} x_0 \\ y_0 \end{pmatrix} - \frac{1}{2x_0 y_0/3} \begin{bmatrix} y_0 & -2y_0 \\ -2x_0/3 & 2x_0 \end{bmatrix} F\begin{pmatrix} x_0 \\ y_0 \end{pmatrix}$$

$$= \begin{pmatrix} 1 \\ 1 \end{pmatrix} - \frac{1}{2/3} \begin{bmatrix} 1 & -2 \\ -2/3 & 2 \end{bmatrix} \begin{pmatrix} 1 \\ -1/6 \end{pmatrix}$$

$$= \begin{pmatrix} -1 \\ 2.5 \end{pmatrix}$$

$$\begin{pmatrix} x_2 \\ y_2 \end{pmatrix} = \begin{pmatrix} x_1 \\ y_1 \end{pmatrix} - \begin{bmatrix} 2x_1 & 2y_1 \\ 2x_1/3 & y_1 \end{bmatrix}^{-1} F\begin{pmatrix} x_1 \\ y_1 \end{pmatrix}$$

$$\doteq \begin{pmatrix} -1 \\ 2.5 \end{pmatrix} - \begin{bmatrix} -1.5 & 3 \\ -0.4 & 1.2 \end{bmatrix} \begin{pmatrix} 6.25 \\ 2.4583 \end{pmatrix}$$

$$\doteq \begin{pmatrix} 1.0001 \\ 2.05 \end{pmatrix}$$

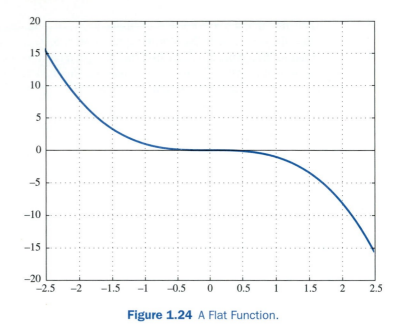

Figure 1.24 A Flat Function.

and so on. Further iterates show that the method is failing to converge; indeed, a sketch of the circle and the ellipse shows that they have no points in common, so there can be no (real) solutions.   ∎

Convergence
Criteria

A small relative error is one commonly used convergence criterion for Newton's method for systems. A preferable method for well-behaved problems[12] is to stop the iteration when

$$\|F(x_k)\| \le \tau_\rho \|F(x_0)\| + \tau_\alpha, \tag{1.18}$$

where τ_ρ is a small tolerance that measures the relative change in the function norm and τ_α is a small tolerance that measures the absolute size of the function norm. The motivation is easier to see when we consider a function $f : \mathbb{R} \to \mathbb{R}$ and initially neglect τ_α. In that case the convergence criterion is $\|f(x_k)\| \le \tau_\rho \|f(x_0)\|$, and we have

$$|f(x_k) - f(x_{k-1})| \le |f'(\theta_k)||x_k - x_{k-1}|$$

by the Mean Value Theorem. If $|f'(\theta_k)|$ is very small, then $|x_k - x_{k-1}|$ could be very large, but $|f(x_k) - f(x_{k-1})|$ could still be small. In fact, if $f'(x)$ is small near the root, then the function looks nearly flat (i.e., constant) near the root, so the knowledge that $f(x_k)$ is approximately zero conveys little information. In fact, the function in Figure 1.24 is $y = -x^3$, and note that at $x = .5$ the residual error is $.5^3 = .125$ but the absolute error is .5. If we had used $y = x^5$ instead, then the residual error would have been $.5^5 = .03125$, but the absolute error would still have been .5. Using $y = x^m$ we could make the residual error arbitrarily small at $x = .5$ while keeping the absolute error $\alpha = .5$.

---

[12] Here *well-behaved* means that the Jacobian of F evaluated at the root is well conditioned in the sense of Section 2.5.

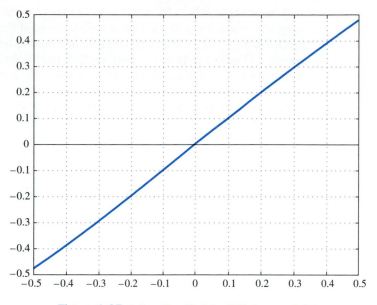

Figure 1.25 A Function That Isn't Flat: $y = \sin(x)$.

But if instead $|f'(x)|$ is, say, about unity near the root x^*, then near x^* we truly have a *linear* approximation

$$f(x_k) \approx f(x^*) + f'(x^*)(x_k - x^*)$$

as opposed to an essentially constant approximation. Since $f(x^*)$ is zero, this becomes

$$f(x_k) \approx f'(x^*)(x_k - x^*),$$

which indicates that the size of $|f(x_k)|$ is indeed a good measure of the size of the absolute error $|x_k - x^*|$. Look at this equation again: It plainly relates the desired true absolute error α to the measurable quantity $f(x_k)$, the residual! This makes geometric sense (Fig. 1.25). If $f'(x^*)$ is not too small, then the function looks pretty much like a straight line crossing the x-axis at an angle that is not too small (so that we don't have the extreme sensitivity of x-values to changes in y-values seen in Figure 1.24). Thus there is a roughly linear relationship between the size of x and the size of $f(x)$ in this region. This is stable; it is not sensitive to small changes in the values of the quantities involved. The convergence criterion

$$\|f(x_k)\| \leq \tau_\rho \|f(x_0)\| + \tau_\alpha$$

of Eq. (1.18) uses this fact to stop the iteration when $\|f(x_k)\|$ is sufficiently small, where small is defined in terms of the initial guess by $\tau_\rho \|f(x_0)\|$. The tolerance τ_α guards against cases where evaluation of f is inaccurate or where $\|f(x_0)\|$ is already very small and so significant further reduction is unlikely. As in any computer program, an upper limit on the number of iterations allowed is a good idea to prevent an infinite loop. In numerical software a common way to achieve this is to place a limit on the maximum number of function evaluations allowed.

Similar arguments in favor of Eq. (1.18) apply in the case of systems of nonlinear equations when the Jacobian $J(x)$ is well-behaved at the root (in a sense that is made precise in Section 2.5). The same idea is sometimes implemented in the form $\|F(x_k)\| \leq \max(\tau_\rho \|F(x_0)\|, \tau_\alpha)$. In this context we often refer to $\|F(x_k)\|$ as the **residual error** or simply the **residual** at iteration k, and we say that our convergence criterion is based on the residuals rather than the errors (i.e., α_k or ρ_k).

Newton's method for systems shares most of the strengths and weaknesses of Newton's method for functions of a single variable, including the ability to find complex zeroes given complex initial guesses and the difficulty of finding and evaluating the Jacobian. The Jacobian can be very expensive to evaluate and/or approximate, and the solution of Eq. (1.17) can be very expensive. This makes the use of the natural general-izations of the finite difference Newton's method and constant-slope Newton's method (from Section 1.5) very important, as well as other approximations of Newton's method (see Section 1.9). The constant-slope Newton's method (or **chord method**)

Chord Method

$$x_{k+1} = x_k - [J(x_0)]^{-1} F(x_k)$$

is a particularly useful alternative version because the Jacobian need only be computed once and the solution of Eq. (1.17),

$$J(x_0)(x_{k+1} - x_k) = -F(x_k),$$

can be made considerably more efficient if we know that we will be using the same matrix $J(x_0)$ repeatedly. (See Section 2.2.) Even though the convergence is only linear, this method may reach a desired tolerance in less time than Newton's method because each iteration is so much less computationally expensive, especially if the tolerance is relatively large.

In practice it is common to restart the chord method every several iterations with a freshly evaluated Jacobian matrix, that is, to use a hybrid strategy that mixes Newton's method and the constant-slope Newton's method. The decision to restart may be made adaptively by checking the progress of the algorithm; if it is taking increasingly small steps and achieving large reductions in the residuals, we might let it go. If we are seeing little change in the size of the residuals or if the steps are so large that the iteration appears to be failing to converge, however, we might choose to re-evaluate $J(x)$ at the current point.

Example 1.8.2   Let's apply the chord method to $(x^4 + y^4, xy + \sin(xy)) = (0, 0)$ with the initial guess $(x_0, y_0) = (1, 2)$. The Jacobian is

$$J(x, y) = \begin{pmatrix} 4x^3 & 4y^3 \\ y + y\cos(xy) & x + x\cos(xy) \end{pmatrix}$$

$$J(1, 2) = \begin{pmatrix} 4 & 32 \\ 2 + 2\cos(2) & 1 + \cos(2) \end{pmatrix}$$

$$\doteq \begin{pmatrix} 4 & 32 \\ 1.1677 & 0.5839 \end{pmatrix}$$

so we have (using $\vec{x} = (x, y)^T$)

$$\vec{x}_0 = \begin{pmatrix} 1 \\ 2 \end{pmatrix}$$

$$\vec{x}_1 = \vec{x}_0 - J^{-1}(\vec{x}_0)F(\vec{x}_0)$$

$$= \begin{pmatrix} 1 \\ 2 \end{pmatrix} - \begin{pmatrix} 4 & 32 \\ 1.1677 & 0.5839 \end{pmatrix}^{-1} F\begin{pmatrix} 1 \\ 2 \end{pmatrix}$$

$$\doteq \begin{pmatrix} -1.3742 \\ 1.7655 \end{pmatrix}$$

$$\vec{x}_2 = \begin{pmatrix} -1.3742 \\ 1.7655 \end{pmatrix} - \begin{pmatrix} 4 & 32 \\ 1.1677 & 0.5839 \end{pmatrix}^{-1} F\begin{pmatrix} -1.3742 \\ 1.7655 \end{pmatrix}$$

$$\doteq \begin{pmatrix} 1.6626 \\ 0.9708 \end{pmatrix}$$

$$\vec{x}_3 = \begin{pmatrix} 1.6626 \\ 0.9708 \end{pmatrix} - \begin{pmatrix} 4 & 32 \\ 1.1677 & 0.5839 \end{pmatrix}^{-1} F\begin{pmatrix} 1.6626 \\ 0.9708 \end{pmatrix}$$

$$\doteq \begin{pmatrix} -.5823 \\ 0.9849 \end{pmatrix}$$

and $\vec{x}_{15} \doteq (0.0036, 0.7337)^T$. The y component is changing very slowly. Let's recompute J at $\vec{x}_{15}$:

$$\vec{x}_{16} = \vec{x}_{15} - J^{-1}(\vec{x}_{15})F(\vec{x}_{15})$$

$$\doteq \begin{pmatrix} 0.0036 \\ 0.7337 \end{pmatrix} - \begin{pmatrix} 0.0000 & 1.5798 \\ 1.4674 & 0.0072 \end{pmatrix}^{-1} F\begin{pmatrix} 0.0036 \\ 0.7337 \end{pmatrix}$$

$$\doteq \begin{pmatrix} 0.0009 \\ 0.5503 \end{pmatrix}$$

$$\vec{x}_{17} = \begin{pmatrix} 0.0009 \\ 0.5503 \end{pmatrix} - \begin{pmatrix} 0.0000 & 1.5798 \\ 1.4674 & 0.0072 \end{pmatrix}^{-1} F\begin{pmatrix} 0.0009 \\ 0.5503 \end{pmatrix}$$

$$\doteq \begin{pmatrix} 0.0005 \\ 0.4922 \end{pmatrix}$$

and $\vec{x}_{20} \doteq (0.0002, 0.4067)^T$. We should update J to improve the speed of convergence of the method to the true solution $(0, 0)^T$. ■

Convergence
Theorem

We give one convergence theorem for Newton's method for systems:

> **Theorem**
>
> If B is an open subset of $\mathbb{R}^n$ and all second-order partial derivatives of $F : B \to \mathbb{R}^n$ exist and are continuous, then for any zero x^* of F in B such that $J(x^*)$ is nonsingular, there exists an open set $V \subseteq B$ containing x^* such that Newton's method with initial guess x_0 converges to x^* for all $x_0 \in V$.

The theorem states that if F is twice continuously differentiable in some region and if the derivative is nonsingular at the zero, then Newton's method converges for any initial guess sufficiently close to the zero. The convergence is quadratic under mild additional conditions, that is, typically we have

$$\|x^* - x_{k+1}\| \approx C\|x^* - x_k\|^2$$

(for some constant $C > 0$ depending only on the particular vector norm used) when using Newton's method for systems.

There are many different convergence theorems for Newton's method for systems, each requiring different hypotheses. These provide guidance in the choice of initial guesses, motivation for the construction of modified versions of the method, and a check on our work. In particular, if we implement this method and use it to solve a problem meeting the hypotheses of the theorem but do not see the type of results promised by the theorem, despite using a variety of initial guesses, then we know that either we have made an error in the implementation *or* the region V guaranteed by the theorem is very small. In the latter case we have gained some measure of insight into the nature of the function F.

PROBLEMS 1.8

1. Use Newton's method for systems to find all points where the hyperbola $y - 1/x = 0$ intersects the ellipse $(x/5)^2 + (y/8)^2 = 1$.

2. **a.** Use fixed point iteration to find a root of $F(x, y, z) = 0$ where $F(x, y, z) = (6x - y - z, x - 5y + z, 2x + 2y - 7z)$ by converting it to the form $v = v + F(v)$ (v is the vector with components (x, y, z)) and using the initial condition $(x_0, y_0, z_0) = (0.5, 0.5, 0.5)$.

   b. What is Newton's method for solving $F(x, y, z) = 0$?

3. What form does Newton's method take when it is applied to a linear system $F(x) = Ax - b = 0$ (where A is an $n \times n$ matrix and b is an n-vector)?

4. If $F : \mathbb{R}^{20} \to \mathbb{R}^{20}$, how many separate derivatives must be found to be able to compute $J(x)$?

5. Why can't the secant method be directly generalized to a method for functions of more than one variable?

MATLAB 1.8

Your local implementation of MATLAB may or may not include the Maple function for solving nonlinear systems of equations. Enter:

```
» help fsolve
» mhelp fsolve
```

to see if it is available for your use. Since it may not be available, we will not make use of it here.

Let's write an M-file that implements Newton's method for systems. Use the edit command to invoke the editor. We will assume there are M-files newtfun.m and newtjac.m already written that compute the function and its Jacobian, respectively; that is, newtfun takes in a vector of length n and returns a column vector of length n, and newtfund takes in a vector of length n and returns an $n \times n$ matrix (the Jacobian). A simple version of Newton's method might read as follows:

```
function out=newtsys(fun,jac,x0,tol)
%NEWTSYS    Newton's method for systems applied to function
%           fun with Jacobian jac and initial condition xo;
%           tol is the tolerance.
d=-feval(jac,x0)\feval(fun,x0);xnew=d+x0;
while norm(x0-xnew)>tol,
  x0=xnew;
  d=-feval(jac,x0)\feval(fun,x0);
  xnew=d+x0;
end
out=xnew;
```

When using this function, we would pass it newtfun and newtfund as arguments, that is, the calling sequence is newtsys(@newtfun,@newtfund,x0,tol).

The norm command gives the norm, or length, of a vector. The line that computes d implements Eq. (1.17) using MATLAB's slash command \ (see help slash and Chapter 2). For example, enter:

```
» jac=[1 2;3 4]
```

This enters the Jacobian matrix jac with entries 1 and 2 in row 1 and entries 3 and 4 in row 2. Matrices of other sizes may be entered in a similar manner, row by row, separated by semicolons. Enter:

```
» jac\[1 1]'
```

to solve the corresponding linear system with right hand side vector $(1, 1)^T$. The line that computes d and the line that follows it could also be expressed as:

```
xnew=x0-inv(feval(jac,x0))*feval(fun,x0);
```

using the MATLAB command inv for inverting a matrix, but this is generally not the best approach (see Chapter 2). Use this program to duplicate the results of Example 1.8.1.

There are many possible criticisms of our program. We should probably check that newtfun.m (fun in the program) and newtjac.m (jac in the program) return results that have the expected sizes (see help size) and that tol is positive; we should certainly use a counter in the while loop to prevent an infinite loop; we should attempt to detect divergence; we should base the convergence criterion on the relative error and require that at least two successive iterations give small errors; and we should check whether the Jacobian is "nearly" singular and issue a warning if it is (see Section 2.5).

Your version and local installation of MATLAB may be able to compute symbolic derivatives and symbolic Jacobians. Type `help jacobian` to see if this functionality is available on your machine. For most problems of practical interest, symbolic differentiation is not a realistic option; it and the evaluation of those derivatives may be too time consuming. More often, however, the function $F(x)$ is itself computed by another program (say, one that solves a PDE numerically) and hence is not symbolically differentiable. For large computing problems, symbolic computation is rarely feasible. In some cases another approach, called **automatic differentiation,** is available. It consists of a special program that reads in your program that computes $F(x)$ and actually applies the rules of differentiation to the formula in your program to produce another program that computes $F'(x)$. This is done in advance and then the program that computes $F'(x)$ is compiled in along with the rest of your programs, making derivative evaluations available. These tools are available for Fortran and C programs.

Type `help numjac` for a function that computes the Jacobian numerically. It uses finite differences to approximate $J(x)$ and has a number of checks programmed in so as to yield an accurate Jacobian (hopefully).

Make some of these changes, then enter a `newtfun.m` and `newtjac.m` and test the program. (Remember to use the command `clear functions` as needed.) Note how compactly an algorithm like this can be expressed in MATLAB; consider what would be involved in writing it in C. Of course, it would run much faster in C, principally because it would be compiled. Rapid prototyping (or rapid development) is an advantage of MATLAB. But while it is possible to create MATLAB executables—see `help mex`—it is often advisable to rewrite programs that will be used repeatedly in C (or C++), Fortran, or a similar language. The mathematical subroutines at `http://www.netlib.org` may be used for specific tasks.

ADDITIONAL PROBLEMS 1.8

6. Use Newton's method to find the points of intersection of the circle of radius 10 centered at the origin and the circle of radius 6 centered at (12, 1).

7. Show that Newton's method for systems reduces to Newton's method if $n = 1$.

8. What happens if you attempt to apply Newton's method for systems to find the point of intersection of three circles? Assume there is a solution.

9. Rewrite the Newton's method for systems program using a `for-end` loop. Exit the loop using the `break` command (see `help break`).

10. a. Use Newton's method to find a root of $(x^2 - 2xyz, x - y^2 - z, 2x - 2y - 2z^3) = (0, 0, 0)$.
  b. Repeat with the constant Jacobian (that is, constant-slope) version, using $J(x_0)$ at every iteration.

11. a. Verify experimentally the linear convergence of the constant Jacobian Newton's method for systems (using $J(x_0)$ at every iteration).

  b. Verify experimentally the quadratic convergence of Newton's method for systems. (Recall that $\|x_k - x^*\|$ is the error that should be converging quadratically to zero.)

12. Use Newton's method to find a simultaneous zero of $xy^2 - 2z + \sin(x) + 2$, $2x^4 + 3xy^2 + yz - 1$, and $2xy + \cos(xy) + 2z^3 - 3$.

13. a. What happens if you apply Newton's method for systems to a system of the form $F(x) = (f_1(x_1), f_2(x_2), \ldots, f_n(x_n))$?
  b. What happens if you apply fixed point iteration in the form $x = x + F(x)$ to a system of the form $F(x) = (f_1(x_1), f_2(x_2), \ldots, f_n(x_n))$?

14. a. A material is considered to be an imperfect dieletric (that is, a poor conductor of electromagnetic energy) if $\sigma/\varpi\varepsilon \ll 1$, where $\sigma > 0$ is the material's conductivity, ϖ is the frequency of the electromagnetic radiation, and ε is the material's permittivity. For such a material the attenuation and phase constants α and β are given by $\alpha \approx \sigma\sqrt{\mu/\epsilon}(1/2 - \sigma^2\varpi^{-2}\epsilon^{-2}/16)$ and $\beta \approx \varpi\sqrt{\mu\epsilon}(1 + \sigma^2\varpi^{-2}\epsilon^{-2}/8)$. The values of α and β are directly measurable, but those of μ and ε must be inferred. Write out Newton's method for solving for μ and ε given α, β, and ϖ.

b. Can μ and ε be found algebraically (without using a numerical method)?

c. A perfect dielectric has $\sigma = 0$ leading to $\alpha = 0$, $\beta = \varpi\sqrt{\mu\epsilon}$. (Since α is zero, all of the electromagnetic energy is attenuated.) What would happen to Newton's method in part a if the parameters were those of a perfect dielctric rather than an imperfect dielectric?

15. a. Modify the Newton's method for systems program to compute the Jacobian only every $p + 1$ iterations, where p will be supplied by the user ($p = 0$ is

Newton's method; $p = \infty$ is the constant-slope Newton's method). See `help inf` for one way to work with the $p = \infty$ case in MATLAB.

b. We can define an iterative method in which each iteration consists of one Newton step followed by p constant-slope Newton's method steps; that is, given x_0, we set $z_{k+1}^{(0)} = x_k - [J(x_k)]^{-1}F(x_k)$ and then compute $z_{k+1}^{(\nu)} = z_{k+1}^{(\nu-1)} - [J(x_k)]^{-1}F(z_{k+1}^{(\nu-1)})$ for $\nu = 1, \ldots, p$, and finally we set $x_{k+1} = z_{k+1}^{(p)}$. Each step of the iteration consists of one Newton's step and p constant-slope steps. This formulation of the constant-slope Newton's method with restarting is sometimes called **Shamanskii's method.** The convergence criterion is usually applied after the computation of either an x-value or a z-value (not just the z-values). What advantages, if any, are gained by this change of point of view?

1.9 Broyden's Method

The theorem in the previous section states that if F is twice continuously differentiable in some region and the Jacobian is nonsingular at the zero, then Newton's method converges for any initial guess sufficiently close to the zero. This fact is easily established by considering the method to be a fixed point iteration

$$x_{k+1} = N_F(x_k)$$

in $\mathbb{R}^n$. However, we turn to the topic of quasi-Newton methods for nonlinear systems, that is, we now consider the higher-dimensional analogue of quasi-Newton's methods (introduced in Section 1.5.)

Suppose we want to solve $F(x) = 0$. When n is not too large, we may use Newton's method for systems

$$x_{k+1} = x_k - J^{-1}(x_k)F(x_k) \tag{1.19}$$

in the form

$$J(x_k)(x_{k+1} - x_k) = -F(x_k) \tag{1.20}$$

with reasonable efficiency. For large n, however, the computation of the $n \times n$ matrix $J(x_k)$ and the solution of the corresponding linear system in Eq. (1.20) may be too expensive or otherwise too difficult, and a quasi-Newton method must be employed. (How large n may be depends on the hardware and software to be used and the function F.) In addition to natural generalizations of the methods already discussed in Section 1.5, *Quasi-Newton* such as the finite difference and constant-slope approaches, there are many quasi-Newton *Methods* methods that construct matrices that approximate $J^{-1}(x_k)$ for use in Eq. (1.19). In other words, for large n we often replace Eq. (1.19) with

$$x_{k+1} = x_k - B_k F(x_k), \tag{1.21}$$

where B_k is some approximation of $J^{-1}(x_k)$, which typically satisfies $B_k \to J^{-1}(x^*)$ as $k \to \infty$. The convergence is generally slower in the sense of taking more iterations to achieve a desired precision but faster overall because each iteration is less expensive.

Broyden's Method

In the context of systems, these quasi-Newton methods are also called **variable metric methods.** One of the most common is a secant-like method called **Broyden's method,** which defines the matrices B_k in Eq. (1.21) as follows: Choose an x_0 that is an initial guess as to the solution of

$$F(x) = 0,$$

and generate a second initial guess x_1 by a single step of Newton's method

$$x_1 = x_0 - J^{-1}(x_0)F(x_0).$$

Let $A_0 = J(x_0)$. We want to find an $A_1 \approx J(x_1)$ that we may use to find x_2 using Eq. (1.21) with $B_1 = A_1^{-1}$. How might we do this? In the one-dimensional case we had the secant method, which used the approximation

$$f'(x_k) \approx \frac{f(x_k) - f(x_{k-1})}{x_k - x_{k-1}} \tag{1.22}$$

but this is not applicable when $x_k - x_{k-1}$ is a vector. However, if we rewrite Eq. (1.22) in the form

$$f'(x_k)(x_k - x_{k-1}) \approx f(x_k) - f(x_{k-1}),$$

it suggests the requirement

$$A_k(x_k - x_{k-1}) = F(x_k) - F(x_{k-1}), \tag{1.23}$$

which is indeed the requirement that is used in Broyden's method. (Eq. (1.23) is called the **secant equation;** methods based on it are referred to as **secant update** methods.[13])

Unfortunately, the secant equation does not define a unique matrix A_k. It only incorporates the requirement that, along the direction from x_{k-1} to x_k, the matrix A_k has an effect that is in some sense similar to the effect the matrix $J(x_k)$ would have. What shall we do about the other $n - 1$ directions in $\mathbb{R}^n$? For simplicity, we add the requirement that if z is any vector orthogonal to $x_k - x_{k-1}$, then

$$A_k z = A_{k-1} z. \tag{1.24}$$

Thus we update A_{k-1} to A_k only with respect to the direction $x_k - x_{k-1}$ and otherwise leave A_{k-1} as it was. It is easily verified, by direct computation, that the matrix

$$A_k = A_{k-1} + \frac{(F(x_k) - F(x_{k-1}) - A_{k-1}(x_k - x_{k-1}))}{\|x_k - x_{k-1}\|^2}(x_k - x_{k-1})^T \tag{1.25}$$

---

[13] We could have chosen a very different requirement on A_k and used it to generate a different method.

satisfies Eq. (1.23) and Eq. (1.24). (see Problem 2). The result is Broyden's method:

Broyden's Method

1. Set $A_0 = J(x_0)$.

2. Compute $x_1 = x_0 - J^{-1}(x_0)F(x_0)$.

3. Begin loop $(k = 1)$:

4. Compute A_k using Eq. (1.25).

5. Compute $x_{k+1} = x_k - A_k^{-1}F(x_k)$.

6. If convergence criterion is not met, increment k and continue, else end.

We may use any desired convergence criterion (or criteria). One such possible criterion might be that the approximate relative error $\rho_k = \|x_k - x_{k-1}\|/\|x_k\|$ be small for two successive iterations.

The method is superlinearly convergent but may actually take much less time to converge than Newton's method if the Jacobian is difficult to evaluate. If it is not computationally feasible to compute $J(x_0)$ in step 1 of the algorithm, then we may approximate it by finite differences or some other method. On the other hand, if it *is* computationally feasible, but expensive, to compute $J(x)$, then it may pay to reset A_k to $J(x_k)$ periodically. This will give a better approximation and therefore a more rapid convergence.

Rank-one Updates Look again at Eq. (1.25), which defines Broyden's method. The formula for computing the updated A_k from A_{k-1} is of the form

$$A_k = A_{k-1} + uv^T$$

where

$$u = \frac{(F(x_k) - F(x_{k-1}) - A_{k-1}(x_k - x_{k-1}))}{\|x_k - x_{k-1}\|^2}, \quad v = (x_k - x_{k-1})$$

are vectors. The product uv^T of two column vectors u, v is called the **outer product** of the vectors and is a square matrix (as opposed to the **inner product** u^Tv of the vectors, which is a scalar; see Fig. 1.26 and Fig. 1.27). For $n \geq 2$ this matrix is necessarily singular, and in fact

$$\text{rank}(uv^T) = 1$$

unless either u or v is the zero vector. Because of this we say that a formula such as Eq. (1.25) represents a **rank-one update** of A_{k-1} to A_k because we add a matrix of rank one to A_{k-1} to obtain A_k. Because the n^2 elements of the matrix uv^T depend on only $2n$ parameters, these methods can be efficient even for large n, but of course they represent a rather limited update of the approximate Jacobian matrix A_{k-1}.

Sherman-Morrison formula There is a mathematically equivalent way of implementing Broyden's method that is usually more efficient. It is based on the **Sherman-Morrison formula,** which states that if A is nonsingular and $v^T A^{-1}u \neq -1$, then $A + uv^T$ is nonsingular, and

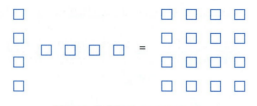

Figure 1.26 Outer Product.

furthermore

$$(A + uv^T)^{-1} = A^{-1} - \frac{A^{-1}uv^T A^{-1}}{1 + v^T A^{-1} u}. \tag{1.26}$$

Note the significance of this formula for Broyden's method: If we are willing to compute

$$A_0^{-1} = J^{-1}(x_0)$$

initially, then we can use Eq. (1.26) to find A_1^{-1}, A_2^{-1}, ..., that is, B_1, B_2, ... This saves us having to solve Eq. (1.20) at each stage; instead we go directly to Eq. (1.21). As we will see in Chapter 2, forming the inverse of a matrix is usually inefficient, and so it is advantageous to have a formula such as this. We incorporate the Sherman-Morrison formula into Broyden's method in the following form. Define $d_k = x_k - x_{k-1}$ and $y_k = F(x_k) - F(x_{k-1})$.

Broyden's Method with Sherman-Morrison Formula

1. Set $B_0 = J^{-1}(x_0)$, $A_0 = J(x_0)$.
2. Compute $x_1 = x_0 - B_0 F(x_0)$.
3. Begin loop ($k = 1$).
4. Compute B_k using $u = \frac{y_k - A_{k-1}d_k}{\|d_k\|^2}$, $v = d_k$.
5. Set $A_k = A_{k-1} + uv^T$.
6. Compute $x_{k+1} = x_k - B_k F(x_k)$.
7. If convergence criterion is not met, increment k and continue, else end.

The formula for the update in step 4 follows from Eq. (1.26) and can be further rearranged for greater computational efficiency. However, we defer the issue of the best way to compute this matrix until after we discuss the solution of linear systems in Chapter 2.

Figure 1.27 Inner Product.

We have developed a quasi-Newton method for nonlinear systems that requires that we compute (or approximate) the Jacobian and its inverse only once, at the start of the iteration. Again, the method benefits from occasional restarts with a computed Jacobian (by setting $B_k = J^{-1}(x_k)$), but these are not necessary.

PROBLEMS 1.9

1. Use Broyden's method to find all points where the hyperbola $y - 1/x = 0$ intersects the ellipse $(x/5)^2 + (y/8)^2 = 1$.

2. Verify that Eq. (1.25) gives a matrix A_k that satisfies Eq. (1.23) and Eq. (1.24).

3. **a.** For $(2\cos(x) - 1 + y, -3\sin(y+1) + 2x) = (0, 0)$, compare three iterations of Newton's method for systems and Broyden's method. How well does the matrix B_1 approximate $J^{-1}(x_1)$? How well does the matrix A_1 approximate $J(x_1)$?

   b. Does it make sense to compare B_2 and $J^{-1}(x_2)$? Why or why not?

4. Show that the update formula in the Broyden's method algorithm with Sherman-Morrison formula follows from Eq. (1.26).

5. Prove that the outer product uv^T of two column vectors always has rank zero or one. When will the rank be zero?

MATLAB 1.9

The matrix is MATLAB's basic (and, until relatively recent versions, only) data type. As mentioned in MATLAB 1.8, matrices may be entered by rows, separated by semicolons. For example, enter:

```
» A=[1 2 3;4 5 6;7 8 9]
A =
     1 2 3
     4 5 6
     7 8 9
```

In every calculation we have done thus far with scalars and vectors, MATLAB has considered them to be special cases of matrices. This is true of strings as well, but not for certain other objects such as inline functions. For example, enter:

```
» size(6)
```

This returns the vector [1 1], indicating that MATLAB treats this number as a 1×1 matrix. (In many operations MATLAB will recognize that a 1×1 matrix is in fact a scalar. This agrees with the mathematical convention but is not what you might expect from experience with other programming languages which consider a 1×1 array to be different from a vector with a single entry, which is in turn different from a floating point number.) Try `size(A)` to see the size of A.

Let's try Broyden's method. We'll use the system $(x^4 + y^4, xy + \sin(xy)) = (0, 0)$ of Example 1.8.2. The Jacobian is

$$J(x, y) = \begin{pmatrix} 4x^3 & 4y^3 \\ y + y\cos(xy) & x + x\cos(xy) \end{pmatrix}$$

and we'll use the initial guess $\vec{x}_0 = (.1, .2)^T$. We'll find a few Newton iterates first. Enter:

```
» x=[.1 .2]';
» f1=inline('sum(x.^4)')
» f2=inline('prod(x)+sin(prod(x))')
» J=[4*x(1)^3 4*x(2)^3;x(2)+x(2)*cos(prod(x)) x(1)+x(1)*cos(prod(x))]
» fx=[f1(x);f2(x)]
» x=x-J\fx;x1=x
» fx1=[f1(x);f2(x)]
» J=[4*x(1)^3 4*x(2)^3;x(2)+x(2)*cos(prod(x)) x(1)+x(1)*cos(prod(x))]
» x=x-J\fx;x2=x
» norm(x2)      %Absolute error (true solution is (0,0)).
```

to get the first two Newton iterates.

Now let's try Broyden's method. Enter:

```
» x=[.1 .2]';

» J=[4*x(1)^3 4*x(2)^3;x(2)+x(2)*cos(prod(x)) x(1)+x(1)*cos(prod(x))]
» B=inv(J);                    %Inverse of matrix.
» fx=[f1(x);f2(x)]
» x1=x-B*fx;                   %Same as previous x1.
» d1=x1-x;
» fx1=[f1(x1);f2(x1)];
» y1=fx1-fx;
» u=(y1-J*d1)*d1'/norm(d1)^2;B1=B-B*u*d1'*B/(1+d1'*B*u);
» x2=x1-B1*fx1
» norm(x2)
```

Broyden's method is performing adequately. For large matrices it would be significantly more efficient per iteration than Newton's method, though we would need more iterations. Perform five more iterations of Newton's method and of Broyden's method, and compare the errors.

ADDITIONAL PROBLEMS 1.9

6. Use Broyden's method to find the points of intersection of the circle of radius 10 centered at the origin and the circle of radius 6 centered at (12, 1).

7. Prove the Sherman-Morrison formula.

8. Demonstrate by specific example the superlinear but nonquadratic convergence of Broyden's method for a nonlinear system of 4 equations in 4 unknowns.

9. a. What is the form of Broyden's method when $n = 1$?
  b. What simplification results if you apply Broyden's method to a system of the form $F(x) = (f_1(x_1), f_2(x_2), \ldots, f_n(x_n))$?

10. a. Use Broyden's method to find a root of $(x^2 - 2xyz, x - y^2 - z, 2x - 2y - 2z^3) = (0, 0, 0)$.

b. Repeat with the Jacobian updated every three iterations (that is, use the rank-one update formula only twice before recomputing the Jacobian at the current point).

11. Write a MATLAB program that inputs the name of an M-file defining a nonlinear system, an initial guess at a zero, and an initial inverse Jacobian, and uses Broyden's method to find and return a zero of the system.

12. Conduct a computational experiment to investigate how sensitive the performance of Broyden's method is to the accuracy of $J^{-1}(x_0)$. Comment.

13. Use Broyden's method to find a simultaneous zero of

$$f(x, y, z) = xy^2 - 2z + \sin(x) + 2,$$

$$g(x, y, z) = 2x^4 + 3xy^2 + yz - 1,$$

$$h(x, y, z) = 2xy + \cos(xy) + 2z^3 - 3.$$

14. **a.** A standard model for a shock absorber leads to the ODE $mx'' + cx' + kx = F(t)$, where m is the car's mass, c is the coefficient of friction (damping) of the shock, and k is the Hooke's Law constant for the shock. The function $F(t)$ represents an imposed force, which is often taken to be sinusoidal, say $F(t) = F_0 \cos(\varpi t)$ for some amplitude $F_0 \neq 0$ and circular frequency $\varpi > 0$. If m, c, and k are positive, this leads to the model $x(t) = A\cos(\varpi t) + B\sin(\varpi t)$ for the steady-state motion of the shock, where $A = \kappa F_0 / [\kappa^2 + c^2 \varpi^2]$, $B = c\varpi F_0 / [\kappa^2 + c^2 \varpi^2]$ ($\kappa = (k - m\varpi^2)$). If $\kappa = 0$ a different model is found (this is the resonant case). Plausible values of the constants are $m = 900$ kg, $c = 3200$ N-s/m, and $k = 60000$ N/m. Suppose the test surface is sinusoidal with amplitude 3 cm and a period of 3 m. Compute A and B.

b. The constants A and B can be found experimentally by driving the car on the test surface and fitting a curve of the form $x(t) = A\cos(\varpi t) + B\sin(\varpi t)$ to the data. If F_0 and ϖ are also assumed known, what is Broyden's method for finding κ and c?

c. Substitute the formula for κ into the formulas for A and B. What is Broyden's method for finding m, c, and k from these expressions?

15. Generalize the Sherman-Morrison formula to find a formula for $(A + UV^T)^{-1}$ where U and V are matrices (not necessarily square). Make any appropriate assumptions. Your result should reduce to the Sherman-Morrison formula when U and V are column vectors. This formula is called the **Sherman-Morrison-Woodbury formula** (or sometimes just the **Woodbury formula**).

2 Linear Systems

2.1 Gaussian Elimination with Partial Pivoting

A S WE STATED PREVIOUSLY, the most commonly occurring problems in numerical analysis are the solution of a linear or nonlinear system of equations and the location of the optimizer of a function. We discussed nonlinear equations in Chapter 1. In this chapter and the next, we turn to the solution of linear systems of equations

$$Ax = b \tag{2.1}$$

where, in general, A is an $m \times n$ matrix (we assume real entries) and $b \in \mathbb{R}^n$. Most often we will assume that the coefficient matrix A is **square,** that is, that $m = n$.

How shall we solve a linear system? In principle we could rewrite Eq. (2.1) in the form

$$Ax - b = 0 \tag{2.2}$$

and apply a method for solving nonlinear systems to $F(x) = Ax - b$. Why don't we? There are a number of reasons. One is that Newton's method for systems requires the solution of an equation like Eq. (2.1) at every iteration, leading to a circularity problem; we need a method for solving Eq. (2.1) before we can use Newton's method on a nonlinear system of equations. Another reason is that, especially if A is not square, there may be no solution or there may be infinitely many solutions, and it is important to be able to determine when this is the case. There are also numerical issues, as we will see.

But the overriding reason that we consider the solution of linear systems separately from the solution of nonlinear systems is size. Linear systems have been studied extensively, and much is known about them; the very use of the term "non-linear" implies "everything else" (all we know about such problems is that they are not linear). Because of what we know about linear systems from linear algebra, we can solve *much* larger *linear* systems, using techniques appropriate for them, than *nonlinear* systems. Large linear systems, with n in the thousands, occur constantly; handling them is MATLAB's principle reason for being. They may arise directly, as in a large linear programming problem, but very often they arise as a subproblem in a numerical method for a different type of problem, such as Newton's method for systems or the discretization of a problem involving a partial differential equation. Large linear systems are ubiquitous in scientific computing.

In this chapter we focus on two approaches to solving Eq. (2.1) (or, equivalently, Eq. (2.2)): The LU decomposition, based on Gaussian elimination, and the QR decomposition. In Chapter 3 we discuss other approaches to solving Eq. (2.1) as well as other aspects of computational matrix algebra.

Gaussian Elimination

Example 2.1.1   Let's review the method of Gaussian elimination. Given an $m \times n$ matrix A and an n-vector b, we write the linear system $Ax = b$ in the form of an augmented matrix $[A \vdots b]$ and attempt to reduce it to the form $[U \vdots \widetilde{b}]$ using only the three **elementary row operations:**

1. Subtracting a multiple of row i from row j and making this the new row j

2. Interchanging rows i and j; and

3. Multiplying a row by a nonzero scalar

These operations leave the solution set unchanged and (augmented) matrices that differ only by some number of these operations having been performed are said to be **(row) equivalent.** (We write $M \sim N$ to indicate that matrices M and N are row equivalent.) The final matrix $[U \vdots \widetilde{b}]$ must have U **upper triangular;** that is, all entries of U below the main diagonal must be zero. If, say, $A = [4\ 2; 2\ 4]$ and $b = (6, 6)^T$, then we have

$$\begin{bmatrix} 4 & 2 & \vdots & 6 \\ 2 & 4 & \vdots & 6 \end{bmatrix} \sim \begin{bmatrix} 4 & 2 & \vdots & 6 \\ 0 & 3 & \vdots & 3 \end{bmatrix}$$

upon performing $R_2 \leftarrow R_2 - \frac{1}{2}R_1$ (where R_i denotes row i). The solution of $Ax = b$ is now easily found by **back substitution** (or **backwards substitution**), that is, since the matrix to the left of the partition is upper triangular, we start from the bottom and solve $3x_2 = 3$ to find $x_2 = 1$, and then proceed to $4x_1 + 2x_2 = 6$ to find $x_1 = (6 - 2 \cdot 1)/4 = 1$. The solution is $x = (1, 1)^T$.   ∎

From now on we will assume, unless otherwise stated, that the matrix A in $Ax = b$ is square. Gaussian elimination as performed above is sometimes called "naive" Gaussian elimination because we do not include any checks for possible numerical problems. Such numerical problems arise too frequently to ignore, however. Consider the linear system $Ax = b$ given by

$$\begin{bmatrix} 0.007 & -0.8 \\ -0.1 & 10 \end{bmatrix} \begin{bmatrix} x_1 \\ x_2 \end{bmatrix} = \begin{bmatrix} 0.7 \\ 10 \end{bmatrix}. \tag{2.3}$$

Naive Gaussian elimination requires that we perform $R_2 \leftarrow R_2 - (-0.1/0.007)R_1$, giving the equivalent (to the precision indicated) system

$$\begin{bmatrix} 0.007 & -0.8 \\ 0 & -1.4286 \end{bmatrix} \begin{bmatrix} x_1 \\ x_2 \end{bmatrix} = \begin{bmatrix} 0.7 \\ 20 \end{bmatrix}. \tag{2.4}$$

The solution is precisely $x_1 = -1500$, $x_2 = -14$ (as you may check by computing Ax). This is fine in principle, but we will be working in finite precision. If either A or b is the result of another calculation and hence has been affected by roundoff errors, we have just magnified those errors by a factor of $-0.1/0.007 \approx 14$ and carried them into Eq. (2.4). To see the effect of this in action, suppose that we are working in three-digit arithmetic (with arbitrary exponent n in the factor 10^n). Note that the original system Eq. (2.3) can be perfectly represented (without representation error) in such a system. We know that the $(2, 1)$ entry of the matrix in Eq. (2.4) must be zero, but the $(2, 2)$ entry is

$$10 - (-0.1/0.007)(-0.8) = 10 - (-14.2857\ldots)(-0.8)$$
$$\doteq 10 - (-14.3)(-0.8)$$
$$= 10 - (11.44)$$
$$\doteq 10 - 11.4$$
$$= -1.40,$$

which seems a reasonable approximation to the correct value -1.43 (to three digits). Note, however, how the subtraction has canceled a digit (we get -1.40, but from $10 - (11.44)$ above it we should have gotten -1.44, which requires only three digits and would be a better approximation).[1] Similarly, the second entry of the vector $\tilde{b}$ in Eq. (2.4) is

$$10 - (-0.1/0.007)(0.7) = 10 - (-14.2857\ldots)(0.7)$$
$$\doteq 10 - (-14.3)(0.7)$$
$$= 10 + (10.01)$$
$$\doteq 10 + 10.0$$
$$= 20.0,$$

which, despite an intermediate roundoff error, is equal to the correct value 20. (Two wrongs have made a right!) Finally, this gives $x_2 = 20/-1.4 \doteq -14.2857 \doteq -14.3$ (to three digits), a so-so approximation of the true value $x_2 = -14$ (the relative error is over 2%), and

$$x_1 = (0.7 - -0.8x_2)/0.007$$
$$\doteq (0.7 - -0.8 \cdot -14.3)/0.007$$
$$= (0.7 - (11.44))/0.007$$
$$\doteq (0.7 - 11.4)/0.007$$
$$= -10.7/0.007$$
$$= -1528.57\ldots$$
$$\doteq -1530,$$

---

[1] In fact, an actual computer has slightly more space for storing numbers in the CPU than in memory, leading to slightly more accuracy than we are indicating.

which is again at best a so-so approximation of the true value $x_1 = -1500$ (the relative error is 2%). Is it because we used three-digit arithmetic? No, though using more digits would give better results. But we can get better results in three-digit arithmetic already. Look again at Eq. (2.3):

$$\begin{bmatrix} 0.007 & -0.8 \\ -0.1 & 10 \end{bmatrix} \begin{bmatrix} x_1 \\ x_2 \end{bmatrix} = \begin{bmatrix} 0.7 \\ 10 \end{bmatrix}.$$

Although every value can be represented exactly in three-digit arithmetic—in fact, every value can be represented exactly in *one*-digit arithmetic—the entries of A range over 5 orders of magnitude. Suppose we rewrite Eq. (2.3) by interchanging the rows:

$$\begin{bmatrix} -0.1 & 10 \\ 0.007 & -0.8 \end{bmatrix} \begin{bmatrix} x_1 \\ x_2 \end{bmatrix} = \begin{bmatrix} 10 \\ 0.7 \end{bmatrix}$$

so that performing the row-reduction step $R_2 \leftarrow R_2 - (0.007/-0.1)R_1$ involves multiplying any errors in row 1 by the quantity $0.007/-0.1 = -0.07$ rather than -14 (approximately); we won't be magnifying any errors. Let's see if this helps. The new $(2, 2)$ entry is

$$-0.8 - (0.007/-0.1)(10) = -0.8 - (-0.070)(10)$$
$$= -0.8 - (-0.700)$$
$$= -0.1,$$

and the new second entry of the vector $\widetilde{b}$ is

$$0.7 - (0.007/-0.1)(10) = 0.7 - (-0.070)(10)$$
$$= 0.7 - (-0.700)$$
$$= 1.40.$$

(The fact that we didn't need to round anything off to three digits is a coincidence. If we had, note that the lost values would have been on the order of thousandths.) The reduced system is

$$\begin{bmatrix} -0.1 & 10 \\ 0 & -0.1 \end{bmatrix} \begin{bmatrix} x_1 \\ x_2 \end{bmatrix} = \begin{bmatrix} 10 \\ 1.4 \end{bmatrix}$$

giving $x_2 = 1.40/-0.1 = -14.0$ (exact), and

$$x_1 = (10 - 10x_2)/-0.1$$
$$\doteq (10 - 10 \cdot -14.0)/-0.1$$
$$= (10 + (140))/-0.1$$
$$= (150)/-0.1$$
$$= -1500,$$

which is again exact. *The use of three-digit arithmetic was not the source of the inaccuracies;* instead the source was the approach to the problem (namely, naive Gaussian elimination). A smarter approach gets the correct answer even when limited to only three digits.

In general we can't expect to get the answer correct to the last digit (or bit). However, we also cannot always save a calculation simply by doubling the precision in which we're working–and even if we can, our calculation will take at least twice as long. We can work smarter instead of harder by generalizing the trick above. The key idea is that at each stage of Gaussian elimination we should interchange rows, if necessary, to make the diagonal entry the largest of all entries in that column (below the diagonal), so that when we perform the $R_j \leftarrow R_j - (a_{j,i}/a_{i,i})R_i$ steps, the quantity $m_{j,i} = a_{j,i}/a_{i,i}$, called the (j, i) **multiplier,** is as small as possible and in fact at most 1 in absolute value. A small multiplier ensures that errors are muted, not magnified. Of course, since new errors are being introduced, we must expect some overall error to remain.

Pivoting   When we are processing column i in Gaussian elimination, the (i, i) position is called the **pivot position,** and the entry in it is called the **pivot entry** (or simply the **pivot**). Algorithms for selecting pivots so as to diminish the effects of roundoff error are called **pivoting strategies.** The idea described above is called (Gaussian elimination with) **partial pivoting.** If A is an $n \times n$ matrix, then the method (as applied to the $n \times (n + 1)$ augmented matrix $[A\vdots b]$) may be described as follows:

Gaussian Elimination with Partial Pivoting

1. Begin loop ($i = 1$ to $n - 1$):

2. Find the largest entry (in absolute value) in column i from row i to row n. If the largest value is zero, signal that a unique solution does not exist and stop.

3. If necessary, perform a row interchange to bring the value from step 2 into the pivot position (i, i).

4. For $j = i + 1$ to $j = n$, perform $R_j \leftarrow R_j - m_{j,i}R_i$ where $m_{j,i} = a_{j,i}/a_{i,i}$.

5. End loop.

6. If the (n, n) entry is zero, signal that a unique solution does not exist and stop. Otherwise, solve for the solution x by back substitution.

(We might replace the tests for a value being equal to zero with a test for it being less than some tolerance.) In practice the row interchanges are usually not performed, but are instead simulated by careful bookkeeping. For large matrices, the time spent moving the rows in memory can be considerable. (Moving data in memory and moving data from memory to the CPU are relatively slow operations, and memory management issues are crucial for intelligent implementation of methods for handling large matrices.) There are a number of other practical programming issues, but for now let us continue to concentrate on the numerics.

Example 2.1.2   Let's use Gaussian elimination with partial pivoting to solve $Ax = b$ with the matrix $A = [1\ 2\ 2; 4\ 4\ 12; 4\ 8\ 12]$ and with $b = (1, 12, 8)^T$. We have:

$$
\begin{bmatrix}
1 & 2 & 2 & \vdots & 1 \\
4 & 4 & 12 & \vdots & 12 \\
4 & 8 & 12 & \vdots & 8
\end{bmatrix}
\sim
\begin{bmatrix}
4 & 4 & 12 & \vdots & 12 \\
1 & 2 & 2 & \vdots & 1 \\
4 & 8 & 12 & \vdots & 8
\end{bmatrix}
$$

$$
\sim
\begin{bmatrix}
4 & 4 & 12 & \vdots & 12 \\
0 & 1 & -1 & \vdots & -2 \\
0 & 4 & 0 & \vdots & -4
\end{bmatrix}
$$

$$
\sim
\begin{bmatrix}
4 & 4 & 12 & \vdots & 12 \\
0 & 4 & 0 & \vdots & -4 \\
0 & 1 & -1 & \vdots & -2
\end{bmatrix}
$$

$$
\sim
\begin{bmatrix}
4 & 4 & 12 & \vdots & 12 \\
0 & 4 & 0 & \vdots & -4 \\
0 & 0 & -1 & \vdots & -1
\end{bmatrix}
$$

($m_{2,1} = 1/4$, $m_{3,1} = 1$, $m_{3,2} = 1/4$). Back substitution gives $x_3 = -1/-1 = 1$, $x_2 = -4/4 = -1$, and $x_1 = (12 - 4x_2 - 12x_3)/4 = (12 - 4(-1) - 12(1))/4 = 1$. The solution is $x = (1, -1, 1)^T$.   ∎

We've kept the multipliers for a reason, as we'll see in the next section. As with interchanging rows, we wouldn't actually form a new matrix $[A \vdots b]$ in a program realizing Gaussian elimination with partial pivoting, but would perform the appropriate operations on b at each step.

There are several other pivoting strategies. **Complete pivoting** (or **maximal pivoting**) searches not just down the column but also to the right through the remaining columns, and it uses a combination of row interchanges (corresponding to renumbering equations) and column interchanges (corresponding to renaming variables) to bring to the pivot position the largest entry in the southeast part of the matrix (that part left to be processed). This is rarely necessary, and good results are usually obtained with partial pivoting. (This is fortunate; complete pivoting is expensive.) It is possible to construct matrices for which partial pivoting gives arbitrarily bad results, using arbitrarily large matrices, but experience shows that these matrices simply do not occur in practice. Partial pivoting or a more sophisticated strategy should *always* be employed when performing Gaussian elimination.

It's common to visualize these types of algorithms by writing generic matrices with an X representing an arbitrary nonzero value and a 0 (or blank) representing a value that must be zero. In this scheme the stages of Gaussian elimination (on, say, a

4×4 coefficient matrix A that is to be reduced to a triangular matrix U) are represented as follows:

$$
\begin{bmatrix} X & X & X & X \\ X & X & X & X \\ X & X & X & X \\ X & X & X & X \end{bmatrix} \sim \begin{bmatrix} X & X & X & X \\ 0 & X & X & X \\ 0 & X & X & X \\ 0 & X & X & X \end{bmatrix} \sim \begin{bmatrix} X & X & X & X \\ 0 & X & X & X \\ 0 & 0 & X & X \\ 0 & 0 & X & X \end{bmatrix} \sim \begin{bmatrix} X & X & X & X \\ 0 & X & X & X \\ 0 & 0 & X & X \\ 0 & 0 & 0 & X \end{bmatrix}
$$

The individual entries represented by Xs may change value from stage to stage. Such a visual representation, called a **Wilkinson diagram,** is said to display the **zero structure** of the matrices, that is, the places where entries are necessarily zero.

PROBLEMS 2.1

1. a. Use Gaussian elimination with partial pivoting and backward substitution to solve by hand (you may use a calculator for the arithmetic, but step through the algorithm) the linear system $Ax = b$, where $A = [1\ 2\ 3; 4\ 5\ 6; 7\ 8\ 8]$ and $b = (1, 1, 1)^T$. Check your answer by computing Ax. List the three multipliers explicitly.

b. Repeat with the same A but with $b = (2, -1, 2)^T$.

c. Repeat with $A = [1\ 2\ 3; 4\ 5\ 6; 7\ 8\ 9]$ and $b = (1, 1, 1)^T$.

2. a. Write a detailed algorithm (pseudocode) for solving a square system by Gaussian elimination with partial pivoting and backward substitution. (You will need to expand considerably on what is in the text.) Assume that the row interchanges are actually performed (not simulated).

b. Draw the Wilkinson diagram for solving a linear system by Gaussian elimination with partial pivoting (assuming a 4×4 coefficient matrix, so that the augmented matrix is 4×5).

3. a. Repeat Example 2.1.2 with maximal pivoting. You will need to keep track of which column corresponds to which variable.

b. Solve the linear system of Eq. (2.3) with maximal pivoting and three-digit arithmetic.

4. a. Solve the linear system $Ax = b$ with $A = [0.0002\ 0.2; 2\ 2]$ and $b = (0.2, 4)^T$ using naive Gaussian elimination and three-digit arithmetic. Compare your result to the true answer $(1.00\overline{1001}, 0.99\overline{8998})^T$.

b. Solve the same system using Gaussian elimination with partial pivoting and three-digit arithmetic.

c. Repeat part (a) with $b = (0.2, 5.6)^T$ (for which $x^* \doteq (1.8018, 0.9982)^T$). Then multiply both sides of $Ax = b$ by the matrix $S = [10\ 0; 0\ 1]$, giving the equivalent system $SAx = Sb$, and then repeat part (a). This corresponds to performing the elementary row operations of multiplying row 1 by a constant and row 2 by a constant before beginning the naive Gaussian elimination. Does it help?

d. We say that a matrix exhibits **artificial ill-conditioning** if its poor behavior with respect to Gaussian elimination is due in large measure to it being poorly scaled: The entries in the matrix vary widely, over several orders of magnitude, which is always a warning sign that we should be on the lookout for poor numerical behavior. Multiply both sides of Eq. (2.3) by $S = [10\ 0; 0\ 1]$, and solve the resulting system by naive Gaussian elimination in three-digit arithmetic. Does this help? (If not, the matrix may be truly, not artificially, ill-conditioned.) This technique is sometimes referred to as **balancing** the matrix, that is, making all entries, or the sums along all rows (in absolute value), more nearly equal.

5. a. How many additions and/or subtractions and how many multiplications and/or divisions, in general, are required to perform back substitution after Gaussian elimination has been applied to an $n \times n$ matrix?

b. How many additions/subtractions and how many multiplications/divisions, in general, are required to perform Gaussian elimination with partial pivoting on an $n \times n$ matrix?

MATLAB 2.1

The MATLAB package was designed for problems like the ones we've been discussing in this section. It was originally intended to be an interactive interface to certain Fortran computational matrix algebra subroutines from the LINPACK and EISPACK subroutine libraries. Through MATLAB 5.3, C language versions of these routines have been the computational core of MATLAB. Starting with version 6, the newer LAPACK routines have replaced their older LINPACK and EISPACK counterparts (see www.netlib.org/lapack for details on LAPACK). The LAPACK routines use newer numerical algorithms in some cases (though generally they are based on the same ideas as before). Just as important, they utilize the Basic Linear Algebra Subroutines (BLAS). These machine-specific subroutines take advantage of the particulars of the computer's architecture, especially its memory structure, to greatly increase the speed of various matrix manipulations. BLAS are divided into three classes: Level 1 (vector–vector operations), Level 2 (matrix–vector operations), and Level 3 (matrix–matrix operations). Higher levels generally give better speed and are superior to the traditional element-by-element manipulations. (Of course, the BLAS themselves must use element-by-element operations on a standard computer; acceleration in this case is achieved by arranging the computations for most efficient processing, including the details of retrieval of data from memory and the attempt to maximize the number of computations performed per retrieval of data from memory. On a vector machine, the effects will be even more noticeable.) Traditionally, MATLAB has used only Level 1 BLAS (for example, multiplying matrices by successive dot products of columns). The LAPACK routines, originally designed for use on supercomputers, use (sub-)blocks of matrices to find these products much faster. The key change in computer architecture that makes these changes worthwhile is the widespread use of *caches,* fast memory near the CPU. Cache management is an important practical issue. By carefully using the BLAS and relying on the computer vendor to supply appropriate implementations optimized for their particular machine, the methods can be (and have been) made portable.

The basic MATLAB matrix solver is implemented in the backslash; see `help slash`. If A is a nonsingular matrix and b is a column vector of the appropriate length, then A\b is the solution of $Ax = b$ as computed by Gaussian elimination (with pivoting). For example, enter:

```
» format long
» A=[.00111 .00112;111 113];b=[.00223 224]';
» A\b
```

(Note that the matrix is entered by rows, delineated by semicolons, and that elements within a row are separated by spaces.) In principle we could use $A^{-1}b$; enter:

```
» inv(A)*b
```

but in general this is less accurate. You may see the difference in this example, although this matrix is so badly scaled that you might even see the opposite result, depending on your machine and your version of MATLAB. The matrix inverse approach is also less efficient, and use of the numerical inverse of a matrix is strongly discouraged. Note that A^{-1} is also badly scaled; enter:

```
» inv(A)
```

Using A^{-1} gives no advantage over the use of A in this case (and in most cases). We can check our results by computing the norm of the **residual** $r = b - Ay$, where y is the computed approximation to x. Enter:

```
» y=A\b;r=b-A*y;norm(r)
```

Of course, it isn't perfectly clear that the fact that $\|r\|$ is small implies that the actual error $\|y - x\|$ is small as well; in fact, as we discuss in a later section, this need not be so. For now note that $\|r\|$ is quite small (it likely underflows to zero on your machine, that is, it's so small that it's set to 0), but enter:

```
» norm(y-[1 1]')
```

to see that $\|y - x\|$ is likely not zero; the absolute error is noticeably larger than the norm of the residual. Recall that sometimes a value in MATLAB displays as though it matches another number exactly, but will fail a test for equality because extra bits retained internally by MATLAB are not displayed. Typically we do not expect equality between quantities computed using floating point numbers but only that they differ by less than some tolerance.

Let's try the rescaling idea suggested in Problem 4(c) in hopes of better balancing the matrix. Enter:

```
» S=[100000 0;0 1]
» M=S*A,b1=S*b
» M\b1
```

Notice that M is very near to being a singular matrix in the sense that changing, say, the $(2, 2)$ entry by 1 to 112 gives a singular matrix; enter:

```
» Q=M;Q(2,2)=112
» det(Q)
```

(Recall that a matrix is singular if and only if its determinant is zero.) Matrices that are nearly singular tend to give poor numerical results. The determinant is not a good way to characterize this property of being nearly singular, though; we discuss an appropriate measure of near-singularity in Section 2.5.

As indicated above with the Q matrix, it is possible to select a single element of a vector or matrix. Enter:

```
» y=[2 4 6 8];
» y(3)
» y(3)=-5
» A=[1 2;3 4];
» A(2,1)=-A(2,2)
```

and note the effects. Indexing single elements out of a vector or matrix is a relatively slow process and is best avoided. Rather than writing a loop that manipulates matrix elements successively, we try to find a corresponding vector command that has the same effect (called "vectorizing" the code).

The MATLAB command `rref` computes the reduced row echelon form of a matrix. To see a demonstration of it, enter:

```
» rrefmovie
```

You will be prompted to press the space bar as the demonstration proceeds. The command `format rat` is used by the `rrefmovie` command to obtain approximate rational (rather than floating point) representation, so enter:

```
» format
```

afterwards to return to the default display format. See `help format` for other display formatting options.

In MATLAB the transpose of a vector or matrix is obtained by using the apostrophe; for complex vectors this gives the conjugate transpose (that is, it performs the Hermitian operation). Enter:

```
» x=[1 2 3]
» x'
» x=[1+i 1-i;2+i 2-i]
» x'
```

(see `help punct` and see also `help transpose` and `help ctranspose`). In MATLAB there is also a dot product command `dot` (`dot(x,y)` is the same as `x'*y` if `x` and `y` are column vectors of the same length). See `help length`.

A few more matrix-oriented MATLAB commands that may be of use in this chapter are: `ones` (a matrix of all ones), `zeros` (a matrix of all zeroes), and `diag` (create a diagonal matrix). See `help elmat` for more matrix commands. Let's try a few. Enter:

```
» ones([3 3])
» size(ans)        %Size of a matrix.
» zeros(4,5)
» diag([1 2 3])
» rand([4 4])
» diag(ans)
» why
```

(Strictly speaking, `why` is not a matrix function.) If you are using a version of MATLAB that predates MATLAB6, then the `flops` command is available and counts the total number of floating point operations (flops) in the current MATLAB session. If you are using MATLAB6 or later, the `flops` command is unavailable, as the BLAS typically do not maintain flop counts. Execution time may then be measured using `tic` and `toc`. Typing `tic` before a sequence of commands and `toc` afterwards gives the time elapsed since the `tic` command. Enter:

```
» tic;for i=1:10000,cos(i);end;toc
```

The elapsed time is displayed. Repeat this command several times. Especially on a shared machine, you will get different results. It's common to average the results of several runs.

(See also `help cputime`.) Enter:

```
» tic;for i=1:10000,cos(i);end;t1=toc
```

This measures the actual run-time for this computation and stores it in the variable `t1`. These times may be used to compare the efficiency of various methods. Re-enter that line and you'll probably get a shorter time due to various efficiencies exploited by MATLAB. Enter:

```
» flops(0)
» M*M
» flops
```

to see how many floating point operations are used in computing this product. Again, if you have the latest edition of MATLAB, this doesn't work. Whenever you see the `flops` command in this text, replace it with a corresponding `tic` and `toc` if you don't have `flops`. If you do have `flops`, enter:

```
» help flops
```

and refer again to Problem 5. The `flops` command is useful for pedagogical purposes but less so in practice.

Counting the number of floating point operations used in matrix manipulations is an important technique for comparing their relative efficiency. There are many caveats, however. Although addition and multiplication are both floating point operations, multiplications (and especially divisions) take longer than additions and subtractions, and often we focus on the number of multiplications/divisions rather than all flops. The square root is usually counted as a single flop despite being relatively slower to compute. Numerical analysts have traditionally used flop counts (the total number of floating point operations required) to compare algorithms, but their importance has lessened considerably nowadays, when floating point operations are faster, computer architectures are more varied, and memory management is much more of an issue in run-time than it used to be. Consider comparing flop counts for standard machines to parallel machines, or even for standard machines to machines with a **fused add/multiply** operation (which computes $\alpha x + \beta$ as a single flop, in essence), or for standard machines with and without use of the BLAS; flop counts and their relevance depend on the machine to be used. For many, perhaps most, large problems, the greatest amount of time is spent waiting for data to be moved in from slow memory. Most of the needed floating point calculations can be done while memory is being moved and hence are "hidden" behind memory moves. In such a case, we should be counting "data movement time" rather than calculation time. Despite all this, flop counts are still a common proxy for total run-time and overall efficiency, so we present them but do not emphasize them.

ADDITIONAL PROBLEMS 2.1

6. a. Let $A = [0.007 \ -0.8; -0.1 \ 10]$ be the matrix of Eq. (2.3). Show that if $P = [0 \ 1; 1 \ 0]$, then PA is the matrix obtained by switching row 1 and row 2 of A.

b. Demonstrate that the MATLAB command `A([2 1],:)` produces PA.

c. Choose a 2×4 matrix B and form PB. What is the effect of premultiplication by P?

d. Choose a 4×2 matrix C and form CP. What is the effect of postmultiplication by P?

7. a. Using $A = [0.007 \ -0.8; -0.1 \ 10]$ and $b = (0.7, 10)^T$ from Eq. (2.3), find the solution of $Ax = b$ in MATLAB (use $y=A \backslash b$).

   b. Find the residual vector r, the norm of the residual, and the absolute error (recall that the true solution is $x_1 = -1500$, $x_2 = -14$).

   c. Compute the ratio of the absolute error to the norm of the residual $\|y - x\|/\|r\|$.

8. a. Solve $Ax = b$ with $A = [0.0002 \ 2; 2 \ 2]$ and $b = (2, 4)^T$ using three-digit arithmetic and naive Gaussian elimination. Compare this to the solution found using exact arithmetic.

   b. Repeat part (a) using Gaussian elimination with partial pivoting.

9. a. Solve $Ax = b$ (by hand) using Gaussian elimination with partial pivoting, where $A = [1 \ 2 \ 3 \ 3; 0 \ 2 \ -1 \ -2; 3 \ 4 \ -4 \ 3; -2 \ -3 \ 3 \ 6]$ and $b = (1, 1, 1, 1)^T$.

   b. Solve $Ax = b$ (by hand) using Gaussian elimination with partial pivoting, where $A = [-4 \ 5 \ 2 \ 1; 1 \ 3 \ -3 \ 0; 5 \ 1 \ 0 \ 0; 1 \ 0 \ 0 \ -3]$ and $b = (-1, 0, 0, 0)^T$.

10. The **Hilbert matrices of order** N ($N = 1, 2, \dots$) form a class of well-known ill-conditioned matrices. The MATLAB command $hilb(N)$ generates the Nth such matrix. Perform a numerical experiment which demonstrates this ill-conditioning for $N = 10, 11, 12$. You may wish to use the $invhilb$ command as well.

11. a. Set $N=2$ and use the $flops$ command, if available, to determine how many flops are required to compute the square $M^2 = MM$ of a 2×2 matrix. (For example, you might use $M=rand(N)$; $flops(0); M\char`^2; flops$. If you cannot use the $flops$ command, use tic and toc to get execution times instead. You'll need to use larger matrices.) Store this value. Then double N and repeat until you have computed the number of flops for squaring a 1024×1024 matrix. (This may take a while.) Plot the number of flops required as a function of N. How rapidly is this number growing (e.g., $O(N)$, $O(N^2)$, $O(N^3)$, $O(N^4)$, ...)?

   b. Repeat part (a) for MATLAB's element-by-element square of the matrix ($M.\char`^2$). Why is this so much faster than squaring the matrix in the matrix-algebra sense of part (a)?

12. In Gauss-Jordan elimination, zeroes are introduced both above and below the main diagonal so as to make the matrix U diagonal if possible. (This is the reduced row echelon form.) In Eq. (2.4), for example, this would mean using the $(2, 2)$ entry -1.4286 to eliminate the $(1, 2)$ entry -0.8. Repeat Problem 1(a) using Gauss-Jordan elimination (by hand). Note that you still may only use values below the pivot position for new pivots without destroying the diagonal structure of the northwest part of the matrix.

13. Write a MATLAB program that implements Gaussian elimination with maximal pivoting. You may assume that the input matrix will be nonsingular, and you may actually switch the rows and columns (this is easier but typically slower than simulating the switches). You may wish to use the fact that the MATLAB command $C([k1,k2],:)=C([k2,k1],:)$ interchanges rows $k1$ and $k2$ of a matrix C, and $C(:, [k1,k2])=C(:,[k2,k1])$ interchanges columns $k1$ and $k2$ of this matrix. (The colon : signifies all columns or all rows, respectively.) The elementary row operation $R_j \leftarrow R_j - mR_i$ may be implemented by a command such as $C(i,:)=C(i,:)-m*C(j,:)$. Your program will need to note which column interchanges have been performed so that the elements of your answer can be put back into the correct order. Demonstrate your program.

14. A standard model for the unforced motion of a mass in a mass-spring system leads to the ODE $mx'' + cx' + kx = 0$, where m is the spring's mass, c is the coefficient of friction (damping) of the medium through which the mass moves, and k is the Hooke's Law constant for the spring. If m, c, and k are positive, this leads to the model $x(t) = \exp(\alpha t)(A \cos(\beta t) + B \sin(\beta t))$ for the motion of the mass, where A and B are determined from the initial position x_0 and velocity v_0 of the mass, and $\alpha \pm i\beta$ are the roots of the characteristic equation $mr^2 + cr + k = 0$.

   a. Compute A and B using Gaussian elimination with partial pivoting if $m = 10$ kg, $k = 400$ N/m, and the force due to friction is proportional to the velocity with proportionality constant $c = .5$. Take $x_0 = 0.2$ m and $v_0 = 0.3$ m/s. Repeat using the same values of m, c, and k, but use the initial data $x(1) = -0.1$ m and $x'(1) = 0.2$ m (with time in seconds).

   b. Compute A and B using Gaussian elimination with partial pivoting if $m = 10$ kg, $k = 40$ N/m, and the force due to friction is proportional to the velocity with proportionality constant $c = .5$. Take $x_0 = 0.2$ m and $v_0 = 0.3$ m/s. Repeat using the same values of m, c, and k, but use the initial data $x(1) = 0.1$ m and $x'(1) = -0.3$ m.

15. a. How many floating point operations are required to compute the determinant $|A|$ of a general $n \times n$ matrix by Laplace expansion (repeatedly expanding along a row or column to break the determinant down to many 2×2 matrices)?

b. Using this method, estimate the time required to find the determinant of a 25×25 matrix on your machine.

c. Roughly how many floating point operations (or how much time) does MATLAB use to compute the determinant det(A) of a general $n \times n$ matrix?

2.2 The LU Decomposition

Gaussian elimination with partial pivoting is a good algorithm for small to medium-sized problems; as usual, it's difficult to set a value for "small" or "medium" across a variety of platforms and needs. In addition, most matrices that people are truly interested in working with possess some sort of **structure.** Structure is a generic term that refers either to the pattern of the locations of the zero elements as opposed to nonzero elements within the matrix, referred to as the **sparsity structure** or simply the **sparsity** of the matrix, or to special properties of the matrix, such as symmetry. A matrix with mostly zero entries is said to be **sparse,** and one with mostly nonzero entries is said to be **dense** (or **full**). There are many special numerical methods for special classes of matrices.

As a trivial case, if the matrix is already upper triangular then we need only perform the back substitution (and if it is lower triangular, that is, if its transpose is upper triangular, then we need only perform forward substitution). Back substitution requires $O(n^2)$ flops, which is reasonable even for large n. (As a rule we can't expect to do much better than that; after all, a general $n \times n$ matrix has n^2 distinct entries, each of which should figure into the solution.) For a general matrix, that is, an unstructured matrix, Gaussian elimination with partial pivoting requires about $2n^3/3$ flops (for large n). That's about $n^3/3$ additions/subtractions and about $n^3/3$ multiplications/divisions.

Because it is common to consider matrices so large that $2n^3/3$ flops is unrealistic or at least very inconvenient, and because Gaussian elimination neither takes advantage of (nor preserves) any structure the matrix might possess, we'll need other methods for large matrices. But for small to medium-sized matrices, Gaussian elimination with a pivoting strategy remains the method of choice; and even though it does not take advantage of the structure of the coefficient matrix A, it does have an advantage in the common situation in which we must solve $Ax = b$ repeatedly for different choices of b. In some cases the b vector plays the role of a forcing vector, and we load the system represented by A with various choices of b; there are many cases in which A represents some system that remains unchanged and b represents an input that will be changed often. Note that if we were to solve the linear system $Ax = b$ once by Gaussian elimination, then we could in principle write down every row operation $R_j \leftarrow R_j - m_{j,i} R_i$ and every pivoting operation $R_k \leftrightarrow R_p$ (where we interchange rows k and p) that is performed to obtain the reduced form

$$[A \vdots b] \sim [U \vdots \widetilde{b}].$$

What if we now wish to solve the related system $Ax = d$ by performing Gaussian elimination with partial pivoting? Note that every decision made about which rows to interchange and what multipliers $m_{j,i}$ to use is based only on the entries of A, and *not* on the entries of b (or d). This means that row-reducing $[A\vdots d]$ must give

$$[A\vdots d] \sim [U\vdots \widetilde{d}]$$

for the same matrix U, arrived at by exactly the same steps. Hence we need only store U and the operations required to produce it from A and then perform the corresponding steps on d. We do not need to reduce A to U again. If n is large, this represents a considerable savings of floating point operations.

Example 2.2.1   Consider the linear system

$$\begin{bmatrix} 1 & 2 \\ 2 & 6 \end{bmatrix} \begin{bmatrix} x_1 \\ x_2 \end{bmatrix} = \begin{bmatrix} 1 \\ -2 \end{bmatrix}.$$

Gaussian elimination with partial pivoting gives

$$\begin{bmatrix} 1 & 2 & \vdots & 1 \\ 2 & 6 & \vdots & -2 \end{bmatrix} \sim \begin{bmatrix} 2 & 6 & \vdots & -2 \\ 1 & 2 & \vdots & 1 \end{bmatrix}$$

$$\sim \begin{bmatrix} 2 & 6 & \vdots & -2 \\ 0 & -1 & \vdots & 2 \end{bmatrix},$$

where we have performed, in order, $R_1 \leftrightarrow R_2$, $R_2 \leftarrow R_2 - \frac{1}{2}R_1$. This gives $x_2 = 2/-1 = -2$ and $x_1 = (-2 - 6x_2)/2 = 5$. If we now wish to solve

$$\begin{bmatrix} 1 & 2 \\ 2 & 6 \end{bmatrix} \begin{bmatrix} x_1 \\ x_2 \end{bmatrix} = \begin{bmatrix} 6 \\ 16 \end{bmatrix},$$

then we need only operate on $b = (6, 16)^T$, performing $R_1 \leftrightarrow R_2$ to get $(16, 6)^T$ followed by $R_2 \leftarrow R_2 - \frac{1}{2}R_1$ to get $(16, 6 - \frac{1}{2}16)^T = (16, -2)^T$. The reduced system is therefore

$$\begin{bmatrix} 2 & 6 & \vdots & 16 \\ 0 & -1 & \vdots & -2 \end{bmatrix},$$

which gives $x_2 = -2/-1 = 2$ and $x_1 = (16 - 6x_2)/2 = 2$. We did not need to reduce A to U again; for a 2×2 matrix this is not a big savings, but for a large matrix it would be. ■

LU
Decomposition

After we've processed the coefficient matrix A once we need not process it again; we need only remember the multipliers $m_{j,i}$, the row interchanges, and the final upper triangular matrix U. There's an efficient way to store this data, which, additionally, relates the method of Gaussian elimination with partial pivoting back to matrix algebra by representing the result as a product of two matrices, namely, a certain lower triangular matrix L and the upper triangular matrix U. There are many ways to do this, and any means of writing a square matrix A as the product

$$A = LU \tag{2.5}$$

of a lower triangular matrix L and an upper triangular matrix U is called an **LU decomposition** of A. This is no more than Gaussian elimination in matrix algebra form, and we largely use the terms Gaussian elimination and LU decomposition interchangeably.

It is a fact (considered in more detail in Section 2.3) that if A is reduced to the upper triangular matrix U without any row interchanges, then we may take L in Eq. (2.5) to be the lower triangular matrix with ones on the main diagonal and the multipliers $l_{j,i} = m_{j,i}$ below the main diagonal. This gives a means of computing the decomposition in such a case.

Example 2.2.2 If $A = [2\ \ 2; 1\ \ 2]$, then no pivoting is actually performed, and we simply row-reduce A to U using $R_2 \leftarrow R_2 - m_{2,1}R_1$ (with $m_{2,1} = 1/2$) to find

$$U = \begin{bmatrix} 2 & 2 \\ 0 & 1 \end{bmatrix}.$$

We may take

$$L = \begin{bmatrix} 1 & 0 \\ m_{2,1} & 1 \end{bmatrix}$$

$$= \begin{bmatrix} 1 & 0 \\ 1/2 & 1 \end{bmatrix}$$

as the lower triangular matrix. Let's check this:

$$LU = \begin{bmatrix} 1 & 0 \\ 1/2 & 1 \end{bmatrix} \begin{bmatrix} 2 & 2 \\ 0 & 1 \end{bmatrix}$$

$$= \begin{bmatrix} 2 & 2 \\ 1 & 2 \end{bmatrix}$$

$$= A.$$

Yes, this checks. We have found an LU decomposition of this matrix. ■

If we wish to solve $Ax = b$ for only one value of b, there is no need to perform an LU decomposition. If we expect to work with A repeatedly, however, an LU decomposition may be advisable. (If A is large we may use another approach, described in Chapter 3.) Suppose we have an LU decomposition of a matrix A. How do we use it? To solve $Ax = b$ we proceed as follows:

$$Ax = b$$

$$LUx = b$$

$$L(Ux) = b$$

$$Ly = b$$

because Ux (which we are now calling y) is simply some unknown vector. We can solve $Ly = b$ by forward substitution to find y, and then solve $y = Ux$, that is,

$$Ux = y$$

for x by back substitution (as usual). This is a very computationally efficient process once the LU decomposition is known.

Example 2.2.3 An LU decomposition of $A = [6\ 4\ 2; 3\ -2\ -1; 3\ 4\ 1]$ may be found as follows:

$$\begin{bmatrix} 6 & 4 & 2 \\ 3 & -2 & -1 \\ 3 & 4 & 1 \end{bmatrix} \sim \begin{bmatrix} 6 & 4 & 2 \\ 0 & -4 & -2 \\ 0 & 2 & 0 \end{bmatrix} \sim \begin{bmatrix} 6 & 4 & 2 \\ 0 & -4 & -2 \\ 0 & 0 & -1 \end{bmatrix}$$

$(m_{2,1} = 1/2, m_{3,1} = 1/2, m_{3,2} = -1/2)$, so

$$U = \begin{bmatrix} 6 & 4 & 2 \\ 0 & -4 & -2 \\ 0 & 0 & -1 \end{bmatrix}$$

$$L = \begin{bmatrix} 1 & 0 & 0 \\ 0.5 & 1 & 0 \\ 0.5 & -0.5 & 1 \end{bmatrix}$$

(check that $LU = A$). To solve

$$Ax = \begin{pmatrix} 12 \\ 0 \\ 8 \end{pmatrix}$$

we first solve $Ly = b$, that is,

$$\begin{bmatrix} 1 & 0 & 0 \\ 0.5 & 1 & 0 \\ 0.5 & -0.5 & 1 \end{bmatrix} \begin{bmatrix} y_1 \\ y_2 \\ y_3 \end{bmatrix} = \begin{pmatrix} 12 \\ 0 \\ 8 \end{pmatrix}$$

by forward substitution, giving $y_1 = 12$, $y_2 = 0 - 0.5y_1 = -6$, $y_3 = 8 - 0.5y_1 + 0.5y_2 = 8 - 6 - 3 = -1$. We then solve $Ux = y$, that is,

$$\begin{bmatrix} 6 & 4 & 2 \\ 0 & -4 & -2 \\ 0 & 0 & -1 \end{bmatrix} \begin{bmatrix} x_1 \\ x_2 \\ x_3 \end{bmatrix} = \begin{pmatrix} 12 \\ -6 \\ -1 \end{pmatrix}$$

by back substitution, giving $x_3 = -1/-1 = 1$, $x_2 = (-6 - -2x_3)/-4 = (-6 + 2)/-4 = 1$, $x_1 = (12 - 4x_2 - 2x_3)/6 = (12 - 4 - 2)/6 = 1$. Hence $x = (1, 1, 1)^T$. ∎

Requiring the diagonal entries of L to be ones and computing the entries of L and U in the order we have described is called **Doolittle's method** of obtaining an LU decomposition. Other choices are possible. Note that A has n^2 entries, and U and L each have

$$1 + 2 + \cdots + n = \frac{n(n+1)}{2}$$

entries (1 in column 1, 2 in column 2, and so on). Hence U and L together have

$$\frac{n(n+1)}{2} + \frac{n(n+1)}{2} = n^2 + n$$

entries, so there are n extra entries between L and U that may be assigned freely. Doolittle's method arbitrarily makes the n diagonal entries of L each be 1; **Crout's method** arbitrarily makes the n diagonal entries of U each be 1 (and changes the order of the computations), and yet another method uses the n constraints that the diagonals of L and U be equal. We continue to focus on Doolittle's method; recall that the numerous variants exist to allow us to take advantage of any structure of the matrix and also the specifics of the machine being used.

Compact Form   One of the advantages of using an LU decomposition is that we may replace the matrix A in memory by L and U; at each stage we overwrite A with the portion of U that has been formed already, and store the multipliers in the lower triangle of the matrix. The Wilkinson diagram would be

$$
\begin{bmatrix} X & X & X & X \\ X & X & X & X \\ X & X & X & X \\ X & X & X & X \end{bmatrix} \rightarrow
\begin{bmatrix} X & X & X & X \\ x & X & X & X \\ x & X & X & X \\ x & X & X & X \end{bmatrix} \rightarrow
\begin{bmatrix} X & X & X & X \\ x & X & X & X \\ x & x & X & X \\ x & x & X & X \end{bmatrix} \rightarrow
\begin{bmatrix} X & X & X & X \\ x & X & X & X \\ x & x & X & X \\ x & x & x & X \end{bmatrix}
$$

where we are using X for an entry of U and x for an entry of L. At any time we can extract L and U explicitly, filling in zeroes and (for L) ones as needed, and use them to recreate $A = LU$. More often we simply write the program in such a way that it draws the needed values from this array. For want of a better term we will refer to this as the **compact form** of the LU decomposition; it is also called an **in place** version because it puts L and U in the same place (in memory) as A. This compact form destroys the matrix A, but A can be reformed if needed from L and U (with some slight loss of accuracy in the reconstructed version, of course).

Example 2.2.4   Consider again the matrix

$$
A = \begin{bmatrix} 6 & 4 & 2 \\ 3 & -2 & -1 \\ 3 & 4 & 1 \end{bmatrix}
$$

$$
= \begin{bmatrix} 1 & 0 & 0 \\ 0.5 & 1 & 0 \\ 0.5 & -0.5 & 1 \end{bmatrix} \begin{bmatrix} 6 & 4 & 2 \\ 0 & -4 & -2 \\ 0 & 0 & -1 \end{bmatrix}
$$

$$
= LU
$$

of Example 2.2.3. We would replace A in memory sequentially, as follows:

$$
\begin{bmatrix} 6 & 4 & 2 \\ 3 & -2 & -1 \\ 3 & 4 & 1 \end{bmatrix} \rightarrow
\begin{bmatrix} 6 & 4 & 2 \\ 0.5 & -2 & -1 \\ 0.5 & 4 & 1 \end{bmatrix} \rightarrow
\begin{bmatrix} 6 & 4 & 2 \\ 0.5 & -4 & -2 \\ 0.5 & -0.5 & -1 \end{bmatrix}
$$

The final matrix has the not necessarily null entries of U in the upper triangle (including the diagonal) and the not necessarily null or unit entries of L in the (strict) lower triangle. ∎

If A is so large that storing two matrices of its size (namely, both L and U) would be problematic, this technique can be useful; we simply overwrite A where it sits in memory. Such storage concerns used to be more important; today memory is usually plentiful. However, this technique is still useful in many cases. For example, rather than passing a matrix A to a subroutine and passing its LU decomposition back, we could pass a pointer to the beginning of A to the subroutine, which could operate on A there, putting L and U in its place using this storage scheme.[2]

An LU decomposition is also called an **LU factorization** because it factors A into a product of matrices (its factors). There are many other matrix factorizations of interest, and it pays to be able to write numerical matrix algebra algorithms in terms of formal matrix algebra, both for analysis and for design of such methods. In the next section we use matrix algebra to justify some of what we've done so far and also to explain why we can form L from the multipliers, and what happens if we do need to perform row interchanges (pivoting), as we usually must.

PROBLEMS 2.2

1. a. Find the determinant of the matrix A of Example 2.2.3 by Laplace expansion.

   b. Find the determinant of the matrix A of Example 2.2.3 by using its LU decomposition and the fact that $|M_1 M_2| = |M_1||M_2|$ for any square matrices M_1 and M_2 and the fact that the determinant of a triangular matrix is the product of the entries on its main diagonal.

2. a. Find the LU decomposition of $A = [8\ 8\ 4; 4\ 2\ -1; 2\ 2\ 2]$.

   b. Write the LU decomposition of A in the compact form of Example 2.2.4.

   c. Solve $Ax = (16, 4, 6)^T$ using the LU decomposition of A.

   d. Solve $Ax = (0, 0, -2)^T$ using the LU decomposition of A.

3. a. Show that if $A = [a\ b; c\ d]$ and $L_1 = [1\ 0; -m\ 1]$, then $L_1 A$ is the matrix obtained from A by performing $R_2 \leftarrow R_2 - mR_1$.

   b. Find L_1^{-1}.

c. If $|a| \geq |c|$ and a is nonzero, show that pivoting is not necessary in row-reducing A and that choosing $m = -c/a$ makes $L_1 A$ an upper triangular matrix U. What is the LU decomposition of A in terms of L_1 and U?

4. a. Additively decompose $A = [1\ 2\ 3; 4\ 5\ 6; 7\ 8\ 9]$ into the sum $A = L + U$ of a lower triangular matrix L and an upper triangular matrix U in such a way that L and U are both nonsingular. Is A nonsingular?

   b. If A is an $n \times n$ matrix, how much freedom is there in your choice of L and U in the decomposition $A = L + U$?

5. a. The matrix $A = [0\ 0\ 1; 0\ 2\ 3; 1\ 4\ -4]$ can't be row-reduced without row interchanges, so our LU decomposition method does not apply. Show that if $P = [0\ 0\ 1; 0\ 1\ 0; 1\ 0\ 0]$, then PA has an LU decomposition. Identify L and U explicitly, and then write them in the form of Example 2.2.4.

   b. Repeat with $A = [0\ 1\ 1; 0\ 2\ 3; 1\ 4\ -4]$ and the same P.

MATLAB 2.2

The MATLAB `lu` command may be used to compute the LU decomposition of a (not necessarily square) matrix. Enter:

```
» A=[8 8 4;4 2 -1;2 2 2]
» [L,U]=lu(A)
```

---

[2] Memory issues are often not as immediately apparent in the highly structured MATLAB environment as when working in C++ or a similar language.

Notice that calling `lu` with two output arguments causes it to return two output arguments; calling it with one (or no) output arguments gives a different result. Enter:

```
» M=lu(A)
```

This is the compact form as in Example 2.2.4. If you use `lu` with a matrix that requires pivoting, you'll get an *L* that is not exactly lower triangular. We explain this in Section 2.3.

If you were using the single output form `M=lu(A)` you could extract the upper and lower triangles using the MATLAB commands `triu` and `tril`. Enter:

```
» U1=triu(M)
» L1=tril(M)
```

and note that `U1` is the same as `U`, but `L1` contains the entire lower triangle of `M`, including the diagonal. We could extract the diagonal if desired as a vector or as a matrix as follows. Enter:

```
» diag(M)
» diag(diag(M))
```

(The `diag` command takes a matrix and returns its diagonal as a vector, or takes a vector and makes a diagonal matrix from it. Think about why this makes `diag(diag(M))` work as it does.)

We need to fix the diagonal of `L1`. There are many ways, including a loop. Enter:

```
» for i=1:size(L1,1);L1(i,i)=1;end
```

However, using a loop is not usually the best approach. We can fix the diagonal of `L1` without loops as follows; enter:

```
» L1=tril(M)      %Reset L1.
» L1=L1-diag(diag(L1))+eye(size(L1,1))
```

which subtracts out the diagonal of `L1` and adds in the identity matrix I_n. While this doesn't have an explicit loop, forming the sparse (that is, mostly full of zeroes) matrices `diag(diag(L1))` and `eye(size(L1,1))` is terribly wasteful if *n* is large. Another possible way to fix the diagonal of `L1` is to initially extract `L1` from `M` as follows. Enter:

```
» L1=tril(M,-1)
```

This starts extracting from one diagonal below the main diagonal (called the **first subdiagonal**). Let's use this idea. Enter:

```
» L1=tril(M,-1)+eye(size(L1,1))
```

to form `L1`. However, if *n* is large we probably don't want to actually create I_n and should consider another approach (possibly the for-loop).

How does the `lu` command know whether to return a single matrix containing both *L* and *U* or the two separate matrices? Two useful permanent variables, `nargin` and `nargout`, are automatically set inside (that is, local to) any program. The value of nargin is the number of inputs to the function, and the value of nargout is the number of output arguments that have been requested. You can see its use in fminsearch; enter:

```
» more on
» type fminsearch
```

and note that in the very first executable statements, the value of nargin is checked and the variable options is set to a default value (the empty vector [], which has no elements) if nargin is less than 3, indicating that a value of options was not supplied by the user.

To demonstrate the use of these variables, suppose that we could access only the compact form, which is the result of using the lu command with a single output, that is, we could call it only in the form M=lu(A). (For example, this might happen if we used MATLAB to call a C or Fortran program that computed the LU decomposition by a different algorithm. MATLAB can call C and Fortran programs and this is frequently useful or even necessary.) We could mimic the behavior of the actual lu command with the following program:

```
function [L,U,x]=ludecomp(A,b)
%LUDECOMP LU decomposition of A and optional solution of Ax=b.
%          Assumes that no pivoting need be performed.
[m n]=size(A);if m~=n | n<2, error('A must be a square matrix.'),end
L=lu(A);x=[];
if nargout>1
    U=triu(L);L=tril(L,-1)+eye(n);
end
if nargin>1 & nargout>1
    if any(size(b)~=[n 1]), error('A and b must be conformable.'),end
    y=L\b;
    x=U\y;
    if nargout==2  %Prepare outputs.
    U=x;           %Assume L,x are desired.
    end
end
end
```

Let's test this program. Enter:

```
» clear all
» A=[8 8 4;4 2 -1;2 2 2]
» ludecomp(A)   %Should just return the overlaid form.
» [L,U]=ludecomp(A)   %Should return L and U.
» [L,x]=ludecomp(A,[1 1 1]')   %Should return L and x.
» [L,U,x]=ludecomp(A,[1 1 1]') %Should return L, U, and x.
» [L,U,x]=ludecomp(A) %Should return L, U, and an empty vector for x.
```

Now let's discuss ludecomp.m. The statement if m~=n | n<2 (equivalent to (m~=n | n<2)) checks for $m \neq n$, indicating a nonsquare matrix, or if the matrix happens to be a scalar. (The symbol | is MATLAB's relational operator *or*; see `help relop`.) The LU decomposition of a scalar is exactly what one would expect. Enter:

```
» [L,U]=lu(7)
L =
    1
U =
    7
```

but we rule out this trivial case in our program for convenience. We then find the LU decomposition of the matrix A and call it L rather than some temporary name to avoid maintaining more matrices than we need. (Overwriting A by `lu(A)` would be sensible too and is often done.)

If more than one output argument has been requested, we will need either both L and U or L and x. We will find x if requested by the LU decomposition, so whenever `nargout` exceeds 1, we will need L and U.

If more than one input argument has been provided, then we must solve $Ax = b$, and we do that using the LU decomposition (which we have already computed and extracted from the output of `lu`). The statement `if any(size(b)~=[n 1])` checks the size of b against the expected size ($n \times 1$). We are checking a 2-vector against a 2-vector here, so the result is a 2-vector of zeroes and ones. For example, enter:

```
» [2 2]~=[2 3]
```

We wish to signal an error if either dimension does not match, so we use the `any` command to check if any element of the result of the comparison is true (that is, is equal to 1). If not, we solve using the backslash command and the LU decomposition.

If `ludecomp` is called with exactly two outputs requested, then we assume that the desired outputs are L and U if the number of input arguments is 1, and that the desired outputs are the result of `lu(A)` and the solution x of $Ax = b$ if the number of input arguments is 2 (that is, if b is provided). After preparing the outputs in this manner, we are done.

The `nargin` and `nargout` commands provide great flexibility in structuring MATLAB calling sequences, and their use should be better documented within the program than they are in our example above. See also `help varargin` and `help varargout`.

The program uses the backslash command to solve the triangular systems $Ly = b$ and $Ux = y$. Is this faster than using A\b? Yes, it is. The verification by MATLAB that no reduction is needed is much quicker than actually performing the reduction. (Partial pivoting requires this much checking of the magnitudes of entries in addition to performing the row operations.) Let's check this; enter:

```
» clear all
» A=rand(1000);b=ones([1000 1]);c=ones([1000 1]);
» tic;[L,U]=ludecomp(A);toc   %May take a while.
» tic;x=A\b;toc
» tic;y=L\c;xx=U\y;toc
```

This test is somewhat unfair in that most matrices of interest are far from random. The variable c addresses the objection that b may have been loaded into fast memory and hence that some of the speed increase may have been due to time saved moving data from memory. This experiment should demonstrate that, once L and U are known, the use of the LU decomposition generally reduces computational time by about one order of magnitude, a considerable advantage. Adding in the cost of performing the initial LU decomposition, it appears that this is worthwhile (for sufficiently large matrices) if we are solving as few as two linear systems involving A.

We used a new variable xx rather than reusing x because there is some speed advantage in having the vector to which the result will be assigned pre-allocated space in memory. By the same token, pre-allocating a matrix as zeros([M N]) is sometimes advantageous within a program. To see this effect, enter:

```
» clear all
» tic;for j=1:500,z(j)=sin(10*j);end;toc
» tic;y=zeros([1 5000]);for i=1:5000,y(i)=cos(10*i);
   end;toc
```

Of course, using explicit indexing into the vector (y(i)) is itself a relatively slow operation; compare t=1:500;y=sin(10*t).

Many MATLAB commands can return more than one output if it is requested. For example, a useful command in writing a program that uses pivoting is the max command with two output arguments. Enter:

```
» [M,ind]=max([4 3 5 2 1])
```

to see that max returns not only the maximum value but its location. Enter:

```
» [M,ind]=max([4 3 5 2 1 5])
```

to see that the first location of the maximum is returned in the index vector. (In pivoting, one must have a rule for breaking ties resulting from more than one entry having maximum modulus.) The commands min, median, and sort function similarly.

Since real matrices can have complex eigenvalues, we'll need to work with complex values on occasion. Enter:

```
» clear all
» i
» j
```

The values of i and j are both set to $i = \sqrt{-1}$ initially. MATLAB handles complex arithmetic automatically. For example, enter:

```
» [z,V]=eig([0 1;-1 0])
» dot(conj(z),z)
```

(The conj command gives the complex conjugate of its argument; the columns of V are the eigenvectors of the matrix in the same order as the eigenvalues appear in z.) See also `help real` and `help imag`. The `lu` command and other such commands work with matrices that have complex entries.

We mention briefly that MATLAB allows arrays with more than two dimensions, that is, you may enter a $2 \times 3 \times 4$ matrix. Enter:

```
» A=reshape(1:24,2,3,4)
```

This is rarely of use in numerical work. See `help shiftdim` and `help squeeze` for some related commands.

In addition, MATLAB allows empty arrays. Enter:

```
» v=[]
» size(v)
```

The variable v is a 0×0 matrix with no elements. Enter:

```
» v=[v,1]
» v=[v,2]
» c="       %Two single quotes, not one double quote.
» size(c)
```

Empty matrices are often used in MATLAB as place holders and to initialize variables used in loops. In many MATLAB commands, entering an empty matrix instructs MATLAB to use default values for the corresponding parameters. This is explained in the help for the command.

ADDITIONAL PROBLEMS 2.2

6. **a.** Find the LU decomposition of the matrix $A =$ [4 5 6; 2 3.5 1; −1 −1 2].

    b. Write the LU decomposition of A in the compact form of Example 2.2.4.

    c. Use the LU decomposition of A to solve the linear system $Ax = (12, 6, 1)^T$.

7. **a.** Find the LU decomposition of the matrix $A =$ [18 3 −6; 6 19 16; −9 3 13.5].

    b. Write the LU decomposition of A in the compact form.

    c. Use the LU decomposition of A to solve the linear system $Ax = (21, 25, 6)^T$.

8. What matrix has the LU decomposition represented by [1 2 1; −0.2 1 0; .4 −0.5 1] in compact form?

9. What matrix has the LU decomposition represented by [5 −1 3; −0.5 2 1; 0.3 0.5 4] in compact form?

10. Use the Doolittle LU decomposition of $A =$ [8 8 4; 4 2 −1; 2 2 2] from Problem 2(a) to find an LU decomposition of A for which the diagonal entries of U are all equal to 1 (but the diagonal entries of L need not be).

11. **a.** Show that A is nonsingular if and only if L and U are both nonsingular.

    b. Show that L is always nonsingular.

    c. Show that if A is nonsingular, then $A^{-1} = U^{-1}L^{-1}$.

    d. Given the LU decomposition of A, what is the LU decomposition of A^T?

    e. Can L and/or U ever be symmetric?

12. **a.** Find the LU decomposition of $A =$ [2 1 0 0; 1 2 1 0; 0 1 2 1; 0 0 1 2].

    b. Find the LU decomposition of $A =$ [2 −1 0 0; −1 2 −1 0; 0 −1 2 −1; 0 0 −1 2].

13. **a.** Solve the linear system in Additional Problem 9 using Gaussian elimination with maximal pivoting, which has roundoff error properties that are superior to those of Gaussian elimination with partial pivoting.

    b. If $A = LU$ and $U = L^T$, show that A is positive semi-definite.

14. A discrete predator–prey model relates the populations of two interacting species, a predator of population size F_i and its sole prey of population size R_i. (We think of the predator and prey as foxes and rabbits, respectively.) These are used, for example, to predict the effect of spraying for Mediterranean fruit flies on the population of aphids in California. The basic form of such a model is $F_{i+1} = \alpha F_i + \beta R_i$, $R_{i+1} = -\gamma F_i + \delta R_i$, where all parameters are positive and $\alpha < 1$ (the predator dies off in the absence of the prey) and $\delta > 1$ (the prey thrives in the absence of the predator). Take i to be in months.

a. If $\alpha = 0.3$, $\beta = 0.25$, $\gamma = 0.4$, and $\delta = 1.3$, compute the population after six months if $R_0 = 1000$, $F_0 = 20$.

b. For the same parameter values, if $R_6 = 900$, $F_6 = 40$, use Gaussian elimination to estimate R_5 and F_5. Repeat until you have an estimate for R_0 and F_0.

15. Write a MATLAB program that accepts as arguments a nonsingular matrix A and one or two vectors b_1, b_2.

If one output argument is requested, the program should return the compact form of the LU decomposition of A if A is the sole input and the solution of the linear system $Ax = b_1$ (found by LU decomposition) otherwise. If two output arguments are requested, the program should return the LU decomposition L and U of A if A is the sole input and the solution of $Ax = b_1$ otherwise. If three output arguments are requested, the program should return the compact form of the LU decomposition of A if A and both b_1, b_2 are given and the LU decomposition L and U of A if A and b_1 are given. If four output arguments are requested, the program should return the LU decomposition L and U of A if A and both b_1, b_2 are given. Signal an error and terminate execution in any case not covered.

2.3 The LU Decomposition with Pivoting

Gaussian elimination is referred to as a **direct method** for solving a linear system; direct methods process the matrix element by element (or row by row), finishing one element (or row) before moving on to the next. This is very different from the methods of Chapter 1; in infinite precision arithmetic, Gaussian elimination would always give us the right answer in finitely many operations (as the quadratic formula does for quadratic equations), whereas Newton's method would always give an approximation (even in infinite precision arithmetic). There are also **iterative methods** for linear systems that are useful for certain types of large systems (as we discuss in Chapter 3).

Our method for finding an LU decomposition works only when the matrix does not require pivoting. It can be shown that, for certain special types of matrices, Gaussian elimination with partial pivoting will in fact never actually pivot (interchange rows). In general, however, a matrix need not have an LU decomposition at all. For example, consider the matrix

$$\begin{bmatrix} 0 & 1 \\ 1 & 1 \end{bmatrix}.$$

This is a square, nonsingular, well-behaved matrix. However, to have

$$\begin{bmatrix} 0 & 1 \\ 1 & 1 \end{bmatrix} = \begin{bmatrix} 1 & 0 \\ m & 1 \end{bmatrix} \begin{bmatrix} a & b \\ 0 & c \end{bmatrix}$$

would require that (upon multiplying the matrices on the RHS) $a = 0$, $b = 1$, $am = 1$, and $mb + c = 1$. But $am = 1$ is not possible, because $a = 0$. Therefore this matrix does not admit an LU decomposition of the form we have been discussing. Of course if we simply interchange the rows then the matrix is essentially its own

LU decomposition:

$$\begin{bmatrix} 1 & 1 \\ 0 & 1 \end{bmatrix} = \begin{bmatrix} 1 & 0 \\ 0 & 1 \end{bmatrix}\begin{bmatrix} 1 & 1 \\ 0 & 1 \end{bmatrix}.$$

(The sole multiplier is zero, and the LU decomposition takes the form $A = IA$.) We certainly want to find a way to include such "nice" matrices in the general scheme of LU decomposition.

Elementary Matrices

To find a way to get a (near) LU decomposition of matrices that require pivoting—which is the typical case, unlike the specially prepared examples in the previous section—let's revisit Gaussian elimination. We perform Gaussian elimination using two of the three elementary row operations. Each elementary row operation corresponds to an elementary matrix that implements that operation by premultiplication; this matrix is always the matrix that arises when the elementary row operation is applied to the identity matrix. That is, if A is an $n \times n$ matrix, then performing $R_i \leftrightarrow R_j$ to A is equivalent to forming the matrix product PA, where P is the matrix obtained from I_n by interchanging rows i and j of it. The other row operations are handled analogously.

Example 2.3.1   Let $A = [1\ 2\ 3; 0\ 5\ 6; 0\ 8\ 9]$. To perform $R_2 \leftrightarrow R_3$, we may use the elementary matrix

$$P = \begin{bmatrix} 1 & 0 & 0 \\ 0 & 0 & 1 \\ 0 & 1 & 0 \end{bmatrix}$$

giving

$$PA = \begin{bmatrix} 1 & 0 & 0 \\ 0 & 0 & 1 \\ 0 & 1 & 0 \end{bmatrix}\begin{bmatrix} 1 & 2 & 3 \\ 0 & 5 & 6 \\ 0 & 8 & 9 \end{bmatrix}$$
$$= \begin{bmatrix} 1 & 2 & 3 \\ 0 & 8 & 9 \\ 0 & 5 & 6 \end{bmatrix}$$

(check this). The matrix P implements $R_2 \leftrightarrow R_3$ for 3×3 matrices. If we now want to use row 2 of PA to eliminate its $(3, 2)$ entry, we may use the elementary matrix corresponding to the operation $R_3 \leftarrow R_3 - (5/8)R_2$, which we find by performing $R_3 \leftarrow R_3 - (5/8)R_2$ on I_3, giving

$$E = \begin{bmatrix} 1 & 0 & 0 \\ 0 & 1 & 0 \\ 0 & -5/8 & 1 \end{bmatrix}.$$

(Notice that E is lower triangular.) Then

$$E(PA) = \begin{bmatrix} 1 & 0 & 0 \\ 0 & 1 & 0 \\ 0 & -5/8 & 1 \end{bmatrix} \begin{bmatrix} 1 & 2 & 3 \\ 0 & 8 & 9 \\ 0 & 5 & 6 \end{bmatrix}$$

$$= \begin{bmatrix} 1 & 2 & 3 \\ 0 & 8 & 9 \\ 0 & 0 & 3/8 \end{bmatrix}$$

(please verify this by hand). The matrix EPA is in echelon (reduced) form; that is, the matrix

$$M = EP$$

$$= \begin{bmatrix} 1 & 0 & 0 \\ 0 & 1 & 0 \\ 0 & -5/8 & 1 \end{bmatrix} \begin{bmatrix} 1 & 0 & 0 \\ 0 & 0 & 1 \\ 0 & 1 & 0 \end{bmatrix}$$

$$= \begin{bmatrix} 1 & 0 & 0 \\ 0 & 0 & 1 \\ 0 & 1 & -5/8 \end{bmatrix}$$

has the effect of triangularizing A, meaning that it transforms A into a row-equivalent upper triangular matrix U:

$$MA = \begin{bmatrix} 1 & 0 & 0 \\ 0 & 0 & 1 \\ 0 & 1 & -5/8 \end{bmatrix} \begin{bmatrix} 1 & 2 & 3 \\ 0 & 5 & 6 \\ 0 & 8 & 9 \end{bmatrix}$$

$$= \begin{bmatrix} 1 & 2 & 3 \\ 0 & 8 & 9 \\ 0 & 0 & 3/8 \end{bmatrix}$$

(check this).　■

The elementary matrices corresponding to the operations $R_j \leftarrow R_j - m_{j,i} R_i$ in Gaussian elimination are *always lower triangular* because j is always greater than i so that its row lies below row i. For example, $R_4 \leftarrow R_4 - m_{4,2} R_2$ would correspond to premultiplication by

$$E_{4,2} = \begin{bmatrix} 1 & 0 & 0 & 0 & 0 \\ 0 & 1 & 0 & 0 & 0 \\ 0 & 0 & 1 & 0 & 0 \\ 0 & -m_{4,2} & 0 & 1 & 0 \\ 0 & 0 & 0 & 0 & 1 \end{bmatrix}$$

($n = 5$). Notice that $E_{4,2}$ is not a specific matrix; it depends on the particular $m_{4,2}$ needed to eliminate the $(4, 2)$ entry of the matrix we are working on.

Now think again about the previous section, where we assumed that no row inter-changes were needed to perform Gaussian elimination. That means that the row-reduction process can be represented algebraically as

$$E_{4,3} E_{4,2} E_{3,2} E_{4,1} E_{3,1} E_{2,1} A = U \tag{2.6}$$

($n = 4$). Look at Eq. (2.6): The first multiplication is by $E_{2,1}$, which eliminates the $(2, 1)$ entry of A. Then comes the multiplication by $E_{3,1}$, which eliminates the $(3, 1)$ entry of A, and then multiplication by $E_{4,1}$ to eliminate the $(4, 1)$ entry of A. This completes the process of introducing zeroes in the first column below a_{11}. We then move on to column 2 and use $E_{3,2}$ and $E_{4,2}$ to make zero the entries beneath a_{22}, successively triangularizing the matrix as we move from left to right across it. Finally we use $E_{4,3}$ to introduce the final needed zero in the $(4, 3)$ position:

$$\begin{bmatrix} X & X & X & X \\ X & X & X & X \\ X & X & X & X \\ X & X & X & X \end{bmatrix} \sim \begin{bmatrix} X & X & X & X \\ 0 & X & X & X \\ X & X & X & X \\ X & X & X & X \end{bmatrix} \sim \begin{bmatrix} X & X & X & X \\ 0 & X & X & X \\ 0 & X & X & X \\ X & X & X & X \end{bmatrix} \sim \begin{bmatrix} X & X & X & X \\ 0 & X & X & X \\ 0 & X & X & X \\ 0 & X & X & X \end{bmatrix}$$

$$\sim \begin{bmatrix} X & X & X & X \\ 0 & X & X & X \\ 0 & 0 & X & X \\ 0 & X & X & X \end{bmatrix} \sim \begin{bmatrix} X & X & X & X \\ 0 & X & X & X \\ 0 & 0 & X & X \\ 0 & 0 & X & X \end{bmatrix} \sim \begin{bmatrix} X & X & X & X \\ 0 & X & X & X \\ 0 & 0 & X & X \\ 0 & 0 & 0 & X \end{bmatrix}.$$

Each step corresponds to a single matrix multiplication. Of course, note that the matrix

$$E_{3,1} E_{2,1}$$

is the same as applying $R_3 \leftarrow R_3 - m_{3,1} R_{21}$ to $E_{2,1}$, and that the multiplier $m_{3,1}$ used isn't affected by the action of $E_{2,1}$, so

$$E_{3,1} E_{2,1} = \begin{bmatrix} 1 & 0 & 0 & 0 \\ 0 & 1 & 0 & 0 \\ -m_{3,1} & 0 & 1 & 0 \\ 0 & 0 & 0 & 1 \end{bmatrix} \begin{bmatrix} 1 & 0 & 0 & 0 \\ -m_{2,1} & 1 & 0 & 0 \\ 0 & 0 & 1 & 0 \\ 0 & 0 & 0 & 1 \end{bmatrix}$$

$$= \begin{bmatrix} 1 & 0 & 0 & 0 \\ -m_{2,1} & 1 & 0 & 0 \\ -m_{3,1} & 0 & 1 & 0 \\ 0 & 0 & 0 & 1 \end{bmatrix}$$

(check the multiplication). By extension,

$$E_{4,1} E_{3,1} E_{2,1} = \begin{bmatrix} 1 & 0 & 0 & 0 \\ -m_{2,1} & 1 & 0 & 0 \\ -m_{3,1} & 0 & 1 & 0 \\ -m_{4,1} & 0 & 0 & 1 \end{bmatrix}$$

$$= L_1.$$

But we cannot include $E_{3,2}$ since the multiplier will depend on the effects on column 2 of having introduced zeroes in column 1. Note that this is a lower triangular matrix; we are using triangular matrices to triangularize A to U. We can write

$$E_{4,2}E_{3,2} = \begin{bmatrix} 1 & 0 & 0 & 0 \\ 0 & 1 & 0 & 0 \\ 0 & -m_{3,2} & 1 & 0 \\ 0 & -m_{4,2} & 0 & 1 \end{bmatrix}$$

$$= L_2$$

and

$$E_{4,3} = \begin{bmatrix} 1 & 0 & 0 & 0 \\ 0 & 1 & 0 & 0 \\ 0 & 0 & 1 & 0 \\ 0 & 0 & -m_{4,3} & 1 \end{bmatrix}$$

$$= L_3$$

and write Eq. (2.6) as

$$L_3 L_2 L_1 A = U \tag{2.7}$$

or simply $MA = U$ with $M = L_3 L_2 L_1$. (Matrices such as L_1, L_2, and L_3 are called **Gauss transformations.**) Now comes a significant point: Every matrix L_i is a lower triangular matrix with ones on the main diagonal (we say that such a matrix is **unit lower triangular**). This means that $\det(L_i) = 1$ and in particular L_i^{-1} always exists. Perhaps surprisingly, L_i^{-1} is itself lower triangular and

$$L_1^{-1} = \begin{bmatrix} 1 & 0 & 0 & 0 \\ m_{2,1} & 1 & 0 & 0 \\ m_{3,1} & 0 & 1 & 0 \\ m_{4,1} & 0 & 0 & 1 \end{bmatrix}$$

$$L_2^{-1} = \begin{bmatrix} 1 & 0 & 0 & 0 \\ 0 & 1 & 0 & 0 \\ 0 & m_{3,2} & 1 & 0 \\ 0 & m_{4,2} & 0 & 1 \end{bmatrix}$$

$$L_3^{-1} = \begin{bmatrix} 1 & 0 & 0 & 0 \\ 0 & 1 & 0 & 0 \\ 0 & 0 & 1 & 0 \\ 0 & 0 & m_{4,3} & 1 \end{bmatrix},$$

as is easily verified by computing, for example, $L_3^{-1}L_3 = I$. (Maybe this isn't so surprising; L_3^{-1} should reverse the action of L_3 and, indeed, L_3 represents the row operation

$R_4 \leftarrow R_4 - m_{4,3}R_3$, and L_3^{-1} represents the row operation $R_4 \leftarrow R_4 + m_{4,3}R_3$, which reverses it.) Hence we have

$$MA = U$$
$$L_3 L_2 L_1 A = U$$
$$L_2 L_1 A = L_3^{-1}U$$
$$L_1 A = L_2^{-1}L_3^{-1}U$$
$$A = L_1^{-1}L_2^{-1}L_3^{-1}U$$
$$= LU,$$

which is the LU decomposition, since a product of unit lower triangular matrices is itself unit lower triangular. The details do not change for a general n.

LU with Pivoting   What happens if we must pivot? In the worst case we might need to pivot at every step. Since the identity matrix I_n represents a trivial row interchange $R_i \leftrightarrow R_i$, we can write Eq. (2.7) as

$$L_3 P_3 L_2 P_2 L_1 P_1 A = U,$$

where each P_i is an elementary matrix that represents a row interchange (as in Example 2.3.1). It may be that $P_i = I$ for some i (and possibly for all i, as in the examples of the previous section). Note that P_i must be its own inverse, since P_i interchanges two rows. Hence $P_i P_i$ interchanges the rows and then switches them back. Therefore $P_i P_i = I$ (the identity transformation) or

$$P_i = P_i^{-1}.$$

Thus we could write

$$L_3 P_3 L_2 P_2 L_1 P_1 A = U$$
$$P_3 L_2 P_2 L_1 P_1 A = L_3^{-1}U$$
$$L_2 P_2 L_1 P_1 A = P_3 L_3^{-1}U$$
$$P_2 L_1 P_1 A = L_2^{-1}P_3 L_3^{-1}U$$
$$L_1 P_1 A = P_2 L_2^{-1}P_3 L_3^{-1}U$$
$$P_1 A = L_1^{-1}P_2 L_2^{-1}P_3 L_3^{-1}U$$
$$A = P_1 L_1^{-1}P_2 L_2^{-1}P_3 L_3^{-1}U,$$

which gives a decomposition of the form

$$A = \widetilde{L}U, \tag{2.8}$$

where U is upper triangular but the matrix $\widetilde{L} = P_1 L_1^{-1}P_2 L_2^{-1}P_3 L_3^{-1}$ is not in general lower triangular. The MATLAB command [L,U]=lu(A) produces $\widetilde{L}$ and U.

Permutation It is not hard to show that it is always the case that $\widetilde{L} = P^T L$, where L is a unit lower
Matrices triangular matrix and $P = P_3 P_2 P_1$ is a **permutation matrix,** that is, P is the result of
permuting (reordering) the rows of the identity matrix. For example,

$$P = \begin{bmatrix} 0 & 0 & 0 & 1 \\ 1 & 0 & 0 & 0 \\ 0 & 0 & 1 & 0 \\ 0 & 1 & 0 & 0 \end{bmatrix}$$

is a permutation matrix. The matrices P_i are special cases of permutation matrices. In
general, if P is a permutation matrix, then P^{-1} is also a permutation matrix, $P^{-1} = P^T$
(permutation matrices are orthogonal), and P has exactly one 1 in each row and in each
column. In addition, PA is equal to A with its rows permuted in the same way as those
of P. For example,

$$\begin{bmatrix} 0 & 0 & 0 & 1 \\ 1 & 0 & 0 & 0 \\ 0 & 0 & 1 & 0 \\ 0 & 1 & 0 & 0 \end{bmatrix} \begin{bmatrix} 1 & 1 & 1 & 1 \\ 2 & 2 & 2 & 2 \\ 3 & 3 & 3 & 3 \\ 4 & 4 & 4 & 4 \end{bmatrix} = \begin{bmatrix} 4 & 4 & 4 & 4 \\ 1 & 1 & 1 & 1 \\ 3 & 3 & 3 & 3 \\ 2 & 2 & 2 & 2 \end{bmatrix}$$

(check this). Hence Eq. (2.8) may be written

$$A = P^T LU$$

or

$$PA = LU. \tag{2.9}$$

This is the form of the LU decomposition for matrices that require pivoting. We also
refer to it as the LU decomposition (since Gaussian elimination is always performed in
the form of Gaussian elimination with pivoting). We may interpret Eq. (2.9) as follows:
For any square matrix A, there is a permutation P of its rows such that PA admits an
LU decomposition. Of course, we do not know P until we perform the actual reduction,
so this is not useful in practice. In addition, we do not form the large and sparse (that is,
comprising nearly all zeroes) matrix P. Instead we form a vector that records the order
in which the rows of I have been permuted to give P and simulate the effects of P. For
example,

$$P = \begin{bmatrix} 0 & 0 & 0 & 1 \\ 1 & 0 & 0 & 0 \\ 0 & 0 & 1 & 0 \\ 0 & 1 & 0 & 0 \end{bmatrix}$$

might be encoded as the vector $p = [4 \ 1 \ 3 \ 2]$ (row 1 of the matrix P has its only
nonzero entry in column 4, row 2 has its only nonzero entry in column 1, etc.).

Example 2.3.2   Let's find the LU decomposition of the matrix $A = [1 \ 2 \ 3; 4 \ 5 \ 6; 7 \ 8 \ 9]$. We begin by performing $R_1 \leftrightarrow R_3$:

$$P_1 A = \begin{bmatrix} 0 & 0 & 1 \\ 0 & 1 & 0 \\ 1 & 0 & 0 \end{bmatrix} \begin{bmatrix} 1 & 2 & 3 \\ 4 & 5 & 6 \\ 7 & 8 & 9 \end{bmatrix}$$

$$= \begin{bmatrix} 7 & 8 & 9 \\ 4 & 5 & 6 \\ 1 & 2 & 3 \end{bmatrix}$$

($p = [3 \ 2 \ 1]$). We now perform the reductions for column 1

$$L_1 P_1 A = \begin{bmatrix} 1 & 0 & 0 \\ -4/7 & 1 & 0 \\ -1/7 & 0 & 1 \end{bmatrix} \begin{bmatrix} 7 & 8 & 9 \\ 4 & 5 & 6 \\ 1 & 2 & 3 \end{bmatrix}$$

$$= \begin{bmatrix} 7 & 8 & 9 \\ 0 & 3/7 & 6/7 \\ 0 & 6/7 & 12/7 \end{bmatrix}$$

(check these multiplications; in MATLAB you may use `format rat` to get the ratio-of-integers form used here). Next we pivot again to obtain

$$P_2 L_1 P_1 A = \begin{bmatrix} 1 & 0 & 0 \\ 0 & 0 & 1 \\ 0 & 1 & 0 \end{bmatrix} \begin{bmatrix} 7 & 8 & 9 \\ 0 & 3/7 & 6/7 \\ 0 & 6/7 & 12/7 \end{bmatrix}$$

$$= \begin{bmatrix} 7 & 8 & 9 \\ 0 & 6/7 & 12/7 \\ 0 & 3/7 & 6/7 \end{bmatrix}$$

(switch the corresponding entries in $p = [3 \ 2 \ 1]$ to get $p = [3 \ 1 \ 2]$). Then

$$L_2 P_2 L_1 P_1 A = \begin{bmatrix} 1 & 0 & 0 \\ 0 & 1 & 0 \\ 0 & -1/2 & 1 \end{bmatrix} \begin{bmatrix} 7 & 8 & 9 \\ 0 & 6/7 & 12/7 \\ 0 & 3/7 & 6/7 \end{bmatrix}$$

$$= \begin{bmatrix} 7 & 8 & 9 \\ 0 & 6/7 & 12/7 \\ 0 & 0 & 0 \end{bmatrix}$$

(note that A is singular since it is row equivalent to a matrix with zero determinant). So

$$U = \begin{bmatrix} 7 & 8 & 9 \\ 0 & 6/7 & 12/7 \\ 0 & 0 & 0 \end{bmatrix}$$

and

$$\begin{aligned}
\widetilde{L} &= (L_2 P_2 L_1 P_1)^{-1} \\
&= P_1^T L_1^{-1} P_2^T L_2^{-1} \\
&= P_1 L_1^{-1} P_2 L_2^{-1} \\
&= \begin{bmatrix} 0 & 0 & 1 \\ 0 & 1 & 0 \\ 1 & 0 & 0 \end{bmatrix} \begin{bmatrix} 1 & 0 & 0 \\ 4/7 & 1 & 0 \\ 1/7 & 0 & 1 \end{bmatrix} \begin{bmatrix} 1 & 0 & 0 \\ 0 & 0 & 1 \\ 0 & 1 & 0 \end{bmatrix} \begin{bmatrix} 1 & 0 & 0 \\ 0 & 1 & 0 \\ 0 & 1/2 & 1 \end{bmatrix} \\
&= \begin{bmatrix} 1/7 & 1 & 0 \\ 4/7 & 1/2 & 1 \\ 1 & 0 & 0 \end{bmatrix},
\end{aligned}$$

which is a permutation of a unit lower triangular matrix $(\widetilde{L} = P^T L)$ as expected. We also have

$$\begin{aligned}
P &= P_2 P_1 \\
&= \begin{bmatrix} 1 & 0 & 0 \\ 0 & 0 & 1 \\ 0 & 1 & 0 \end{bmatrix} \begin{bmatrix} 0 & 0 & 1 \\ 0 & 1 & 0 \\ 1 & 0 & 0 \end{bmatrix} \\
&= \begin{bmatrix} 0 & 0 & 1 \\ 1 & 0 & 0 \\ 0 & 1 & 0 \end{bmatrix}
\end{aligned}$$

in agreement with the order specified by the permutation vector $p = [3\ 1\ 2]$. To find L, we'll use $\widetilde{L} = P^T L$ to find

$$\begin{aligned}
L &= P\widetilde{L} \\
&= \begin{bmatrix} 0 & 0 & 1 \\ 1 & 0 & 0 \\ 0 & 1 & 0 \end{bmatrix} \begin{bmatrix} 1/7 & 1 & 0 \\ 4/7 & 1/2 & 1 \\ 1 & 0 & 0 \end{bmatrix} \\
&= \begin{bmatrix} 1 & 0 & 0 \\ 1/7 & 1 & 0 \\ 4/7 & 1/2 & 1 \end{bmatrix}
\end{aligned}$$

so that

$$PA = LU$$

$$\begin{bmatrix} 0 & 0 & 1 \\ 1 & 0 & 0 \\ 0 & 1 & 0 \end{bmatrix} \begin{bmatrix} 1 & 2 & 3 \\ 4 & 5 & 6 \\ 7 & 8 & 9 \end{bmatrix} = \begin{bmatrix} 1 & 0 & 0 \\ 1/7 & 1 & 0 \\ 4/7 & 1/2 & 1 \end{bmatrix} \begin{bmatrix} 7 & 8 & 9 \\ 0 & 6/7 & 12/7 \\ 0 & 0 & 0 \end{bmatrix}$$

$$\begin{bmatrix} 7 & 8 & 9 \\ 1 & 2 & 3 \\ 4 & 5 & 6 \end{bmatrix} = \begin{bmatrix} 7 & 8 & 9 \\ 1 & 2 & 3 \\ 4 & 5 & 6 \end{bmatrix},$$

which checks. We have found an LU decomposition of A. ∎

Storage

There are many practical implementation issues (like the use of the vector p rather than the matrix P) that we do not address here. One crucial issue, however, that we must address is this: Some programming languages store matrices by writing successive rows to memory (called storage in **row-major** form), whereas others store matrices by writing successive columns to memory (called **column-major** form). All matrix algorithms come in row-oriented and column-oriented versions, and using the appropriate version[3] will speed execution by (very) roughly a factor of two for matrices of modest size. (The reason is that it is faster to retrieve data near recently retrieved data; if matrices are stored by rows, then a_{11} and a_{12} are close. But if matrices are stored by columns, they need not be, although a_{11} and a_{21} will be close. When a particular datum is requested, nearby data is automatically loaded into the fast cache memory, and under a row-major storage scheme nearby means nearby when tracing by rows, not nearby as seen when visually inspecting the matrix as a two-dimensional array.) Another issue is the desire to use as many Level 3 BLAS as feasible by appropriately partitioning the matrix into block form (or Level 2 or Level 1 BLAS by designing appropriate vector-oriented versions of the method).

The MATLAB command $[L,U,P]=lu(A)$ produces the matrices L, U, and P of the LU decomposition of a general square matrix. The relation $L = P\tilde{L}$ means that if $[L,U,P]=lu(A)$ and $[L1,U1]=lu(A)$, then U is equal to U1 and L is equal to P*L1. Note that the LU decomposition is not unique, so this command gives *an* LU decomposition of the matrix, not *the* LU decomposition of the matrix.

Using the Decomposition

Once we know L, U, and P, we may solve the linear system $Ax = b$ in essentially the same manner as before. We pre-multiply by P (again, although we would typically not form the matrix P, it is useful for deriving and analyzing the method) to obtain

$$PAx = Pb$$
$$(PA)x = d \tag{2.10}$$
$$LUx = d$$

$(d = Pb)$ and proceed as before, solving $Ly = d$ and then $Ux = y$. Premultiplication by P simply reorders the equations that constitute the linear system.

For special matrices it may be possible to simplify or otherwise improve upon this scheme, and there are many variations of the LU decomposition. For example, if A is positive definite, then we may choose $U = L^T$ and $P = I_n$, giving $A = LL^T$ (this L need not be *unit* lower triangular). In some cases it is convenient to use an **LDU decomposition** in which A (or PA) is factored into the product $A = LDU$, where L is a (possibly permuted) lower triangular matrix, D is a diagonal matrix, and U is an upper triangular matrix.

Inverses

We close this section with a few words on the matrix inverse. This is almost never needed in computation, and whenever a matrix inverse is encountered in a formula it pays to study the equation to see if it is possible to rewrite it so that an equivalent linear system is solved rather than an inverse matrix computed.[4] In practice this is almost always possible—exceptions are exceedingly rare. Certainly in the formula

$$x = A^{-1}b$$

---

[3] G.W. Stewart notes that "both [FORTRAN90 and C++] include powerful features that make it easy to write inefficient code."

[4] The same goes for matrices that may be the products of (simpler or better structured) matrices earlier on in a derivation. Bill Gragg states that whenever one encounters a matrix, one would do well to ask from whence it came.

we would want to solve $Ax = b$ using the LU decomposition or some similar approach. For $X = A^{-1}B$, where B is a matrix, we can solve $AX = B$ column by column. Experience shows that many people feel that they need to compute a matrix inverse, but few if any actually do.[5] However, on those occasions when one wishes to compute $x = A^{-1}b$ in a way that is both less accurate and significantly less efficient than the use of the LU decomposition, the usual way to do so[6] is to use the fact that $A = LU$ implies that

$$A^{-1} = U^{-1}L^{-1}$$

(and similarly if $PA = LU$). One way to compute this is to recall that column i of A^{-1} is the solution of

$$Ac_i = e_i,$$

where e_i is column i of the identity matrix; that is, e_i is the column n-vector that is entirely zero except for entry i, which is equal to one. We simply solve

$$LUc_i = e_i$$

in the usual way for $i = 1, \ldots, n$, and then form $A^{-1} = [c_1 \cdots c_n]$ from the results. We will still need to do a matrix-vector multiplication afterwards to find $A^{-1}b$. There are algorithms for finding the inverse in place.

PROBLEMS 2.3

1. a. Compute (by hand) the products L_1L_2 and L_2L_1 of $L_1 = [1\ 0\ 0; -1/2\ 1\ 0; 1/2\ 0\ 1]$ and $L_2 = [1\ 0\ 0; 0\ 1\ 0; 0\ 1/4\ 1]$.

b. If A is a 3×3 matrix, describe the row operations that would be performed on A if it were premultiplied by L_1; if it were premultiplied by L_2; and if it were premultiplied by L_2L_1.

c. Find the inverses of L_1 and L_2.

d. Let $A = [1\ 1\ 1; 1/2\ 3/2\ 3/2; -1/2\ -3/4\ 1/4]$. Compute L_2L_1A.

e. What is the LU decomposition of A? Explain how you are using your answers from the previous parts of this problem to answer this question.

2. a. Find the LU decomposition of the matrix $A = [1\ 2\ 3; 4\ 5\ 6; 7\ 8\ 8]$ (by hand; follow Example 2.3.2).

b. Use the LU decomposition of A to solve the linear system $Ax = b$, where $b = (1, 2, 3)^T$.

3. Prove that a product of unit lower triangular matrices must be unit lower triangular. (*Hint:* Consider a typical dot product of a row from the first matrix and a column from the second matrix.)

4. a. Prove that the product of two elementary matrices that represent row interchanges is a permutation matrix.

b. Prove that a permutation matrix is nonsingular and in fact orthogonal.

5. Write a MATLAB program that accepts as arguments a nonsingular matrix A and a vector b (check that it is conformable) and solves $Ax = b$ by using the command `[L,U,P]=lu(A)` followed by the method of Eq. (2.10). (Use the backslash to solve the triangular systems $Ly = Pb$ and $Ux = y$.) Signal an error if U is found to be singular (use `prod(diag(U))` rather than `det(U)` to check the determinant). Return x if only one output is requested, and return x and the compact form of the LU decomposition (given by `tril(L,-1)+triu(U)`) if two output arguments are requested.

---

[5] G.W. Stewart suggests that one exception is when a researcher wishes to inspect an inverse matrix "to get a feel for its structure."

[6] For a general matrix–as always, there are specialized methods for matrices with certain types of structure.

MATLAB 2.3

We mentioned `format rat` in the reading; note that using this format causes numbers to be printed as ratios of *small* integers, meaning that sometimes the values displayed are approximations. In particular, this is not computation with arbitrarily many digits (as can be done in Maple, for example). Enter:

```
» format rat
» pi
```

The displayed value is $355/113$. However:

```
» sin(ans)
» sin(355/113)
```

We see that only the display is affected, not the actual values. Another useful format command is `format compact`, which suppresses extra linefeeds in the display of results. This may be useful when displaying modest-sized matrices on the screen. Enter:

```
» A=rand(13)
» format compact
» A
» format loose
```

to see the difference. The `format loose` command changes back to the default display with respect to linefeeds. Other format settings (e.g., `format rat`) are not affected, whereas simply entering `format` resets all formatting options to their defaults.

The MATLAB command `prod` used in Problems 2.3 computes the product $\prod_{i=1}^{n} x_i$ of the elements of a vector, much as `sum` computes the sum $\sum_{i=1}^{n} x_i$ of the elements of a vector. For a triangular matrix the determinant is the product of its diagonal entries `prod(diag(U))`, that is, $\prod_{i=1}^{n} u_{i,i}$. In this case, MATLAB notation is significantly simpler than standard mathematical notation.[7]

As mentioned in the reading, the `lu` command with three outputs requested returns the L, U, and P of the LU decomposition. Enter:

```
» A=[1 2 3;4 5 6;7 8 9]
» [L1,U1]=lu(A)
» [L,U,P]=lu(A)
```

to see the LU decomposition of Example 2.3.2. The matrix `L1` is clearly a permuted unit lower triangular matrix. Enter:

```
» P*L1
» L==ans
```

to see that $L = P\widetilde{L}$ as claimed, and enter:

```
» P*A,L*U
```

---

[7] The programming language APL (now known as J in its modern form) was initially developed as a mathematical notation and later implemented as a computer language. It had many MATLAB-like features, including simple notation for sums, products, and similar operations, and a vector and array orientation.

to see that $PA = LU$ as claimed. Enter:

```
» [L2,U2]=lu(P*A)
```

to see that PA can be row-reduced without pivoting, as claimed; indeed, L2 is lower triangular (as opposed to permuted lower triangular matrix, as it would be if pivoting had been performed). In fact, if we request the values of L, U, and P by typing:

```
» [L2,U2,P2]=lu(P*A)
```

we see that P2 is the identity matrix (I_3), indicating that no pivoting has been performed in row-reducing PA to triangular form.

In experimenting with permutation matrices, you may find the command `randperm` to be useful. This command generates a (pseudo-)random permutation of the integers $1, \ldots, n$. Try:

```
» randperm(6)
» randperm(6)
```

You may also have commands `permute` and `ipermute`. From Version 5 on, MATLAB can create arrays with more than two dimensions. For example:

```
» rand(3,3,3)
```

creates a $3 \times 3 \times 3$ array (loosely, a three-dimensional matrix). While this could be useful for simulating spatial phenomena, we will not make use of it. The `permute` and `ipermute` commands are used to change the structure of such a matrix. To permute the entries of a vector we may index it in the desired order. For example, enter:

```
» v=2*(1:8);v(8:-1:1),v([2 4 6 8 1 3 5 7])
```

The `sort` command can make use of this feature (as discussed in MATLAB 2.6). Enter:

```
» y=rand([1 8])
» [s,index]=sort(y)
» y(index)
```

Note that `y(index)` is equal to s. We may work with matrices in a similar way. Enter:

```
» A=[1 2 3 4;5 6 7 8;9 10 11 12;13 14 15 16]
» A([1 3 2 4],:)
» A(:,[1 3 2 4])
```

In `A([1 3 2 4],:)` and `A(:,[1 3 2 4])`, the colon signifies all columns and all rows, respectively. The vector `[1 3 2 4]` is interpreted as a permutation vector, and the rows or columns are permuted according to it.

Gaussian elimination with partial pivoting—that is, LU decomposition—stands with Newton's method as one of the most widely used numerical algorithms in existence. (It is somewhat atypical of numerical methods in that it always "converges" after finitely many operations.) While in principle it can exaggerate errors, in practice it does not. However, we will need to develop other methods for solving linear systems, especially large ones. For such matrices the $O(n^3)$ operation count of this method may be too expensive. In addition, in most cases of interest, large matrices have a structure and in particular are sparse: Most of their entries (more than 95%, say) are zeroes. This *should* save us a lot of work, much as symmetry should in general cut our work in half. What happens when Gaussian elimination with partial pivoting is applied to a matrix with a structured pattern of null entries? Enter:

```
» A=eye(10);A(1,:)=ones([1 10]);A(:,1)=ones([10 1])
```

to create such a matrix. This is a symmetric matrix with entirely integer entries. Enter:

```
» eig(A)
» sum(sum(A>0))/prod(size(A))
```

to see some other properties of A and to compute the percentage of A that is nonzero (28%). Enter:

```
» format rat
» A1=inv(A)
```

On the one hand, the inverse matrix has an obvious pattern; on the other hand, while A is 28% nonzero, its inverse A1 is 100% nonzero. The inverse of a sparse matrix is typically not sparse. (As usual, there are special classes of matrices that are exceptions to this general rule; the most obvious one is diagonal matrices.) This is another reason that we avoid inverting a matrix: There are special methods of storing and manipulating sparse matrices that give considerable speed advantages, and these advantages are typically lost if the matrix is inverted. Enter:

```
» format
» norm(A1*A-eye(10))
```

to see that the inverse is nonetheless quite accurate normwise. Now enter:

```
» [L,U,P]=lu(A)
```

Note that L and U are each as full as they could be, save for one null entry. Their inverses have the same property. The act of performing Gaussian elimination with partial pivoting on the matrix A has destroyed its sparsity structure and with it any advantages in speed or storage that we might have had. For small matrices this may be acceptable, and for small to medium n, we typically use Gaussian elimination with partial pivoting for both sparse and dense matrices, unless the matrix has some other structure we can make use of to get a better algorithm. (Even in these cases, we usually just use a variant of the LU decomposition.) For large sparse matrices we can do better, as is discussed in Chapter 3, where we consider iterative methods for linear systems. These methods do not in general converge in finitely many steps. Large dense problems are difficult.

A matrix like the matrix A is sometimes called an **arrowhead matrix** (or **arrow matrix**). To see why, enter:

```
» spy(A)
```

The spy command indicates graphically the location of the nonzero entries of a matrix (its sparsity structure or sparsity pattern). In fact the term arrowhead matrix is more commonly used to mean the matrix obtained as follows. Enter:

```
» B=flipud(fliplr((A)))
» spy(B)
```

The flip commands flip a matrix or vector up-down or left-right. For example, enter:

```
» fliplr(1:10)
» flipud(1:10)
```

(Recall that `1:10` is a 1×10 matrix to MATLAB.) The command `rot90` rotates a matrix through a 90° angle. Enter:

```
» spy(rot90(A))
» spy(rot90(A,2))
```

(The command `rot90(A,2)` rotates A through two right angles; that is, it is the same as `rot90(rot90(A))`.) To try `spy` on a bigger matrix, we may use the `sprandn` command, which generates a pseudo-random sparse matrix. (There are other commands to generate such matrices; see `help sprandn`.) Enter:

```
» S=sprandn(100,100,.05);
» spy(S)
```

to generate a 100×100 matrix that has about 5% nonzero entries. If you look at the matrix S, you will see it displayed in a different form than usual; this is because MATLAB knows that matrices generated by `sprandn` should be treated as sparse matrices. MATLAB stores and manipulates them in a more efficient way. The `sparse` command tells MATLAB to change the representation of a matrix to sparse form, and the `full` command changes it back to the standard form. Enter:

```
» S
» F=full(S)
```

The matrices S and F are equal but are stored and handled differently. Enter:

```
» tic;S*S;toc
» tic;F*F;toc
```

to see the difference. The matrices S*S and F*F are the same, but the sparse form is more efficient. This is even more so when the sparsity pattern is not random as it is here.

ADDITIONAL PROBLEMS 2.3

6. a. Find the LU decomposition of the matrix $A =$ [1 0 − 2; 4 3 8; 8 8 − 3] (by hand).

b. Use the LU decomposition of A to solve the linear system $Ax = (1, -1, 1)^T$.

7. Give two LU decompositions of the zero matrix (with L unit lower triangular) and two LU decompositions of the identity matrix (with L unit lower triangular in at least one of the decompositions).

8. Describe the set of all 3×3 unit lower triangular matrices L such that LU is an LU decomposition of $A = [1\ 0\ 0; 0\ 0\ 0; 0\ 0\ 0]$ (take $U = A$).

9. Show that if L is unit lower triangular, then so is L^{-1}.

10. a. Consider again the equation $L_3 P_3 L_2 P_2 L_1 P_1 A = U$ representing the general case of row-reducing a 4×4 matrix to upper triangular form. Define $\Lambda_3 = L_3$, $\Lambda_2 = P_3 L_2 P_3^{-1}$, $\Lambda_1 = P_3 P_2 L_1 P_2^{-1} P_3^{-1}$, and $P = P_3 P_2 P_1$. Show that Λ_1, Λ_2, and Λ_3 are unit lower triangular and hence $\Lambda = \Lambda_3 \Lambda_2 \Lambda_1$ is unit lower triangular.

b. Show that $L_3 P_3 L_2 P_2 L_1 P_1 A = \Lambda_3 \Lambda_2 \Lambda_1 P (= \Lambda P)$.

c. Justify the transition from Eq. (2.8) to Eq. (2.9) using the relation $\Lambda P A = U$ derived above.

d. Let A be $n \times n$. Show that A has an LU decomposition $PA = LU$ with L unit lower triangular (that is, justify Eq. (2.8) and Eq. (2.9) starting from the first step of Gaussian elimination in this general case).

11. a. Find (by hand) the LU decomposition of $A = [2 \ -1 \ 1; -1 \ 2 \ -1; 1 \ -1 \ 2]$.

 b. Find (by hand) a decomposition of A of the form $A = LDL^T$, where L is unit lower triangular and D is diagonal with strictly positive diagonal entries.

 c. Show that if $A = LDL^T$, where L is unit lower triangular and D is diagonal with strictly positive diagonal entries, then A is positive definite. (In fact A is positive definite if and only if it has such a representation.)

 d. Find (by hand) a decomposition of A of the form $A = LL^T$, where L is lower triangular with nonzero diagonal entries.

 e. Show that if $A = LL^T$, where L is lower triangular with nonzero diagonal entries, then A is positive definite. (In fact A is positive definite if and only if it has such a representation.)

12. For the matrix $A = [1 \ 2 \ 3 \ 4; 5 \ 6 \ 7 \ 8; 9 \ 10 \ 11 \ 12; 13 \ 14 \ 15 \ 16]$, write out all elementary matrices involved in row-reducing A to upper triangular form, and indicate the order in which they would be applied to A (similar to Eq. (2.6)).

13. a. If A is square, then it is possible to write it as $A = UTU^{-1}$, where U is unitary ($U^{-1} = U^T$) and T is upper triangular with the eigenvalues of A on its main diagonal. (This is called the **Schur decomposition**.) Note that U and T may be complex-valued even though A is real. Use the MATLAB commands `[U1,T1]=schur(A);[U,T]=rsf2csf(U1,T1)` to find the Schur decomposition of $A = [0 \ 1 \ 0; -1 \ 0 \ 0; 0 \ 0 \ 1]$. (The `rsf2csf` command converts the output of `schur` to the form described above.)

 b. If you had the Schur decomposition of A pre-computed, how would you solve $Ax = b$? Assume that complex arithmetic is implemented automatically. (*Note:* The Schur decomposition is not in fact used to solve linear systems; it is used to numerically compute eigenvalues.)

c. Use the MATLAB commands `lu` and `chol` to find the LU and Cholesky decompositions of $A = [2 \ -1 \ 1; -1 \ 2 \ -1; 1 \ -1 \ 2]$. The Cholesky decomposition is an LU decomposition that applies only to positive definite matrices; L is not necessarily *unit* lower triangular but $L^T = U$. Form the products in each case ($L_1 U$ and $L_2 L_2^T$, respectively) to verify that they are correct.

 d. Use the Cholesky decomposition of A to solve $Ax = (1, -2, 1)^T$.

14. In the analysis of linear systems in electrical engineering it is frequently necessary to find the roots of a polynomial that appears in the denominator of a rational function, the transfer function of the system. (In many cases it is necessary to determine only whether these roots, called **poles**, have positive or negative real part.) A common approach for high-degree monic polynomials $x^n + p_{n-1}x^{n-1} + \ldots + p_1 x + p_0$ is to form the **companion matrix** of the polynomial, which can be written as the matrix with first row $[-p_{n-1} \ -p_{n-2} \ \ldots \ -p_1 \ -p_0]$ and all other rows zero, save the subdiagonal entries, which are unities (ones). For example, $x^3 + 4x^2 + 2x + 3$ would have companion matrix $C = [-4 \ -2 \ -3; 1 \ 0 \ 0; 0 \ 1 \ 0]$ (see `help compan` in MATLAB). The eigenvalues of the companion matrix are the same as the roots of the polynomial. A scalar λ is an eigenvalue of C if and only if $Cx = \lambda x$ has a nonzero solution x, that is, if and only if $(C - \lambda I)x = 0$ admits a nontrivial solution.

 a. For the polynomial $x^4 - 10x^3 + 35x^2 - 50x + 24$, use the LU decomposition to determine which of the following are eigenvalues of C and hence roots of the polynomial: $-5, -4, -3, -2, -1, 0, 1, 2, 3, 4, 5$.

 b. Is there a convenient way to use the LU decomposition of $C - \lambda_1 I$ to find the LU decomposition of $C - \lambda_2 I$?

15. Use MATLAB to find the LU decomposition of `ones([10 10])`. Explain why L, U, and P have the form they do in terms of the Gaussian elimination with partial pivoting algorithm.

2.4 The Cholesky Decomposition

When we know something special about a matrix A involved in a computational linear algebra problem, we can often exploit it for additional efficiency. The two most commonly occurring cases are those in which we know that the matrix is sparse, that is, most of

Positive Definite Matrices

its entries are zeroes, and those in which we know that the matrix is symmetric, that is, that $A = A^T$. In this section we focus on symmetric matrices that have an additional property: If x is a nonzero vector then

$$x^T A x > 0.$$

A symmetric matrix with this property is said to be **positive definite.**[8] An equivalent characterization is that a matrix is positive definite if and only if it is symmetric and all of its eigenvalues are strictly positive. A symmetric matrix with the property that $x^T A x \geq 0$ for all x is said to be **positive semi-definite,** and all its eigenvalues must be nonnegative.

Positive definite matrices appear in practice more frequently than one might expect. The quantity $x^T A x$ is called a **quadratic form** and is the natural generalization of the scalar quantity ax^2; in this context it occurs in the generalization of Taylor series to functions of more than one variable, as we'll see in Chapter 7 (on nonlinear optimization). Positive definite matrices also appear in least squares curve-fitting problems (see Section 2.6) and in the numerical solution of partial differential equations.

Since positive definite matrices are symmetric, they contain only about half as many distinct entries as a general matrix of the same order, and so we ought to be able to save about half the work and half the storage when dealing with them. However, an arbitrarily selected method will usually not take advantage of this structure. For example, the LU decomposition $A = LU$ of a symmetric matrix cannot have L or U symmetric in general, for if $L = L^T$ and L is lower triangular, then L is in fact diagonal. Using the methods of the previous section, we cannot even hope for $L = U^T$ since L is *unit* lower triangular. If we were to have $L = U^T$, then U would be unit upper triangular, and so we would have

$$\det(LU) = \det(L)\det(U)$$
$$= 1 \cdot 1$$
$$= 1,$$

that is, $\det(A) = 1$, which is certainly not true of a general symmetric matrix. We need a smarter approach; in the case of positive definite matrices, there is indeed a straightforward procedure that produces an LU decomposition of the matrix in about half the time and using about half the storage, as we would expect.

Cholesky Decomposition

The method is called the **Cholesky decomposition,** or **Cholesky factorization,** of the matrix A, and it has the form $A = LL^T$, where L is a lower triangular matrix. (Either L or $U = L^T$ may be referred to as the **Cholesky factor** of the matrix.) The matrix L will not in general be *unit* lower triangular. Clearly, once we have the decomposition it suffices to store only L, and so we can cut our storage requirements about in half.

Let A be a positive definite $n \times n$ matrix. Since A is symmetric, it's orthogonally diagonalizable; that is,

$$A = SDS^T,$$

---

[8] Many authors do not include symmetry in the definition of a positive definite matrix. The Cholesky decomposition requires that A both be symmetric and satisfy $x^T A x > 0$.

where S is the matrix whose columns are the orthonormalized eigenvectors of A, and D is a diagonal matrix with the eigenvalues of A along the main diagonal. This is sometimes called the **eigenvalue decomposition** of A. Since $D = diag([\lambda_1 \; \lambda_2 \cdots \lambda_n])$ (mixing MATLAB and traditional notation) with each $\lambda_i > 0$, we may define $H = diag([\sqrt{\lambda_1} \; \sqrt{\lambda_2} \cdots \sqrt{\lambda_n}])$ and write this as

$$A = SHHS^T$$
$$= SHH^TS^T$$
$$= (SH)(SH)^T$$
$$= MM^T$$

($M = SH$). It's very unlikely that M will be lower triangular, however, so this is not the decomposition we seek. In fact a more useful way to write this is as

$$A = SHHS^T$$
$$= SH(S^TS)HS^T$$
$$= (SHS^T)(SHS^T)$$
$$= H_0H_0$$
$$= H_0^2,$$

and we say that $H_0 = SHS^T$ is the **matrix square root** of A. Note that H_0 is itself positive definite; its eigenvalues are the positive numbers $\sqrt{\lambda_1}, \sqrt{\lambda_2}, \cdots, \sqrt{\lambda_n}$, and it is symmetric, for we have

$$H_0^T = (SHS^T)^T$$
$$= (S^T)^T H^T S^T$$
$$= SHS^T.$$

The matrix square root appears in a number of physical applications, but we will use it as a tool to find an algorithm for computing the Cholesky decomposition.

Elementary Matrices and Symmetry

The key idea for finding a Cholesky decomposition is this: When A is symmetric, any elementary matrix E used in row-reducing A to upper triangular form by performing EA has the analogous effect on the columns of A if we perform AE^T. We can maintain symmetry while reducing A if we form a product of the form EAE^T at each step.

Example 2.4.1   Consider the positive definite matrix $A = [4 \; 2 \; 1; 2 \; 3 \; 1; 1 \; 1 \; 4]$. The first step in finding an LU decomposition of A is to perform $A \to E_1 A$, where

$$E_1 = \begin{bmatrix} 1 & 0 & 0 \\ -1/2 & 1 & 0 \\ -1/4 & 0 & 1 \end{bmatrix}$$

is the product of the two elementary matrices that perform $R_2 \leftarrow R_2 - \frac{1}{2}R_1$ and $R_3 \leftarrow R_3 - \frac{1}{4}R_1$. This gives

$$E_1 A = \begin{bmatrix} 1 & 0 & 0 \\ -1/2 & 1 & 0 \\ -1/4 & 0 & 1 \end{bmatrix} \begin{bmatrix} 4 & 2 & 1 \\ 2 & 3 & 1 \\ 1 & 1 & 4 \end{bmatrix}$$

$$= \begin{bmatrix} 4 & 2 & 1 \\ 0 & 2 & 1/2 \\ 0 & 1/2 & 15/4 \end{bmatrix}$$

as expected. But then

$$E_1 A E_1^T = \begin{bmatrix} 4 & 2 & 1 \\ 0 & 2 & 1/2 \\ 0 & 1/2 & 15/4 \end{bmatrix} \begin{bmatrix} 1 & -1/2 & -1/4 \\ 0 & 1 & 0 \\ 0 & 0 & 1 \end{bmatrix}$$

$$= \begin{bmatrix} 4 & 0 & 0 \\ 0 & 2 & 1/2 \\ 0 & 1/2 & 15/4 \end{bmatrix}$$

(check this). We started with a symmetric matrix A, performed a step of Gaussian elimination and got a nonsymmetric matrix $E_1 A$, and then postmultiplied by E_1^T to get a symmetric matrix $E_1 A E_1^T$ once again. The next step gives

$$E_2 E_1 A E_1^T = \begin{bmatrix} 1 & 0 & 0 \\ 0 & 1 & 0 \\ 0 & -1/4 & 1 \end{bmatrix} \begin{bmatrix} 4 & 0 & 0 \\ 0 & 2 & 1/2 \\ 0 & 1/2 & 15/4 \end{bmatrix}$$

$$= \begin{bmatrix} 4 & 0 & 0 \\ 0 & 2 & 1/2 \\ 0 & 0 & 29/8 \end{bmatrix}$$

$$E_2 E_1 A E_1^T E_2^T = \begin{bmatrix} 4 & 0 & 0 \\ 0 & 2 & 1/2 \\ 0 & 0 & 29/8 \end{bmatrix} \begin{bmatrix} 1 & 0 & 0 \\ 0 & 1 & -1/4 \\ 0 & 0 & 1 \end{bmatrix}$$

$$= \begin{bmatrix} 4 & 0 & 0 \\ 0 & 2 & 0 \\ 0 & 0 & 29/8 \end{bmatrix},$$

and so if we define

$$\tilde{L} = E_2 E_1$$

$$= \begin{bmatrix} 1 & 0 & 0 \\ 0 & 1 & 0 \\ 0 & -1/4 & 1 \end{bmatrix} \begin{bmatrix} 1 & 0 & 0 \\ -1/2 & 1 & 0 \\ -1/4 & 0 & 1 \end{bmatrix}$$

$$= \begin{bmatrix} 1 & 0 & 0 \\ -1/2 & 1 & 0 \\ -1/8 & -1/4 & 1 \end{bmatrix},$$

then $\tilde{L}^T = (E_2 E_1)^T = E_1^T E_2^T$, and we have $\tilde{L} A \tilde{L}^T = D_0$ where D_0 is a diagonal matrix with strictly positive diagonal entries (though these are not the eigenvalues of A). Since D_0 is (trivially) positive definite, it has a matrix square root $D_0 = H_0^2$, which is also a diagonal matrix with strictly positive diagonal entries. Hence we may write

$$\tilde{L} A \tilde{L}^T = D_0$$
$$A = \tilde{L}^{-1} D_0 (\tilde{L}^T)^{-1}$$
$$= \tilde{L}^{-1} H_0^2 (\tilde{L}^{-1})^T$$
$$= L_0 H_0^2 L_0^T,$$

where $L_0 = \tilde{L}^{-1}$ is lower triangular since it is the inverse of a lower triangular matrix. (We have also used the fact that if a matrix B is nonsingular then $(B^T)^{-1} = (B^{-1})^T$.) Hence

$$A = L_0 H_0 H_0^T L_0^T$$
$$= L_0 H_0 (L_0 H_0)^T$$
$$= L L^T,$$

where $L = L_0 H_0$. Since postmultiplication by a diagonal matrix simply rescales columns, L is lower triangular; this is a Cholesky decomposition $A = L L^T$ of A. In our case we have

$$\tilde{L} = \begin{bmatrix} 1 & 0 & 0 \\ -1/2 & 1 & 0 \\ -1/8 & -1/4 & 1 \end{bmatrix}$$

$$L_0 = \tilde{L}^{-1}$$
$$= \begin{bmatrix} 1 & 0 & 0 \\ 1/2 & 1 & 0 \\ 1/4 & 1/4 & 1 \end{bmatrix}$$

$$H_0 = \begin{bmatrix} \sqrt{4} & 0 & 0 \\ 0 & \sqrt{2} & 0 \\ 0 & 0 & \sqrt{29/8} \end{bmatrix}$$
$$= \begin{bmatrix} 2 & 0 & 0 \\ 0 & \sqrt{2} & 0 \\ 0 & 0 & \frac{1}{2}\sqrt{29/2} \end{bmatrix}$$

so

$$L = L_0 H_0$$
$$= \begin{bmatrix} 1 & 0 & 0 \\ 1/2 & 1 & 0 \\ 1/4 & 1/4 & 1 \end{bmatrix} \begin{bmatrix} 2 & 0 & 0 \\ 0 & \sqrt{2} & 0 \\ 0 & 0 & \frac{1}{2}\sqrt{29/2} \end{bmatrix}$$

$$\doteq \begin{bmatrix} 2 & 0 & 0 \\ 1 & 1.4142 & 0 \\ 0.5 & 0.3536 & 1.9039 \end{bmatrix}.$$

Let's check:

$$LL^T = \begin{bmatrix} 2 & 0 & 0 \\ 1 & 1.4142 & 0 \\ 0.5 & 0.3536 & 1.9039 \end{bmatrix} \begin{bmatrix} 2 & 0 & 0 \\ 1 & 1.4142 & 0 \\ 0.5 & 0.3536 & 1.9039 \end{bmatrix}^T$$

$$= \begin{bmatrix} 2 & 0 & 0 \\ 1 & 1.4142 & 0 \\ 0.5 & 0.3536 & 1.9039 \end{bmatrix} \begin{bmatrix} 2 & 1 & 0.5 \\ 0 & 1.4142 & 0.3536 \\ 0 & 0 & 1.9039 \end{bmatrix}$$

$$= \begin{bmatrix} 4 & 2 & 1 \\ 2 & 3 & 1 \\ 1 & 1 & 4 \end{bmatrix},$$

which checks. This is the desired Cholesky factorization of A. ∎

The method above is entirely general, *assuming* we don't need to pivot at any stage. We introduce the needed zeroes in a column of the working matrix, and then do the same on the corresponding row. When we are done, the matrix

$$D_0 = E_{n-1} \cdots E_2 E_1 A E_1^T E_2^T \cdots E_{n-1}^T$$

will be diagonal with positive diagonal entries. (This is one reason that we need positive definiteness, not just symmetry, for A: to guarantee that D_0 will have positive diagonal entries.) Then if

$$\tilde{L} = E_{n-1} \cdots E_2 E_1$$

we have

$$\tilde{L} A \tilde{L}^T = D_0$$
$$A = \tilde{L}^{-1} H_0^2 (\tilde{L}^{-1})^T$$
$$= LL^T$$

with $L = \tilde{L}^{-1} H_0$. A positive definite matrix is nonsingular (since no eigenvalue may be zero) so this process completes, giving a Cholesky factorization of A. If A is positive definite, then there is exactly one lower triangular matrix L having positive diagonal entries for which $A = LL^T$.

What if we must pivot? It can be shown that naive (unpivoted) Gaussian elimination can always be performed on a positive definite matrix and that a zero pivot will never be encountered. In fact, all the pivots will be positive. Of course, for a general matrix, we use partial pivoting not just because of the possibility of a zero pivot but also because it controls the growth of roundoff errors. However, when A is positive definite, partial pivoting is not necessary to control errors; naive Gaussian elimination may be safely employed and will not amplify roundoff errors significantly. (This is by no means obvious.) Hence the method described above need not be modified to use pivoting.

Deriving the
Algorithm

As usual, the matrix formulation given above is useful for analytical work but would be inefficient if implemented literally. We want to compute L directly, not its inverse. We need a computationally efficient algorithm. In the trivial case, where A is a 1×1 matrix

$$A = (a_{11})$$

(with $a_{11} > 0$), the decomposition must have $L = (\sqrt{a_{11}})$. (Recall that the decomposition is unique if we require the diagonal entries of L to be positive.) For a 2×2 matrix

$$A = \begin{pmatrix} a_{11} & a_{12} \\ a_{12} & a_{22} \end{pmatrix}$$

(where we have used the fact that $a_{21} = a_{12}$), we need a decomposition of the form

$$\begin{pmatrix} a_{11} & a_{12} \\ a_{12} & a_{22} \end{pmatrix} = \begin{pmatrix} l_{11} & 0 \\ l_{21} & l_{22} \end{pmatrix} \begin{pmatrix} l_{11} & l_{21} \\ 0 & l_{22} \end{pmatrix},$$

which means that we must have

$$a_{11} = l_{11}^2$$

$$a_{12} = l_{11}l_{21} \tag{2.11}$$

$$a_{22} = l_{21}^2 + l_{22}^2.$$

It appears that we may use the decomposition from the 1×1 case here; using the already known $l_{11} = \sqrt{a_{11}}$ from the 1×1 case, we can solve $a_{12} = l_{11}l_{21}$ for l_{21} and then use it to solve $a_{22} = l_{21}^2 + l_{22}^2$ for l_{22}.

More generally, suppose that we wish to find the Cholesky decomposition of an $n \times n$ positive definite matrix. Maybe we can generalize the approach in Eq. (2.11). We can write the decomposition in the form $A = R^T R$, where $R = L^T$ is upper triangular (also called **right triangular;** hence the use of the letter R). Define A_p to be the $p \times p$ **leading principal minor** of A, that is, the northwest $p \times p$ submatrix of A. A matrix is positive definite if and only if each leading principal minor of the matrix is also positive definite. Let's try to find a relationship between the Cholesky decompositions of $A_1, A_2, A_3, \ldots,$ $A_n = A$. We know that the case

$$A_1 = (a_{11})$$

has the decomposition $R_1 = \sqrt{a_{11}}$. Hence suppose that for some $p \geq 2$ we have a Cholesky decomposition $A_{p-1} = R_{p-1}^T R_{p-1}$ of the $(p-1) \times (p-1)$ leading principal minor of A. We need a decomposition of the $p \times p$ submatrix

$$A_p = \begin{pmatrix} A_{p-1} & c_{p-1} \\ c_{p-1}^T & a_{pp} \end{pmatrix},$$

where a_{pp} is a scalar (which must be positive) and c_{p-1} is a column vector with $(p-1)$ entries. That is, we need to find a column vector γ_{p-1} with $(p-1)$ entries and a positive scalar r_{pp} such that

$$\begin{pmatrix} A_{p-1} & c_{p-1} \\ c_{p-1}^T & a_{pp} \end{pmatrix} = \begin{pmatrix} R_{p-1}^T & 0 \\ \gamma_{p-1}^T & r_{pp} \end{pmatrix} \begin{pmatrix} R_{p-1} & \gamma_{p-1} \\ 0 & r_{pp} \end{pmatrix}$$

is the Cholesky decomposition of A. Analogous to Eq. (2.11), we have

$$A_{p-1} = R_{p-1}^T R_{p-1}$$
$$c_{p-1} = R_{p-1}^T \gamma_{p-1}$$
$$c_{p-1}^T = \gamma_{p-1}^T R_{p-1}$$
$$a_{pp} = \gamma_{p-1}^T \gamma_{p-1} + r_{pp}^2,$$

$$(2.12)$$

which we would like to solve for γ_{p-1} and $r_{pp} > 0$. The first equation $A_{p-1} = R_{p-1}^T R_{p-1}$ is known to be satisfied; we do not need to consider it. The next two equations are redundant, for if $c_{p-1} = R_{p-1}^T \gamma_{p-1}$, then $c_{p-1}^T = (R_{p-1}^T \gamma_{p-1})^T = \gamma_{p-1}^T R_{p-1}$. Thus we need to solve the equations

$$c_{p-1} = R_{p-1}^T \gamma_{p-1}$$
$$a_{pp} = \gamma_{p-1}^T \gamma_{p-1} + r_{pp}^2$$

for γ_{p-1} and r_{pp}. But this can be done, and it can be done very efficiently; for, the system

$$R_{p-1}^T \gamma_{p-1} = c_{p-1}$$

is a triangular nonsingular system that may be solved by forward substitution for γ_{p-1} (as R_{p-1} and c_{p-1} are known), and then

$$r_{pp}^2 = a_{pp} - \gamma_{p-1}^T \gamma_{p-1}$$

gives

$$r_{pp} = \sqrt{a_{pp} - \gamma_{p-1}^T \gamma_{p-1}}.$$

One of the properties of a positive definite matrix is that $a_{pp} - \gamma_{p-1}^T \gamma_{p-1}$ is always positive, and so r_{pp} is real and positive. In summaries, the algorithm for finding the Cholesky decomposition of A from Eq. (2.12) is as follows:

Cholesky Decomposition Algorithm:

1. Set $R_1 = \sqrt{a_{11}}$.

2. Begin loop ($p = 2$ to n):

3. Solve $R_{p-1}^T \gamma_{p-1} = c_{p-1}$ for γ_{p-1} by forward substitution.

4. Set $r_{pp} = \sqrt{a_{pp} - \gamma_{p-1}^T \gamma_{p-1}}$.

5. Set $R_p = \begin{pmatrix} R_{p-1} & \gamma_{p-1} \\ 0 & r_{pp} \end{pmatrix}$.

6. End loop.

7. Set $L = R_n^T$.

Again, it can be shown that in infinite precision arithmetic step 4 will always give a positive r_{pp} and that each A_p is positive definite and hence has its own Cholesky decomposition. Notice that R_p differs from R_{p-1} only by the addition of a last row and last column, so that in forming the factor R_p of A_p we do not change the entries of R_{p-1} but simply add more entries.

The flops count for this method is about half that of Doolittle's LU decomposition, as would be expected since U is determined from L in this case. Square roots are typically counted as a single flop, although they are significantly more expensive than, say, an addition. As with any problem of significant interest, there are other algorithms for finding the Cholesky decomposition of a positive definite matrix.

PROBLEMS 2.4

1. a. Use the Cholesky Decomposition Algorithm (by hand) to find the Cholesky decomposition of the matrix $A = [4\ 2\ 1; 2\ 3\ 1; 1\ 1\ 4]$. Compare your results to Example 2.4.1.
  b. Use the Cholesky decomposition of A to solve the linear system $Ax = (3, 0, 4)^T$.

2. Use the Cholesky Decomposition Algorithm to find the Cholesky decomposition of the matrix $A = [4\ 1\ 0\ 1; 1\ 4\ 2\ -1; 0\ 2\ 4\ -2; 1\ -1\ -2\ 4]$.

3. Draw the Wilkinson diagram for the Cholesky Decomposition Algorithm applied to a 4×4 positive definite matrix.

4. Write a detailed algorithm (pseudocode) for performing the Cholesky Decomposition Algorithm in place (that is, overwriting A or part of it with L). Explicitly include the back substitution steps.

5. a. Show that if A is symmetric then EAE^T is symmetric.
  b. Show by example that it is possible for a nonsymmetric matrix to satisfy $x^T Ax > 0$ for all nonzero x.

MATLAB 2.4

The MATLAB command `chol` finds the Cholesky factor R. The command may also be used to test for positive definiteness. Enter:

```
» R=chol([4 2 1;2 3 1;1 1 4])
» R'*R
» [R,p]=chol([4 2 1;2 3 1;1 1 1])
» [R,p]=chol([4 2 1;2 3 1;1 1 0])
```

The first matrix is positive definite, and its right triangular factor R is returned. If the `chol` command is used with two output arguments R and p, then `chol` returns zero for p if the input is a positive definite matrix; if `chol` encounters a problem while performing the decomposition, indicating that A is not positive definite, then it sets p to a positive integer indicating when it encountered the problem, and returns an R that is the factor of A_{p-1} in the notation of this section. For example,

```
» [R,p]=chol(-2)
```

returns an empty matrix for R and $p = 1$ (error encountered on the very first submatrix), and

```
» [R,p]=chol([2 1;1 -1])
```

returns $R_1 = \sqrt{2}$ and $p = 2$ (the Cholesky Decomposition Algorithm failed while attempting to factor A_2; the fact that the $(2, 2)$ entry of the matrix is negative shows that A cannot be positive definite, but $A_1 = (2)$ is positive definite).

We've already looked at some of the numerical issues associated with the Cholesky decomposition, so let's briefly mention some other MATLAB matrix commands that may be useful. First, recall that the ellipsis (. . .), entered as three periods, may be used as a continuation character when entering long vectors or matrices by hand. Within an M-file this may not be necessary. To see an example, enter:

```
» type rosser
```

Also recall that when dealing with a large matrix it is often advisable to pre-allocate memory for it using a command of the form A=zeros([m n]). For sparse matrices there is a special command, spalloc, which may be used to pre-allocate memory.

The transpose operation A' is actually the **Hermitian** operation; that is, it is the complex conjugate transpose of A (often denoted A^*). For the non-conjugate transpose of a complex matrix, if needed, you may use A. ' instead. For example, enter:

```
» v=eig([1 -1;1 1])
» v',v.'
```

The conj command returns the complex conjugate of its argument.

Often it is possible to rearrange a formula algebraically so as to avoid actually transposing the matrix, and this can be valuable. Enter:

```
» clear all
» A=rand(1000);
» tic;A=A';toc
```

to see that transposition is not without cost. Suppose that A is stored but we must solve $A^T x = b$. Rather than using A'\b we might rewrite the equation as $x^T A = b^T$ and use the forward slash command b'/A to find x^T, and then transpose it to find x=(b'/A)'. (See help slash for the forward slash.) This requires two vector transpositions which is certainly preferable to a matrix transposition in the general case. Enter:

```
» clear all
» A=randn(1000);b=randn([1000 1]);   %Use normal dist.
» tic;C=A'\b;toc
» clear C
» tic;C=(b'/A)';toc     %Use forward slash /.
```

The difference may not be dramatic and may not be perfectly consistent, but if you repeat the experiment several times it should be noticeable. Use a larger random matrix if necessary. The command whos (a more informative version of who) details memory usage information for your current variables.

The poly command, when applied to a matrix, returns the coefficients of its characteristic polynomial. Enter:

```
» A=rand(3);
» eig(A)
» roots(poly(A))
» det(A)
» prod(roots(poly(A)))
```

(the eigenvalues of A are the roots of the characteristic polynomial, and the determinant of A is the product of those roots). The determinant and characteristic polynomial occur infrequently in numerical work; the fact that the roots of a polynomial may be viewed as the eigenvalues of a related matrix is useful however. The matrix typically used to find roots of a polynomial is the **companion matrix** of the polynomial, which may be found using the MATLAB command compan. The eigs command may be used to find some but not all eigenvalues of a matrix; often we need only the largest or smallest, and if the matrix is large, then it is more efficient to use eigs rather than eig.

The reshape command may be used to change the shape of a matrix. For example, a 4×4 matrix could be reshaped to be 8×2. Enter:

```
» A=rand(4)        %4x4 matrix.
» reshape(A,8,2)   %8x2 matrix.
```

The repmat command may be used to create matrices that have a repetitive structure. The kron command forms a Kronecker product of matrices. There are numerous sparse matrix commands; type help sparfun for a list of them (and see Section 3.2).

It is also possible to form matrices from blocks of other matrices in MATLAB, if the blocks conform. Enter:

```
» A11=[1 2;4 5]
» A12=[3 6]'
» A21=[7]
» A22=[8 9]
» A=[A11 A12;A21 A22]
```

Note that A does not retain information about the subblocks from which it was formed, however. There are more complicated structures in MATLAB (starting with Version 5); see help struct and help cell, for example.

The trace command finds the trace of a matrix, that is, the sum of its diagonal elements. The pinv command finds the pseudo-inverse of a matrix. The hess command orthogonally reduces a matrix to **upper Hessenberg** form (where the lower triangle is zero except possibly for the first subdiagonal).

If you have certain MATLAB toolboxes installed, you may have many other matrix functions available. Type help for a list of topics. One useful toolbox for matrices is the

Image Processing Toolbox (`help images`). The Signal Processing Toolbox (`help signal`) has many useful vector commands.

ADDITIONAL PROBLEMS 2.4

6. a. Use the Cholesky Decomposition Algorithm to find the Cholesky decomposition of the cross-product matrix $A^T A$, where $A = [1\ 0\ 1; 1\ 0\ -1; 1\ 1\ 0; 1\ 1\ 1]$.

   b. Use your Cholesky decomposition from part (a) to solve $A^T A x = A^T b$, where $b = (1, -1, 1, -1)^T$.

7. a. Prove that if A is nonsingular, then, $(A^T)^{-1} = (A^{-1})^T$.

   b. Prove that if A is positive definite, then every leading principal minor of A is positive definite. (*Hint:* Recall that a symmetric matrix is positive definite if and only if $x^T A x > 0$ for all nonzero x. Partition A and choose an appropriate x.)

   c. Prove that if A is positive definite then it has a factorization of the form $A = LDL^T$, where L is unit lower triangular and D is a diagonal matrix with positive diagonal entries. (You may use the fact that A has a Cholesky decomposition.)

8. Write a MATLAB program that implements the Cholesky Decomposition Algorithm. Attempt to mimic the behavior of the `chol` command by checking for errors and returning a p value that indicates how far the method has proceeded if an error occurs.

9. a. Use the eigenvalue decomposition to show that a symmetric matrix is positive definite if and only if all its eigenvalues are positive, and is positive semi-definite if and only if all its eigenvalues are nonnegative.

   b. Show that a symmetric matrix A is positive definite if and only if it has an LU factorization $A = LU$, where L is unit lower triangular and U has only positive diagonal entries.

10. a. Prove that if every leading principal minor of a symmetric matrix A is positive definite, then A is positive definite.

   b. Prove that the diagonal elements of a positive definite matrix are positive.

   c. Prove that every leading principal minor of a positive definite matrix has a positive determinant.

11. a. Use the `spy` command and the matrices of Example 2.4.1 to generate a Wilkinson diagram for the Cholesky decomposition applied to a 3×3 matrix.

   b. Use the `spy` command to generate a Wilkinson diagram for the Cholesky decomposition applied to a 6×6 matrix. You will need to generate a 6×6 positive definite matrix. One way to do this is to use the eigenvalue decomposition $A = SDS^T$ with a D having positive diagonal entries. Note that the `orth` or `qr` commands may be used to find an orthogonal S if applied to a nonsingular 6×6 matrix.

12. a. The Cholesky Decomposition Algorithm as we have given it is called the inner product form of the algorithm. Derive the outer product form of the algorithm by writing $A = R^T R$ as

$$\begin{pmatrix} a & s \\ s^T & A_1 \end{pmatrix} = \begin{pmatrix} r & 0 \\ \rho^T & R_1^T \end{pmatrix} \begin{pmatrix} r & \rho \\ 0 & R_1 \end{pmatrix},$$

where a is a scalar, r is a scalar, and s and ρ are appropriately sized row vectors. By equating blocks on the LHS and RHS, find an equation for r and ρ (the first row of R) and an equation relating $R_1^T R_1$, A_1, and an outer product. Explain how this technique may be applied iteratively to determine R.

   b. Write a MATLAB program that implements this method. Attempt to mimic the behavior of the `chol` command by checking for errors and returning a p value that indicates how far the method has proceeded if an error occurs.

13. a. Create a 100×100 positive definite matrix A by using the eigenvalue decomposition $A = SDS^T$, with D having positive diagonal entries, and the MATLAB command `S=orth(rand(100))`. Use the `chol` command to factor A. Find the error in $R^T R$.

   b. Create a 100×100 positive definite matrix with known Cholesky decomposition by using the sequence of commands `R=eye(100)+triu(rand(100));A=R'*R;` and compare the computed Cholesky decomposition (using `chol`) to the known Cholesky factor R.

   c. Recall that a matrix is positive definite if and only if it can be written in the form $R^T R$, where R is a square upper triangular matrix with positive diagonal entries. Repeat the sequence of commands `R=triu(rand(100));A=R'*R;[R,p]=chol`

(A);p at least 10 times. Are all these matrices found to be positive definite by the chol command? (Probably not.) Why not? (*Hint:* For one possibility, consider min(diag(R)) and see if the change R=1000*R;A=R'*R; improves matters when p is found to be nonzero.)

14. **a.** In the numerical solution of partial differential equations (e.g., the numerical modeling of heat flow), it is common to encounter matrices like $M_1 =$ [4 −1 0 0 0; −1 4 −1 0 0;0 −1 4 −1 0;0 0 −1 4 −1; 0 0 0 −1 4] or $M_2 =$ [4 −1 −1 0 0;−1 4 −1 −1 0;−1 −1 4 −1 − 1;0 −1 −1 4 −1;0 0 −1 −1 4]. That is, M_1 is tridiagonal with −1 on the super- and subdiagonals and 4 on the main diagonal, and M_2 is pentadiagonal with −1 on the first two super- and first two subdiagonals and 4 on the main diagonal. Of course, the matrices are typically much larger—on the order of thousands by thousands or more—and depending on the shape of the boundary of the material, they may vary slightly from the form given. Argue that a matrix like M_1 must be positive definite. What can you say about M_2?

b. When a matrix like M_2 is used to model heat flow, each x_i represents a grid point on the surface of a thin metal plate. Consider a square plate. Cover it with a 3 × 3 grid labeled $x_1, \ldots, x_9$ for the temperatures at those points. Draw the grid and label the points. Every entry of $x = (x_1, \ldots, x_9)^T$ except x_5 represents a point on the boundary; points 1, 2, and 3 are on the top, 4 is on the middle of the left side, 6 is on the middle of the right side, and points 7, 8, and 9 are on the bottom. Point 5 is in the middle. We want to know the steady-state temperature at each of these points if the edges are held at a given temperature(s). It is a fact that the temperature at a point is the average of the temperatures along any circle centered at that point, so $x_5 = (x_2 + x_4 + x_6 + x_8)/4$. Suppose that the corners of the plate are held at 5 degrees and that the middles of the edges are held at 10 degrees. Argue that the steady-state temperatures at the points are given by the solution of $Mx = b$, where M is the identity matrix, except that the 5th row is (0 −1/4 0 −1/4 1 −1/4 0 − 1/4 0), and where $b = (5, 10, 5, 10, 0, 10, 5, 10, 5)^T$.

c. Solve this system. What is x_5?

d. Write the corresponding system for a 4 × 4 grid. For a very large grid, would the coefficient matrix look something like M_2 of part (a)? Would it be positive definite?

15. **a.** Prove that every symmetric matrix A has a factorization of the form LDL^T, where L is unit lower triangular.

b. Write a detailed algorithm (pseudocode) for decomposing a positive definite matrix into the form $A = LDL^T$, where L is unit lower triangular and D is a diagonal matrix with positive diagonal entries.

c. Show that if $A = LDL^T$, where L is unit lower triangular and D has positive diagonal entries, then A has a Cholesky decomposition.

2.5   Condition Numbers

Although Gaussian elimination with partial pivoting usually destroys the sparsity structure of a matrix, it's still the method of choice for small to medium n. The rapid growth of error that can happen in principle simply does not occur in practice. One reason is that there is some cancellation of errors due to the fact that some will be high (positive error) and some will be low (negative error).[9] This is not the only reason, however, and numerical analysts do not fully understand why the method performs as well as it does.

Gaussian elimination with partial pivoting does not solve the linear system $Ax = b$ with the same degree of accuracy for every $n \times n$ matrix A, however. Clearly $Ix = b$ will always be solved exactly, apart from representation error, the error that's due to entering the components of b into the machine. This is of course not typical. To understand how the quality of the solution of $Ax = b$ depends on the coefficient matrix A, we must extend

---

[9] In fact, there is a statistical theory of error analysis.

the concept of a norm to matrices. This will involve a fair amount of new terminology but the concept is indispensable for analyzing the algorithms of computational matrix algebra.

Norms

Recall that a vector norm on $\mathbb{R}^n$ is a real-valued function $\|x\|$ defined for all $x \in \mathbb{R}^n$ that is positive definite ($\|x\| > 0$ unless $x = 0$ in which case $\|x\| = 0$) and that satisfies $\|\alpha x\| = |\alpha| \|x\|$ for all scalars α and the triangle inequality $\|x + y\| \leq \|x\| + \|y\|$ ($x, y \in \mathbb{R}^n$). A vector norm is a notion of length of vectors. The most commonly used vector norms are the **Hölder p-norms**

$$\|x\|_p = \left[\sum_{i=1}^{n} |x_i|^p \right]^{1/p}$$

($p \geq 1$). These are also called the l_p **norms.** The three cases of greatest interest are the l_1 norm

$$\|x\|_1 = \sum_{i=1}^{n} |x_i|$$

and the l_2 norm

$$\|x\|_2 = \left[\sum_{i=1}^{n} x_i^2 \right]^{1/2}$$

which is simply the Euclidean root-mean-square (RMS) norm for which we also write $\| \cdot \|_E$, and the limiting case as $p \to \infty$, which can be shown to give a valid vector norm

$$\|x\|_\infty = \max_{i=1}^{n}(|x_i|)$$

called the l_∞ or **max** or **sup** (for supremum) norm. Each of these norms may be used for measuring the size of an error vector such as the residual from solving a linear system

$$r = b - A\widehat{x}$$

(where $\widehat{x}$ is an approximate solution of $Ax = b$); r is a vector, so its norm $\|r\|$ gives a single scalar value that may be compared to some tolerance. (Note that the computation of r involves the subtraction of nearly equal quantities so cancellation of significant figures is an issue here.) The l_1 norm measures the total error, the l_2 norm measures the RMS error, and the max norm measures the worst-case error over all components.

For a fixed n, all vector norms on $\mathbb{R}^n$ are **equivalent,** meaning that for any two norms $\| \cdot \|_\alpha, \| \cdot \|_\beta$ there exist positive scalars r_l and r_u, independent of x, such that

$$r_l \|x\|_\beta \leq \|x\|_\alpha \leq r_u \|x\|_\beta$$

for every $x \in \mathbb{R}^n$. (Again, note that the constants r_l and r_u depend only on the norms $\| \cdot \|_\alpha$ and $\| \cdot \|_\beta$ but do *not* depend on the specific vector x.) In particular, if a sequence converges (or diverges) in one norm, it does so in all norms.

The norm of a vector is a measure of its size. For example, if $\|x_k\| \to 0$, then $x_k \to 0$. We need a similar measure of size for (square) matrices. We could treat an $n \times n$ matrix as a vector in $\mathbb{R}^{n^2}$ by unraveling it row by row into a vector of length n^2, but this neglects an important difference between vectors and matrices: Matrices can be multiplied; vectors cannot. In addition to the triangle inequality for addition, we want a similar result for products of matrices as well.

A real-valued function $\| \cdot \|$ defined for all $n \times n$ matrices is said to be a **matrix norm** if it has the following properties:

1. $\|A\| > 0$ unless A is the zero matrix, in which case $\|A\| = 0$ (positive definiteness)
2. $\|\alpha A\| = |\alpha|\|A\|$ for all scalars α (homogeneity)
3. $\|A + B\| \leq \|A\| + \|B\|$ (the triangle inequality)
4. $\|AB\| \leq \|A\|\|B\|$ (the submultiplicativity property)

(where A, B are $n \times n$ matrices). Unraveling the matrix to an n^2 long vector and using a vector norm on $\mathbb{R}^{n^2}$ gives a function that satisfies the first three properties (called a **matrix subnorm**) but that is not in general submultiplicative. If $\| \cdot \|$ is a matrix norm, then $d(A, B) = \|A - B\|$ defines a distance between matrices. In addition, note that submultiplicativity immediately gives

$$\|A^2\| = \|AA\| \leq \|A\|\|A\| = \|A\|^2$$

and, inductively, $\|A^k\| \leq \|A\|^k$ ($k = 1, 2, \ldots$).

We'll also need to work with matrix-vector products. If $\| \cdot \|_v$ is a vector norm on $\mathbb{R}^n$ and $\| \cdot \|_M$ is a matrix norm on $n \times n$ matrices, then we say that the vector norm and the matrix norm are **consistent** (or **compatible**) if

$$\|Ax\|_v \leq \|A\|_M \|x\|_v$$

(similar to the submultiplicativity property). If we have consistent vector and matrix norms, then we may estimate the size of Ax from the sizes of A and x. This will prove useful.

How do we find matrix norms? If A is an $n \times n$ matrix with entries a_{ij}, then the function

$$\|A\|_F = \sqrt{\sum_{i=1}^{n} \sum_{j=1}^{n} a_{ij}^2}$$

defines a matrix norm, called the **Frobenius norm.** It can be shown that

$$\|A\|_F = \sqrt{\text{tr}(A^T A)},$$

where $\text{tr}(M)$ is the **trace** of M, that is, the sum of the diagonal entries of M. The most important matrix norm, however, is the **spectral norm**

$$\|A\|_s = \sqrt{\rho(A^T A)},$$

where $\rho(M)$ is the **spectral radius** of M, that is, the largest eigenvalue of M in absolute value. The square roots of the eigenvalues of $A^T A$ (which must be nonnegative) are called the **singular values** of A so we can also say that $\|A\|_s$ is equal to the largest singular value of A.

The motivation for the Frobenius norm is clear, but where does the spectral norm come from? In fact, every vector norm induces a matrix norm. If $\|\cdot\|_v$ is a vector norm on $\mathbb{R}^n$, then the function

$$\|A\|_M = \sup_{x \neq 0}(\|Ax\|_v/\|x\|_v)$$
$$= \max_{\|x\|_v=1}(\|Ax\|_v)$$

is a matrix norm, called the **induced norm** (or **natural norm**) associated with, or induced by, the vector norm $\|\cdot\|_v$. An induced matrix norm is always consistent with the vector norm that induces it. In other words

$$\|Ax\|_v \leq \|A\|_M \|x\|_v$$

if $\|\cdot\|_v$ induces $\|\cdot\|_M$. In addition, if $\|\cdot\|_\mu$ is any other matrix norm consistent with $\|\cdot\|_v$, then for every $n \times n$ matrix A,

$$\rho(A) \leq \|A\|_M \leq \|A\|_\mu \tag{2.13}$$

so that $\rho(A)$ is a lower bound on $\|A\|_M$ for any natural norm $\|\cdot\|_M$. Furthermore the natural norm gives the smallest value of all norms consistent with a given vector norm. This is a desirable property.

The spectral norm arises as the natural norm induced by the Euclidean norm, and this is why it is of interest. The Frobenius norm is also consistent with the Euclidean vector norm, but by Eq. (2.13) it must always be the case that

$$\|A\|_s \leq \|A\|_F. \tag{2.14}$$

(The Frobenius norm is not induced by any vector norm.) Because of this when we use the Frobenius norm it is only because it is easier to compute than the spectral norm, which is relatively expensive to compute.

Example 2.5.1   Let $A = [2\ 1\ 0; 1\ 1\ 0; 0\ 0\ -1]$. The Frobenius norm of A is $\|A\|_F = [2^2 + 1^2 + 0^2 + 1^2 + 1^2 + 0^2 + 0^2 + 0^2 + (-1)^2]^{1/2} = \sqrt{8} \doteq 2.8284$, and the spectral norm of A, which may be found from the MATLAB command `sqrt(max(eig(A'*A)))` to be 2.6180, is indeed not more than $\|A\|_F$ (in accordance with Eq. (2.14)). It is also the same as the spectral radius `max(eig(A))` of A, in agreement with Eq. (2.13). (The `norm` command can be used to compute these quantities.)

Let $x = (5, -4, 3)^T$ (for which $\|x\|_2 = [5^2 + (-4)^2 + (-3)^2]^{1/2} = \sqrt{50} \doteq 7.0711$). We could estimate $\|Ax\|_2$ by $\|A\|_F \|x\|_2 = \sqrt{8}\sqrt{50} = 20$ or by $\|A\|_s \|x\|_2 = 2.6180\sqrt{50} \doteq 18.5121$. In fact $Ax = (5, 0, -3)^T$, and so $\|Ax\|_2 = [5^2 + 0^2 + (-3)^2]^{1/2} = \sqrt{34} \doteq 5.8310$. ■

We almost always need consistent matrix norms because we are usually working with matrix-vector products (e.g., Ax, $A^{-1}b$), and whenever possible we choose natural norms because they give the best (that is, smallest) estimates of the sizes of these quantities. The spectral radius is not a norm so we cannot use it.

Quality of Solutions   We're now ready to apply the matrix norm to help us understand how the nature of the matrix A affects the quality of the computed solution $\widehat{x}$ to $Ax = b$, for which

$x = A^{-1}b$ is the true solution. (We are assuming that A is nonsingular.) Consider the linear system

$$Ax = b.$$

No matter what method we use to solve it, we will find an approximation $\widehat{x}$ to x. We would like to say something about the absolute error

$$\alpha = \|x - \widehat{x}\|$$

or the relative error

$$\rho = \|x - \widehat{x}\|/\|x\|$$

(if x is nonzero) in our computed solution, but since we do not know x, we cannot do this directly. An obvious substitute measure of error is the norm of the residual

$$r = b - A\widehat{x}$$

since $\|r\| = 0$ if $x = \widehat{x}$ and, by continuity, $r \to 0$ as $x \to \widehat{x}$. But now we must ask the following crucial question: Is it the case that if $\|r\|$ is small then the absolute error $\alpha = \|x - \widehat{x}\|$ is also small? Remember, the residual measures the difference in the values of the function

$$y = Ax$$

at the true solution x (where we are given that $y = b$) and the computed solution (assuming that $y = A\widehat{x}$ is computed accurately). In root-finding problems we stated that we could not safely use the reasoning that if $f(x_0)$ was nearly zero, then x_0 was nearly a root of $f(x) = 0$, for example. Is it different here, when we are solving the root-finding problem for the linear equation $Ax - b = 0$?

Conditioning   The answer is both yes and no. *Conditioning*—the sensitivity of the solution of a problem to small changes in the given data that leads to poor behavior of numerical methods on those problems—can be defined for a very general class of problems. Non-linear root-finding problems in particular can be well-conditioned (not sensitive to small changes in the problem) or ill-conditioned (highly sensitive to small charges in the problem); roots of multiplicity greater than 1, for which the derivative of the function is 0 at the root, are the most common ill-conditioned problems of this sort. In this sense there is nothing special about the case $Ax - b = 0$. Indeed, several of our methods for nonlinear root-finding were based on linearizing the function f to obtain a linear approximant. As a practical matter, however, the more useful answer is that the condition of A plays a special role in solving the *linear* system $Ax = b$.

Let's refine the notion of conditioning for square linear systems. If our computed solution is $\widehat{x}$, then the residual

$$r = b - A\widehat{x}$$

$$= Ax - A\widehat{x}$$

$$= A(x - \widehat{x})$$

is an easily computable measure of the error. Take norms on both sides using any consistent vector and matrix norm to find

$$\|r\|_v = \|A(x - \widehat{x})\|_v$$

$$\leq \|A\|_M \|x - \widehat{x}\|_v$$

(by consistency of the norms). But this inequality goes the wrong way as far as we are concerned; $\|r\|_v$ is what we can compute, and we want to use it to bound $\alpha = \|x - \widehat{x}\|_v$ or $\rho = \|x - \widehat{x}\|_v / \|x\|_v$. Let's try again:

$$r = b - A\widehat{x}$$

$$= Ax - A\widehat{x}$$

$$A^{-1}r = x - \widehat{x}$$

$$\|A^{-1}r\|_v = \|x - \widehat{x}\|_v$$

$$\|A^{-1}\|_M \|r\|_v \geq \|x - \widehat{x}\|_v.$$

This is better. If we know or can estimate $\|A^{-1}\|_M$, then we can put an upper bound on the absolute error α. For the relative error we have

$$\frac{\|A^{-1}\|_M \|r\|_v}{\|x\|_v} \geq \frac{\|x - \widehat{x}\|_v}{\|x\|_v} \tag{2.15}$$

and from $Ax = b$ we have

$$\|Ax\|_v = \|b\|_v$$

$$\|A\|_M \|x\|_v \geq \|b\|_v$$

$$\|x\|_v \geq \frac{\|b\|_v}{\|A\|_M}.$$

Thus Eq. (2.15) becomes

$$\frac{\|A^{-1}\|_M \|r\|_v}{\left(\dfrac{\|b\|_v}{\|A\|_M}\right)} \geq \frac{\|x - \widehat{x}\|_v}{\|x\|_v}.$$

That is,

$$\frac{\|x - \widehat{x}\|_v}{\|x\|_v} \leq \|A\|_M \|A^{-1}\|_M \frac{\|r\|_v}{\|b\|_v}, \tag{2.16}$$

which gives a bound on the relative error $\|x - \widehat{x}\|_v / \|x\|_v$ using the values of $\|r\|_v$ and $\|b\|_v$, which are easily computed, and the matrix norms of A and A^{-1}. Since we are usually more interested in ρ than α, we define the **condition number** of A (with respect to $\| \cdot \|_M$) to be

$$\kappa(A) = \|A\|_M \|A^{-1}\|_M$$

(also written cond(A)). To simplify the notation, from here on we'll drop the subscripts on the norms and simply write $\kappa(A) = \|A\| \|A^{-1}\|$. It should be clear from context whether a vector or matrix norm is intended. (Typically we use the Euclidean vector norm and the spectral matrix norm.) The condition number of a singular matrix is taken to be infinity. The condition number of a nonsingular matrix is always at least 1, for

$$AA^{-1} = I$$

$$\|AA^{-1}\| = \|I\|$$

$$\|A\| \|A^{-1}\| \geq \|I\|$$

and the relation $\|A^2\| \leq \|A\|^2$ with $A = I$ gives $\|I\|^2 \geq \|I^2\| = \|I\|$ so that $\|I\| \geq 1$ (recall that only the zero matrix can have a zero norm). Hence $\kappa(A) = \|A\|\|A^{-1}\| \geq 1$. If $\kappa(A)$ is near 1, we say that A is well-conditioned. If $\kappa(A)$ is much larger than 1, we say that A is ill-conditioned; there is no cutoff value of $\kappa(A)$ for a matrix to be considered well-conditioned as opposed to ill-conditioned.

Consider again Eq. (2.16). We may write this equation in terms of the condition number as

$$\frac{\|x - \widehat{x}\|}{\|x\|} \leq \kappa(A)\frac{\|r\|}{\|b\|}$$

or

$$\rho \leq \kappa(A)\frac{\|r\|}{\|b\|}. \tag{2.17}$$

For simplicity, suppose that $\|b\| = 1$. Since $\kappa(A) \geq 1$, Eq. (2.17) states that the relative error in our computed solution $\widehat{x}$ may be larger than the error as measured by the residual. In fact, it may be larger by a factor of $\kappa(A)$. If A is well-conditioned ($\kappa(A) \approx 1$), then we may justly reason that a small residual implies a small relative error in $\widehat{x}$. But if A is ill-conditioned ($\kappa(A) \gg 1$), then knowing that the residual is small tells us very little about the relative error in $\widehat{x}$.

Example 2.5.2 Let's look at the effect predicted by Eq. (2.17). Set $\epsilon = 0.1$ and $\varpi = 2\ln(\epsilon)$, and define

$$A = \begin{bmatrix} \cosh(\varpi) & \sinh(\varpi) \\ \sinh(\varpi) & \cosh(\varpi) \end{bmatrix}.$$

From MATLAB (using the command `cond(A)`) the condition number of A is 10^4. (The MATLAB functions `sinh` and `cosh` may be used to enter the hyperbolic trig functions.) Let's take $b = (1/\sqrt{2}, 1/\sqrt{2})^T$ (for which $\|b\| = 1$). The true solution is

$$x = \begin{bmatrix} \cosh(\varpi) & \sinh(\varpi) \\ \sinh(\varpi) & \cosh(\varpi) \end{bmatrix}^{-1} \begin{pmatrix} 1/\sqrt{2} \\ 1/\sqrt{2} \end{pmatrix}$$

$$= \frac{1}{\cosh^2(\varpi) - \sinh^2(\varpi)} \begin{bmatrix} \cosh(\varpi) & -\sinh(\varpi) \\ -\sinh(\varpi) & \cosh(\varpi) \end{bmatrix} \begin{pmatrix} 1/\sqrt{2} \\ 1/\sqrt{2} \end{pmatrix}$$

$$= (1/\sqrt{2}) \begin{pmatrix} \cosh(\varpi) - \sinh(\varpi) \\ \cosh(\varpi) - \sinh(\varpi) \end{pmatrix}$$

$$= (1/\sqrt{2}) \begin{pmatrix} \exp(-\varpi) \\ \exp(-\varpi) \end{pmatrix}$$

$$= (1/\sqrt{2}) \begin{pmatrix} 1 \\ 1 \end{pmatrix} \epsilon^{-2}$$

so that

$$x = \frac{1}{\sqrt{2}\epsilon^2} \begin{pmatrix} 1 \\ 1 \end{pmatrix} \tag{2.18}$$

and so $x = (70.71067811865474, 70.71067811865474)^T$ for $\epsilon = 0.1$. (Note the division by a small number in the formula for x.) From MATLAB, A\b is

$\widehat{x} = (70.71067811864299, 70.71067811864299)^T$. The relative error is $\|x - \widehat{x}\|/\|x\|$ or about 1.66×10^{-13} and the norm of the residual $\|b - A\widehat{x}\|$ is about 3.45×10^{-13}. Despite a condition number of 10^4 the residual and the relative error are on the same order of magnitude. Note however that $\widehat{x}$ is accurate to only 12 digits (70.7106781186) and not to the full 16 digits of x; we have lost about 4 digits of accuracy ($16 - 12 = 4$) in performing a calculation in which cond$(A) \approx 10^4$.

Let's try again with $\epsilon = 0.01$. We find that cond(A) is essentially 10^8 and $x = (7071.067811865475, 7071.067811865475)^T$. (Note that this is just the previous x rescaled by a factor of 100, as per Eq. (2.18).) From MATLAB, A\b is $\widehat{x} = (7071.06791978500, 7071.06791978500)^T$. The relative error is $\|x - \widehat{x}\|/\|x\|$ or about 2.16×10^{-8}, and the norm of the residual $\|b - A\widehat{x}\|$ is about 1.04×10^{-8}. The relative error is larger than the norm of the residual, though only by a factor of about 2 (far from the worst case of 10^8). However, the entries of $\widehat{x}$ agree with those of x only to 7 digits (7071.067). We have lost about 8 digits of accuracy ($16 - 7 = $ about 8) in performing a calculation in which cond$(A) \approx 10^8$. ■

In both cases in Example 2.5.2 the norm of the residual is on the same order of magnitude as the relative error. As indicated by Eq. (2.17), this need not always be the case; between Eq. (2.17) and the subtraction of nearly equal quantities performed when computing r, we must be very careful in drawing conclusions about ρ based on it. Also in both cases in Example 2.5.2 we lose about p digits of accuracy in the solution of $Ax = b$ when the condition number of A is on the order of 10^p. This is typical. Although better results will be obtained for certain choices of b, both theory and experience show that:

If the condition number of A is on the order of 10^k, about k significant figures will be lost in solving $Ax = b$.

(Commit the statement above to memory.) Note that this rule of thumb does *not* state that about k significant figures will be lost in solving $Ax = b$ by Gaussian elimination with partial pivoting; it states that about k significant figures will be lost by *any* method.

The reason is that Eq. (2.17) is a statement about the sensitivity of the solution x of the system $Ax = b$; in fact, it is more a statement about the sensitivity of the system $Ax = b$ to perturbations of A than it is a statement about numerical analysis. The very act of entering the matrix A on the computer almost always causes some representation error, and so rather than solving $Ax = b$ we are in fact solving $A_1 x = b_1$, where $A \approx A_1$ and $b \approx b_1$. (These quantities are approximately equal both componentwise and normwise). Hence the best we can possibly hope for is to solve

$$A_1 \xi = b_1$$

exactly for its solution ξ. How close is ξ to x? This is exactly the question that the condition number answers, and the answer is Eq. (2.17) and the guideline above. Even supposing that $b = b_1$, it is not hard to show that if A is nonsingular and the individual entries of A_1 differ by no more than ϵ from those of A, then

$$\frac{\|\xi - x\|}{\|x\|} \leq \kappa(A)\epsilon \qquad (2.19)$$

for $\epsilon > 0$ sufficiently small. (Recall that ξ is the *exact* solution of the perturbed system!) For example, if $\epsilon \approx 10^{-16}$ is the machine epsilon and $\kappa(A) \approx 10^k$, then

$$\frac{\|\xi - x\|}{\|x\|} \lesssim 10^k 10^{-16} = 10^{-16+k},$$

meaning that, generally, ξ and x may have components that differ in the $(16 - k)$th place (e.g., the tenth place if $k = 6$; the smaller entries of the vectors ξ and x may differ even sooner, but they contribute less to the norm.) We can't possibly hope to do better than get the exact solution of the closest system to $Ax = b$ that can be represented on the machine; we can only expect that we might do worse. Of course Eq. (2.19) is an inequality, not an equality, so we will not get results this poor every time, but we certainly can and typically do get results like that, as seen in Example 2.5.2, and we should expect this.

It's worth repeating: The loss of about k significant figures when the condition number is roughly 10^k is a property of A, not a property of the numerical method used to solve $Ax = b$. It is not a failing of the method or the machine but rather an inherent property

Error Analysis   of the matrix—namely, its condition. In fact, we usually consider a method for solving $Ax = b$ "good" if it computes a solution $\widehat{x}$ with the property that

$$(A + E)\widehat{x} = b \tag{2.20}$$

for some matrix E with small norm. This equation states that the computed solution $\widehat{x}$ of $Ax = b$ is the *exact* solution of a "nearby" problem involving the matrix $A + E$, which is close to A in the sense that $\|(A + E) - A\| = \|E\|$ is small. A result such as Eq. (2.20) is called a **backward error analysis** in that it refers the errors backward to the coefficient matrix; if the errors in $\widehat{x}$ may be accounted for by a slight perturbation of A, then unless we know A to great precision, we cannot blame the algorithm for failing to find the desired solution x. A **forward error analysis** generally refers to a procedure for estimating the worst-case effects of roundoff error as a computation proceeds step by step through the algorithm. Backward error analyses are preferred for a number of reasons; one is that the worst-case effects of roundoff error are almost never seen in practice. Some errors are positive, some are negative, and they will largely cancel. For this reason forward error analyses often give extremely large bounds which are irrelevant in an actual computation.

A method that satisfies an equation such as Eq. (2.20), that is, one with a backward error analysis, is said to be **backwards stable.** *Stability* refers to the tendency of a method to produce answers that are about as good as the conditioning will allow. *Instability* means that roundoff errors are magnified to the point where the returned answer isn't even close (as measured with respect to the conditioning). The LU decomposition with complete pivoting is stable; the LU decomposition with partial pivoting is not, strictly speaking, but in practice it behaves as though it were. Systems that demonstrate the instability of Gaussian elimination with partial pivoting are almost never encountered in practice.

For matrices with a given condition number it is still true that some solution methods are superior to others, and there are techniques for improving an estimate $\widehat{x}$ of x (see Section 3.3). But when solving a linear system it is always useful to know the condition number of the coefficient matrix A. This can be relatively easy to compute for some matrix norms. For others, such as the spectral norm, the condition number of the coefficient matrix A is hard to compute but not necessarily hard to approximate. Since the order of magnitude of $\kappa(A)$ is all we really need, an estimate is usually sufficient (and saves us from having to compute A^{-1}, which would be unreasonable). Using the Frobenius norm or some other norm generally gives an overestimate (that is, an upper bound) on the condition number with respect to the spectral norm, but if that estimate is small enough then we need not compute $\kappa(A)$ more precisely.

We've covered a lot of ground in this section, and if matrix norms are new to you, it may take some time to adjust to them. Remember however that MATLAB can compute $\kappa(A)$ and the solution of $Ax = b$, and you now know how to interpret these quantities in an informed manner.

PROBLEMS 2.5

1. a. Given a norm $\| \cdot \|_v$ on $\mathbb{R}^n$ we call the pair $(\mathbb{R}^n, \| \cdot \|_v)$ a **normed space.** By definition, a circle in $(\mathbb{R}^n, \| \cdot \|_v)$ is the set of all $x \in \mathbb{R}^n$ such that $\|x\| = c$ for some $c > 0$. Sketch the unit circle ($c = 1$) for $\mathbb{R}^n$ with the l_1, l_2, and l_∞ vector norms.

b. We define distance in a normed space by $d(x, y) = \|x - y\|_v$. Find $d((2, 1), (0, 0))$ for $\mathbb{R}^2$ with the l_1, l_2, and l_∞ vector norms.

c. The distance function on the normed space $(\mathbb{R}^2, l_1)$ is also called the **taxicab distance** (or **Manhattan distance**). Explain why.

2. a. The matrix norm induced by the l_1 vector norm is $\|A\|_\gamma = \max_{j=1}^n \{\sum_{i=1}^n |a_{ij}|\}$, the maximum column sum. The matrix norm induced by the l_∞ vector norm is $\|A\|_\rho = \max_{i=1}^n \{\sum_{j=1}^n |a_{ij}|\}$, the maximum row sum. For $A = [1\ 2\ 3; 4\ 5\ 6; 7\ 8\ 9]$, find (by hand) $\|A\|_F, \|A\|_\gamma, \|A\|_\rho$.

b. Find $\|A\|_s$ by finding the largest eigenvalue of $A^T A$ (use `max(eig(A'*A))`).

3. a. Show that if $\|A\| < 1$ in any matrix norm, then $A^k \to 0$ (the zero matrix) as $k \to \infty$. (*Note:* A vector or matrix norm is always a continuous function of the elements of the vector or matrix.)

b. Show that the spectral radius $\rho(A)$ is not a matrix norm. (*Hint:* Find a nonzero matrix for which $\rho(A) = 0$.)

c. Show that if A is nonsingular, then $\|A^{-1}\| \geq \|I\|/\|A\|$ in any matrix norm.

d. Show that $\|I\| = 1$ for any natural norm.

4. Show that $\kappa_s(A) \leq \kappa_F(A)$ for any nonsingular matrix A, where κ_s is the condition number with respect to the spectral norm and κ_F is the condition number with respect to the Frobenius norm.

5. Use Eq. (2.15) to show that $\|x - \widehat{x}\| \leq \kappa(A)\|r\|/\|A\|$ is a bound on the absolute error in the computed solution $\widehat{x}$ of $Ax = b$.

MATLAB 2.5

Let's start with some relevant MATLAB commands. The `norm` command computes vector and matrix norms. For example, enter:

```
» help norm
» A=rand(5);
» norm(A)            %Spectral norm.
» norm(A,'fro')      %Frobenius norm.
» norm(A,1)          %l1 (max. column sum) norm.
» norm(A,'inf')      %l-infinity (max. row sum) norm.
» v=1:10;p=3;
» norm(v,p)          %Holder p-norm for vectors.
```

For large matrices, the function `normest` may be used to estimate the spectral norm of a matrix. It is faster but less accurate `then norm`.

A definition of the spectral norm is that it is equal to the square root of the largest eigenvalue of $A^T A$. Enter:

```
» sqrt(max(eig(A'*A)))
» norm(A)
```

The square roots of the eigenvalues of $A^T A$ are by definition the singular values of A, which may be found by the `svd` command. Enter:

```
» svd(A)
» max(ans)
```

to see this. The norm of A and the norm of A^{-1} may differ by several orders of magnitude.

The command `cond` computes the condition number of A with respect to the spectral norm. Enter:

```
» cond(A)
» norm(A)*norm(inv(A))   %Definition of cond(A).
```

(The `cond` command uses the singular value decomposition, which is more accurate and more efficient than the above approach.) There is also a `condest` command, which estimates the condition number of A with respect to the $\| \cdot \|_\gamma$ norm (see Problem 2). The definition of condition number may be extended to nonsquare matrices, and the `cond` command works for such matrices.

The **Hilbert matrix of order** n is the $n \times n$ matrix with entries $a_{ij} = 1/(i + j - 1)$, and this family of matrices is known to be poorly conditioned. Enter:

```
» B=hilb(5)
» norm(B)
» norm(inv(B))
» cond(B)
```

for the 5×5 case. How badly conditioned is it? The condition number $\kappa(A)$ is sometimes called the condition of A with respect to matrix inversion because of its connection to the solution of $Ax = b$, which is (theoretically) equivalent to finding $A^{-1}b$. Enter:

```
» H=hilb(10);
» cond(H)
» inv(H)-invhilb(10)
» norm(ans)
```

The command `invhilb` produces the *exact* inverse of H (if n is sufficiently small, which it is here). The errors in the numerical computation of H^{-1} by `inv(H)` are *huge;* note the leading factor of 10^8, or enter:

```
» format bank
» inv(H)-invhilb(10)
```

to see just how large these errors are. Enter:

```
» format
» cond(invhilb(10))
» max(max(invhilb(10)))
```

From the size of the largest element of H^{-1} we see that the absolute errors in `inv(H) -` `invhilb(10)` are not quite as bad as they may seem at first. In fact, enter:

```
» format long
» inv(H)*H
» norm(ans)        %Should be 1.
» invhilb(10)*H
» norm(ans)        %Should be 1.
```

to see that the net effect of using the computed inverse is not as bad as expected; the errors in H^{-1} are worse than those we saw in its application (similar to the effect we saw with the LU decomposition). Enter:

```
» b=ones([10 1]);
» x1=inv(H)*b              %Computed solution of Hx=b.
» x=invhilb(10)*b          %Solution of Hx=b.
» norm(x-x1)/norm(x)       %Relative error.
» x2=H\b                   %Solution by Gaussian elimination.
» norm(x-x2)/norm(x)       %Relative error.
» r=b-H*x2                 %Residual.
» cond(H)*norm(r)/norm(b)  %Upper bound on relative error.
```

(see Eq. (2.17)). The relative error in $\widehat{x}$ (i.e., x2) is nearly 10^6 times larger than the absolute error in $A\widehat{x}$ (as measured by $\|r\|$). Problem 5 gives the bound $\|x - \widehat{x}\| \le \kappa(A)\|r\|/\|A\|$ on the absolute error; enter:

```
» cond(H)*norm(r)/norm(H)
» norm(x-x2)
```

and apparently the absolute error $\|x - \widehat{x}\|$ is quite close to the limit. The norm of the residual is a terrible estimate of the size of the error in the computed solution for this matrix; the large condition number serves as our warning.

Recall that some matrices are artificially ill-conditioned. For example, the condition number of any matrix of the form $A = [1\ 0; 0\ \epsilon]$ is always $1/\epsilon$ (if $\epsilon > 0$), which may be made arbitrarily small by taking ϵ as small as desired; however, A will be well-behaved in almost any computation. This is technically an ill-conditioned matrix for small ϵ, but the row equivalent matrix $[1\ 0; 0\ 1]$ is not.

Let's look again at the arrowhead matrix of MATLAB 2.3. Enter:

```
» A=eye(10);A(1,:)=ones([1 10]);A(:,1)=ones([10 1])
» [L,U,P]=lu(A)
» cond(A)
» cond(L),cond(U)
```

to form A and find its LU decomposition. The condition numbers of L and U are each larger than that of A, though they would still be considered small. Enter:

```
» cond(P'*L*U)     %This should equal cond(A).
» cond(P*A)        %PA=LU.
```

We might have expected that since L and U have larger condition numbers their product should too, but of course this cannot be the case since their product is A (actually, PA). This is related to a slightly subtle issue: When performing an LU decomposition, the error in the product LU tends to be much less than the errors in L and U individually. The errors are correlated in such a way that the product is a better approximation to PA than the individual factors are to L and U.

ADDITIONAL PROBLEMS 2.5

6. a. Solve $Ax = b$, where A is the Hilbert matrix of order 8 and $b = (1, -1, 1, -1, 1, -1, 1, -1)^T$, using the LU decomposition (in MATLAB, this may be done by using A\b).

b. What is $\kappa(A)$? Use the `invhilb` command to solve $Ax = b$. Is the relative error in your solution from part (a) what you would expect?

c. Repeat parts (a) and (b) for the Hilbert matrix of order 12 and $b = (1, -1, 1, -1, 1, -1, 1, -1, 1, -1, 1, -1)^T$.

7. For $A = [1\ 2\ 2; 2\ -1\ 1; 2\ 1\ -2]$ find $\|A\|_s$, $\|A\|_F$, $\|A\|_\gamma$, $\|A\|_\rho$, and $\|A\|_1 = \sum_{i=1}^n \sum_{j=1}^n |a_{ij}|$, and the corresponding condition numbers $\kappa_s(A)$, $\kappa_F(A)$, $\kappa_\gamma(A)$, $\kappa_\rho(A)$, and $\kappa_1(A)$.

8. a. Show that $\kappa(A) = \kappa(cA)$ for any nonzero scalar c.

b. Show that $\kappa(A) = \kappa(A^{-1})$ for any nonsingular matrix A.

9. a. Gaussian elimination with partial pivoting is generally well-behaved but can in principle give poor results for certain matrices. The matrix $A = [1\ 0\ 0\ 0\ 1; -1\ 1\ 0\ 0\ 1; -1\ -1\ 1\ 0\ 1; -1\ -1\ -1\ 1\ 1; -1\ -1\ -1\ -1\ 1]$ is one of the matrices for which it behaves poorly. Use MATLAB to find the LU decomposition of A and the condition numbers of A, L, and U.

b. Set n=10 and use the sequence of commands
```
A=eye(n)-tril(ones([n n]),-1);A(:,n)
=ones([n 1]);
```
to generate the 10×10 version of the matrix of part (a). Find the condition numbers of A, L, and U.

c. Set n=80 and use the same sequence of commands
```
A=eye(n)-tril(ones([n n]),-1);A(:,n)
```
`=ones([n 1]);` to generate the 80×80 version of the matrix of part (a). Find the condition numbers of A, L, and U.

d. Use the matrix A from part (c) and set x=ones ([n 1]);b=A*x;. Solve $Ax = b$ using both x1=A\b and y=L\b;x2=U\y;. Look at x1 and x2; do they seem like good approximations of x (a vector of all ones)? Compute norm(x1-x) and norm(x2-x). How bad are these solutions?

e. Compute norm(x1-x,1) and norm(x2-x,1) which measures the total error from all elements, that is, norm(a-b,1) is equal to sum(abs (a-b)). (This is the l_1 norm $\|a - b\|_1 = \sum_{i=1}^n |a_i - b_i|$.) How bad are these solutions?

f. This matrix represents a worst-case scenario for Gaussian elimination with partial pivoting. Set B=rand(80) and find its LU decomposition, and then find the condition numbers of B, L, and U.

10. a. An orthogonal matrix satisfies $U^T U = I$. Show that $\|Ux\|_2 = \|x\|_2$ for all x if U is orthogonal. (*Hint:* Consider the quadratic form $x^T Ax$ with $A = U^T U$.)

b. Show that an orthogonal matrix U has $\|U\|_2 = 1$ and $\kappa_s(U) = 1$.

11. Conduct an experiment in MATLAB that compares the determinant and the condition number as measures of near-singularity. Is the determinant a useful measure of near-singularity for numerical purposes?

12. a. Conduct an experiment in MATLAB to determine the expected condition number of an elementwise uniformly distributed (on [0, 1]) random $N \times N$ matrix (use rand(N) to form the matrices), using $N = 10$ and $N = 100$.

b. Conduct an experiment in MATLAB to determine the expected condition number of an elementwise normally distributed random 10×10 matrix (use `A=randn(N)` to form the matrices) for $N = 10$ and $N = 100$.

13. a. Prove that the matrix norm induced by the l_1 vector norm is $\|A\|_\gamma = \max_{j=1}^{n}\{\sum_{i=1}^{n} |a_{ij}|\}$.

b. Prove that the matrix norm induced by the l_∞ vector norm is $\|A\|_\rho = \max_{i=1}^{n}\{\sum_{j=1}^{n} |a_{ij}|\}$.

14. Show that the Hölder p-norms $\|A\|_p = [\sum_{i=1}^{n} |a_{ij}|^p]^{1/p}$ are matrix norms if and only if $1 \leq p \leq 2$. (*Hint:* You may wish to use the **Hölder inequality** $\sum_{k=1}^{n} |x_k y_k| \leq (\sum_{k=1}^{n} |x_k|^p)^{1/p} (\sum_{k=1}^{n} |y_k|^p)^{1/p}$, where $p \geq 1, q \geq 1$, and $1/p + 1/q = 1$.)

15. a. Show that $\max\{|a_{ij}|\}$ is not a matrix norm (where the maximum is taken over all elements of the matrix).

b. Show that $n \max\{|a_{ij}|\}$ is a matrix norm on $n \times n$ matrices.

2.6 The QR Decomposition

QR Decomposition

The MATLAB backslash command \ (see `help slash`) uses Gaussian elimination with pivoting (in essence, the LU decomposition) to solve $Ax = b$ when A is square. For large square matrices we need another approach, namely, one that does not require $O(n^3)$ flops. We discuss such methods in Chapter 3. For now let us look at the problem of solving $Ax = b$ when A is not necessarily square. When A is $m \times n$ and $m \neq n$, the MATLAB backslash command uses the **QR decomposition**

$$A = QR$$

of A, where Q is an $m \times m$ orthogonal matrix ($Q^T = Q^{-1}$) and R is an $m \times n$ upper triangular matrix. For example, if A is 5×3, then

$$
\begin{bmatrix} X & X & X \\ X & X & X \\ X & X & X \\ X & X & X \\ X & X & X \end{bmatrix} = \begin{bmatrix} X & X & X & X & X \\ X & X & X & X & X \\ X & X & X & X & X \\ X & X & X & X & X \\ X & X & X & X & X \end{bmatrix} \begin{bmatrix} X & X & X \\ 0 & X & X \\ 0 & 0 & X \\ 0 & 0 & 0 \\ 0 & 0 & 0 \end{bmatrix}
$$

is the Wilkinson diagram of the QR decomposition. This decomposition is of great importance in numerical linear algebra.

Suppose we have a QR decomposition for a *square* matrix A. We can solve $Ax = b$ efficiently as follows:

$$Ax = b$$
$$QRx = b$$
$$Rx = Q^T b.$$

Because R is a square upper triangular matrix, the last equation can be solved by back substitution, provided that no diagonal entry of R is zero. Since an orthogonal matrix has determinant ± 1, we have

$$\det(A) = \det(QR)$$
$$= \det(Q)\det(R)$$
$$= \pm\det(R).$$

Therefore if A is nonsingular $(\det(A) \neq 0)$, then $\det(R)$ is nonzero. But R is upper triangular, so $\det(R)$ is equal to the product of the diagonal entries of R; if $\det(R) \neq 0$, then $r_{ii} \neq 0$ for each $i = 1, \ldots, n$. This shows that the back substitution can be performed whenever A is nonsingular. In fact, if A is nonsingular, then a QR decomposition of A must exist.

Let's consider the problem of solving $Ax = b$ when the $m \times n$ coefficient matrix A is not necessarily square. The nonsquare case of greatest interest is when $m > n$, that is, when there are more equations than unknowns. Since the product Ax is always a linear combination of the columns of A, the linear system $Ax = b$ has a solution (that is, the linear system is consistent) exactly when b may be written as a linear combination of the columns of A. This means that we must have

$$b \in \text{Col}(A)$$

for consistency. (The linear space $\text{Col}(A)$ is the column space of A, the set of all linear combinations of the columns of A considered as vectors in $\mathbb{R}^m$.) Looked at another way, $Ax = b$ has a solution exactly when the function

$$y = Ax$$

can take on the value $y = b$ for some choice of $x \in \mathbb{R}^n$; that is, b must be in the range of A (the set of all $y \in \mathbb{R}^m$ such that $y = Ax$ for some $x \in \mathbb{R}^n$). If b is not in the range of A, then the system is inconsistent, and so there is no solution x of $Ax = b$.

Inconsistent   What this means is that if $m > n$ then we expect that $Ax = b$ will be inconsistent for
Linear Systems   most choices of b. Will we let the fact that no solution exists stop us from finding one?

Example 2.6.1   Consider an experiment to determine the spring constant k of a spring using Hooke's law $F = k\Delta$, where F is the force applied to the spring and Δ is the resulting deflection from its equilibrium position. We attach an object of known mass to the spring ($F = -mg$) and measure the resulting displacement Δ of the end of the spring (which will be negative). Then $k = F/\Delta$ is an estimate of the spring constant.

But using one measurement is clearly inferior to using several, since each contains some random error. Suppose we take three measurements and find the (Δ, F) data $(0.98, 2), (1.20, 2.5), (1.45, 3)$ in some units. We have three estimates of K: $2/1 \doteq 2.0408, 2.5/1.2 \doteq 2.0833$, and $3/1.6 \doteq 2.0690$. Which is correct? Probably none of them. Averaging them is one way to get a better estimate of h. Fundamentally what we have is a linear system

$$\begin{bmatrix} 0.98 \\ 1.20 \\ 2.5 \end{bmatrix} [k] = \begin{pmatrix} 2 \\ 2.5 \\ 3 \end{pmatrix}.$$

of three equations in one unknown (k). The system is inconsistent, but we certainly want to find a value of k nonetheless. ■

The problem in Example 2.6.1 is much too simple. But problems with $m > n$ occur all the time and are said to be **overdetermined** (if $m < n$ we say that the problem, or system, is **underdetermined**). We have too much data, and, because of measurement or other error in the data, we cannot fit an exact straight line to it. As another example, if we were processing nuclear magnetic resonance (NMR) data, then we might need to estimate the τ_1 relaxation time constant c from the relation

$$y = a + b\exp(-t/c)$$

given a long string of (t_i, y_i) data $(i = 1, \ldots, m)$. In other words, we would need to find the values of a, b, and c such that

$$a + b\exp(-t_1/c) = y_1$$
$$a + b\exp(-t_2/c) = y_2$$
$$\vdots \qquad\qquad (2.21)$$
$$a + b\exp(-t_m/c) = y_m$$

where typically $m \gg 3$. This is an overdetermined *nonlinear* system of m equations in 3 unknowns, and since no choice of a, b, and c will provide an exact solution for experimental data, we would like to find the best (or most likely) values of a, b, and c for the given data. For a nonlinear system like this, we must use the nonlinear optimization methods of Chapter 7 to find the best choice of a, b, and c (that is, the choice that minimizes the error in some sense). This can be difficult.

What about overdetermined *linear* systems $Ax = b$ $(m > n)$? These systems can arise when we attempt to fit a polynomial

$$y = a_n t^n + a_{n-1}t^{n-1} + \cdots + a_1 t + a_0$$

Least Squares Solutions

to experimental data (m data pairs (t_i, y_i)) since the polynomial y is linear in its coefficients $a_n, \ldots, a_0$. It is common to define the "best" solution of $Ax = b$ in this case to be that choice of x that minimizes

$$\|b - Ax\| \qquad\qquad (2.22)$$

(the value of x for which the residual $r = b - Ax$ is as small as possible). For a variety of reasons we almost always use the Euclidean norm in Eq. (2.22). This is called the **linear least squares solution** of the overdetermined system $Ax = b$. Strictly speaking it is a solution of the minimization problem (Eq. (2.22)) and not the linear system, but we refer to it as the solution of $Ax = b$ in the sense of least squares.

Example 2.6.2   Suppose we wish to fit the straight line $y = \alpha x + \beta$ to the data $(1, 0.9)$, $(2, 2.1)$, $(3, 2.9)$. This means we are seeking α and β such that

$$\begin{bmatrix} 1 & 1 \\ 2 & 1 \\ 3 & 1 \end{bmatrix} \begin{bmatrix} \alpha \\ \beta \end{bmatrix} = \begin{pmatrix} 0.9 \\ 2.1 \\ 2.9 \end{pmatrix},$$

but no such α and β exist. The least squares solution is the value of $(\alpha, \beta)^T$ for which the residual

$$r = \begin{pmatrix} 0.9 \\ 2.1 \\ 2.9 \end{pmatrix} - \begin{bmatrix} 1 & 1 \\ 2 & 1 \\ 3 & 1 \end{bmatrix} \begin{bmatrix} \alpha \\ \beta \end{bmatrix}$$

$$= \begin{pmatrix} 0.9 - \alpha - \beta \\ 2.1 - 2\alpha - \beta \\ 2.9 - 3\alpha - \beta \end{pmatrix}$$

has the smallest possible norm

$$\|r\| = \left[(0.9 - \alpha - \beta)^2 + (2.1 - 2\alpha - \beta)^2 + (2.9 - 3\alpha - \beta)^2 \right]^{1/2}$$

$$= \left[13.63 - 27.6\alpha - 11.8\beta + 14\alpha^2 + 12\alpha\beta + 3\beta^2 \right]^{1/2}$$

(as simplified by Maple). This expression will be minimized when

$$f(\alpha, \beta) = 13.63 - 27.6\alpha - 11.8\beta + 14\alpha^2 + 12\alpha\beta + 3\beta^2$$

is a minimum. To find the optimal α and β we could use the MATLAB nonlinear optimization routine `fminsearch` or take the partial derivatives of f with respect to α and β and set them to zero. The latter approach gives the *square* linear system

$$28\alpha + 12\beta - 27.6 = 0$$
$$6\beta + 12\alpha - 11.8 = 0$$

that is,

$$28\alpha + 12\beta = 27.6$$
$$12\alpha + 6\beta = 11.8$$

for the solution $(\alpha, \beta)^T$ of the least squares problem. The solution is

$$\alpha = 1$$
$$\beta = -1/30$$

so $y = x - 1/30$ is the best line (in the least squares sense). The norm of the residual is

$$\|r\| = \left[(0.9 - 1 + 1/30)^2 + (2.1 - 2 + 1/30)^2 + (2.9 - 3 + 1/30)^2 \right]^{1/2}$$

$$\doteq 0.1633,$$

which should be the smallest possible. By contrast, if we were to take $(\alpha, \beta)^T = (1.1, -1/20)^T$ instead, then we would have

$$\|r\| = \left[(0.9 - 1.1 + 1/20)^2 + (2.1 - 2.2 + 1/20)^2 + (2.9 - 3.3 + 1/20)^2 \right]^{1/2}$$

$$\doteq 0.3841,$$

which is indeed larger (worse). Note that $Ax \doteq (0.9667, 1.9667, 2.9667)^T$, which as we expected is different from b. ∎

How are we to find least squares solutions of linear systems in the general case? We'll sketch the details. In linear algebra the solution of

$$\min_{x \in \mathbb{R}^n} \|b - Ax\|$$

(Eq. (2.22)) is shown to be that value of x that satisfies $Ax = Pb$, where P is the projection matrix from $\mathbb{R}^m$ to the range of A. This implies that the residual r must be orthogonal to every vector in the range of A. Since the range of A is precisely the column space of A, some subset of the columns of A spans it. This means that the dot product of r with each column of A must be zero:

$$r^T A = 0.$$

It's customary to write this last equation in the equivalent form

$$A^T r = 0$$
$$A^T(b - Ax) = 0$$
$$A^T Ax = A^T b$$

and to call the square linear system $A^T Ax = A^T b$ the **normal equation** (or **normal equations**) for the system $Ax = b$.

From here on, unless stated otherwise, we'll assume that $m \geq n$ (the system is either square or overdetermined) and that A has full rank (meaning rank$(A) = n$ since $m \geq n$). The underdetermined case may be handled in essentially the same way that square or overdetermined cases are handled in the following discussion, except that underdetermined cases use a QR decomposition of A^T rather than of A.

Solving the Normal Equation

We now have a means of transforming an overdetermined linear system into a square linear system of the form $A^T Ax = A^T b$. In one sense, we have reduced the problem of solving a nonsquare system to that of solving a square system, and the solution of a square linear system is a problem that we have already addressed. It can be shown that if A has full rank, then the $n \times n$ matrix $A^T A$ is nonsingular and in fact positive definite. (Furthermore, if $m \gg n$, then the resulting matrix $A^T A$ is small relative to the size of A itself.) Therefore to solve $Ax = b$ when $m > n$, we may form the normal equation $A^T Ax = A^T b$ and then find an LU decomposition of $A^T A$. Since $A^T A$ is positive definite, it is possible to choose $L = U^T$ and compute this accurately without pivoting (that is, the permutation matrix P may be taken to be I_n). This means that we may decompose $A^T A$ as

$$A^T A = L^T L.$$

This decomposition is the **Cholesky decomposition** (of $A^T A$), as discussed in Section 2.4. The matrix L is not in general *unit* lower triangular, but it will be lower triangular and nonsingular. We then solve

$$A^T Ax = A^T b$$
$$L^T Lx = A^T b$$

for $x = (A^T A)^{-1} A^T b$ in the usual way:

$$L^T y = A^T b$$
$$Lx = y.$$

The Cholesky decomposition may be computed using about half the flops needed for a general LU decomposition (due to the symmetry of $A^T A$).

This method of finding least squares solutions by Cholesky decomposition is widely used, but forming $A^T A$ (sometimes called the **cross-product matrix** of A) can be inconvenient. In addition, the solution of the normal equation is sensitive to roundoff errors. (Consider how much data gets packed into the 4 elements of a 2×2 matrix if we have $m = 1000$ data points and $n = 2$ unknowns.) This sensitivity is enough to force us to consider other approaches.

Example 2.6.3 Let H=hilb(20) and A=H(1:20,1:10) (A is 20×10). Set x=ones([10 1])- .5 and b=A*x (b is a 10×1 vector; we ignore the errors introduced in b by this computation). If we use the MATLAB command A\b, which uses the QR decomposition, then the relative error in the computed solution is $4.5779e - 006$. Since $\kappa(A) \approx 2.6 \times 10^{11}$ we may have to live with this relatively poor quality. If we use the Cholesky decomposition approach (A'*A)\(A'*b) (MATLAB employs the Cholesky decomposition method automatically here), then the relative error in the computed solution is 3.0453. That's not a typo—the relative error is greater than 3. The absolute error in the l_∞ norm is 2.9121, meaning that at least one component of the computed solution differs from the correct solution x by nearly 3 units! This matches expectations in one sense, since $\kappa(A^T A) \approx 5.2 \times 10^{17}$ meaning that we should expect to lose about 17 digits (out of a possible 16) in performing this computation. ■

The case of Example 2.6.3 is extreme; still, the Cholesky decomposition approach can amplify errors beyond what the condition number of A would predict because it works with $A^T A$, not A. In fact, use of the QR decomposition of A generally gives more accurate results than use of the LU decomposition of A, even when we are not concerned about the additional roundoff errors (and expense) associated with the formation of $A^T A$. This is because $\kappa(A^T A) \approx \kappa(A)^2$, in general.

Solving with QR   Consider again the normal equation $A^T Ax = A^T b$. If we knew a QR decomposition of A, then we could write this as

$$A^T Ax = A^T b$$
$$(QR)^T (QR)x = (QR)^T b$$
$$R^T Q^T QRx = R^T Q^T b$$
$$R^T IRx = R^T Q^T b$$
$$R^T Rx = R^T Q^T b$$

since Q is orthogonal ($Q^T Q = I$). (Under our assumptions a QR decomposition of A must exist.) We'd like to conclude that the equation

$$Rx = Q^T b$$

must be satisfied by the solution of $A^T A x = A^T b$, but because in general R is not even square, we cannot use multiplication by $(R^T)^{-1}$ to arrive at this conclusion. In fact, it is not true in general that the solution of $Rx = Q^T b$ even exists; after all, $Ax = b$ is equivalent to $QRx = b$, that is, to $Rx = Q^T b$, so $Rx = Q^T b$ can have an actual solution x only if $Ax = b$ does. However, we are getting close to finding the least squares solution. We need to find a way to simplify the expression $R^T Rx = R^T Q^T b$.

The matrix R is upper triangular, and because we have restricted ourselves to the case $m \geq n$, we may write the $m \times n$ matrix R as

$$R = \begin{pmatrix} R_1 \\ 0 \end{pmatrix}$$

in partitioned (block) form, where R_1 is an upper triangular $n \times n$ matrix and 0 represents an $(m - n) \times n$ zero matrix. Since rank$(R) = n$, it must be the case that rank$(R_1) = n$, so that R_1 is nonsingular. Hence every diagonal entry of R_1 must be nonzero. Now we may write $R^T Rx = R^T Q^T b$ as

$$\begin{pmatrix} R_1 \\ 0 \end{pmatrix}^T \begin{pmatrix} R_1 \\ 0 \end{pmatrix} x = \begin{pmatrix} R_1 \\ 0 \end{pmatrix}^T Q^T b$$

$$\begin{pmatrix} R_1^T & 0^T \end{pmatrix} \begin{pmatrix} R_1 \\ 0 \end{pmatrix} x = \begin{pmatrix} R_1^T & 0^T \end{pmatrix} Q^T b$$

$$R_1^T R_1 x = \begin{pmatrix} R_1^T & 0^T \end{pmatrix} (Q^T b)$$

(verify the conformability of the matrices and the sizes of the results). Note that multiplying by the block 0^T (an $n \times (m - n)$ zero matrix) on the RHS simply means that the last $(m - n)$ components of $Q^T b$ do not affect the computation. Since R_1 is nonsingular, we have

$$R_1 x = (R_1^T)^{-1} \begin{pmatrix} R_1^T & 0^T \end{pmatrix} (Q^T b)$$

$$= \begin{pmatrix} I_n & 0^T \end{pmatrix} (Q^T b).$$

The LHS, $R_1 x$, is $(n \times n) \times (n \times 1) \to n \times 1$, and the RHS is $(n \times (n + (m - n)) \times (m \times m) \times (m \times 1) \to n \times 1$; this checks. In fact, this is the equation we want. If we define the vector q to be equal to the first n components of $Q^T b$, then this becomes

$$R_1 x = q \tag{2.23}$$

which is a square linear system involving a nonsingular upper triangular $n \times n$ matrix. That's about as simple as we could hope for, and we refer to Eq. (2.23) as the **QR equation.** Its solution

$$x = R_1^{-1} q$$

(found by back substitution) is the least squares solution of $Ax = b$. We repeat that $Ax = b$, that is, $QRx = b$, will not usually have a solution in the strict sense when $m > n$.

This is important; the QR equation (Eq. (2.23)) states that the least squares solution of $Ax = b$ is precisely the solution of $R_1 x = q$ as found by back substitution, where $A = QR$ is the QR decomposition of A and q is essentially $Q^T b$. Because we do not need to form $A^T A$ and because Q and R can be found accurately, the resulting computed solution is generally more accurate than the solution of the normal equation as found by Cholesky decomposition. There's actually a deeper connection; $R_1^T R_1$ is the Cholesky decomposition of $A^T A$ and so the QR decomposition approach may be viewed as simply a more accurate means of employing the Cholesky decomposition approach. We do not take this point of view however.

Example 2.6.4   Consider again Example 2.6.2, where we wished to fit the straight line $y = \alpha x + \beta$ to the data $(1, 0.9)$, $(2, 2.1)$, $(3, 2.9)$. This led to the overdetermined system

$$\begin{bmatrix} 1 & 1 \\ 2 & 1 \\ 3 & 1 \end{bmatrix} \begin{bmatrix} \alpha \\ \beta \end{bmatrix} = \begin{pmatrix} 0.9 \\ 2.1 \\ 2.9 \end{pmatrix}$$

in which the coefficient matrix A clearly has full rank. Let's use the QR decomposition approach on this problem. The MATLAB command `[Q,R]=qr(A)` produces:

```
Q =
   -0.2673   0.8729   0.4082
   -0.5345   0.2182  -0.8165
   -0.8018  -0.4364   0.4082
R =
   -3.7417  -1.6036
         0   0.6547
         0         0
```

so that $R_1 = [-3.7417 \ -1.6036; 0 \ 0.6547]$. We find $Q^T b = (-3.6882, -0.0218, -0.1633)^T$ so $q = (-3.6882, -0.0218)^T$. Hence we must solve $R_1 x = q$, that is,

$$\begin{bmatrix} -3.7417 & -1.6036 \\ 0 & 0.6547 \end{bmatrix} \begin{bmatrix} \alpha \\ \beta \end{bmatrix} = \begin{pmatrix} -3.6882 \\ -0.0218 \end{pmatrix} \tag{2.24}$$

giving $\alpha \doteq 1.0000$, $\beta \doteq -0.0333$ as expected (when all computations are performed with 16 digits; solving Eq. (2.24) in four-digit arithmetic gives $\alpha \doteq 0.9714$). ■

We still haven't discussed how to find a QR decomposition. We do that in the next section. For now we mention that, as the methods are usually implemented, finding the least squares solution of $Ax = b$ by Cholesky decomposition requires about half as many flops as using the QR decomposition when $m \gg n$; both methods require about $4n^3/3$ flops if $m = n$ (and n is large). Since $m \gg n$ in typical of cases of interest, the Cholesky decomposition approach is usually twice as fast. On the other hand, the QR decomposition is likely to be more accurate because it is less sensitive to rounding errors, and a loss factor of 2 increase in computation time may be a reasonable price to pay for this increased accuracy. In fact, the QR decomposition is the preferred approach for least squares problems.

Uniqueness of the QR Decomposition   The QR decomposition is not unique; after all, if $A = QR$ then $A = (-Q)(-R)$, and $-Q$ is orthogonal if Q is orthogonal. However, under our assumptions ($m \geq n$ and rank$(A) = n$), there exists a unique QR decomposition of A for which the diagonal entries of R are positive. It's conventional to add the requirement that the diagonal entries of R must be positive to the definition of a QR decomposition (i.e., $A = QR$ where Q is orthogonal and R is upper triangular with positive diagonal entries) when A has full rank.

Finally, note that the QR decomposition (or **QR factorization**) of A results in an $m \times n$ matrix R that typically contains a large block of zeroes that will be removed when we actually use R; that is, if we know m and n then we really need only R_1 to reconstruct R. Similarly, in forming q from the first n components of $Q^T b$, we are in effect partitioning the $m \times m$ matrix Q as

$$Q = [Q_1 \ Q_0] \tag{2.25}$$

where Q_1 is an $m \times n$ matrix with orthonormal columns and Q_0 is an $m \times (m - n)$ matrix with orthonormal columns, since

$$Qb = [Q_1 \ Q_0]b$$
$$= [Q_1 b \ Q_0 b]$$
$$= [q \ Q_0 b]$$

so that $q = Q_1 b$. In addition,

$$QR = [Q_1 \ Q_0]\begin{pmatrix} R_1 \\ 0 \end{pmatrix}$$
$$= Q_1 R_1 + Q_0 0$$
$$= Q_1 R_1$$

(verify the conformability for each of these products). That is, $A = Q_1 R_1$. Hence we may write the QR equation (Eq. (2.23)) as

$$R_1 x = Q_1^T b,$$

which (under our assumptions) is a square system involving a nonsingular upper triangular matrix R_1. We say that $A = Q_1 R_1$ is the **reduced QR decomposition** (or **reduced QR factorization**) of A, and that $A = QR$ is the **full QR decomposition** (or **full QR factorization**) of A. The reduced QR factorization is the version commonly used in practice.

PROBLEMS 2.6

1. a. If A is a 7×4 matrix with full rank, what are the sizes of x and b in $Ax = b$?
   b. What are the sizes of Q, R, Q_1, R_1, and q?
   c. What are the Wilkinson diagrams for the relations $A = QR$ and $A = Q_1 R_1$?

2. a. If A is a 4×7 matrix with with rank 3, what are the sizes of x and b in $Ax = b$?
   b. What are the sizes of Q, R, Q_1, R_1, and q?
   c. What are the Wilkinson diagrams for the relations $A = QR$ and $A = Q_1 R_1$?

3. Derive the QR equation $R_1 x = Q_1^T b$ by substituting the reduced QR factorization of A into the normal equation $A^T A x = A^T b$.

4. a. What matrix A has $Q_1 = [1/\sqrt{2} \ 0; 0 \ 1; -1/\sqrt{2} \ 0]$ and $R_1 = [1 \ 2; 0 \ 3]$ as its reduced QR factorization?
   b. What is the full QR decomposition of A? (*Hint:* The only orthogonal matrices that have the columns of Q_1 as their first two columns are $[1/\sqrt{2} \ 0 \ 1/\sqrt{2}; 0 \ 1 \ 0; -1/\sqrt{2} \ 0 \ 1/\sqrt{2}]$ and $[1/\sqrt{2} \ 0 \ -1/\sqrt{2}; 0 \ 1 \ 0; -1/\sqrt{2} \ 0 \ -1/\sqrt{2}]$.)

c. Use the reduced QR factorization of A to find the least squares solution of $Ax = (1, 1, 1)^T$. What is the norm of the residual (Eq. (2.22))?

d. Verify that $R^T R = R_1^T R_1 = A^T A$.

e. Find the least squares solution of $Ax = (1, 1, 1)^T$ by forming the normal equation and using the Cholesky decomposition.

5. a. Let $Q = [1/\sqrt{2} \ 1/\sqrt{2} \ 0; 0 \ 0 \ 1; 1/\sqrt{2} \ -1/\sqrt{2} \ 0]$, $R = [1 \ 2 \ 2; 0 \ 2 \ -1; 0 \ 0 \ 2]$. Find the determinant of $A = QR$ (do not form A).

b. Solve $Ax = (1, -1, 1)^T$ (do not form A).

c. Find A.

MATLAB 2.6

If you haven't done so already, type `help slash` to read a description of the slash command. Note that there is also a forward slash operator / which may be used to solve problems in the form $y^T A = b$. Both commands may also be used with matrices. For example, if $AB = C$, then B=A\C (in the least squares sense if necessary).

The MATLAB command qr computes the full QR decomposition of a matrix. For example, enter:

```
» [Q,R]=qr(rand([7 4]))
```

The qr command does not force r_{ii} to be positive. The reduced QR factorization may be found using the qr command as well; enter:

```
» [Q1,R1]=qr(rand([7 4]),0)
```

to find the factors in the reduced form. The qr command also has an option to introduce pivoting in the algorithm, which can increase the accuracy.

The MATLAB command chol produces the Cholesky decomposition of a matrix; see Section 2.4 for more details. Enter:

```
» A=rand([5 3])
» M=A'*A
» X=chol(M)
» X'*X              %Should equal M.
» [Q,R]=qr(A)
» R'*R              %Should equal M.
» [Q1,R1]=qr(A,0)
» R1'*R1            %Should equal M.
» norm(M-X'*X)      %Error in M from Cholesky.
» norm(M-R'*R)      %Error in M from QR.
» norm(M-R1'*R1)    %Error in M from reduced QR.
```

For this small matrix all the errors are in the level of noise.

Let's step through the details of Example 2.6.3 in MATLAB. (Look again at Example 2.6.3 first.) Enter:

```
» H=hilb(20);
» A=H(1:20,1:10)    %A is an ill-conditioned 20x10 matrix.
» cond(A)
```

```
» x=ones([10 1])-.5;
» b=A*x
» xqr=A\b                    %Solve Ax=b by QR decomposition.
» xchol=(A'*A)\(A'*b)        %Solve Ax=b by Cholesky decomposition.
» norm(xqr-x)/norm(x)
» norm(xchol-x)/norm(x)
» norm(xchol-x,'inf')
» cond(A'*A)
```

In this case, the QR decomposition (used by the slash command when A is nonsquare) gives a much more accurate solution than solving the normal equation by Cholesky decomposition (used by the slash command for the square matrix $A^T A$). Bear in mind, however, that this is an especially ill-conditioned example.

Let's find the least squares solution of an inconsistent overdetermined linear system by the reduced QR factorization step by step. (The slash command would do this for us automatically.) Enter:

```
» A1=magic(5)        %5x5 magic square.
» A2=pascal(5)       %5x5 Pascal's triangle as a matrix.
» A=[A1;A2]          %Concatenate along vertical axis.
» b=ones([10 1]);
» [Q1,R1]=qr(A,0)
» x=R1\(Q1'*b)       %Solve R1*x=Q1'*b.
» norm(b-A*x)        %Residual.
```

Now let's see the floating point operations count difference between the two approaches and compare them. Enter:

```
» clear all
» rand('state',0)
» A=rand([500 10]);b=rand([500 1]);
» %QR decomposition:
» %N.B.: Use tic, toc, and a larger matrix if you don't have flops.
» flops(0);A\b;flops
» clear all
» rand('state',0)
» A=rand([500 10]);b=rand([500 1]);
» %Cholesky decomposition:
» %N.B.: Use tic, toc, and a larger matrix if you don't have flops.
» flops(0);(A'*A)\(A'*b);flops
```

In this experiment, the QR decomposition uses about half again as many flops as the Cholesky decomposition, but should be more accurate. The difference would be closer to a factor of 2 if the cross-product matrix $A^T A$ were computed more efficiently (since it must be symmetric we can compute it in about half the flops required by the use of the command (A'*A) above). Another complication is that A\b uses a pivoting procedure in the QR decomposition to increase accuracy, which increases its flop count.

As we've mentioned before, the flops count can be a misleading indicator of an algorithm's efficiency. Here's another reason why this can be so. Enter `type hilb` to see that forming the $n \times n$ Hilbert matrix in the manner used by MATLAB requires n^2 divisions and a like number of additions and subtractions (`H = E./(I+J-1)`, that is, $h_{ij} = 1/(i + j - 1)$); this means that the operation of forming the matrix H already requires $O(n^2)$ flops. If the entries a_{ij} of the matrix A in $Ax = b$ are given by a more complicated function than this, then the act of forming A, not the actual solution of A, may dominate the computation.

We mention a few other MATLAB commands (see `help matfun`) that you may find useful for least squares problems. The `rank` command determines the rank of a matrix (see `help rank` and Chapter 3 for details). The problem of numerically determining the rank of a matrix is more difficult than one might imagine. The command `orth(A)` returns an orthonormal matrix with the same range (column space) as A. The `lsqnonneg` (or `nnls` in older versions) command may be used to minimize Eq. (2.22), subject to a nonnegativity constraint, that is, to find $\min_{x \geq 0} \|b - Ax\|$.

ADDITIONAL PROBLEMS 2.6

6. a. What matrix A has $Q_1 = [1/\sqrt{3} \; 0; 1/\sqrt{3} \; 1/\sqrt{2}; -1/\sqrt{3} \; 1/\sqrt{2}]$ and $R_1 = [2 \; 2; 0 \; 1]$ as its reduced QR factorization?

b. What is the full QR decomposition of A?

c. Use the reduced QR factorization of A to find the least squares solution of $Ax = (1, -2, 1)^T$. What is the norm of the residual?

d. Verify that $R^T R = R_1^T R_1 = A^T A$.

e. Find the least squares solution of $Ax = (1, -2, 1)^T$ by forming the normal equation and using the Cholesky decomposition.

7. a. If A is an upper triangular matrix of full rank with at least as many rows as columns, what is its unique QR decomposition for which r_{ii} is positive for all i?

b. If A is an orthogonal matrix, what is its unique QR decomposition for which r_{ii} is positive for all i?

c. Show that if an $m \times n$ matrix A for which $m \geq n$ has a QR decomposition, then it has a QR decomposition in which all diagonal entries of R are nonnegative.

8. a. Show that if Q is orthogonal, then $\det(Q) = \pm 1$.

b. Show that if Q is orthogonal, then $-Q$ is orthogonal.

c. Show that if Q_1 is an $m \times n$ matrix with orthonormal columns, then $Q_1^T Q_1 = I_n$.

9. For which choices of b is $Ax = b$ consistent if $A = [1 \; 2 \; 2; -1 \; 2 \; -1; 0 \; 4 \; 1; 2 \; 0 \; -2]$?

10. As with the LU decomposition, it is not uncommon to find that the computed Q and R of a QR decomposition, call them Q^* and R^*, are relatively poor approximations in the sense that $\|Q - Q^*\|$ and $\|R - R^*\|$ are large but are good approximations in the sense that $\|A - Q^* R^*\|$ is small. (The errors in Q^* and R^* are correlated.) Construct an example that demonstrates this effect.

11. A more careful operation count for Cholesky decomposition is approximately $mn^2 + \frac{1}{3}n^3$ flops (if the symmetry in $A^T A$ is exploited), and for the QR decomposition it is approximately $2mn^2 - \frac{2}{3}n^3$ flops, neglecting lower order terms. For which choices $m \geq n$ is the Cholesky decomposition more efficient than the QR decomposition by this count?

12. a. Show that if u and v are orthogonal vectors, then $\|u + v\|^2 = \|u\|^2 + \|v\|^2$ for the Euclidean norm. (*Hint:* Recall that $\|x\|^2 = x^T x$.)

b. Show that if the column vector v is partitioned as $v = (v_1^T : v_2^T)^T$, then $\|v\|^2 = \|v_1\|^2 + \|v_2\|^2$.

c. Consider the overdetermined linear system $Ax = b$. Since orthogonal matrices Q satisfy $\|Qx\| = \|x\|$ for the Euclidean norm, the norm of the residual $\|r\| = \|b - Ax\|$ satisfies $\|r\|^2 = \|b - Ax\|^2 = \|Q^T(b - Ax)\|^2$ (where $A = QR$ is the QR decomposition of A). Simplify $\|r\|^2 = \|Q^T(b - Ax)\|^2$ to the form $\|r\|^2 = \|q - R_1 x\|^2 + \|Q_0 b\|^2$ using Eq. (2.25) and part b.

d. Use the result of part (c) to argue that the solution of the QR equation $R_1 x = q$ is the least squares solution of $Ax = b$. What formula does this give for the residual?

13. Write a MATLAB program that accepts three positive integers, m, n, and N ($m \geq n$), and compares the flops required for solving a random $m \times n$ linear system by Cholesky decomposition and QR decomposition, using N trials. Your program should set reasonable default values for each of the inputs, should produce graphical output, and should return an appropriate value. Comment your code in detail, and demonstrate it for at least three choices of inputs.

14. Show that if A is positive definite, then there is a positive definite matrix S such that $S^2 = A$. (This is called

the matrix square root of A; see Section 2.4.) Use the MATLAB command sqrtm to compute the matrix square root of $A = [4\ 2\ 1; 2\ 3\ 1; 1\ 1\ 4]$.

15. Suggest a method of using the QR decomposition of A^T to solve the underdetermined linear system $Ax = b$ when it is consistent using the QR decomposition of A^T. (Consider making the unitary change of variables $y = Q^T x$.) Typically there are infinitely many solutions, and we seek the one that minimizes $\|x\|$.

2.7 Householder Triangularization and the QR Decomposition

In the last section we saw that the QR decomposition is a useful direct method for solving overdetermined linear systems. It is also used in algorithms to find eigenvalues.

There are two major approaches to actually computing the QR decomposition of a matrix. We describe one of them here. It is the less intuitive but more commonly employed approach; the second major approach, based on the Gram-Schmidt process, is discussed in the next section.

A Different View of LU

We continue to assume (unless stated otherwise) that A is an $m \times n$ matrix with $m \geq n$ and full rank n. Consider again the case of the LU decomposition where pivoting is not needed as discussed in Section 2.3. We start with a matrix A that we want to reduce to triangular form using lower triangular matrices, so that we have $MA = U$ when we are finished, with M lower triangular. We can then solve for $A = LU$ (where $L = M^{-1}$ is also lower triangular). The first step has the form

$$L_1 A = \begin{bmatrix} 1 & 0 & 0 \\ X & 1 & 0 \\ X & 0 & 1 \end{bmatrix} \begin{bmatrix} X & X & X & X \\ X & X & X & X \\ X & X & X & X \end{bmatrix} = \begin{bmatrix} X & X & X & X \\ 0 & X & X & X \\ 0 & X & X & X \end{bmatrix}.$$

(When we studied this problem previously, we restricted ourselves to square matrices, but the LU decomposition may be applied to nonsquare matrices as well.) At the next stage we really need to process only the 2×3 block in the southeast using a 2×2 lower triangular matrix. We may represent this as

$$\begin{bmatrix} 1 & {}_1 0_2 \\ {}_2 0_1 & L_2 \end{bmatrix} \begin{bmatrix} X & X \\ {}_2 0_1 & A_1 \end{bmatrix} = \begin{bmatrix} X & X & X & X \\ 0 & X & X & X \\ 0 & 0 & X & X \end{bmatrix}, \tag{2.26}$$

where L_2 is the 2×2 unit lower triangular matrix $L_2 = [1\ 0; -m_{32}\ 1]$ and A_1 is the southeast 2×3 block of the result $L_1 A$ of the first step. The matrix ${}_k 0_p$ represents a $k \times p$ zero matrix.

Verify the conformability of the matrices in Eq. (2.26). It is important to be able to multiply matrices when they are partitioned into blocks of submatrices, as we saw in the previous section. Note how this emphasizes the iterative nature of Gaussian elimination— the same process is applied to smaller and smaller blocks of the current matrix.

In the more general case, a typical step of the LU decomposition on an $m \times n$ matrix with $m \geq n$ (for which pivoting is not needed) has the form

$$
\begin{bmatrix} I_r & {}_r 0_{m-r} \\ {}_{m-r} 0_r & L_{r+1} \end{bmatrix}
\begin{bmatrix} X_a & X_b \\ 0 & X_c \end{bmatrix}
=
\begin{bmatrix} X_\alpha & X_\beta \\ {}_{m-r-1} 0_{r+1} & X_\gamma \end{bmatrix}.
\tag{2.27}
$$

We have processed r rows and are beginning to work on row $r + 1$ using the $(m - r) \times (m - r)$ unit lower triangular matrix L_{r+1}. Note that the entire matrix

$$
\begin{bmatrix} I_r & {}_r 0_{m-r} \\ {}_{m-r} 0_r & L_{r+1} \end{bmatrix}
$$

is unit lower triangular. The matrix to which it is applied,

$$
\begin{bmatrix} X_a & X_b \\ {}_{m-r} 0_r & X_c \end{bmatrix},
$$

is partway to being upper triangular; the matrix X_a is $r \times r$ and is upper triangular (it and the zeroes below it represent the completed part of the matrix). The matrix X_b is $r \times (m - r)$ and represents the remaining entries of the first r rows, which are no longer being used in the processing of A. The matrix X_c ($(m - r) \times (m - r)$) is the part of the original matrix A, now changed by the row operations that have brought us this far, that must still be triangularized. Performing the multiplication gives the result

$$
\begin{bmatrix} X_\alpha & X_\beta \\ {}_{m-r-1} 0_{r+1} & X_\gamma \end{bmatrix},
$$

where X_α is $(r + 1) \times (r + 1)$ (we have gained an additional column which is in upper triangular form; that is, it has all entries below the diagonal entry zero), X_β is $(r + 1) \times (m - r - 1)$, and X_γ is $(m - r - 1) \times (m - r - 1)$. The block X_γ, the part that must still be triangularized, is one row and one column smaller than X_c was ($(m - (r + 1)) \times (m - (r + 1))$) rather than $(m - r) \times (m - r)$).

Once again, please carefully verify the conformability of the matrices in Eq. (2.27). This block matrix form of the LU decomposition is useful for analyzing the method and preparing to make use of options such as Level-3 BLAS (based on matrix-matrix operations). We have omitted pivoting only to emphasize the ideas behind Gaussian elimination without the details.

One of the key ideas is this: Gaussian elimination (or the LU decomposition) may be viewed as a process of using successive (lower) triangular matrices to (upper) triangularize a matrix. Gaussian elimination works because the process used to make A into the triangular matrix U is based on multiplications by matrices of exactly the form we hope to obtain when we are done (lower triangular). The process may be described as one of *triangular triangularization,* that is, triangularization by triangular matrices.

Finding Q and R

What does this have to do with the QR decomposition? It suggests a way to find a method for computing the decomposition. What if we could find an orthogonal matrix Q_1 that behaves like the unit lower triangular matrix in Eq. (2.27), namely, that it acts on A to return a matrix $Q_1 A$ which is one step closer to being upper triangular? Similar to Eq. (2.27) we would have an iterative process of the form

$$Q_{r+1} \begin{bmatrix} X & X & X & X & X \\ 0 & X & X & X & X \\ 0 & 0 & X & X & X \\ 0 & 0 & X & X & X \\ 0 & 0 & X & X & X \end{bmatrix} = \begin{bmatrix} X & X & X & X & X \\ 0 & X & X & X & X \\ 0 & 0 & X & X & X \\ 0 & 0 & 0 & X & X \\ 0 & 0 & 0 & X & X \end{bmatrix}.$$

That is,

$$Q_{r+1} \begin{bmatrix} X_a & X_b \\ {}_{m-r+1}0_r & X_c \end{bmatrix} = \begin{bmatrix} X_\alpha & X_\beta \\ {}_{m-r}0_{r+1} & X_\gamma \end{bmatrix}$$

for some orthogonal matrix Q_{r+1}. (The matrix Q_{r+1} would likely have a block structure of its own.) If so then we might be able to find a sequence of such matrices that would triangularize A,

$$Q_{m-1} \cdots Q_2 Q_1 A = R, \tag{2.28}$$

in which case

$$\begin{aligned} A &= (Q_{m-1} \cdots Q_2 Q_1)^{-1} R \\ &= \left(Q_1^T Q_2^T \cdots Q_{m-1}^T \right) R \\ &= QR \end{aligned}$$

is a **QR** decomposition of A. This would be a process of *orthogonal triangularization* of A (that is, making A triangular using orthogonal matrices).

Can we carry out such a program? And if so, can we do it in a manner that does not amplify roundoff errors to the extent that the method becomes useless on an actual machine? Yes.

Example 2.7.1 Consider a 2×2 matrix with rank 2. Making it upper triangular requires nothing more than eliminating the $(2, 1)$ entry. If $A = [a \ b; c \ d]$ then we seek an orthogonal matrix $Q_1 = [q_{11} \ q_{12}; q_{21} \ q_{22}]$ such that $Q_1 A$ is upper triangular. The $(2, 1)$ entry of this product is the dot product of row 2 of Q_1 with column 1 of A, namely $(q_{21}, q_{22}) \cdot (a, c) = aq_{21} + cq_{22} = 0$. If c is nonzero (the only case of interest), then we may write this equation as $q_{22} = -aq_{21}/c$. The only other condition that must be satisfied is the orthogonality of Q_1. It is a fact that every real 2×2 orthogonal matrix is either of the form $H = [-\cos(\theta) \ \sin(\theta); \sin(\theta) \ \cos(\theta)]$ or of the form $G = [\cos(\theta) \ -\sin(\theta); \sin(\theta) \ \cos(\theta)]$ for some angle θ. In either case, the condition $q_{22} = -aq_{21}/c$ means $\cos(\theta) = -a \sin(\theta)/c$ or $\cot(\theta) = -a/c$.

For example, if $A = [1 \ 2; 3 \ 4]$ then $H = [-\cos(\theta) \ \sin(\theta); \sin(\theta) \ \cos(\theta)]$ with $\theta = \cot^{-1}(-1/3) \doteq -1.2490$, so $H = [-0.3162 \ -0.9487; -0.9487 \ 0.3162]$. This gives $HA = [-3.1623 \ -4.4272; 0.0000 \ -0.6325]$, which is upper triangular as expected (call it R_H).

Using G instead gives $G = [0.3162 \ 0.9487; -0.9487 \ 0.3162]$, so $GA = [3.1623 \ 4.4272; 0.0000 \ -0.6325]$, which again is upper triangular as expected (call it R_G).

Both $HA = R_H$ and $GA = R_G$ define QR decompositions $A = H^T R_H$ and $A = G^T R_G$ of A. Neither has r_{11} and r_{22} positive; in fact, R_H has both diagonal entries negative. Hence (using $(-I)^2 = I$, the matrix analogue of $(-1)^2 = 1$) we may write

$$A = H^T R_H$$
$$= H^T I R_H$$
$$= H^T (-I)(-I) R_H$$
$$= H^T (-I)(-I) R_H$$
$$= (-H^T)(-R_H)$$

to obtain a QR decomposition of the desired form. The orthogonal matrix $-H^T$ corresponds to $[-\cos(\theta_1) \ \sin(\theta_1); \sin(\theta_1) \ \cos(\theta_1)]$ where $\theta_1 = \cot^{-1}(-1/3) + \pi$.

Nothing changes if the matrix to be decomposed is $2 \times n$; for example ($n = 3$) if $B = [1 \ 2 \ -1; 3 \ 4 \ 2]$ then the same H as before gives $HB = [-3.1623 \ -4.4272 \ -1.5811; 0.0000 \ -0.6325 \ 1.5811]$, which is upper triangular. Hence $B = (-H^T)(-HB)$ is a QR decomposition of B with positive diagonal entries in R. ∎

Now that we have a means of finding a QR decomposition for 2×2 matrices, we need to generalize it to a method for finding the QR decomposition of $m \times n$ matrices. Methods based on generalizing the H matrices (which have $\det(H) = -1$ and represent a reflection in the plane) are different from methods based on generalizing the G matrices (which have $\det(G) = 1$ and represent a rotation in the plane). We generalize the H matrices first.

Householder Matrices   A **Householder matrix** (or **Householder reflector** or **Householder reflection** or **elementary reflector**) is a matrix of the form

$$H_w = I_m - 2ww^T$$

for some unit vector $w \in \mathbb{R}^m$. Householder matrices have a number of interesting properties: They are symmetric and orthogonal (which implies that $H_w^2 = I$).[10] In addition, if w is nonzero, then $H_w x$ is the vector obtained by reflecting x across a certain hyperplane, namely, the hyperplane through the origin that is orthogonal to w. (Recall from the calculus that a point—here the origin—and a nonzero vector determine a plane.) A Householder reflector algebraically performs the act of reflecting a vector across a plane.

We can choose a w that gives a desired result for the product $H_w x$. If u and v are distinct vectors in $\mathbb{R}^m$ and $\|u\|_2 = \|v\|_2$, and if we take w to be the normalized vector from u to v,

$$w = \frac{v - u}{\|v - u\|_2}, \tag{2.29}$$

then

$$H_w u = v.$$

---

[10] If $M^2 = I$, then we say that M is **idempotent**.

This is precisely the result we need. The first step of our scheme (Eq. (2.28)) should construct an orthogonal matrix Q_1, which zeroes out every entry below the $(1, 1)$ entry of A:

$$\begin{bmatrix} X & X & X \\ X & X & X \\ X & X & X \end{bmatrix} \begin{bmatrix} X & X & X \\ X & X & X \\ X & X & X \end{bmatrix} = \begin{bmatrix} X & X & X \\ 0 & X & X \\ 0 & X & X \end{bmatrix}$$

(the RHS is $Q_1 A$). Write A in the partitioned form $A = [a_1 \ A_{12}]$, where a_1 is the first column of A. If a_1 is the zero vector, we may take $Q_1 = I$ (that is, nothing needs to be done so we do nothing) and move on. Otherwise, we need Q_1 to be an orthogonal matrix that maps a_1 to $\alpha_1 e_1$ (for some scalar α_1, with e_1 the first column of I_m). Let's take $\alpha_1 = \pm \|a_1\|_2$, for then the vectors a_1 and $\alpha_1 e_1$ have the same length, and so from Eq. (2.29) a matrix that maps a_1 to $\alpha_1 e_1$ is H_w with

$$w = \frac{\alpha_1 e_1 - a_1}{\|\alpha_1 e_1 - a_1\|_2}$$

(for either choice of α_1). Then

$$H_w a_1 = (I - 2ww^T)a_1$$
$$= \alpha_1 e_1$$

(and $H_w A_{12}$ is some matrix so that $H_w A = [\alpha_1 e_1 \ H_w A_{12}]$). We have constructed the desired orthogonal matrix Q_1 needed for Eq. (2.28).

Example 2.7.2   Consider the matrix $A = [1 \ 2 \ 3; 4 \ 5 \ 6; 7 \ 8 \ 9]$. For the first step of QR decomposition using orthogonal triangularization by Householder reflectors, we set $a_1 = (1, 4, 7)^T$, for which $\alpha_1 = \pm[1^2 + 4^2 + 7^2]^{1/2} = \pm\sqrt{66} \doteq \pm 8.1240$. Since we must form the difference $\alpha_1 e_1 - a_1$ to find H_w, we may as well take $\alpha_1 < 0$ so that the only nonzero entry of $\alpha_1 e_1$, the first entry, is opposite in sign to the corresponding entry in a_1. This means that no subtraction (and hence potential cancellation of significant figures) actually occurs. We find

$$w = \frac{[(-\sqrt{66}, 0, 0)^T - (1, 4, 7)^T]}{\|(-\sqrt{66}, 0, 0)^T - (1, 4, 7)^T\|}$$
$$= \frac{-(\sqrt{66} + 1, 4, 7)^T}{\| - (\sqrt{66} + 1, 4, 7)^T \|}$$
$$\doteq (-0.7494, -0.3285, -0.5749)^T,$$

and so

$$H_w = I - 2(-0.7494, -0.3285, -0.5749)^T(-0.7494, -0.3285, -0.5749)$$
$$\doteq \begin{bmatrix} -0.1231 & -0.4924 & -0.8616 \\ -0.4924 & 0.7841 & -0.3777 \\ -0.8616 & -0.3777 & 0.3389 \end{bmatrix},$$

and $H^T H = I$ checks. Then

$$H_w A = \begin{bmatrix} -0.1231 & -0.4924 & -0.8616 \\ -0.4924 & 0.7841 & -0.3777 \\ -0.8616 & -0.3777 & 0.3389 \end{bmatrix} \begin{bmatrix} 1 & 2 & 3 \\ 4 & 5 & 6 \\ 7 & 8 & 9 \end{bmatrix}$$

$$\doteq \begin{bmatrix} -8.1240 & -9.6011 & -11.0782 \\ 0.0000 & -0.0860 & -0.1719 \\ 0.0000 & -0.9004 & -1.8009 \end{bmatrix},$$

which has the expected zeroes in the first column ($Q_1 = H_w$).

Let's do another step. We want to operate on the southeast 2×2 block

$$A_{22} = \begin{bmatrix} -0.0860 & -0.1719 \\ -0.9004 & -1.8009 \end{bmatrix}.$$

The new a_1 is $(-0.0860, -0.9004)^T$ with $\alpha_1 = \pm 0.9045$. This time we should take $\alpha_1 > 0$ to avoid subtraction. We have

$$\begin{aligned} w_2 &= \frac{[(0.9045, 0)^T - (-0.0860, -0.9004)^T]}{\|(0.9045, 0)^T - (-0.0860, -0.9004)^T\|} \\ &= \frac{(0.9045 + 0.0860, 0.9004)^T}{\|(0.9045 + 0.0860, 0.9004)^T\|} \\ &\doteq \frac{(0.9905, 0.9004)^T}{1.3386} \\ &\doteq (0.7400, 0.6727)^T, \end{aligned}$$

and

$$\begin{aligned} H_{w_2} &= I - 2(0.7400, 0.6727)^T (0.7400, 0.6727) \\ &\doteq \begin{bmatrix} -0.0951 & -0.9955 \\ -0.9955 & 0.0951 \end{bmatrix}, \end{aligned}$$

and finally

$$\begin{aligned} H_{w_2} A_{22} &= \begin{bmatrix} -0.0951 & -0.9955 \\ -0.9955 & 0.0951 \end{bmatrix} \begin{bmatrix} -0.0860 & -0.1719 \\ -0.9004 & -1.8009 \end{bmatrix} \\ &\doteq \begin{bmatrix} 0.9045 & 1.8091 \\ 0.0000 & -0.0001 \end{bmatrix}, \end{aligned}$$

which has the expected form. Note that we can put this in the form of Eq. (2.28) by defining

$$\begin{aligned} Q_2 &= \begin{bmatrix} 1 & {}_1 0_2 \\ {}_2 0_1 & H_{w_2} \end{bmatrix} \\ &= \begin{bmatrix} 1 & 0 & 0 \\ 0 & -0.0951 & -0.9955 \\ 0 & -0.9955 & 0.0951 \end{bmatrix} \end{aligned}$$

because then the action of H_{w_2} on the sub-block A_{22} of $Q_1 A$ may be represented as $Q_2(Q_1 A)$. We have $Q_2 Q_1 A = R$ (in accordance with Eq. (2.28)) so that $A = QR$ where

$$R = \begin{bmatrix} -8.1240 & -9.6011 & -11.0782 \\ 0.0000 & 0.9045 & 1.8091 \\ 0.0000 & 0.0000 & -0.0001 \end{bmatrix}$$

and $Q = (Q_2 Q_1)^{-1} = Q_1^{-1} Q_2^{-1} = Q_1^T Q_2^T$, giving

$$Q = \begin{bmatrix} -0.1231 & -0.4924 & -0.8616 \\ -0.4924 & 0.7841 & -0.3777 \\ -0.8616 & -0.3777 & 0.3389 \end{bmatrix}^T \begin{bmatrix} 1 & 0 & 0 \\ 0 & -0.0951 & -0.9955 \\ 0 & -0.9955 & 0.0951 \end{bmatrix}^T$$

$$\doteq \begin{bmatrix} -0.1231 & 0.9046 & 0.4082 \\ -0.4924 & 0.3015 & -0.8165 \\ -0.8616 & -0.3015 & 0.4083 \end{bmatrix}.$$

And it is easy to check that $Q^T Q = I_3$. We now have a QR decomposition of A. (The $(3, 3)$ entry of R should have been exactly zero because the original matrix is singular.) To make R have $r_{ii} > 0$, we could write $A = QJJR$ where $J = [-1 \ 0 \ 0; 0 \ 1 \ 0; 0 \ 0 \ -1]$; note that J satisfies $J^2 = I$. Then $A = (QJ)(JR)$, where JR is of the desired form and $(QJ)^T(QJ) = J^T Q^T QJ = J^T IJ = J^T J = I$ so that QJ is orthogonal. ∎

QR with Householder Matrices

This approach is entirely general. Similar to Eq. (2.27) for the LU decomposition, a typical step of QR decomposition by Householder triangularization has the form

$$\begin{bmatrix} I_r & {}_r 0_{m-r} \\ {}_{m-r} 0_r & H_{r+1} \end{bmatrix} \begin{bmatrix} X_a & X_b \\ 0 & X_c \end{bmatrix} = \begin{bmatrix} X_\alpha & X_\beta \\ {}_{m-r-1} 0_{r+1} & X_\gamma \end{bmatrix}$$

where H_{r+1} is an $(m - r) \times (m - r)$ Householder reflector that will eliminate (make zero) all the entries in the first column of X_c save the first entry. The result of this process is R, and we can collect the matrices $Q_1, \ldots, Q_{m-1}$ to form Q. Since a zero column is not a problem—we simply take $Q_i = I$ for that step—this process may be applied to any $m \times n$ matrix, even if it does not have full rank. (Note that we didn't actually use the assumption that A had full rank.) However, if A does have full rank, then the QR decomposition with $r_{ii} > 0$ is unique.

Choosing the appropriate sign for the constant that multiplies e_1, as in Example 2.7.2, is in fact more important than we have indicated; if cancellation of significant figures occurs then we may get very inaccurate results. Note that the computed R, even if inaccurate, will certainly be upper triangular (as we will set to zero those entries we know must be zero), but this is not necessarily the case for the orthogonality property of Q. Choosing the sign of α_1 opposite to that of the first component of a_1 gives an algorithm that is well-behaved with respect to roundoff errors (i.e., which is stable).

In many applications the matrix Q is not explicitly required. Even if it is, constructing each Householder matrix is inefficient. Since

$$
\begin{aligned}
H_w x &= (I - 2ww^T)x \\
&= Ix - 2ww^T x \\
&= x - 2w(w^T x) \\
&= x - 2w(w^T x),
\end{aligned}
$$

we can compute the product $H_w x$ using only the vector w, and furthermore we can compute it efficiently: The factor $w^T x$ is just a dot product. For m-vectors, evaluating $H_w x$ in this way requires $O(m)$ flops, rather than the $O(m^2)$ required for explicitly premultiplying x by H_w (and does not require the formation of a potentially large matrix). This is a significant gain. In a similar way, if we store the w vector at each step then $Q^T b$ and Qy (if needed) may be formed without explicitly forming Q. The Q matrix may be formed by applying the technique for finding Qy successively to $e_1, \ldots, e_m$.

We haven't yet generalized the matrix G of Example 2.7.1; we do so in MATLAB 2.7. That class of matrices provides a variant of the orthogonal triangularization approach to computing the QR decomposition that we have developed in this section. In Section 2.8 we discuss a procedure based on the Gram-Schmidt process that finds the QR decomposition by *triangular orthogonalization* of A.

PROBLEMS 2.7

1. a. Show that the matrices H and G of Example 2.7.1 are orthogonal, and find their determinants.

   b. Show that every 2×2 orthogonal matrix corresponds to H or G for some angle θ.

   c. Show that a Householder matrix H_w ($w \in \mathbb{R}^m$) is symmetric and orthogonal, and that it satisfies $H^2 = I_m$.

2. Repeat Example 2.7.2 for the matrix $A = [2\ 2\ 3;$ $4\ 5\ 6; 7\ 8\ 9]$. (Supply all intermediate details as in the example; use MATLAB for the multiplications.) Include a check of your final result ($A = QR$).

3. a. Suppose that in the process of performing QR decomposition by Householder triangularization on some 8×6 matrix B we arrive at the matrix $\tilde{B} = [I_5\ 0; 0\ A]$ after some step, where $A = [1\ 2\ 3;$ $4\ 5\ 6; 7\ 8\ 9]$ is the matrix of Example 2.7.2. Write out explicitly (that is, not in block form) the 8×8 matrix Q_6 that would be applied to $\tilde{B}$ to find the next matrix $Q_6 \tilde{B} = [I_6\ 0; 0\ A_{next}]$ in this process and the matrix $Q_6 \tilde{B}$.

   b. Find $Q_6 \tilde{B}$ using the formula $H_w x = x - 2w(w^T x)$ rather than matrix multiplication.

4. Find the QR decomposition of $A = [1\ 2\ 3\ 4;\ 5\ 6\ 7$ $8; 9\ 10\ 11\ 12; 13\ 14\ 15\ 16]$ by Householder triangularization (follow Example 2.7.2).

5. a. Partition the $n \times n$ matrix A into the block matrix $A = [A_{11}\ A_{12}; A_{21}\ A_{22}]$, where each $A_{i,j}$ is a submatrix of A and A_{11} is an $m \times m$ nonsingular matrix ($1 \le m < n$). Define the block matrix $E = [I_p\ 0; -A_{21}A_{11}^{-1}\ I_q]$, where I is an identity matrix of the appropriate order and 0 represents a zero matrix of the appropriate size. Give the sizes of A_{12}, A_{21}, A_{22}, I_p, the zero matrix 0, $-A_{21}A_{11}^{-1}$, and I_q.

   b. Show that $EA = [A_{11}\ A_{12}; 0\ A_{22} - A_{21}A_{11}^{-1}A_{12}]$. What are the sizes of the zero matrix and the submatrix $A_{22} - A_{21}A_{11}^{-1}A_{12}$ (called the **Schur complement** of A_{11})?

   c. Draw the Wilkinson diagram for passing from A to EA if $n = 6$ and $m = 3$.

   d. What is the significance of this observation? (Think in terms of Gaussian elimination and the use of Level-3 BLAS, which perform matrix-matrix operations. You may wish to refer to MATLAB 2.1.)

MATLAB 2.7

The Householder matrix $H_w = I - 2ww^T$ corresponding to a given w may be generated as follows; enter:

```
» w=[1 1 1]';w=w/norm(w);
» H=eye(3)-2*w*w'
```

Note that if w is a row vector, rather than a column vector as above, then w*w' will be a scalar (the dot, or inner, product) and MATLAB will automatically subtract 2w*w' from every entry of I_3; this will give incorrect results. Where w is a column vector, as here, the quantity w*w' is a matrix, called the **outer product** (more generally, if x and y are column vectors then the matrix xy^T is their outer product). Let's verify that the formula $Hx = x - 2w(w^T x)$ may be used to compute the product Hx without forming H. Enter:

```
» x=[2 1 2]'
» H*x              %Compute product using matrix.
» x-2*w*(w'*x)     %Compute product using vectors only.
```

How much more efficient is the latter approach than forming $H_w x$? Let's use a much larger example. Matrices with thousands of rows are not uncommon in practice. Enter:

```
» w=rand([1000 1]);w=w/norm(w);x=rand([1000 1]);
» tic;H=eye(1000)-2*w*w';toc
```

If the `flops` command is not available omit it and just use `tic` and `toc`. Enter:

```
» flops(0);tic;H*x;toc,flops
» flops(0);tic;x-2*w*(w'*x);toc,flops
```

The time it takes to form H is already nontrivial. Doing this 999 times while factoring a 1000×1000 matrix would be very time-consuming. (The size of the H_w matrices would be decreasing, of course, though the size of the Q_i matrices in which they are embedded would not.) The time for performing Hx is variable, but the flops count should be about 2 million ($O(n^2)$). The time for performing $x - 2w(w^T x)$ is almost certainly negligible and requires about 5000 flops ($O(n)$). This is a considerable difference; even if H is known, using it requires about 400 times as many floating point operations as using the alternative formula $x - 2w(w^T x)$.

Let's generalize the matrices G of Example 2.7.1. The Householder matrices H_w ($w \in \mathbb{R}^m$) represent reflections in $\mathbb{R}^m$ across $(m - 1)$-dimensional hyperplanes defined by the one-dimensional vector w. The matrices $G = [\cos(\theta) -\sin(\theta); \sin(\theta) \cos(\theta)]$ represent rotations through a counterclockwise angle of θ in the plane and are called **plane rotations** (or **plane rotation matrices**). If we were to use the definition $[\cos(\theta) \sin(\theta); -\sin(\theta) \cos(\theta)]$ (equivalent to replacing θ with $-\theta$) instead then the direction of the rotation would be clockwise. Enter:

```
» clear all
» th=pi;
» G=[cos(th) -sin(th);sin(th)  cos(th)]
```

```
» G*[1 0]'
» G*[1 1]'
» compass([1 -1],[1 1]),grid
```

for a simple example (90° CCW rotation); the `compass` command gives a visual display of x and Gx. (See `help compass`.) Try another value of `th` and verify that the vector is rotated appropriately.

If x is a 2-vector with its second entry nonzero, then clearly there exists a θ such that a rotation of x through the angle θ lies along the x-axis. For example, if we start with the vector $x = [-4 \ 3]$' then there must be a rotation that gives the result $G_1 x = (5, 0)^T$ and another one that gives the result $G_2 x = (-5, 0)^T$ (recall that G_i preserves lengths since it is orthogonal). To visualize these choices, enter:

```
» compass(-4,3,'b')
» hold on
» compass(5,0,'r')
» compass(-5,0,'y')
```

Notice that G_1 maps the blue vector to the red one, and G_2 maps the blue vector to the yellow one.

The MATLAB command `planerot` generates such plane rotations for a given x. (Computing the elements of G requires some care, and `planerot` handles this issue.) Enter:

```
» x=[-4 3]';
» G=planerot(x)
» G*x
```

to find a plane rotation G that maps x to a vector with second component zero and to verify that it is in fact G_1. Enter:

```
» [G,y]=planerot(x)
```

to obtain both G and Gx. Enter:

```
» [G,y]=planerot([1 0]')
» [G,y]=planerot([-1 0]')
```

to see that $G = I_2$ if the vector to be rotated already lies along the x-axis. This means that if A is a 2×2 matrix, then we can find a G to orthogonally triangularize it as follows; enter:

```
» A=rand([2 2])
» G=planerot(A(:,1))      %Use first column of A.
» G'*G     %Check orthogonality.
» R=G*A
» G'*R     %Should be A.
```

This is a QR decomposition with $Q = G^T$, and it is truly different from the Householder approach (though it is still an orthogonal triangularization). We'd like to generalize it to

$m \times n$ matrices. This is straightforward, and we will demonstrate it using an example. Enter:

```
» clear all
» A=rosser
```

The command `rosser` takes no input arguments and returns the Rosser test matrix, a symmetric 8×8 matrix used to test numerical eigenvalue routines. (We are just using it for convenience in this example.) We want to orthogonally triangularize it using rotations. Let's start by eliminating the (2, 1) entry 196. If we were concerned only with the upper 2×2 submatrix [611 196;196 899] then applying `planerot` would suffice; enter:

```
» A1=A(1:2,1)      %Entries (1,1) and (2,1) of A.
» G1=planerot(A1)
» G1*A1
```

to see the result. But if we simply embed G in an 8×8 identity matrix, similar to Eq. (2.27) but with G in the northwest corner, we will get the desired effect. Enter:

```
» I=eye(8);Q1=I;Q1(1:2,1:2)=G1
» Q1'*Q1      %Check orthogonality.
» R1=Q1*A
```

Note that the second entry of the first column of A is now zero. Let's continue. We now want to eliminate (or annihilate) the (3, 1) entry of R1. Enter:

```
» A2=R1([1 3],1)      %Entries (1,1) and (3,1) of R1.
» G2=planerot(A2)
» Q2=I;Q2([1 3],[1 3])=G2
```

Look carefully at the northwest 3×3 submatrix of this matrix. The 4 elements of G2 have been inserted in the (1, 1), (3, 1), (1, 3), and (3, 3) entries of the current working matrix R1. What will happen when we apply Q2 to R1? Enter:

```
» Q2'*Q2      %Check orthogonality.
» R2=Q2*R1
```

As desired, the effect of multiplying R1 by Q2 is to eliminate the (3, 1) entry of R1. (Note that Q2 would not have this effect on other matrices—it was constructed to have this effect only on this particular matrix.) Let's try again. Enter:

```
» A3=R2([1 4],1)      %Entries (1,1) and (4,1) of R2.
» G3=planerot(A3)
» Q3=I;Q3([1 4],[1 4])=G3
» R3=Q3*R2
```

(We should really be overwriting some of these variables, of course.) The matrix R3 has zeroes in its (2, 1) *and* (3, 1) entries; we've introduced a new desired zero without losing the previous one. Let's do one more; enter:

```
» Q4=I;Q4([1 5],[1 5])=planerot(R3([1 5],1))
» R4=Q4*R3
```

This is easier to type, but enter:

```
» R1==R2
```

to see that relatively few entries of the working matrix R_i are changing each time (as would be expected, since Q_i always has identity matrix blocks). There is a more efficient implementation of the action of the Q_i that could be used.

A matrix such as the Q_i above, consisting of I_m with a plane rotation matrix inserted in its (k, k), (k, p), (p, k), and (p, p) entries in the natural way, is called a **Givens matrix** (or **Givens rotation**); the 2×2 matrix of Example 2.7.1 is a special case. For an $m \times n$ matrix with $m \geq n$, we might in principle need $(m - 1) + (m - 2) + \ldots + 1 = m(m - 1)/2$ such matrices (working west to east across the matrix) to introduce all the zeroes needed to drive A to triangular form. This will give $Q_N Q_{N-1} \cdots Q_1 A = R$ ($N = m(m - 1)/2$), or $A = QR$ with $Q = Q_1^T Q_2^T \cdots Q_N^T$ orthogonal and R upper triangular. This is the method of QR decomposition using Givens rotations.

The traditional implementation of QR decomposition using Givens rotations is more expensive than the QR decomposition using Householder reflections (and the former requires the computation of square roots whereas the Householder version does not). However, there is a fast implementation of QR decomposition using Givens rotations whose computational cost is comparable to the Householder version. The error properties of the Givens and Householder schemes are similar. The MATLAB `qr` command is based on Householder triangularization (as is the QR decomposition used in the slash command, which also uses column pivoting for improved accuracy), and the Householder triangularization approach is used more often than the Givens rotation approach. However, the QR decomposition using Givens rotations is important for a certain class of matrices (those that are upper Hessenberg, meaning that every entry with $i > j + 1$ is zero), and Givens rotations have other applications as well.

ADDITIONAL PROBLEMS 2.7

6. Find (step by step) the QR decomposition of $A = [0\ 0\ 1; 0\ 1\ 0; 1\ 0\ 0]$ using Householder reflectors.

7. a. What unit vector $w(\theta) \in \mathbb{R}^2$ corresponds to the 2×2 Householder matrix $H = [-\cos(\theta)\ \sin(\theta); \sin(\theta)\ \cos(\theta)]$?

   b. Let $w = (1, 0, 1)^T$ and $x = (1, 1, 1)^T$. Sketch w, the plane in $\mathbb{R}^3$ determined by w, x, and $H_w x$. Explain geometrically why $H_w x$ is the reflection of x in that plane.

8. a. Show that no 2×2 Householder reflector is also a Givens rotation. (See Example 2.7.1.)

   b. Show that a Givens rotation is orthogonal. Can it be symmetric?

c. How many rows of an $m \times n$ matrix A might be affected by premultiplying it by a Householder reflector? How many rows of A might be affected by premultiplying it by a Givens rotation?

9. Find the QR decomposition of $A = [1\ 2\ 3\ 4; 5\ 6\ 7\ 8; 9\ 10\ 11\ 12; 13\ 14\ 15\ 16]$ by Givens rotations (see Problem 4).

10. a. Find the QR decomposition of the Hilbert matrix of order $N = 4$. Use it to solve $QRx = b$, where b is a vector of ones. Find the relative error in your answer (use `invhilb(A)*b` to determine the true solution). Give the condition numbers of the Hilbert matrix, Q, and R.

   b. Repeat for $N = 5, 6, 7, 8, 9, 10, 11, 12$. Comment.

11. a. Find the QR decomposition of the Hadamard matrix of order $N = 4$. (Use the MATLAB command A=hadamard(N) to generate the matrix.) Use it to solve $QRx = b$, where b is a vector of ones. Find the relative error in your answer (to determine the true solution, use the fact that $A^T A = NI_N$ if A is a Hadamard matrix). Give the condition numbers of the Hadamard matrix, Q, and R.

b. Repeat for $N = 8, 12, 16, 20$. Comment.

12. a. Show that the Givens rotation that takes the nonzero vector $(x_1, x_2)^T$ to a vector on the positive x-axis may be found without computing θ using the formulas $\cos(\theta) = x_1/\sqrt{x_1^2 + x_2^2}$ and $\sin(\theta) = -x_2/\sqrt{x_1^2 + x_2^2}$.

b. The formulas in part (a) may produce an overflow in the computation of $x_1^2 + x_2^2$, even though the final result would not overflow. This is undesirable. Underflows are also a concern for this method. One way to address these problems is to set $s = |x_1| + |x_2|$ and then compute $\sqrt{x_1^2 + x_2^2}$ as $s\sqrt{(x_1/s)^2 + (x_2/s)^2}$ if s is nonzero, else take $\cos(\theta) = 1$, $\sin(\theta) = 0$. (A technique such as this should be used when you are using Givens rotations.) Show that these expressions are mathematically equivalent.

c. What problem is avoided by using $s\sqrt{(x_1/s)^2 + (x_2/s)^2}$ in the computation? Give a numerical example in which the use of this trick is beneficial.

d. What problem is avoided by checking whether $s = 0$, even though $(x_1, x_2)^T$ is known to be nonzero? Give a numerical example in which the use of this trick is beneficial.

e. The MATLAB command planerot computes the quantity $\sqrt{x_1^2 + x_2^2}$ using the norm command. Does the norm command seem to have a safeguarding technique like that in part (b) built into it? Justify your answer with the output of several MATLAB computations.

13. Recall that a matrix is said to be upper Hessenberg if every entry below the first subdiagonal (that is, every entry with $i > j + 1$) is zero; such a matrix is "nearly" upper triangular. Show that if A is upper Hessenberg, then the QR decomposition using Givens rotations is more efficient than the QR decomposition using Householder reflectors.

14. Write a MATLAB program that performs the QR decomposition using Givens rotations. Compare the results of your program with those of the qr command.

15. Let A be an $m \times n$ matrix with $m \geq n$. Prove that if $A = QR$ is a QR decomposition of A and A has full rank, then the rows of Q form an orthonormal basis for Col(A) (the column space of A).

2.8 Gram-Schmidt Orthogonalization and the QR Decomposition

Blocking

We've been placing a greater emphasis on looking at numerical linear algebra algorithms in terms of sub-blocks of the matrices involved. This is important for many reasons: Design and analysis of algorithms and use of the BLAS and/or the special architecture of the machine are chief among them. (It would be convenient to block problems into chunks of data that fit in the fast cache, for example.) Often if we can analyze one step in the iterative process of reducing a matrix to a special form in terms of simple matrix algebra operations, usually but not always moving (north)west to (south)east across the matrix, then we can gain a great deal of understanding of the method, including the effects of roundoff error on the results.

Putting algorithms in blocked form is not as simple as dividing matrices into blocks. For example, the matrix

$$A = \begin{bmatrix} 1 & 0 & 0 & 0 \\ 0 & 0 & 0 & 1 \\ 0 & 0 & 1 & 0 \\ 0 & 1 & 0 & 0 \end{bmatrix}$$

certainly has an LU decomposition (after all, it's just a permutation of I_4), but if we block it in the form

$$A = \begin{bmatrix} 1 & 0 & \vdots & 0 & 0 \\ 0 & 0 & \vdots & 0 & 1 \\ \ldots & \ldots & \vdots & \ldots & \ldots \\ 0 & 0 & \vdots & 1 & 0 \\ 0 & 1 & \vdots & 0 & 0 \end{bmatrix}$$

then every block is singular, and so block Gaussian elimination fails even with complete pivoting. There is more to constructing a blocked algorithm than simply partitioning A into blocks.

To a certain extent ideas like blocking straddle numerical analysis and computer science, because determining the best way to block a matrix for a particular application depends on software and hardware issues as well as mathematical ones. The term *scientific computation* is sometimes used to describe the practical issues that arise when one thinks about coding a particular algorithm for use on a particular machine.[11]

The purpose of this text is not to make you a programmer of scientific software but rather an educated user of such programs who can understand new methods and, if needed, modify older methods as the need arises. An important part of this process is studying different algorithms for the same mathematical problem and learning why some methods are preferable in certain cases and others are stronger in other cases.

In Section 2.7, we considered Householder triangularization as a means of computing a QR decomposition. In this section, we now discuss a second major approach to computing a QR decomposition, which is based on the Gram-Schmidt process. In some ways, this second approach is more intuitive.

Although the Householder triangularization (or the related Givens rotation) method is usually superior, there is at least one special case in which the Gram-Schmidt approach to computing a QR decomposition is the superior method.

Gram-Schmidt Process

Let's begin our exploration of the Gram-Schmidt approach with a review of the Gram-Schmidt process from linear algebra.

Example 2.8.1

If $v_1, v_2, \ldots, v_k$ are linearly independent vectors, then their span is some vector space $V = \text{span}(v_1, v_2, \ldots, v_k)$, for which $\{v_1, v_2, \ldots, v_k\}$ is a basis. We seek an orthonormal basis for V. The Gram-Schmidt process finds an orthonormal basis $\{u_1, u_2, \ldots, u_k\}$ for V from $\{v_1, v_2, \ldots, v_k\}$ as follows:

$$u_1 = \frac{v_1}{\|v_1\|}$$

$$u_2' = v_2 - \left(v_2^T u_1\right) u_1$$

---

[11] In fact, commercial software is usually written and tested by *teams* of individuals with strengths in various aspects of computing (as well as in the scientific problems to which the programs will ultimately be applied).

$$u_2 = \frac{u_2'}{\|u_2'\|}$$

$$u_3' = v_3 - \left(v_3^T u_2\right) u_2 - \left(v_3^T u_1\right) u_1$$

$$u_3 = \frac{u_3'}{\|u_3'\|}$$

$$\vdots$$

$$u_k' = v_k - \left(v_k^T u_{k-1}\right) u_{k-1} - \cdots - \left(v_k^T u_1\right) u_1$$

$$u_k = \frac{u_k'}{\|u_k'\|}$$

and if $\{v_1, v_2, \ldots, v_k\}$ is a linearly independent set, then the process will complete and $\{u_1, u_2, \ldots, u_k\}$ will be an orthonormal set with the same span. Note that the terms $(v_2^T v_1)$, etc., are inner products and the terms $(v_2^T u_1)u_1$, etc., are projections along the various vectors; the Gram-Schmidt process simply subtracts off the nonorthogonal parts from the current vector. For example, if $\{v_1, v_2, v_3\} = \{(1, 0, 1)^T, (-1, 1, 1)^T, (0, 1, 1)^T\}$, then we have

$$u_1 = \frac{v_1}{\|v_1\|}$$

$$= \frac{(1, 0, 1)^T}{\sqrt{2}}$$

$$= \left(\frac{1}{\sqrt{2}}, 0, \frac{1}{\sqrt{2}}\right)^T$$

$$u_2' = v_2 - \left(v_2^T u_1\right) u_1$$

$$= (-1, 1, 1)^T - \left((-1, 1, 1) \cdot \left(\frac{1}{\sqrt{2}}, 0, \frac{1}{\sqrt{2}}\right)\right) \left(\frac{1}{\sqrt{2}}, 0, \frac{1}{\sqrt{2}}\right)^T$$

$$= (-1, 1, 1)^T - (0) \left(\frac{1}{\sqrt{2}}, 0, \frac{1}{\sqrt{2}}\right)^T$$

$$= (-1, 1, 1)^T$$

$$u_2 = \frac{(-1, 1, 1)^T}{\|(-1, 1, 1)^T\|}$$

$$= \left(\frac{-1}{\sqrt{3}}, \frac{1}{\sqrt{3}}, \frac{1}{\sqrt{3}}\right)^T$$

$$u_3' = v_3 - \left(v_3^T u_2\right) u_2 - \left(v_3^T u_1\right) u_1$$

$$= (0, 1, 1)^T - \left((0, 1, 1) \cdot \frac{(-1, 1, 1)}{\sqrt{3}}\right) \frac{(-1, 1, 1)^T}{\sqrt{3}} - \left((0, 1, 1) \cdot \frac{(1, 0, 1)}{\sqrt{2}}\right) \frac{(1, 0, 1)^T}{\sqrt{2}}$$

$$= (0, 1, 1)^T - \left(\frac{2}{\sqrt{3}}\right)\frac{(-1, 1, 1)^T}{\sqrt{3}} - \left(\frac{1}{\sqrt{2}}\right)\frac{(1, 0, 1)^T}{\sqrt{2}}$$

$$= (0, 1, 1)^T - \left(\frac{2}{3}\right)(-1, 1, 1)^T - \left(\frac{1}{2}\right)(1, 0, 1)^T$$

$$= \left(\frac{1}{6}, \frac{1}{3}, -\frac{1}{6}\right)^T$$

$$u_3 = \frac{\left(\frac{1}{6}, \frac{1}{3}, -\frac{1}{6}\right)^T}{\left\| \left(\frac{1}{6}, \frac{1}{3}, -\frac{1}{6}\right)^T \right\|}$$

$$= \frac{\left(\frac{1}{6}, \frac{1}{3}, -\frac{1}{6}\right)^T}{\sqrt{\frac{1}{6}}}$$

$$= \left(\frac{\sqrt{6}}{6}, \frac{\sqrt{6}}{3}, -\frac{\sqrt{6}}{6}\right)^T.$$

So

$$\{u_1, u_2, u_3\} = \{(1/\sqrt{2}, 0, 1/\sqrt{2})^T, (-1/\sqrt{3}, 1/\sqrt{3}, 1/\sqrt{3})^T, (\sqrt{6}/6, \sqrt{6}/3, -\sqrt{6}/6)^T\}$$

is an orthonormal set with the same span (in this case, $\mathbb{R}^3$). To check this, we can form a matrix Q with columns u_1, u_2, u_3,

$$Q = \begin{bmatrix} 1/\sqrt{2} & -1/\sqrt{3} & \sqrt{6}/6 \\ 0 & 1/\sqrt{3} & \sqrt{6}/3 \\ 1/\sqrt{2} & 1/\sqrt{3} & -\sqrt{6}/6 \end{bmatrix} \tag{2.30}$$

and see whether it is orthogonal:

$$Q^T Q = \begin{bmatrix} 1/\sqrt{2} & 0 & 1/\sqrt{2} \\ -1/\sqrt{3} & 1/\sqrt{3} & 1/\sqrt{3} \\ \sqrt{6}/6 & \sqrt{6}/3 & -\sqrt{6}/6 \end{bmatrix} \begin{bmatrix} 1/\sqrt{2} & -1/\sqrt{3} & \sqrt{6}/6 \\ 0 & 1/\sqrt{3} & \sqrt{6}/3 \\ 1/\sqrt{2} & 1/\sqrt{3} & -\sqrt{6}/6 \end{bmatrix}$$

$$= \begin{bmatrix} 1 & 0 & 0 \\ 0 & 1 & 0 \\ 0 & 0 & 1 \end{bmatrix}.$$

This checks. We might have expected to find the standard basis for $\mathbb{R}^3$, but in general this will not be the case. ■

Gram-Schmidt and QR

Let's return to the QR decomposition. Remember from the previous section that this is a triangular orthogonalization approach. It's easiest to consider a square matrix; let A be an $m \times m$ matrix with rank$(A) = m$. Then Col(A) is the span of the columns $a_1, \ldots, a_m$ of A, and $\{a_1, \ldots, a_m\}$ is a linearly independent set. (In fact, Col$(A) = \mathbb{R}^m$ in this case.) Hence the Gram-Schmidt process may be used to generate an orthonormal basis $\{u_1, u_2, \ldots, u_m\}$ for $\text{Col}(A)$. In fact, note from Example 2.8.1 that we can say something a bit stronger: The span of a_1 will be the same as the span of u_1 (they are multiples of each other, after all); the span of a_1 and a_2 will be the same as the span of u_1 and u_2 (u_1 and u_2 are linear combinations of a_1 and a_2); and so on.

Since the product Mx of a matrix and a vector is a linear combination of the columns of the matrix, we may express this relationship as follows: Let Q be the matrix with columns $u_1, u_2, \ldots, u_m$. Then

$$a_1 = Qr_1,$$

where r_1 is nonzero only in its first entry (a_1 is a linear combination of u_1 only). Also

$$a_2 = Qr_2,$$

where r_2 is nonzero only in its first and second entry (a_2 is a linear combination of u_1 and u_2 only). We could write

$$[a_1 \ a_2] = Q[r_1 \ r_2],$$

where $[a_1 \ a_2]$ is an $m \times 2$ matrix consisting of the first two columns of A and $[r_1 \ r_2]$ is also an $m \times 2$ matrix. More generally $A = QR$ where R is an upper triangular matrix. The diagonal entries of R are nonzero; in fact, according to the Gram-Schmidt process, they are the nonzero values $1/\|u_i'\|$ ($i = 1, \ldots, m$).

This is the Gram-Schmidt orthogonalization approach to the QR decomposition, then, also called the **classical Gram-Schmidt orthogonalization** method (or **classical Gram-Schmidt iteration**). As above, we construct the orthogonal matrix Q column by column from the matrix A by the (inherently triangular) Gram-Schmidt process.

Example 2.8.2   Refer back to Example 2.8.1; we're going to redo it in matrix form to show the close connection between the Gram-Schmidt process and the QR decomposition. Continue referring to Example 2.8.1 as you study this example.

The vectors from Example 2.8.1 are used to form the A matrix

$$A = \begin{bmatrix} 1 & -1 & 0 \\ 0 & 1 & 1 \\ 1 & 1 & 1 \end{bmatrix}$$

($A = [v_1|v_2|v_3]$), and the first step in orthogonalizing A is to rescale its first column so that it is a column vector. Rescaling a column requires that we post-multiply the matrix:

$$\begin{aligned} Q_1 &= AR_1 \\ &= \begin{bmatrix} 1 & -1 & 0 \\ 0 & 1 & 1 \\ 1 & 1 & 1 \end{bmatrix} \begin{bmatrix} 1/\sqrt{2} & 0 & 0 \\ 0 & 1 & 0 \\ 0 & 0 & 1 \end{bmatrix} \\ &= \begin{bmatrix} 1/\sqrt{2} & -1 & 0 \\ 0 & 1 & 1 \\ 1/\sqrt{2} & 1 & 1 \end{bmatrix} \end{aligned}$$

(note that Q_1 is not orthogonal; rather, it is the matrix we are working on with the goal of *making* it orthogonal).

Next we need to make column 2 of AR_1 orthogonal to column 1 of AR_1. Referring to Example 2.8.1, we may accomplish this by multiplying column 1 by 0 (the columns are already orthogonal) and then normalizing by $\sqrt{3}$. Hence we perform

$$Q_2 = AR_1R_2$$

$$= \begin{bmatrix} 1/\sqrt{2} & -1 & 0 \\ 0 & 1 & 1 \\ 1/\sqrt{2} & 1 & 1 \end{bmatrix} \begin{bmatrix} 1 & 0 & 0 \\ 0 & 1/\sqrt{3} & 0 \\ 0 & 0 & 1 \end{bmatrix}$$

$$= \begin{bmatrix} 1/\sqrt{2} & -1/\sqrt{3} & 0 \\ 0 & 1/\sqrt{3} & 1 \\ 1/\sqrt{2} & 1/\sqrt{3} & 1 \end{bmatrix},$$

which now has two orthonormal columns. Note that postmultiplying by these upper triangular matrices has the effect of performing a sequence of elementary column operations on the matrix, just as premultiplying lower triangular matrices had the effect of performing elementary row operations on the matrix in Gaussian elimination.

We have one last column to process. Referring to Example 2.8.1, we need to take the third column a_3 of Q_2 (which is also the third column of A) and subtract from it $1/\sqrt{2}$ times the first column u_1 of Q_2 and $2/\sqrt{3}$ times the second column u_2 of Q_2, and divide the result by $1/\sqrt{6}$. That is, we need to form

$$\frac{\left(a_3 - \frac{2}{\sqrt{3}}u_2 - \frac{1}{\sqrt{2}}u_1\right)}{\sqrt{\frac{1}{6}}} = \sqrt{6}a_3 - 2\frac{\sqrt{6}}{\sqrt{3}}u_2 - \frac{\sqrt{6}}{\sqrt{2}}u_1$$

$$= \sqrt{6}a_3 - 2\sqrt{2}u_2 - \sqrt{3}u_1$$

and so we continue using triangular matrices to drive A to an orthogonal matrix by performing

$$Q_3 = AR_1R_2R_3$$

$$= \begin{bmatrix} 1/\sqrt{2} & -1/\sqrt{3} & 0 \\ 0 & 1/\sqrt{3} & 1 \\ 1/\sqrt{2} & 1/\sqrt{3} & 1 \end{bmatrix} \begin{bmatrix} 1 & 0 & -\sqrt{3} \\ 0 & 1 & -2\sqrt{2} \\ 0 & 0 & \sqrt{6} \end{bmatrix}$$

$$= \begin{bmatrix} 1/\sqrt{2} & -1/\sqrt{3} & \sqrt{6}/6 \\ 0 & 1/\sqrt{3} & \sqrt{6}/3 \\ 1/\sqrt{2} & 1/\sqrt{3} & -\sqrt{6}/6 \end{bmatrix}.$$

The matrix Q_3 is in fact the desired orthogonal matrix Q (compare the matrix Q in Example 2.8.1, Eq. (2.30)), and the orthogonalizing matrix $\tilde{R}$ is the upper triangular matrix

$$\tilde{R} = R_1 R_2 R_3$$

$$= \begin{bmatrix} 1/\sqrt{2} & 0 & 0 \\ 0 & 1 & 0 \\ 0 & 0 & 1 \end{bmatrix} \begin{bmatrix} 1 & 0 & 0 \\ 0 & 1/\sqrt{3} & 0 \\ 0 & 0 & 1 \end{bmatrix} \begin{bmatrix} 1 & 0 & -\sqrt{3} \\ 0 & 1 & -2\sqrt{2} \\ 0 & 0 & \sqrt{6} \end{bmatrix}$$

$$= \begin{bmatrix} 1/\sqrt{2} & 0 & -\sqrt{6}/2 \\ 0 & 1/\sqrt{3} & -2\sqrt{6}/3 \\ 0 & 0 & \sqrt{6} \end{bmatrix}.$$

We have $Q = A\tilde{R}$ (that is, postmultiplying by the triangular matrix $\tilde{R}$ orthogonalizes A), and this method guarantees that all diagonal entries of $\tilde{R}$ are strictly positive; hence the inverse of $\tilde{R}$ exists and $A = Q\tilde{R}^{-1}$. Since the inverse of an upper triangular matrix with positive diagonal entries is itself an upper triangular matrix with positive diagonal entries, this is a QR decomposition of A with $R = \tilde{R}^{-1}$. Let's check:

$$QR = \begin{bmatrix} 1/\sqrt{2} & -1/\sqrt{3} & \sqrt{6}/6 \\ 0 & 1/\sqrt{3} & \sqrt{6}/3 \\ 1/\sqrt{2} & 1/\sqrt{3} & -\sqrt{6}/6 \end{bmatrix} \begin{bmatrix} \sqrt{2}/2 & 0 & -\sqrt{6}/2 \\ 0 & \sqrt{3}/3 & -2\sqrt{6}/3 \\ 0 & 0 & \sqrt{6} \end{bmatrix}^{-1}$$

$$= \begin{bmatrix} 1/\sqrt{2} & -1/\sqrt{3} & \sqrt{6}/6 \\ 0 & 1/\sqrt{3} & \sqrt{6}/3 \\ 1/\sqrt{2} & 1/\sqrt{3} & -\sqrt{6}/6 \end{bmatrix} \begin{bmatrix} \sqrt{2} & 0 & 1/\sqrt{2} \\ 0 & \sqrt{3} & -2/\sqrt{3} \\ 0 & 0 & 1/\sqrt{6} \end{bmatrix}$$

$$= \begin{bmatrix} 1 & -1 & 0 \\ 0 & 1 & 1 \\ 1 & 1 & 1 \end{bmatrix}$$

$$= A.$$

This checks. Clearly, we would not compute the inverse matrix in an actual computation; a simple reorganization of the method above allows us to form R directly without ever forming $\tilde{R}$.   ■

The classical Gram-Schmidt orthogonalization method is a natural way to find an orthogonal matrix Q such that $A = QR$, and as indicated we may view the effect of the R_i matrices as elementary column operations that are applied to A (in general one R_i matrix will perform several elementary column operations). Note that the columns of Q are generated directly; we do not need to form Q, after the reduction, from individual transformations. (In fact the same is true of R, though we have not brought that fact out.) The flops count is similar to that of the Householder triangularization approach (and if Q is needed explicitly, the classical Gram-Schmidt orthogonalization method is more efficient). This is an excellent example of a simple, intuitive, straightforward, and efficient method that is guaranteed to converge in infinite precision arithmetic (given our assumptions) and that *does not work*.

Errors

There are two principal problems with the classical Gram-Schmidt orthogonalization approach to the QR decomposition: amplification of roundoff errors (similar to unpivoted Gaussian elimination) and loss of the orthogonality property of Q. The problem is that in a computation such as

$$u_3' = v_3 - \left(v_3^T u_2\right) u_2 - \left(v_3^T u_1\right) u_1$$

it may be that v_3 is nearly in the span of u_1 and u_2, meaning that we will be subtracting nearly equal quantities and hence causing the cancellation of significant figures. The classical Gram-Schmidt orthogonalization method can amplify errors significantly and therefore should not be used to compute QR decompositions.

Was it a waste of time to introduce the Gram-Schmidt orthogonalization method? No. It's a useful theoretical framework for understanding both the QR decomposition and the Gram-Schmidt process itself, and as we shall see here and in Chapter 3 there are sometimes reasons why we would use a quick but relatively inaccurate method to solve a linear system (see Section 3.4). In addition, we can modify this method to get one with better error properties.

Let's look again at the classical Gram-Schmidt orthogonalization method. Let A be an $m \times n$ matrix with $m \geq n$ and $\text{rank}(A) = n$. We might write the Gram-Schmidt algorithm more efficiently as follows (using MATLAB notation for the indexing):

CGS Algorithm:

1. Set $Q = A$.

2. Set $R(1, 1) = \| Q(:, 1) \|$.

3. Normalize column 1 of Q.

4. Begin loop ($k = 2$ to n):

5. Set $p = 1 : (k - 1)$.

6. Set $R(p, k) = Q(:, p)^T Q(:, k)$.

7. Set $Q(:, k) = Q(:, k) - Q(:, p)R(p, k)$.

8. Normalize column k of Q; store normalization constant $\| Q(:, k) \|$ in $R(k, k)$.

9. End loop.

(Note that p is a vector representing the rows containing the superdiagonal entries of R for a given column k.) We interpret setting $Q = A$ to mean that A is to be overwritten by Q; we generally wouldn't want to make two copies of A to start. As with any algorithm discussed in this text, we are omitting myriad implementation details that a practical program must include to be efficient (and to safeguarde against bad inputs, divisions by zeroes, etc.).

Modified Method

The **modified Gram-Schmidt orthogonalization method** (or **modified Gram-Schmidt iteration**) for finding the QR decomposition of such a matrix has the following form:

> **MGS Algorithm:**
> 1. Set $Q = A$.
> 2. Set $R(1, 1) = \|Q(:, 1)\|$.
> 3. Normalize column 1 of Q.
> 4. Begin loop ($k = 2$ to n):
> 5. Begin loop ($i = 1$ to $k - 1$):
> 6. Set $R(i, k) = Q(:, i)^T Q(:, k)$.
> 7. Set $Q(:, k) = Q(:, k) - R(i, k)Q(:, i)$.
> 8. End i loop.
> 9. Normalize column k of Q; store normalization constant $\|Q(:, k)\|$ in $R(k, k)$.
> 10. End k loop.

Rather than use the index vector p of the classical method, we step through p (using the i loop) in the updates of both R (step 6 of the classical method) and Q (step 7 of the classical method). In the classical method, step 6 ends before step 7 begins, and we change column k of Q only once (apart from the final normalization). In the modified method we change Q every time we compute an entry of R in step 6 (as an inner product, like $v_2^T u_1$ from Example 2.8.1). Nonetheless, the methods are equivalent in infinite precision arithmetic. (We omit the demonstration, which is based on viewing the calculation of a column of Q as a single projection in the classical method and as a series of projections in the modified method.) They also have similar flops counts (roughly $2mn^2$ for large m, n). However, they behave differently in finite precision arithmetic.

The modified Gram-Schmidt orthogonalization method has roundoff error properties similar to those of Householder triangularization; in this sense it is a considerable improvement over the classical Gram-Schmidt orthogonalization method.[12] However, loss of the orthogonality property of Q can still occur in the modified method, though it is not as severe as in the classical method. If an accurate orthogonal matrix Q is needed, Householder triangularization is usually preferable, but it is possible to use a "reorthogonalization" procedure with either Gram-Schmidt method to improve the quality of Q.

The modified Gram-Schmidt orthogonalization method as we have presented it is sometimes called the column version of the method since it fills in R by columns. There is a row version that fills in R by rows and that is more amenable to the use of higher level BLAS.

Note that whereas our version of the classical Gram-Schmidt orthogonalization method is written using matrix-vector products such as $Q(:, p)^T Q(:, k)$ and $Q(:, p)R(p, k)$ (recall that p is a vector of indices, so $Q(:, p)$ and $R(p, k)$ are matrix blocks), they do not appear in our modified Gram-Schmidt orthogonalization algorithm. Early in this section we said that there is a special circumstance in which we might prefer the classical method, and this is it: The classical method is vector-oriented, and if we are

---

[12] These comments also apply to the problem of making a basis into an orthonormal basis; this problem is simply that of finding a QR decomposition where we do not care about R.

using a parallel machine, then the speed benefits of using the classical method may make up for the loss of accuracy in some circumstances (particularly if we need only R, not Q, say because we wish to compute $\det(A)$ or $\text{rank}(A)$). We can apply a reorthogonalization procedure if necessary.

We'll see this happen again as we continue studying numerical linear algebra in Chapter 3: Advanced architecture machines can make older methods of computation that are less accurate or less efficient (in the serial machine sense) become attractive options once again. For most purposes, however, the modified Gram-Schmidt orthogonalization method should be used rather than the classical version.

PROBLEMS 2.8

1. a. Use the Gram-Schmidt process (as in Example 2.8.1) to find an orthonormal basis for the space spanned by $\{(1, 0, 1, 0, 1)^T, (2, 2, 1, 2, 2)^T, (1, -1, 1, 0, 0)^T\}$.

b. Use the Gram-Schmidt process (as in Example 2.8.1) to find an orthonormal basis for the space spanned by $\{(1, -1, 1, 0, 0)^T, (2, 2, 1, 2, 2)^T, (1, 0, 1, 0, 1)^T\}$.

2. a. Apply the classical Gram-Schmidt method (as in Example 2.8.2) to find a QR decomposition of the matrix $A = [2\ 1\ 1; 1\ 2\ 1; 1\ 1\ 2]$.

b. Apply the CGS Algorithm (by hand) to find a QR decomposition of A.

c. Apply the MGS Algorithm (by hand) to find a QR decomposition of A.

3. Apply the CGS Algorithm (by hand) to find an orthonormal basis for the space spanned by $\{(1, 0, 1, 0, 1)^T, (2, 2, 1, 2, 2)^T, (1, -1, 1, 0, 0)^T\}$.

4. a. Write a MATLAB program that implements the CGS Algorithm. Demonstrate it on the matrix $A = [2\ 1\ 1; 1\ 2\ 1; 1\ 1\ 2]$.

b. Find a matrix A for which your program returns a Q that demonstrates the loss of orthogonality.

5. a. Write a MATLAB program that implements the MGS Algorithm. Demonstrate it on the matrix $A = [2\ 1\ 1; 1\ 2\ 1; 1\ 1\ 2]$.

b. Demonstrate your program on the example you found for Problem 4(b). Does the MGS Algorithm perform better?

MATLAB 2.8

The `orth` command finds an orthonormal basis for the column space of a matrix (that is, the space spanned by its columns), and the `null` command finds an orthonormal basis for its null space (that is, the set of all x such that $Ax = 0$); enter:

```
» type orth
» type null
```

to see that each uses the `svd` command (see Section 2.9). Previous versions of these commands used the `qr` command. (See the commented-out block at the bottom. The SVD command implements another matrix decomposition and is discussed in Section 2.9.) The QR decomposition is a versatile technique.

Let's look at a rank-deficient problem. We'll make a random matrix whose first and third columns are the same. Enter:

```
» A=rand(3);A(:,3)=A(:,1)
```

Since the range of A is a two-dimensional space, $Ax = b$ will be inconsistent for most $b \in \mathbb{R}^3$. Enter:

```
» [Q,R]=qr(A)
```

Notice that R, like A, is singular (since $R(3, 3)$ is zero), but the decomposition is still correct. Enter:

```
» A,Q*R
» norm(A-ans)
```

The first two columns of Q span the same space as the first two columns of A. Let's do a check; enter:

```
» w=cross(A(:,1),A(:,2))
```

to generate a vector orthogonal to the column space of A (which is a plane in $\mathbb{R}^3$ spanned by $A(:, 1)$ and $A(:, 2)$). Enter:

```
» dot(w,Q(:,1))
» dot(w,Q(:,2))
```

These are essentially zero, as expected; that checks (vectors orthogonal to the span of the first two columns of A are orthogonal to the span of the first two columns of Q). Enter:

```
» dot(w,Q(:,3))
```

This is not zero. Recall that the third column of Q is an arbitrary vector orthonormal to the first two columns of Q. The reduced factorization is:

```
» [Q1,R1]=qr(A,0)
```

This is the same as the QR decomposition because A is square. Now enter:

```
» clear all
» A=rand([6 3])
» A(:,4)=A(:,1)       %Create fourth column (equal to first).
» [Q,R]=qr(A)
» [Q1,R1]=qr(A,0)
```

Once again R is singular. In the square case we said that R was singular because A was singular but we now see that the real reason R is singular in each case is that A does not have full rank. In the current case, A is a 6×4 matrix with rank$(A) = 3$. The reduced QR factorization matrix Q_1 is a nonsquare matrix with orthonormal columns; the QR decomposition matrix Q agrees with Q_1 for the first four columns and then has two added orthonormal columns.

The first 3 columns of Q_1 are an orthonormal basis for the column space of A; all the other columns are just there to fill out the Q_1 (or Q) matrix. For example, enter:

```
» v1=A(:,1);            %First column of A.
» q1=Q1(:,1);
» v1/norm(v1)           %Should be q1 or -q1.
» v2=A(:,2);q2=Q1(:,2); %Second columns.
» w=cross(v1,v2);       %Orthogonal to v1, v2.
» dot(q1,w)             %Should be zero.
» dot(q2,w)             %Should be zero.
```

Similarly for column 3. The fourth column of Q_1 is just there for multiplicative conformability; it is an arbitrary extension of the orthonormal basis for Col(A) contained in $Q_1(:, 1 : 3)$. The fifth and sixth columns of Q are present for the same reason.

The QR decomposition is being computed column by column. Because of this, you can efficiently find the decomposition of the matrix that is formed by deleting a column from A when you are given the QR decomposition of A. (This is true whether the matrices Q and R are found by orthogonal triangularization or triangular orthogonalization.) The MATLAB command qrdelete may be used to do this. Enter:

```
» clear all
» format compact
» A=pascal(6)
» [Q,R]=qr(A);
» B=A;
» B(:,3)=[]        %Eliminate column 3 of B.
» [QB,RB]=qr(B);
» Q,QB            %Compare the entries of Q and QB.
» Q==QB           %Compare the entries of Q and QB.
» R,RB            %Compare the entries of R and RB.
» R(:,1:5)==RB    %Compare the entries of R and RB.
```

(We shouldn't really be testing for exact equality here, of course.) We recomputed the QR decomposition of B; the qrdelete command is more efficient. Enter:

```
» [QC,RC]=qrdelete(Q,R,3);
» abs(QC-QB)<1E-10     %Compare the entries of QC and QB.
» abs(RC-RB)<1E-10     %Compare the entries of RC and RB.
» norm(QC-QB)
» norm(RC-RB)
```

It appears that the matrices QB and QC and the matrices RB and RC are quite close. Enter:

```
» B
» QB*RB
» QC*RC
```

to see that these are both QR decompositions of B. If we already have a QR decomposition of A, however, the qrdelete approach is much more efficient. (There is also a qrinsert command and a qrupdate command.) There are many techniques for efficiently updating decompositions of a given matrix when the matrix undergoes a change of a prescribed form.

The MATLAB command B(:,k)=[] is an efficient way to delete a column of a matrix in MATLAB. We can also represent such deletions using matrix multiplications for analytical purposes. For example, enter:

```
» A=[1 2 3 4;5 6 7 8;9 10 11 12;13 14 15 16]
» E=eye(4);E(3,:)=[]
» E*A
» A*E'
```

The matrix E is sometimes called a **deletion matrix;** it deletes a row if used to premultiply a matrix or a column if its transpose is used to postmultiply a matrix. Again, this would be used for analytical purposes only.

We make one final point about the QR decomposition. As with the LU decomposition, the errors in the computed Q and R matrices do not lead (as a rule) to comparably sized errors in their product QR; the errors are somehow correlated. Enter:

```
» clear all
» Q=orth(rand(100));R=triu(rand(100));
» A=Q*R;              %Matrix A has a known QR decomposition.
» [QCOMP,RCOMP]=qr(A);
» ACOMP=QCOMP*RCOMP;  %Computed A.
» norm(Q-QCOMP)
» norm(R-RCOMP)
» norm(A-ACOMP)
```

The error in ACOMP is quite small despite the large error in QCOMP and in RCOMP. Enter:

```
» norm(Q-QCOMP,'inf')
» norm(R-RCOMP,'inf')
» norm(A-ACOMP,'inf')
```

to see the maximum amount by which an entry of each computed value differs from its true value. In all likelihood the error in QCOMP was on the order of ones or tens, the error in RCOMP was on the order of tens or hundreds, and the error in ACOMP, which depends only on QCOMP and RCOMP, was on the order of 10^{-14}. The result is many orders of magnitude better than we had any right to expect. This phenomenon is not fully understood.

ADDITIONAL PROBLEMS 2.8

6. a. Apply the CGS Algorithm (by hand) to find a QR decomposition of the matrix $A = [1\ 2\ 3\ 4;$ $5\ 6\ 7\ 8; 9\ 10\ 11\ 12; 13\ 14\ 15\ 16]$.

   b. Apply the MGS Algorithm (by hand) to find a QR decomposition of A.

7. a. Apply the CGS Algorithm (by hand) to find a QR decomposition of the matrix $A = [1\ 0\ 1\ 0;$ $0\ 1\ 0\ 1; 1\ 0\ 0\ 1; 0\ 0\ 1\ 1]$. Use it to find $\det(A)$.

   b. Apply the MGS Algorithm (by hand) to find a QR decomposition of A.

8. a. If the $m \times n$ matrix A $(m \geq n)$ is of full rank, then we define its **Moore-Penrose pseudo-inverse** to be the square matrix $A^+ = (A^T A)^{-1} A^T$. (The MATLAB command pinv computes the pseudo-inverse.) Show that the least squares solution of the

overdetermined linear system $Ax = b$ is $x = A^+ b$ if A has full rank.

   b. Show that $A^+ A = I$ and $AA^+ y = y$ for all conformable vectors y.

   c. Show that $(A^+)^+ = A$. Why is the term pseudo-inverse appropriate for A^+?

   d. Suppose $A = QR$ is a QR decomposition of A. Express A^+ in terms of Q and R.

   e. What is the Moore-Penrose pseudo-inverse of the zero matrix?

   f. Show that if A is symmetric, then A^+ is symmetric.

   g. Show that $(A^k)^+ = (A^+)^k$.

   h. If $A = [1\ 2; 2\ 1; -1\ 2]$, find A^+ and use it to find the least squares solution of $Ax = (2, 2, 2)^T$. Also, find the condition number of A, defined by $\kappa(A) = \|A\| \|A^+\|$.

9. **a.** Assuming A is nonsingular, express $\|A\|_s$ in terms of the spectral norms of its QR factors Q and R.

   b. Assuming A is nonsingular, express $\kappa_s(A)$ in terms of the condition numbers of its QR factors Q and R.

   c. Do the results of parts (a) and (b) hold when the quantities are computed in MATLAB? Experiment to determine this.

10. **a.** Prove that the MGS Algorithm is mathematically equivalent to the CGS Algorithm.

    b. Give an exact floating point operations count for the CGS Algorithm and for the MGS Algorithm.

11. **a.** Using your CGS Algorithm program from Problem 4 and your MGS Algorithm program from Problem 5, demonstrate experimentally the numerical superiority of the MGS Algorithm. Explain the reasoning behind your design of the experiment.

    b. Using your MGS Algorithm program from Problem 5, compare the accuracy of the MGS Algorithm to that of the Householder triangularization approach (as implemented in the MATLAB qr command). Explain the reasoning behind your design of the experiment.

12. **a.** Prove that if the $m \times n$ matrix A $(m \geq n)$ is of full rank, then the CGS Algorithm will produce an orthogonal Q and an upper triangular R with positive entries on the main diagonal.

    b. Prove that if the $m \times n$ matrix A $(m \geq n)$ is of full rank, then the MGS Algorithm will produce an orthogonal Q and an upper triangular R with positive entries on the main diagonal.

13. **a.** If the $m \times n$ matrix A $(m \leq n)$ is of full rank, then we define its Moore-Penrose pseudo-inverse to be the square matrix $A^+ = A^T(AA^T)^{-1}$. Show that the least squares solution of $Ax = b$ is given by $x = A^+b$ (when the underdetermined system is consistent, its least squares solution is the one for which $\|x\|$ is smallest).

    b. Repeat Problem 8 parts (b)–(g) for this case, if possible. Not all cases will be true! For example, A^+A need not equal I, though $AA^+A = A$ and $A^+AA^+ = A^+$.

14. Explain how the QR decomposition may be used to find an orthonormal basis for the null space of a matrix A.

15. Develop a triangular triangularization approach to the LU decomposition that uses column reduction rather than row reduction (as would be desirable if matrices were stored in column-major form).

2.9 The Singular Value Decomposition

SVD

We have considered two principal techniques for solving $Ax = b$: the LU decomposition and its variants, and the QR decomposition. In the next chapter we discuss iterative methods for this problem. But there is one other decomposition in common use: the **singular value decomposition (SVD)**

$$A = U\Sigma V^T \tag{2.31}$$

of an $m \times n$ matrix A. Here U is an $m \times m$ orthogonal matrix, V is an $n \times n$ orthogonal matrix, and Σ is an $m \times n$ matrix that has nonzero entries only on its main diagonal

$$
\begin{bmatrix}
X & X & X \\
X & X & X \\
X & X & X \\
X & X & X \\
X & X & X
\end{bmatrix}
=
\begin{bmatrix}
X & X & X & X & X \\
X & X & X & X & X \\
X & X & X & X & X \\
X & X & X & X & X \\
X & X & X & X & X
\end{bmatrix}
\begin{bmatrix}
X & 0 & 0 \\
0 & X & 0 \\
0 & 0 & X \\
0 & 0 & 0 \\
0 & 0 & 0
\end{bmatrix}
\begin{bmatrix}
X & X & X \\
X & X & X \\
X & X & X
\end{bmatrix}
$$

(a 5×3 example). The diagonal entries of Σ are called the **singular values** of A and are necessarily nonnegative. The singular values are denoted

$$\sigma_i = \Sigma_{ii}$$

and are ordered so that $\sigma_1 \geq \sigma_2 \geq \cdots \geq \sigma_p$ (where there are $p = \min(m, n)$ singular values). Every matrix has a singular value decomposition. The singular value decomposition occurs in many applications, though we are able to present only a brief overview of its use here.

It is a fact that the nonzero singular values of A are the square roots of the nonzero eigenvalues of AA^T, which are the same as the nonzero eigenvalues of $A^T A$. There are exactly $r = \text{rank}(A)$ positive singular values.

Suppose that A is square and has full rank. Then if $Ax = b$, we have

$$U \Sigma V^T x = b$$
$$U^T U \Sigma V^T x = U^T b$$
$$\Sigma V^T x = U^T b$$
$$V^T x = \Sigma^{-1} U^T b$$
$$V V^T x = V \Sigma^{-1} U^T b$$
$$x = V \Sigma^{-1} U^T b$$

(since $U^T U = I$, $V V^T = I$ by orthogonality). If A has full rank, all of its eigenvalues are nonzero, and therefore all of its singular values are nonzero as well, so the square diagonal matrix Σ is nonsingular and Σ^{-1} is trivial to compute. Hence if we can compute the SVD accurately, then we can solve $Ax = b$ very efficiently.

Similarly, consider the problem of finding the least squares solution of the overdetermined linear system $Ax = b$. The least squares solution of $Ax = b$ is the solution of $A^T Ax = A^T b$ (see Section 2.6), that is, the solution of

$$(U \Sigma V^T)^T U \Sigma V^T x = (U \Sigma V^T)^T b$$
$$V \Sigma^T U^T U \Sigma V^T x = V \Sigma^T U^T b$$
$$V \Sigma^T \Sigma V^T x = V \Sigma^T U^T b$$
$$V^T V \Sigma^T \Sigma V^T x = V^T V \Sigma^T U^T b \qquad (2.32)$$
$$\Sigma^T \Sigma V^T x = \Sigma^T U^T b$$
$$\Sigma V^T x = U^T b$$
$$V^T x = \Sigma^{-1} U^T b$$
$$x = V \Sigma^{-1} U^T b$$

(some additional justification is needed to remove the factor Σ^T in going from $\Sigma^T \Sigma V^T x = \Sigma^T U^T b$ to $\Sigma V^T x = U^T b$). This is the same formal solution that we found for the linear system $Ax = b$, but recall that A is no longer a square matrix.

One advantage of the SVD is clear: We can efficiently compute the (least squares) solution $x = V \Sigma^{-1} U^T b$ once the SVD is known. In addition, since the condition number of an orthogonal matrix is always unity, we can do so very accurately.

LU, QR, and SVD
Unfortunately, when m and n are of similar size, the SVD is significantly more expensive to compute than the QR factorization (if $m \gg n$ then the work is comparable),

and the QR factorization in turn is more expensive to compute than the LU decomposition. If m and n are equal, then solving a least squares problem by the SVD is about an order of magnitude more costly than using the QR factorization. For many applications the LU decomposition has perfectly acceptable accuracy, but for least squares problems it is generally advisable to use the QR factorization. When a least squares problem is known to be a difficult[13] one, using the SVD is probably justified. (Recall that the condition number for solving $A^T A x = A^T b$ is roughly the square of that for solving $Ax = b$ so these problems require extra care.) As always, the choice of decomposition method depends on the user's needs as well as available hardware and software.

We do not present the details of computing the SVD. Many packages will compute the **reduced singular value decomposition** $A = U_1 \Sigma_1 V^T$ with U_1 an $m \times n$ matrix with orthonormal columns, V an $n \times n$ matrix with orthonormal columns, and Σ_1 a diagonal $n \times n$ matrix. (The SVD in Eq. (2.31) is called the **full singular value decomposition.**) The reduced SVD removes the zero rows at the bottom of Σ, if any, as they do not affect any computations.

We briefly mention a few interesting facts about the SVD: If $r = \text{rank}(A)$ is positive, then the first r columns of U form a basis for the column space of A and the first r columns of V form a basis for the row space of A. The Frobenius norm of a square matrix A is equal to $\sqrt{\sigma_1^2 + \cdots + \sigma_p^2}$, and the spectral norm is given by $\|A\|_2 = \sigma_1$ (the largest singular value of A). These results are explored further in Additional Problems 2.9.

The SVD is important in many more applications, including finding the rank of a matrix, improving the conditioning of an ill-conditioned matrix, information retrieval by search engines, where the matrices may be on the order of millions by millions, analyzing genetic data, image processing, and many others. However, exploring them would require additional material from linear algebra, so we focus instead on gaining facility with using the SVD in MATLAB.

PROBLEMS 2.9

1. Find an SVD of I_4. Is it unique?

2. What matrix has $U = [1/\sqrt{2}\ 0\ 1/\sqrt{2}; 0\ 1\ 0; 1/\sqrt{2}\ 0 -1/\sqrt{2}]$, $V = [1/\sqrt{2} -1/\sqrt{2}; 1/\sqrt{2}\ 1/\sqrt{2}]$, and $\Sigma = [2\ 0; 0\ 1; 0\ 0]$ as the factors in its SVD? What are its singular values? What is its rank?

3. Carefully justify the derivation in Eq. (2.32). Pay attention to the sizes of the matrices involved.

4. Prove that the rank of a matrix is equal to the number of nonzero singular values it has.

5. Prove that the nonzero singular values of A are the square roots of the nonzero eigenvalues of AA^T and of $A^T A$.

MATLAB 2.9

The MATLAB command for computing the SVD of a matrix is `[U,S,V]=svd(A)`, which returns the SVD factors U, Σ, and V. The command `[U,S,V]=svd(A,0)` gives the reduced SVD of A. Note that the U of the SVD is different from the U of the LU decomposition.

---

[13] Here difficult generally means that A is rank-deficient or nearly so.

Let's solve a linear least squares problem using the SVD. We'll use a 100×10 matrix (100 equations in 10 unknowns). If you have flops, you might also look at the amount of computation effort required. Enter:

```
» A=rand([100 10]);
» b=rand([100 1]);
» [U,S,V]=svd(A);
» x=V*(S\(U'*b));           %Solution.
» norm(A*x-b)               %Residual.
» [U0,S0,V0]=svd(A,0);
» x0=V0*(S0\(U0'*b));       %Solution.
» norm(A*x0-b)             %Residual.
```

Let's check the SVD itself. Enter:

```
» norm(A-U*S*V')
```

to check how well USV^T reconstructs A. Now let's compare the three methods (LU, QR, SVD) on a square system. Enter:

```
» A=gallery('chebvand',1:12);
» cond(A)
» x=ones([12 1]);
» b=A*x;
» norm(b-A*x)          %Check.
```

This last is worth checking because there is some error in computing Ax, and it is worse for an ill-conditioned matrix. Enter:

```
» [L,U1]=lu(A);
» norm(A-L*U1)
» [Q,R]=qr(A);
» norm(A-Q*R)
» [U2,S,V]=svd(A);
» norm(A-U2*S*V')
```

None of the reconstructed matrices are very good approximations, though the LU decomposition is noticeably better. Let's solve $Ax = b$. Enter:

```
» xlu=U1\(L\b);
» norm(x-xlu)
» xqr=R\Q'*b;
» norm(x-xqr)
» xsvd=V*inv(S)*U2'*b;
» norm(x-xsvd)
```

All of these answers are very bad, but we are using a matrix with a condition number on the order of 10^{18} and expect to lose 18 out of a possible 16 digits of accuracy. The SVD gives the least erroneous results. Let's try a different example. Enter:

```
» A=gallery('chebvand',1:8);
» cond(A)
» x=ones([8 1]);
» b=A*x;
» [L,U1]=lu(A);
» [Q,R]=qr(A);
» [U2,S,V]=svd(A);
» xlu=U1\(L\b);
» xqr=R\Q'*b;
» xsvd=V*inv(S)*U2'*b;
» norm(x-xlu)
» norm(x-xqr)
» norm(x-xsvd)
```

Now the LU decomposition gives an absolute error on the order of 10^8 while the QR and SVD approaches give errors on the order of 10^{-5} (the SVD error is slightly smaller). Now enter:

```
» A=A*A;
» format long
```

and repeat this experiment. The errors are worse, as expected ($\kappa(A^2) \approx \kappa(A)^2$) but QR and SVD still give better results. Once again the SVD error is smaller, though only slightly. In any individual case it's quite possible for any of the three methods to give superior results, but as a rule the SVD is best for difficult systems.

One of the many computational applications of the SVD is in finding the rank of a matrix numerically. (Defining the numerical rank of a matrix is an issue in itself.) Enter:

```
» help rank
```

to see that MATLAB computes the rank of a matrix A by finding its SVD and counting the number of singular values that are significantly greater than zero. For example, enter:

```
» rank(A)
» diag(S)       %Singular values of A.
» S1=S;S1(10,10)=0;diag(S1)
» A1=U2*S*V';
» rank(A1)
```

Setting a singular value to zero reduces the rank of the reconstructed matrix. This is used to produce lower-rank approximations of A.

ADDITIONAL PROBLEMS 2.9

6. If A is a 6×4 matrix, what are the sizes of U, Σ, and V in its full SVD? What are the sizes of U_1, Σ_1, and V in its reduced SVD?

7. a. Write a MATLAB program that computes the rank of a matrix by finding its SVD (use the MATLAB svd command) and finding the number of singular values that exceed a user-supplied tolerance.

b. Write a MATLAB program that computes the rank of a matrix by finding its QR decomposition (use the MATLAB qr command) and finding the number of diagonal entries of R having magnitudes that exceed a user-supplied tolerance.

c. Compare your programs on several test matrices. Can you explain why the SVD rather than the QR decomposition is used in practice?

8. Construct the matrix for fitting a degree 15 polynomial to $\sin(x)$ on 200 equally spaced nodes on $[0, 1]$. Solve for the coefficients using the LU decomposition, the QR decomposition, and the SVD. Give the residual errors.

9. Construct the matrix for fitting a degree 20 polynomial to $\sin(x)$ on 400 equally spaced nodes on $[0, 1]$. Solve for the coefficients using the LU decomposition, the QR decomposition, and the SVD. Give the residual errors. Comment.

10. Prove that $\det(A) = \pm \sigma_1 \cdots \sigma_p$.

11. a. Prove that if $r = \text{rank}(A)$ is positive, then the first r columns of U form a basis for the column space of A.

b. Prove that if $r = \text{rank}(A)$ is positive, then the first r columns of V form a basis for the row space of A.

12. Prove that the Frobenius norm of a square matrix A is equal to $\sqrt{\sigma_1^2 + \cdots + \sigma_p^2}$.

13. a. It is a fact that $\|A\|_2 = \sigma_1$ (the largest singular value of A). What is $\kappa(A)$ in terms of the singular values of A? What does this imply about the numerical significance of the sizes of the singular values of A? Demonstrate this by using the SVD to create matrices with large condition numbers.

b. Write a MATLAB program that computes the condition number of a matrix using the fact in part (a) and the svd command.

14. How could the SVD be used to find A^{-1}? Is this computationally practical?

15. a. It is a fact that $A = \sum_{i=1}^{i=r} \sigma_i u_i v_i^T$ where u_i and v_i are the columns of U and V, respectively. Verify this for three matrices.

b. Verify for three matrices that if $A_k = \sum_{i=1}^{i=k} \sigma_i u_i v_i^T$ $(k = 1, \ldots r)$ then $\|A - A_k\|$ is a monotonically decreasing function of k.

3 Iterative Methods

3.1 Jacobi and Gauss-Seidel Iteration

Direct Methods

I N THE PREVIOUS CHAPTER we discussed direct methods for solving linear systems. These are the methods of choice for small to moderate-sized problems. Computing the LU decomposition of an $n \times n$ matrix, for example, requires about $\frac{2}{3}n^3$ floating point operations. If $n = 100$, this is about 6.7×10^5 floating point operations, a task that takes well under a second to execute on a standard desktop computer. If $n = 1000$, however, this is about 6.7×10^8 flops, a task that takes considerably longer to finish (due to memory management issues in addition to the thousand-fold extra flops required). Since in practice matrices as large as tens of thousands by tens of thousands are common (in problems involving the numerical solution of partial differential equations such as in meteorology) and matrices as large as hundreds of thousands by hundreds of thousands are not uncommon (for example, applications involving the analysis of genetic data), more efficient methods are clearly needed.

We will have little to say about large dense matrices. If approximating such a matrix with a simpler matrix is not acceptable, then the computation will take a long time. Moving entries of the matrix from memory to the processor(s) will likely be more time-consuming than the actual computations.

Fortunately, in practice large matrices are commonly sparse. For large sparse matrices there are a number of iterative methods that—when used in combination with a smart storage system for the sparse matrix—can considerably reduce computation times. As a rule, direct methods are $O(n^3)$ and iterative methods are in the cases in which they are appropriate $O(n^2)$. The goal for computing with sparse matrices is always to get a method that is $O(N)$, where N is the number of nonzero entries in the matrix.

In this section we discuss two classical methods for the iterative solution of linear systems.

Matrix
Splittings

Consider a square linear system $Ax = b$. We seek an iteration of the form $x^{k+1} = F(x^k)$, where an initial guess $x^0 \in \mathbb{R}^n$ is given and F is simple to compute. One way to find such an iteration is based on additively decomposing A into its upper triangle, lower triangle, and diagonal parts, called a **matrix splitting:**

$$A = U + L + D \tag{3.1}$$

where U is a square matrix with the strict upper triangle of A in its upper triangle and is zero otherwise, L is a square matrix with the strict lower triangle of A in its lower triangle and is zero otherwise, and D is a diagonal matrix containing the main diagonal of A. For example,

$$\begin{pmatrix} 1 & 2 & 3 \\ 4 & 5 & 6 \\ 7 & 8 & 9 \end{pmatrix} = \begin{pmatrix} 0 & 2 & 3 \\ 0 & 0 & 6 \\ 0 & 0 & 0 \end{pmatrix} + \begin{pmatrix} 0 & 0 & 0 \\ 4 & 0 & 0 \\ 7 & 8 & 0 \end{pmatrix} + \begin{pmatrix} 1 & 0 & 0 \\ 0 & 5 & 0 \\ 0 & 0 & 9 \end{pmatrix}$$

$$= U + L + D$$

is a splitting of the form of Eq. (3.1). Now we can write

$$Ax = b$$

$$(U + L + D)x = b \tag{3.2}$$

$$Dx = -(U + L)x + b$$

$$x = -D^{-1}(U + L)x + D^{-1}b$$

(if no diagonal element of A is zero, which we assume throughout this section). This equation has the form $x = g(x)$ of a fixed point iteration; perhaps

$$x^{k+1} = -D^{-1}(U + L)x^k + D^{-1}b \tag{3.3}$$

Jacobi Iteration

will be a useful iteration. Indeed, Eq. (3.3) is called **Jacobi iteration.** Note that D is diagonal so the computation of D^{-1} is trivial.

Example 3.1.1

Let's apply Jacobi iteration to the system $Ax = (3, -1, 4)^T$ with the matrix $A = [4\ 2\ 1; 1\ 3\ 1; 1\ 1\ 4]$. From Eq. (3.2) we form $Dx = -(U + L)x + b$, which is equivalent to moving the nondiagonal entries to the RHS; that is,

$$4x_1 + 2x_2 + x_3 = 3$$

$$x_1 + 3x_2 + x_3 = -1$$

$$x_1 + x_2 + 4x_3 = 4$$

becomes

$$4x_1 = 3 - 2x_2 - x_3$$

$$3x_2 = -1 - x_1 - x_3$$

$$4x_3 = 4 - x_1 - x_2$$

corresponding to the matrix-vector form $Dx = -(U + L)x + b$. We obtain Eq. (3.3)

$$x_1^{k+1} = \frac{1}{4}\left(3 - 2x_2^k - x_3^k\right)$$

$$x_2^{k+1} = \frac{1}{3}\left(-1 - x_1^k - x_3^k\right)$$

$$x_3^{k+1} = \frac{1}{4}\left(4 - x_1^k - x_2^k\right)$$

by dividing out the diagonal entries and iterating. Let's take $x^0 = (0, 0, 0)^T$ as the initial guess. Then we have

$$x_1^1 = \frac{1}{4}(3 - 2 \cdot 0 - 0)$$

$$= \frac{3}{4}$$

$$x_2^1 = \frac{1}{3}(-1 - 0 - 0)$$

$$= -\frac{1}{3}$$

$$x_3^1 = \frac{1}{4}(4 - 0 - 0)$$

$$= 1$$

$$x_1^2 = \frac{1}{4}\left(3 - 2 \cdot \frac{-1}{3} - 1\right)$$

$$\doteq 0.6667$$

$$x_2^2 = \frac{1}{3}\left(-1 - \frac{3}{4} - 1\right)$$

$$\doteq -0.9167$$

$$x_3^2 = \frac{1}{4}\left(4 - \frac{3}{4} - \frac{-1}{3}\right)$$

$$\doteq 0.8958$$

which seems to be slowly converging to the true solution $x_1 = 1$, $x_2 = -1$, $x_3 = 1$. The method does not recognize that x_3^1 is exact, but notice that the absolute errors for these estimates are $\alpha_1 = \|x^1 - x\| \doteq .7120$ and $\alpha_2 = \|x^2 - x\| \doteq .3590$, so the method is certainly reducing the overall error. We would continue iterating until some convergence criterion was met. ■

The formula for Jacobi iteration may also be written in component form. If x_i^k is used to denote the ith component of x^k, then Jacobi iteration corresponds to solving equation

i for the diagonal entry x_i,

$$a_{ii}x_i = b_i - \sum_{\substack{j=1 \\ j \neq i}}^{n} a_{ij}x_j$$

$$x_i = \frac{b_i}{a_{ii}} - \frac{1}{a_{ii}} \sum_{\substack{j=1 \\ j \neq i}}^{n} a_{ij}x_j$$

and then iterating

$$x_i^{k+1} = \frac{b_i}{a_{ii}} - \frac{1}{a_{ii}} \sum_{\substack{j=1 \\ j \neq i}}^{n} a_{ij}x_j^k$$

until some convergence criterion is met. The convergence criterion used for Jacobi iteration may be that the absolute error, relative error, or residual error

$$r_k = \|b - Ax_k\|$$

be less than some tolerance. We will use the approximate relative error

$$\rho_k = \frac{\|x^k - x^{k-1}\|}{\|x^k\|}$$

for the convergence criterion. Often the tolerance τ is set as some small percentage of $\|x^0\|$ (but not smaller than some $\tau_\alpha > 0$; see Section 1.8).

We now ask the standard questions: Does Jacobi iteration (Eq. (3.3)) converge for all matrices and all initial guesses x^0? How rapidly does it converge? Is the method stable? And can we accelerate the convergence?

Analysis   Experience quickly shows that Jacobi iteration can diverge for some initial guesses for some matrices. In order to explore the convergence properties of this method, let's write Eq. (3.3) as

$$x^{k+1} = Mx^k + \beta,$$

where the matrix $M = -D^{-1}(U + L)$ and vector $\beta = D^{-1}b$ are known. Any iteration that can be written in the form $x^{k+1} = Mx^k + \beta$ is said to be a **stationary method** (since M and β do not depend on k). Note that

$$\|x^{k+1}\| = \|Mx^k + \beta\|$$

$$\leq \|M\|\|x^k\| + \|\beta\|$$

for the natural norm induced by the vector norm (see Section 2.5). So

$$\|x^{k+1}\| \leq \|M\| \|x^k\| + \|\beta\|$$

$$\leq \|M\| (\|M\| \|x^{k-1}\| + \|\beta\|) + \|\beta\|$$

$$= \|M\|^2 \|x^{k-1}\| + \|M\| \|\beta\| + \|\beta\|$$

$$= \|M\|^2 \, \|x^{k-1}\| + (\|M\| + 1) \, \|\beta\|$$

$$\leq \|M\|^2 \, (\|M\| \, \|x^{k-2}\| + \|\beta\|) + (\|M\| + 1) \, \|\beta\|$$

$$= \|M\|^3 \, \|x^{k-2}\| + (\|M\|^2 + \|M\| + 1) \, \|\beta\|$$

$$\vdots$$

$$\leq \|M\|^{k+1} \, \|x^0\| + (\|M\|^k + \cdots + \|M\| + 1) \, \|\beta\|$$

and so if $\|M\| < 1$, then

$$\|x^{k+1}\| \leq \|M\|^{k+1} \, \|x^0\| + \frac{1}{1 - \|M\|} \, \|\beta\| \tag{3.4}$$

since $\|M\|^k + \cdots + \|M\| + 1$ is a partial sum of the geometric series

$$\sum_{k=0}^{\infty} \|M\|^k = \frac{1}{1 - \|M\|}. \tag{3.5}$$

Because the term $\|M\|^{k+1} \to 0$ as $k \to \infty$ if $\|M\| < 1$, we suspect from Eq. (3.4) that $\|M\| < 1$ will give convergence. While this is true, there is a more precise result. Recall from Section 2.5 that the spectral radius of a matrix M is

$$\rho(M) = \max_{i=1}^{n}(|\lambda_i|),$$

where $\lambda_1, \ldots, \lambda_n$ are the eigenvalues of M. It is a fact that if $\rho(M) < 1$ then M is **convergent:** that is, $M^k \to 0$ (the zero matrix) as $k \to \infty$, and also

$$\sum_{k=0}^{\infty} M^k = (I - M)^{-1}$$

(an analogue of Eq. (3.5)). The quantity $(I - M)^{-1}$ is called the **resolvent** of M; note that M itself need not be invertible for the resolvent to exist. Now, consider again the linear fixed point iteration

$$x^{k+1} = Mx^k + \beta$$

$$= M(Mx^{k-1} + \beta) + \beta$$

$$= M^2 x^{k-1} + (M + I)\beta$$

$$= M^2(Mx^{k-2} + \beta) + (M + I)\beta$$

$$= M^3 x^{k-2} + (M^2 + M + I)\beta$$

$$\vdots$$

$$= M^{k+1} x^0 + (M^k + \cdots + M + I)\beta.$$

So, if M is convergent, we have

$$\lim_{k \to \infty} x^{k+1} = \lim_{k \to \infty} (M^{k+1}x^0 + (M^k + \cdots + M + I)\beta)$$

$$= 0 + (I - M)^{-1}\beta$$

$$= (I - M)^{-1}\beta$$

for any initial guess x^0. In fact, the iteration $x^{k+1} = Mx^k + \beta$ converges to this unique value for every initial guess if and only if M is convergent. (If $\rho(M) \geq 1$, the method can still converge for some x^0, in principle, but not for every x^0. For such an M the method is unstable however.) Indeed, $x = (I - M)^{-1}\beta$ is a fixed point of the method, for

$$Mx + \beta = M(I - M)^{-1}\beta + \beta$$

$$= M \sum_{k=0}^{\infty} M^k \beta + \beta$$

$$= \sum_{k=0}^{\infty} M^{k+1}\beta + \beta$$

$$= \sum_{k=1}^{\infty} M^k \beta + I\beta$$

$$= \sum_{k=0}^{\infty} M^k \beta$$

$$= (I - M)^{-1}\beta$$

$$= x$$

(as $M^0 = I$ by convention). In summary, if M is convergent, then $x = Mx + \beta$ has a unique fixed point at $x = (I - M)^{-1}\beta$, and fixed point iteration always converges to this value.

Note the similarlity to the fixed point analysis we performed on Newton's method in Section 1.4. Here the requirement that $\rho(M) < 1$ replaces the requirement that $|g'(x)| < 1$. Indeed, M is the derivative of the iteration function $Mx + \beta$ with respect to x.

Hence, Jacobi iteration, or any other matrix splitting technique, will converge if the matrix $A = U + L + D$ leads to an M that is a convergent matrix. Since the iteration will converge for *any* initial guess, stability is immediate (a perturbation of a given x^k will necessarily perturb it to another value from which the method converges). The speed of convergence can be shown to be like $\rho(M)^k$, that is,

$$\frac{\left\| x^k - x \right\|}{\left\| x^0 - x \right\|} = O(\rho(M)^k)$$

as $k \to \infty$. (This is linear convergence.) Hence a small spectral radius is desirable, and if $\rho(M)$ is near unity, then we must expect very slow convergence.

Diagonal
Dominance

Clearly, A is not always such that $M = -D^{-1}(U + L)$ is convergent. However, there is an important class of matrices for which this is always the case. We say that a square matrix A is **diagonally dominant** if

$$|a_{ii}| \geq \sum_{\substack{j=1 \\ j \neq i}}^{n} |a_{ij}|$$

$(i = 1, \ldots, n)$, that is, if the diagonal element of each row exceeds in absolute value the sum of the absolute values of all other entries in that row. If the inequality is strict we say that the matrix is **strictly diagonally dominant,** and if it is weak we say that the matrix is **weakly diagonally dominant.** If A is strictly diagonally dominant, then $M = -D^{-1}(U + L)$ is convergent and Jacobi iteration will converge. In fact, the method will frequently converge if A is weakly diagonally dominant. Diagonally dominant matrices occur frequently in applications involving the numerical solution of partial differential equations.

If A is not diagonally dominant, then in principle we must check $\rho(M)$ to see if the method is applicable. This is usually too expensive, however, and so we use the fact that

$$\rho(M) \leq \|M\|$$

for any natural norm. If $\|M\| < 1$ in some natural norm, then M is convergent and we may use Jacobi iteration.

Example 3.1.2   The matrix $A = [1\ 1\ 3; 1\ 3\ 1; 3\ 1\ 1]$ is not strictly diagonally dominant, but interchanging the first and last rows gives $A_1 = [3\ 1\ 1; 1\ 3\ 1; 1\ 1\ 3]$ which is strictly diagonally dominant. Jacobi iteration will converge if applied to A_1.

The matrix $M = [0.3\ 0.2\ 0.1; 0.2\ 0.2\ -0.2; 0.4\ -0.5\ 0]$ has Frobenius norm (see Section 2.5) $\|M\| = \sqrt{.3^2 + .2^2 + \cdots + (-.5)^2 + 0^2} \doteq .8185$ so $\rho(M) < 1$ (in fact, $\rho(M) \doteq .4531$). Hence, iteration of $x^{k+1} = Mx^k + c$ will converge for any c and any x^0.   ■

The easiest norm to use in checking whether $\|M\| < 1$ is the matrix norm that is induced by the l_∞ vector norm (see Section 2.5),

$$\|M\|_\rho = \max_{i=1}^{n} \left\{ \sum_{j=1}^{n} |m_{ij}| \right\}$$

that is, the maximum row sum of M. This matrix norm is called the **max norm** or **inf norm.** The spectral norm $\|M\|_s$ will be closer to $\rho(M)$ but is harder to compute. For the matrix M in Example 3.1.2, the row sums are 0.6, 0.6, and 0.9, so $\|M\| = .9$. This is larger than the Frobenius norm $\|A\|_F \doteq .8185$ and the spectral norm $\|A\|_s \doteq .6419$, and all exceed the spectral radius $\rho(M) \doteq .4531$, as they must. Basing our estimate only on the max norm, we estimate that the error decreases to about 90% of its previous level each iteration; basing it on the Frobenius norm, about 82%; on the spectral norm, about 64%. The spectral radius gives the correct value, about 45%. The spectral radius may be estimated if needed.

If $\rho(M)$ is near unity, convergence will be slow. Can we speed it up? One possibility arises from considering again what we did in Example 3.1.1.

Example 3.1.3 Consider again the system $Ax = (3, -1, 4)^T$ with the matrix $A = [4\ 2\ 1; 1\ 3\ 1; 1\ 1\ 4]$. We have from Eq. (3.3)

$$x_1^{k+1} = \frac{1}{4}\left(3 - 2x_2^k - x_3^k\right)$$

$$x_2^{k+1} = \frac{1}{3}\left(-1 - x_1^k - x_3^k\right)$$

$$x_3^{k+1} = \frac{1}{4}\left(4 - x_1^k - x_2^k\right),$$

and we again take $x^0 = (0, 0, 0)^T$ as the initial guess. Then we have

$$x_1^1 = \frac{1}{4}(3 - 2\cdot 0 - 0)$$

$$= \frac{3}{4}$$

$$x_2^1 = \frac{1}{3}\left(-1 - x_1^0 - x_3^0\right).$$

It may now occur to us that we have presumably improved the estimate of the true value of x_1, namely x_1^1, and we may wish to use this better estimate in place of x_1^0. Let's do that:

$$x_2^1 = \frac{1}{3}\left(-1 - x_1^1 - x_3^0\right)$$

$$= \frac{1}{3}\left(-1 - \frac{3}{4} - 0\right)$$

$$= -\frac{7}{12},$$

which is a better estimate of $x_2 = -1$ than the previous $x_2^1 = -1/3$. Let's use the same trick for x_3^1:

$$x_3^1 = \frac{1}{4}\left(4 - x_1^1 - x_2^1\right)$$

$$\frac{1}{4}\left(4 - \frac{3}{4} - \frac{-7}{12}\right)$$

$$= \frac{23}{24}$$

$$\doteq 0.9583$$

which is close to the previous estimate of $3/4$. Continuing in this way, using new estimates as soon as they become available, we have

$$x_1^2 = \frac{1}{4}\left(3 - 2 \cdot \frac{-7}{12} - \frac{23}{24}\right)$$

$$\doteq 0.8021$$

$$x_2^2 = \frac{1}{3}\left(-1 - 0.8021 - \frac{23}{24}\right)$$

$$\doteq -0.9201$$

$$x_3^2 = \frac{1}{4}(4 - 0.8021 - -0.9201)$$

$$\doteq 1.0295,$$

which is superior to the estimate $x^2 = (0.7292, -0.8333, 0.6458)^T$ from Jacobi iteration in every component (recall that the solution is $x = (1, -1, 1)^T$).   ■

Gauss-Seidel Iteration

The method of Example 3.1.3 is referred to as **Gauss-Seidel iteration.** It simply uses newer information as soon as it becomes available (a simple and widely applicable idea). Gauss-Seidel iteration corresponds to the matrix splitting

$$Ax = b$$

$$(U + L + D)x = b$$

$$(L + D)x = -Ux + b$$

$$x = -(L + D)^{-1}Ux + (L + D)^{-1}b$$

(i.e., $M = -(L + D)^{-1}U$ if $(L + D)^{-1}$ exists), giving the iteration

$$x^{k+1} = -(L + D)^{-1}Ux^k + (L + D)^{-1}b. \tag{3.6}$$

Of course, we would not form $(L + D)^{-1}$ explicitly but would instead proceed as in Example 3.1.3. In component form,

$$x_i^{k+1} = \frac{b_i}{a_{ii}} - \frac{1}{a_{ii}}\sum_{j=1}^{i-1}a_{ij}x_j^{k+1} - \frac{1}{a_{ii}}\sum_{j=i+1}^{n}a_{ij}x_j^k,$$

where by convention an empty sum is zero. Again, we assume throughout that a_{ii} is nonzero ($i = 1, \ldots, n$).

Comparison

Typically, if Jacobi iteration converges for a given matrix A, then Gauss-Seidel iteration also converges and is faster (that is, the spectral radius of its iteration matrix M is smaller). However, this is not always the case. If A is strictly diagonally dominant, then Gauss-Seidel iteration will converge for any initial guess. There are block forms of both algorithms.

Gauss-Seidel iteration is generally superior to Jacobi iteration. One exception might be on a parallel machine: If $x \in \mathbb{R}^n$ and there are n processors available, Jacobi iteration can be performed very efficiently (processor i computes the updated x_i), whereas Gauss-Seidel does not gain much benefit. However, the number p of processors is usually much less than n, so the acceleration is not as great as indicated. In that case we might have each processor compute n/p of the entries of x using the idea of Gauss-Seidel iteration (that is, making use of any updated variables available to it) but might or might not try to pass updated values between processors. There are a number of strategies in common use for performing Gauss-Seidel iteration on a parallel machine.

Note that the particular iterates in Jacobi or Gauss-Seidel iteration depend on the ordering of the unknowns. If we write the same linear system in a different order we generate a different Jacobi or Gauss-Seidel sequence.

For many years, these methods were used to solve large linear systems arising from the discretization of partial differential equations, among other applications. Today, however, the Jacobi and Gauss-Seidel iterations are used most often in conjunction with another iterative method, such as the technique that we discuss in Section 3.3.

PROBLEMS 3.1

1. **a.** Perform another three iterations of the method in Example 3.1.1. Compute the relative error of your answer.

   b. Perform another three iterations of the method in Example 3.1.3. Compute the relative error of your answer.

2. **a.** Find the spectral radius of the Jacobi iteration matrix for Example 3.1.1, and use it to estimate the size of the error after 5 iterations. Compare this to the estimate found by using the max, Frobenius, and spectral norms.

   b. Find the spectral radius of the Gauss-Seidel iteration matrix for Example 3.1.3, and use it to estimate the size of the error after 5 iterations. Compare this to the estimate found by using the max, Frobenius, and spectral norms.

   c. Compare your estimates with the results from Problems 1(a) and (b).

3. **a.** Prove that Jacobi iteration must converge for a strictly diagonally dominant matrix. (*Hint:* Show that $\|M\| < 1$ for some convenient norm.)

   b. Prove that Gauss-Seidel iteration must converge for a strictly diagonally dominant matrix.

4. **a.** Verify that Eq. (3.6) is equivalent to the scalar form of Gauss-Seidel iteration as described in Example 3.1.3.

   b. Jacobi iteration is also known as the **method of simultaneous displacements,** while Gauss-Seidel iteration is also known as the **method of successive displacements.** Why are these descriptions appropriate?

5. **a.** Prove that $\rho(A) \leq \|A\|$ for any natural matrix norm.

   b. Show that if $\rho(M) < 1$, then the resolvent $(I - M)^{-1}$ of M exists.

   c. Show that the Gauss-Seidel matrix $-(L + D)^{-1}U$ must be singular. Is this also true of the Jacobi iteration matrix?

MATLAB 3.1

In principle we could implement Jacobi iteration using Eq. (3.3), $x^{k+1} = -D^{-1}(U + L)x^k + D^{-1}b$, and Gauss-Seidel iteration using Eq. (3.6), $x^{k+1} = -(L + D)^{-1}Ux^k + (L + D)^{-1}b$, but because n is generally large in these applications solving even the triangular system $(L + D)x^{k+1} = -Ux^k + b$ for Gauss-Seidel iteration may be too time consuming. In fact, it is often the case that we avoid ever forming A, L, U, or D explicitly, owing to memory concerns and the fact that A is typically sparse. Instead we write a program that returns selected entries of A or that computes Ax (given x). We then implement the updates as separate formulas for $x_1^{k+1}, \ldots, x_n^{k+1}$.

For convenience, however, let us use the matrix forms for these iterations here. Enter:

```
» A=4*eye(10);for i=2:9;A(i,[i-1 i+1])=[1 1];end
» A(10,1)=1;A(1,10)=1;A(1,2)=1;A(10,9)=1
```

Matrices like this occur frequently in applications involving partial differential equations. Enter:

```
» D=diag(diag(A));L=tril(A,-1);U=triu(A,1);
```

to split the matrix. Let's compare the Jacobi and Gauss-Seidel iteration to solve $Ax = b$. Enter:

```
» b=6*ones([10 1]);
```

which makes the true solution a vector of all ones. Enter:

```
» x0j=zeros([10 1]);x0gs=x0j;        %Initial guess.
» xj=D\(-(U+L)*x0j+b);rj=b-A*xj      %Jacobi iteration.
» xgs=(L+D)\(-U*x0gs+b);rgs=b-A*xgs  %Gauss-Seidel iteration.
» norm(rj),norm(rgs)
» x0j=xj;x0gs=xgs;
```

Repeat this for several iterations. (Be sure to display the residual vectors each time.) Note that Gauss-Seidel iteration is reducing the residual more rapidly than Jacobi iteration; note also that `rgs` always has a zero component. Enter:

```
» alpha_j=norm(xj-ones([10 1]))
» alpha_gs=norm(xgs-ones([10 1]))
```

to compute the absolute error in the solution. Generally `alpha_gs` should be smaller than `alpha_j` but a smaller residual does not guarantee this; compare the residuals and absolute errors for several more iterations.

We can accelerate the convergence of Gauss-Seidel iteration using a technique similar to the damping used in Newton's method for systems (see Section 1.5). We rewrite Gauss-Seidel iteration as $x^{k+1} = x^k + \Delta^k$, where the vector Δ^k is the difference between x^k and x^{k+1}. Then we introduce a new parameter ϖ and write $x^{k+1} = x^k + \varpi \Delta^k$. If $\varpi = 1$ we have the standard Gauss-Seidel iteration method. If $0 < \varpi < 1$ we say that we are using **under-relaxation,** and if $\varpi > 1$ we say that we are using **over-relaxation;** the term **successive over-relaxation** (or **SOR**) is used to refer to both cases. Under-relaxation may be used in some cases to force Gauss-Seidel iteration to converge when it is diverging. More commonly over-relaxation ($\varpi > 1$) is used to accelerate convergence. The idea is that if Δ^k is a step from x^k toward x^{k+1}, then it's likely to be a step in the right direction so we should take a larger one. The right value of ϖ can be difficult to determine, but a good choice of ϖ can give much faster convergence. (A poor choice of ϖ may cause divergence.) The SOR method can be written in the form $x^{k+1} = Mx^k + c$, where $M = (D + \varpi L)^{-1}((1 - \varpi)D - \varpi U)$ and $c = \varpi (D + \varpi L)^{-1}b$.

For example, let's use SOR on the system we have been solving. Enter:

```
» x0gs=zeros([10 1]);x0SOR=x0gs;w=1.5;
» xgs=(L+D)\(-U*x0gs+b);rgs=b-A*xgs; %Gauss-Seidel iteration.
» xSOR=(D+w*L)\((1-w)*D-w*U)*x0SOR+w*(D+w*L)\b;rSOR=b-A*xSOR; %SOR.
```

```
» norm(rgs),norm(rSOR)
» x0gs=xgs;x0SOR=xSOR;
```

Repeat for several iterations. The SOR method seems to be inferior to the Gauss-Seidel iteration. Let's check the spectral radius of the two iteration matrices. Enter:

```
» max(abs(eig((L+D)\(-U))))             %Gauss-Seidel.
» max(abs(eig((D+w*L)\((1-w)*D-w*U))))   %SOR.
```

to find the values of $\rho(M)$ in each case. We have $\rho(M) \doteq .3093$ for Jacobi iteration and $\rho(M) \doteq .6135$ for SOR, so it is not surprising that SOR performed as it did. Enter:

```
» bestz=Inf;bestw=0;
» for w=1:.005:2;z=max(abs(eig((D+w*L)\((1-w)*D-w*U))));
»    if z<bestz;bestz=z;bestw=w;end;
» end
» bestw
```

to see that $\varpi \approx 1.07$ appears to be optimal in this case. Enter:

```
» w=1.07;
» max(abs(eig((D+w*L)\((1-w)*D-w*U))))
```

to see that $\rho(M) \doteq .2335$ for this choice of ϖ. This is a considerable improvement over Gauss-Seidel iteration. Compare Gauss-Seidel iteration to SOR with this value of ϖ.

It can be shown that a necessary condition for the SOR method to converge for all x^0 is that no diagonal entry of A be zero and $0 < \varpi < 2$. If A is positive definite and $0 < \varpi < 2$, then the SOR method will converge for any x^0. (As a special case, Gauss-Seidel iteration converges for a positive definite matrix as it corresponds to $\varpi = 1$.) In practice we would usually let $\varpi = \varpi_k$ with $\varpi_k \to 1$ as $k \to \infty$. The best value of ϖ can be determined for certain special matrices, but in general it must be found by trial and error. Finding a good ϖ is worthwhile when the same matrix is to be used repeatedly for different choices of b, which is a common occurrence.

ADDITIONAL PROBLEMS 3.1

6. Write a MATLAB program that performs the SOR method on a given system. The user should provide A, b, x^0, ϖ, and any additional parameters needed (such as tolerances), and the program should return an estimate of the solution.

7. a. Perform 5 iterations of Jacobi SOR on the system in Example 3.1.1 using $\varpi = 1.1, 1.3, 1.5$. Compare your results to your results from Problem 1(a).

b. Perform 5 iterations of Gauss-Seidel SOR on the system in Example 3.1.3 using $\varpi = 1.1, 1.3, 1.5$. Compare your results to your results from Problem 1(b).

8. Construct a chart that shows the advantage of a method with $\rho(M) = .3$ over a method with $\rho(M) = .5$.

9. a. Compute (by hand) the spectral, Frobenius, and max norms of the $n \times n$ identity matrix, and its spectral radius.

b. Compute (by hand) the spectral, Frobenius, and max norms of the matrix $A = [2\ 1; 1\ 2]$, and its spectral radius.

10. Let A be a 10×10 tridiagonal matrix with 4 on the main diagonal and -1 on the superdiagonal and subdiagonal, and let b be a vector of all ones. Solve $Ax = b$ to a relative error of 10^{-6} using Jacobi iteration,

Gauss-Seidel iteration, and SOR using an appropriate ϖ (determined by trial-and-error). Comment.

11. Generate 20 random 100×100 matrices and compare $\rho(M)$ for both Jacobi iteration and Gauss-Seidel iteration. (Use a script file to do this.) Comment.

12. **a.** Verify experimentally that $\rho(M) \geq |\varpi - 1|$ for SOR. Why does this imply that $0 < \varpi < 2$ is a necessary condition for convergence of SOR?

    b. If A is a positive definite tridiagonal matrix, then the optimal ϖ for SOR has $\rho(M) = \varpi - 1$. Verify this experimentally (as in MATLAB 3.1).

    c. Prove that if the main diagonal of A contains no zero entries, then $\rho(M) \geq |\varpi - 1|$ for the iteration matrix M of the SOR method.

13. Consider the formula $\sum_{k=0}^{\infty} M^k = (I - M)^{-1}$. Comment on the efficiency of using partial sums of this series to approximate the resolvent $(I - M)^{-1}$.

14. **a.** The simplest possible matrix splitting method for $Ax = b$ is the **Richardson iteration** $x^{k+1} = (I - A)x^k + b$. Under what conditions on A will it converge?

    b. Give a direct proof that $\|M\| < 1$ implies convergence of $x^{k+1} = Mx^k + c$ for any c and any x^0 by taking norms on both sides of $x^{k+1} - x = Mx^k + c - x$, where x is the solution. (*Hint*: Note

that $x = Mx + c$ and that $\alpha_k = \|x^k - x\|$ is the absolute error.)

15. **a.** A commonly occurring system of equations in the numerical study of heat flow takes the form $u_{ij} = \frac{1}{4}(u_{i-1,j} + u_{i+1,j} + u_{i,j-1} + u_{i,j+1})$ where the u_{ij} are the unknowns ($i = 1, \ldots n, j = 1, \ldots m$). Write this as a linear system in matrix form. Is the matrix sparse?

    b. This system could be reindexed $x_1 = u_{11}, x_2 = u_{12}, \ldots$, but it is convenient to retain the u_{ij}. Explain how the system could be solved by Jacobi or Gauss-Seidel iteration in place by treating the unknowns u_{ij} as a matrix and never forming the coefficient matrix of the system in part (a). Is this more efficient?

    c. A strategy for partially parallelizing the Gauss-Seidel iteration is **red-black Gauss-Seidel iteration,** where we imagine the entries u_{ij} with $i + j$ even to be "red" and the entries u_{ij} with $i + j$ odd to be "black" (imagine the U as a checker board). We compute u_{ij}^{k+1} from u_{ij}^k by first updating all red entries and then updating all black entries. Compare this to standard Gauss-Seidel iteration.

    d. Write a MATLAB program to perform red-black Gauss-Seidel iteration for this system. Test your program.

3.2 Sparsity

The iterative methods discussed in the previous section will be sufficiently fast for large matrices only if the matrices are sparse. One common type of sparse matrix is a tridiagonal matrix. Such a matrix is essentially composed of three vectors—the vector $d = (a_{ii})_{i=1}^{n}$ of diagonal elements, the vector $s = (a_{i+1,i})_{i=1}^{n-1}$ of subdiagonal elements, and the vector $t = (a_{i,i+1})_{i=1}^{n-1}$ of superdiagonal elements:

$$A = \begin{pmatrix} d_{11} & t_{12} & & & & \\ s_{21} & d_{22} & t_{23} & & & \\ & s_{32} & d_{33} & t_{34} & & \\ & & s_{43} & d_{44} & t_{45} & \\ & & & s_{54} & d_{55} & t_{56} \\ & & & & s_{65} & d_{66} \end{pmatrix}.$$

A matrix such as this can have at most $(n - 1) + n + (n - 1) = 3n - 2$ nonzero entries, which is considerably fewer than the n^2 possible nonzero entries for a dense matrix. How can we realize storage and speed gains for a matrix like this?

For such a specialized case we could write a program that inputs a vector x and returns Ax, computed efficiently, and that operates similarly for other computations involving

A. But, what if the sparse matrix does not have a simple and recognizable structure? In the general case we might store a sparse matrix using three vectors: a vector r of row indices, a vector c of column indices, and a vector v of values. For example, for the unstructured sparse matrix

$$A = \begin{pmatrix} 8 & 7 & 0 & 0 & 0 & 8 \\ 0 & 0 & 0 & 0 & 0 & 7 \\ 0 & 9 & 0 & 0 & 8 & 0 \\ 8 & 0 & 7 & 0 & 0 & 7 \\ 0 & 0 & 0 & 9 & 0 & 8 \\ 0 & 7 & 9 & 0 & 0 & 0 \end{pmatrix}$$

we would have

$$r = (1, 1, 1, 2, 3, 3, 4, 4, 4, 5, 5, 6, 6)$$
$$c = (1, 2, 6, 6, 2, 5, 1, 3, 6, 4, 6, 2, 3) \qquad (3.7)$$
$$v = (8, 7, 8, 7, 9, 8, 8, 7, 7, 9, 8, 7, 9)$$

Coordinate Scheme

as our representation of the matrix, called the **coordinate scheme.** A representation such as this is called a **packed** form of the matrix, and the operation of putting it into such a form is called a **gather** operation.

To understand how the coordinate scheme encodes information about the matrix, look at the fourth entry in each vector in Eq. (3.7):

$$r = (1, 1, 1, 2, 3, 3, 4, 4, 4, 5, 5, 6, 6)$$
$$c = (1, 2, 6, 6, 2, 5, 1, 3, 6, 4, 6, 2, 3)$$
$$v = (8, 7, 8, 7, 9, 8, 8, 7, 7, 9, 8, 7, 9).$$

We see that the intersection of row 2 and column 6 corresponds to the value 7; that is, the $(2, 6)$ entry of the matrix is 7. Similarly, the $(5, 4)$ entry is 9. Any entry not listed above is taken to be zero. Since rows or columns consisting entirely of zeroes are possible, we need to store separately the total number of rows and of columns. We have listed the rows in order and the columns in order within the rows, but this is not essential. In fact, while it is obviously desirable to have the vectors in this form, it is undesirable to have to maintain this form if a new nonzero entry is added to the matrix.

In Eq. (3.7) each vector has 13 entries, so we are using 39 entries to store the nonzero entries of a 6×6 matrix. Such a matrix has only 36 entries (including the zeroes) and so this is not efficient.[1] However, suppose that matrix A was 1000×1000 and had only 3000 nonzero entries. In this case, the coordinate scheme uses nine thousand entries whereas storing the entire matrix requires one million entries. That is a considerable savings of memory and of time required to access it.

There are more efficient ways to store matrices in packed form. Most such schemes use linked lists. What form is best may depend on the application; for example, the coordinate scheme of Eq. (3.7) would be very inconvenient for an algorithm that accesses matrices

---

[1] Of course, 26 of the 39 entries here are indices and so must be small integers, which can be represented more compactly than a floating point number.

Using Sparse
Matrices

by columns, as a search of c would be required to find all entries in a given column. However for purposes of illustration we continue to use this form.

How do we perform operations involving sparse matrices (and vectors)? Suppose A is stored in packed form and we wish to compute Ax where x is also packed. (Packing a vector x requires only a single index vector.) We might first expand x into a full vector with zeroes in appropriate places, called a **scatter** operation. Then we could, for each row of A, multiply the nonzero entries of A, as found from the vector c, by the corresponding entries in x and sum them:

$$(Ax)_i = \sum v_j x_j \tag{3.8}$$

where the sum is over all indices j found in the vector c that correspond to row i (from r). After all rows have been processed, the resulting vector may be gathered into packed form. If it is convenient to access the packed form of A by columns, then it may be easier to use the formula

$$Ax = \sum_{i=1}^{n} x_i a_i \tag{3.9}$$

where a_i represents column i of A. (We are using the fact that a matrix-vector product is a linear combination of the columns of the matrix). Of course, we skip columns of A that are entirely full of zeroes.

While we benefit from manipulating many fewer entries, finding those entries requires searching, and indexing entries out of, several vectors. This is a relatively slow operation. We generally benefit from using the sparse form only for matrices that are significantly sparse; a common rule of thumb is that the matrix should have at least 95% null entries. Treating a matrix as a sparse matrix can make a considerable difference in speed of execution. If the technique is used appropriately speed of execution can be accelerated, but if it is used for a matrix that might better be treated as if it were full, execution can be slowed.

Much more could be said about the storage and manipulation of sparse matrices and vectors. We explore these issues further in MATLAB 3.2. Many times, however, you may be working in Fortran or C++. In this case, to perform an LU decomposition, say, you will generally need a routine that packs the matrix into sparse storage followed by a routine that operates on the matrix to find its LU factors in that particular packed form. You may then need to scatter the matrix back into unpacked form. Coordinating these steps may make for a programming challenge, even if the subprograms to perform the individual steps are available.

Recall that the goal for sparse matrices is always to get a method that is $O(N)$ where N is the number of nonzero entries in the matrix. Can we do this for tridiagonal matrices? Consider such a matrix T,

$$T = \begin{pmatrix} d_1 & t_1 & & & & \\ s_2 & d_2 & t_2 & & & \\ & s_3 & d_3 & t_3 & & \\ & & s_4 & d_4 & t_4 & \\ & & & s_5 & d_5 & t_5 \\ & & & & s_6 & d_6 \end{pmatrix},$$

where we have switched to singly indexing the entries. A simple scheme might be to store T as three vectors—its superdiagonal t, its diagonal d, and its subdiagonal s. Whether or not this is the best form to use to store T depends on what we intend to do with T.

Since there are about $3n$ nonzero entries, we expect that we should be able to solve $T_x = b$ in $O(N)$ operations, where $N \approx 3n$. One algorithm for doing so is:

Tridiagonal Solver:

1. Set $\varpi_1 = d_1, \rho_1 = t_1/\varpi_1, \varsigma_1 = b_1/\varpi_1$.

2. For $i = 2 : n$:

3. Set $\varpi_i = d_i - s_i\rho_{i-1}$.

4. Set $\rho_i = t_i/\varpi_i$.

5. Set $\varsigma_i = (b_i - s_i\varsigma_{i-1})/\varpi_i$.

6. End loop.

7. Set $x_n = \varsigma_n$.

8. For $k = (n-1) : -1 : 1$:

9. Set $x_k = \varsigma_k - \rho_k x_{k+1}$.

10. End loop.

This algorithm uses $8n - 6 \approx (8/3)N$ flops, which is certainly $O(N)$. It requires three temporary vectors (ϖ, v, and ς), in addition to the vectors s, d, t, b, and the solution x. Evidently, storing T as the three vectors s, d, and t is reasonable if solving the system $Tx = b$ is our goal.

PROBLEMS 3.2

1. Write the matrix $A = [1 \ 0 \ 1 \ 0; -1 \ 0 \ 0 \ 0; 0 \ 5 \ 0 \ 0; 0 \ 0 \ 0 \ -2]$ in packed form using the coordinate scheme. Is this an efficient representation of A?

2. If $r = (1, 1, 2, 2, 2, 3, 3, 4, 5, 5, 5, 6, 8)$, $c = (1, 3, 5, 6, 8, 2, 3, 1, 4, 6, 8, 6, 1)$, and $v = (-1, 7, 2, 3, 4, -5, 8, -7, -1, -5, 3, -4, 6)$ for a matrix stored in the coordinate scheme, what is a_{32}? What is a_{61}? What row of A contains the most nonzero entries? What column of A contains the most nonzero entries? Are there any zero rows or columns? What can you say about the size of A? Is this an efficient representation of A?

3. Write a detailed algorithm (pseudocode) for storing a matrix in packed form using the coordinate scheme.

4. a. Write a detailed algorithm (pseudocode) for performing the multiplication of a packed matrix times a packed vector using Eq. (3.8). Assume that there is a command such as the MATLAB `zeros` command that creates a full vector of all zeroes. Do not assume that the entries in the r vector are ordered.

b. Write a detailed algorithm (pseudocode) for performing the multiplication of a packed matrix times a packed vector using Eq. (3.9).

5. If entries of A, r, c, and v all require the same amount of memory, when is it storage-efficient to use the coordinate scheme? What if the entries of r and c require only half as much memory as an entry of v (or A)? What if the entries of r and c require only one-quarter as much memory as an entry of v (or A)?

MATLAB 3.2

Sometimes a routine for storing matrices in packed form must be written because a matrix with a very specialized structure is being manipulated. However, there are programs available (at www.netlib.org, for example) that are appropriate for general use. In MATLAB sparse matrix support is provided. For a listing of sparse matrix functions, enter:

```
» help sparfun
```

Enter:

```
» A=[1 0 2 0 0]'*[1 0 2 0 0]
» S=sparse(A)
» whos
```

To enter a full matrix A and then convert it to sparse form (S). Notice the difference in bytes used from the whos command. Note that MATLAB displays the matrix using the coordinate scheme, sorted by columns. In fact, we could have used that scheme to define it; enter:

```
» sparse([1 3 1 3],[1 1 3 3],[1 2 2 4])
```

(this has the form sparse(r,c,v) in the notation of Eq. (3.7)). To convert it back to full form, enter:

```
» full(ans)
```

Note that MATLAB has no way of knowing that this should be a 5×5 matrix padded by zero rows and columns.

There are a number of useful commands for sparse matrices (by which we mean matrices stored as though they were sparse, whether or not they are truly sparse). Enter:

```
» nnz(S)        %Number of nonzero entries in S.
» spy(S)        %Wilkinson diagram.
» nonzeros(S)   %The vector v of nonzero values.
» S(1,3)
» S(1,3)=0      %Note, r, c, v are updated automatically.
» S(1,3)=2;     %Reset this entry.
» issparse(S)   %Check for sparse storage.
» issparse(A)   %Check for sparse storage.
```

We are focusing on iterative methods in this chapter, but sparse matrix techniques are also used in conjunction with direct methods. Let's create a sparse arrowhead matrix and find its LU decomposition. Enter:

```
» clear all
» S=speye(10)
» full(S)
» S(1,1:10)=ones([1 10])
» S(1:10,1)=ones([10 1])
```

```
» full(S)
» [L,U]=lu(S)
» nnz(S),nnz(L),nnz(U)
» spy(S)
» spy(L)
» spy(U)
```

Note that the factors L and U are not truly sparse, although they are stored as though they are. Enter:

```
» full(U)
» whos
```

to see that there is still some advantage in storing U as though it were sparse. (The full form of U appears as ans.) This phenomenon is known as **fill-in**: A sparse matrix fills in the zero entries when Gaussian elimination is performed on it, so that sparsity is not preserved by Gaussian elimination.

To see that a simple row interchange operation can improve the degree of fill-in considerably, enter:

```
» S1=S([10,2:9,1],:)
» full(S1)
» [L1,U1]=lu(S1)
» nnz(S1)
» nnz(L1)
» nnz(U1)
» whos          %Compare L and L1, U and U1.
» spy(L)
» spy(U)
» spy(S1)
» spy(L1)
» spy(U1)
```

The reordering algorithms listed under help sparfun are used to find an ordering of the rows and columns of the matrix that will reduce fill-in, based on the pattern of the nonzero elements of the matrix. For example, enter:

```
» p=symrcm(S)    %New ordering.
» S2=S(p,p);
» [L2,U2]=lu(S2);
» whos           %Compare L1 and L2, U1 and U2.
```

to see that this ordering, generated by a method known as the **reverse Cuthill-McKee algorithm,** further reduces the amount of storage required by L. Of course, searching and reordering the matrix both cost something in terms of computing time.

If it is known that a sparse matrix will have new nonzero elements added to it at a later point, memory can be allocated for these future entries using the sparse command or the spalloc command. There are also sparse versions of rand (sprand), randn (sprandn), ones (spones), eye (speye), and other commands.

ADDITIONAL PROBLEMS 3.2

6. Compare the time and/or flops required for MATLAB to solve a 300×300 linear system stored in sparse form to the same system stored in full form when the matrix is approximately 0.1% full; 0.5% full; 1% full; 2% full; 5% full; and then in increments of 5 percentage points to 50% full. (You may wish to use the `sprandn` command to create the matrices.) Solve the systems using the slash command.

7. Consider the arrowhead matrix of the MATLAB subsection. What is the optimal reordering of the rows and columns for minimizing fill-in when Gaussian elimination is performed on it?

8. **a.** One strategy to decrease fill-in in the LU decomposition of a sparse matrix A is to use as a pivot that value a_{ij} in the active submatrix with the smallest **Markowitz count** $(r_i - 1)(c_j - 1)$, where r_i is the number of nonzero entries in row i, called the **row count,** and c_j is the number of nonzero entries in column j, called the **column count.** Write a MATLAB program that performs Gaussian elimination on a matrix with the pivots chosen to minimize the Markowitz count. Test your program. Does it decrease fill-in?

   b. In practice this method won't be stable since the size of the pivot isn't being taken into account. For this reason it is used in conjunction with **threshold pivoting,** where we insist that the new pivot not only minimize the Markowitz count but that it also have magnitude at least $\alpha \max(|a_{ij}|)$, where $0 < \alpha < 1$ and the max is taken over all entries in the active submatrix. In this way the new pivot may not be the largest possible pivot but if α is not too small, it should not amplify errors significantly. If no potential pivot satisfies both the thresholding and Markowitz count criteria, we allow the count to be larger than the minimal value. Modify your MATLAB program to use threshold pivoting. Test your program and comment.

   c. For a large matrix this method requires too much searching and comparing, and so it is common to use heuristics such as searching only for k rows and columns from the current position or taking the first entry that meets the thresholding requirement and has a suitably small Markowitz count. Suggest a modification along these general lines, and implement it as an option in your program. Test your program and comment.

9. **a.** Write a detailed algorithm (pseudocode) for updating r, c, and v to reflect the deletion of a single entry from the matrix.

   b. Write a detailed algorithm (pseudocode) for updating r, c, and v to reflect the deletion of a single row from the matrix.

10. **a.** Another scheme for storing a sparse matrix stores its elements as a sparse vector. The entries of A are read into the vector v by rows, first all entries of row 1, then all entries of row 2, and so on. A second vector c contains the column in which the corresponding entry in v occurs. A third vector l contains the length of the rows, in order; note that this vector may be shorter than c and v. Alternatively (or, for convenience, additionally) a vector s may be stored that indicates where in v each row starts. For example, if the first row of A has four nonzero entries and the second row has three, then $s(1) = 1$, $s(2) = 5$ (the values for row 2 start in entry 5 of v), $s(3) = 8$, and $l(1) = 4$, $l(2) = 3$. Rewrite the matrix of Eq. (3.7) and the arrowhead matrix of the MATLAB subsection in this format.

    b. What are the advantages and disadvantages of this scheme?

11. **a.** A common storage scheme for sparse matrices is the **row-linked list,** where we store the values in a vector v and the columns of those values in a vector c of the same length. In addition, a vector s stores the start of the ith row in its ith entry (compare Problem 10). However, rather than listing the entries in v by rows, we store a fourth vector λ of links. The vector λ has the same length as v, and $\lambda(i)$ points to the next entry in row i (or is zero to indicate the end of a row). For example, if $v = (-1, -2, -3, -4, -5)$, $c = (2, 3, 3, 1, 3)$, $s = (1, 3, 5)$, and $\lambda = (4, 0, 0, 2, 0)$, then we reconstruct the matrix A as follows: Row 1 starts at $s(1) = 1$, for which $c(1) = 2$ and $v(1) = -1$, so $a_{12} = -1$. The link points to $\lambda(1) = 4$, for which $c(4) = 1$ and $v(4) = -4$, so $a_{11} = -4$. The link points to $\lambda(4) = 2$, for which $c(2) = 3$ and $v(2) = -2$, so $a_{13} = -2$. The link points to $\lambda(2) = 0$, so we have reached the end of row 1. Similarly, row 2 starts at $s(2) = 3$, giving $a_{23} = -3$, and as $\lambda(3) = 0$, this is the end of the row; finally, $a_{33} = -5$. An advantage of the row-linked list is that it is easy to add new entries to the matrix. Rewrite the matrix of Eq. (3.7)

and the arrowhead matrix of the MATLAB subsection in this format.

b. Rewrite the matrix of Eq. (3.7) and the arrowhead matrix of the MATLAB subsection using the **column-linked list** format, where we store links to the next entries in columns rather than rows.

c. If we may need to access a packed matrix both by its rows and its columns, then we sometimes store both the row and column links. Comment on the efficiency of this scheme with respect to storage.

12. a. Create a 100×100 arrowhead matrix such as the one in MATLAB 3.2, and compare the sparsity of its LU and QR factors as given and after reordering using the results of the symrcm and colmmd commands.

b. Repeat part (a) using several tridiagonal matrices.

c. Repeat part (a) using several matrices created by sprandn.

13. Write a detailed algorithm (pseudocode) for performing Gaussian elimination on a sparse matrix using the coordinate scheme. (Do not use the MATLAB sparse matrix functions; manipulate r, c, and v directly.) Assume the matrix is already packed.

14. Give several examples of matrices whose structures ensure that Gaussian elimination will create no fill-in, no matter what nonzero values occupy those positions.

15. a. Write a MATLAB program that performs Jacobi iteration on a sparse matrix.

b. Write a MATLAB program to perform Gauss-Seidel iteration on a sparse matrix.

c. Write a MATLAB program to perform SOR on a sparse matrix.

d. Test your programs on several large sparse matrices. Compare your results to the use of the MATLAB slash command. Comment.

3.3 Iterative Refinement

The Jacobi, Gauss-Seidel, and SOR methods of Section 3.1 used to be widely employed for solving large sparse systems. The modern approach is different: We use such a method to prime another iterative technique. This priming takes two forms, which we explore in this section and the next.

The technique we discuss here is based on the observation that if x_0 is an estimate of the true solution x of $Ax = b$, then the residual r satisfies

$$r = b - Ax_0$$
$$= Ax - Ax_0$$
$$= A(x - x_0)$$

Iterative Refinement

(since $Ax = b$). But $e = x - x_0$ is precisely the error in estimating x using x_0; we have found a linear system satisfied by the error vector,

$$Ae = r, \qquad (3.10)$$

and in principle we can solve Eq. (3.10) for e and set $x = x_0 + e$ to determine x. In practice of course we will have error in e as well, but $x_1 = x_0 + e$ may still be an improved estimate of x. This technique is called **iterative refinement** (or **iterative improvement**). It uses the current x_0 to predict a correction e to be applied to it.

We could use iterative refinement simply to recover some of the accuracy that is lost in solving $Ax = b$ by some other method. For example, it is reasonable to take the approximate solution of $Ax = b$ as found by LU decomposition and perform one or two iterations of iterative improvement on it to clean it up. As the LU decomposition of A is already known from solving $Ax = b$ to get the approximate solution, this can be done efficiently. Since iterative improvement requires only $O(n^2)$ operations if we save the LU factors of A and reuse them (whereas solving $Ax = b$ in the first place requires $O(n^3)$ operations), this is an inexpensive measure we can employ to improve a solution. For well-conditioned matrices, one iteration is likely to suffice. Also, if we spend $O(n^3)$ operations and gain an inaccurate solution, possibly owing to ill-conditioning, then spending a mere $O(n^2)$ additional operations to improve it may be wise (we are "saving" the computation, hopefully).

However, we can also use iterative refinement as our solution method. We generate an initial guess x_0 that is suitably close to the true solution—say, by performing several iterations of Gauss-Seidel iteration to generate x_0—and perform iterative improvement on it until the error ceases to be reduced. In fact, it is not uncommon to use Gaussian elimination *without pivoting* to generate the initial guess! Iterative refinement takes the inaccurate but relatively rapidly generated result and improves it.

Example 3.3.1   Let $A = [4\ 2\ 1; 1\ 3\ 1; 1\ 1\ 4]$ and let $b = (3, -1, 2)^T$ be the system from Example 3.1.1, for which $x = (1, -1, 1)$ is the true solution. Two iterations of Jacobi iteration gave the approximation $(0.6667, -0.9167, 0.8958)^T$ which we take as the initial guess x_0 for iterative improvement. We have $r_0 = b - Ax_0 \doteq (1.2708, 0.1876, .6668)^T$ for the residual error ($\|r_0\| \doteq 1.4473$). Applying iterative refinement, we solve $Ae_1 = r_0$, giving $e_1 = (0.3333, -0.0833, 0.1042)^T$, and hence $x_1 = x_0 + e_1 = (1, -1, 1)^T$ to the precision available. The residual error is now $r_1 = b - Ax_1 = 0$ to the precision available ($\|r_1\| = 0.0$ to about 16 decimal places). This reduction in the residual and absolute errors cannot be improved upon with the available precision.   ■

For a well-conditioned matrix it is not unreasonable to expect that the absolute error α may be reduced to the order of machine precision by repeated application of this technique; for ill-conditioned matrices we expect less dramatic but still significant improvement, unless $\kappa(A)$ is on the order of 10^p or larger, where p is the number of digits of precision. However, to achieve this reduction in x, the computation of the residual r, which involves extreme cancellation of significant figures, must be done with extra precision. (The small matrix in Example 3.3.1 had small integer entries and so is not typical of matrices to which this method is applied.)

Precision   If the other computations are being done in single precision, the computation of

$$r_k = b - Ax_k \tag{3.11}$$

(which should be nearly zero if x_k is a good estimate of x) should be in done in double precision, and if we are using double precision for the other computations, then we should use **extended precision,** which uses at least 63 bits for the mantissa (and at least 15 bits for the exponent), for computing r_k. Availability of extended precision varies from machine to machine, but it can always be simulated in software. It is not uncommon to have the facility to compute inner products of vectors in extended precision readily available.

In addition to the extra care used in computing the residuals we should use the original A in the calculation of Ax_k in Eq. (3.11), as opposed to LUx_k (which would introduce additional errors). This means that we cannot overwrite A with its LU factors. The resulting technique is referred to as **mixed precision iterative improvement.** Without the extra precision, iterative improvement is much less successful in reducing, the error, though for moderately ill-conditioned matrices ($\kappa(A)$ less than order of 10^p) it may still yield a worthwhile gain in accuracy.

When using this method and comparing the (measurable) norm of the residual error $\|r_k\|$ to the (unknown) relative error ρ_k, recall the formula

$$\rho \le \kappa(A)\frac{\|r\|}{\|b\|}$$

(Eq. (2.5.5)), that is,

$$\frac{\|x_k - x^*\|}{\|x^*\|} \le \kappa(A)\frac{\|r_k\|}{\|b\|}, \tag{3.12}$$

which bounds the relative error in the approximation x_k of x in terms of the condition number of A, the residual, and the constant vector b. If $\kappa(A)$ can be estimated, then this formula may be used to check the relative error in our approximate solution.

At this point it may be worthwhile to consider that many problems of practical interest involve inexact data, and that it may not be sensible to seek great accuracy in their solution. In solving a partial differential equation numerically it is common to end up with a linear system $Ax = b$ where A is known exactly (a sparse matrix of small integers) but b reflects imprecisely known boundary data. Given that we are therefore solving the equation

$$Ax = b + \delta b$$

(where δb is the error in our knowledge of the true b vector), rather than the desired problem $Ax = b$, we may not be justified going to extra effort to obtain a more accurate solution of this inaccurate system of equations. Users of numerical software commonly want "more power" in the form of higher precision used in the computations (which then will take longer to complete), more accuracy in the solution (which means a longer time to achieve a desired tolerance), more detailed models, and so on, but often a single precision computation to a few digits of precision is all that is justified by the data and model.

PROBLEMS 3.3

1. Solve $Ax = b$ where $A = [2\ 1; 1\ 1]$, $b = (0.5, 0.5)^T$ using mixed precision iterative improvement. Use three-digit floating point arithmetic as single precision and six-digit floating point arithmetic as double precision. Generate an initial guess using a single Jacobi iteration step starting from $(1, 1)^T$.

2. Solve $Ax = b$ where $A = [20\ 1; 1\ 0.1]$ and $b = (0.5, 0.5)^T$ using mixed precision iterative improvement. Use three-digit floating point arithmetic as single precision and six-digit floating point arithmetic as double precision. Generate an initial guess using a single Jacobi iteration step starting from $(1, 1)^T$.

3. a. Solve the system in Problem 1 using Jacobi iteration with the given initial guess (in three-digit floating point arithmetic). How many iterations

are required to achieve the same accuracy as in Problem 1?

b. Repeat part (a) using Gauss-Seidel iteration.

4. a. Solve the system in Problem 2 using Jacobi iteration with the given initial guess (in three-digit floating point arithmetic). How many iterations are required to achieve the same accuracy as in Problem 2?

b. Repeat part (a) using Gauss-Seidel iteration.

5. Construct a sequence of increasingly ill-conditioned matrices in MATLAB, with condition numbers ranging up to at least 10^{20}, and solve systems involving them (for which you know the true solution) using two iterations of Jacobi iteration followed by as many iterations of iterative improvement as seem justified. Record the relative errors. Comment.

MATLAB 3.3

We do not attempt to access variable precision arithmetic in MATLAB as it may or may not be available in your installation (see `help vpa`.) Enter:

```
» help vpa
» vpa(2.814+2.814,3)
» vpa(vpa(2.814,3)+vpa(2.814,3),3)
```

If you do have variable precision arithmetic, consider why the last two commands above give different results. For numbers that exceed 15 or 16 digits, it's necessary to use the `sym` command to prevent them from being stored in shorter form.

Although we do not use variable precision arithmetic, we do use the **fixed precision iterative improvement** method, where the same precision (double, in this case) is used for all computations. (We emphasize that mixed precision iterative improvement is the appropriate technique to use when feasible.) Let's use this technique to recover some of the accuracy that is lost in solving $Ax = b$ when A is the Hilbert matrix of order 10. Enter:

```
» b=ones([10 1]); H=hilb(10);
» x=invhilb(10)*b            %True solution.
» x2=H\b                     %Approximate solution.
» r=b-H*x2
» e=H\r;
» xnew=x2+e;
» rnew=b-H*xnew;
» norm(rnew)
» norm(x-xnew)/norm(x)
```

The change in $\|r\|$ is not great, but the relative error is almost an order of magnitude smaller. Let's iterate; enter:

```
» e=H\rnew;
» xnew2=xnew+e;
» rnew2=b-H*xnew2;
» norm(rnew2)
» norm(x-xnew2)/norm(x)
```

This time there has been a very small change in the relative error, though $\|r\|$ has decreased. With a condition number of roughly 10^{13}, and without extended precision, this may not be a surprise.

Let's try this with a better conditioned matrix, say, a condition number on the order of 10^5, which is large but not nearly as bad as the previous example. Enter:

```
» clear all
» A=hilb(5)
» cond(A)
» b=[2 -2 1 -1 2]';
» x1=A\b
» x=invhilb(5)*b
» norm(x-x1)/norm(x)         %Relative error.
```

```
» r=b-A*x1
» norm(r)
```

The relative error in x1 is already on the order of 10^{-12}, which is as expected (16 digits of precision minus 5 lost because of a condition number on the order of 10^5 means that we expect roughly 11 digits of accuracy left). Let's do one iteration of iterative improvement. Enter:

```
» e=A\r                    %Can use LU decomposition here.
» x2=x1+e
» norm(x-x2)/norm(x)
```

This gave some improvement but not as much as we might have hoped. Unless we can compute r more accurately, we probably won't do much better. If you have Maple or if your version of MATLAB has access to it, you may be able to experiment with this.

Having to retain A to compute r (and not recompute it from L and U, which will be used to solve $Ae = r$ in the form $LUe = r$) and needing extended precision for the computation of r represent significant drawbacks of this method. Yet in principle it can give good improvements at relatively small computational cost. Iterative improvement is a general-purpose tool for improving the quality of a solution.

ADDITIONAL PROBLEMS 3.3

6. Write a MATLAB program that accepts a square matrix A, a conformable vector b, and an optional positive integer k and returns the solution of $Ax = b$ as found by MATLAB's backslash command followed by k iterations of iterative improvement (use $k = 1$ if k is not provided by the user). Demonstrate your program on well-conditioned and ill-conditioned matrices.

7. Let $A = [2\ 1\ 1; 1\ 2\ 1; 1\ 1\ 2]$ and $b = (4, 4, 4)^T$ so that $Ax = b$ has the solution $x = (1, 1, 1)^T$. Use iterative improvement to solve $Ax = b$ starting from an initial guess of $x_0 = 10^m(1, -2, 3)^T$ for $m = 1, 2, \ldots$, until m is so large that convergence is no longer achieved. Comment.

8. Write a MATLAB program that solves $Ax = b$ using Gaussian elimination to a desired tolerance using Eq. (3.12). Have your program apply iterative improvement to ensure that the tolerance is met and return both the solution and the final upper bound on ρ.

9. Write a MATLAB program that solves $Ax = b$ using QR decomposition to a desired tolerance using Eq. (3.12). Have your program apply iterative improvement to ensure that the tolerance is met and return both the solution and the final upper bound on ρ.

10. Write a MATLAB program that solves $Ax = b$ using Gauss-Seidel iteration to a desired tolerance using Eq. (3.12). Have your program apply one round of iterative improvement after the tolerance is met and return both the solution and the final upper bound on ρ (after the iterative improvement step).

11. If you have access to a system with arbitrary precision arithmetic (such as Maple, available through MATLAB's Symbolic Toolbox), repeat Problem 5 using very high precision. Comment on your results, including the price paid in execution speed for using higher precision.

12. a. Under reasonable assumptions, fixed precision iterative improvement reduces the relative error $\|x_k - x\|_\infty / \|x\|_\infty$ at each step by a factor of about $2n\epsilon\kappa_\infty(A)$, where ϵ is the machine epsilon. Verify this experimentally.

   b. For mixed precision iterative improvement, the relative error is reduced by a factor of about ϵ at each step. Verify this experimentally.

   c. How much better is mixed precision iterative improvement than fixed precision iterative improvement?

13. A common means of solving a moderately large sparse system is to use Gaussian elimination with thresholding (see Problem 8 of Section 3.2) and then improve the result using iterative improvement or another

iterative technique. We choose the threshold sufficiently high that we will pivot only rarely. In fact,
one might skip pivoting entirely, thereby generating
a relatively inaccurate result relatively quickly. Write a
MATLAB program that performs Gaussian elimination
without pivoting followed by iterative improvement.
Test it on several ill-conditioned matrices.

14. Preserving the sparsity structure of a large sparse matrix is often important; all the more so if the scheme
used to store the sparse matrix makes adding a new
nonzero entry time consuming. For this reason one
might design a method as follows: Perform Gaussian
elimination with or without pivoting, but whenever

an operation would create fill-in in the matrix, ignore the result of that operation and leave the entry as
zero. This technique is known as **incomplete Gaussian
elimination.**

Write a MATLAB program that implements incomplete Gaussian elimination without pivoting followed
by iterative improvement. Test it on several large sparse
matrices.

15. If you have access to a system with arbitrary precision arithmetic (such as Maple, available through
MATLAB's Symbolic Toolbox), write a program that
implements mixed precision iterative improvement.
Test your program.

3.4 Preconditioning

Iterative improvement is one way in which we can prime an iterative method using the
ideas of the Jacobi iteration

$$x^{k+1} = -D^{-1}(U + L)x^k + D^{-1}b, \tag{3.13}$$

or the Gauss-Seidel iteration

$$x^{k+1} = -(L + D)^{-1}Ux^k + (L + D)^{-1}b \tag{3.14}$$

Preconditioning   (where $A = U + L + D$), or SOR. However, another way that is standard nowadays is
preconditioning, where we take a linear system $Ax = b$ and transform it to an equivalent
system of the form

$$M_1 A M_2 y = \tilde{b}$$

(where $y = M_2^{-1}x$ and $\tilde{b} = M_1 b$), for which

$$\kappa(M_1 A M_2) << \kappa(A),$$

so that $M_1 A M_2$ is significantly better conditioned than A itself.[2] We refer to M_1 as
a **left preconditioner** and M_2 as a **right preconditioner.** If the costs of finding and
using M_1 and M_2 do not negate the gains from the reduction in the condition number,
preconditioning can be very beneficial.

Preconditioning followed by an iterative method is the standard approach for solving
large sparse linear systems. In fact, an iteration or two of Jacobi or Gauss-Seidel iteration
followed by iterative improvement (see Section 3.3) is considered an example of this
approach; the Jacobi or Gauss-Seidel iteration is considered a form of preconditioning.

In some cases it is important to use both a right preconditioner and a left preconditioner; for example, if A is positive definite, then $M_1 A$ may not be, but $M_1 A M_2$ can be
made to be positive definite. This is likely to be desirable. However, for simplicity we
look only at left preconditioners (so that $M_2 = I$).

---

[2] In some applications we might want $\rho(I - M_1 A M_2) << \rho(I - A)$, or some other requirement involving
the eigenvalues, and we use the term preconditioning to refer to this as well.

It is convenient to write the preconditioner as $P = M_1^{-1}$ so that the linear system $Ax = b$ becomes

$$P^{-1}Ax = P^{-1}b \qquad (3.15)$$

after preconditioning by P. Of course, we will not actually be inverting P at any point unless doing so is trivial.

One of the simplest preconditioners is also one of the most widely used. It is motivated in part by Eq. (3.13), Jacobi iteration, where D^{-1} is used to rescale all the nondiagonal entries of the matrix A. Perhaps $P^{-1} = D^{-1}$, that is, $P = D$, will yield a useful preconditioner? Indeed,

$$D^{-1}Ax = D^{-1}b,$$

where D is the matrix of the diagonal entries of A, is often a good preconditioner and is called the **Jacobi preconditioner** (we say that we are using **Jacobi preconditioning**). That is, it is frequently the case that if A is ill-conditioned, then $D^{-1}A$ is better conditioned than A.

Example 3.4.1   Consider $A = [2\ 1; 0.1\ 0.01]$. Then $\kappa(A) \doteq 62.6103$ but $\kappa(D^{-1}A) \doteq 25.5233$ ($D = [2\ 0; 0\ 0.01]$ so $D^{-1}A = [1\ 0.5; 10\ 1]$). Jacobi preconditioning has reduced the condition number to less than half of what it was. Of course, we need to reduce it by an order of magnitude to see a meaningful difference in the accuracy of the solution of $Ax = b$ (recall that if $\kappa(A) \approx 10^k$, then we expect to lose about k digits of accuracy in solving $Ax = b$). If $A = [2\ 1; 0.01\ 0.01]$ then $\kappa(A) \doteq 500.0180$, but $\kappa(D^{-1}A) \doteq 6.3423$ ($D = [2\ 0; 0\ 0.01]$ so $D^{-1}A = [1\ 0.5; 1\ 1]$), a considerable improvement. If $A = [2\ 1; 0.0001\ 0.0001]$ then $\kappa(A) \doteq 50000.0$ ($5.0E4$), but again $\kappa(D^{-1}A) \doteq 6.3423$ ($D = [2\ 0; 0\ 0.01]$ so $D^{-1}A = [1\ 0.5; 1\ 1]$). In the last case Jacobi preconditioning could gain us 4 digits of accuracy! ∎

Balancing   The Jacobi preconditioner is a type of **diagonal preconditioner** (in which P is a diagonal matrix). Sometimes we use an even simpler diagonal preconditioner, with $P = cI$ for some nonzero constant c. We might also use a diagonal preconditioner designed to **balance** (or **equibalance**) the matrix, meaning that we attempt to make all row vectors of the matrix have about the same length with respect to some vector norm. It is rarely obvious how best to choose the entries of P to achieve the desired effect.

The simple and inexpensive nature of Jacobi preconditioning makes it worth trying in many cases. However, there are a number of other preconditioners in common use. One is the **Gauss-Seidel preconditioner** $P = (L + D)$ (from Eq. (3.14); the minus sign is irrelevant here); SOR is another. Here the preconditioning matrix is not quite as simple as before, though it is lower triangular. As we look at more computationally expensive preconditioners, note from Eq. (3.15)

$$P^{-1}Ax = P^{-1}b$$

that the trivial preconditioner $P = I$ has no effect, whereas the choice $P = A$ (so that $P^{-1} = A^{-1}$) solves the system immediately but at prohibitive cost. (Recall that sparse matrices typically have full inverses.) We would like to choose a P that is simple to use, like a diagonal matrix. In particular, systems of the form $Px = c$ should be easy to solve. But we also want a P that is somehow "near" A^{-1} so that $P^{-1}A$ is nearer to I than A was. This is desirable because I has unit condition number and is easy to manipulate.[3] These two conditions are in tension; only in exceptional circumstances can both P and $P^{-1}A$ be simple.

Suppose that A is large and sparse. What keeps us from solving $Ax = b$ by the LU decomposition? It isn't just that the method is $O(n^3)$, because if A is very sparse we have relatively few nonzero entries to handle and could write a program to make use of this fact. But we also have fill-in. The LU factors of A are apt to be dense even if A is sparse. What if we form the LU decomposition of A approximately, so that $A \approx \widetilde{L}\widetilde{U}$? We could then use the approximate LU decomposition $P = \widetilde{L}\widetilde{U}$ as a preconditioner. If the approximation is good enough, perhaps $P^{-1}A$ will be near enough to I to represent an improvement.

ILU Methods   One way to use the approximate LU decomposition $P = \widetilde{L}\widetilde{U}$ as a preconditioner is simply to prohibit fill-in. We allow an entry of $\widetilde{L}$ or $\widetilde{U}$ to be nonzero only if the corresponding entry of A is nonzero. More generally, we might specify a range of entries of $\widetilde{L}$ and $\widetilde{U}$ that may be filled in (e.g., up to the first three subdiagonals and up to the first three superdiagonals). Any such factorization is known as **incomplete LU factorization** leading to an **incomplete LU preconditioner** $P = \widetilde{L}\widetilde{U}$ (often called simply an **ILU** method). The corresponding technique for positive definite matrices is **incomplete Cholesky factorization** and the **incomplete Cholesky preconditioner.**

Example 3.4.2   Consider

$$A = \begin{pmatrix} 10 & 0.1 & 0.1 & 0.1 \\ 0.1 & 0.1 & 0 & 0 \\ 0.1 & 0 & 0.1 & 0 \\ 0.1 & 0 & 0 & 0.1 \end{pmatrix},$$

which has condition number $\kappa(A) \doteq 103.1553$. Its LU decomposition is (to the precision indicated)

$$L = \begin{pmatrix} 1 & 0 & 0 & 0 \\ 0.1 & 1 & 0 & 0 \\ 0.1 & -0.0101 & 1 & 0 \\ 0.1 & -0.0101 & -0.0102 & 1 \end{pmatrix}$$

$$U = \begin{pmatrix} 10 & 0.1 & 0.1 & 0.1 \\ 0 & 0.099 & -0.001 & -0.001 \\ 0 & 0 & 0.099 & -0.001 \\ 0 & 0 & 0 & 0.099 \end{pmatrix},$$

and we see that both L and U have completely filled in. The incomplete LU factorization,

---

3 This is sometimes called an **approximate inverse** preconditioner, as opposed to preconditioning for, say, some change in the eigenvalues of the preconditioned matrix.

allowing no nonzero entries where A has zero entries, is

$$\widetilde{L} = \begin{pmatrix} 1 & 0 & 0 & 0 \\ 0.1 & 1 & 0 & 0 \\ 0.1 & 0 & 1 & 0 \\ 0.1 & 0 & 0 & 1 \end{pmatrix}$$

$$\widetilde{U} = \begin{pmatrix} 10 & 0.1 & 0.1 & 0.1 \\ 0 & 0.099 & 0 & 0 \\ 0 & 0 & 0.099 & 0 \\ 0 & 0 & 0 & 0.099 \end{pmatrix}$$

(notice that the replaced entries were all relatively small in magnitude). Then

$$\widetilde{L}\widetilde{U} \doteq \begin{pmatrix} 10 & 0.1 & 0.1 & 0.1 \\ 0.1 & 0.1 & 0.001 & 0.001 \\ 0.1 & 0.001 & 0.1 & 0.001 \\ 0.1 & 0.001 & 0.001 & 0.1 \end{pmatrix}$$

and so

$$(\widetilde{L}\widetilde{U})^{-1} A \doteq \begin{pmatrix} 1 & 0.0002 & 0.0002 & 0.0002 \\ 0 & 1 & -0.0101 & -0.0101 \\ 0 & -0.0101 & 1.0001 & -0.0101 \\ 0 & -0.0101 & -0.0101 & 1.0002 \end{pmatrix}$$

is the ILU preconditioned matrix, which has $\kappa((\widetilde{L}\widetilde{U})^{-1} A) \doteq 1.0310$. This is a considerable improvement in condition number but at a significant computational cost. ∎

The term **incomplete LU factorization with thresholding** refers to the technique of discarding small elements in L and U. (Thresholding can also refer to a pivoting strategy, as described in Section 3.2.) This gives a decomposition $A = \widehat{L}\widehat{U} + E$ where the entries of E, the discarded entries, are small in magnitude, and therefore $\|E\|$ is small. We then use $P = \widehat{L}\widehat{U}$ as the preconditioner. If the entries of E are truly negligible, then $P^{-1} A$ should be close to the identity matrix.[4]

Using the Preconditioner
Clearly, we will not form $P^{-1} A$ for a preconditioner like this. We will need to restructure our algorithms so that we solve a matrix involving P to simulate the effect of forming $P^{-1} A$. For example, suppose we need to form the residual of a preconditioned system $P^{-1} Ax = P^{-1} b$. We have

$$r = P^{-1} b - P^{-1} Ax$$
$$r = P^{-1} (b - Ax)$$
$$Pr = b - Ax,$$

so we find r by computing the unpreconditioned residual $\rho = b - Ax$ and then solving $Pr = \rho$ for r. This is why we write the preconditioner as P^{-1}: We need to solve systems involving P. We see an example of this in MATLAB 3.5.

---

[4] A statement like this always begs the question, "*Close* in what sense?" Close in norm ($\|P^{-1} A - I\|$) is the obvious sense, but not the only one that might be of interest.

What method should we apply to the preconditioned system $P^{-1}Ax = \tilde{b}$? In practice we usually have an iterative method in mind and choose a preconditioner that is appropriate for that method. Common iterative methods include iterative refinement (Section 3.3), GMRES (Section 3.5), and conjugate gradients (Section 7.7). In principle one could precondition adaptively, that is, use a different preconditioner P_i at each step of the main method, but this is rarely done. For some algorithms it will be something other than a reduction in the condition number that will do the most to improve the speed and accuracy of the computation (namely, the location of its eigenvalues or singular values).

Preconditioners are also used for other problems in numerical linear algebra, most notably eigenvalue problems (discussed later in this chapter). Efficient and effective preconditioning algorithms are extremely important in practice.[5]

PROBLEMS 3.4

1. a. Create three different 3×3 matrices for which Jacobi preconditioning improves the condition number. Also compare $\|A - I\|$ to $\|P^{-1}A - I\|$ for each case.

  b. Create three different 3×3 matrices for which Gauss-Seidel preconditioning improves the condition number. Also compare $\|A - I\|$ to $\|P^{-1}A - I\|$ for each case.

2. Create a large ($n \geq 100$) matrix for which ILU preconditioning improves the condition number. Simulate the incomplete LU factorization by performing the LU decomposition and then explicitly making appropriate entries of the matrix zero.

3. Write a complete algorithm (pseudocode) for *efficiently* performing incomplete LU factorization with no fill-in allowed.

4. Suggest a method for using SOR as a preconditioner.

5. Solve $Hx = b$, where H is the Hilbert matrix of order 10 and b is a vector of all ones, using the LU decomposition. Repeat using Jacobi preconditioning and then again using Gauss-Seidel preconditioning. Compare the errors and the efficiency.

MATLAB 3.4

Here we look at the effects of preconditioning but leave the practical implementation until Section 3.5.

Let's look again at the first matrix of Example 3.4.1. Enter:

```
» A=[2 1;.1 .01]
» cond(A)
» AJ=inv(diag(diag(A)))*A
» cond(AJ)
```

to duplicate the results in the example. Now let's try Gauss-Seidel preconditioning. Enter:

```
» AGS=inv(tril(A))*A
» cond(AGS)
```

Not only is the condition number for the Gauss-Seidel preconditioner smaller than that for the Jacobi preconditioner, but the resulting matrix is more nearly equibalanced: The max norms of the rows are closer, and the entries of the matrix vary less in magnitude.

---

[5] Trefethen and Bau write, "The name of the new game [in numerical linear algebra] is *iteration with preconditioning.* Increasingly often it is not optimal to solve a problem exactly in one pass; instead, solve it approximately, then iterate."

Let's try this with a bigger matrix. We'll use the Hilbert matrix of order 10. Enter:

```
» H=hilb(10);
» cond(H)
» HJ=inv(diag(diag(H)))*H;
» cond(HJ)
» HGS=tril(H)\*H;          %More accurate than inv(tril(H))*H.
» cond(HGS)
```

The Jacobi preconditioner reduces the condition number by about an order of magnitude, and the more expensive Gauss-Seidel preconditioner reduces it by about another order of magnitude. Again, in practice we would not actually invert these matrices but would instead solve a system involving them.

There are commands in MATLAB for incomplete LU and incomplete Cholesky factorizations (luinc and cholinc, respectively). Enter:

```
» S=sprand(100,100,.2);
» cond(S)                          %Ignore the warning about condest.
» [L1,U1,P]=luinc(S,'0');          %ILU factorization with no fill-in.
» spones(L1)~=spones(tril(P*S))    %Where do L and A differ in pattern?
» spones(U1)~=spones(triu(P*S))    %Where do U and A differ in pattern?
```

The ILU factors should differ only in their patterns of nonzero elements along the main diagonal (which is expected to be full of nonzeroes for both L and U) and possibly in places where L or U has gained an additional zero entry by cancellation. Enter:

```
» norm(full(P'*L1*U1-S))    %How well does L1*U1 approximate PS?
» nnz(inv(P'*L1*U1))/10000  %How sparse is the approx. inverse?
```

Clearly we do not want to form $(P^T LU) \approx A^{-1}$. We will see in MATLAB 3.5 how the ILU method may be used effectively and efficiently.

ADDITIONAL PROBLEMS 3.4

6. a. The MATLAB command cgs(A,b,[],[],P) attempts to solve $P^{-1}Ax = P^{-1}b$ by an iterative method. Use this to experiment with various preconditioners P. Comment.

b. The MATLAB command bicg(A,b,[],[],P) attempts to solve $P^{-1}Ax = P^{-1}b$ by an iterative method. Use this to experiment with various preconditioners P. Comment.

c. The MATLAB command bicgstab(A,b,[], [],P) attempts to solve $P^{-1}Ax = P^{-1}b$ by an iterative method. Use this to experiment with various preconditioners P. Comment.

7. a. Find a diagonal preconditioner that minimizes the condition number of $P^{-1}A$ if $A = [10 \ 1; 0.1 \ 0.2]$.

b. Let S=sprandn(100,100,.2). Use trial and error to find a good diagonal preconditioner for S.

8. Write a MATLAB program that computes an ILU factorization with thresholding for a sparse matrix. Compare your approach to that in luinc (with drop tolerance).

9. Could you use a unitary matrix as a preconditioner? Why or why not?

10. Solve $Hx = b$, where H is the Hilbert matrix of order N and b is a vector of all ones, using the LU decomposition for $N = 5, 6, \ldots, 15$. Repeat using Jacobi preconditioning and then again using Gauss-Seidel preconditioning. Comment on the errors and efficiency.

11. **a.** Solve $Ax = b$, where A is the prolate matrix of order N (use the MATLAB command `A=gallery('prolate',N)`) and b is a vector such that the true solution x is known, using the LU decomposition for $N = 5, 6, \ldots, 15$. Repeat using Jacobi preconditioning and then again using Gauss-Seidel preconditioning. Comment on the errors.

    b. The prolate matrices are **Toeplitz matrices,** meaning that every diagonal is constant. A common preconditioner for Toeplitz matrices is an appropriate **circulant matrix,** that is, a Toeplitz matrix for which each row is found from the row above it by pushing the entries one entry to the right, with wraparound. The MATLAB command `gallery('circul',V)` creates the circulant matrix with first row V. Use trial and error to find a useful circulant preconditioner for the prolate matrix of order 8.

12. **a.** Write a MATLAB program that computes the incomplete Cholesky factorization with no fill-in allowed of a sparse positive definite matrix. Compare your approach to that in `cholinc`.

    b. Write a MATLAB program that computes the incomplete Cholesky factorization with thresholding of a sparse positive definite matrix. Compare your approach to that in `cholinc` (with drop tolerance).

13. The MATLAB command `gallery('dorr',N)` creates the **Dorr matrix** of order N, an ill-conditioned sparse tridiagonal matrix. Compare Jacobi, Gauss-Seidel, and ILU preconditioning of the Dorr matrix for $N = 10, 50, 100$.

14. **a.** Compare the estimates returned by `cond(A,1)` and `condest(A)` for both accuracy and speed.

    b. Compare the estimates returned by `norm(A,1)` and `normest1(A)` for both accuracy and speed.

15. Experience shows that preconditioning is more effective on structured matrices than on unstructured matrices. See if you can verify this experimentally by preconditioning a number of matrices of the form `S=sprand(N,N,p)` and of the form `S=sprandsym(N,p)` (sparse symmetric matrices).

3.5 Krylov Space Methods

Krylov Spaces

Many iterative methods for solving linear systems $Ax = b$ and for finding eigenvalues and eigenvectors of a matrix A are based on the **Krylov space**

$$K_k = \text{span}\{b, Ab, A^2b, \ldots, A^{k-1}b\} \tag{3.16}$$

associated with A, often called a **Krylov subspace** (of $\mathbb{R}^n$). For solving $Ax = b$, the general idea is this: Given the linear system $Ax = b$ we might first try to find an approximate solution x_1 that is a multiple of b. We might then look for a next iterate x_2 that is a linear combination of b and Ab, that is, an element of K_2; and we might continue in this way, so that the kth approximation x_k is an element of K_k. Since

$$K_n = \mathbb{R}^n$$

(for a typical A and b) it appears that, if a solution exists, it is in K_n. We hope to find a good approximate solution in K_k for $k \ll n$, as in the cases of interest n will be very large (and A will be sparse).

There are many ways to build such a method. In some cases it will be convenient to take the Krylov subspace to be of the form

$$\hat{K}_k = \text{span}\{z, Az, A^2z, \ldots, A^{k-1}z\}$$

for some vector $z \neq b$, but in this section we focus on a method that uses Eq. (3.16). To begin, we choose an initial estimate x_0 of the solution of $Ax = b$. Then we define

$$V_k = x_0 + K_k$$

to be the set of all vectors of the form $x_0 + z$, where x_0 is the initial guess and z is an element of K_k. (Frequently we take $x_0 = 0$ so that $V_k = K_k$.) We say that V_k is an **affine space,** meaning a vector space shifted by the vector x_0. Note that if $x_0 \neq 0$, then this is not in fact a linear space. At each stage of the iteration we choose from V_k a new approximation x_k of the true solution of $Ax = b$.

Minimizing the Residual   The natural way to define an approximate solution x_k of $Ax = b$ drawn from V_k is to let x_k be the value that minimizes the residual

$$\|b - Ax\|$$

over $x \in V_k$. This is equivalent to

$$x_k = \min_{x \in V_k} \|b - Ax\|^2, \tag{3.17}$$

and we see that x_k solves a least squares problem over a restricted part of the entire space $\mathbb{R}^n$, namely, the affine space V_k. Note that $z_k = x_k - x_0$ satisfies

$$z_k = \min_{z \in K_k} \|b - A(z + x_0)\|^2$$

$$= \min_{z \in K_k} \|b - Ax_0 - Az\|^2$$

$$= \min_{z \in K_k} \|r_0 - Az\|^2 \tag{3.18}$$

(where $r_0 = b - Ax_0$ is the initial residual) because $x_k - x_0$ is an element of the Krylov space K_k. Since K_k, unlike V_k, is a vector space, this form is often easier to work with.

GMRES   Clearly if we were to solve for $k = 1, 2, \ldots, n$, we would eventually find the least squares solution of $Ax = b$, which is the true solution x if A is nonsingular; this would be a grossly inefficient way to solve $Ax = b$. The method, known as **GMRES** (for *g*eneralized *m*inimum *res*idual), succeeds because it is easier to solve Eq. (3.17) over a smaller-dimensional space than a larger-dimensional one, and because it is frequently the case that an acceptable solution can be found for $k \ll n$. This justifies thinking of the method as an iterative method even though k cannot possibly exceed n; n will be so large in practice that k will never be nearly as big, and we imagine iterating for $k = 1, 2, 3 \ldots$ until some convergence criterion is met. We will solve Eq. (3.18) for a one-dimensional vector space K_1, then over a two-dimensional space K_2, and so on, until we decide to stop.

We may use any of our usual termination criteria with GMRES. One commonly employed criterion is that the **relative residual**

$$\frac{\|r_k\|}{\|b\|}$$

be less than some specified tolerance, where as usual $r_k = b - Ax_k$ denotes the residual after the kth iteration. It can be shown that if A is diagonalizable and

$$\mu = \|A - I\|$$

is less than unity, then

$$\|r_k\| \le \mu^k \|r_0\|$$

so that we may estimate the number of iterations required to achieve a desired decrease in the residual. Since $\mu < 1$ is not true of a general matrix, we certainly want to try to find an approximate inverse preconditioner P such that

$$\left\| P^{-1}A - I \right\| < 1$$

(or a right preconditioner, or both a left and a right preconditioner) when using GMRES, though preconditioning is not strictly necessary for convergence.

The algorithm in outline, then, is to choose an x_0 and successively solve Eq. (3.17) or Eq. (3.18) until convergence is achieved.

How shall we solve the least squares problem at each iteration? It's natural to think of using the QR decomposition. Define

$$\Gamma_k = \begin{bmatrix} b \mid Ab \mid A^2 b \mid \cdots \mid A^{k-1}b \end{bmatrix}$$

called the kth **Krylov matrix.** Every vector in K_k is some linear combination of the k columns of Γ_k, and every linear combination of the columns of Γ_k is in K_k, so there must be some vector $y \in \mathbb{R}^k$ such that

$$x_k - x_0 = \Gamma_k y.$$

In terms of y, Eq. (3.18) becomes the problem of finding the solution y of

$$\min_{y \in \mathbb{R}^k} \|r_0 - A\Gamma_k y\|^2 ; \tag{3.19}$$

that is,

$$\min_{y \in \mathbb{R}^k} \|r_0 - My\|^2$$

where $M = A\Gamma_k$. This is a standard least squares problem over all of $\mathbb{R}^k$, and it could be solved using the QR decomposition of M (see Section 2.6).

However, this approach is both unstable and inefficient. Part of the problem is that the Krylov matrix Γ_k tends to be very ill-conditioned; this problem is inherited by the R factor in the QR factorization of Γ_k. We will use a closely related approach based on using the Gram-Schmidt process (see Section 2.8) to find the orthonormal basis Q for the Krylov space K_k. This will allow us to avoid the formation and use of R. When applied to K_k, the Gram-Schmidt process is called the **Arnoldi process,** and it may be summarized for our case as follows:

Arnoldi Process Algorithm

1. Set $q_1 = (b - Ax_0)/\|b - Ax_0\|$.
2. Begin loop ($m = 1$ to $k - 1$):
3. Set $v_{m+1} = Aq_m - \sum_{i=1}^{m}(q_m^T Aq_i)q_i$.
4. Set $q_{m+1} = v_{m+1}/\|v_{m+1}\|$.
5. End loop.

If it should happen that $\|q_m\| = 0$ for some m, then the process cannot be completed. However, it is a fact that if $\|q_m\| = 0$, then the true solution x of $Ax = b$ lies in $V_m = x_0 + K_m$, and hence we have already found the true solution. Otherwise, $\{q_1, \ldots, q_k\}$ is the desired orthonormal basis for K_k. Let

$$Q_k = [q_1 \mid q_2 \mid q_3 \mid \cdots \mid q_k]$$

be the corresponding matrix. This is the factor Q in the reduced QR factorization of K_k. Using the same reasoning that led us to Eq. (3.19), we can now rephrase our problem as

$$\min_{y \in \mathbb{R}^k} \|r_0 - AQ_k y\|^2 \tag{3.20}$$

(note, this is not the same variable y as in Eq. (3.19)). Eq. (3.20) will be much better behaved because Q_k has orthonormal columns and hence is well-conditioned, whereas K_k in Eq. (3.19) was likely to be ill-conditioned. We will solve Eq. (3.20) for y_k and then set $x_k = x_0 + Q_k y$.

Example 3.5.1 Let $A = [2\ 1\ -1; 0\ 2\ 2; -2\ 1\ 2]$ and $b = (2, 4, 1)^T$. To solve $Ax = b$, we'll take $x_0 = 0$ and use Eq. (3.20). We have $r_0 = b - Ax_0 = b$, $\Gamma_1 = b$, and so the Arnoldi process gives $q_1 = b/\|b\| \doteq (0.4364, 0.8729, 0.2182)^T$. Hence we must solve for

$$y_1 = \min_{y \in \mathbb{R}^k} \|r_0 - AQ_1 y\|^2$$

$$= \min_{y \in \mathbb{R}^k} \|r_0 - Aq_1 y\|^2$$

$$\doteq \min_{y \in \mathbb{R}^k} \|(2, 4, 1)^T - (1.5275, 2.1822, 0.4364)^T y\|^2$$

for $y_1 \in \mathbb{R}$. We need the least squares solution of

$$\begin{pmatrix} 1.5275 \\ 2.1822 \\ 0.4364 \end{pmatrix} y_1 = \begin{pmatrix} 2 \\ 4 \\ 1 \end{pmatrix},$$

and we use the reduced QR decomposition of $(1.5275, 2.1822, 0.4364)^T$,

$$Q \doteq \begin{pmatrix} -0.5659 \\ -0.8085 \\ -0.1617 \end{pmatrix}$$

$$R \doteq -2.6992 \tag{3.21}$$

(from MATLAB, using [Q,R]=qr(A*q1,0)) to find

$$y_1 = R^{-1}Q^T r_0$$

$$\doteq 1.6773$$

(see Section 2.6). Our current estimate of the solution of $Ax = b$ is $x_1 = Q_1 y_1 = q_1 y_1 \doteq (0.7320, 1.4641, 0.3660)^T$, for which $r_1 = b - Ax_1 \doteq (-0.5621, 0.3399, 0.2680)^T$ ($\|r_1\| \doteq .7094$, compared to $\|r_0\| \doteq 4.5826$).

Let's do a second iteration of the method. First we need v_2. From the Arnoldi process, we have

$$v_2 = Aq_1 - \sum_{i=1}^{1} \left(q_i^T Aq_i \right) q_i$$

$$= \begin{pmatrix} 1.5275 \\ 2.1822 \\ 0.4364 \end{pmatrix} - \left[\begin{pmatrix} 0.4364 \\ 0.8729 \\ 0.2182 \end{pmatrix}^T A \begin{pmatrix} 0.4364 \\ 0.8729 \\ 0.2182 \end{pmatrix} \right] \begin{pmatrix} 0.4364 \\ 0.8729 \\ 0.2182 \end{pmatrix}$$

$$\doteq \begin{pmatrix} 0.3637 \\ -0.1455 \\ -0.1455 \end{pmatrix}$$

$$q_2 = \frac{\begin{pmatrix} 0.3637 \\ -0.1455 \\ -0.1455 \end{pmatrix}}{\left\| \begin{pmatrix} 0.3637 \\ -0.1455 \\ -0.1455 \end{pmatrix} \right\|}$$

$$\doteq \begin{pmatrix} 0.8704 \\ -0.3482 \\ -0.3482 \end{pmatrix}$$

so

$$Q_2 = [q_1 \mid q_2]$$

$$= \begin{pmatrix} 0.4364 & 0.8704 \\ 0.8729 & -0.3482 \\ 0.2182 & -0.3482 \end{pmatrix}$$

is the orthonormal basis of the Krylov subspace K_2. We must solve

$$y_2 = \min_{y \in \mathbb{R}^k} \| r_0 - AQ_2 y \|^2$$

for $y_2 \in \mathbb{R}^2$; note that we always use r_0 in the formula determining y_k, not r_k. Once again we use the reduced QR factorization of AQ_2,

$$Q \doteq \begin{pmatrix} -0.5659 & 0.5899 \\ -0.8085 & -0.2600 \\ -0.1617 & -0.7645 \end{pmatrix}$$

$$R \doteq \begin{pmatrix} -2.6992 & 0.5911 \\ 0 & 3.5182 \end{pmatrix}$$

(3.22)

(compare the Q and R factors in Eq. (3.21) and in Eq. (3.22)) applied to the system

$AQ_2 y = r_0$, that is, $QRy = r_0$, giving

$$y_2 = R^{-1} Q^T r_0$$

$$\doteq \begin{pmatrix} 1.6384 \\ -0.1776 \end{pmatrix}$$

(note that the first component of y_2 is not equal to y_1, though it is close). We have $x_2 = Q_2 y_2 \doteq (0.5605, 1.4919, 0.4194)^T$, for which $r_2 = b - A x_2 \doteq (-0.1935, 0.1774, -0.2097)^T$ ($\|r_2\| \doteq .3360$, compared to $\|r_1\| \doteq .7094$ and $\|r_0\| \doteq 4.5826$). ∎

In fact, at stage $k + 1$ of GMRES we are searching for an approximate x over a subspace K_{k+1} (or more generally an affine space V_{k+1}), which includes the subspace K_k over which we searched at the previous stage, so the approximation can only improve or stay the same; it cannot get worse. If there were no better approximation in K_{k+1}, after all, then we could use the approximation previously found in K_k because $K_k \subset K_{k+1}$. Hence, the residuals $\{r_k\}$ must be nonincreasing:

$$\|r_{k+1}\| \le \|r_k\|.$$

(Recall that, as per Eq. (3.17), it is the residual r_k that we are minimizing at each step, even though it is r_0 that appears explicitly in Eq. (3.20).) If A is nonsingular, then GMRES will converge in at most n steps, but again, this theoretical guarantee is useless for the cases in which GMRES is applied because n is so large. We need convergence in many fewer iterations than n.

Improving Efficiency

As discussed in Example 3.5.1, the implementation of GMRES can be made significantly more efficient than what we have described. At each iteration, define the matrix H_k by

$$H_k = Q_k A Q_k^T.$$

The matrix H_k will be upper Hessenberg, that is, almost upper triangular save that the first subdiagonal may be nonzero. Then it can be shown that

$$AQ_k = Q_{k+1} H_k,$$

which we may use in Eq. (3.20), giving

$$y_k = \min_{y \in \mathbb{R}^k} \|r_0 - Q_{k+1} H_k y\|^2,$$

which may be simplified as follows (we omit the justifications)

$$y_k = \min_{y \in \mathbb{R}^k} \|r_0 - Q_{k+1} H_k y\|^2$$

$$= \min_{y \in \mathbb{R}^k} \left\| Q_{k+1} (Q_{k+1}^T r_0 - H_k y) \right\|^2 \tag{3.23}$$

$$= \min_{y \in \mathbb{R}^k} \left\| Q_{k+1}^T r_0 - H_k y \right\|^2$$

$$= \min_{y \in \mathbb{R}^k} \|\rho e_1 - H_k y\|^2$$

where $\rho = \|r_0\|$ and e_1 is the first standard basis vector. In GMRES we solve the least squares problem

$$\min_{y \in \mathbb{R}^k} \|\rho e_1 - H_k y\|^2 \qquad (3.24)$$

or equivalently

$$\min_{y \in \mathbb{R}^k} \|\rho e_1 - H_k y\|$$

at each iteration, using QR factorization (on H_k).[6] It is a fact that

$$r_k = Q_{k+1}(\rho e_1 - H_k y_k),$$

so we need not form $x_k = x_0 + Q_k y_k$ at each iteration to check the residual but can wait and form only the final x_k. In addition, as you might have guessed from comparing Eqs. (3.21) and (3.22), there is an efficient way to find the QR factors of H_{k+1} from those of H_k. This is called an **updating** procedure because it updates the old Q and R.

The Algorithm   If you look carefully at what we've discussed and at Example 3.5.1, you'll see that we need not perform the entire Arnoldi procedure first before going to the minimization step. We can find an orthonormal basis for K_k, solve Eq. (3.24), then return to the Arnoldi process to get the next needed vector (for the orthonormal basis for K_{k+1}), and then solve Eq. (3.24) with H_{k+1}, and so on until the convergence criterion is met. In broad outline the GMRES algorithm is:

GMRES Algorithm (Outline)

1. Compute ρ.

2. Begin loop ($k = 1$ to n):

3. Perform a step of the Arnoldi process.

4. Form Q_k and H_k.

5. Solve $\min_{y \in \mathbb{R}^k} \|\rho e_1 - H_k y\|$ using the QR decomposition.

6. If convergence criterion is met, set $x_k = x_0 + Q_k y_k$ and terminate.

7. End loop.

In step 5 we can use the updating procedure to get the QR factors of H_k from the QR factors of H_{k-1} (don't confuse this Q with the matrix Q_k, which is a factor of the Krylov matrix Γ_k). An algorithm that implements GMRES is:

GMRES Algorithm

1. Set $r_0 = b - Ax$, $\rho = \|r_0\|$, $q_1 = r_0/\rho$.

2. Begin loop ($k = 1$ to n):

---

[6] We might use the Givens rotation method because the matrix is upper Hessenberg.

3. Begin loop ($p = 1$ to k):
4. Set $h_{pk} = q_k A^T q_p^T$.
5. End loop.
6. Set $t_{k+1} = Aq_k - \sum_{p=1}^{k} h_{pk}q_p$.
7. Set $h_{k+1,k} = \|t_{k+1}\|$.
8. Set $q_{k+1} = t_{k+1}/h_{k+1,k}$.
9. Set Q and R to be the reduced QR factors of H_k.
10. Set $y_k = \rho R^{-1}Q^T e_1$.
11. If convergence criterion is met or maximum iteration count is exceeded, set $x_k = x_0 + Q_k y_k$ and terminate.
12. End loop.

(For clarity, we have left out the updating procedure.) If the convergence criterion we are using is based on the residual r_k, which is almost certainly the case, we may use

$$\|r_k\| = \|\rho e_1 - H_k y_k\|$$

to compute it after y_k has been found, without having to find $r_k = b - Ax_k = b - AQ_k y_k$. Note that although we do not need to retain the values of the temporary vectors t_k, for example, we must retain $\{q_i\}$ throughout the iteration.

Reorthogonali-
zation

There are other things we must do to get a good program. We should be using the modified Gram-Schmidt process, for instance, and even then the ill-conditioning of Γ_k means that we may lose the orthogonality of the eigenvectors. Because of this potential loss of orthogonality we periodically **reorthogonalize** the basis for Γ_k (typically by applying the modified Gram-Schmidt process to the current basis). There are heuristics for detecting loss of orthogonality.

The advantages of GMRES are principally that it is applicable to matrices without special properties[7] and that it depends on A only through matrix-vector products such as the computation of Ax_0 in finding the residual, and the computation of products like Aq_m in the Arnoldi process. This fact can be useful when A is so large that storing it and working with it directly are impractical but we have a formula for computing a_{ij}. (This is a common case, especially in the numerical solution of partial differential equations.)

Matrix-Free
Methods

We may write a special program that computes Ax from the entries of A without ever creating a copy of A. For this reason the method is said to be **matrix-free.** Matrix-free algorithms are often convenient for large sparse systems, but to use them the method must access A only in this way. This means that products such as $A^T y$ cannot be used (the program that computes Ax, which may be supplied by someone else, will not compute $A^T y$), and so an inner product such as

$$h_{pk} = q_k A^T q_p^T$$

must be computed as

$$h_{pk} = \left(Aq_k^T\right)^T q_p^T$$

---

[7] However, it is a fact that GMRES works particularly well for normal matrices.

to keep the method matrix-free. This is no inconvenience, but we must be alert for opportunities to rewrite our algorithms so as to take advantage of efficiencies like this one.

The disadvantages of GMRES include computational expense (especially when the matrix-vector products are expensive) and the need to store a basis for K_k. The latter is usually the biggest concern: If A is very large, we may be able to store it efficiently as a sparse matrix or avoid storing it at all by using a program to compute the matrix-vector products. The entries in an orthonormal basis for K_k, however, form an $n \times k$ matrix that is likely to have almost no zero entries. As k increases, the storage cost to store Q_k, needed to find x_k from

$$x_k = x_0 + Q_k y_k$$

will increase, often to the point where it is impractical to continue. Maintaining orthogonality will also become more and more difficult.

GMRES(k)   For these reasons it is common to use a **restarting** provision, where we periodically stop the iteration and begin it again using the most current estimate, x_k, as the new initial guess. This means that we start over again with a one-dimensional subspace and build up a new $K_1, K_2, \ldots$, until convergence or the next restart. A common version of this restarted GMRES algorithm is known as **GMRES(k),** which restarts after every k iterations. A restarted version of GMRES generally has worse convergence properties than GMRES but requires less memory.

The theory of GMRES and other Krylov space methods is related to the theory of polynomials in a fascinating way. We quote one theorem among many to give an idea of the flavor of these results:

Theorem 3.5.1

If A is a nonsingular matrix, then the residuals generated by the GMRES method satisfy

$$\|r_k\| = \min_{p \in P_k^1} (\|p(A)r_0\|),$$

where P_k^1 is the set of all polynomials of degree at most k with the property that $p(0) = 1$.

In this context, the set P_k^1 is sometimes called the set of **residual polynomials** of degree k; $p(A)$ is the polynomial $p(z)$ evaluated at $z = A$ in the obvious manner. It may be helpful to use the Cayley-Hamilton theorem, which states that every matrix satisfies its own characteristic equation, to generate a residual polynomial to use to estimate $\|r_k\|$; a polynomial with roots at the eigenvalues of A is also frequently useful. When we use polynomials in this way to derive bounds on $\|r_k\|$ using Theorem 3.5.1 or a similar theorem, we say that we are using a **test polynomial.**

We mention again that GMRES is typically used with preconditioning. The GMRES algorithm tends to perform better when the eigenvalues of A are **clustered** in the complex plane, that is, when they tend to group around some (nonzero) point, and so clustering the eigenvalues is a goal of preconditioning for GMRES.

PROBLEMS 3.5

1. Perform one more iteration in Example 3.5.1, and verify that you get the true solution.

2. Let $A = [-2\ 1\ 2\ 4; 1\ 0\ -1\ 2; -3\ 2\ -1\ -1; 0\ 1\ -2\ 1]$ and $b = (1, 1, 1, 1)^T$. Approximate the solution of $Ax = b$ using three iterations of GMRES (as in Example 3.5.1), starting from $x_0 = (1, 0, -1, 0)^T$.

3. a. Write a MATLAB program that implements GMRES.
b. Write a MATLAB program that implements GMRES(k).

4. a. Let $A = [2\ 2\ 1\ -1\ 3; 1\ 0\ -1\ -3\ 1; 0\ -1\ 3\ 2\ -1; 1\ 0\ -1\ 2\ 1]$ and $b = (1, 1, 1, 1, 1)^T$.

Approximate the solution of $Ax = b$ using four iterations of GMRES.

b. Approximate the solution of $Ax = b$ using two iterations of GMRES(2) (that is, perform two iterations of GMRES, restart, and then perform two more iterations of GMRES). Compare with your answer from part (a).

5. If A is diagonalizable, nonsingular, and has $p < n$ distinct eigenvalues, then GMRES will converge in at most p iterations. Demonstrate this for two full 4×4 matrices, having one and two distinct eigenvalues, respectively.

MATLAB 3.5

For the very large sparse matrices we're talking about, one would ordinarily use (or write) a special-purpose program in Fortran, C, or the like, that would call subroutines from Netlib or a similar source of high-quality numerical subroutines. In fact, MATLAB started as an interactive way of using such Fortran subroutines. Fortran remains popular today largely because in the 1970s and 1980s a great many scientific computation subroutines were created in it. Additionally, it is still used on supercomputers.

Let's step through Example 3.5.1 in MATLAB. Compare the results to those in the example. Enter:

```
» A=[2 1 -1;0 2 2;-2 1 2]
» b=[2 4 1]'
» r0=b                  %Recall that x0=0 here.
» q1=b/norm(b)
» AQ=A*q1
» [Q,R]=qr(AQ,0)
» y1=R\Q'*b             %Solution of minimization problem.
» x1=q1*y1
» r1=b-A*x1
» norm(r1)
» norm(x1-[1 1 1]')  %Abs. error; true solution is [1 1 1]'.
» clear Q R             %Start the second iteration:
» v2=A*q1-(q1'*A*q1)*q1;q2=v2/norm(v2)
» Q2=[q1,q2]
» AQ2=A*Q2
» [Q,R]=qr(AQ2,0)
» y2=R\Q'*b
» x2=Q2*y2
» r2=b-A*x2
» norm(r2)
» norm(x2-[1 1 1]')   %Abs. error.
```

Notice that the absolute error has increased slightly, even though the residual has decreased considerably. Unfortunately in a real application of the method, we can monitor only the residual error, not the absolute error. We must rely on formulas like $\rho_k \leq \kappa(A)\,\|r_k\|\,/\,\|b\|$ from Section 2.5 to bound the relative error ρ_k in terms of the residual, or the related result $\alpha_k/\alpha_0 \leq \kappa(A)\,\|r_k\|\,/\,\|r_0\|$ for the absolute error.

How would we implement preconditioning? Suppose we are using a left preconditioner P so that the system we want to solve is now $P^{-1}Ax = P^{-1}b$. If P is the Jacobi preconditioner we might simply perform the multiplication and perform GMRES on $P^{-1}A$. For most other preconditioners this would not be feasible, so we simulate it. Note that for the preconditioned system, the residuals are of the form $r_k = P^{-1}b - P^{-1}Ax_k = P^{-1}(b - Ax_k)$. Hence, $Pr_k = b - Ax_k$, which can be solved for r_k (remember that one criterion for a good preconditioner is that systems involving P should be easy to solve). Let's try using the Gauss-Seidel preconditioner on this example; we'll have to substitute $P^{-1}A$ for A at each step. Enter:

```
» P=tril(A)              %Preconditioner.
» r0=P\b
» q1=b/norm(b)
» AQ=P\A*q1
» [Q,R]=qr(AQ,0)
» y1=R\Q'*b              %Solution of minimization problem.
» x1=q1*y1
» r1=P\(b-A*x1)
» norm(r1)
» norm(x1-[1 1 1]')   %Abs. error; true solution is [1 1 1]'.
```

After a single iteration of preconditioned GMRES, the residual norm $\|r_1\|$ is about the same as the residual norm after two iterations of unpreconditioned GMRES. Of course, we have added work, which makes this preconditioned iteration slower.

The Jacobi and Gauss-Seidel preconditioners are not usually used with GMRES; we have used them for simplicity. Remember that we have in mind a matrix A that is sparse and very large.

There is a GMRES command in MATLAB, gmres. Enter help gmres and note that you may enter a program that returns Ax rather than a matrix A. You may also pass a preconditioner to gmres and have it restart periodically (that is, it incorporates GMRES(k) as well). The routine also accepts an initial guess x_0 and a maximum number of iterations. The help suggests the following example using GMRES(10); enter:

```
» A=gallery('wilk',21); b=sum(A,2);
» tol=1e-12;maxit=15;M1=diag([10:-1:1 1 1:10]);
» x=gmres(A,b,10,tol,maxit,M1,[],[]);
» norm(b-A*x)/norm(b)    %Relative residual.
» norm(b-A*x)            %Residual.
» norm(x-ones(size(x)))  %Absolute error.
```

Note that the preconditioner M1 used in this example is essentially the Jacobi preconditioner, with 1 substituted where the diagonal of A has a zero entry. Let's try again with the ILU method; enter:

```
» A=sparse(A);
» [L,U,P]=luinc(A,'0');
» M1=P'*L*U;
» x=gmres(A,b,10,tol,maxit,M1);
» norm(x-ones(size(x)))    %Absolute error.
```

The relative residual is about three orders of magnitude smaller than it is with the Jacobi preconditioner, at the level of the machine epsilon. The absolute error is also about three orders of magnitude smaller. Using a better preconditioner has gained us 3 additional decimal places of accuracy but has been more computationally expensive.

What happens if we use no preconditioning? Enter:

```
» x=gmres(A,b,10,tol);
» norm(b-A*x)/norm(b)      %Relative residual.
» norm(x-ones(size(x)))    %Absolute error.
```

The relative residual is on the order of 10^{-9}, and the absolute error is on the order of 10^{-8}. This is much worse, and the routine indicates that convergence is not achieved (tol is 10^{-12}).

In fact, if you look at the help for gmres you will see that it is set up to use the ILU method in a more efficient form than we used it above. Enter:

```
» x=gmres(A,b,10,tol,maxit,P'*L,U);
```

to have gmres use the same preconditioner without actually forming $P^T LU$. Instead, gmres solves systems such as $P^T LUx = c$ in the usual LU decomposition two step manner. Using these two triangular solves is more efficient (and more accurate, but then the decomposition is already intentionally inaccurate).

Repeat this experiment using A=sprandn(100,100,.2); solve using no preconditioner, the Jacobi preconditioner, and the ILU method. Repeat for a few different matrices A. Your results will likely indicate that preconditioning is more effective, as a rule, on structured matrices than unstructured ones. There are preconditioners that are specialized to certain highly structured problems.

The gmres command with default tolerance and maximum number of iterations and no restarts may be entered in the form gmres(A,b,[],[],[],M). In this routine MATLAB interprets the empty vectors as a signal to use the default values. Enter type gmres and see how this is implemented. Enter help minres and help qmr to see details of two methods related to GMRES.

ADDITIONAL PROBLEMS 3.5

6. a. Let $A = [-2\ 1\ 2\ 4; 0\ 1\ -1\ 2; -3\ 2\ -1\ -1; 0\ 1\ -2\ 1]$, $b = (1, 1, 1, 1)^T$, and $x_0 = (1, 0, -1, 0)^T$ as in Problem 2. Approximate the solution of $Ax = b$ using three iterations of precon-

ditioned GMRES using the Jacobi preconditioner. Do not use gmres; step through the computation.

b. Repeat part (a) with the Gauss-Seidel preconditioner.

238

7. Use `sprandn` to generate a 100×100 sparse matrix A that is about 10% dense. Pick a solution x and generate the corresponding b. Approximate the solution using: four iterations of GMRES; two iterations of GMRES(2); four iterations of preconditioned GMRES using the Jacobi preconditioner; and four iterations of preconditioned GMRES using the Gauss-Seidel preconditioner. Use $x_0 = 0$ in each case. Compare your answers and the efficiency of each method.

8. **a.** Use `sprandn` to generate a 500×500 sparse matrix A that is about 5% dense. Pick a solution x and generate the corresponding b. Approximate the solution using: ten iterations of GMRES; two iterations of GMRES(5); ten iterations of preconditioned GMRES using the Gauss-Seidel preconditioner; and ten iterations of preconditioned GMRES using the ILU preconditioner. Use $x_0 = 0$ in each case. Compare your answers and the efficiency of each method.

   b. Repeat part (a), but rather than limit the number of iterations, continue until a relative residual of less than 10^{-8} is achieved.

9. Carefully justify the steps in Eq. (3.23).

10. It is possible to compute the QR factors of H_{k+1} from those of H_k using one Givens matrix. Suggest a method

for doing so (for a hint, enter `type qrinsert` in MATLAB).

11. **a.** Write a MATLAB program for performing GMRES using the modified Gram-Schmidt method (from the MGS algorithm in Section 2.8).

    b. Compare the performance of GMRES with the modified Gram-Schmidt method to the performance of GMRES as given in the text. Find a matrix for which the former gives noticeably better results.

12. If A is nonsingular and normal and b is a linear combination of m linearly independent eigenvectors of A, then GMRES will converge in at most m iterations. Verify this for three different (nontrivial) normal matrices.

13. Verify Theorem 3.5.1 for the iteration in Example 3.5.1 for $k = 1$ and 2.

14. Prove Theorem 3.5.1. (*Hint:* Show that if $x_k \in x_0 + K_k$, then $x_k = x_0 + \sum_{i=0}^{k} c_i A^i r_0$, and then use this in $r_k = b - Ax_k$.)

15. Write an efficient MATLAB program that implements GMRES with preconditioning. If a preconditioner is not supplied by the user, the program should use a reasonable default preconditioner.

3.6   Numerical Eigenproblems

In Chapters 2 and 3 we've focused on solving the linear system $Ax = b$. There are other types of matrix computations that are of interest, such as computing $\|A\|$ or finding $\det(A)$ or decomposing A in some manner, yet, overwhelmingly the two main types of matrix problems involve solving the linear system $Ax = b$ and finding the eigenvalues of A. Most other matrix problems are solved in the service of one of these two goals.

Recall that the spectrum of A, $sp(A)$, is the set of all eigenvalues of A, that is, the set of all complex numbers λ such that

$$Ax = \lambda x$$

for some nonzero vector x, called an eigenvector of A associated with λ. These are important in many physical and mathematical applications, such as determining whether an engineering control system is stable, or finding the singular values and hence condition number of a matrix (since the nonzero singular values of A are the square roots of the eigenvalues of $A^T A$; see Section 2.9).

Nature of Eigenproblems   All methods for finding the eigenvalues of a general matrix are iterative methods, because finding the eigenvalues of an $n \times n$ matrix is equivalent to finding the roots of its characteristic polynomial

$$c(\lambda) = \lambda^n + a_{n-1}\lambda^{n-1} + \cdots + a_1\lambda + a_0,$$

and there is no way to find the roots of a general polynomial of degree 5 or higher without using iterative methods.[8] Since finding eigenvalues is equivalent to finding the roots of $c(\lambda)$, the same must be true of eigenvalue problems. (In fact, sometimes we find the zeroes of a polynomial by constructing a matrix that has that polynomial as its characteristic polynomial and then finding the eigenvalues of the matrix.) Hence, we will not have a finite-step method like Gaussian elimination for numerical eigenproblems; unlike the case for linear systems, we do not choose between direct methods and iterative methods.

Power Method

There are a number of ways to find the eigenvalues of a matrix. The simplest is the **power method,** which proceeds as follows: Pick an estimate v_0 of an eigenvector of A associated with a largest eigenvalue of A (in modulus) and such that $\|v_0\|_\infty = 1$, and compute

$$
\begin{aligned}
v_k &= \frac{Av_{k-1}}{\mu_k} \\
&= \frac{A^k v_0}{\mu_k \mu_{k-1} \cdots \mu_1}
\end{aligned}
\tag{3.25}
$$

($k = 1, 2, \ldots$), where μ_k is an entry of the vector in the numerator Av_{k-1} that has maximum modulus. This ensures that $\|v_k\|_\infty = 1$. (There are other ways to normalize this iteration). What happens when we iterate the power method, Eq. (3.25)? Suppose that A has a full set of linearly independent eigenvectors[9] $\{x_1, \ldots, x_n\}$ associated, in that order, with the eigenvalues $\lambda_1, \ldots, \lambda_n$, where $|\lambda_1| \geq |\lambda_2| \geq \cdots \geq |\lambda_n|$. Then

$$
v_0 = \alpha_1 x_1 + \cdots + \alpha_n x_n
$$

for some coefficients $\alpha_1, \ldots, \alpha_n$. Then

$$
\begin{aligned}
Av_0 &= A\left(\alpha_1 x_1 + \cdots + \alpha_n x_n\right) \\
&= \alpha_1 Ax_1 + \cdots + \alpha_n Ax_n \\
&= \alpha_1 \lambda_1 x_1 + \cdots + \alpha_n \lambda_n x_n
\end{aligned}
$$

because $Ax_i = \lambda_i x_i$ ($i = 1, \ldots, n$). So

$$
\begin{aligned}
A^2 v_0 &= A(Av_0) \\
&= \alpha_1 \lambda_1 Ax_1 + \cdots + \alpha_n \lambda_n Ax_n \\
&= \alpha_1 \lambda_1^2 x_1 + \cdots + \alpha_n \lambda_n^2 x_n
\end{aligned}
$$

and in general

$$
\begin{aligned}
A^k v_0 &= \alpha_1 \lambda_1^k x_1 + \cdots + \alpha_n \lambda_n^k x_n \\
&= \lambda_1^k \left(\alpha_1 x_1 + \alpha_2 \frac{\lambda_2^k}{\lambda_1^k} x_2 + \cdots + \alpha_n \frac{\lambda_n^k}{\lambda_1^k} x_n \right) \\
&= \lambda_1^k \left(\alpha_1 x_1 + \alpha_2 \left(\frac{\lambda_2}{\lambda_1}\right)^k x_2 + \cdots + \alpha_n \left(\frac{\lambda_n}{\lambda_1}\right)^k x_n \right).
\end{aligned}
$$

---

[8] For every polynomial of degree at least 1, there is a matrix that has it as its characteristic polynomial.
[9] Recall that this is necessarily so in the commonly occurring case that A is symmetric.

Now, if it happens that $|\lambda_1| > |\lambda_2|$ (in which case we say that the matrix has a **dominant eigenvalue** λ_1), then $A^k v_0 \approx \alpha_1 \lambda_1^k x_1$ for large k; $A^k v_0$ is tending toward a vector in the direction of an eigenvector associated with the largest eigenvalue of A (in magnitude), and the ratio of $\|A^k v_0\|_\infty$ and $\|A^{k+1} v_0\|_\infty$ is $|\lambda_1|$, the size of that eigenvalue.

In Problem 3.6 you'll be asked to show that the normalization by μ_k in Eq. (3.25) is just what is needed to ensure that

$$
\begin{aligned}
v_k &\to x_1 \\
\mu_k &\to \lambda_1
\end{aligned}
\tag{3.26}
$$

as $k \to \infty$. Clearly, the convergence is linear, with rate λ_2/λ_1; the more widely separated the top two eigenvalues, the smaller this ratio and the faster the convergence.

What could go wrong? First, if A does not have a dominant eigenvalue, it is still possible to extract some information from the iterates v_k, but fundamentally the method fails. (Fortunately in many applications it is known or exceedingly probable that there is a dominant eigenvalue.) Second, if α_1 is zero, then we've had the incredibly bad luck to choose an initial vector v_0 that is orthogonal to x_1. Even if this should happen—and it's very unlikely—roundoff errors will quickly introduce a component along x_1 and the method will recover. (Note, roundoff error is actually *beneficial* here!) Usually, we make little effort to ensure that the initial guess v_0 is a good guess at x_1; we choose as the initial guess any vector with no zero entries.

If we are principally interested in the eigenvalue, not the eigenvector, then we may compute the **Rayleigh quotient**

$$
R_k = \frac{v_k^T A v_k}{v_k^T v_k},
$$

which can be shown to converge to the eigenvalue quadratically. Other acceleration techniques for linearly convergent sequences could also be applied (see Section 1.4).

Example 3.6.1   Consider the matrix $A = [1 \ 2; 2 \ 1]$. The eigenvalues are -1 and 3, so there is a dominant eigenvalue. Let's use $v_0 = (2, 1)^T$. We have

$$
\begin{aligned}
v_1 &= \frac{A v_0}{\mu_1} \\
&= \frac{1}{\mu_1} \begin{pmatrix} 1 & 2 \\ 2 & 1 \end{pmatrix} \begin{pmatrix} 2 \\ 1 \end{pmatrix} \\
&= \frac{1}{\mu_1} \begin{pmatrix} 4 \\ 5 \end{pmatrix} \\
&= \begin{pmatrix} 4/5 \\ 1 \end{pmatrix}
\end{aligned}
$$

($\mu_1 = 5$). Then

$$v_2 = \frac{A v_1}{\mu_2}$$

$$= \frac{1}{\mu_2} \begin{pmatrix} 1 & 2 \\ 2 & 1 \end{pmatrix} \begin{pmatrix} 4/5 \\ 1 \end{pmatrix}$$

$$= \frac{1}{\mu_2} \begin{pmatrix} 14/5 \\ 13/5 \end{pmatrix}$$

$$= \begin{pmatrix} 1 \\ 13/14 \end{pmatrix}$$

($\mu_2 = 14/5$). Since the dominant eigenvalue is 3, $\mu_2 = 2.8$ is already a fair approximation; the corresponding eigenvector is $(1, 1)^T$, and $(1, 13/14)^T \doteq (1, 0.9286)^T$ is also a decent approximation for only two iterations. The Rayleigh quotients are

$$R_1 = \frac{v_1^T A v_1}{v_1^T v_1}$$

$$= \frac{\begin{pmatrix} 4/5 \\ 1 \end{pmatrix}^T \begin{pmatrix} 1 & 2 \\ 2 & 1 \end{pmatrix} \begin{pmatrix} 4/5 \\ 1 \end{pmatrix}}{\begin{pmatrix} 4/5 \\ 1 \end{pmatrix}^T \begin{pmatrix} 4/5 \\ 1 \end{pmatrix}}$$

$$\doteq 2.9512$$

and

$$R_2 = \frac{v_2^T A v_2}{v_2^T v_2}$$

$$= \frac{\begin{pmatrix} 1 \\ 13/14 \end{pmatrix}^T \begin{pmatrix} 1 & 2 \\ 2 & 1 \end{pmatrix} \begin{pmatrix} 1 \\ 13/14 \end{pmatrix}}{\begin{pmatrix} 1 \\ 13/14 \end{pmatrix}^T \begin{pmatrix} 1 \\ 13/14 \end{pmatrix}}$$

$$\doteq 2.9945,$$

and these are, as expected, much better approximations of $\lambda_1 = 3$ (the relative error in R_2 is .0018 or about two-tenths of one percent). ∎

Inverse Power Method

A simple trick allows us to find the smallest eigenvalue (in modulus) of a nonsingular matrix A. Note that if (λ_i, x_i) are an eigenpair

$$A x_i = \lambda_i x_i$$

and no eigenvalue is zero, then

$$\frac{1}{\lambda_i} x_i = A^{-1} x_i$$

that is, the eigenvalues of A^{-1} are the reciprocals of those of A. Hence, the largest eigenvalue of A^{-1} is the smallest eigenvalue of A, and so applying the power method to A^{-1} will locate it. Of course, as should go without saying, we do not actually compute A^{-1}; rather we compute the quantity

$$v_k = \frac{A^{-k}v_{k-1}}{\mu_k} \tag{3.27}$$

by solving $Ay = v_k$ for the next numerator in Eq. (3.27) at each step. (Because we will be solving a system involving the same A many times, it would be sensible to use a decomposition of it, or possibly even to transform A to a similar[10] matrix B such that linear systems involving B are easier to solve, for example, if B were sparse or otherwise structured.) The process of using Eq. (3.27) to find the smallest eigenvalue of A is known as the **inverse power method.**

The power method is useful if we need only the largest eigenvalue of A. This would allow us, for example, to determine the spectral radius

$$\rho(A) = \max\{|\lambda_i|\}$$

of the matrix. It is relatively rare, however, to need *only* the largest eigenvalue of a matrix; yet in many problems only the *largest several* eigenvalues of a matrix are needed. For example, many applications involving systems of differential equations require only the largest three or so eigenvalues.

How can we find more eigenvalues? Deflation is an obvious approach.[11] Note that if λ is an eigenvalue of A with associated eigenvector x, then $(0, x)$ is an eigenpair of

$$A - \lambda I_n$$

because

$$
\begin{aligned}
(A - \lambda I_n)x &= Ax - \lambda I_n x \\
&= \lambda x - \lambda x \\
&= 0 \\
&= 0 \cdot x.
\end{aligned}
$$

So if λ_1 is the largest eigenvalue in modulus of A, then λ_2 is the largest eigenvalue in modulus of

$$A - \lambda_1 I_n$$

and if in addition $|\lambda_2| > |\lambda_3|$, then λ_2 is the dominant eigenvalue of $A - \lambda_1 I_n$ and the power method applied to $A - \lambda_1 I_n$ should converge to λ_2. This process could then be repeated for λ_3, λ_4, etc.

We don't discuss deflation in any detail. It has the usual drawbacks; it produces relatively low-quality estimates, with error growing as the process continues, and its

---

[10] Recall that matrices A and B are said to be *similar* if $B = P^{-1}AP$ for some matrix P; similar matrices have the same spectrum.

[11] The term deflation is also used to refer to a method for splitting an eigenvalue problem into smaller problems. We do not discuss this sense of deflation.

results should be cleaned up by another method. It is not usually used with the identity matrix but is used instead in the form

$$A - \lambda_1 \Lambda, \tag{3.28}$$

where Λ is a rank 1 matrix that is formed as the outer product of (the approximate eigenvector) x_1 and another vector that determines the method of deflation used: $\Lambda = x_1 c^T$ for some vector c.

Shifts
On a related note, if σ is a given value, then the eigenvalues of $A - \sigma I_n$ are related to the eigenvalues λ_i of A as follows:

$$(A - \sigma I_n) x = Ax - \sigma I_n x$$

$$= \lambda x - \sigma x$$

$$= (\lambda - \sigma) x.$$

That is, $\tau_i = \lambda_i - \sigma$ are the eigenvalues of $A - \sigma I_n$. Applying the power method to $A - \sigma I_n$ to find its largest eigenvalue is known as the **shifted power method** (with shift σ.).

Most often the power method is applied in the following way: We obtain an initial estimate of the eigenvalue λ_i that we seek, which may or may not be the largest or smallest eigenvalue of A. We then apply the inverse power method to $A - \sigma I_n$. Since the eigenvalues of this matrix are

$$\frac{1}{\lambda_i - \sigma}$$

(assuming $\sigma \notin \mathrm{sp}(A)$), the largest eigenvalue of $(A - \sigma I_n)^{-1}$ corresponds to the eigenvalue λ_i of A, which is closest to σ. Hence, this approach, called the **inverse shifted power method**[12] or **inverse iteration,** allows us to find the eigenvalue of A closest to a given value σ. This is the form in which the power method is most commonly seen, unless it is being used to get an initial estimate of an eigenvalue. Note that the power method with deflation may be used to get an estimate of the second-largest, third-largest, etc., eigenvalues for use in this method.

The inverse iteration method typically converges much more rapidly than the power method (per iteration, but of course iterations are more expensive now that we must solve a linear system at each step). Of course the choice of shift affects this; if σ is very close to the eigenvalue, then $1/(\lambda_i - \sigma)$ is likely to be very large and hence far from the next nearest eigenvalue, so rapid convergence of the method can be expected.

In the spirit of the Gauss-Seidel iteration (see Section 3.1), a natural idea is to update the shift at each step of the shifted or inverse shifted power method with the estimate provided by the Rayleigh quotient, that is, to set $\sigma_k = R_{k-1}$ and use $A - \sigma_k I_n$ at each step. This is sensible because R_k is our best available estimate of the eigenvalue. The inverse shifted power method with this modification is called **Rayleigh quotient iteration** and yields very rapid convergence of the eigenvalue.

We might worry for all shifted methods that as $\sigma \to \lambda$ the matrix $A - \sigma I_n$ may become ill-conditioned with respect to the solution of linear systems. This is so, but

---

[12] Many authors simply call this the inverse power method.

the net effect on the resulting eigenvalue estimates is less than would be expected. The errors tend to align with the direction of the approximate eigenvector, but because any nonzero multiple of an eigenvector is itself an eigenvector, the resultant is just another approximate eigenvector.

Inverse iteration is a good technique for improving the accuracy of an eigenvalue or eigenvector, for finding an eigenvector corresponding to a known eigenvalue, or for finding a single eigenvalue near a given value σ. If more than just a few eigenpairs of A are sought, however, there are significantly more efficient methods to find them.

PROBLEMS 3.6

1. **a.** Apply three iterations of the power method to estimate the largest eigenvalue of $A = [2\ 1; 1\ 2]$.
   b. Compute the three Rayleigh quotients.

2. Apply three iterations of the shifted power method to estimate an eigenvalue of $A = [2\ 1; 1\ 2]$ using the shift $\sigma = 1.25$.

3. Apply three iterations of the inverse power method to estimate the smallest eigenvalue of $A = [2\ 1; 1\ 2]$.

4. **a.** Why must a dominant eigenvalue be real?
   b. What happens if the largest eigenvalue of A is a multiple eigenvalue but all other eigenvalues of A are smaller in modulus?
   c. If x is an eigenvector of A, what can you say about the Rayleigh quotient $R(x) = x^T A x / x^T x$?

5. Verify that the results in Eq. (3.26) are correct.

MATLAB 3.6

We have already seen the `eig` command. If A is a square matrix, `[V,D]=eig(A)` finds matrices such that `A*V=V*D`; that is, V is the matrix of eigenvectors and D is a diagonal matrix containing the corresponding eigenvalues on the main diagonal. To see the options, enter:

```
» help eig
```

In particular, note that by default a balancing procedure is used to help improve the condition of the matrix. You can turn off this procedure if you believe that it may be making matters worse.

Recall that, although we have been focusing in this text on the condition number of a matrix with respect to the solution of a linear system $Ax = b$ involving it, the idea of a condition number is more general and can be discussed with respect to other problems. For nonlinear root-finding problems, ill-conditioning is associated with multiple roots. An eigenvalue problem is ill-conditioned when A is near a matrix with multiple eigenvalues (which would correspond to multiple roots of the characteristic polynomial of the matrix). The MATLAB command `condeig` computes the condition number of a matrix's eigenvalues. Enter:

```
» H=hilb(10);
» cond(H)
» condeig(H)
```

Each eigenvalue of the 10×10 Hilbert matrix is very well-conditioned with respect to the eigenvalue problem, even though the matrix is very poorly conditioned with respect to the solution of linear systems. Enter:

```
» A=[2 1;0 2]
» cond(A)
» condeig(A)
```

This matrix is well-conditioned with respect to the solution of linear systems, but since it is defective (as it has only one linearly independent eigenvector), it is very poorly conditioned with respect to the eigenvalue problem.

The eigenvalue condition number depends on the matrix of eigenvectors and its inverse, similar to the way in which the condition number with respect to the solution of linear systems depends on A and A^{-1}. Recall that if A is symmetric, then the matrix of eigenvectors is orthogonal and hence its inverse is easy to compute. To see how the eigenvalue condition number is computed in MATLAB, enter:

```
» type condeig
```

Note from the help for `condeig` that you may use it to compute the eigenvalues, eigenvectors, and condition numbers all at once.

The MATLAB command `poly` may be used to find the characteristic polynomial of A. However, this is a slow process. Enter:

```
» type poly
```

and note that MATLAB finds the characteristic polynomial by using the `eig` command to find its roots and then constructing the coefficients of the polynomial. Finding the coefficients in $c(\lambda)$ without knowing the roots of the characteristic equation is prohibitively expensive in the general case. Even if we could do that, the corresponding root-finding problem $c(\lambda) = 0$ can be ill-conditioned (as a root-finding problem) even when the eigenvalue problem itself is well-conditioned (that is, when the eigenvalue condition number is small). Using techniques intended to find eigenvalues of matrices directly is the best approach in essentially all cases.

ADDITIONAL PROBLEMS 3.6

6. a. Apply three iterations of the inverse shifted power method to estimate the eigenvalue of $A = [2\ 1; 1\ 2]$ nearest to 1.2.

   b. Apply three iterations of the inverse shifted power method to estimate the eigenvalue of $A = [2\ 1; 1\ 2]$ nearest to 1.1.

   c. Apply three iterations of the inverse shifted power method to estimate the eigenvalue of $A = [2\ 1; 1\ 2]$ nearest to 1.05. Comment on the effect of the shift on the convergence of the method.

7. What is the formula for the eigenvalue condition number used in the `condeig` program?

8. Write a MATLAB program for performing the power method using the Rayleigh quotient. Attempt to detect failure to converge (owing to the lack of a dominant eigenvalue). The user should be asked to supply only the matrix. Return an estimate of both the eigenvalue and an associated eigenvector.

9. Apply the power method to the matrix $A = [-5\ -4; 4\ 5]$. Explain your results.

10. a. Apply five iterations of the power method to estimate the largest eigenvalue of $A = [3\ 1\ 0; 1\ 3\ 0; 0\ 0\ 1]$.

   b. Compute the Rayleigh quotient of the last estimate of the eigenvalue.

   c. Use deflation in the form $A - \lambda I_2$ to approximate the next-smallest eigenvalue of A using five iterations of the power method.

  d. Compute the Rayleigh quotient of the last estimate of this eigenvalue.

11. The method of **Wielandt deflation** uses Eq. (3.28) with $\Lambda = x_1 c^T$ where $c = A_i/(\lambda_1 \xi_i)$. Here A_i is the ith row of A, written as a column vector; λ_1 is the estimate of the largest eigenvalue of A; and ξ_i is the ith entry of x_1, the estimate of the associated eigenvector. Repeat Problem 10 (c) and Problem 10 (d) using Wielandt deflation. Is it a better technique than using $\Lambda = I_n$?

12. Write a MATLAB program for performing the inverse shifted power method using the Rayleigh quotient. Attempt to detect failure to converge (owing to the lack of a dominant eigenvalue). The user should be asked to supply only the matrix. Return an estimate of both the eigenvalue and an associated eigenvector.

13. a. Use the power method with deflation to find all eigenvalues of the Hilbert matrix of order 10 to an accuracy of at least 10^{-4}.

  b. Repeat with the inverse shifted power method, choosing shifts in a reasonable way based on the information available (perhaps by using the Gerschgorin Circle Theorem). Comment.

14. What happens in the power method if the largest eigenvalue of A is complex?

15. a. Prove that the Rayleigh quotient converges to the dominant eigenvalue.

  b. Prove that the convergence is quadratic.

4 Polynomial Interpolation

4.1 Lagrange Interpolating Polynomials

S O FAR WE'VE DISCUSSED two of the three most common problems in numerical analysis: root-finding for nonlinear equations and the solution of linear systems. (We address the third, nonlinear optimization, in Ch. 7.) These types of problems are important in their own right. But other type of problems often require, at each step, the solution of a problem from one of these classes. For example, Newton's method for systems (Section 1.8) and Newton's method for nonlinear optimization (Section 7.3) both require that a linear system be solved at every step. We'll make frequent use of techniques for solving root-finding problems and linear systems while solving other computational problems.

In this chapter we discuss the problem of polynomial interpolation, that is, of fitting a polynomial curve through a given set of points. Polynomial interpolation is of interest in and of itself, but it is also of interest as a theoretical tool to devise and analyze numerical methods. We've already seen how linear interpolation (for example, in the method of false position, Section 1.1) and quadratic interpolation (for example, in Brent's method, Section 1.6) are useful for deriving methods. Interpolation has also been a useful tool for arguing that the methods should work well for sufficiently smooth functions. We start by developing this powerful tool somewhat more formally, and then we look at related techniques for finding an equation of a smooth curve through a given set of points.

Suppose we have a set of points $\{x_0, x_1, \ldots, x_n\}$ ordered so that $x_0 < x_1 < \cdots < x_n$, and either a continuous function $f(x)$ defined on $[x_0, x_n]$ or a set of y-values $y_0, y_1, \ldots, y_n$ corresponding to the x-values (that is, (x_i, y_i) is a pair).

Polynomial
Interpolation

The polynomial interpolation problem is to find a polynomial $p(x)$ of degree at most n that interpolates the data $(x_0, y_0), (x_1, y_1), \ldots, (x_n, y_n)$:

$$y_0 = p(x_0)$$

$$y_1 = p(x_1) \tag{4.1}$$

$$\vdots$$

$$y_n = p(x_n)$$

and we say that p interpolates f (or the data) at $x_0, x_1, \ldots, x_n$, and that p is an interpolant. We stress that an interpolant must agree with the function f or the values $y_0, y_1, \ldots, y_n$ at the corresponding points $x_0, x_1, \ldots, x_n$, which are sometimes called the **nodes** (or **breakpoints**).

The obvious technique for finding the coefficients in a polynomial interpolant is as follows: Let $x_0 < x_1 < \cdots < x_n$ and $y_0, y_1, \ldots, y_n$ be given, and let

$$p(x) = a_n x^n + a_{n-1} x^{n-1} + \cdots + a_1 x + a_0$$

represent the interpolant. We must find $a_n, \ldots, a_1, a_0$. We may represent the interpolation requirements of Eq. (4.1) as

$$a_n x_0^n + a_{n-1} x_0^{n-1} + \cdots + a_1 x_0 + a_0 = y_0$$

$$a_n x_1^n + a_{n-1} x_1^{n-1} + \cdots + a_1 x_1 + a_0 = y_0$$

$$\vdots$$

$$a_n x_n^n + a_{n-1} x_n^{n-1} + \cdots + a_1 x_n + a_0 = y_0$$

that is

$$\begin{bmatrix} 1 & x_0 & x_0^2 & \cdots & x_0^n \\ 1 & x_1 & x_1^2 & \cdots & x_1^n \\ 1 & x_2 & x_2^2 & \cdots & x_2^n \\ \vdots & \vdots & \vdots & \ddots & \vdots \\ 1 & x_n & x_n^2 & \cdots & x_n^n \end{bmatrix} \begin{bmatrix} a_0 \\ a_1 \\ \vdots \\ a_n \end{bmatrix} = \begin{pmatrix} y_0 \\ y_1 \\ \vdots \\ y_n \end{pmatrix}$$

where the matrix

$$V = \begin{bmatrix} 1 & x_0 & x_0^2 & \cdots & x_0^n \\ 1 & x_1 & x_1^2 & \cdots & x_1^n \\ 1 & x_2 & x_2^2 & \cdots & x_2^n \\ \vdots & \vdots & \vdots & \ddots & \vdots \\ 1 & x_n & x_n^2 & \cdots & x_n^n \end{bmatrix}$$

Vandermonde
Matrices

contains the known x-values. A matrix with the form of V, where each row has entries $\alpha^0, \alpha^1, \ldots, \alpha^n$ for some α, is called a **Vandermonde matrix,** and we say that a system involving it is a **Vandermonde system.** If the x_i are distinct then it is nonsingular, which implies that the polynomial interpolant exists and is unique. The coefficients of the interpolant are then given by the solution of

$$V \begin{bmatrix} a_0 \\ a_1 \\ \vdots \\ a_n \end{bmatrix} = \begin{pmatrix} y_0 \\ y_1 \\ \vdots \\ y_n \end{pmatrix},$$

and we may solve this linear system by any method desired. (Not surprisingly, there are special methods for solving systems involving Vandermonde matrices, and these should be used; we omit details.) We arrive at a linear system because while a polynomial in the variable x is in general *nonlinear* in x, it is always *linear* in its coefficients—and it is the coefficients we seek.

Example 4.1.1 Suppose we wish to interpolate a polynomial to the data points $(0, 0)$, $(\pi/2, 1)$, $(\pi, 0)$, $(3\pi/2, -1)$ from the sine curve. We have $\{x_0, x_1, x_2, x_3\} = \{0, \pi/2, \pi, 3\pi/2\}$, $\{y_0, y_1, y_2, y_3\} = \{0, 1, 0, -1\}$, and so we must solve

$$\begin{bmatrix} 1 & 0 & 0 & 0 \\ 1 & \frac{\pi}{2} & \frac{\pi^2}{4} & \frac{\pi^3}{8} \\ 1 & \pi & \pi^2 & \pi^3 \\ 1 & \frac{3\pi}{2} & \frac{9\pi^2}{4} & \frac{27\pi^3}{8} \end{bmatrix} \begin{bmatrix} a_0 \\ a_1 \\ a_2 \\ a_3 \end{bmatrix} = \begin{pmatrix} 0 \\ 1 \\ 0 \\ -1 \end{pmatrix}$$

for a_0, a_1, a_2, a_3. Using $V\backslash y$ in MATLAB gives

$$\begin{bmatrix} a_0 \\ a_1 \\ a_2 \\ a_3 \end{bmatrix} \doteq \begin{bmatrix} 0 \\ 1.6977 \\ -0.8106 \\ 0.0860 \end{bmatrix}$$

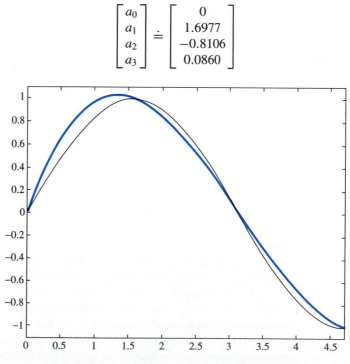

Figure 4.1 Sine Function (Blue) and Interpolant.

that is,

$$p(x) = 0.0860x^3 - 0.8106x^2 + 1.6977x$$

is the interpolant (see Fig. 4.1). It is easy to check that Eq. (4.1) is satisfied by $p(x)$ (up to roundoff error). ∎

Why might we want to use a polynomial interpolant to a function? We might need to find a simple approximation for the function. After all, to evaluate

$$f(x) = \sin(x)$$

on a computer, we must approximate it by a function using only arithmetic operations, and a polynomial interpolant is one possible way to do this. Another approach is to use the Taylor series, but this is rarely done; while the Taylor series is of great use in deriving and analyzing numerical methods, the series itself usually provides a poor approximation of the function, except in a very small interval about its center, and computing it requires derivative information that is usually inconvenient to find or unavailable.

Difficulties with Polynomial Interpolation
But polynomial interpolation is often a poor way to approximate a function also. The Vandermonde matrix is frequently ill-conditioned. Even if we do solve it accurately, the error in evaluating the polynomial

$$p(x) = a_n x^n + a_{n-1} x^{n-1} + \cdots + a_1 x + a_0$$

can be considerable: If n is large and x is large, then any error in x will be amplified greatly in raising x to the nth power. Cancellation could be a problem as well, particularly if the signs of the coefficients alternate. There are tricks for addressing these problems, at least in part, but there is another complication: Polynomial interpolants of high degree tend to be oscillatory, that is, they often must make large twists and turns to go through the nodes. An example is provided by the **Runge function**

$$f(x) = \frac{1}{1 + 25x^2} \tag{4.2}$$

($-1 \leq x \leq 1$). In Figure 4.2, the Runge function is plotted along with a polynomial interpolant of degree 10 (the nodes are the 11 points $-1:.2:1$). Note the large oscillations near the endpoints. Unfortunately, this type of behavior is typical. For the Runge function, the amplitude of the turns actually increases as n increases—that is, as n increases the approximation gets worse, in the sense that $\max |f(x) - p(x)|$ grows and in fact diverges.

This situation can be improved by using nodes (if we are free to choose the nodes) that are not equally spaced. But the fact remains that interpolation by high-degree polynomials is rarely useful in practice. Its principal use for us will be in deriving other numerical methods, such as the root-finding methods in Chapter 1 and the numerical integration procedures that we consider in the next chapter.

Deriving and understanding other methods is certainly an important application, so we consider one more aspect of the subject before turning to more practical methods of approximating a function.

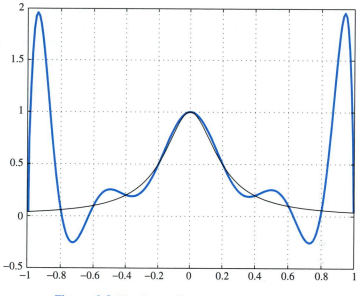

Figure 4.2 The Runge Function and Interpolant.

Lagrange
Polynomials

Suppose we wish to interpolate a line to two distinct points x_a, x_b. Define the functions $L_a(x)$ and $L_b(x)$ by

$$L_a(x) = \frac{x - x_b}{x_a - x_b}$$

$$L_b(x) = \frac{x - x_a}{x_b - x_a}$$

and note that

$$L_a(x_a) = 1, \, L_a(x_b) = 0$$

$$L_b(x_a) = 0, \, L_b(x_b) = 1$$

and that $L_a(x)$ and $L_b(x)$ are each linear functions of x. Given $y_a = f(x_a)$ and $y_b = f(x_b)$ we see that

$$\ell(x) = y_a L_a(x) + y_b L_b(x) \tag{4.3}$$

has the property that

$$\ell(x_a) = y_a L_a(x_a) + y_b L_b(x_a)$$

$$= y_a \cdot 1 + y_b \cdot 0$$

$$= y_a$$

$$\ell(x_b) = y_a L_a(x_b) + y_b L_b(x_b)$$

$$= y_a \cdot 0 + y_b \cdot 1$$

$$= y_b.$$

That is, $\ell(x)$ interpolates f at (x_a, y_a) and (x_b, y_b). Since $\ell(x)$ is the sum of two linear functions it is also linear (possibly constant), and since there is a unique line between any two points with distinct abscissas, $\ell(x)$ must be that line. The functions $L_a(x)$ and $L_b(x)$ appearing in Eq. (4.3) would be convenient to use if we knew that x_a and x_b were likely to stay the same while the y-values varied.

Let's generalize this technique to an arbitrary list of $n + 1$ distinct nodes $x_0, x_1, \ldots, x_n$ (ordered so that $x_0 < x_1 < \cdots < x_n$). Define the functions

$$L_{n,i}(x) = \frac{(x - x_0)(x - x_1) \cdots (x - x_{i-1})(x - x_{i+1}) \cdots (x - x_n)}{(x_i - x_0)(x_i - x_1) \cdots (x_i - x_{i-1})(x_i - x_{i+1}) \cdots (x_i - x_n)}$$

$$= \prod_{\substack{k=0 \\ k \neq i}}^{n} \frac{(x - x_k)}{(x_i - x_k)}$$

$(i = 0, \ldots, n)$. These are polynomials of precise degree n with the property that

$$L_{n,i}(x_j) = 0$$

if $j \neq i$ and

$$L_{n,i}(x_i) = 1$$

(see Fig. 4.3). These functions are called the **Lagrange polynomials** (or **Lagrange interpolating polynomials**). Note that they depend not only on n and $i \in \{0, 1, \ldots, n\}$ but also on the nodes $x_0, x_1, \ldots, x_n$.

Since a sum of polynomials of degree n is a polynomial of degree at most n, we can easily find the interpolating polynomial $p(x)$ of degree at most n through the points $(x_0, y_0), (x_1, y_1), \ldots, (x_n, y_n)$ in terms of the Lagrange polynomials:

$$p(x) = y_0 L_{n,0}(x) + y_1 L_{n,1}(x) + \cdots + y_n L_{n,n}(x)$$

$$= \sum_{i=0}^{n} y_i L_i(x).$$

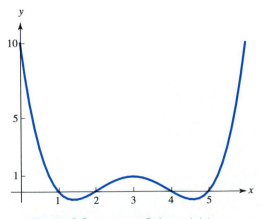

Figure 4.3 Lagrange Polynomial $L_{4,3}$.

(If n is understood we usually omit it in $L_{n,i}$ and simply write L_i.) Note that $p(x)$ is a polynomial of degree n (or possibly less) with the property that

$$p(x_j) = \sum_{i=0}^{n} y_i L_i(x_j)$$

$$= y_0 L_0(x_j) + y_1 L_1(x_j) + \cdots + y_n L_n(x_j)$$

$$= y_j \cdot 1$$

$$= y_j$$

as $L_i(x_j)$ is zero for all $i \neq j$. Hence, p is the desired polynomial interpolant, and we sometimes say that it is in the Lagrange form. By uniqueness of the interpolant, it is the same polynomial that would be found by use of the Vandermonde matrix.

Example 4.1.2 Again, suppose we wish to interpolate a polynomial to the data points $(0, 0)$, $(\pi/2, 1)$, $(\pi, 0)$, $(3\pi/2, -1)$ from the sine curve. We have $\{x_0, x_1, x_2, x_3\} = \{0, \pi/2, \pi, 3\pi/2\}$, $\{y_0, y_1, y_2, y_3\} = \{0, 1, 0, -1\}$, and so

$$L_0(x) = \frac{(x - x_1)(x - x_2)(x - x_3)}{(x_0 - x_1)(x_0 - x_2)(x_0 - x_3)}$$

$$= \frac{\left(x - \frac{\pi}{2}\right)(x - \pi)\left(x - \frac{3\pi}{2}\right)}{\left(0 - \frac{\pi}{2}\right)(0 - \pi)\left(0 - \frac{3\pi}{2}\right)}$$

$$= -\frac{4}{3\pi^3}\left(x - \frac{\pi}{2}\right)(x - \pi)\left(x - \frac{3\pi}{2}\right)$$

$$L_1(x) = \frac{(x - x_0)(x - x_2)(x - x_3)}{(x_1 - x_0)(x_1 - x_2)(x_1 - x_3)}$$

$$= \frac{(x - 0)(x - \pi)\left(x - \frac{3\pi}{2}\right)}{\left(\frac{\pi}{2} - 0\right)\left(\frac{\pi}{2} - \pi\right)\left(\frac{\pi}{2} - \frac{3\pi}{2}\right)}$$

$$= \frac{4}{\pi^3}x(x - \pi)\left(x - \frac{3\pi}{2}\right)$$

$$L_2(x) = \frac{(x - x_0)(x - x_1)(x - x_3)}{(x_2 - x_0)(x_2 - x_1)(x_2 - x_3)}$$

$$= \frac{(x - 0)(x - \frac{\pi}{2})(x - \frac{3\pi}{2})}{(\pi - 0)\left(\pi - \frac{\pi}{2}\right)\left(\pi - \frac{3\pi}{2}\right)}$$

$$= -\frac{4}{\pi^3}x\left(x - \frac{\pi}{2}\right)\left(x - \frac{3\pi}{2}\right)$$

$$L_3(x) = \frac{(x - x_0)(x - x_1)(x - x_2)}{(x_3 - x_0)(x_3 - x_1)(x_3 - x_2)}$$

$$= \frac{(x - 0)\left(x - \frac{\pi}{2}\right)(x - \pi)}{\left(\frac{3\pi}{2} - 0\right)\left(\frac{3\pi}{2} - \frac{\pi}{2}\right)\left(\frac{3\pi}{2} - \pi\right)}$$

$$= \frac{4}{3\pi^3}x\left(x - \frac{\pi}{2}\right)(x - \pi)$$

are the Lagrange polynomials. Hence

$$p(x) = 0 \cdot L_0(x) + 1 \cdot L_1(x) + 0 \cdot L_2(x) + (-1) \cdot L_3(x)$$

$$= L_1(x) - L_3(x)$$

$$= \frac{4}{\pi^3}x(x - \pi)\left(x - \frac{3\pi}{2}\right) - \frac{4}{3\pi^3}x\left(x - \frac{\pi}{2}\right)(x - \pi)$$

$$\doteq 0.0860x^3 - 0.8106x^2 + 1.6977x$$

is the interpolating polynomial, in agreement with the result of Example 4.1.1. ∎

It is trivial to find the coefficients needed for the Lagrange form of the polynomial interpolant; they are the given values $y_0, y_1, \ldots, y_n$ or the values of a given function f at the given nodes $x_0, x_1, \ldots, x_n$. It is harder to find the coefficients for the polynomial written in the natural form $a_n x^n + a_{n-1}x^{n-1} + \cdots + a_1 x + a_0$ since we must solve a linear system involving a dense and frequently ill-conditioned linear system.

On the other hand, if we have the polynomial in the form $a_n x^n + a_{n-1}x^{n-1} + \cdots + a_1 x + a_0$, then it is easy to evaluate $p(x)$ at a given x. But to evaluate $p(x)$ in the Lagrange form $p(x) = y_0 L_0(x) + y_1 L_1(x) + \cdots + y_n L_n(x)$, we must find the Lagrange polynomials

$$L_0, L_1, \ldots, L_n$$

for the given nodes $x_0, x_1, \ldots, x_n$, and this involves some work (in addition to concerns about overflow and underflow in intermediate calculations). The natural form is easy to evaluate but hard to find, and the Lagrange form is just the opposite.

Newton Form   There is another form, the **Newton form,** that is based on writing the polynomial interpolant as

$$p(x) = b_n(x - x_{n-1}) \cdots (x - x_1)(x - x_0) + \cdots + b_2(x - x_1)(x - x_0) + b_1(x - x_0) + b_0 \tag{4.4}$$

and for which computing the coefficients $b_0, b_1, \ldots, b_n$ is easier than for the natural form and evaluating the resulting interpolant is easier than (and as accurate as for) the Lagrange form (see Additional Problem 13 for more details).

It is common to need only the values of the interpolant at some point or points. In such cases we do not need the coefficients at all, in principle, and there are efficient techniques for computing the value of $p(x)$ at a point x without first computing an explicit expression for $p(x)$. As with any computation, it pays to ask at the start what we actually *need* and to compute only what is needed.

Bases

The terms *natural form, Lagrange form*, and *Newton form* are based on the notion that the interpolating polynomial $p(x)$ is an element of the linear (vector) space P_n of all polynomials of degree at most n, for which

$$\{1, x, x^2, \ldots, x^n\}$$

is called the natural basis, but for which

$$\{L_0, L_1, \ldots, L_n\}$$

and

$$\{1, (x - x_0), (x - x_1)(x - x_0), \ldots, (x - x_{n-1}) \cdots (x - x_1)(x - x_0)\}$$

are also bases. (That is, every polynomial of degree at most n may be written as a linear combination of the elements of these sets, and that combination is unique.) The different ways of writing the interpolating polynomial are based on different choices of a basis for the space P_n, and lead to different coefficients and easier or harder ways of finding these coefficients. We sometimes refer to the problem of interpolating a polynomial to a function, or to data, as the **Lagrange interpolation** problem (regardless of the form in which we write that interpolant).

Error Estimate

Finally, we present a theorem concerning the quality of a polynomial interpolant and a theorem concerning polynomial approximation. It's convenient to use the notation $C^k(I)$ for the set (in fact, linear space) of all functions defined on an interval I that are k-times continuously differentiable on that interval. Often we write this as $C^k(\alpha, \beta)$ or $C^k[\alpha, \beta]$ to indicate the interval $I = (\alpha, \beta)$ or $I = [\alpha, \beta]$, respectively. The case $k = 0$ is written $C(I)$ and represents the set of all continuous function on I.

Theorem 4.1.1 (Cauchy Remainder Theorem for Polynomial Interpolation)
Let $a \leq x_0 < x_1 < \cdots < x_n \leq b$ and f in $C^{n+1}[a, b]$ be given. Then the polynomial interpolant $p(x)$ to f at $x_0, x_1, \ldots, x_n$ satisfies

$$f(x) - p(x) = \frac{f^{(n+1)}(\xi)}{(n+1)!}(x - x_0)(x - x_1) \cdots (x - x_n)$$

for any $x \in [a, b]$, for some $\xi = \xi(x)$ in (a, b).

Proof.

Fix $x \notin \{x_0, x_1, \ldots, x_n\}$ and define $\varpi(x) = (x - x_0)(x - x_1) \cdots (x - x_n)$. Let

$$\Phi(x) = \frac{f(x) - p(x)}{\varpi(x)}$$

$$\Omega(y; x) = f(y) - p(y) - \varpi(y)\Phi(x)$$

and note that $\Omega(y; x) = 0$ if $y \in \{x_0, x_1, \ldots, x_n\}$ or if $y = x$. Hence by the generalized

Rolle's theorem, there exists a ξ in (a, b) such that $\Omega^{(n+1)}(\xi; x) = 0$. But

$$\frac{d^{n+1}}{dy^{n+1}} \Omega(y; x) = \frac{d^{n+1}}{dy^{n+1}} \left(f(y) - p(y) - \varpi(y)\Phi(x) \right)$$

$$= f^{(n+1)}(y) - 0 - \Phi(x)\frac{d^{n+1}}{dy^{n+1}} \varpi(y)$$

$$= f^{(n+1)}(y) - (n+1)!\Phi(x)$$

and so $\Omega^{(n+1)}(\xi; x) = 0$ means that

$$0 = f^{(n+1)}(\xi) - (n+1)!\Phi(x)$$

$$\Phi(x) = \frac{f^{(n+1)}(\xi)}{(n+1)!}$$

$$\frac{f(x) - p(x)}{\varpi(x)} = \frac{f^{(n+1)}(\xi)}{(n+1)!}$$

$$f(x) - p(x) = \varpi(x)\frac{f^{(n+1)}(\xi)}{(n+1)!}$$

for any $x \notin \{x_0, x_1, \ldots, x_n\}$. But if $x \in \{x_0, x_1, \ldots, x_n\}$, then $f(x) - p(x) = 0$ and $\varpi(x) = 0$, so the result holds for any x. ∎

Note that Theorem 4.1.1 may be used to estimate the error in the interpolating polynomial within the range of its data $x_0 < x_1 < \cdots < x_n$. (Compare this error term with that from the Taylor series with remainder.) The error typically grows very rapidly outside $[x_0, x_n]$, and it is therefore not advisable to use an interpolant to approximate values of the function outside of the range of the data (that is, for $x < x_0$ or $x > x_n$). Interpolants, polynomial or otherwise, should be used only to approximate values within the range of the data on which they were based, if possible. Extrapolated values are highly suspect.

Theorem 4.1.2 (Weierstrass Approximation Theorem)

If f is in $C[a, b]$ then for every $\epsilon > 0$ there exists a polynomial $p(x)$ such that

$$|f(x) - p(x)| \leq \epsilon$$

for every $x \in [a, b]$.

The Weierstrass Approximation Theorem is one of the most important theorems in approximation theory; it asserts that every continuous function can be approximated arbitrarily well by a polynomial of sufficiently high degree.[1] Of course, it need not be the case that $p(x)$ is equal to $f(x)$ for some x: This is a theorem about approximation,

---

[1] This is an existence theorem. There is a constructive proof, but the construction that is usually used, involving Bernstein polynomials, does not lend itself to numerical work.

not interpolation. Still, it justifies the belief that approximation by polynomials can be a successful approach to the approximation problem.

It's worth emphasizing once more that we have focused on methods that find the coefficients of the interpolating polynomial because that is what we will need in this text. If all that is needed in a certain application are the values of the interpolant, then there are much more efficient and accurate methods available to find them.

PROBLEMS 4.1

1. Use the Vandermonde matrix approach and then the Lagrange interpolating polynomial approach to find the equation $y = \alpha x^2 + \beta x + \gamma$ of the quadratic through the points $\{(0, 1), (1, 2), (2, 1)\}$.

2. a. Approximate $f(x) = e^{x/2}$ over $[1, 9]$ by a fourth-degree polynomial in two ways: using the Lagrange form of the interpolating polynomial with the nodes 1, 3, 5, 7, and 9, and using a Taylor polynomial centered at $x = 5$.

b. Plot the error estimate for these approximants (from Theorem 4.1.1 and from the remainder form of Taylor series) for $x \in [0, 12]$.

c. Plot the actual error for these approximants for $x \in [0, 12]$.

d. Find the actual error for both approximants at $x = 1.5 : 0.5 : 8.5$. Comment.

e. Find the actual error for both approximants at $x = 4.7 : 0.1 : 5.3$. Comment.

3. a. Prove that if $p(x)$ and $q(x)$ are polynomials of degree at most n that interpolate a function f at the distinct points $x_0, x_1, \ldots, x_n$, then $p = q$. Use the

function $h(x) = p(x) - q(x)$ (not the nonsingularity of the corresponding Vandermonde matrix).

b. Show that a polynomial of degree m is its own polynomial interpolant of degree at most n ($n \geq m$) no matter how the distinct points $x_0, x_1, \ldots, x_n$ are chosen.

c. Argue that a Vandermonde matrix is nonsingular if the points $x_0, x_1, \ldots, x_n$ on which it is based are distinct by showing that it maps only the zero vector to the zero vector.

4. A sine table is desired. It is to be such that linear interpolation ($n = 1$) between neighboring entries will always give a result that is correct to at least 4 decimal places. The table will be for equally spaced angles in $[0, \pi/2]$ and will give sine values correct to 10 decimal places. Use the error formula from Theorem 4.1.1 to suggest a suitable spacing between the nodes.

5. a. Find the interpolating polynomial for $f(x) = x^4 - 2x^3 + 2x - 1$ based on the nodes $\{0, 1, 2, 3\}$. Use the Lagrange method, but write your final answer in the natural form.

b. Write your answer in the Newton form (Eq. (4.4)).

MATLAB 4.1

There are a number of MATLAB commands for performing interpolation. Let's redo Example 4.1.1 in MATLAB. Enter:

```
» x=[0 pi/2 pi 3*pi/2];y=[0 1 0 -1]';
» V=vander(x)
» V=fliplr(V)
```

The MATLAB command `vander` sets up a Vandermonde matrix, but the MATLAB convention differs from ours. Enter:

```
» p=V\y
```

to find the coefficients of the polynomial. Note that $p(1)$ is the constant term and $p(4)$ is the coefficient of x^3. Again, the MATLAB convention is the opposite, so let's flip p around. Enter:

```
» p=flipud(p)'
```

to put p in the appropriate form for use in other MATLAB commands. (Had we set up the problem to conform with MATLAB's notion of a Vandermonde matrix, this would not be necessary.) The MATLAB command `polyval` may be used to evaluate a polynomial given its coefficients. Enter:

```
» z=rand;p(1)*z^3+p(2)*z^2+p(3)*z+p(4)
» polyval(p,z)
```

The values should be the same. In fact we may use the `polyval` command to evaluate the polynomial at a vector. Enter:

```
» z=linspace(0,2*pi,100);
» zy=polyval(p,z);    %Polynomial evaluated at z.
» plot(z,zy,'g',z,sin(z),'r'),grid
```

The actual curve is in red and the approximant is in green. Enter:

```
» z=linspace(0,4*pi,200);
» zy=polyval(p,z);
» plot(z,zy,'g',z,sin(z),'r'),grid
```

The interpolant can be expected to give reasonable results only where it had data (in our case, 0 to $3\pi/2$); extrapolating outside of this range is likely to give poor results.

There is a built-in command for performing the interpolation, and it should generally be used if a polynomial interpolant is desired. Enter:

```
» x,y        %Data.
» pnew=polyfit(x,y,3)
» p          %Should be the same.
```

The form of the `polyfit` command is `polyfit(x,y,n)` where x and y are the data to be interpolated and n is the degree of the polynomial. The assumption throughout this section is that n is equal to `length(x)-1`; if this is not so, then the `polyfit` command will give a least squares fit. (See Section 3.5.) For another interpolation command, see `help interp1`.

The poor behavior shown in Figure 4.2 is typical for Lagrange interpolation using equally spaced nodes. Enter:

```
» x=linspace(0,2*pi);n=9;
» plot(x,abs(sin(x)),'y')   %Note the plot's inaccuracy near pi.
» nodes1=linspace(0,2*pi,n+1);  %Choose 10 equally spaced nodes.
» ynodes1=abs(sin(nodes1));     %Corresponding y-values.
» p=polyfit(nodes1,ynodes1,n);
» y1=polyval(p,x);     %Evaluate p(x) on a finer grid.
» hold on;plot(x,y1,'g')
```

This isn't very good, though we are using only 10 points. Let's see if we can improve it. Enter:

```
» nodes1        %Current nodes.
» plot(nodes1,zeros([1 n+1]),'wo') %Locate them as white 'o's.
» cheby=cos((2*(n-(0:n))+1)*pi/(2*n+2)) %Chebyshev nodes on [-1,1].
» nodes2=cheby*pi+pi;       %Rescale to [0,2*pi].
» plot(nodes2,zeros([1 n+1]),'mx')   %Locate them as magenta 'x's.
```

Notice that the second set of nodes is not equally spaced; in particular, notice how they are more closely packed near the endpoints. Enter:

```
» ynodes2=abs(sin(nodes2));      %Corresponding y-values.
» p2=polyfit(nodes2,ynodes2,n);
» y2=polyval(p2,x);     %Evaluate p2(x) on a finer grid.
» plot(x,y2,'c')
```

The approximation is worse in the very middle but is considerably better everywhere else. Try again with a larger value of n. Equally spaced nodes are much easier to use, but unequally spaced nodes typically give better results. The **Chebyshev nodes** $x_i = \cos((2(n-i)+1)\pi/(2n+2))$ $(i = 0, 1, \ldots, n)$ are often a good choice on $[-1, 1]$ (or rescaled to the appropriate interval), but there is no guarantee that they will give good results.

We should address the issue of accurate evaluation of polynomials. For a polynomial of degree n, we must compute x^n, and if n is large and $|x| > 1$, then errors could be magnified considerably. For example, enter:

```
» clear all
» N=20;y=10^N,y1=(10*(1+2*eps))^N
» abs(y1-y)      %Absolute error.
» ans/y          %Relative error.
```

The absolute error is quite large, though the relative error is small. Larger perturbations and larger exponents would give worse results. Cancellation is also a potential problem; enter:

```
» x=linspace(.995,1.005,200);
» plot(x,(x-1).^8)
```

to plot $f(x) = (x - 1)^8$ for $x \in [.995, 1.005]$. Then enter:

```
» g=x.^8-8*x.^7+28*x.^6-56*x.^5+70*x.^4-56*x.^3+28*x.^2-8*x+1;
» plot(x,g),grid
```

to plot $g(x) = x^8 - 8x^7 + 28x^6 - 56x^5 + 70x^4 - 56x^3 + 28x^2 - 8x + 1$ over the same range. It is a fact that $f(x) = g(x)$ for all x; $g(x)$ is just the expanded version of $f(x)$. However, cancellation of significant figures caused by the subtractions lead to a very noisy function near $x = 1$. (Imagine trying to find the sole root $x^* = 1$ of this function using a root-finding method!) There is a way to address the cancellation issue. One aspect of it is buried in the Lagrange and Newton forms; if we know that we will be evaluating a polynomial $p(x)$ near $x = x_0$, then it usually makes sense to write it as $p(x) = b_n(x - x_0)^n + \cdots + b_1(x - x_0) + b_0$ since then we will be raising the small quantity $(x - x_0)$ to the nth power rather than the large quantity x.

The other aspect of evaluating a polynomial accurately is **nested evaluation** (or **Horner's method**), which we illustrate by example. If $g(z) = 3z^3 - 6z^2 + 4z - 5$ (possibly $z = x - x_0$), then we could evaluate it directly; enter:

```
» z=pi;
» %Omit the flops command if you do not have it.
» flops(0),3*z^3-6*z^2+4*z-5,flops
```

Now we rewrite $g(z)$ in the mathematically equivalent form $g(z) = ((3z - 6)z + 4)z - 5$ and evaluate it as follows; enter:

```
» %Omit the flops command if you do not have it.
» flops(0),((3*z-6)*z+4)*z-5,flops
```

Note that the nested form uses fewer flops. This is true in general, and the nested form typically gives a more accurate result as well. Horner's method should generally be used to evaluate polynomials. If you have the MATLAB Symbolic Toolbox, type `help horner` for a useful command.

We mention that the `conv` command (convolution) may be used to find polynomial products; that is, if `p1` and `p2` are vectors representing coefficients of the polynomials $p_1(x)$ and $p_2(x)$, then `conv(p1,p2)` is a vector that contains the coefficients of the polynomial $p_1(x)p_2(x)$. More generally `conv(x,y)` convolves the vectors `x` and `y`. The `deconv` command may be used to divide polynomials, and the `polyder` command to differentiate polynomials (again, in the form of a vector of coefficients).

The help for `polyfit` mentions that there are things to try when an interpolant seems poor: removing repeated or nearly repeated points; centering the data (that is, shifting it so that the average value of the abscissas, and possibly the ordinates, is zero); and rescaling the data. These may work in certain cases, and in fact centering is usually a good initial strategy, but the fundamental problems of polynomial interpolation remain.

ADDITIONAL PROBLEMS 4.1

6. a. Consider again the Runge function (Eq. (4.2)). Reproduce Figure 4.2 by finding the polynomial of degree $n = 10$ that interpolates it at equally spaced points in $[-1, 1]$. Approximate the maximum error by evaluating the Runge function and the interpolant on a fine grid and finding the largest absolute difference.

   b. Repeat for $n = 15$.

   c. Repeat for $n = 20$.

   d. Repeat for $n = 50$. Does raising the degree of the interpolating polynomial necessarily give a better approximation?

   e. Find, by trial and error, a polynomial of degree $n = 10$ that interpolates the Runge function reasonably well over $[-1, 1]$ by using unequally spaced nodes. (*Hint:* Place more nodes near the endpoints ± 1 of the interval.)

7. **a.** Using `polyfit` and `polyval`, find a good approximation for $\sin(x)$ on $[0, 2\pi]$ by choosing an interpolating polynomial of degree at most 8. The nodes need not be equally spaced. Plot the polynomial and $\sin(x)$ on a single graph.

  b. Use Theorem 4.1.1 to estimate the worst-case error in your approximation for $x \in [0, 2\pi]$.

  c. Plot $\sin(x)$ and your approximant for $x \in [-2\pi, 4\pi]$.

8. A sine table is desired. It is to be such that quadratic interpolation ($n = 2$) between neighboring entries will always give a result that is correct to at least 4 decimal places. The table will be for equally spaced angles in $[0, \pi/2]$ and will give sine values correct to 10 decimal places. Use the error formula from Theorem 4.1.1 to suggest a suitable spacing between the nodes. Compare your answer to Problem 4.

9. **a.** How many flops are required to compute a value of a polynomial of degree n by the obvious method, counting x^n as $n - 1$ multiplications?, How many are required counting each exponentiation x^n as a single flop (which is usual)? How many are required by Horner's method?

  b. Using `tic` and `toc`, experiment with Horner's method. Comment on its efficiency.

10. Write a MATLAB program that accepts an n-vector and produces labeled plots of $L_{n,0}, \ldots, L_{n,n}$. Each plot should have its own figure window; use `pause` to display the separate graphs briefly as they are produced. The program should return some appropriate quantity.

11. Plot $\frac{(1+x)-1}{x}$ for $x \in (0, 10^{-k}]$ for $k = 12, 13, 14, 15, 16$. Comment on these graphs.

12. **a.** Write a MATLAB program that performs inverse interpolation (see Section 1.6) for given data consisting of two vectors of length $n + 1$.

  b. Write a MATLAB program that performs root-finding by inverse interpolation based on $n + 1$ nodes; that is, given an initial bracket, the method chooses $n - 1$ additional points within the bracket, performs inverse interpolation with a polynomial of degree at most n, and uses that as a new point,

discarding an older one, and then performs inverse interpolation again on the new set of $n + 1$ points until some convergence criterion is met.

13. **a.** For $n = 4$, use Eq. (4.4) and the conditions of Eq. (4.1) to write a lower triangular matrix system for the coefficients $b_0, \ldots, b_4$ of the Newton form of the interpolating polynomial.

  b. Write out the solution of the system found in part (a) using forward substitution.

  c. Note that b_0 may be found directly in terms of $y_0 = f(x_0)$. Write b_1 as a difference of two y-values divided by a difference of two x-values. Then write b_2 as a difference of two terms of this form $(\Delta y/\Delta x)$ divided by a difference of x-values. Continue for b_3 and b_4. This is known as the **divided differences** technique for finding the Newton form.

  d. Write a MATLAB program that computes the interpolatory polynomial of degree at most n for given data consisting of two vectors of length $n + 1$ in the Newton form by the divided differences technique. (The MATLAB `diff` command may be useful.) Demonstrate your program.

14. **a.** In some cases we are given data of the form (x_i, y_i, y_i') $(i = 0, \ldots, n)$, where $y_i = f(x_i)$ and $y_i' = f'(x_i)$ and we seek a polynomial interpolant of degree at most $2n + 1$ to the data (x_i, y_i), which also has the prescribed derivatives; that is, $p(x_i) = y_i$ (Eq. (4.1)) and also $p'(x_i) = y_i'$. This is called the **Hermite interpolation** problem. If the x_i are distinct, must such a polynomial exist for arbitrary choices of y_i and y_i'? If so, is it unique?

  b. Solve the Hermite interpolation problem for the sine function using the nodes $\{x_0, x_1, x_2, x_3\} = \{0, \pi/2, \pi, 3\pi/2\}$. Compare your result to Example 4.1.1.

15. **a.** What is the change-of-basis matrix for going from the natural basis of the space P_n to the Lagrange form basis?

  b. What is the change-of-basis matrix for going from the natural basis of the space P_n to the Newton form basis?

4.2 Piecewise Linear Interpolation

There are many reasons that we might want to approximate a function. On most standard machines, anything that is to be computed must be broken down, at some level, to addition, subtraction, multiplication, or division (plus bookkeeping operations).[2] Therefore when a calculator returns a value for $\sin(3)$ it is only because the function $y = \sin(x)$ has been approximated by a rational function (that is, a ratio of polynomials). At a higher level, we often need to approximate special functions that occur in particular problems. In these cases it is far from clear that we need an interpolant, which is required to pass through certain points; we really just need to control the error in our approximation. We discuss approximation in more generality in Chapter 8.

Another common situation that calls for approximation of a function is the numerical solution of an ODE (or the numerical integral of a function), which yields a discrete set of points through which we would like to draw a smooth curve. We might also have measured data through which we would like to pass a curve (say, from a digitized curve or from tracking a moving object). In these cases it is usually desirable to pass the curve through the known data points, so an interpolant is needed.

In the previous section, we said that polynomial interpolants are usually not the right choice for approximating a function. The oscillatory nature of high-order polynomial interpolants, plus the errors in evaluating x^n for large n, prevent them from being useful as a general-purpose tool. An oscillatory interpolant makes a perfect interpolant ($p(x_i) = y_i$) but a very poor approximation, and we always want to get a good approximation of the underlying function. Taylor polynomials are worse; they are guaranteed to interpolate only at a single point, their center, and while they are an excellent approximation there the quality of the approximation drops off rapidly. In addition, Taylor polynomials require derivative information about the function, which is rarely available. Polynomial interpolants and Taylor polynomials are of great use in numerical analysis but they are principally used to derive and analyze methods, not as methods in and of themselves. We'll see examples of their usefulness to numerical integration and numerical solution of ODEs in the next two chapters.

Hermite Interpolation

One way to improve the fidelity of the approximant is to require not only that the polynomial interpolate the function but also that the derivative of the polynomial interpolate the derivative of the function as well; that is, we could seek an interpolant $p(x)$ such that

$$p(x_i) = f(x_i)$$
$$p'(x_i) = f'(x_i)$$

($i = 0, 1, \ldots, n$). This is called the **Hermite interpolation** problem and, like Lagrange interpolation, there are special polynomials that may be used to solve it. Derivative information is seldom available, however, and the degree of p in the Hermite interpolation must be about twice the degree of the corresponding Lagrange interpolant since twice as many conditions must be satisfied. This is inconvenient, even though we expect better accuracy since making the derivatives match forces the shape of the interpolant to more nearly match that of the function.

A Different Approach

We should mention an important point which was alluded to in the previous section: The difficulties with polynomial interpolation are made that much worse by using equally spaced points. Choosing the nodes intelligently can give a much less oscillatory fit. Of course, we would like to automate the process as much as possible so that an M-file may be written that does not need help from the user in the middle of its run (especially

---

[2] Of course, we are oversimpilfying matters.

since sooner or later some other program will certainly be calling it to perform some computation), and so we would need a technique for choosing the points. These exist; but oscillations can still occur, evaluating x^n for large n is still an issue, an error in any coefficient affects the values of the polynomial everywhere, and there are better and more efficient methods.

How shall we find a better method? We must give up either "polynomial" or "interpolation," and we know that interpolation is sometimes desired. (For cases where we need only approximation and can sacrifice interpolation, the techniques of Chapter 8 are appropriate.) Evidently we have to look to non-polynomial functions. For example, there are trigonometric and rational interpolants. Still, polynomials were attractive in the first place because they are simple, familiar, easily computed, easily differentiated and integrated, and so on, and it would be nice to be able to use them. Fortunately, there is a compromise–and we have been using it since Section 1.1. Rather than use functions that are polynomials in the strict sense, we will use functions defined piecewise that are equal to polynomials on subintervals of the interval of interest. This is called **piecewise polynomial interpolation,** and the subintervals are often referred to as **elements** or **panels.**

The simplest approach is **piecewise linear interpolation,** in which each polynomial piece is linear. This is what the MATLAB `plot` function does: Given a set of points, it "connects the dots" by straight line segments. Between any two points the curve is a (linear) polynomial, but over the entire interval it is not a polynomial. The plot takes on the correct values at the nodes (that is, it interpolates). We've already seen that if we choose sufficiently many points the result looks like a nice, smooth curve that approximates the function; every time we've plotted $\sin(x)$, for example, we have been using this technique and have been viewing a piecewise linear interpolant. This simple method bears closer attention.

Basis Functions   It's convenient to define an analogue of the Lagrange polynomials for this case. There are two ways we might proceed: Given the $n + 1$ nodes $x_0, x_1, \ldots, x_n$ (ordered so that $x_0 < x_1 < \cdots < x_n$), we might define a separate linear function on each of the n subintervals $[x_i, x_{i+1}]$ $(i = 0, \ldots, n - 1)$ by

$$m_i(x) = s_i x + b_i$$

on the subinterval $[x_i, x_{i+1}]$, and $m_i(x) = 0$ outside this subinterval. We then choose the constants s_i and b_i on each subinterval according to the interpolation condition

$$s_i x_i + b_i = y_i$$
$$s_i x_{i+1} + b_i = y_{i+1}$$

(4.5)

$(i = 0, \ldots, n - 1)$. This gives a system of $2n$ equations (2 per element, n elements) in $2n$ unknowns (2 per element, n elements), and this system is trivially broken down into n 2×2 blocks. (Eq. (4.5)).

A more natural analogue of the Lagrange polynomials, however, is obtained by choosing a basis $\Lambda_0, \ldots, \Lambda_{n-1}$ of functions with the property that Λ_i is a piecewise linear function satisfying

$$\Lambda_i(x_j) = \begin{cases} 1 & \text{if } j = i \\ 0 & \text{if } j \neq i \end{cases}$$
$$= \delta_{ij}$$

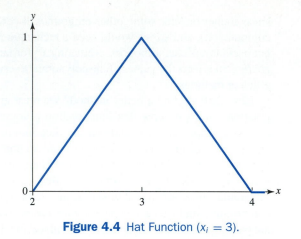

Figure 4.4 Hat Function ($x_i = 3$).

($i = 0, \ldots, n - 1$), where δ_{ij} is the **Kronecker delta function** that is equal to 1 if $i = j$, and is equal to 0 otherwise. The obvious choice for $\Lambda_i(x)$ is the **hat function** (or **chapeau function**), which is zero everywhere except on the subintervals to the immediate left and right of x_i, where it goes from 0 at x_{i-1} to 1 at x_i and back down to 0 at x_{i+1} (see Fig. 4.4, based on the nodes $\{1, 2, 3, 4, 5\}$). For the leftmost subinterval $[x_0, x_1]$ and the rightmost subinterval $[x_{n-1}, x_n]$ we omit the line segments that would fall outside the interval $[x_0, x_n]$.

We use the functions $\{\Lambda_0, \ldots, \Lambda_{n-1}\}$ (called the **hat basis** or **chapeau basis**) in exactly the way we used the Lagrange polynomials for (true) polynomial interpolation. The piecewise linear polynomial interpolant with the nodes $x_0, x_1, \ldots, x_n$ and corresponding function values $y_0, y_1, \ldots, y_n$ is

$$p(x) = y_0 \Lambda_0 + \cdots + y_n \Lambda_n. \tag{4.6}$$

(We call $\Lambda_0, \ldots, \Lambda_{n-1}$ the **piecewise linear Lagrange interpolating polynomials** for these nodes.) Clearly, the interpolant is unique, so this is the same solution that we would

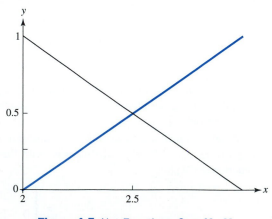

Figure 4.5 Hat Functions Over $[2, 3]$.

find from Eq. (4.5), although the coefficients are easier to compute in this case. On the other hand, evaluating $p(x)$ by Eq. (4.6) within a panel requires that we evaluate two piecewise Lagrange interpolating polynomials, that is, the two linear functions that are summed to find the linear segment for that subinterval (see Fig. 4.5). This is twice the work required to evaluate the interpolant as given by Eq. (4.5).

Example 4.2.1 Recall from the previous section that the Runge function

$$f(x) = \frac{1}{1 + 25x^2}$$

is poorly approximated by a polynomial interpolant of degree 10 (which uses 11 nodes). To see the corresponding piecewise linear interpolant, all we need to do is plot this function using 11 points; the commands x=linspace(-1,1,11); plot (x,1./(1+25*x.^2),'r'), grid accomplish this. To compare it to the actual Runge function, we may use the MATLAB commands hold on; y=linspace (-1,1,200); plot(y,1./(1+25*y.^2),'b') (see Fig. 4.6). Because of Theorem 4.2.1 (below), this should be a good approximation to the actual curve.

To construct the actual approximant, note that $x_0 = -1$ and $x_i = x_0 + ih$ ($i = 0, 1, \ldots, 10$) where $h = 0.2$. The first piecewise linear Lagrange interpolating polynomial Λ_0 must be equal to 1 at $x_0 = -1$, equal to 0 for $x \geq x_1 = -0.8$, and linear between x_0 and x_1. An appropriate function (using the Lagrange interpolating polynomials from Eq. (4.3)) is

$$\Lambda_0(x) = 1 \cdot \frac{x - (-0.8)}{-1 - (-0.8)} + 0 \cdot \frac{x - (-1)}{-0.8 - (-1)}$$
$$= -5(x + 0.8)$$

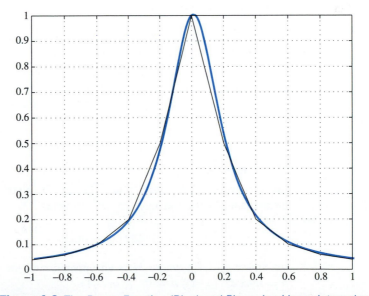

Figure 4.6 The Runge Function (Blue) and Piecewise Linear Interpolant.

for $x \in [x_0, x_1]$ (and zero elsewhere). (Sketch $\Lambda_0(x)$.) Similarly, again using the Lagrange interpolating polynomials from Eq. (4.3),

$$\Lambda_1(x) = 0 \cdot \frac{x - (-0.8)}{-1 - (-0.8)} + 1 \cdot \frac{x - (-1)}{-0.8 - (-1)}$$

$$= 5(x + 1)$$

for $x \in [x_0, x_1] = [-1, -0.8]$ and

$$\Lambda_1(x) = 1 \cdot \frac{x - (-0.6)}{-0.8 - (-0.6)} + 0 \cdot \frac{x - (-0.8)}{-0.6 - (-0.8)}$$

$$= -5(x + 0.6)$$

for $x \in [x_1, x_2] = [-0.8, -0.6]$, and is zero elsewhere. (Note that, as promised, the Lagrange interpolating polynomials of the previous section are useful tools in other, more practical methods.) You should sketch $\Lambda_1(x)$.

Hence, using the functions $\Lambda_0(x), \Lambda_1(x), \ldots, \Lambda_{10}(x)$, we can write the interpolant in the form

$$p(x) = f(x_0)\Lambda_0(x) + f(x_1)\Lambda_1(x) + \cdots + f(x_{10})\Lambda_{10}(x),$$

which, being piecewise defined, is equal to 10 different linear segments on 10 different subintervals. On the first subinterval $[x_0, x_1] = [-1, -0.8]$ it can be written as

$$p(x) = f(x_0)\Lambda_0(x) + f(x_1)\Lambda_1(x)$$

$$= \frac{1}{1 + 25(-1)^2}[-5(x + 0.8)] + \frac{1}{1 + 25(-0.8)^2}[5(x + 1)]$$

$$\doteq 0.1018x + 0.1403$$

and similarly for the other subintervals. ∎

Error Estimate   Notice that equally spaced nodes are not a problem in this approach; in addition, an error in one piece of the interpolant has only a local effect (it does not degrade the quality of the interpolant over the entire data range, as happens for polynomial interpolation). It is a fact that any continuous function on a closed and bounded interval may be approximated arbitrarily well by a piecewise linear interpolant on a sufficiently fine grid. In fact, we have the following theorem:

Theorem 4.2.1

Let $x_0 < x_1 < \cdots < x_n$ and f in $C^2[x_0, x_n]$ be given. Then the piecewise linear interpolant $p(x)$ to f at $x_0, x_1, \ldots, x_n$ satisfies

$$|f(x) - p(x)| \leq \frac{Mh^2}{8} \tag{4.7}$$

for any $x \in [a, b]$, where M is an upper bound on $|f''(x)|$ for $x \in [a, b]$ and $h = \max(x_{i+1} - x_i)$ $(i = 0, \ldots, n - 1)$.

This formula gives an estimate of the worst-case error in the approximation; it may be employed over any smaller interval within $[x_0, x_n]$ by taking M to be a bound for $|f''(x)|$ on just that interval. Note that the larger the second derivative $f''(x)$ is, the worse the linear approximation might be—as you might expect, since this indicates a greater degree of curvature. Looked at another way, the smaller M is, the closer f'' is to being zero, and hence the closer f is to being linear (and thus the closer it is to being well-approximated by a line segment). Theorem 4.2.1 follows from Theorem 4.1.1.

Often we must use the nodes we are given. For example, they may be measured data or may be experimental data, and it is often infeasible to get additional data, as this would require sending out a team to collect additional data in the field or rerunning the experiment, often at prohibitive expense and delay. (In these cases we do not have an explicit formula for $f(x)$.) In other cases, however, we *can* select the nodes—for example, when we are writing a subprogram to approximate a special function of interest. It seems clear from Eq. (4.6) that we should pick more points where the curvature of $f(x)$ is greater so that we get a smaller h in that region and therefore a lower overall error bound. Making such a selection is called selecting the nodes **adaptively.** If we have a formula for f then we may do so using the same approach that we used in deciding how best to construct a sine table in the previous section; if not, f'' can be estimated (as discussed in Section 6.1). The key idea is that we use some heuristic to detect regions where the function is changing more rapidly and then place relatively more points there.

Adaptivity

Example 4.2.2   Let's look at plotting $y = \sin(x)$ over $[0, \pi]$. We have $y'' = -\sin(x)$. If we use, say, 10 equally spaced points in the subinterval $0 \le x \le 0.1$ then the error bound $Mh^2/8$ from Eq. (4.2) gives $(M = \sin(0.1), h = 0.01)$ $E \le \sin(0.1)(0.01)^2/8 \doteq 1.2479E - 6$ on this interval. Note that this means that the approximant is good to within about $1.25E - 6$ for *every* $x \in [0, 0.1]$. How many equally spaced points would we have to put in the subinterval $[1.4, 1.5]$ to get the same accuracy? Here $M = \sin(1.5) \doteq 0.9975$, so we need to choose h such that

$$Mh^2/8 \le 1.25E - 6$$

$$h^2 \le \frac{8(1.25E - 6)}{\sin(1.5)}$$

$$h \le 0.0032,$$

meaning we need about $0.1/0.0032$ or more than 300 points in this subinterval to get the same guaranteed accuracy. It's unfortunate that we need so many nodes, but at least the error bound gives us a means of guaranteeing that a given accuracy is achieved. ∎

An adaptive routine for constructing a piecewise linear interpolant would typically take a step of a certain size, use some heuristic to test the error or the curvature, and then refine the grid if necessary. If it seems that a larger step could be taken, then the step size would be relaxed. (Just as we want a finer grid for improved accuracy when needed, we want to use a coarser grid, where possible, for efficiency. This efficiency is often what allows us to place more nodes in regions where the function is changing rapidly, because there is often a limit on the number of function evaluations allowed. We are saving our limited number of function evaluations for where they're truly needed.) We consider this idea in more detail when we consider numerical integration and the numerical solution of ODEs.

Notice that if we construct a piecewise linear interpolant for a function and decide to add a few more points, then relatively little work is required to construct the new interpolant; the new points affect the interpolant only in the subintervals in which they lie, and we need to recompute the interpolant only in these regions. Compare this to a polynomial interpolation problem to which we add a single node: In that case, every coefficient of the polynomial will change, in general.

There is an evaluation issue that we have overlooked until now. If the nodes are irregularly spaced, then given an x we must determine in which element $[x_i, x_{i+1}]$ the node lies before we can evaluate $p(x)$. There are a number of ways to handle this efficiently; the easiest method is to treat it like a root-finding problem and apply the method of bisection (binary search). For example, if $n = 101$ and the nodes $x_0 < x_1 < \cdots < x_{100}$ are stored in a list, then to determine the subinterval containing a given $x \in [x_0, x_{100}]$, we might check whether $x < x_{50}$. If it is, then we might check whether $x < x_{25}$. If it isn't, then we know that $x_{25} \leq x < x_{50}$. Our next test might be whether $x < x_{37}$, and so on until we determine the interval in which x lies.

PROBLEMS 4.2

1. a. Sketch the hat functions $\Lambda_0, \ldots \Lambda_4$ for the nodes $\{1, 3, 4, 6, 7\}$.

b. Find the formulas for the hat functions $\Lambda_0, \ldots \Lambda_4$ using the Lagrange interpolating polynomials (as in Example 4.2.1). Be sure to indicate where the functions are zero.

c. Use the hat basis to express the piecewise linear interpolant to $\sin(x)$ at these points.

2. a. What spacing (assuming equally spaced nodes) should be used to plot $2\sin(x)$ over the interval $[0, \pi]$ to ensure that the error in the piecewise linear interpolant is no more than .01?

b. What selection of nodes should be used to plot $2\sin(x)$ over the interval $[0, \pi]$ to ensure that the error in the piecewise linear interpolant is no more than .01? Use the following procedure to answer this question: Set $x_0 = 0$ and $h = 0.1$. Generate a test point by taking a step of size h into the interval. Use Theorem 4.2.1 to check the error over that interval. If the error is too large, cut h in half, and try again; if the predicted error is less than .005 (half the tolerance), double h and try again. Repeat until you find an acceptable node, and then use that value of h in

the next step. You may write a program or script file to do this if you wish.

3. a. Plot Figure 4.6 from Example 4.2.1 using the MATLAB commands x=linspace(-1,1,11); plot (x,1./(1+25*x.^2)),grid,hold on; y=linspace(-1,1,200); plot(y,1./(1 +25*y.^2)).

b. Repeat with 10 equally spaced points.

c. How many points must you use before the curve looks like a smooth curve and not a piecewise linear curve?

4. Use Theorem 4.1.1 to prove Theorem 4.2.1.

5. Consider the nodes $\{0, \pi/2, \pi\}$ and the function $y = \sin(x)$. Fit a piecewise cubic interpolant $c_1(x)$ to this function by choosing a cubic for the subinterval $[0, \pi/2]$ which not only interpolates y at the endpoints but also has the property that the derivative of the cubic interpolates y'. That is, the cubic $c_1(x)$ should satisfy $c_1(0) = y(0)$, $c_1(\pi/2) = y(\pi/2)$, $c_1'(0) = y'(0)$, $c_1'(\pi/2) = y'(\pi/2)$. Then do the same with a second cubic $c_2(x)$ on the subinterval $[\pi/2, \pi]$. Plot the resulting approximant.

MATLAB 4.2

Up to now, we've been focusing on using MATLAB as a tool for performing numerical experiments, yet, the emphasis in MATLAB and other computation-oriented languages on vectorization actually affects the development of numerical algorithms as well. Because we haven't focused as much on some of the other tools available in MATLAB, let's take this opportunity to explore its plotting capabilities in greater detail. It is not uncommon for those who work in other languages to import the results of their calculations into MATLAB for display (we speak of "visualization" of data).

We've used the `plot` command often. Let's look at a more sophisticated application. Enter:

```
» close all
» th=linspace(0,2*pi);
» fig1=plot(th,sin(th),'g',th,cos(th),'b:')
» grid on
```

The `plot` command returns a vector; each entry, called a handle, identifies an object within the plot. We can use these handles to determine properties of these objects. To see the properties of the first line, enter:

```
» get(fig1(1))
```

The color is [0 1 0]; that is, no Red, some Green, and no Blue in the RGB color scheme. To see the properties of the second (dashed) line, enter:

```
» get(fig1(2))
```

The color is [0 0 1]; that is, no Red, no Green, and some Blue, and the LineStyle is dashed. What about the figure itself? It's the first figure, and therefore its handle is 1. To see some of its properties, enter:

```
» get(1)
```

For example, if the color is [0 0 0], this means the background is black; if it's [0.8 0.8 0.8], this means the background is white (there are equal amounts of Red, Green, and Blue). To see a display of possible settings for this figure window, enter:

```
» set(1)
```

Let's make the background red. Enter:

```
» set(1,'color',[1 0 0])
» figure(1)
```

That's too red. Let's try again. Enter:

```
» set(1,'color',[.8 0 0])
» figure(1)
```

We can mix colors, too. Enter:

```
» set(1,'color',[.8 .6 .4])
» figure(1)
```

Maybe a white background would be better. Enter:

```
» set(1,'color',[1 1 1])
» figure(1)
```

We can adjust the colors and thickness of the plotted lines, too. To change the shade of green used on the first curve and to thicken it, enter:

```
» set(fig1(1),'color',[0 .5 0])
» set(fig1(1),'LineWidth',8)
» figure(1)
```

You may enter `set(fig1(1))` to see what else about the sine curve's plot may be changed using `set`. We can delete a curve as well. To delete just the cosine curve from the plot, enter:

```
» delete(fig1(2))
```

The `refresh` command may be used to refresh a plot.

Let's get a new figure window. We'll leave the previous one where it is. Enter:

```
» H=figure
```

to open a new figure window and store its handle in `H`. This window will remain the active plot unless we select the previous figure window (or a new one) by a MATLAB command or by clicking on it. For example, enter:

```
» gcf    %Get current figure's handle.
```

(this should be 2), and then click on the first figure window (containing the sine curve) to make it active. Enter:

```
» gcf
```

again; it should be 1. Let's make the empty figure window active again. Enter:

```
» figure(2)
» gcf
```

Now let's plot a circle in it. Enter:

```
» plot(sin(th),cos(th),'y-',sin(th),cos(th),'wo')
» figure(H)
```

The discrete points are plotted as white circles, and the yellow line interpolates those circles. (The circle is a function of neither x nor y, so this is a more general piecewise linear interpolation than we have considered in the reading.) To make it look circular, enter:

```
» axis equal
```

(Note that the `axes` command is different from the `axis` command. We want the latter command.) Let's enlarge the box around the circle a bit; enter:

```
» axis([-1.1 1.1 -1.1 1.1]),figure(H)
```

Now let's title and label it. You can use certain TeX commands. For example, enter:

```
» title('Plot of x=sin(\theta), y=cos(\theta)')
» figure(H)
```

and note that the `\theta` is displayed as the Greek letter θ. (In Version 4 it displays literally as written above.) You can display the other Greek letters in the same way; for those for which the capital letter is also available, it may be obtained as `\Theta` (etc.). There are many other TeX commands that may be used; enter:

```
» title('Plot of {\itx}=sin(\theta), {\ity}=cos(\theta)')
» figure(H)
```

to have the x and y written in italics (the braces limit the scope of the italic switch). Other TeX commands may be used to give other common mathematical symbols (e.g., `\infty` for ∞, `\int` for $\int$) and effects (e.g., subscripts and superscripts). Enter:

```
» xlabel('{\itx} axis','color','red')
» ylabel('{\ity} axis','color','blue')
```

to label the axes in red and blue. (Changing colors is not based on the TeX mathematical typesetting system, so it works in Version 4.) Other properties of the title and labels may be set as well, including the style and size of font used.

The `text` command may be used to place text within a plot. Enter:

```
» htext=text(-.6,0,'This is a circle.')
» get(htext)
» figure(H)
```

to write the indicated text starting at the point $x = -.6$, $y = 0$ on the current axes. Everything listed by the `get` command is something we can change. To make some changes, enter:

```
» set(htext,'color',[0 0 1],'FontUnderline','on')
» figure(H)
```

Let's write it smaller and better centered. Enter:

```
» delete(htext)
» figure(H)      %Text should be gone
```

```
» text(-.1,0,'This is a circle.','color', ...
[0 0 1],''FontSize',6,FontUnderline','on')
```

Recall that the ellipsis (...) means continuation of the current line onto the next. We did not ask for a handle this time, so none is returned.

All of the properties we have discussed, and others, may be used with `title`, `xlabel`, `ylabel`, and `text`. More than one piece of text may be written. Enter:

```
» text(0,.9,'\uparrow','color',[1 1 1])
» text(-.05,.8,'Top','color',[1 0 0])
```

to point to the top of the circle, from within it. To add text by the mouse, use the `gtext` command. Enter:

```
» gtext('Hello world!')
```

and then click on some point within the figure window. The text should appear at the point where you clicked the mouse. The `gtext` command returns a handle (after the click) if one is requested. The `ginput` command may be used to collect the location of a mouse click; enter:

```
» [x,y]=ginput(2)
```

and then click twice in the figure window. The x and y vectors collect the x and y coordinates of those mouse clicks. If used in the form `[x,y]=ginput` an unlimited number of points may be gathered.

We can also add a legend to the plot that indicates which line type corresponds to what curve. To add the legend, enter:

```
» legend('y-','Circle: y','wo','Dots: o')
```

The legend may be dragged to a new location using the mouse. (See `help legend` for more options.) The command `legend off` removes the legend from the plot.

There is much more which can be done; see a MATLAB manual and a TeX manual for details. It is possible to make very professional-looking plots (two dimensional and three dimensional) in MATLAB.

We briefly mention some other plot-related commands; you may look up the details using `help` if you need these capabilities. The `reset` command resets properties set by `set`. The `clf` and `cla` commands clear figures and axes. (Many of these commands are most useful when embedded in a MATLAB program that makes many plots; see the `demo` command, or `expo` in Version 4, for example.) The `axes` command positions the axes. The `axis` command has more options than we have discussed. The `subplot` command may be used to put more than one plot in a single figure window. For example, enter:

```
» clf      %Clear figure 2.
» subplot(2,1,1),plot(th,sin(th))
» subplot(2,1,2),plot(th,cos(th))
```

The figure window may be subdivided further than this. The `semilogx`, `semilogy`, and `loglog` commands may be used for logarithmic plots. The `polar` command may be used for polar plots. The `line` command may be used to draw lines. The `fplot` command is essentially an interface to `plot` but can be convenient for plotting a function; see `help fplot`. The `plot3` command is a three-dimensional analogue of `plot`. For example, enter:

```
» t=0:pi/50:10*pi;
» plot3(sin(t),cos(t),t);
```

(This example is from the `plot3` help.) The `view` command may be used to view a plot from another angle. Enter:

```
» view([10 100 10])
» plot(t,sin(t))
» view(10,20)
```

See `help view` for details. Plots in three dimensions may be rotated by using the mouse. See also MATLAB 7.3.

The `patch` and `fill` commands may be used to create filled-in polygons in a plot. Enter:

```
» close all
» t=t/max(t);
» plot(t,sin(t)),hold on
» fill([0 .5 .5 0],[0 0 .5 .5],'g')
```

to draw a filled-in green polygon on this plot, with successive vertices at $(0, 0)$, $(.5, 0)$, $(.5, .5)$, $(0, .5)$ (in that order).

The `print` command may be used (in lieu of the figure's drop-down commands) to print a figure from MATLAB to the printer or to a file. The print command has many options; see also `printopt` and `orient`. See also the `saveas` command.

There's a lot more plotting power in MATLAB; we haven't even touched on three-dimensional plots in this section and have only hinted at the color options. See `help graphics` and `help graph2D`, `help graph3d`, `help colormap` (or in Version 4 `help plotxy`, `help plotxyz`, `help color`) for more details.

ADDITIONAL PROBLEMS 4.2

6. (Refer to Problem 3 (a)) Plot Figure 4.6 from Example 4.2.1. Include an appropriate title, axis labels, and a legend. Use the `text` or `gtext` command to note on the graph the point or points where the approximation is worst.

7. Choose an efficient selection of nodes to plot the error function `erf(x)` over the interval $[0, 1]$ with error in the piecewise linear interpolant of no more than .01. Give the nodes and a plot of `erf(x)` and the approximant.

8. Choose an efficient selection of nodes to plot the function `sin(12x)` over the interval $[0, 1]$ with error in the piecewise linear interpolant no more than .01. Give the nodes and a plot of `sin(12x)` and the approximant.

9. Write a MATLAB program that accepts an inline function as an input argument, solicits nodes from the user using `ginput`, and then plots the corresponding hat basis functions. Plot five hat functions per figure window, each a different color, and pause between opening new windows. The windows should be titled and labeled appropriately; you may use a command like `title(['Numbers ',num2str(N),' to ',num2str(N+4),'.'])`, for example.

10. Write a MATLAB program that accepts an inline function as an input argument, solicits nodes from the user using `ginput`, and then plots the piecewise linear interpolant for the function using those nodes. (Ignore the y-values collected by `ginput`.) Note that you may use the figure command to open a window and `text` or `title` to display a request asking that the user enter points. Your function should plot the function and the approximant on a single graph; plot the function using 5 times as many points as there are nodes. Return the nodes as output. Demonstrate your program on the Runge function.

11. Write a detailed algorithm (pseudocode) for evaluating a piecewise linear interpolant by performing binary search. Assume that the ordered list of nodes, the corresponding function values, and a point x are given; perform the search, evaluate the interpolant at x, and return the value of the interpolant or an error message if appropriate.

12. Write a MATLAB program that accepts an inline function and a number of subintervals and plots a piecewise linear interpolant with that number of equally spaced subintervals. The program should then prompt the user to specify a subinterval by clicking on the plot; the region beneath the linear segment on the selected subinterval should then be filled in. If an output argument is requested, then the number of the selected subinterval should be returned, counting from zero.

13. Write a MATLAB program that performs piecewise linear interpolation using the technique of Eq. (4.5). Your program should take as inputs the nodes and the function or a vector of y-values (use some test to decide which has been supplied), and return the coefficients in a 2–column matrix. Write a second program that evaluates the interpolant at a given point.

14. Write a MATLAB program that accepts a vector of nodes the length of which is a multiple of 3 and a function or a vector of y-values (use some test to decide which has been supplied), and returns the coefficients of a piecewise quadratic interpolant as a 3–column matrix. Determine the quadratics by fitting the first quadratic through the first three points x_0, x_1, x_2, the next quadratic through the points x_2, x_3, x_4, the next quadratic through the points x_4, x_5, x_6, and so on. Your program should have an optional input argument that requests a plot of the interpolant.

15. **a.** Write a MATLAB program that approximates the definite integral of a function using a piecewise linear interpolant. Your program should input the function, a desired number of nodes, and limits of integration, and should output an approximation of the integral. Your program should have an optional input argument that requests a plot of the function (using `fplot`) and the interpolant on the same graph, with the area under the interpolant filled in. Choose colors and ordering so that the function is visible over the filled-in region.

b. Experiment with your program. How many nodes are needed to get an error of no more than 1% for some common functions?

4.3 Cubic Splines

Piecewise linear interpolation is a useful tool. However, while the resulting interpolant is necessarily continuous, it is not smooth (differentiable). For many applications we would like to have a smooth interpolant. (Think of video game graphics for which the characters have angular, gem-faceted faces, and compare them to more sophisticated graphics that produce smooth, rounded, natural-looking features.) Taking a finer and finer grid improves the visual appearance of a piecewise linear interpolant but is computationally expensive, is not always possible—if the nodes are measured data, for example—and still doesn't produce an approximating function that is truly differentiable. We want to be able to produce a smooth interpolant using a reasonable number of nodes.

Piecewise Polynomial Interpolation   The idea of piecewise linear interpolation may be generalized to piecewise polynomial interpolation using quadratics, cubics, and so on, as the pieces. For example, given the nodes $\{0, \pi/2, \pi\}$ and the function $y = \sin(x)$, we could get a differentiable interpolant by fitting a quadratic to the three points (in effect treating the interval from 0 to π as a single element over three nodes), or by fitting a quadratic on $\{0, \pi/2\}$ and another quadratic on $\{\pi/2, \pi\}$ and making each have the correct derivative in the middle. That is, if the two quadratics are $q_1(x) = a_1 x^2 + b_1 x + c_1$ and $q_2(x) = a_2 x^2 + b_2 x + c_2$, we could choose the coefficients so that

$$q_1(0) = 0$$

$$q_1\left(\frac{\pi}{2}\right) = 1$$

$$q_1'\left(\frac{\pi}{2}\right) = 0$$

$$q_2\left(\frac{\pi}{2}\right) = 1$$

$$q_2'\left(\frac{\pi}{2}\right) = 0$$

$$q_2(\pi) = 0,$$

that is,

$$c_1 = 0$$

$$a_1\left(\frac{\pi}{2}\right)^2 + b_1\left(\frac{\pi}{2}\right) + c_1 = 1$$

$$2a_1\left(\frac{\pi}{2}\right) + b_1 = 0$$

$$a_2\left(\frac{\pi}{2}\right)^2 + b_2\left(\frac{\pi}{2}\right) + c_2 = 1$$

$$2a_2\left(\frac{\pi}{2}\right) + b_2 = 0$$

$$a_2\pi^2 + b_2\pi + c_2 = 0,$$

for which the solution is

$$a_1 = -0.4053$$

$$b_1 = 1.2732$$

$$c_1 = 0$$

$$a_2 = -0.4053$$

$$b_2 = 1.2732$$

$$c_2 = 0$$

(see Fig. 4.7). The two quadratics happen to be the same due to the symmetry; in general they are not. We have forced them to give a continuous and differentiable curve on $[0, \pi]$ by requiring that the derivatives have the same value where the quadratics meet—namely, the true value of $y'(x)$ at that point. Fitting a quadratic between each pair of nodes is called **piecewise quadratic interpolation.**

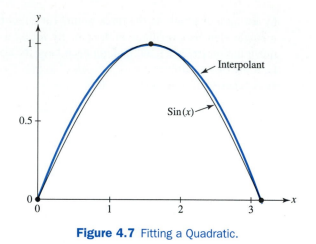

Figure 4.7 Fitting a Quadratic.

If there were another node to the right of π (for example, if the nodes were augmented to become $\{0, \pi/2, \pi, 3\pi/2\}$), then we wouldn't have another free coefficient to match the derivative at the node at π. The obvious thing to do is to use cubics on each section, for then we have four freely selectable coefficients on each subinterval. We write

$$c_i(x) = \alpha_i x^3 + \beta_i x^2 + \gamma_i x + \delta_i \tag{4.8}$$

on subinterval i and require

$$
\begin{aligned}
c_i(x_i) &= y_i \\
c_i'(x_i) &= y_i' \\
c_i(x_{i+1}) &= y_{i+1} \\
c_i'(x_{i+1}) &= y_{i+1}'
\end{aligned}
\tag{4.9}
$$

at the left and right endpoints, x_i and x_{i+1}, respectively, of the subinterval. This gives four equations in the four unknowns $\alpha_i, \beta_i, \gamma_i, \delta_i$ for each of the n subintervals, and if the nodes are distinct then there is a unique solution for every choice of function and derivative values. Fitting a cubic between each pair of nodes is called **piecewise cubic interpolation.**

More generally, we could use a polynomial of any degree on a given element, or even of different degrees on different elements; this is called **piecewise polynomial interpolation.** If we require that an appropriate number of derivative values be matched, as above, then it is called **piecewise polynomial Hermite interpolation.** For the reason indicated above, polynomials of odd degree (especially linear, cubic, and quintic) are the most commonly employed.

Piecewise cubic Hermite interpolation (using Eq. (4.8) and Eq. (4.9)) has an attractive property: The resulting interpolant is differentiable. In general it will not be twice differentiable. For many problems, however, having a twice differentiable interpolant is important. If we have discrete observations of a moving particle (say, a satellite that reports its position once per second) and we wish to recreate its orbit, then interpolating the data is a reasonable approach. However, the velocity and acceleration of the particle are certainly continuous functions as well, so on physical grounds we would like our interpolant to be at least twice continuously differentiable. If velocity and acceleration data are also reported, we could use a piecewise quintic interpolant, and this is probably a good approach because it uses all of the data. If velocity and acceleration data are not reported, however, we cannot use piecewise polynomial Hermite interpolation since we don't have the needed derivative data.

How can we get a twice differentiable curve, then? We could choose to not interpolate the data and instead find a best-fit ellipse for the satellite's path, similar to the least squares lines discussed in Section 2.6. This curve-fitting approach generally requires a nonlinear optimization to find the coefficients, but it is useful if forcing the curve to go through every data point isn't important. If the data contains significant measurement errors or other uncertainties, curve-fitting may be the best approach.

Piecewise Polynomials without Derivative Values

If we do require interpolation (as we likely would in many cases involving a moving particle or similar data), then we have two options to get a sufficiently smooth interpolant: Lagrange interpolation, which as we have seen can give a very strange-looking path (think of the Runge function), or piecewise polynomial interpolation, where we select values for the derivatives that will give a smooth curve. Let's explore the latter approach.

Example 4.3.1 Let's fit a twice continuously differentiable curve to the data $\{(-1, 0.3679), (0, 1), (2, 7.3891)\}$. To do so, we need to choose polynomials $p_1(x)$ (on $[-1, 0]$) and $p_2(x)$ (on $[0, 2]$) that will satisfy the conditions

$$p_1(-1) = 0.3679$$

$$p_1(0) = 1$$

$$p_1'(0) = p_2'(0)$$

$$p_1''(0) = p_2''(0)$$

$$p_2(0) = 1$$

$$p_2(2) = 7.3891$$

at the nodes -1, 0, and 2. The first two conditions and the last two conditions ensure interpolation, and the middle two ensure differentiability at the middle node 0, where the polynomials meet. We have a total of six conditions. We should be able to use two quadratics $p_1(x) = ax^2 + bx + c$ and $p_2(x) = \alpha x^2 + \beta x + \gamma$ since this gives a total of six unknowns a, b, c, α, β, and γ. We have the requirements

$$a - b + c = 0.3679$$

$$c = 1$$

$$b = \beta$$

$$2a = 2\alpha$$

$$\gamma = 1$$

$$4\alpha + 2\beta + \gamma = 7.3891$$

upon substituting in the equations for p_1 and p_2. Clearly, $a = \alpha$, $b = \beta$, and $c = \gamma = 1$, so $p_1 = p_2$. The first and last equation then give

$$a - b + 1 = 0.3679$$

$$4a + 2b + 1 = 7.3891,$$

and the solution is $[1 \ -1; 4 \ 2] \backslash [-0.6321; 6.3891]$ or $a = 0.8542, b = 1.4862$. Hence $p_1(x) = p_2(x) = 0.8542x^2 + 1.4862x + 1$ defines the interpolant.

We never actually set the values for the derivatives at the node 0; we just required that they be equal. They have taken the values

$$p'_1(0) = 1.4862$$

$$p''_1(0) = 2(.8542)$$

$$= 1.7083$$

to meet this requirement. In fact, the data is from the function $y = e^x$, for which $y'(0) = y''(0) = 1$. The derivative is not well approximated, but the interpolant is twice continuously differentiable. Indeed, since $p_1(x) = p_2(x)$, it is infinitely differentiable, but typically we get only as much derivative agreement as we explicitly require. ∎

We now have a means of taking data $\{(x_0, y_0), \ldots, (x_n, y_n)\}$ and fitting a smooth curve to it. The data may be measured data (possibly provided directly to the computer by another device, e.g., a digitizer reading in discrete points along the boundary of some object of interest like the body of an automobile) or may be the output of another program that provides such points (say, a program that numerically solves an ODE by finding the solution only on a discrete grid). Let's formalize this approach. Consider again Example 4.3.1. If we had had 4 grid points instead of 3, then we would have had 3 elements. Nothing changes for the first and last element, but the middle element has to match derivatives across two nodes rather than just one. A quadratic won't work here; we need more parameters in the polynomial for that section. This is true for most subintervals unless n, the number of subintervals, is trivially small.

Typically we use a piecewise cubic interpolant on every subinterval (even the ones at the ends). Each cubic has 4 coefficients for a total of $4n$ parameters over the entire interpolant. How many conditions are there that must be satisfied? Each of the n cubics must interpolate at 2 points (its left and right endpoints), giving $2n$ conditions; in addition, at each of the $n - 1$ internal nodes we place 2 conditions, namely, first differentiability and second differentiability. This gives a total of $2n + 2(n - 1) = 4n - 2$ constraints (equations) in the $4n$ parameters (unknowns). We need two additional conditions to have a uniquely determined interpolant.

Boundary Conditions   Using quadratics on the end subintervals would reduce the number of unknowns to $4n - 2$, but it's convenient to have a piecewise cubic interpolant rather than a mixed-degree interpolant. Instead we add two conditions at the end subintervals, called **boundary conditions.** There are a number of standard boundary conditions. Let $p_0(x)$ and $p_{n-1}(x)$ be the leftmost and rightmost cubic. The **free boundary conditions** are

$$p''_0(x_0) = 0$$

$$p''_{n-1}(x_n) = 0$$

(also called the **natural boundary conditions**). The **clamped boundary conditions** are

$$p_0'(x_0) = s_0$$

$$p_{n-1}'(x_n) = s_n,$$

where s_0 and s_n are given values; typically we take s_0 and s_n to be the derivatives $s_0 = f'(x_0)$ and $s_n = f'(x_n)$ of the function $y = f(x)$ or approximations of them. Of course, if the data $\{(x_0, y_0), \ldots, (x_n, y_n)\}$ is random, say, due to additive error, there might not even *be* a deterministic functional relationship $y = f(x)$ between x and y.

Let $S(x)$ be the interpolant; that is, $S(x)$ is equal to $p_0(x)$ on $[x_0, x_1]$, $p_1(x)$ on $[x_1, x_2]$, $\ldots$, $p_{n-1}(x)$ on $[x_{n-1}, x_n]$. The **not-a-knot boundary conditions** are that $p_0(x) = p_1(x)$ for all x and $p_{n-2}(x) = p_{n-1}(x)$ for all x (almost as if the nodes x_1 and x_{n-2} were not being used, although note that $S(x)$ must still interpolate at x_1 and x_{n-2}). An equivalent condition is that S is three times continuously differentiable at the knots x_1 and x_{n-2}. If the derivative values at the endpoints are not available and not easily approximated, this condition is commonly employed.

Example 4.3.2 Let's find a twice continuously differentiable interpolant of this form for $y = e^x$ using the nodes $\{(-1, 0.3679), (0, 1), (2, 7.3891), (4, 54.5982)\}$. Since we know the function, we'll use the clamped boundary conditions. We need to find 3 cubics $p_0(x) = a_0 x^3 + b_0 x^2 + c_0 x + d_0$, $p_1(x) = a_1 x^3 + b_1 x^2 + c_1 x + d_1$, and $p_2(x) = a_2 x^3 + b_2 x^2 + c_2 x + d_2$. The conditions are:

$$p_0(-1) = 0.3679 \qquad p_0(0) = 1 \qquad p_1(2) = 7.3891 \qquad p_2(4) = 54.5982$$

$$p_0'(-1) = 0.3679 \qquad p_1(0) = 1 \qquad p_2(2) = 7.3891 \qquad p_2'(4) = 54.5982$$

$$p_0'(0) = p_1'(0) \qquad p_1'(2) = p_2'(2)$$

$$p_0''(0) = p_1''(0) \qquad p_1''(2) = p_2''(2)$$

or, in terms of the 12 unknown coefficients,

$$-a_0 + b_0 - c_0 + d_0 = 0.3679$$

$$3a_0 - 2b_0 + c_0 = 0.3679$$

at the node at -1,

$$d_0 = 1$$

$$d_1 = 1$$

$$c_0 = c_1$$

$$2b_0 = 2b_1$$

at the node at 0,

$$8a_1 + 4b_1 + 2c_1 + d_1 = 7.3891$$

$$8a_2 + 4b_2 + 2c_2 + d_2 = 7.3891$$

$$12a_1 + 4b_1 + c_1 = 12a_2 + 4b_2 + c_2$$

$$12a_1 + 2b_1 = 12a_2 + 2b_2$$

at the node at 2, and

$$64a_2 + 16b_2 + 4c_2 + d_2 = 54.5982$$

$$48a_2 + 8b_2 + c_2 = 54.5982$$

at the node at 4. This gives a linear system involving a 12×12 coefficient matrix, though we could clearly reduce the order by inspecting the above relations and using $d_0 = 1$, $d_1 = 1$, $c_0 = c_1$, and $b_0 = b_1$ to eliminate four of the unknowns. The solution of this system is

$$a_0 = 0.1803, \quad b_0 = 0.6249, \quad c_0 = 1.0766, \quad d_0 = 1.0000$$

$$a_1 = 0.2170, \quad b_1 = 0.6249, \quad c_1 = 1.0766, \quad d_1 = 1.0000$$

$$a_2 = 3.3924, \quad b_2 = -18.4275, \quad c_2 = 39.1813, \quad d_2 = -24.4031$$

(using MATLAB); we plot this in the MATLAB subsection. ■

Cubic Splines

Notice that the equations really are coupled; for example, c_0 is coupled to c_1, and another equation couples c_1 and c_2. The interpolation conditions are local to the elements, but the differentiability conditions are not local; every value affects every other one, in the general case. This is different from the piecewise cubic interpolant with known values of the derivatives, where each cubic depends only on data from the nodes at either end of its subinterval. We refer to any twice continuously differentiable piecewise cubic interpolant to the data $\{(x_0, y_0), \ldots, (x_n, y_n)\}$ as a **cubic spline.** We call it a **natural (or free), clamped,** or **not-a-knot cubic spline** according to the boundary conditions used. The clamped cubic spline is also called a **complete cubic spline.**

Note that a piecewise cubic interpolant that is used to interpolate both f and f' at some nodes (a piecewise cubic Hermite interpolant) uses the same number of coefficients as a cubic spline for f at those nodes but requires twice as much data, namely, the values of both $f(x_i)$ and $f'(x_i)$, and is only *once* continuously differentiable. On the other hand, since the piecewise cubic Hermite interpolant uses more data we expect it to give a better fit in the quantitative sense of deviating less from the true function even though it may give a worse fit in the qualitative sense of not being *twice* differentiable.

Splines of other orders may be defined as well. The piecewise linear interpolants of the previous section are considered **linear splines.** In cases where a thrice continuously differentiable interpolant is needed, a **quintic spline,** with degree five polynomial sections interpolated to the data $\{(x_0, y_0), \ldots, (x_n, y_n)\}$, may be used. However, linear and cubic splines are by far the most commonly used types of splines. We may also use other boundary conditions (for example, if the function is known to have some property such as periodicity).

It appears that we will need to solve a $4n \times 4n$ system to find a cubic spline for $n + 1$ data points. This is not the case, however. By arranging the computation carefully we can reduce the $4n \times 4n$ system to a much smaller one. We discuss how to arrange the computation in the next section.

PROBLEMS 4.3

1. a. Fit a piecewise quadratic interpolant to $y = \cos(x)$ at the nodes $\{0, 1, 2\}$. (Match the derivative of $y(x)$ at the center node.)

  b. Fit a piecewise cubic Hermite interpolant to $y = \cos(x)$ at the nodes $\{0, 1, 2\}$. (Match the derivatives of $y(x)$ at each node.) Is it a spline (that is, does the second derivative of the interpolant exist at $x = 1$)?

  c. Fit a natural cubic spline interpolant to $y = \cos(x)$ at the nodes $\{0, 1, 2\}$. Plot it, $\cos(x)$, and your piecewise cubic interpolant from part (b) on a single graph.

2. Let $f(x) = \exp(x)$. Find the piecewise cubic interpolant that interpolates both f and f' at $\{0, 0.1, 0.2, 0.3\}$ and the natural cubic spline that interpolates f. Plot them on a single graph along with $f(x)$.

3. Find the natural and clamped cubic splines for $f(x) = \log(x)$ at the nodes $\{1, 2, 3\}$.

4. Can a piecewise quadratic interpolant be used to find a differentiable interpolant to a function at an arbitrary list of nodes? If so, it is called a **quadratic spline** (or **parabolic spline**). What boundary conditions might need to be imposed?

5. Suppose a quintic spline $S(x)$ is to be fit to the function $f(x)$ at the nodes $\{x_0, x_1, \ldots, x_n\}$. What conditions must S satisfy? Use the natural boundary conditions.

MATLAB 4.3

Let's look again at Example 4.3.2, where we found a cubic spline interpolant for $y = \exp(x)$ at the nodes $\{-1, 0, 2, 4\}$. Enter the coefficients as a vector:

```
» p=[-0.6333 -1.0024 0.2630 1.0000 1.2341 -1.0024 ...
    0.2630 1.0000 2.2737 -7.2401 3.3819 11.3963]
```

The first four entries of p are the coefficients in $p_0(x) = a_0 x^3 + b_0 x^2 + c_0 x + d_0$, and so on. Let's plot the interpolant. The first panel is $[-1, 0]$. To form a vector of x-values from -1 to 4 and corresponding y-values, enter:

```
» x=linspace(-1,0);y=polyval(p(1:4),x);
» xtemp=linspace(0,2);y=[y,polyval(p(5:8),xtemp)];x=[x,xtemp];
» xtemp=linspace(2,4);y=[y,polyval(p(9:12),xtemp)];x=[x,xtemp];
```

(We are using piecewise linear interpolation to plot the cubic spline.) To plot the interpolant and the function, enter:

```
» plot(x,y,'y',x,exp(x),'g'),grid
```

This is a good fit (recall that we used only 4 nodes). Do the derivatives truly match? Let's check at $x = 2$. To find the first derivatives there, enter:

```
» p1d=polyder(p(5:8)),p2d=polyder(p(9:12))
```

Enter:

```
» exp(2)
» polyval(p1d,2),polyval(p2d,2)
```

to verify that they are equal, though they are not equal to $y'(2) = \exp(2)$. (The piecewise cubic Hermite interpolant would have the correct value here, since it would have taken that as data.) Similarly, enter:

```
» p1dd=polyder(p1d),p2dd=polyder(p2d)
» polyval(p1dd,2),polyval(p2dd,2)
```

to verify that the second derivatives match across this node, as expected, although they do not match $y''(2) = \exp(2)$. The piecewise cubic Hermite interpolant would not generally have had a second derivative here.

There are a number of built-in spline functions in MATLAB, as well as an optional Spline Toolbox. The `spline` command takes as arguments a vector x of nodes, a vector y of corresponding y-values, and a finer grid xi of values, and returns the values of the spline function at the points in xi. The not-a-knot boundary condition is used. Enter:

```
» x=[0 1 2 3];y=cos(x);       %Nodes and y-values.
» xi=linspace(min(x),max(x),300);
» yi=spline(x,y,xi);
» plot(x,y,'yo',xi,yi,'b'),grid
```

This evaluates the spline at the 300 points in xi and uses those points to plot the spline; the nodes are plotted as yellow circles. Note that the coefficients of the cubics that constitute the spline are not returned, just the values of the spline interpolant. The spline interpolates at the nodes, as expected, and has a smooth appearance. Enter:

```
» hold on
» plot(xi,cos(xi),'r')    %Compare to true function.
» plot(x,y,'g')           %Compare piecewise linear interp.
```

Note how well the piecewise linear interpolant fits in the middle section, which stretches across $\pi/2$; this is because the function $y = \cos(x)$ being interpolated has $y''(\pi/2) = -\cos(\pi/2) = 0$ in the center of this section, so a line is a good approximation near it.

The command `interp1` may also be used to interpolate values. What if we want the coefficients of the spline? The `spline` command may be used to obtain this information, in a special form called the *pp*-representation (piecewise polynomial representation). See `help` for `spline`, `mkpp`, `unmkpp`, and `ppval` for more information.

One of the biggest uses of splines is to draw a smooth (and hence physically plausible) curve through measured data, or data generated discretely by some other program. Let's simulate measured data for a trajectory. Enter:

```
» t=1+sort(rand([1 100])); %Random nodes on [1,2], sorted.
» y=-(t-1).*(t-2)+(rand([1 100])-.5)/50; %Trajectory plus noise.
» plot(t,y,'y',t,-(t-1).*(t-2),'r')
» hold on
» tt=linspace(1,2,600);yy=spline(t,y,tt);
» plot(tt,yy,'b')    %Cubic spline.
```

The cubic spline is worse than the linear spline! Even splines can suffer from some of the difficulties associated with high-order polynomial interpolation. Because of the additive noise, which is not small compared to the data (especially near $t = 1$ and $t = 2$, where y is zero), the values of y do not form a smooth curve. In fact, the relation $y(t) = -(t-1)(t-2) + e(t)$, where $e(t)$ is uniformly distributed noise on $[-.5, .5]$, does not even represent a deterministic functional relationship, and the resulting curves are nondifferentiable. Unless the noise is sufficiently small, fitting a twice continuously differentiable function may not be wise.

Often the noise is not so large as to make this a problem. As another example, let's fit a cubic spline to data generated from the numerical solution of an ODE. The MATLAB command ode23 may be used to numerically solve ODEs, as we discuss in Chapter 6. Enter:

```
» clear all
» close all
» g=inline('exp(y).*sin(t.*y.^2)')
» [t,y]=ode23(g,[0 3],1);
» plot(t,y,'b'),grid
```

to solve the ODE IVP $y' = g(t, y) = e^y \sin(ty^2)$, $y(0) = 1$ numerically and plot that solution using a linear spline. The ode23 command returns a vector of nodes t and the approximate values y of $y(t)$ at those nodes. To plot the cubic spline interpolant to the numerical solution of the ODE IVP, enter:

```
» tt=linspace(0,3,600);yy=spline(t,y,tt);
» figure(2);plot(tt,yy,'g'),grid
```

Compare the plots; the cubic spline is smoother, especially near the origin and the hump on the graph. This gives a more natural-looking fit; of course, without knowing the true solution $y(x)$, we can't assert that it is in fact a better approximation to the solution.

ADDITIONAL PROBLEMS 4.3

6. a. Repeat Example 4.3.2 using the natural boundary conditions. Compare your result to the clamped spline found in Example 4.3.2.

b. Repeat Example 4.3.2 using the not-a-knot boundary conditions.

7. If a function is known to be periodic on $[x_0, x_n]$ then we might use the **cyclic** (or **periodic**) **boundary conditions** $p_0'(x_0) = p_{n-1}'(x_n)$, $p_0''(x_0) = p_{n-1}''(x_n)$. Create a cyclic spline for $\sin(2x)$ using the nodes $\{0, 1, 2, \pi\}$. List the three cubics, and plot the interpolant and $\sin(2x)$ on a single graph.

8. a. Write a MATLAB program that performs piecewise cubic Hermite interpolation. The input arguments should be a vector of nodes, a vector of corresponding y-values, and a vector of corresponding y'-values. The output should be a matrix with one row of 4 coefficients for each panel.

b. Write a MATLAB program that inputs the coefficients from your program of part (a) and the nodes plus a vector of x-values and returns the y-values of the spline at those x-values (similar to the MATLAB spline command).

9. a. Write a MATLAB program that performs piecewise quadratic interpolation using elements based on 3 nodes; that is, fit a quadratic to x_0, x_1, x_2, then another quadratic to x_2, x_3, x_4, and so on. The input arguments should be a vector of $n + 1$ nodes where n is even and a vector of corresponding y-values. The output should be a matrix with one row of three coefficients for each of the $n/2$ elements.

b. Write a MATLAB program that inputs the coefficients from your program of part (a) and the nodes plus a vector of x-values and returns the y-values of the interpolant at those x-values (similar to the MATLAB spline command).

10. a. The **quadratic boundary conditions** for a cubic spline require the leftmost cubic $p_0(x)$ and the rightmost cubic $p_{n-1}(x)$ to be quadratics. Repeat problem 7 using this boundary condition.

b. Experiment with the natural, clamped (with the correct derivative values), not-a-knot, and quadratic boundary conditions for a variety of functions. Comment.

c. Experiment with the natural, not-a-knot, and quadratic boundary conditions for randomly generated data. Comment.

11. Prove that the condition that the spline S is three times continuously differentiable at the knots x_1 and x_{n-2} is equivalent to the not-a-knot requirement that $p_0(x) = p_1(x)$ for all x and $p_{n-2}(x) = p_{n-1}(x)$ for all x.

12. a. Find the clamped cubic spline interpolant $S(x)$ for $y = e^{-x} \cos(2x)$ at the nodes $\{0, 0.1, 0.2, 0.3\}$. Plot $S(x)$ and $y(x)$ on the same graph.

b. Plot $S'(x)$ and $y'(x)$ on the same graph.

c. Plot $S''(x)$ and $y''(x)$ on the same graph.

13. a. Write a MATLAB program that performs piecewise quintic Hermite interpolation. The input arguments

should be a vector of nodes, a vector of corresponding y-values, a vector of corresponding y'-values, and a vector of corresponding y''-values. The output should be a matrix with one row of 6 coefficients for each element.

b. Write a MATLAB program that inputs the coefficients from your program of part (a) and the nodes plus a vector of x-values and returns the y-values of the spline at those x-values (similar to the MATLAB `spline` command).

14. Use the MATLAB `spline` command to plot an approximation of $y = e^{2x} \cos(\ln(x))$ for $x \in [1, 7]$. Try to use as few nodes as possible to get a good fit.

15. Prove that if $y(x)$ is a cubic, then it is equal to its piecewise cubic Hermite interpolant and to its clamped cubic spline. Does it equal its natural and not-a-knot cubic splines? Does it equal its piecewise quintic Hermite interpolant and clamped quintic spline?

4.4 Computation of the Cubic Spline Coefficients

Cubic splines are widely used. When data from the profile of a physical object like the hood of a car is scanned in, it consists of a discrete set of points that must be smoothly interpolated. The fact that cubic splines are twice differentiable ensures that the resulting curve has a realistic, natural look.[3]

Form of the Polynomial Pieces

We need to consider the accuracy of the spline approximant and also discuss how to compute the spline coefficients efficiently. These topics involve a lot of little details, but the results are worth it in the end. Let's start with an improved representation of the cubic pieces. As before, let $S(x)$ be the spline and let $p_0(x), p_1(x), \ldots, p_{n-1}(x)$ be the cubics on $[x_0, x_1], [x_1, x_2], \ldots, [x_{n-1}, x_n]$. Rather than writing $p_i(x) = a_i x^3 + b_i x^2 + c_i x + d_i$, let's write

$$p_i(x) = \alpha_i(x - x_i)^3 + \beta_i(x - x_i)^2 + \gamma_i(x - x_i) + \delta_i \qquad (4.10)$$

$(i = 0, 1, \ldots, n - 1)$. (Compare Eq. (4.4), the Newton form of the Lagrange interpolant, from Section 4.1.) There are two immediate advantages to using this form. One is that if x is large, then a small error in x will be magnified considerably in the computation of the x^3 term in $a_i x^3 + b_i x^2 + c_i x + d_i$, but if the subintervals are not too large, then the term $(x - x_i)^3$ in the equivalent form of Eq. (4.10) will be relatively small, and therefore the effect of an error in x will be lessened. (In a similar way, any error in a_i would be multiplied by the large value x^3, but an error in α_i would be multiplied by the

---

[3] For the profile of a car, say, we might use three splines—one each for the hood, roof/windshields, and trunk—so that we could get the hood and windshield to meet at an angle (nonmatching first derivatives) and similarly for the trunk and the back windshield.

smaller value $(x - x_i)^3$.) Hence, this form should result in more accurate evaluations of the spline.

The second benefit of using this form is that the interpolation condition $p_i(x_i) = y_i$ (where $y_i = f(x_i)$ are given values) immediately gives

$$
\begin{aligned}
y_i &= p_i(x) \\
&= \alpha_i(x_i - x_i)^3 + \beta_i(x_i - x_i)^2 + \gamma_i(x_i - x_i) + \delta_i \\
&= \delta_i
\end{aligned}
$$

so that the values of $\delta_0, \ldots, \delta_{n-1}$ are trivially determined. Recall that in the previous section we found the spline coefficients by solving a system of $4n$ equations in $4n$ unknowns. This representation of the cubics reduces the number of unknowns to $3n$ while also giving a final result that is more accurate when evaluated at a given x. Remember that the direct solution methods we've discussed take $O(N^3)$ floating point operations to solve an $N \times N$ system; for $N = 4n$ this means about $c(4n)^3$ flops for some $c > 0$ (if N is large), whereas for $N = 3n$ this means about $c(3n)^3$ flops for some c. That means that solving the reduced system takes about $3^3/4^3$ or $27/64$ as many flops. We've saved half the work at no cost. In graphics applications it isn't uncommon to have hundreds of thousands of nodes, so this is a big deal.

Another Improvement
We can do even better. Let's suppose that the spline exists (we'll justify this assumption later). Then $S''(x)$ is a well-defined piecewise linear interpolant to the unknown values $S''(x_0), S''(x_1), \ldots, S''(x_n)$ at the nodes $x_0, x_1, \ldots, x_n$. Let's write $\sigma_i = S''(x_i)$ for $i = 0, 1, \ldots, n$. In terms of these unknown values, it must be the case that

$$
S''(x) = \sum_{i=0}^{n} \sigma_i \Lambda_i(x_i) \tag{4.11}
$$

in terms of the piecewise linear Lagrange interpolating polynomials. (This is just Eq. (4.6) from Section 4.2.) If we can determine $\sigma_0, \sigma_1, \ldots, \sigma_n$, then we can find an expression for $S''(x)$. From Eq. (4.10),

$$
\begin{aligned}
p_i''(x) &= 6\alpha_i(x - x_i) + 2\beta_i \\
p_i''(x_i) &= 2\beta_i,
\end{aligned}
$$

but $p_i''(x_i)$ is just $S''(x_i)$, which by definition is σ_i. In other words, if we can find $\sigma_0, \sigma_1, \ldots, \sigma_n$, then we can find $\beta_0, \beta_1, \ldots, \beta_{n-1}$ trivially from

$$
\beta_i = \frac{\sigma_i}{2}.
$$

Can we also relate the values of the remaining coefficients α_i and γ_i ($i = 0, 1, \ldots, n - 1$) to the values $\sigma_0, \sigma_1, \ldots, \sigma_n$ (and possibly the known x-values and y-values)? If so, then we would only need to solve a matrix system for the $n + 1$ unknowns $\sigma_0, \sigma_1, \ldots, \sigma_n$.

It will be convenient to write $h_i = x_{i+1} - x_i$. Consider Eq. (4.11) on a single element $[x_i, x_{i+1}]$. Proceeding as in Example 4.2.1, we have

$$S''(x) = \sigma_i \Lambda_i(x) + \sigma_{i+1} \Lambda_{i+1}(x)$$

$$= \sigma_i \frac{x - x_{i+1}}{x_i - x_{i+1}} + \sigma_{i+1} \frac{x - x_i}{x_{i+1} - x_i}$$

$$= -\sigma_i \frac{x - x_{i+1}}{h_i} + \sigma_{i+1} \frac{x - x_i}{h_i}$$

on this element. Integrating,

$$S'(x) = -\sigma_i \frac{(x - x_{i+1})^2}{2h_i} + \sigma_{i+1} \frac{(x - x_i)^2}{2h_i} + \tau_i \tag{4.12}$$

for some constant of integration τ_i, and

$$S(x) = -\sigma_i \frac{(x - x_{i+1})^3}{6h_i} + \sigma_{i+1} \frac{(x - x_i)^3}{6h_i} + \tau_i(x - x_i) + \kappa_i \tag{4.13}$$

for some constants of integration τ_i and κ_i. (You are asked to verify this formula in Problems 4.4. You may wish to complete the squares in the numerators, after integrating, to get the form in Eq. (4.12).) But from Eq. (4.13), if we take $x = x_i$, we have

$$S(x_i) = -\sigma_i \frac{(x_i - x_{i+1})^3}{6h_i} + \sigma_{i+1} \frac{(x_i - x_i)^3}{6h_i} + \tau_i(x_i - x_i) + \kappa_i$$

$$= -\sigma_i \frac{(x_i - x_{i+1})^3}{6h_i} + \kappa_i$$

$$= \sigma_i \frac{h_i^3}{6h_i} + \kappa_i$$

$$= \sigma_i \frac{h_i^2}{6} + \kappa_i$$

$$= y_i$$

by the interpolation condition. That is,

$$\kappa_i = y_i - \frac{\sigma_i h_i^2}{6}$$

so that if we can find the σ_i then we can find the κ_i. Using Eq. (4.13) again, if we take $x = x_{i+1}$, we have

$$S(x_{i+1}) = -\sigma_i \frac{(x_{i+1} - x_{i+1})^3}{6h_i} + \sigma_{i+1} \frac{(x_{i+1} - x_i)^3}{6h_i} + \tau_i(x_{i+1} - x_i) + \kappa_i$$

$$= \sigma_{i+1} \frac{(x_{i+1} - x_i)^3}{6h_i} + \tau_i(x_{i+1} - x_i) + \kappa_i$$

$$= \sigma_{i+1}\frac{h_i^3}{6h_i} + \tau_i h_i + \kappa_i$$

$$= \sigma_{i+1}\frac{h_i^2}{6} + \tau_i h_i + \kappa_i$$

$$= y_{i+1}$$

by the interpolation condition. That is,

$$\sigma_{i+1}\frac{h_i^2}{6} + \tau_i h_i + \kappa_i = y_{i+1}$$

or

$$\tau_i h_i = y_{i+1} - \sigma_{i+1}\frac{h_i^2}{6} - \kappa_i$$

$$\tau_i = \frac{\left(y_{i+1} - \sigma_{i+1}\dfrac{h_i^2}{6} - \kappa_i\right)}{h_i}$$

$$= \frac{\left(y_{i+1} - \sigma_{i+1}\dfrac{h_i^2}{6} - \left(y_i - \sigma_i\dfrac{h_i^2}{6}\right)\right)}{h_i}$$

$$= \frac{y_{i+1} - y_i}{h_i} - \frac{h_i}{6}(\sigma_{i+1} - \sigma_i) \tag{4.14}$$

($i = 0, 1, \ldots, n-1$), which gives the values of τ_i in terms of the σ_i and the known y-values and the known spacings h_i between the nodes.

Notice from Eq. (4.13) that the cubic polynomial on the element i is completely determined by knowledge of the σ_i, τ_i, and κ_i (plus the known grid spacings), and we now have formulas for τ_i and κ_i in terms of the unknowns σ_i plus the known y- and h-values; we only need to find the $n+1$ values $\sigma_0, \sigma_1, \ldots, \sigma_n$ in order to completely determine the spline. It's a trivial matter to compare Eq. (4.10) and Eq. (4.13) to find the needed expressions for the α_i and γ_i (recall that we already know that $\delta_i = y_i$ and $\beta_i = \sigma_i/2$). In fact,

$$\alpha_i = \frac{\sigma_{i+1} - \sigma_i}{6h_i}$$

$$\gamma_i = \frac{y_{i+1} - y_i}{h_i} - \frac{h_i}{6}(\sigma_{i+1} + 2\sigma_i) \tag{4.15}$$

as you are asked to verify in Problems 4.4.

Focusing on σ_i All we need now is a way to determine $\sigma_0, \sigma_1, \ldots, \sigma_n$. We have ensured that the second derivative of $S(x)$ exists by piecewise linear interpolation (Eq. (4.11)) and have been using the interpolation conditions that S must satisfy; we haven't really made use of $S'(x)$. The requirement that $S'(x)$ be continuous means that at $x_1, \ldots, x_{n-1}$ we must have

$$p'_{i-1}(x_i) = p'_i(x_i)$$

(convince yourself that the subscripts are correct); that is,

$$3\alpha_{i-1}(x_i - x_{i-1})^2 + 2\beta_{i-1}(x_i - x_{i-1}) + \gamma_{i-1} = 3\alpha_i(x_i - x_i)^2 + 2\beta_i(x_i - x_i) + \gamma_i$$

or

$$3\alpha_{i-1}h_{i-1}^2 + 2\beta_{i-1}h_{i-1} + \gamma_{i-1} = \gamma_i$$

for the $n-1$ interior nodes $i = 1, \ldots, n-1$. Substituting from Eq. (4.15) and using $\beta_i = \sigma_i/2$ gives

$$3\frac{\sigma_i - \sigma_{i-1}}{6h_{i-1}}h_{i-1}^2 + \frac{2\sigma_{i-1}h_{i-1}}{2} = \frac{y_{i+1} - y_i}{h_i} - \frac{h_i}{6}(\sigma_{i+1} + 2\sigma_i)$$
$$- \left[\frac{y_i - y_{i-1}}{h_{i-1}} - \frac{h_{i-1}}{6}(\sigma_i + 2\sigma_{i-1}) \right] \quad (4.16)$$

or

$$3\frac{\sigma_i - \sigma_{i-1}}{h_{i-1}}h_{i-1}^2 + 6\sigma_{i-1}h_{i-1} = 6\frac{y_{i+1} - y_i}{h_i} - h_i(\sigma_{i+1} + 2\sigma_i)$$
$$- \left[6\frac{y_i - y_{i-1}}{h_{i-1}} - h_{i-1}(\sigma_i + 2\sigma_{i-1}) \right]$$

or, after considerable simplification,

$$\varpi_i\sigma_{i-1} + 2\sigma_i + (1 - \varpi_i)\sigma_{i+1} = r_i, \quad (4.17)$$

where

$$\varpi_i = \frac{h_{i-1}}{h_{i-1} + h_i}$$
$$r_i = \frac{6}{h_i + h_{i-1}} \left(\frac{y_{i+1} - y_i}{h_i} - \frac{y_i - y_{i-1}}{h_{i-1}} \right) \quad (4.18)$$

(again, you are asked to fill in the details in Problems 4.4). Note the similarity of the equation determining r_i to a difference equation for the second derivative (it looks like a difference of two approximations of a first derivative). Our linear system now consists of the $n-1$ equations represented by Eq. (4.17) for $i = 1, \ldots, n-1$, plus the 2 boundary conditions, for a total of $n+1$ equations in $n+1$ unknowns. For example, note that the natural boundary conditions (second derivatives constrained to be zero at the endpoints of the spline) correspond to the two additional conditions $\sigma_0 = 0$, $\sigma_n = 0$.

We've gone through a lot of detailed algebra to get here, and we're not done yet. Let's take stock. We started with a $4n \times 4n$ linear system (from the end of the previous section). We've come to an $(n+1) \times (n+1)$ linear system (and the small cost of using Eq. (4.15) to find α_i and γ_i plus the comparatively negligible cost of forming δ_i and β_i). This reduction of a $4n \times 4n$ system to a $(n+1) \times (n+1)$ system represents a considerable benefit with respect to the amount of work we must perform to find the spline interpolant, at the cost of our having had to wade through a modest amount of algebra. This is a good thing.

Example 4.4.1 Consider the data $\{(-1, -1), (0, 1), (1, 1)\}$. Let's interpolate a natural spline to the data using the method we've just developed. There are 3 nodes ($n = 2$), so we need to find the 3 values σ_0, σ_1, and σ_2. The natural boundary conditions give $\sigma_0 = 0$, $\sigma_2 = 0$, and Eq. (4.17) gives

$$\varpi_1 \sigma_0 + 2\sigma_1 + (1 - \varpi_1)\sigma_2 = r_1$$

$$\frac{h_0}{h_0 + h_1}\sigma_0 + 2\sigma_1 + \left(1 - \frac{h_0}{h_0 + h_1}\right)\sigma_2 = \frac{6}{h_0 + h_1}\left(\frac{y_2 - y_1}{h_1} - \frac{y_1 - y_0}{h_0}\right)$$

$$\frac{1}{2}\sigma_0 + 2\sigma_1 + \left(1 - \frac{1}{2}\right)\sigma_2 = \frac{6}{2}\left(\frac{1 - 1}{1} - \frac{1 - -1}{1}\right)$$

$$\frac{1}{2}\sigma_0 + 2\sigma_1 + \frac{1}{2}\sigma_2 = -6$$

(using Eq. (4.18) and the data). Hence we must solve the system

$$\begin{pmatrix} 1 & 0 & 0 \\ \frac{1}{2} & 2 & \frac{1}{2} \\ 0 & 0 & 1 \end{pmatrix} \begin{pmatrix} \sigma_0 \\ \sigma_1 \\ \sigma_2 \end{pmatrix} = \begin{pmatrix} 0 \\ -6 \\ 0 \end{pmatrix}$$

for σ_0, σ_1, and σ_2. (We're not using the fact that σ_0 and σ_2 are already determined.) This is our $(n + 1) \times (n + 1)$ system. We find the solution easily: $\sigma_0 = 0$, $\sigma_1 = -3$, and $\sigma_2 = 0$.

To actually construct the spline, we need to find the coefficients. Since there are two elements, we are looking for two cubics. We have

$$\delta_0 = y_0$$

$$= -1$$

$$\delta_1 = y_1$$

$$= 1$$

$$\beta_0 = \frac{\sigma_0}{2}$$

$$= 0$$

$$\beta_1 = \frac{\sigma_1}{2}$$

$$= -\frac{3}{2}$$

and from Eq. (4.15),

$$\alpha_0 = \frac{\sigma_1 - \sigma_0}{6h_0}$$

$$= \frac{(-3 - 0)}{(6 \cdot 1)}$$

$$= -\frac{1}{2}$$

$$\alpha_1 = \frac{\sigma_2 - \sigma_1}{6h_1}$$

$$= \frac{(0 - -3)}{(6 \cdot 1)}$$

$$= \frac{1}{2}$$

$$\gamma_0 = \frac{y_1 - y_0}{h_0} - \frac{h_0}{6}(\sigma_1 + 2\sigma_0)$$

$$= \frac{(1 - -1)}{1} - \left(\frac{1}{6}\right)(-3 + 2 \cdot 0)$$

$$= \frac{5}{2}$$

$$\gamma_1 = \frac{y_2 - y_1}{h_1} - \frac{h_1}{6}(\sigma_2 + 2\sigma_1)$$

$$= \frac{(1 - 1)}{1} - \left(\frac{1}{6}\right)(0 + 2 \cdot -3)$$

$$= 1$$

so that

$$p_0(x) = \alpha_0(x - x_0)^3 + \beta_0(x - x_0)^2 + \gamma_0(x - x_0) + \delta_0$$

$$= -\frac{1}{2}(x + 1)^3 + 0(x + 1)^2 + \frac{5}{2}(x + 1) - 1$$

$$= -\frac{1}{2}(x + 1)^3 + \frac{5}{2}(x + 1) - 1$$

is the cubic on the first element $[-1, 0]$ and

$$p_1(x) = \alpha_1(x - x_1)^3 + \beta_1(x - x_1)^2 + \gamma_1(x - x_1) + \delta_1$$

$$= \frac{1}{2}(x - 0)^3 - \frac{3}{2}(x - 0)^2 + 1(x - 0) + 1$$

$$= \frac{1}{2}x^3 - \frac{3}{2}x^2 + x + 1$$

is the cubic on the second element $[0, 1]$. Verify that $p_0(-1) = -1$, $p_0(0) = 1$, $p_1(0) = 1$, and $p_1(1) = 1$ (interpolation). Note also that at the node $x_1 = 0$ we have $p_0'(0) = 1$, $p_1'(0) = 1$ (these match as expected) and $p_0''(0) = -3$, $p_1''(0) = -3$ (these match and furthermore are equal to σ_1, as expected). ■

Matrix Form   We still must put Eq. (4.17) in matrix form and discuss the other boundary conditions. The natural spline is easy; the linear system has the form

$$
\begin{bmatrix}
1 & 0 & 0 & 0 & 0 & 0 \\
\varpi_1 & 2 & 1-\varpi_1 & 0 & 0 & 0 \\
0 & \varpi_2 & 2 & 1-\varpi_2 & 0 & 0 \\
0 & 0 & \varpi_3 & 2 & 1-\varpi_3 & 0 \\
 & & & \vdots & & \\
0 & 0 & 0 & \varpi_{n-1} & 2 & 1-\varpi_{n-1} \\
0 & 0 & 0 & 0 & 0 & 1
\end{bmatrix}
\begin{pmatrix}
\sigma_0 \\ \sigma_1 \\ \vdots \\ \sigma_{n-1} \\ \sigma_n
\end{pmatrix}
=
\begin{pmatrix}
0 \\ r_1 \\ \vdots \\ r_{n-1} \\ 0
\end{pmatrix},
\qquad (4.19)
$$

where the coefficient matrix T is tridiagonal, that is, it has nonzero entries only on the main diagonal and the first superdiagonal and first subdiagonal. In addition, note from Equation (4.18) that $0 < \varpi_i < 1$, and hence $0 < 1 - \varpi_i < 1$ as well. This means that the matrix T has the property that the diagonal entry of each row is greater than the sum $\varpi_i + (1 - \varpi_i) = 1$ of the off-diagonal entries in that row. Recall from Section 3.1 that any square matrix A with the property that

$$
|a_{ii}| \geq \sum_{\substack{j=1 \\ j \neq i}}^{n} |a_{ij}|
$$

for each row i is said to be a *diagonally dominant matrix*, and if the inequality is strict it is said to be a *strictly diagonally dominant matrix*. Strictly diagonally dominant matrices, such as the matrix T in Eq. (4.19), have many interesting and useful properties, including nonsingularity and the property that Gaussian elimination may be performed on them without the need for pivoting (meaning that pivoting is not necessary because there is no possibility of a zero pivot, and it is not needed to control the growth of errors). The matrix T has other desirable properties as well. For example, it has the positive definiteness property $x^T T x > 0$ if $x \neq 0$ (though it is not symmetric).

So the linear system in Eq. (4.19) has a unique solution (the natural spline exists and is unique), and we may find it accurately using a direct method. The fact that T is tridiagonal suggests that we should be able to find a very efficient way of solving the system if we take advantage of this special structure, and indeed this is so; there are $O(n)$ techniques for such systems. For now let's look at the other boundary conditions, however. The first and last equations are trivial and we might rewrite this as an $(n-1) \times (n-1)$ system in $\sigma_1, \ldots, \sigma_{n-1}$, but we'll leave it in the form of Eq. (4.19).

Physical Splines   The term *spline* is a drafting term that originally referred to a thin, pliable strip of wood that was passed through pins stuck through paper to allow a smooth curve to be drawn through the points marked by the pins (by tracing along the spline). Sometimes clamps or weights (called *ducks*) were used to adjust the angle at which the spline passed through certain points, if desired. If no clamps were used, the spline would take on a straight shape to the left of the leftmost pin and to the right of the rightmost pin, where it was no longer subject to the forces exerted by the pins. The natural (or free) boundary conditions $S''(x_0) = 0$, $S''(x_n) = 0$ simulate this case (the zero second derivative corresponds to linearity). The clamped spline, where a derivative is specified at the endpoints, corresponds to clamping the spline at the leftmost and rightmost pins to force it to enter and leave at a prescribed angle. Clearly, the clamped spline will be more accurate in general, since it uses additional information about the desired shape of the spline. Of course, this information is not always available. On the other hand, the natural boundary conditions impose two conditions ($S''(x_0) = 0$, $S''(x_n) = 0$) that are almost certainly incorrect. For this reason the not-a-knot boundary conditions are usually preferred when the data needed for the clamped spline is not available (or cannot be accurately estimated).

Clamped BCs   For the clamped boundary conditions, the only changes in Eq. (4.19) are the first and last rows of T and the vector on the right-hand side. The conditions $S'(x_0) = s_0$, $S'(x_n) = s_n$ may be applied to Eq. (4.12); at $x = x_0$, for example, we have

$$S'(x_0) = -\sigma_0 \frac{(x_0 - x_1)^2}{2h_0} + \sigma_1 \frac{(x_0 - x_0)^2}{2h_0} + \tau_0$$

$$s_0 = \frac{-\sigma_0 h_0}{2} + \frac{\left(y_1 - \sigma_1 \frac{h_0^2}{6} - \kappa_0\right)}{h_0}$$

(using Eq. (4.14) to find τ_0). Substituting in the expression for κ_0 gives

$$s_0 = \frac{-\sigma_0 h_0}{2} + \frac{\left(y_1 - \sigma_1 \frac{h_0^2}{6} - \kappa_0\right)}{h_0}$$

$$= \frac{-\sigma_0 h_0}{2} + \frac{\left(y_1 - \sigma_1 \frac{h_0^2}{6} - \left(y_0 - \sigma_0 \frac{h_0^2}{6}\right)\right)}{h_0}$$

$$= \frac{-\sigma_0 h_0}{2} + \frac{(y_1 - y_0)}{h_0} + \frac{(\sigma_0 - \sigma_1)h_0}{6}$$

$$= \frac{(y_1 - y_0)}{h_0} - \frac{\sigma_0 h_0}{3} - \frac{\sigma_1 h_0}{6},$$

which is a single equation in the 2 unknowns σ_0 and σ_1. Writing it in a form similar to Eq. (4.17) gives

$$2\sigma_0 + \sigma_1 = \frac{6(y_1 - y_0)}{h_0^2} - \frac{6s_0}{h_0},$$

which becomes the new first row of Eq. (4.19) for this boundary condition. In a similar way we find the equation

$$\sigma_{n-1} + 2\sigma_n = \frac{6s_n}{h_{n-1}} - \frac{6(y_n - y_{n-1})}{h_{n-1}^2}$$

from Eq. (4.12) evaluated at $x = x_n$. This gives the linear system

$$
\begin{bmatrix}
2 & 1 & 0 & 0 & 0 & 0 \\
\varpi_1 & 2 & 1-\varpi_1 & 0 & 0 & 0 \\
0 & \varpi_2 & 2 & 1-\varpi_2 & 0 & 0 \\
0 & 0 & \varpi_3 & 2 & 1-\varpi_3 & 0 \\
& & & \vdots & & \\
0 & 0 & 0 & \varpi_{n-1} & 2 & 1-\varpi_{n-1} \\
0 & 0 & 0 & 0 & 1 & 2
\end{bmatrix}
\begin{pmatrix}
\sigma_0 \\ \sigma_1 \\ \vdots \\ \\ \sigma_{n-1} \\ \sigma_n
\end{pmatrix}
=
\begin{pmatrix}
\frac{6(y_1-y_0)}{h_0^2} \frac{-6s_0}{h_0} \\
r_1 \\
\vdots \\
\\
r_{n-1} \\
\frac{6s_n}{h_{n-1}} - \frac{6(y_n-y_{n-1})}{h_{n-1}^2}
\end{pmatrix}
$$

$$(4.20)$$

for the complete spline. Once again, the coefficient matrix is tridiagonal, diagonally dominant, and (nonsymmetric) positive definite, giving us many opportunities to increase the efficiency and accuracy of our solution.

We could also put the linear system for the not-a-knot spline in matrix form, but this derivation has been detailed enough for now. It will likely pay to re-read this section. The big point is: Spending a small amount of time setting up a problem and formulating it properly can lead to big gains in efficiency. In this case, not only have we reduced the system from a $4n \times 4n$ system (that would require $O(N^3)$ flops for its solution, where $N = 4n$) to an $(n+1) \times (n+1)$ structured system (with many special properties, and that may be handled in $O(n)$ flops), but also Eq. (4.10) will be more accurate when we actually need to evaluate $S(x)$ for some x that is not a node.

We can define basis functions for splines as we did with Lagrange interpolating polynomials in Section 4.1 and piecewise Lagrange interpolating polynomials in Section 4.2. In fact, the hat basis of Section 4.2 is a set of basis functions for linear splines.

We close with two theorems. The notation is as used elsewhere in this section.

Theorem 4.4.1

If $f \in C^4[x_0, x_n]$ and there is an $M > 0$ such that $|f^{(iv)}(x)| \le M$ for $x \in [x_0, x_n]$, then

$$
\max_{x \in [x_0, x_n]} \{|f(x) - S(x)|\} \le \frac{5M}{384} \max_{i=0}^{n-1} \{|h_i^4|\}
$$

for the clamped cubic spline interpolant $S(x)$ to $f(x)$.

Note that the error in the clamped cubic spline decreases as $O(h^4)$, where h is the maximum distance between nodes. In particular, the spline converges to the function as $h \to 0$ if the function has a bounded fourth derivative (justifying refinement of the grid as a means of obtaining an improved approximant). There is an $O(h^3)$ error formula for $\max\{f'(x) - S'(x)\}$, and so on, justifying the use of splines for numerical differentiation. Note also that there is no assumption of equal spacing, and as usual equal spacing is not likely to be the best choice. Adaptive selection of knots is useful, but we are not always free to choose these values.

> **Theorem 4.4.2 (Minimum Curvature Property of Natural Splines)**
>
> If $g \in C^2[x_0, x_n]$ is any function that interpolates $f(x)$ at the nodes $x_0, \ldots, x_n$ and $S(x)$ is the free cubic spline interpolant to $f(x)$ at those nodes, then
>
> $$\int_{x_0}^{x_n} [S''(x)]^2 dx \leq \int_{x_0}^{x_n} [g''(x)]^2 dx,$$
>
> and if $g(x)$ is not equal to $S(x)$, then the inequality is strict.

Note that g need not be a spline (or even a polynomial) and that no assumption is made about $f(x)$ other than that it is defined at the nodes. Theorem 4.4.2 states that, amongst all sufficiently smooth interpolants to a given function, the natural spline has minimum total curvature (as measured by the second derivative). It can be shown that this means that it has approximately minimum strain energy of all such curves through those nodes. In this sense the mathematical spline mimics the physical spline, which assumes the least strain shape. Although this is an interesting property, it does not alter the fact that the clamped and not-a-knot boundary conditions are generally preferable–or possibly other boundary conditions, if we know something special about the function f (e.g., that it is periodic).

PROBLEMS 4.4

1. Fill in the details in going from Eq. (4.11) to Eq. (4.13).

2. Derive Eq. (4.15) by comparing Eq. (4.13) and Eq. (4.10).

3. Derive Eq. (4.17) and Eq. (4.18) from Eq. (4.16).

4. a. Use Eq. (4.19) to fit a natural cubic spline to the data $\{(0, 1), (1, 2), (2, 1), (3, 2)\}$. Form and solve the 4×4 matrix by hand. Write the three cubics (Eq. (4.10)) explicitly.

　b. Use your spline to interpolate values at $x = 0.5, 1.5, 2.5$.

5. a. Use Eq. (4.19), Eq. (4.20), and MATLAB to fit a natural cubic spline and a clamped cubic spline to the function $y = e^{-x} \cos(2x)$ at the nodes $\{0, 0.1, 0.2, 0.3, 0.4, 0.5\}$. Write the five cubics (Eq. (4.10)) explicitly. Plot the function and the splines on a single graph. Comment.

　b. Repeat (part a) with the nodes $\{0, 0.05, 0.18, 0.32, 0.45, 0.5\}$.

　c. Use Theorem 4.4.1 to bound the error in the clamped splines in parts (a) and (b).

MATLAB 4.4

The matrices in Eq. (4.19) and Eq. (4.20) are sparse; they have $(n + 1) + 2n = 3n + 1$ nonzero entries out of a total of n^2 entries, so roughly $3/n$ of the entries are nonzero. It's wasteful to form an $n \times n$ matrix to hold roughly $3n$ entries—not only in terms of memory usage but also in terms of the time spent forming the matrix initially and then retrieving rows from memory as needed. If we only stored the $3n + 1$ needed entries, the whole matrix might fit in fast memory.

　For this reason the tridiagonal matrices in Eq. (4.19) and Eq. (4.20) would never be formed at all, unless they were small. We could achieve this by writing a program that uses Eq. (4.17) directly and that never works explicitly with a matrix, or by storing the matrix in sparse form. (Recall the `sparse` command, which stores and manipulates sparse matrices efficiently.) In either case we obtain speed and storage benefits.

The MATLAB backslash command recognizes certain special matrices and uses a more efficient method for them. Enter:

```
» b=ones([4 1]);
» A=rand(4)
» flops(0);A\b;flops
```

(If you don't have the flops command, use a much larger matrix and `tic,toc`.) Repeat this several times; your answers will vary slightly. Now enter:

```
» A2=diag(rand([4 1]))
» flops(0);A2\b;flops    %Special structure (diagonal).
» A2(1,4)=1
» flops(0);A2\b;flops    %Special structure (upper triangular).
» A2(4,1)=1
» flops(0);A2\b;flops  %No special structure recognized.
```

In fact the final A2 matrix does have an obvious structure, and matrices that are tridiagonal except for two corner entries such as in A2 do occur in practice (for example, for periodic splines), but MATLAB does not recognize this structure. A person looking at A2 would see that the middle entries can be solved for immediately and that only the first and last row require any real effort, amounting to a 2×2 linear system in the first and last unknowns, but MATLAB uses about as many flops for the final A2 as for the full matrix A. Clearly, if A2 were large, we would want to write a special routine to handle it or use the `sparse` command. Enter:

```
» SA2=sparse(A2)
» flops(0);SA2\b;flops
```

to do so. This is not optimal (and hides the fact that there is some cost associated with forming and manipulating the sparse representation) but is certainly an improvement.

Does MATLAB recognize tridiagonal matrices as a special case? Let's find out. Again, if you don't have the flops command, use a much larger matrix and `tic,toc`. Enter:

```
» b=ones([7 1]);
» A3=rand(7);A3=A3-triu(A3,2)-tril(A3,-2)
» flops(0);SA2\b;flops
» A3(1,7)=1;A3(7,1)=1;
» flops(0);A3\b;flops
» A=rand(7);
» flops(0);A\b;flops
```

Many fewer flops are required for the tridiagonal matrix than for the tridiagonal matrix with two additional entries, which is about the same as for an arbitrary dense matrix. However, there are methods for solving $n \times n$ tridiagonal systems in about $8n$ flops, and we are certainly not getting performance that good. Let's try using `sparse`. Enter:

```
» SA3=sparse(A3);
» flops(0);SA3\b;flops
```

This is an improvement, but if we want to handle large tridiagonal matrices we should write our own code. As mentioned above, the inefficiency of forming a matrix like A3 is reason enough to use `sparse` or a specially written program. The `sparse` command can be used to form a matrix like SA3 without ever actually forming the A3 matrix. For example, enter:

```
» rows=[1 1 2 2 2 3 3 3 4 4 4 5 5 5 6 6];
» cols=[1 2 1 2 3 2 3 4 3 4 5 4 5 6 5 6];
» T=sparse(rows,cols,.5*ones([16 1]))
» full(T)     %Standard form.
» T=T+diag(1.5*ones([6 1]))
» T(1,2)=1;T(6,5)=1;
» full(T)
```

creates the matrix T of Eq. (4.20) if $\varpi_i = 1/2$. Note that MATLAB knows to retain the sparse form when adding a sparse matrix like `diag(1.5*ones([6 1]))` to another sparse matrix.

We don't present the details for a tridiagonal solver here. Instead, we consider how we might present a table of interpolated values using MATLAB. If we had the data $\{(0, 0), (.1, .0998), (.2, .1987)\}$ from the sine function and wished to interpolate values at $x_i = .01i$ ($i = 0, 1, \ldots, 20$) then we could do the following; enter:

```
» x=0:.01:.2
» y=spline([0 .1 .2],sin([0 .1 .2]),x)   %List y values.
» disp('   x   y'),disp([x' y'])   %9 spaces before x,y.
```

(The `spline` command uses a not-a-knot spline.) The display of the y-values is adequate. What if we want a 5 place table, though? Enter:

```
» header='        x        y'  %6 spaces, x, 8 spaces, y.
» s_table=sprintf('%5.5f %5.5f\n',[x' y'])
» disp(header),disp(s_table)
```

(The `sprintf` command formats a matrix according to the conventions of the C programming language). For another example, enter:

```
» format long
» z=exp(10)
» disp(sprintf('The value of z is ',z)) %No format.
» disp(sprintf('The value of z is %5.3f',z))   %Floating pt. format.
» disp(sprintf('The value of z is %5.2f',z))
» disp(sprintf('The value of z is %5.1f',z))
» disp(sprintf('The value of z is %5.0f',z))
» disp(sprintf('The value of z is %20.8f',z))
```

```
» disp(sprintf('The value of z is %5.3e',z)) %Exponential format.
» disp(sprintf('The value of z is %5.2e',z))
» disp(sprintf('The value of z is %5.0e',z))
» disp(sprintf('z=%5.3f units and z^2=%5.3f units.',z, z^2))
» disp(sprintf('z=%5.3f units\nz^2=%5.3f units.',z,z^2))
```

The \n formats a newline. A specification such as %5.3f represents a format of 5 total spaces for the number, of which 3 are allotted to the values after the decimal point (hence the extra spaces when %20.8f was used). The total number of spaces used may be more if the format does not allow for the non-fractional part of the number. Use of the sprintf command (or the fprintf command if writing to a file) allows careful control over the format of your output; this is useful for creating table displays. Note that the sprintf command actually returns a string variable, so we use disp to display it in order to suppress the MATLAB "ans =" formatting of displayed values.

ADDITIONAL PROBLEMS 4.4

6. a. Use Eq. (4.19) to fit a natural cubic spline to the function $y = \sin(x^2)$ using the nodes $0, .1, \ldots, 1$. Give the coefficients and plot your result.

  b. Use Eq. (4.20) to fit a clamped cubic spline to the function $y = \sin(x^2)$ using the nodes $0, .1, \ldots, 1$. Give the coefficients and plot your result.

7. a. Use Eq. (4.19) to fit a natural cubic spline to the function $y = x^9 - 5x^7 + x^4 - 2x^2 + 1$ using the nodes $0, .1, \ldots, 1$. Give the coefficients and plot your result.

  b. Use Eq. (4.20) to fit a clamped cubic spline to the function $y = x^9 - 5x^7 + x^4 - 2x^2 + 1$ using the nodes $0, .1, \ldots, 1$. Give the coefficients and plot your result.

8. If a function is periodic on $[x_0, x_n]$, then we may use the cyclic boundary conditions $p_0'(x_0) = p_{n-1}'(x_n)$, $p_0''(x_0) = p_{n-1}''(x_n)$. Give the matrix form for the cyclic spline equations.

9. a. Write a MATLAB program that approximates the definite integral of a given function between given endpoints using a cubic spline based on n equally spaced nodes, where n is an optional input argument. Demonstrate your program and discuss its accuracy.

  b. Write a MATLAB program that approximates the derivative of a given function using a cubic spline based on n equally spaced nodes, where n is an optional input argument; use a second optional argument to request a plot of the function and its derivative. Your output should be the approximate derivatives at the interior nodes. Demonstrate your program and discuss its accuracy.

10. Write a MATLAB program that inputs a function and a vector of nodes and displays a six-digit table of the function values at the nodes and at the midpoints of the subintervals between the nodes. Return the y-values from the table as your output.

11. Derive the systems corresponding to Eq. (4.19) and Eq. (4.20) for quintic splines.

12. Give the matrix form for the not-a-knot spline equations.

13. a. Derive an efficient algorithm for solving a tridiagonal system.

  b. Derive an efficient algorithm for solving a positive definite tridiagonal system.

  c. Show that a symmetric diagonally dominant matrix that has positive diagonal entries is necessarily positive definite. (*Hint:* Use Gershgorin's Circle Theorem.) What happens if the matrix is not symmetric?

14. Verify Theorem 4.4.1 using MATLAB experiments.

15. a. Demonstrate Theorem 4.4.2 using MATLAB experiments.

  b. Prove Theorem 4.4.2.

5 Numerical Integration

5.1 Closed Newton-Cotes Formulas

ANY DEFINITE INTEGRALS of interest can't be evaluated analytically. Probably the best-known example is the integral that gives the area under the standard bell-shaped curve, given by

$$F(x) = \frac{1}{2} + \frac{1}{\sqrt{2\pi}} \int_0^x e^{-z^2/2} \, dz. \tag{5.1}$$

This integral appears very frequently in probability and statistics and is extensively tabulated; every statistics book contains a table of its values. The integral is tabulated because it is a fact that there is no way to express the antiderivative of $\exp(-z^2)$ in terms of elementary functions. Because of cases like this we need methods to perform approximate integration; for other cases it may be more convenient to use a numerical method than a symbolic one. Often we're given values of $f(x)$ at various points but not a formula for f and so have no choice but to use a numerical method. This is true of data from an experiment, for example.

Throughout this chapter, unless otherwise mentioned, we assume that the integrand f is continuous on the finite interval $[a, b]$. We'll see some methods for integrals on unbounded intervals as well.

There are many analytical techniques for approximating integrals. We might imagine approximating the definite integral

$$I = \int_a^b f(x) \, dx$$

by expanding $f(x)$ in a Taylor or other series, and then integrating that series term by term to find a series for I itself. Most of the methods we consider, however, have the

Weighted
Average Rules

form of a **weighted average rule**

$$\int_a^b f(x)\,dx \approx w_0 f(x_0) + w_1 f(x_1) + \cdots + w_n f(x_n) \tag{5.2}$$

for some weights $w_0, w_1, \ldots, w_n$ and some nodes $x_0, x_1, \ldots, x_n$ (which won't always lie in $[a, b]$). The selection of weights and nodes defines the method. Techniques for performing numerical integration are also called **numerical quadrature** methods.

For example, in the calculus you likely encountered several numerical integration techniques, including the **midpoint rule**

$$\int_a^b f(x)\,dx \approx (b - a)f\left(\frac{a+b}{2}\right)$$

($w_0 = b - a$, $x_0 = (a + b)/2$), which approximates f by a constant, namely, its value at the midpoint of the interval of integration, and the **trapezoidal rule**

$$\int_a^b f(x)\,dx \approx \frac{b-a}{2}(f(a) + f(b)) \tag{5.3}$$

($w_0 = w_1 = (b - a)/2$, $x_0 = a$, $x_1 = b$), which approximates f by linear interpolation over the interval. (See Fig. 5.1, which shows a constant and a linear interpolant to the same function.) Geometrically, we can think of the midpoint rule as approximating the area under f by the area of a rectangle and the trapezoidal rule as approximating the area under f by the area of a trapezoid.

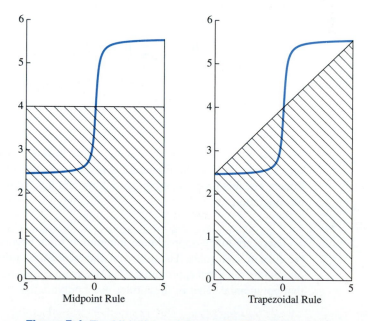

Figure 5.1 The Midpoint and Trapezoidal Rule Approximants.

Example 5.1.1   Consider Eq. (5.1). It is usual to evaluate the integral in this formula in terms of a special function known as the **error function**

$$\text{erf}(x) = \frac{2}{\sqrt{\pi}} \int_0^x e^{-z^2} dz$$

(or another, similar special function). Note that

$$F(x) = \frac{1}{2}\left(1 + \text{erf}\left(\frac{x}{\sqrt{2}}\right)\right)$$

(this is valid for all x). Hence we can find values of $F(x)$ by evaluating the error function, which again must be done numerically. We do not necessarily need to perform numerical quadrature; there are ways to approximate the function $y = \text{erf}(x)$ directly. (We could use a spline, for example.) However, let's try using the midpoint and trapezoidal rules to approximate erf(1). We have

$$\text{erf}(1) = \frac{2}{\sqrt{\pi}} \int_0^1 e^{-z^2} dz$$

$$\approx \frac{2}{\sqrt{\pi}} \exp\left(-\left(\frac{1}{2}\right)^2\right)$$

$$\doteq .8788$$

from the midpoint rule, since $x = 1/2$ is the midpoint of the interval, and

$$\text{erf}(1) = \frac{2}{\sqrt{\pi}} \int_0^1 e^{-z^2} dz$$

$$\approx \frac{2}{\sqrt{\pi}}\left(\frac{1-0}{2}\right)(\exp(-(0)^2) + \exp(-(1)^2))$$

$$\doteq .7717$$

from the trapezoidal rule. The actual value to four places (using the MATLAB `erf` function) is .8427. From Figure 5.2 it is clear why the trapezoidal rule gives an underestimate: For this function, the linear interpolant lies below the function over the interval of integration. ∎

There are many approximate integration rules beyond these two; in fact there are families of such rules. The midpoint and trapezoidal rules are members of a family of quadrature rules that approximate $f(x)$ by an interpolating polynomial and then integrate that polynomial. That is, these rules use a polynomial

$$p(x) = c_0 + c_1 x + \cdots + c_n x^n,$$

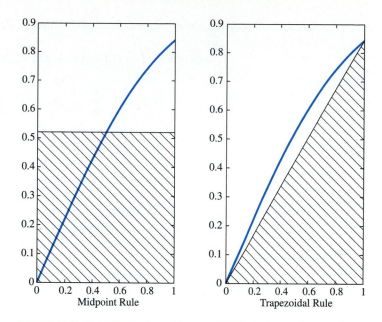

Figure 5.2 The Midpoint and Trapezoidal Rule Approximants for Example 5.1.1.

where $p(x) \approx f(x)$ over the interval of integration, and then use the rule

$$\int_a^b f(x)\,dx \approx \int_a^b p(x)\,dx$$

$$= c_0 x + \frac{c_1}{2}x^2 + \cdots + \frac{c_n}{(n+1)!}x^{n+1}\Big|_a^b$$

$$= c_0(b-a) + \frac{c_1}{2}(b-a)^2 + \cdots + \frac{c_n}{(n+1)!}(b-a)^{n+1}$$

where the constants $c_0, \ldots, c_n$ depend on the nodes $x_0, \ldots, x_n$, the limits of integration a and b, and values of f at appropriate points. Rules of this type—formed by polynomially interpolating f and then integrating that interpolant exactly—are called **interpolatory rules**,[1] and if the nodes are equally spaced then they are called **Newton-Cotes rules.**

Newton-Cotes Rules

For example, the trapezoidal rule is the Newton-Cotes rule found by using an interpolant of degree 1 with the nodes $x_0 = a$, $x_1 = b$. Recall from Section 4.1 that we may write this interpolant as

$$p(x) = f(a)L_a(x) + f(b)L_b(x),$$

where

$$L_a(x) = \frac{x-b}{a-b}$$

$$L_b(x) = \frac{x-a}{b-a}$$

---

[1] We could of course interpolate with some function other than polynomials, but this is rare.

are the appropriate Lagrange interpolating polynomials. Then

$$\int_a^b p(x)\,dx = \int_a^b (f(a)L_a(x) + f(b)L_b(x))\,dx$$

$$= f(a)\int_a^b \frac{x-b}{a-b}\,dx + f(b)\int_a^b \frac{x-a}{b-a}\,dx$$

$$= f(a)\left(\frac{b-a}{2}\right) + f(b)\left(\frac{b-a}{2}\right)$$

$$= \frac{b-a}{2}(f(a) + f(b))$$

in agreement with Eq. (5.3). Again, with respect to Eq. (5.2) we have weights $w_0 = w_1 = (b-a)/2$ and nodes $x_0 = a$, $x_1 = b$.

Let's explore the Newton-Cotes rules in more detail. Notice that there is no reason that we must have $x_0 = a$ and $x_n = b$, or even that all nodes must be contained in $[a, b]$ (although usually we do not assume that f is known outside of this interval). If it is the case that $x_0 = a$ and $x_n = b$ we say that the rule is a **closed Newton-Cotes rule** (based on $(n+1)$ points). The trapezoidal rule is closed but the midpoint rule is not; its only node in $[a, b]$ is $x_0 = (a+b)/2$. Note that the $n+1$ points of a closed Newton-Cotes rule divide $[a, b]$ into n subintervals.

We can easily derive the formula for the closed Newton-Cotes rule based on $(n+1)$ points using the methods of Section 4.1. The interpolant is

$$p(x) = f_0 L_{n,0}(x) + f_1 L_{n,1}(x) + \cdots + f_{n+1} L_{n,n}(x),$$

where $f_i = f(x_i)$, $i = 0, \ldots, n$. Hence

$$\int_a^b p(x)dx = \int_a^b (f_0 L_{n,0}(x) + f_1 L_{n,1}(x) + \cdots + f_{n+1} L_{n,n}(x))dx$$

$$= \sum_{i=0}^n f_i \left(\int_a^b L_{n,i}(x)\,dx\right)$$

$$= \sum_{i=0}^n B_{n,i} f_i,$$

where the weights

$$B_{n,i} = \int_a^b L_{n,i}(x)dx$$

$$= \int_a^b \frac{(x-x_0)(x-x_1)\cdots(x-x_{i-1})(x-x_{i+1})\cdots(x-x_n)}{(x_i-x_0)(x_i-x_1)\cdots(x_i-x_{i-1})(x_i-x_{i+1})\cdots(x_i-x_n)}\,dx$$

do not have a simple formula, despite being merely the definite integrals of polynomials. The trapezoidal rule has $B_{1,0} = B_{1,1} = (b-a)/2$, for example. We let

$$h = \frac{b-a}{n} \tag{5.4}$$

be the width of each of the n subintervals of $[a, b]$ so that the trapezoidal rule weights may be written as $B_{1,0} = B_{1,1} = h/2$.

Common Rules   There are tables of values of $\{B_{n,i}\}_{i=0}^{n+1}$ for various n. Some of the more frequently used closed Newton-Cotes rules are **Simpson's rule**

$$\int_a^b f(x)\,dx \approx \frac{h}{3}(f(x_0) + 4f(x_1) + f(x_2))$$

$(n + 1 = 3)$, **Simpson's 3/8 rule**

$$\int_a^b f(x)\,dx \approx \frac{3h}{8}(f(x_0) + 3f(x_1) + 3f(x_2) + f(x_3))$$

$(n + 1 = 4)$, and **Boole's rule** (or **Milne's rule**)

$$\int_a^b f(x)\,dx \approx \frac{2h}{45}(7f(x_0) + 32f(x_1) + 12f(x_2) + 32f(x_3) + 7f(x_4))$$

$(n + 1 = 5)$. In each case the value of h is given by Eq. (5.4). Although all the coefficients of $f(x_i)$ are positive in these formulas, for higher n they are of mixed sign. In addition, they become increasingly large.

Error Estimates   What is the approximation error involved in using one of these rules? Consider Theorem 4.1.1, which states that, if f is suitably differentiable, then the error in the interpolant is

$$f(x) - p(x) = \frac{f^{(n+1)}(\xi)}{(n+1)!}(x - x_0)(x - x_1)\cdots(x - x_n)$$

for any $x \in [a, b]$ and for some $\xi = \xi(x)$ in (a, b). Since this formula is valid for any x in the interval, we have

$$E = \int_a^b f(x)\,dx - \int_a^b p(x)\,dx$$

$$= \int_a^b \frac{f^{(n+1)}(\xi(x))}{(n+1)!}(x - x_0)(x - x_1)\cdots(x - x_n)\,dx \tag{5.5}$$

for the approximation error. This cannot be integrated exactly because ξ is an unknown function of x. Nonetheless, it can be shown that

$$E = \frac{h^{n+2} f^{(n+1)}(\gamma)}{(n+1)!} \int_0^n \varpi(x)\,dx \tag{5.6}$$

for n odd and

$$E = \frac{h^{n+3} f^{(n+2)}(\gamma)}{(n+2)!} \int_0^n x\varpi(x)\,dx \tag{5.7}$$

for n even, where

$$\varpi(x) = x(x - 1)(x - 2)\cdots(x - n) \tag{5.8}$$

and $\gamma \in (a, b)$. Note from the expressions for E that the error for $n = 2$ (that is, Simpson's rule) is $O(h^5)$, and that the error for $n = 3$ (Simpson's 3/8 rule) is the same, $O(h^5)$. In fact, all the closed Newton-Cotes rules based on an odd number of points (even number

n of subintervals) have the same order of error as the rule that follows them (based on an even number of points and odd number n of subintervals).

But there is another interesting consequence of Eq. (5.7) and Eq. (5.6). Since we are approximating $f(x)$ by a polynomial interpolant of degree n and then integrating that polynomial *exactly*, if $f(x)$ should happen to be a polynomial of degree at most n then $f(x) = p(x)$ and

$$\int_a^b f(x)\,dx = \int_a^b p(x)\,dx$$

apart from rounding error. This is reflected in Eq. (5.6), which shows that if n is even and

$$f^{(n+1)}(x) = 0$$

over $[a, b]$, then certainly $f^{(n+1)}(\gamma) = 0$ and so $E = 0$. A polynomial of degree n or less has $f^{(n+1)}(x)$ identically zero so it is integrated exactly, just as expected. But now consider the case of n even; Eq. (5.7) shows that $E = 0$ if

$$f^{(n+2)}(x) = 0$$

over $[a, b]$, so if n is even, then the rule integrates polynomials of degree at most $n + 1$ exactly! This is quite a surprise—Simpson's rule, which fits a quadratic to three points, nonetheless integrates cubics exactly (up to roundoff error).

Example 5.1.2   Let $f(x) = 2x^2 - 3x + 2$ and consider $\int_1^2 f(x)\,dx$. Simpson's rule gives

$$\int_1^2 f(x)\,dx \approx \frac{h}{3}(f(x_0) + 4f(x_1) + f(x_2))$$

$$= \frac{1/2}{3}(f(1) + 4f(1.5) + f(2))$$

$$= \frac{1}{6}(1 + 4 \cdot 2 + 4)$$

$$= \frac{13}{6},$$

which you can easily verify as the correct answer. Let $g(x) = 3x^3 - 4x^2 + 2x + 1$ and consider $\int_1^2 g(x)\,dx$. Then Simpson's rule gives

$$\int_1^2 g(x)\,dx \approx \frac{h}{3}(g(x_0) + 4g(x_1) + g(x_2))$$

$$= \frac{1/2}{3}(g(1) + 4g(1.5) + g(2))$$

$$= \frac{1}{6}\left(2 + 4 \cdot \frac{41}{8} + 13\right)$$

$$= \frac{71}{12},$$

which again you can easily verify as the correct answer.   ■

We say that a numerical quadrature rule has **precision** or **degree of accuracy** n if it integrates x^i exactly for $i = 0, \ldots, n$ but does not integrate x^{n+1} exactly. If a rule has precision n then it integrates all polynomials of degree at most n exactly (up to roundoff error). If n is odd, the closed Newton-Cotes rule based on $n + 1$ points has precision n and is of order $O(h^{n+2})$. But $n - 1$ is even in this case, and so the rule based on n points has the same precision n and the same order $O(h^{n+2})$ as the rule based on $n + 1$ points but uses one point less, and has smaller coefficients (which will amplify errors less). Hence rules based on n even are usually preferred in applications, especially if f is costly to evaluate. In fact, in the next section we show that

$$E = -\frac{h^5}{90} f^{(4)}(\gamma_1) \tag{5.9}$$

for Simpson's rule, and it can also be shown that

$$E = -\frac{3h^5}{80} f^{(4)}(\gamma_2)$$

for Simpson's 3/8 rule. So, even the asymptotic error constant 1/90 of Simpson's rule is smaller than the asymptotic error constant 3/80 of Simpson's 3/8 rule.

What do we do if we need to integrate a function over a large interval of integration? On the one hand, we cannot expect Simpson's rule, based on three points, to do well over an interval like $[0, 10]$; the behavior of Eq. (5.9) won't become apparent until $h = (b - a)/2$ is less than 1. On the other hand, we know that interpolating by a high-degree polynomial is generally a bad idea; the high oscillations would introduce a great deal of error (see Fig. 5.3). In fact, closed Newton-Cotes rules need not converge as $n \to \infty$ even if the integrand is analytic on $[a, b]$.

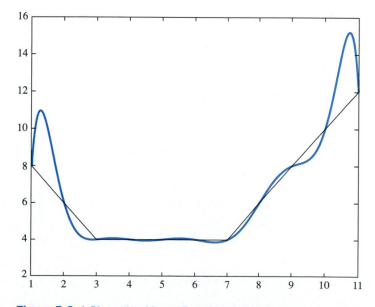

Figure 5.3 A Piecewise Linear Function and Its Degree 10 Polynomial Interpolant.

Composite
Rules

For a large interval of integration, then, we should use the fact that we may break down any integral into a sum of integrals over smaller regions using the relation

$$\int_a^b f(x)\,dx = \int_a^c f(x)\,dx + \int_c^b f(x)\,dx$$

and apply the rule to each of the integrals over the smaller intervals. This is called the **composite** (or **compound**) form of the rule; until now, we have used the **simple** form. As before, we divide the interval $[a, b]$ into nodes $x_0 = a, x_1, \ldots, x_N = b$, but now we apply a simple rule over every several points. For example, if we take $h = (b - a)/N$ then the composite trapezoidal rule is

$$\int_a^b f(x)\,dx \approx \frac{x_1 - x_0}{2}(f(x_0) + f(x_1)) + \frac{x_2 - x_1}{2}(f(x_1) + f(x_2)) + \cdots$$

$$+ \frac{x_N - x_{N-1}}{2}(f(x_{N-1}) + f(x_N))$$

$$= \frac{h}{2}(f(x_0) + f(x_1)) + \frac{h}{2}(f(x_1) + f(x_2)) + \cdots + \frac{h}{2}(f(x_{N-1}) + f(x_N))$$

$$= \frac{h}{2}(f(x_0) + f(x_1) + f(x_1) + f(x_2) + \cdots + f(x_{N-1}) + f(x_N))$$

$$= \frac{h}{2}(f(x_0) + 2f(x_1) + 2f(x_2) + \cdots + 2f(x_{N-1}) + f(x_N))$$

$$= \frac{h}{2}\left(f(a) + 2\sum_{i=1}^{N-1} f(x_i) + f(b)\right),$$

and the composite Simpson's rule is

$$\int_a^b f(x)\,dx \approx \frac{(x_2 - x_0)/2}{3}(f(x_0) + 4f(x_1) + f(x_2)) + \cdots$$

$$+ \frac{(x_N - x_{N-2})/2}{3}(f(x_{N-2}) + 4f(x_{N-1}) + f(x_N))$$

$$= \frac{h}{3}(f(x_0) + 4f(x_1) + f(x_2)) + \frac{h}{3}(f(x_2) + 4f(x_3) + f(x_4)) + \cdots$$

$$+ \frac{h}{3}(f(x_{N-2}) + 4f(x_{N-1}) + f(x_N))$$

$$= \frac{h}{3}(f(x_0) + 4f(x_1) + f(x_2)) + f(x_2) + 4f(x_3) + f(x_4) + \cdots$$

$$+ f(x_{N-2}) + 4f(x_{N-1}) + f(x_N))$$

$$= \frac{h}{3}(f(x_0) + 4f(x_1) + 2f(x_2) + 4f(x_3) + 2f(x_4) + \cdots$$

$$+ 2f(x_{N-2}) + 4f(x_{N-1}) + f(x_N))$$

$$= \frac{h}{3}\left(f(a) + 4\sum_{\substack{i=1 \\ i\ odd}}^{N-1} f(x_i) + 2\sum_{\substack{i=1 \\ i\ even}}^{N-1} f(x_i) + f(b)\right)$$

$$= \frac{h}{3}\left(f(a) + 4\sum_{k=1}^{N/2} f(x_{2k-1}) + 2\sum_{k=1}^{N/2-1} f(x_{2k}) + f(b)\right)$$

if N is even. Note how both of these rules give less weight to the values of f at the endpoints a, b than to the interior points, and that the composite Simpson's rule gives them even less weight than the composite trapezoidal rule does. The endpoint information is less reliable—we do not know what the function does to the left of x_0, although we know what it does to the left and right of x_1 because we have data there (see also Fig. 5.3 and note that the fit is worse near the endpoints)—so we weight these points less.

Error for Composite Rules

Clearly we will almost always use composite rules, not simple rules, in practice. What is the error associated with a composite rule? Let's look at Simpson's rule. The error of the simple rule is

$$E = -\frac{h^5}{90}f^{(4)}(\gamma)$$

(from Eq. (5.9)). In the case of the composite rule we have $h = (b-a)/N$, so

$$E_i = -\frac{(b-a)^5}{N^5 90}f^{(4)}(\gamma_i)$$

on the ith subinterval. But when we use the composite rule we add up N terms

$$E_1 + \cdots + E_n = -\frac{(b-a)^5}{N^5 90}f^{(4)}(\gamma_1) + \cdots + -\frac{(b-a)^5}{N^5 90}f^{(4)}(\gamma_N)$$

or, if $f^{(4)}(x)$ is roughly constant on $[a, b]$, say, $f^{(4)}(x) \approx K$,

$$E_1 + \cdots + E_n \approx -\frac{(b-a)^5}{N^5 90}K + \cdots + -\frac{(b-a)^5}{N^5 90}K$$

$$= -N\frac{(b-a)^5}{N^5 90}K$$

$$= -\frac{(b-a)^5}{N^4 90}K$$

$$= -\frac{(b-a)h^4}{90}K,$$

so that we expect the order of the method to be reduced to $O(h^4)$. Indeed, this is what happens, and it can be shown that

$$E = -\frac{(b-a)h^2}{12}f''(\gamma) \tag{5.10}$$

for the composite trapezoidal rule (compare Eq. (5.7) for $n = 1$), and

$$E = -\frac{(b-a)h^4}{180}f^{(4)}(\gamma) \tag{5.11}$$

for the composite Simpson's rule. Note that the degree of accuracy is not affected; only the order of convergence is affected (as $h \to 0$). The formulas in Eq. (5.10) and Eq. (5.11), not the error formulas for the simple versions of the rules, are the ones that will be used to estimate errors in any practical case.

Example 5.1.3 How large must N be if we want to use the composite trapezoidal rule to approximate the integral of $f(x) = \ln(x)$ over $1 \le x \le 2$ with an error of no more than $.5 \cdot 10^{-6}$? Using Eq. (5.10), we have

$$|E| \le .5 \cdot 10^{-6}$$

$$\frac{(b-a)h^2}{12}M \le .5 \cdot 10^{-6},$$

where M is a bound on $|f''(x)|$ over $[1, 2]$. Since $f''(x) = -x^{-2}$ we can take $M = 1$, so we have

$$\frac{(2-1)h^2}{12} \cdot 1 \le .5 \cdot 10^{-6}$$

$$h^2 \le 6 \cdot 10^{-6}$$

$$h \le .0025$$

(rounded up from $h \le .002449\ldots$). We need h to be $.0025$ or smaller, that is, $N \ge 1/h = 400$ panels ($N + 1 = 401$ points). Fortunately function evaluations are not very expensive for this function. For the composite Simpson's rule we have (with $M = 6$ now a bound on $|f^{(4)}(x)|$)

$$\frac{(b-a)h^4}{180}M \le .5 \cdot 10^{-6}$$

$$h^4 \le 90 \cdot \frac{10^{-6}}{6}$$

$$h \le .0039$$

(rounded up again), or $N \ge 1/h \doteq 258.1989$ giving $N = 259$. Since we must evaluate f at $N + 1$ points using either method, this is much more efficient if the cost of function evaluations is our biggest concern. ∎

We can apply these methods to any continuous function but the error estimates will not apply unless we have sufficient differentiability. We should expect worse performance of the methods for functions that have fewer continuous derivatives.

Total Error   We have been talking about the approximation error E of closed Newton-Cotes quadrature rules, defined in Eq. (5.5) as

$$E = \int_a^b f(x)\,dx - \int_a^b p(x)\,dx,$$

which is also called the **truncation error** because it arises from truncating a term from the exact formula

$$\int_a^b f(x)\,dx = \int_a^b p(x)\,dx + \int_a^b \frac{f^{(n+1)}(\xi(x))}{(n+1)!}(x-x_0)(x-x_1)\cdots(x-x_n)\,dx$$

for $\int_a^b f(x)\,dx$. We also need to consider the effects of roundoff error, that is, the issue of stability. We define the **total error** to be the sum

$$E_{Total} = E_{Tr} + E_R$$

of the error that results from truncation—the quality of our method from an analytical perspective—and the error that results from the effects of using finite precision arithmetic. Note that the act of truncation implies that there will be some error in our computations, so we must make sure that the error doesn't grow too large.

From Section 1.7 we know how to bound the error in a single arithmetic computation. However, f may be supplied by another program or may be given as data (with no functional relationship provided). This is a common type of numerical integration problem: Measured data is provided as a list of x- and y-values, and so exact integration is not an option. The data may be the result of a laboratory experiment, for example. Whether the values of $f(x_i)$ are found by computation or measurement, we assume that the x_i are known exactly and that the error in the values of $f(x_i)$ is bounded,

$$|f(x_i) - f_i| \le \varepsilon,$$

where f_i is the computed or measured value of $f(x_i)$ and $\varepsilon > 0$ is a constant. Consider a weighted average rule as in Eq. (5.2),

$$\int_a^b f(x)\,dx = w_0 f(x_0) + w_1 f(x_1) + \cdots + w_n f(x_n) + E_{Tr},$$

where E_{Tr} represents the truncation error. The rule itself is

$$A_f = w_0 f(x_0) + w_1 f(x_1) + \cdots + w_n f(x_n),$$

but we will be computing

$$\tilde{A}_f = w_0 f_0 + w_1 f_1 + \cdots + w_n f_n \tag{5.12}$$

instead. (The multiplications $w_i f_i$ introduce a small error, but because they are typically small with respect to the errors in f, we neglect them for now.) We have

$$
\begin{aligned}
E_R &= |A_f - \widetilde{A}_f| \\
&= |w_0 f(x_0) + w_1 f(x_1) + \cdots + w_n f(x_n) - (w_0 f_0 + w_1 f_1 + \cdots + w_n f_n)| \\
&= |w_0(f(x_0) - f_0) + w_1(f(x_1) - f_1) + \cdots + w_n(f(x_n) - f_n)| \\
&\leq |w_0|\varepsilon + |w_1|\varepsilon + \cdots + |w_n|\varepsilon \\
&= (|w_0| + |w_1| + \cdots + |w_n|)\varepsilon \\
&= \Omega_n \varepsilon
\end{aligned}
$$

(where $\Omega_n = |w_0| + |w_1| + \cdots + |w_n|$), which depends on the coefficients of the simple rule. What if we use a composite rule over N panels? Notice that in each of the methods we have seen so far, Ω_n is proportional to h, where

$$ h = \frac{b - a}{N}. $$

So the error over N panels will be bounded by $\Omega_n \varepsilon \cdot N$ if $|f(x_i) - f_i| \leq \varepsilon$ over all of $[a, b]$. But $\Omega_n = \alpha h$ for some constant of proportionality α, so in the composite case

$$
\begin{aligned}
E_R &\leq \Omega_n N \varepsilon \\
&= \alpha h N \varepsilon \\
&= \alpha(b - a)\varepsilon
\end{aligned}
$$

since $hN = b - a$. But this bound on E_R is independent of the number of panels N! Compound rules of this sort are certainly stable with respect to reducing h because h has no effect on this bound.

However, an additional complication occurs if the weights w_i can be negative. For $n = 9$ and $n \geq 11$ the closed Newton-Cotes rules have weights of mixed sign. In this case the computation of

$$ \widetilde{A}_f = w_0 f_0 + w_1 f_1 + \cdots + w_n f_n $$

will likely involve the subtraction of nearly equal quantities, since $f_{i+1} \approx f_i$ by continuity. Then we must modify Eq. (5.12) to include the effects of errors in the addition of the various terms. Cancellation of significant figures will be a serious problem. Furthermore, in the closed Newton-Cotes rules the size of

$$ \Omega_n = |w_0| + |w_1| + \cdots + |w_n| $$

grows without bound as the order n of the method increases, so the error

$$ E_R = \Omega_n \varepsilon $$

can be large even if ε is small. In fact, Ω_n serves as a condition number for the problem.

Stability   What we see from all this is that the closed Newton-Cotes formula cannot be stable for large n. However, weighted-average rules like Eq. (5.2) *do* have desirable roundoff error properties if the weights w_i are nonnegative. The composite versions of closed Newton-Cotes rules for $n \leq 8$ may be safely applied. We expect more accuracy at a slightly higher computational cost for the higher-degree rules.

Note also that Simpson's rule requires an even number of panels (odd number of data points), Simpson's 3/8 rule requires that the number of panels be divisible by 3 (the number of data points must be $3n + 1$), and so on. We will discuss ways to circumvent these limitations.

PROBLEMS 5.1

1. Estimate erf(1) using the simple Simpson's, Simpson's 3/8, and Boole's rules. Construct a simple graph plotting the error vs. the number of points $n + 1$ used (include the midpoint and trapezoidal rule errors from Example 5.1.1).

2. **a.** Estimate the number of subintervals needed to approximate $\int_0^1 \sin(x)dx$ to within 10^{-3} using the trapezoidal rule, and then apply the trapezoidal rule with that number of subdivisions. What is the actual error in your method?

   b. Repeat with Simpson's rule and with Boole's rule.

3. Compare the errors in using Simpson's rule and Simpson's 3/8 rule to approximate $\int_0^1 \cos(x)dx$,

$\int_1^{10} \ln(x)dx$, and $\int_{-1}^1 (x^7 - 2x^3 + 1)dx$ with $N = 6, 12, 18$ panels.

4. The error formula for the trapezoidal rule assumes that f is at least twice continuously differentiable. Use the trapezoidal rule to approximate $\int_{-1}^1 |x^3|dx$ and $\int_{-1}^1 g(x)dx$, where $g(x) = 0$ if $x < 0$ and $g(x) = x^2$ if $x \geq 0$. Use $N = 5, 9, 15$. Comment.

5. Write a MATLAB program that accepts a function, an interval, a number of subintervals, and a choice of method (trapezoidal rule, Simpson's rule, Simpson's 3/8 rule, or Boole's rule) and returns the appropriate approximate integral of the function over the interval.

MATLAB 5.1

The MATLAB commands for numerical integration are quad (as in quadrature), which uses Simpson's rule in an adaptive manner, choosing the number of panels to fit the local difficulty in estimating the integral, and quadl, which uses a different interpolatory quadrature method based on unequally spaced nodes. The quad command is recommended for relatively low accuracies or relatively difficult integrals, and the quadl command is recommended for relatively high accuracies or relatively easy integrals (that is, relatively well-behaved integrands). If you are using a previous version of MATLAB, you should have quad8 rather than quadl; quad8 uses the 9-point closed Newton-Cotes rule. The command quad8 is still available in current version of MATLAB. Enter:

```
» more on
» type quad8
```

and look for the line defining the weights w, which are indeed of mixed sign. We'll emphasize the current commands quad and quadl. Enter:

```
» more off
» f=inline('1./x')
```

(these commands expect functions that accept vector arguments). Enter:

```
» format long
» q=quad(f,1,10)
» ql=quadl(f,1,10)
» q8=quad8(f,1,10)
» a=log(10)            %Answer.
» norm(q-a),norm(ql-a),norm(q8-a)
```

The result from quad8 has error on the order of 10^{-6}; quad gives a result that has error on the order of 10^{-8}, and for quadl the error is on the order of 10^{-9}. Note that each program meets or exceeds its default error tolerance ($1E - 3$ for quad8 and $1E - 6$ for quad and quadl), so each routine has succeeded. Let's try another function. Enter:

```
» g=inline('abs(x-1)+abs(x+1)+sin(x)')
» q=quad(g,1,10)
» ql=quadl(g,1,10)
» q8=quad8(g,1,10)
```

If you have the Symbolic Toolbox, enter:

```
» syms x
» G=int(abs(x-1)+abs(x+1)+sin(x),x)
```

to find the symbolic antiderivative of $g(x)$, which MATLAB (via Maple) gives as $.5(|x - 1|(x - 1) + |x + 1|(x + 1)) - \cos(x)$ (after slight rearrangement). This allows us to find the analytical value of the integral very accurately; enter:

```
» x=1;y1=.5*(abs(x-1)*(x-1)+abs(x+1)*(x+1))-cos(x);
» x=-2;y2=.5*(abs(x-1)*(x-1)+abs(x+1)*(x+1))-cos(x);
» a=y1-y2;
» norm(q-a),norm(ql-a),norm(q8-a)
```

Now quad is the most accurate and quadl is the least accurate, in agreement with the advice that quad is preferable to quadl for nonsmooth integrands such as this one. Again, any time one of these programs meets the requested error tolerance, which can be entered as an optional argument, it must be deemed to have been successful.

Error estimates as given in the text are bounds on the worst case, and typically the methods do much better than indicated. For example, in Example 5.1.3 we estimated that using the composite trapezoidal rule to approximate the integral of $f(x) = \ln(x)$ over $1 \leq x \leq 2$ with an error of no more than $.5 \times 10^{-6}$ would require $N = 400$ panels. Let's see. If you have the Symbolic Toolbox, enter:

```
» syms z
» int(log(z),z)
```

to see that the antiderivative is $x \ln(x) - x$, so the correct value of the integral is $2 \ln(2) - 1$. Enter:

```
» A=2*log(2)-1
» quad8(@log,1,2)                        %Check.
```

(for mnemonic reasons you may find it convenient to make your own M-file `ln.m` that simply evaluates `log(x)`). Enter:

```
» a=1;b=2;f=inline('log(x)');
» T=.5*(b-a)*(f(a)+f(b))                    %Simple rule.
» x1=1.5;
» T=.5*(x1-a)*(f(a)+f(x1))+.5*(b-x1)*(f(x1)+f(b)) %Two panels.
» N=3;h=(b-a)/N;
» S=2*sum(f((a+h):h:(b-h)));S=h*(f(a)+f(b)+S)/2 %Comp. Trap. Rule.
```

Let's try $N = 400$ as in Example 5.1.3. Enter:

```
» N=400;h=(b-a)/N;
» S=2*sum(f((a+h):h:(b-h)));S=h*(f(a)+f(b)+S)/2
» norm(A-S)
```

The actual error is about $2.6E - 7$, about half the guarantee provided by the error bound. Since the error bound reflects the worst case over *all* sufficiently differentiable functions, any given function is likely to have an error that is rather smaller. Enter:

```
» h^2                    %Error is O(h^2).
```

The error is roughly $O(h^2)$, as predicted. In fact, the error being roughly $O(h^2)$ means that, for large N, $E \approx ch^2$ for some c (treating $f''(x)$ as roughly constant). To estimate c, enter:

```
» c1=norm(A-S)/h^2
» N=800;h=(b-a)/N;
» S=2*sum(f((a+h):h:(b-h)));S=h*(f(a)+f(b)+S)/2
» norm(A-S)
» c2=norm(A-S)/h^2
```

These two estimates agree to the number of digits displayed. That means that we can estimate the error for $N = 1600$. Enter:

```
» N=1600;h=(b-a)/N;
» c2*h^2                      %Estimate.
» S=2*sum(f((a+h):h:(b-h)));S=h*(f(a)+f(b)+S)/2
» norm(A-S)
```

This is excellent agreement with our prediction! Using this idea we could make an estimate, tailored to this function (rather than using the general-purpose Eq. (5.10)), of how many more subintervals would be needed to achieved a desired error tolerance. Indeed, this is how adaptive methods such as `quad` attempt to locally estimate the error and choose more subintervals if they are needed. (There are other ways of doing so.) Enter:

```
» c3=norm(A-S)/h^2
```

to see that the estimate of the asymptotic error constant $-(b-a)f''(\gamma)/12$ of Eq. (5.10) is unchanged.

What do we do if we want to use Simpson's rule but the number of panels is odd? There are several possible approaches we might take. If you have the Symbolic Toolbox, enter:

```
» syms x
» int(x.^8-3*x.^5+4*x.^2+2+sin(x),x)
```

The antiderivative is $F(x) = x^9/9 - x^6/2 + 4x^3/3 + 2x - \cos(x)$, so the integral of the function from 1 to 2 is $F(2) - F(1)$. Enter:

```
» clear all
» x=1;y1=1/9*x^9-1/2*x^6+4/3*x^3+2*x-cos(x);
» x=2;y2=1/9*x^9-1/2*x^6+4/3*x^3+2*x-cos(x);
» A=y2-y1
» f=inline('x.^8-3*x.^5+4*x.^2+2+sin(x)')
» N=9;h=1/N;              %N=9 panels.
» xval=1:h:2              %Nodes.
» fval=f(xval)            %Function evaluated at nodes.
» Simp=dot([1 4 2 4 2 4 2 4 1],fval(1:9))*h/3
```

This gives the Simpson's rule estimate over the first 8 panels. Let's check its error; enter:

```
» x=xval(end-1);y2=1/9*x^9-1/2*x^6+4/3*x^3+2*x-cos(x);A2=y2-y1
» norm(A2-Simp)
```

The absolute error in estimating the integral up to $x = 1.8$ is about .006. We might imagine using the trapezoidal rule over the last panel; enter:

```
» Trap=h*(fval(end-1)+fval(end))/2
» Aest=Simp+Trap                    %Estimated area.
» norm(A-Aest)
```

The absolute error is about .3! We had an estimate that was good to about .006 over [1, 1.8] and ended up with one that was only good to about .3 over [1, 2] because we contaminated our earlier $O(h^4)$ results with an $O(h^2)$ estimate. As you might guess, this is definitely a bad idea. Instead, let's try an approach that maintains the same order of the error. Enter:

```
» Simp2=dot([1 4 2 4 2 4 1],fval(1:7))*h/3
```

This is the Simpson's rule estimate over the first 6 of the 9 panels. Now let's use the (simple) Simpson's 3/8 rule, which is $O(h^4)$, over the last 3 panels. Enter:

```
» Simps38=dot([1 3 3 1],fval((end-3):end))*3*h/8
» Aest2=Simp2+Simps38
» norm(A-Aest2)
```

While this isn't as small as we'd like, it's an order of magnitude better than before. The step size h isn't small enough yet for the $O(h^4)$ behavior of the error to fully kick in. To see why the trapezoidal rule had difficulty getting an accurate estimate at this step size, enter:

```
» z=1:.01:2;plot(z,f(z),'r'),grid
» line([2-h 2],[f(2-h) f(2)])
```

(note the vertical scale), then enter:

```
» line([1 1+h],[f(1) f(1+h)])
```

to see that the fitted line would have been a better approximant near $x = 1$. Of course, because we have stored the f values in fval we could get a better estimate by taking additional nodes at the midpoints of each panel and then using those points together with those in fval to get an estimate at resolution $h/2$. This would save us recomputing f at the original nodes, which is important if computing f is expensive. If f is measured data, there may be a literal expense involved in repeating the experiment or requesting that additional field measurements be taken.

In addition to the adaptive recursive Simpson's rule in quad (see also quaddemo), MATLAB provides the trapezoidal rule via the command trapz and the cumulative trapezoidal rule (simulating indefinite integration) in cumtrapz. Enter:

```
» x=0:.1:1;
» f=inline('2*x-3')      %Integral from 0 to 1 is -2.
» trapz(x,f(x))          %Quadrature from 0 to 1.
» cumtrapz(x,f(x))       %Cumulative quadrature from 0 to 1.
» plot(x,ans)            %Numerical antiderivative of f.
```

The trapezoidal rule is provided because of its use in the numerical solution of ODEs and its high accuracy for certain special quadrature problems. If you have the Symbolic Toolbox, enter mhelp int [numerical] or mhelp simpson for details.

ADDITIONAL PROBLEMS 5.1

6. a. Create a 4-digit table of values of $\text{erf}(x)$ for $x = 0, .1, .2, \ldots, 3$ using Simpson's rule. Your table entries should be accurately rounded to the 4-digits listed. Determine the appropriate number of panels to use from Eq. (5.11).

b. How many panels would you have needed to create the table using the trapezoidal rule?

7. a. Use the trapezoidal, Simpson's, and Simpson's 3/8 rules to approximate $\int_0^{20} x^5 \ln(x + 1)dx$ to within 10^{-6}. Comment on the relative efficiency of the methods.

b. Use the trapezoidal, Simpson's, and Simpson's 3/8 rules to approximate $\int_0^{20} (|x - 2| + |x - 5| + |x - 18|) \ln(x + 1)dx$ to within 10^{-6}. Comment on the relative efficiency of the methods.

c. Use the trapezoidal, Simpson's, and Simpson's 3/8 rules to approximate $\int_0^{20} x \ln(\sin(x) + 1.01)dx$ to within 10^{-6}. Comment on the relative efficiency of the methods.

d. What are Ω_n and α for the trapezoidal, Simpson's, and Simpson's 3/8 rules?

8. a. What is the degree of accuracy of the rule $\int_{-1}^{1} f(x)dx = f(-1/\sqrt{3}) + f(1/\sqrt{3})$?

b. Experiment with this rule, and compare it to the trapezoidal rule, which is also based on two points. Which seems to perform better?

c. How could you use this rule to approximate $\int_a^b \phi(x)dx$?

9. a. Derive Simpson's rule and Simpson's 3/8 rule

by performing the appropriate integrations $B_{n,i} = \int_a^b L_{n,i}(x)dx$ analytically.

b. What are the closed Newton-Cotes rules based on 6 and 7 points? (The rule based on 7 points is called **Weddle's rule**.) You may integrate numerically to find the coefficients, but will need to transform $\int_a^b L_{n,i}(x)dx$ to, say, $\int_0^1 L_{n,i}(z)dz$ first, and then transform back to find the $B_{n,i}$ in terms of a and b.

10. a. Cubic splines interpolate a function with a piecewise cubic function. Does interpolating a function with a cubic spline and then integrating the interpolant give the same result as the Simpson's 3/8 rule, which also corresponds to cubic interpolation?

b. Perform an experiment to compare the results of interpolating free, clamped, and not-a-knot cubic splines and integrating the splines exactly. Which seems to work best? How do they compare with Simpson's rule and Simpson's 3/8 rule?

11. a. Approximate $\pi = 4 \arctan(1)$ using the fact that $\arctan(x) = \int_0^x (1 + z^2)^{-1}dz$ $(x \geq 0)$. Use `quad` and `quadl`.

b. Find the positive solution of $\text{erf}(x) = x$ using Newton's method. Evaluate $\text{erf}(x)$ using Simpson's rule applied to $\text{erf}(x) = \frac{2}{\sqrt{\pi}} \int_0^x e^{-z^2}dz$.

12. a. Use the trapezoidal rule to estimate $\int_0^1 \sqrt{x} \sin(x)dx$.

What does the error estimate suggest for this integrand?

b. Make the change of variables $x = z^2$ to get $\int_0^1 2z^2 \sin(z^2)dz$. Use the trapezoidal rule to estimate the value of this integral. What does the error estimate suggest for this integrand?

13. a. The function $\varpi(x)$ in Eq. (5.8) appears because of the following formula for the Lagrange interpolating polynomials with respect to the nodes $x_0, \ldots, x_n$: If $\varpi(x) = \prod_{i=0}^n (x - x_0)$, then $L_{n,i}(x) = \varpi(x)/[\varpi'(x)(x - x_i)]$. Prove this.

b. Prove that the interpolatory rule is the unique rule of the form of Eq. (5.2) with $x_0 < x_1 < \cdots < x_n$ which has the property that it integrates the monomials $f(x) = 1, x, x^2, \ldots, x^n$ exactly.

14. Use Simpson's rule to approximate $\iint_R \sin(x^3 + y^2)dA$, where R is the unit square $0 \leq x \leq 1$, $0 \leq y \leq 1$, by treating it as an iterated integral $\int_{y=0}^{y=1}(\int_{x=0}^{x=1} \sin(x^3 + y^2)\,dx)\,dy$. For fixed values of y, find $\int_{x=0}^{x=1} \sin(x^3 + y^2)\,dx$ numerically to get a series of values of $F(y) = \int_{x=0}^{x=1} \sin(x^3 + y^2)dx$. Then find $\int_{y=0}^{y=1} F(y)dy$.

15. Construct an experiment to verify that the trapezoidal rule has $O(h^2)$ error and Simpson's rule has $O(h^4)$ error. Produce appropriate plots.

5.2 Open Newton-Cotes Formulas and Undetermined Coefficients

Open Rules

In the previous section, we discussed the closed Newton-Cotes formulas. In this section, we discuss the other type of Newton-Cotes formulas, the **open Newton-Cotes rules** (based on $n + 1$ points). These approximate the value of $\int_a^b f(x)dx$ by interpolating a polynomial of degree n to the points

$$x_0 = a + h, x_1 = a + 2h, \ldots, x_n = a + (n + 1)h$$

(note that $x_n = b - h$) and then integrating that polynomial over $[a, b]$. (See Fig. 5.4.) The methods use only interior points, not the endpoints, with spacing

$$h = \frac{b - a}{n + 2}$$

(note that this h is slightly smaller than the corresponding h for a closed Newton-Cotes rule based on $n + 1$ points, which was $(b - a)/n$). Examples include the midpoint rule

$$\int_a^b f(x)\,dx \approx 2hf(x_0)$$

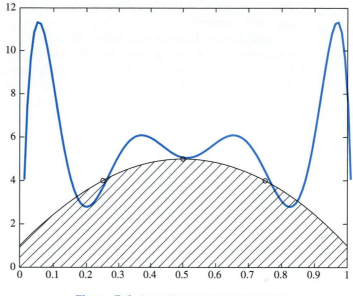

Figure 5.4 Open Newton-Cotes Formula.

where $(x_0 = (a + b)/2)$, which corresponds to $n = 0$ and has error

$$E = \frac{h^3}{3} f''(\gamma)$$

$(\gamma \in (a, b))$, the $n = 1$ case

$$\int_a^b f(x)\, dx \approx \frac{3h}{2} \left(f(x_0) + f(x_1) \right)$$

with error

$$E = \frac{3h^3}{4} f''(\gamma),$$

and the $n = 2$ case

$$\int_a^b f(x)\, dx \approx \frac{4h}{3} \left(2f(x_0) - f(x_1) + 2f(x_2) \right)$$

with error

$$E = \frac{14h^5}{45} f^{(4)}(\gamma).$$

The corresponding composite rules are $O(h^2)$, $O(h^2)$, and $O(h^4)$, respectively. The weights w_i are given once again by

$$w_i = \int_a^b L_{n,i}(x)\, dx \tag{5.13}$$

$(i = 0, 1, \ldots, n)$, though note that the nodes themselves are different (and $L_{n,i}(x)$ depends on the locations of the nodes). Therefore, these weights will not be the same as the closed Newton-Cotes weights. The weights w_i in a Newton-Cotes rule are also called the **Cotes numbers.**

Open Newton-Cotes formulas share the properties of the closed formulas; those for which n is even are more accurate than might be expected, for example. There are special situations where methods that do not use the endpoints are needed but generally speaking the open formulas are used much less often than the closed formulas.

Finding
Coefficients
In the previous section we gave a formula for the coefficients in the closed Newton-Cotes rule based on $n + 1$ points. This formula, which is the same as that for the open rules (Eq. (5.13)), involves the integrals of the Lagrange interpolating polynomials. Now let's look at a different approach for finding coefficients that applies to both the open and closed rules. One characterization of the Newton-Cotes rules is that they are the unique rules based on $n + 1$ equally spaced points in $[a, b]$ for which

$$\int_a^b x^i \, dx$$

is found exactly for $i = 0, 1, \ldots, n$. Let's use this fact to find the coefficients in Simpson's rule. Simpson's rule is a weighted-average rule

$$\int_a^b f(x) \, dx \approx w_0 f(x_0) + w_1 f(x_1) + w_2 f(x_2)$$

based on the three points

$$x_0 = a, x_1 = \frac{a+b}{2}, \quad x_2 = b,$$

which must be exact for each of the monomials $1, x, x^2$. So we must have that

$$w_0 \cdot 1 + w_1 \cdot 1 + w_2 \cdot 1 = \int_a^b 1 \, dx$$
$$= b - a$$
$$w_0 \cdot a + w_1 \cdot \frac{a+b}{2} + w_2 \cdot b = \int_a^b x \, dx$$
$$= \frac{1}{2}(b^2 - a^2)$$
$$w_0 \cdot a^2 + w_1 \cdot \left(\frac{a+b}{2}\right)^2 + w_2 \cdot b^2 = \int_a^b x^2 \, dx$$
$$= \frac{1}{3}(b^3 - a^3),$$

which, for fixed a and b, is a linear system in the unknown weights w_0, w_1, w_2. In particular,

$$\begin{pmatrix} 1 & 1 & 1 \\ a & \frac{a+b}{2} & b \\ a^2 & \left(\frac{a+b}{2}\right)^2 & b^2 \end{pmatrix} \begin{pmatrix} w_0 \\ w_1 \\ w_2 \end{pmatrix} = \begin{pmatrix} b - a \\ \frac{1}{2}(b^2 - a^2) \\ \frac{1}{3}(b^3 - a^3) \end{pmatrix},$$

which is a Vandermonde system[2] (see Section 4.1), and so it is nonsingular if $a \neq b$. For fixed a and b it is easy to solve this system; for general a and b we assert that the solution is

$$w_0 = \frac{b-a}{6}, \quad w_1 = \frac{2(b-a)}{3}, \quad w_2 = \frac{b-a}{6} \tag{5.14}$$

in agreement with Simpson's rule. Of course, although we require that this rule be exact for 1, x, and x^2, we know that it is also exact for x^3.

Undetermined Coefficients

This technique is known as the **method of undetermined coefficients.** Let's apply it to a specific problem. Suppose we are using Simpson's rule to approximate the integral of some function $f(x)$ for which we have only measured values $y_i = f(x_i)$ at equally spaced points $x_0, \ldots, x_n$. If n is even we can approximate

$$\int_{x_0}^{x_{n-1}} f(x) \, dx$$

using Simpson's rule, but to find

$$\int_{x_0}^{x_n} f(x) \, dx$$

we will need to approximate

$$\int_{x_{n-1}}^{x_n} f(x) \, dx$$

as well. We know that using the trapezoidal rule is a bad idea as it will contaminate our approximation of $\int_{x_0}^{x_{n-1}} f(x)dx$ with its $O(h^2)$ error. We'd like a $O(h^4)$ rule for the single panel $[x_{n-1}, x_n]$ and in fact one can be found in the following form:

$$\int_{x_{n-1}}^{x_n} f(x) \, dx \approx w_{n-2} f(x_{n-2}) + w_{n-1} f(x_{n-1}) + w_n f(x_n).$$

A rule like this, intended to take care of the extra panel problem of Simpson's rule, is called a **semi-simp rule** (or **half-simp rule**). It uses the value of f to the immediate left of the point x_{n-1} to help build a model for f and thereby get a better approximation over the interval $[x_{n-1}, x_n]$. Let's ask that it be exact for 1, x, and x^2 again. We have

$$w_0 \cdot 1 + w_1 \cdot 1 + w_2 \cdot 1 = \int_{x_{n-1}}^{x_n} 1 \, dx$$

$$= x_n - x_{n-1}$$

$$w_0 \cdot x_{n-2} + w_1 \cdot x_{n-1} + w_2 \cdot x_n = \int_{x_{n-1}}^{x_n} x \, dx$$

$$= \frac{1}{2} \left(x_n^2 - x_{n-1}^2 \right)$$

---

[2] Strictly speaking this is the transpose of a Vandermonde matrix as we have defined it. Other texts define a matrix such as this one to be a Vandermonde matrix.

$$w_0 \cdot x_{n-2}^2 + w_1 \cdot x_{n-1}^2 + w_2 \cdot x_n^2 = \int_{x_{n-1}}^{x_n} x^2 \, dx$$

$$= \frac{1}{3} \left(x_n^3 - x_{n-1}^3 \right),$$

which gives the Vandermonde system

$$\begin{pmatrix} 1 & 1 & 1 \\ x_{n-2} & x_{n-1} & x_n \\ x_{n-2}^2 & x_{n-1}^2 & x_n^2 \end{pmatrix} \begin{pmatrix} w_0 \\ w_1 \\ w_2 \end{pmatrix} = \begin{pmatrix} x_n - x_{n-1} \\ \frac{1}{2} \left(x_n^2 - x_{n-1}^2 \right) \\ \frac{1}{3} \left(x_n^3 - x_{n-1}^3 \right) \end{pmatrix}$$

to be solved for w_0, w_1, w_2. The solution may be found using the fact that the determinant of a Vandermonde matrix

$$A = \begin{pmatrix} 1 & 1 & 1 \\ \alpha & \beta & \gamma \\ \alpha^2 & \beta^2 & \gamma^2 \end{pmatrix} \tag{5.15}$$

is $\det(A) = (\beta - \alpha)(\gamma - \alpha)(\gamma - \beta)$, and Cramer's rule. (Cramer's rule is not useful as a numerical method but can be useful for symbolic purposes such as this.) Recall that Cramer's rule asserts that if A is nonsingular, then the solution of $Ax = b$ is

$$x_i = \frac{\det(A_i)}{\det(A)}$$

$(i = 1, \ldots, n)$, where A_i is equal to A with its ith column replaced by b. In this case we have

$$\det(A) = (x_{n-1} - x_{n-2})(x_n - x_{n-2})(x_n - x_{n-1})$$

$$= h \cdot 2h \cdot h$$

$$= 2h^3$$

$(h = x_n - x_{n-1})$. Also

$$\det(A_1) = \begin{vmatrix} x_n - x_{n-1} & 1 & 1 \\ \frac{1}{2} \left(x_n^2 - x_{n-1}^2 \right) & x_{n-1} & x_n \\ \frac{1}{3} \left(x_n^3 - x_{n-1}^3 \right) & x_{n-1}^2 & x_n^2 \end{vmatrix}$$

$$= -\frac{1}{6} (x_{n-1} - x_n)^4$$

$$= -\frac{1}{6} h^4$$

$$\det(A_2) = \begin{vmatrix} 1 & x_n - x_{n-1} & 1 \\ x_{n-2} & \frac{1}{2} \left(x_n^2 - x_{n-1}^2 \right) & x_n \\ x_{n-2}^2 & \frac{1}{3} \left(x_n^3 - x_{n-1}^3 \right) & x_n^2 \end{vmatrix}$$

$$= \frac{1}{6} (x_n - x_{n-2}) (x_{n-1} - x_n)^2 (2x_{n-1} + x_n - 3x_{n-2})$$

$$= \frac{1}{6} \cdot 2h \cdot h^2 \cdot (2(x_{n-2} + h) + (x_{n-2} + 2h) - 3x_{n-2})$$

$$= \frac{1}{6} \cdot 2h \cdot h^2 \cdot (2h + 2h)$$

$$= \frac{4}{3} h^4$$

$$\det(A_3) = \begin{vmatrix} 1 & 1 & x_n - x_{n-1} \\ x_{n-2} & x_{n-1} & \frac{1}{2}\left(x_n^2 - x_{n-1}^2\right) \\ x_{n-2}^2 & x_{n-1}^2 & \frac{1}{3}\left(x_n^3 - x_{n-1}^3\right) \end{vmatrix}$$

$$= \frac{1}{6}(x_{n-1} - x_{n-2})(x_{n-1} - x_n)^2(x_{n-1} - 3x_{n-2} + 2x_n)$$

$$= \frac{1}{6} \cdot h \cdot h^2 \left((x_{n-2} + h) - 3x_{n-2} + 2(x_{n-2} + 2h)\right)$$

$$= \frac{1}{6} \cdot h \cdot h^2 \cdot (h + 4h)$$

$$= \frac{5}{6} h^4$$

(using Maple to take the symbolic determinants). So

$$w_0 = \frac{-\frac{1}{6}h^4}{2h^3}$$

$$= -\frac{1}{12}h$$

$$w_1 = -\frac{\frac{4}{3}h^4}{2h^3}$$

$$= \frac{2}{3}h$$

$$w_2 = \frac{\frac{5}{6}h^4}{2h^3}$$

$$= \frac{5}{12}h$$

are the coefficients, and the half-simp rule is

$$\int_{x_{n-1}}^{x_n} f(x)\,dx \approx \frac{h}{12}(-f(x_{n-2}) + 8f(x_{n-1}) + 5f(x_n)).$$

We can now employ Simpson's rule and if we encounter an unmatched last panel we can use the half-simp rule. This is especially useful if the data is being integrated in real time.

Example 5.2.1   Let's use Simpson's rule and the half-simp rule to approximate $\int_0^{2.5} \exp(x)\,dx$ using $N = 5$ panels. We have $x_0 = 0, x_1 = 0.5, x_2 = 1, x_3 = 1.5, x_4 = 2, x_5 = 2.5$. Simpson's rule gives

$$\int_0^2 \exp(x)\,dx \approx \frac{.5}{3}\left(f(0) + 4f(.5) + 2f(1) + 4f(1.5) + f(2)\right)$$

$$\doteq 6.3912$$

(the correct value is $\exp(2) - \exp(0) \doteq 6.3891$). The half-simp rule gives

$$\int_2^{2.5} \exp(x)\,dx \approx \frac{.5}{12}\left(-f(1.5) + 8f(2) + 5f(2.5)\right)$$

$$\doteq 4.8143$$

(the correct value is $\exp(2.5) - \exp(2) \doteq 4.7934$). Hence

$$\int_0^{2.5} \exp(x)\,dx \approx 6.3912 + 4.8143$$

$$\doteq 11.1846$$

(the correct value of $\exp(2.5) - \exp(0) \doteq 11.1825$). This is an error of about .002, which isn't bad considering that we used only 6 points. ∎

We could create similar special methods for other Newton-Cotes formulas that may have unmatched panels, such as Simpson's 3/8 rule. Simpson's rule is by far the most popular of the closed Newton-Cotes rules, however, and so this is rarely done.

Error Estimates   How accurate is the half-simp rule? Before answering that, let's look at another method of deriving the simple Simpson's rule. We expand the integrand $f(x)$ as a Taylor series about the leftmost point:

$$\int_{x_0}^{x_2} f(x)\,dx = \int_{x_0}^{x_2} \left(f(x_0) + f'(x_0)(x - x_0) + \frac{f''(x_0)}{2!}(x - x_0)^2\right.$$

$$\left. + \frac{f'''(x_0)}{3!}(x - x_0)^3 + \frac{f^{(4)}(x_0)}{4!}(x - x_0)^4 + \cdots\right)dx$$

$$= \left(xf(x_0) + \frac{f'(x_0)}{2}(x - x_0)^2 + \frac{f''(x_0)}{3 \cdot 2!}(x - x_0)^3\right.$$

$$\left. + \frac{f'''(x_0)}{4 \cdot 3!}(x - x_0)^4 + \frac{f^{(4)}(x_0)}{5 \cdot 4!}(x - x_0)^5 + \cdots\right)\Big|_{x_0}^{x_2}$$

$$= (x_2 - x_0)f(x_0) + \frac{f'(x_0)}{2}(x_2 - x_0)^2 + \frac{f''(x_0)}{6}(x_2 - x_0)^3$$

$$+ \frac{f'''(x_0)}{24}(x_2 - x_0)^4 + \frac{f^{(4)}(x_0)}{5 \cdot 4!}(x_2 - x_0)^5 + \cdots$$

$$= 2hf(x_0) + 2h^2 f'(x_0) + 8h^3\frac{f''(x_0)}{6} + 16h^4\frac{f'''(x_0)}{24}$$

$$+ 32h^5\frac{f^{(4)}(x_0)}{120} + \cdots$$

$$= 2hf(x_0) + 2h^2 f'(x_0) + \frac{4}{3}h^3 f''(x_0) + \frac{2}{3}h^4 f'''(x_0)$$

$$+ \frac{4}{15}h^5 f^{(4)}(x_0) + \cdots$$

$$= \frac{h}{3}(f(x_0) + 4f(x_0) + f(x_0)) + \frac{h}{3}\left(4f'(x_0) + 1 \cdot 2f'(x_0)\right)h$$

$$+ \frac{h}{3}\left(4 \cdot \frac{1}{2}f''(x_0) + 1 \cdot 2f''(x_0)\right)h^2 + \frac{h}{3}\left(4 \cdot \frac{1}{6}f'''(x_0) + 1 \cdot \frac{4}{3}f'''(x_0)\right)h^3$$

$$+ \frac{h}{3}\left(4 \cdot \frac{1}{24}f^{(4)}(x_0) + 1 \cdot \frac{2}{3}f^{(4)}(x_0)\right)h^4 - \frac{1}{90}f^{(4)}(x_0)h^5 + \cdots$$

$$= \frac{h}{3}f(x_0) + \frac{4h}{3}\left(f(x_0) + f'(x_0)h + \frac{1}{2}f''(x_0)h^2 + \frac{1}{6}f'''(x_0)h^3\right.$$

$$\left. + \frac{1}{24}f^{(4)}(x_0)h^4 + \cdots\right) + \frac{h}{3}\left(f(x_0) + 2f'(x_0)h + 2f''(x_0)h^2\right.$$

$$\left. + \frac{4}{3}f'''(x_0)h^3 + \frac{2}{3}f^{(4)}(x_0)h^4 + \cdots\right) - \frac{1}{90}f^{(4)}(x_0)h^5 + \cdots$$

$$= \frac{h}{3}f(x_0) + \frac{4h}{3}f(x_1) + \frac{h}{3}(f(x_0) + f'(x_0)(2h) + \frac{1}{2}f''(x_0)(2h)^2$$

$$+ \frac{1}{6}f'''(x_0)(2h)^3 + \frac{1}{24}f^{(4)}(x_0)(2h)^4 + \cdots) - \frac{1}{90}f^{(4)}(x_0)h^5 + \cdots$$

$$= \frac{h}{3}f(x_0) + \frac{4h}{3}f(x_1) + \frac{h}{3}f(x_2) - \frac{1}{90}f^{(4)}(x_0)h^5 + \cdots$$

$$= \frac{h}{3}(f(x_0) + 4f(x_1) + f(x_2)) - \frac{1}{90}f^{(4)}(x_0)h^5 + \cdots.$$

(In the last several lines note that the terms indicated by $+\cdots$ within parentheses represent terms in h^6 and higher since they are multiplied by the h outside the parentheses.) So the truncation error in the simple Simpson's rule is

$$E = -\frac{1}{90}f^{(4)}(x_0)h^5 + \cdots \tag{5.16}$$

in agreement with Eq. (5.9), where a different analysis has yielded

$$E = -\frac{1}{90}f^{(4)}(\gamma)h^5 \tag{5.17}$$

(exactly) for some unknown $\gamma \in (x_0, x_2)$. We have shown that the simple Simpson's rule is $O(h^5)$ as $h \to 0$.

Look at what we did in deriving Eq. (5.16): We expanded the integrand in a Taylor series; integrated that series term by term; grouped terms to recover the rule on the RHS; and then identified the error term. Let's do the same for the half-simp rule. Note that the integral is from x_{n-1} to x_n even though the rule uses x_{n-2}. We have

$$\int_{x_{n-1}}^{x_n} f(x)\,dx = \int_{x_{n-1}}^{x_n} \left(f(x_{n-1}) + f'(x_{n-1})(x - x_{n-1}) + \frac{f''(x_{n-1})}{2!}(x - x_{n-1})^2 \right.$$

$$\left. + \frac{f'''(x_{n-1})}{3!}(x - x_{n-1})^3 + \frac{f^{(4)}(x_{n-1})}{4!}(x - x_{n-1})^4 + \cdots \right) dx$$

$$= \left(x f(x_{n-1}) + \frac{f'(x_{n-1})}{2}(x - x_{n-1})^2 + \frac{f''(x_{n-1})}{3 \cdot 2!}(x - x_{n-1})^3 \right.$$

$$\left. + \frac{f'''(x_{n-1})}{4 \cdot 3!}(x - x_{n-1})^4 + \frac{f^{(4)}(x_{n-1})}{5 \cdot 4!}(x - x_{n-1})^5 + \cdots \right)\Big|_{x_{n-1}}^{x_n}$$

$$= (x_n - x_{n-1}) f(x_{n-1}) + \frac{f'(x_{n-1})}{2}(x_n - x_{n-1})^2$$

$$+ \frac{f''(x_{n-1})}{6}(x_n - x_{n-1})^3 + \frac{f'''(x_{n-1})}{24}(x_n - x_{n-1})^4$$

$$+ \frac{f^{(4)}(x_{n-1})}{5 \cdot 4!}(x_n - x_{n-1})^5 + \cdots$$

$$= h f(x_{n-1}) + \frac{f'(x_{n-1})}{2} h^2 + \frac{f''(x_{n-1})}{6} h^3 + \frac{f'''(x_{n-2})}{24} h^4$$

$$+ \frac{f^{(4)}(x_{n-2})}{120} h^5 + \cdots$$

$$= \frac{h}{12}\left(-f(x_{n-1}) + 8 f(x_{n-1}) + 5 f(x_{n-1}) \right)$$

$$+ \frac{h}{12}\left(-1 \cdot -1 f'(x_{n-1}) + 5 f'(x_{n-1}) \right) h$$

$$+ \frac{h}{12}\left(-1 \cdot \frac{1}{2} f''(x_{n-1}) + 5 \cdot \frac{1}{2} f''(x_{n-1}) \right) h^2$$

$$+ \frac{h}{12}\left(-1 \cdot \frac{-1}{6} f'''(x_{n-1}) + 5 \cdot \frac{1}{6} f'''(x_{n-1}) \right) h^3$$

$$+ \frac{h}{12}\left(-1 \cdot \frac{1}{24} f^{(4)}(x_{n-1}) + 5 \cdot \frac{1}{24} f^{(4)}(x_{n-1}) \right) h^4$$

$$+ \frac{-19}{120} f^{(4)}(x_{n-1}) h^5 + \cdots$$

$$= \frac{-h}{12}\left(f(x_{n-1}) - f'(x_{n-1}) h + \frac{1}{2} f''(x_{n-1}) h^2 - \frac{1}{6} f'''(x_{n-1}) \right.$$

$$\left. + \frac{1}{24} f^{(4)}(x_{n-1}) - \cdots \right) + \frac{8h}{12} f(x_{n-1}) + \frac{5h}{12}\left(f(x_{n-1}) + f'(x_{n-1}) h \right.$$

$$\left. + \frac{1}{2} f''(x_{n-1}) h^2 + \frac{1}{6} f'''(x_{n-1}) + \frac{1}{24} f^{(4)}(x_{n-1}) + \cdots \right)$$

$$+ \frac{-19}{120} f^{(4)}(x_{n-1}) h^5 + \cdots$$

$$= \frac{h}{12}\left(-f(x_{n-2}) + 8 f(x_{n-1}) + 5 f(x_n) \right) + \frac{-19}{120} f^{(4)}(x_{n-1}) h^5 + \cdots,$$

where all neglected terms are $O(h^6)$ or higher. Hence the truncation error for the half-simp rule is $O(h^5)$, the same as the truncation error for the simple Simpson's rule, so we are justified in using the half-simp rule with the $O(h^4)$ composite Simpson's rule. Incidentally, note that the half-simp rule is exact for cubics (because $f^{(4)}(x) = 0$ for cubics) despite being based on a quadratic approximation, just like Simpson's rule.

The method of undetermined coefficients is useful for deriving rules but is less useful for computing the needed coefficients for large n. For one thing, note that in the 3×3 case the determinant of the Vandermonde matrix is h^3, which for small h is near zero; this is just one symptom of the fact that Vandermonde matrices based on equally spaced points are apt to be ill-conditioned. The closed Newton-Cotes formulas form a very popular family of quadrature rules, but finding efficient means of generating the weights requires some ingenuity. We have given the weights as integrals and as solutions of a linear system, but there are faster ways of evaluating them numerically.

Symbolic Methods

We have been discussing approximate integration, but there is another computational tool available for integration. Symbolic integration, as provided by Maple or Mathematica, for example, is a powerful tool for integrals that can be solved by formula. Even then, however, we may get an answer like

$$\int_a^b \frac{1}{x}\,dx = \ln(b) - \ln(a),$$

and $\ln(x)$ is itself approximated in the software. Since the function $\ln(x)$ is generally provided, it is convenient to use it, but we should remember that its values are generated by a numerical method and are therefore subject to both approximation error and the rounding error of the arithmetic operations involved in using that approximation. Thus for a more complicated integral with a nonpolynomial integrand, we might consider simply using numerical quadrature in the first place rather than finding an antiderivative that must then be evaluated approximately. But for many integrals, and for all cases involving experimental data or function values generated by another program (so that f itself is unavailable), we need an approximate integration rule.

PROBLEMS 5.2

1. Use Cramer's rule to derive Eq. (5.14), and verify that these are the weights of Simpson's rule as given in the previous section.

2. Use Simpson's rule with the half-simp rule to approximate $\int_0^1 f(x)\,dx$ for $f(x) = \sin(x^2)$ and $f(x) = x^7$ using $N = 9$ and $N = 21$ panels. Compare your answers to those found by using Simpson's 3/8 rule over the last three panels rather than the half-simp rule over the last panel.

3. What is the half-simp rule for integrating over the first (not last) panel? Use the method of undetermined coefficients.

4. **a.** What are the degrees of accuracy of the first three open Newton-Cotes formulas ($n = 0, 1, 2$)? Directly show that they are exact for the appropriate monomials.

   b. Directly show that Simpson's rule and the half-simp rule are exact for constants, linear functions, quadratics, and cubics, but not quartics.

5. Prove that Eq. (5.13) gives the correct Cotes numbers for the open Newton-Cotes rules.

MATLAB 5.2

The MATLAB routine `quad` uses Simpson's rule adaptively. (If you don't have `quad`, `quad8` is similar.) Let's study it and see how it uses some of the ideas we have discussed. Enter:

```
» more on
» type quad
```

to see that most of the work is actually done by a subprogram `quadstep`. Since `quadstep` is a subprogram within `quad.m`, entering `type quadstep` won't display it. Look at `quadstep`; it uses the simple Simpson's rule (two panels) over $[a, b]$ in the form `Q1=(h/6)*(fa+4*fc+fb)` (called "three point Simpson's rule" in the comments) and then the composite Simpson's rule on four panels `Q2=(h/12)*(fa+4*fd+2*fc+4*fe+fb)` (called "five point Simpson's rule" in the comments) over the same interval $[a, b]$. Note how the values `fa`, `fb`, and `fc` are reused rather than recomputed for efficiency. The next step combines these estimates, `Q=Q2+(Q2-Q1)/15` (the weighted sum $\frac{16}{15}Q_2 - \frac{1}{15}Q_1$), to get its estimate of the area Q over this interval. We discuss this technique later in this chapter, but for now we ask you to accept that it is typically a more accurate estimate than either `Q1` or `Q2`. Note the accuracy check that follows the computation of Q: `if abs(Q2-Q)<=tol` (then end).

What happens if the accuracy check fails? The `else` of the `if` calls `quadstep` twice more, on the intervals $[a, b/2]$ and $[b/2, b]$ (i.e., h is replaced by $h/2$). Since the same program, `quadstep`, is being called, it will have its own check on its own Q over its smaller interval, and will call itself again if the estimated error isn't small enough. A program that calls itself is said to be **recursive.** Recursion is one programming technique that may be used (if the programming language allows it) to implement the repeated subdivision of a panel and the repeated application of the same rule in the same way on the new subinterval.

Look carefully at the logic in `quadstep` and in `quad`. Notice the checks for invalid or insufficient data and the check for the possibility that the integral is improper because the integrand is infinite at one of the endpoints; a heuristic is used if this is the case. Notice the use of a minimum step size and a maximum recursion level, and how values of the function f are passed and reused rather than recomputed.

A method such as this parallelizes easily, as we can divide the number of panels by the number of processors and ship out to each processor an appropriately sized region on which it will perform the quadrature. Of course, if one processor happens to get a difficult region that requires a disproportionate amount of recursion, that process may require much more time to complete than the others will.

Now `type quad8` and study it. You will see that similar techniques are used. Notice that if it exceeds its recursion limit it warns that a singularity is likely. There are a number of specialized techniques for dealing with singularities.

If there is a singularity at an endpoint, then the open formulas can be very inaccurate. But if it is some derivative of the integrand that is singular at the endpoint, open rules are usually preferred to closed rules as they avoid this singularity.

Let's look at function with an interesting singularity[3], namely, the function $f(x) = 3x^2 + \ln((\pi - x)^2)/\pi^4 + 1$. Enter:

```
» f=inline('3*x.^2+log((pi-x).^2)/pi^4+1')
» x=0:.00001:5;
» y=f(x);
» plot(x,y),grid
```

Where is the singularity that should occur when $x = \pi$ (giving $\ln(0)$)? Let's check for it; enter:

```
» f(pi)
» min(y)
```

The singularity is there, but even at this fine resolution the smallest value we see is greater than 1, even though f is not bounded from below on this interval! (The smallest value near $x = \pi$ is even larger.) All the negative values must lie in an extremely small interval about $x = \pi$. Let's try plotting it again. Enter:

```
» x=(pi-1E-8):1E-10:(pi+1E-8);
» y=f(x);
» plot(x,y),grid
» min(y)
» s=y(isfinite(y));          %Remove the infinite value.
» min(s)
```

This is a little better, but still no (finite) negative values. Let's try one more time. Enter:

```
» x=(pi-10*eps):eps:(pi+10*eps);
» y=f(x);
» plot(x,y),grid
» min(y)
» s=y(isfinite(y));
» min(s)
```

The plot is not terribly informative except to show that the function is still not very small. In fact, $f(x) = 3x^2 + \ln((\pi - x)^2)/\pi^4 + 1$ is positive for every IEEE standard double precision floating point number $x > 0$. We have seen this in our f(x) (which differs from $f(x)$ because, for example, pi is not equal to π and log(x) is not equal to $\ln(x)$). This singularity is not detectable numerically (except by interval methods). Enter:

```
» quad(f,2,4)
» quadl(f,2,4)
» quad8(f,2,4)
```

---

[3] From Krommer and Ueberhuber, 1998 (see Bibliography).

In fact $f(x)$ is integrable, and the MATLAB routines cannot see the singularity anyway so they do not notice any difficulty (we say that we are "ignoring the singularity"). But, enter:

```
» g=inline('x.^(-.99)')
» quad(g,0,1)                    %Should be about 1.
» quadl(g,0,1)
» quad8(g,0,1)
```

This function is also singular and integrable, and all three routines recognize that this function is also singular and integrable, and they correctly terminate with warnings and highly inaccurate answers. Let's try another singular function. Enter:

```
» h=inline('sin(1./x)./x')
» quad(h,0,1)                    %Should be about .6247.
» quadl(h,0,1)
» quad8(h,0,1)
```

Perhaps this isn't so surprising since $h(0)$ is undefined. Let's try the idea of "avoiding the singularity"; enter:

```
» quad(h,eps,1)                  %Should be about .6247.
» quadl(h,eps,1)
» quad8(h,eps,1)
```

Maybe eps is too small. Enter:

```
» quad(h,1E-4,1)                 %Should be about .6247.
» quadl(h,1E-4,1)
» quad8(h,1E-4,1)
» ezplot(h,0,1)
```

In fact, $h(x)$ is much more ill-behaved near $x = 0$ than a plot could ever show. But a simple change of variables shows that $h(x) = \int_1^\infty \text{sinc}(x)dx$, so if we have a routine for integrals on unbounded domains, we may be able to evaluate $h(x)$. Enter:

```
» quad('sin(x)./x',1,1000)
» quad('sin(x)./x',1,10000)
```

to see that we now get plausible answers. We could continue to increase the upper limit until the values returned by the routine cease to differ appreciably.

Recall that a function like $\text{sinc}(x) = \sin(x)/x$ may appear to be singular (in this case at $x = 0$), but in fact in the limit as x approaches the apparent singularity the function may be well-defined ($\text{sinc}(0) = 1$) and hence not singular. Of course, the naive evaluation of $\sin(x)/x$ at $x = 0$ would not give its correct value.

Although weighted-average rules are stable, subdividing the interval too finely means we are performing many operations. This is inefficient. In addition, for a large sum and a small h we run the risk of eventually adding small numbers (from the last few intervals) to a large number (the area up to that point) if we do not take some care in how we form the sum. Taking too many panels ("overcomputing") will increase the error.

Stability means only that the error won't grow too large too fast, not that it won't occur. Enter:

```
» k=0;
» f=inline('sin(2*pi*x)');
» k=k+1;h=10^-k;x=0:h:1;
» trapz(x,f(x))                    %Should be zero.
» k=k+1;h=10^-k;x=0:h:1;
» trapz(x,f(x))
» k=k+1;h=10^-k;x=0:h:1;
» trapz(x,f(x))
```

The error remains on the order of 10^{-17}. An error of this size is certainly acceptable, given that the machine epsilon is about 10^{-16}, but it has still increased, even though h has decreased by an order of magnitude. Enter:

```
» k=k+1;h=10^-k;x=0:h:1;
» trapz(x,f(x))
» k=k+1;h=10^-k;x=0:h:1;
» trapz(x,f(x))
» k=k+1;h=10^-k;x=0:h:1;
» trapz(x,f(x))
```

Because the rule is stable, roundoff error is growing slowly, but even slow-growing error degrades our results.

If the error for small h ($k = 1$) seemed smaller than you expected from the trapezoidal rule, which is $O(h^2)$, you're right; the trapezoidal rule sometimes gives unexpectedly good results. This phenomenon is a consequence of the Euler-Maclaurin formula.

ADDITIONAL PROBLEMS 5.2

6. a. Derive the half-simp rule in the following way: Find a rule of the form $\int_{-1}^{1} f(x)dx \approx w_0 f(x_0) + w_1 f(x_1) + w_2 f(x_2)$ that is exact for $f(x) = 1, x, x^2$ by the method of undetermined coefficients, and then use a transformation that allows you to apply it to integrals of the form $\int_a^b \phi(x)dx$.

b. Derive a rule that could be used with Simpson's 3/8 rule if there is a single panel left.

c. What rule would you use for Simpson's 3/8 rule with two panels left?

7. Why do all the integration formulas that we've seen for approximating $\int_a^b f(x)dx$ have the property that $\sum_{i=0}^{n} w_i = b - a$?

8. Construct an experiment to compare the closed Newton-Cotes rules based on $n + 1$ points with the open Newton-Cotes rules based on $n + 1$ points. Is one type of rule consistently better than the other?

9. We stated in the text that Cramer's rule isn't useful as a numerical method. However, one can imagine highly specialized cases where the structure of A makes it easy to accurately find the determinants, and where only a few componenets x_i of x are needed. Such a situation occurs very rarely in practice, but suppose that A is a large nonsingular upper triangular matrix and that $b = e_1$. If only the first component x_1 of $Ax = b$ is needed, is Cramer's rule more efficient than backward solution of the triangular system? What numerical issues arise in computing $\det(A) = \prod_{i=1}^{n} a_{ii}$ by such a method? Suggest a method for scaling in this computation to avoid underflow and overflow and to maintain accuracy.

10. a. Derive the error term for the midpoint and trapezoidal rules using Taylor series.

b. Derive the error term for the Simpson's 3/8 rule using Taylor series.

c. Derive the error term for Simpson's rule using Taylor series with remainder and an appropriate mean value theorem.

11. Show that Eq. (5.16) can be written in the form Eq. (5.17).

12. a. Consider evaluating $\ln(x)$ for $x \geq 1$ using the rule $\int_1^x t^{-1}dt = \ln(x)$. How many points would you need to evaluate $\ln(2)$ to within 10^{-15} using Simpson's rule? How about with Boole's rule?

b. The closed Newton-Cotes rule based on 7 points has error term $E = -9h^9 f^{(8)}(\gamma)/1400$. How many points would be required for this rule?

13. a. Show that the determinant of the matrix in Eq. (5.15) is $(\beta - \alpha)(\gamma - \alpha)(\gamma - \beta)$.

b. Generalize this to a formula for the determinant of an $n \times n$ Vandermonde matrix. If you can't prove it correct, verify it experimentally.

14. a. Write a MATLAB program that performs approximate integration for measured data (that is, the input will be a vector y of function values and a step size h) using Simpson's rule and, when needed, the half-simp rule.

b. Evaluate $\int_0^1 \sin(x)dx$ using Simpson's rule and, when necessary, the half-simp rule, using $n = 5$, $6, \ldots 16$ panels. Comment on the differences, if any, between using an odd and even number of panels.

15. a. Derive the open Newton-Cotes rule based on 4 points using the method of undetermined coefficients.

b. Show that the error term is $E = 95h^5 f^{(4)}(\gamma)/144$ using Taylor series.

c. Derive the closed Newton-Cotes rule based on 7 points using the method of undetermined coefficients.

d. Show that the error term is $E = -9h^9 f^{(8)}(\gamma)/1400$ using Taylor series.

5.3   Gaussian Quadrature

The Newton-Cotes formulas use a set of equally spaced nodes to which they interpolate a polynomial. The composite rules may be thought of as using a piecewise polynomial interpolant. These rules are widely used, though we most commonly see from this class of methods closed Newton-Cotes rules of low order. (We see the open rules in the numerical solution of ordinary differential equations.) But we know that interpolating to equally spaced nodes can be problematic. Can we do better with unequally spaced nodes? Yes, we can, if what we mean by *better* is a higher degree of accuracy. Here's an example: The rule

$$\int_{-1}^{1} f(x)dx = f\left(\frac{-1}{\sqrt{3}}\right) + f\left(\frac{1}{\sqrt{3}}\right) \tag{5.18}$$

has degree of accuracy 3, whereas the Newton-Cotes rules based on 2 points both have degree of accuracy 1. Since

$$\int_a^b g(t)dt = \frac{b-a}{2} \int_{-1}^{1} g(t(x))dx, \tag{5.19}$$

where $t(x) = ((b-a)x + b + a)/2$, we see that this technique is not restricted to the interval $[-1, 1]$. Think about it: This is a rule based on only 2 points that evaluates all cubics correctly. That's pretty impressive.

Example 5.3.1   Let's try this method on $\int_{-1}^{1} x^6 dx = 2/7$. The trapezoidal rule uses 2 points and gives $\int_{-1}^{1} x^6 dx \approx f(-1) + f(1) = 2$ ($E \doteq 1.7143$). The open Newton-Cotes rule for

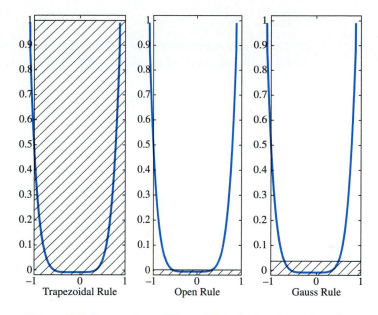

Figure 5.5 Comparison of Three 2-Point Rules for $f(x) = x^6$.

$n = 1$ uses 2 points and gives $\int_{-1}^{1} x^6 dx \approx f(-1/3) + f(1/3) = .0027$ ($E \doteq 0.2830$). Gaussian quadrature also uses 2 points and gives $\int_{-1}^{1} x^6 dx \approx f(-1/\sqrt{3}) + f(1/\sqrt{3}) \doteq .0741(E \doteq .2116)$. See Figure 5.5; the area under the curve $f(x) = x^6$ is approximated by the area under the straight line for each rule. ■

How do we find rules like Eq. (5.18)? Suppose we decide that in the general weighted-average rule

$$\int_a^b f(x)dx \approx w_0 f(x_0) + w_1 f(x_1) + \cdots + w_n f(x_n) \qquad (5.20)$$

we are free to choose not only the weights w_i but also the locations of the nodes x_i. Then we have $2n + 2$ degrees of freedom rather than $n + 1$. We will try to choose these quantities so as to maximize the method's degree of accuracy.

Interpolation and Accuracy   It's clear that any interpolatory rule based on $n + 1$ points has degree of accuracy at least n because we are interpolating a polynomial of degree at most n to the data; if the function is itself a polynomial, we have a perfect fit. In the other direction we have the following theorem:

Theorem 5.3.1

A weighted-average rule based on $n + 1$ points that has degree of accuracy at least n is an interpolatory rule.

Proof.

The proof is essentially the method of undetermined coefficients. If a rule of the form of Eq. (5.20) has degree of accuracy at least n, then at the least we have

$$w_0 \cdot 1 + w_1 \cdot 1 + \cdots + w_n \cdot 1 = \int_a^b 1 dx$$

$$w_0 \cdot x_0 + w_1 \cdot x_1 + \cdots + w_n \cdot x_n = \int_a^b x dx$$

$$w_0 \cdot x_0^2 + w_1 \cdot x_1^2 + \cdots + w_n \cdot x_n^2 = \int_a^b x^2 dx$$

$$\vdots$$

$$w_0 \cdot x_0^n + w_1 \cdot x_1^n + \cdots + w_2 \cdot x_n^n = \int_a^b x^n dx,$$

and if the x_i are distinct, then this is a nonsingular Vandermonde system and so there is one and only one solution. But any interpolatory rule based on $n + 1$ points has degree of accuracy at least n, so the interpolatory rule based on $x_0, x_1, \ldots, x_n$ is a solution. Hence, it is the unique solution. ∎

This is a useful theorem, for now we know that since we seek a rule based on $n + 1$ points with degree of accuracy greater than n, we will necessarily be using an interpolatory rule. That means the only question before us is how to position the nodes so as to maximize the degree of accuracy. The coefficients in an interpolatory rule are always of the form

$$w_i = \int_a^b L_{n,i}(x) \, dx$$

$(i = 0, 1, \ldots, n)$, no matter the location of the nodes (but recall that $L_{n,i}(x)$ depends on the locations of the nodes).

A Two-Point Rule

How shall we find $x_0, x_1, \ldots, x_n$? We could try the method of undetermined coefficients. Let's try this for $n = 1$ (a method based on 2 points). Since there are 4 degrees of freedom (w_0, w_1, x_0, x_1) in the rule

$$\int_a^b f(x) \, dx \approx w_0 f(x_0) + w_1 f(x_1),$$

we ask that the method be exact for the monomials $1, x, x^2, x^3$. This gives

$$w_0 \cdot 1 + w_1 \cdot 1 = \int_a^b 1 dx$$

$$= b - a$$

$$w_0 \cdot x_0 + w_1 \cdot x_1 = \int_a^b x \, dx$$

$$= \frac{1}{2}(b^2 - a^2)$$

$$w_0 \cdot x_0^2 + w_1 \cdot x_1^2 = \int_a^b x^2 \, dx$$

$$= \frac{1}{3}(b^3 - a^3)$$

$$w_0 \cdot x_0^3 + w_1 \cdot x_1^3 = \int_a^b x^3 \, dx$$

$$= \frac{1}{4}(b^3 - a^3)$$

which is a nonlinear system of 4 equations in the 4 unknowns w_0, w_1, x_0, x_1,

$$w_0 + w_1 = b - a$$

$$w_0 x_0 + w_1 x_1 = \frac{1}{2}(b^2 - a^2)$$

$$w_0 x_0^2 + w_1 x_1^2 = \frac{1}{3}(b^3 - a^3) \tag{5.21}$$

$$w_0 x_0^3 + w_1 x_1^3 = \frac{1}{4}(b^3 - a^3)$$

which we must solve. For $a = -1$, $b = 1$ it is not hard to show that the solution is $w_0 = 1$, $w_1 = 1$, $x_0 = -1/\sqrt{3}$, $x_1 = 1/\sqrt{3}$ as in Eq. (5.18). However, for larger n it's clear that this approach, based on solving an $n \times n$ nonlinear system, will be difficult to apply. Fortunately there's another way to find the locations of the nodes.

Gauss Rules   It's easiest to describe the approach in terms of **product integration rules,** which are weighted-average rules of the form

$$\int_a^b w(x) f(x) \, dx \approx w_0 f(x_0) + w_1 f(x_1) + \cdots + w_n f(x_n) \tag{5.22}$$

for some weight function $w(x)$ that is nonnegative on $[a, b]$.[4] Every rule we've seen so far has been of this form with $w(x) = 1$. One advantage of writing a rule as a product integration rule is that if we need to integrate $g(x) = w(x) f(x)$ and $w(x)$ is poorly behaved (e.g., highly oscillatory, unbounded at some point), then we may be able to handle the poor behavior of $g(x)$ analytically—burying its effect in the weights w_i—and only have to evaluate $f(x)$ numerically. We say that a rule of the form of Eq. (5.22) is a **Gaussian quadrature rule** (or **Gauss rule**) if it integrates all monomials of degree at most $2n + 1$ exactly, that is, if

$$\int_a^b w(x) p(x) \, dx = w_0 p(x_0) + w_1 p(x_1) + \cdots + w_n p(x_n)$$

---

[4] We also require that $\int_a^b w(x) x^k \, dx$ converge for $k = 0, 1, 2, \ldots$.

for all polynomials p of degree less than or equal to $2n + 1$. Note that it's actually the integral of the function $w(x)p(x)$ that is found by the product rule, but we say that the product rule integrates polynomials exactly, not that it integrates the weight function times polynomials exactly (though the latter is precisely what it does). All Gauss rules are **open** rules; they do not use the endpoints of the interval of integration.

Example 5.3.2   Let $w(x) = (1 - x^2)^{-1/2}$. This weight function is positive over $(-1, 1)$ and integrable over $[-1, 1]$ but is singular at $x = \pm 1$. The product integration rule

$$\int_{-1}^{1} w(x)f(x)dx \approx \frac{\pi}{n + 1} \sum_{k=0}^{n} f\left(x_{k,n}\right),$$

where

$$x_{k,n} = \cos\left(\frac{(k + \frac{1}{2})\pi}{n + 1}\right),$$

is a Gauss rule, to be discussed in the next section. Hence it should integrate

$$\frac{x^2}{\sqrt{1 - x^2}}$$

(corresponding to $f(x) = x^2$) exactly. Let's take $n = 1$, which should be exact for polynomials of degree at most $2n + 1 = 3$. We have $x_{0,1} = \cos(\pi/4) = 1/\sqrt{2}$ and

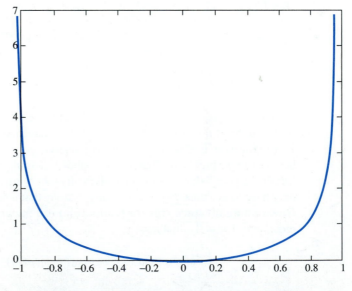

Figure 5.6 Singular Integrand of Example 5.3.2.

$x_{1,1} = \cos(3\pi/4) = -1/\sqrt{2}$, so

$$\int_{-1}^{1} \frac{x^2}{\sqrt{1-x^2}} dx \approx \frac{\pi}{2}(f(x_{0,1}) + f(x_{1,1}))$$

$$= \frac{\pi}{2}\left(f\left(\cos\left(\frac{\pi}{4}\right)\right) + f\left(\cos\left(\frac{3\pi}{4}\right)\right)\right)$$

$$= \frac{\pi}{2}\left(\cos^2\left(\frac{\pi}{4}\right) + \cos^2\left(\frac{3\pi}{4}\right)\right)$$

$$= \frac{\pi}{2}\left(\frac{1}{2} + \frac{1}{2}\right)$$

$$= \frac{\pi}{2},$$

and indeed it can be shown that

$$\int_{-1}^{1} \frac{x^2}{\sqrt{1-x^2}} dx = \frac{\pi}{2}$$

so that the rule has integrated $f(x) = x^2$ exactly using only 2 points and without needing to manipulate the singular function $w(x)$. The integrand is plotted in Figure 5.6. ■

Product integration rules are useful when $w(x)f(x)$ is hard to approximate but $f(x)$ isn't. After all, if a polynomial of low to moderate order can't approximate $w(x)f(x)$ well, then none of the methods we've seen so far are likely to be successful. In principle we could approximate $w(x)f(x)$ by something other than an interpolant, such as a Taylor or Fourier series, but the product rule approach is generally simpler.

Inner Product Spaces   Describing the nodes of Gauss rules with weight $w(x)$ requires a digression. We define the **inner product** of two functions f, g with respect to the weight $w(x)$ over the interval $[a, b]$ by

$$(f, g) = \int_a^b f(x)g(x)w(x)dx. \tag{5.23}$$

This has the usual properties of an inner product: positive definiteness,

$$(f, f) \geq 0 \text{ and } (f, f) = 0 \text{ iff } f = 0$$

symmetry,

$$(f, g) = (g, f)$$

and linearity

$$(\alpha f + \beta g, h) = \alpha(f, h) + \beta(g, h)$$

($\alpha, \beta \in \mathbb{R}$), where f, g, and h are integrable functions over $[a, b]$. Two functions are said to be orthogonal with respect to this inner product if their inner product is zero.

Let P_n be the set of all polynomials in x of degree at most n. Then P_n is a linear space, for the sum of two polynomials in x of degree at most n is a polynomial in x of degree at most n, and also, a scalar times a polynomial in x of degree at most n is a polynomial in x of degree at most n. Every element of P_n is integrable over any interval $[a, b]$, so

Eq. (5.23) defines an inner product on P_n, making it an **inner product space** (a linear space together with an inner product).

Since P_n is a linear space, it has a basis. The obvious basis is the set $M = \{1, x, x^2, \ldots, x^n\}$ of monomials, but it's always convenient to have an orthonormal basis. The Gram-Schmidt process can always be used to make a basis into an orthogonal basis. We need only set

$$p_0(x) = m_0(x)$$
$$= 1$$

and apply the Gram-Schmidt process (see Section 2.8):

$$p_1(x) = m_1(x) - \frac{(p_0, m_1)}{(p_0, p_0)} p_0(x)$$

$$= x - \frac{1}{b-a} \left(\int_a^b 1 \cdot x \cdot w(x) dx \right) \cdot 1$$

$$= x - \frac{1}{b-a} \int_a^b x w(x) dx \tag{5.24}$$

$$p_2(x) = m_2(x) - \frac{(p_0, m_2)}{(p_0, p_0)} p_0(x) - \frac{(p_1, m_2)}{(p_1, p_1)} p_1(x)$$

$$= x^2 - \frac{1}{b-a} \left(\int_a^b 1 \cdot x^2 \cdot w(x) dx \right) \cdot 1 -$$

$$\frac{1}{(p_1, p_1)} \left(\int_a^b p_1(x) \cdot x^2 \cdot w(x) dx \right) \cdot p_1(x) \tag{5.25}$$

and so on. For a specific choice of $w(x)$, each of the definite integrals is just a scalar and so, for example, Eq. (5.24) shows that

$$p_1(x) = x - c$$

for some constant c, and so

$$p_2(x) = x^2 - c_1 x - c_2$$

(for some c_1, c_2) by Eq. (5.25). These polynomials are **monic,** that is, the coefficient of their leading terms is always unity, and by construction they are orthogonal,

$$(p_k, p_l) = \int_a^b p_k(x) p_l(x) w(x) dx = 0$$

if $k \neq l$. In fact, note that if $g(x)$ is a polynomial of degree at most m, then

$$g(x) = c_0 p_0(x) + \cdots + c_n p_m(x)$$

by the fact that $\{p_0, \ldots, p_m\}$ forms a basis for P_m, and so

$$(p_{m+1}, g) = (p_{m+1}, c_0 p_0(x) + \cdots + c_n p_m(x))$$

$$= c_0(p_{m+1}, p_0(x)) + \cdots + c_n(p_{m+1}, p_m(x))$$

$$= 0 + \cdots + 0$$

$$= 0$$

Orthogonal
Polynomials

(by the properties of an inner product). That is, the polynomial p_{m+1} is orthogonal to *every* polynomial of degree at most m. We give an example in MATLAB 5.3.

There's no reason that we can't go on indefinitely, getting an orthogonal basis for P_n for larger and larger values of n, and thereby defining an orthogonal family of polynomials

$$\{p_i(x)\}_{i=0}^{\infty}$$

(for a fixed interval and weight function). In summary, we have an infinite sequence $p_0, p_1, p_2, \ldots$ of monic orthogonal polynomials.

So what? Well, it turns out that the zeroes of any member of such a family are real and distinct and located in the interior of $[a, b]$. That is, p_{n+1} has $n + 1$ zeroes $a < x_0 < x_1 < \cdots < x_n < b$. Our Gauss rule

$$\int_a^b w(x)f(x)dx = w_0 f(x_0) + w_1 f(x_1) + \cdots + w_n f(x_n)$$

will use the zeroes of p_{n+1} as its nodes and will have the weights

$$w_i = \int_a^b L_{n,i}(x)w(x)dx \tag{5.26}$$

$(i = 0, 1, \ldots, n)$. Let's prove this fact.

Theorem 5.3.2

Let $\{p_i\}_{i=0}^{\infty}$ be a family of orthogonal polynomials with respect to the weight function $w(x)$ over $[a, b]$. Let $x_0, x_1, \ldots x_n$ be the zeroes of p_{n+1}. Then the quadrature rule

$$\int_a^b w(x)f(x)dx \approx w_0 f(x_0) + w_1 f(x_1) + \cdots + w_n f(x_n),$$

where

$$w_i = \int_a^b L_{n,i}(x)w(x)dx$$

$(i = 0, 1, \ldots, n)$, integrates $f(x) = x^k$ exactly for $k = 0, 1, \ldots, 2n + 1$.

Proof.

Since the weights w_i are the weights found by replacing f with an interpolating polynomial of degree n, the method must integrate $f(x) = x^k$ exactly for $k = 0, 1, \ldots, n$. Suppose that $f(x)$ is any polynomial of degree at most $2n + 1$. Then

$$f(x) = Q(x)p_{n+1}(x) + R(x),$$

where $Q(x)$ is the quotient upon (synthetic) division by $p_{n+1}(x)$ and $R(x)$ is the remainder. Both $Q(x)$ and $R(x)$ must have degree at most n because $p_{n+1}(x)$ has degree $n + 1$.

Then applying the quadrature rule gives

$$w_0 f(x_0) + w_1 f(x_1) + \cdots + w_n f(x_n) = \sum_{i-0}^{n} w_i (Q(x_i) p_{n+1}(x_i) + R(x_i))$$

$$= \sum_{i-0}^{n} w_i R(x_i)$$

because we chose the nodes so that $p_{n+1}(x_i) = 0$ $(i = 0, 1, \ldots, n)$. But the rule is exact for polynomials of degree at most n, so

$$\sum_{i-0}^{n} w_i R(x_i) = \int_a^b w(x) R(x) dx$$

$$= \int_a^b w(x) R(x) dx + \int_a^b w(x) Q(x) p_{n+1}(x) dx$$

since $(p_{n+1}(x), Q(x)) = 0$ because $Q(x)$ is of degree at most n. Pulling this all together we have

$$w_0 f(x_0) + w_1 f(x_1) + \cdots + w_n f(x_n) = \int_a^b w(x) R(x) dx + \int_a^b w(x) Q(x) p_{n+1}(x) dx$$

$$= \int_a^b w(x) (Q(x) p_{n+1}(x) R(x)) dx$$

$$= \int_a^b w(x) f(x) dx$$

if $f(x)$ is a polynomial of degree at most $2n + 1$. ∎

Accuracy

This proof shows that the degree of accuracy of a Gauss rule is at least $2n + 1$. In fact no weighted-average rule

$$\int_a^b w(x) f(x) dx \approx w_0 f(x_0) + w_1 f(x_1) + \cdots + w_n f(x_n)$$

can have degree of accuracy $2n + 2$, so Gauss rules are optimal in this sense. It is also a fact that the weights w_i satisfy $w_i \in [0, 1]$, which is beneficial with respect to roundoff error (in particular, $w_i > 0$). Gauss rules are not strictly optimal with respect to absolute error but have excellent error properties. The error formula is

$$E = \frac{f^{(2n+2)}(\gamma)}{(2n + 2)!} (p_{n+1}, p_{n+1}) \tag{5.27}$$

for some $\gamma \in (a, b)$. Of course, these rules, like the Newton-Cotes rules, can also be used in composite form.

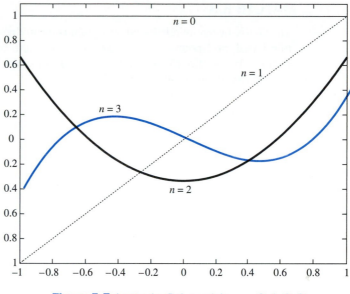

Figure 5.7 Legendre Polynomials, $n = 0, 1, 2, 3$.

We have reduced the problem of finding rules with degree of accuracy as high as possible to choosing a weight $w(x)$, generating the relevant orthogonal polynomials, finding their roots, and then finding the weights from Eq. (5.26),

$$w_i = \int_a^b L_{n,i}(x)w(x)dx$$

($i = 0, 1, \ldots, n$). But we know that finding all roots of a polynomial isn't always easy; even in a case like this, where the roots are real, simple, and located in a known interval, for large n the roots near the endpoints of the interval may not be well separated. We'll discuss more efficient techniques for generating these values in the next two sections.

The case $w(x) = 1$ is obviously of special interest. The orthogonal polynomials in this case are known as the **Legendre polynomials** (if $[a, b] = [-1, 1]$; see Figure 5.7) and the quadrature rule derived from it is called **Gauss-Legendre quadrature.** The formula in Eq. (5.18) is the Gauss-Legendre rule for $n = 1$, and the midpoint rule is the $n = 0$ case.

PROBLEMS 5.3

1. Show that Eq. (5.19) is correct. Use it to approximate $\int_2^4 \sin(x^2)dx$ using Eq. (5.18).

2. Show that every interpolatory rule for $\int_a^b w(x)f(x)dx$ has the weights $w_i = \int_a^b L_{n,i}(x)w(x)dx$.

3. Show that for $a = -1$, $b = 1$ the solution of Eq. (5.21) is $w_0 = 1$, $w_1 = 1$, $x_0 = -1/\sqrt{3}$, $x_1 = 1/\sqrt{3}$.

4. The inner product (f, g) defines a norm by $\|f\| = (f, f)^{1/2}$. For $w(x) = 1$ and $[a, b] = [-1, 1]$, find $\|1\|$, $\|x\|$, and $\|\sin(x)\|$.

5. What are the first three Legendre polynomials? Show that the midpoint rule is the Gauss-Legendre rule for $n = 0$ and that Eq. (5.18) is the Gauss-Legendre rule based on $n + 1 = 2$ points.

MATLAB 5.3

The Gauss-Legendre rule based on 1 point is the midpoint rule, and the Gauss-Legendre rule based on 2 points is Eq. (5.18). Let's find the rule based on 3 points. We take $p_0(x) = 1$; from Eq. (5.24), $p_1(x) = x$, and from Eq. (5.25), $p_2(x) = x^2 - 1/3$. If you have the Symbolic Toolbox, enter:

```
» syms x p2
» p2=x^2-1/3;
» %Recall that the ellipsis '...' is the line continuation symbol.
» p3=x^3-int(1*x^3,x,-1,1)/int(1,x,-1,1)-...
   int(x*x^3,x,-1,1)*x/int(x^2,x,-1,1)-...
   int(p2*x^3,x,-1,1)*x/int(p2^2,x,-1,1)
```

to see that $p_3(x) = x^3 - \frac{3}{5}x$. Let's check:

```
» clear all
» p=inline('x.^3-.6*x')
» quad('x.^3-.6*x',-1,1)
» quad('x.*(x.^3-.6*x)',-1,1)
» quad('x.^2.*(x.^3-.6*x)',-1,1)
```

Yes, $p_3(x)$ appears to be orthogonal to $p_0(x)$, $p_1(x)$, and $p_2(x)$. Enter:

```
» nodes=roots([1 0 -.6 0])
```

to get the nodes ($x_0 = -\sqrt{3/5}$, $x_1 = 0$, $x_2 = \sqrt{3/5}$). Now let's generate the weights using the Lagrange interpolating polynomials. Enter:

```
» w0=quad('x.*(x-sqrt(.6))./((-sqrt(.6))*(-sqrt(.6)-sqrt(.6)))',-1,1)
» w1=quad('(x+sqrt(.6)).*(x-sqrt(.6))./((sqrt(.6))*(-sqrt(.6)))',-1,1)
» w2=quad('x.*(x+sqrt(.6))./((sqrt(.6))*(sqrt(.6)+sqrt(.6)))',-1,1)
» format rat
» w0,w1,w2
» format
```

The weights appear to be 5/9, 8/9, and 5/9. (Since the functions are just polynomials it would be easy to integrate them analytically or symbolically and verify this.) Let's check; we have used $n = 2$ so we should be able to integrate polynomials of degree at most 5 exactly. Enter:

```
» nodes=sort(nodes)                        %Reorder the nodes.
» g=inline('3*x.^5-7*x.^4+2*x.^3-5*x.^2-8*x+3')
» w0*g(nodes(1))+w1*g(nodes(2))+w2*g(nodes(3)) %Gauss-Legendre rule.
» quad(g,-1,1)
```

The answers agree, so this checks. The Gauss-Legendre rule based on 3 points is $\int_a^b f(x)dx \approx \frac{5}{9}f(-\sqrt{3/5}) + \frac{8}{9}f(0) + \frac{5}{9}f(\sqrt{3/5})$.

Let's plot the first three Legendre polynomials. Some patterns already seem clear (for example, every other term is missing). Enter:

```
» z=-1:.01:1;
» plot(z,1,'b'),hold on
» plot(z,z,'r')
» plot(z,z.^2-1/3,'g')
» plot(z,z.^3-3*z/5,'y')
» axis([-1 1 -1.1 1.1])
» grid
```

The polynomials appear to be constrained to take on values that remain within $[-1, 1]$. Indeed, this is the case, and for this reason the change of variables $x = \cos(\phi)$ is often used to simplify formulas involving Legendre polynomials. The orthogonality is difficult to see from the plot as it represents the fact that $\int_a^b p_k(x)p_l(x)dx = 0$ if $k \neq l$, but you may be able to imagine how the areas cancel.

The Legendre polynomials as we have defined them are orthogonal but not orthonormal on $[a, b]$. You may see the Legendre polynomials defined in other texts as constant multiples of the monic ones given here. This does not affect the location of the roots.

ADDITIONAL PROBLEMS 5.3

6. Prove that no weighted-average formula for $\int_a^b w(x)f(x)dx$ can have degree of accuracy $2n + 2$. (*Hint:* Consider the polynomial $(x - x_0)^2(x - x_1)^2 \cdots (x - x_n)^2$.)

7. Use the Gauss-Legendre rules based on 2 and 3 points to approximate $\int_0^2 (1 + e^x)^{-2}dx$. Bound the errors using Eq. (5.27).

8. a. Determine the Gauss-Legendre rule based on 4 points.

b. Determine the Gauss-Legendre rule based on 5 points. Did the work you did in part (a) simplify these calculations?

c. Use the Gauss-Legendre rules based on N points, $N = 1, 2, 3, 4, 5$, to approximate $\int_{-1}^1 x^3 \ln(x)dx = -20\ln(2) + 14$.

d. Repeat part (c) for $\int_{-1}^1 x^{m/2}dx$, $m = 1, 3, 5$.

e. Bound the error in your answers to part (c) using Eq. (5.27).

9. Conduct an experiment to compare the open Newton-Cotes, closed Newton-Cotes, and Gauss-Legendre rules based on n points for all n for which you have formulas. Discuss your results.

10. a. Use the method of undetermined coefficients to derive a product integration rule of the form $\int_0^{2\pi} f(x)\cos(x)dx \approx w_0 f(0) + w_1 f(\pi) + w_2 f(2\pi)$. This is the first **Filon cosine formula**. For which monomials is it exact?

b. Compare this rule to Simpson's rule, which is also based on 3 points, for several choices of f.

c. Use the method of undetermined coefficients to derive a product integration rule of the form $\int_0^{2\pi} f(x)\sin(x)dx \approx w_0 f(0) + w_1 f(\pi) + w_2 f(2\pi)$. This is the first **Filon sine formula**. For which monomials is it exact?

d. Compare this rule to Simpson's rule and the Gauss-Legendre rule based on 3 points for several choices of f.

11. Let $x = \cos(\phi)$ and write $p_n(x) = p_n(\cos(\phi))$ for the nth Legendre polynomial. Plot $p_n(\cos(\phi))$ as a function of ϕ for $n = 0, 1, \ldots, 10$. Comment on the qualitative properties of these graphs.

12. a. Let $w(x) = \exp(-x^2)$ and $a = -\infty$, $b = \infty$. The orthogonal polynomials generated by the inner product $(f, g) = \int_{-\infty}^{\infty} f(x)g(x)\exp(-x^2)dx$ are the

Hermite polynomials (see Section 4.2). Find the first three Hermite polynomials.

b. The quadrature rule for $\int_{-\infty}^{\infty} f(x)\exp(-x^2)dx$, which these polynomials define, is called **Gauss-Hermite quadrature**. Find the first three Gauss-Hermite quadrature rules.

c. Use the first three Gauss-Hermite quadrature rules to approximate the value of $\int_{-\infty}^{\infty} \cos(x)\exp(-x^2)dx$.

13. Use composite Gauss-Legendre integration based on 3 points to approximate the indefinite integral $\int_0^x \sin(t)dt$

at $x = 0, 0.1, 0.2, \ldots, 6.4$. Plot your integral. Use linear interpolation of these values to estimate the value at $x = 2\pi$.

14. For $n = 0, 1, 2, 3$, show that the Legendre polynomial $y = p_n(x)$ satisfies **Legendre's differential equation** $(1 - x^2)y'' - 2xy' + n(n + 1)y = 0$. (This is true in general.)

15. Normalize the Legendre polynomials p_0, p_1, p_2, p_3 by dividing them by their respective norms $(p_i, p_i)^{1/2}$.

5.4 Gauss-Chebyshev Quadrature

Gauss-Legendre rules are the most popular Gauss rules because $w(x) = 1$ is so convenient; in fact, the term *Gauss rule* is often used to mean Gauss-Legendre rule. For a general-purpose routine like the quad commands in MATLAB, a Gauss rule is clearly a good choice: A routine is needed that will work on as broad a class of integrands as possible, because it's intended to be used by a wide class of users, not all of whom will have training in numerical analysis.

However, it's important to have special rules for special cases: noisy functions, non-smooth functions, functions singular at points within the interval, highly oscillatory integrands, infinite intervals of integration, and so on. There are many such rules that may be used for difficult quadrature problems. Many Gauss rules are of this sort, because they use an interval of integration that is unbounded. One example is **Gauss-Laguerre quadrature**, which is based on the **Laguerre polynomials**, generated by the weight function

$$w(x) = \exp(-x)$$

on the interval $[0, \infty)$. This provides a rule for approximating $\int_0^\infty f(x)\exp(-x)dx$, which could be used for the numerical calculation of Laplace transforms, for example.

Gauss Rules and Orthogonal Polynomials　　Let's continue to explore Gaussian quadrature. We say that a weight function is **admissible** if it is nonnegative on $[a, b]$ (possibly equal to positive infinity at some points) and if

$$\int_a^b w(x)x^k dx$$

converges for $k = 0, 1, 2, \ldots$. Often we normalize $w(x)$ so that

$$\int_a^b w(x)\,dx = 1,$$

but this is not essential. Every admissible weight function that is positive on (a, b) generates a sequence of orthogonal polynomials and hence a Gauss rule.[5] The orthogonal

---

[5] Sometimes we allow $w(x)$ to be of mixed sign. Such rules, if they exist for a given $w(x)$, can have degree of accuracy even greater than Gauss rules.

polynomials may be generated by the Gram-Schmidt process, as described in the previous section,

$$p_1(x) = m_1(x) - \frac{(p_0, m_1)}{(p_0, p_0)} p_0(x)$$

$$p_2(x) = m_2(x) - \frac{(p_0, m_2)}{(p_0, p_0)} p_0(x) - \frac{(p_1, m_2)}{(p_1, p_1)} p_1(x)$$

$$p_3(x) = m_3(x) - \frac{(p_0, m_3)}{(p_0, p_0)} p_0(x) - \frac{(p_1, m_3)}{(p_1, p_1)} p_1(x) - \frac{(p_2, m_3)}{(p_2, p_2)} p_2(x)$$

$$\vdots$$

where $m_i(x) = x^i$ $(i = 0, 1, 2, \ldots)$ and $p_0(x) = 1$. Notice that these equations are of the form

$$p_1(x) = m_1(x) - c_1 p_0(x)$$

$$p_2(x) = m_2(x) - c_2 p_0(x) - c_3 p_1(x)$$

$$p_3(x) = m_3(x) - c_4 p_0(x) - c_5 p_1(x) - c_6 p_2(x)$$

$$\vdots$$

for some constants c_i that are formed from inner products of monomials with orthogonal polynomials. We might expect some of these constants to be zero by orthogonality and indeed, it is always possible to generate the orthogonal polynomials corresponding to a given weight function $w(x)$ and interval by

$$p_{n+1}(x) = xp_n(x) - \alpha_{n+1} p_n(x) - \beta_{n+1} p_{n-1}(x), \tag{5.28}$$

which is called a **three-term recurrence relation** because the terms p_{n+1}, p_n, and p_{n-1} appear in it. All orthogonal polynomials satisfy a three-term recurrence relation of this form with

$$\alpha_{n+1} = \frac{(p_n, xp_n)}{(p_n, p_n)}$$

$$= \frac{\int_a^b xp_n^2(x)w(x)dx}{\int_a^b p_n^2(x)w(x)dx}$$

$$\beta_{n+1} = \frac{(p_n, xp_{n-1})}{(p_{n-1}, p_{n-1})}$$

$$= \frac{\int_a^b xp_n p_{n-1}(x)w(x)dx}{\int_a^b p_{n-1}^2(x)w(x)dx}$$

$(n = 0, 1, \ldots)$, where we define $p_{-1}(x) = 0$ so that $\beta_1 = 0$. Every polynomial generated in this way, for every choice of $w(x)$, has only real, simple zeroes, and they lie entirely in (a, b). If the weight function is symmetric with respect to the midpoint of the interval $[a, b]$, then the roots are also located symmetrically about $(a + b)/2$ and the Gauss rule weights for the points $\pm x_i$ are the same.

In fact, there are formulas for the weights in a Gauss rule. One formula for the weights in a Gauss rule based on $n + 1$ points is

$$w_i = -\frac{(p_{n+1}, p_{n+1})}{p_{n+2}(x_i)p'_{n+1}(x_i)} \tag{5.29}$$

$(i = 0, 1, \ldots, n)$, where the x_i are the zeroes of $p_{n+1}(x)$.

Example 5.4.1   The first two Legendre polynomials are $p_0(x) = 1$ and $p_1(x) = x$, so the next Legendre polynomial is, by Eq. (5.28),

$$p_2(x) = xp_1(x) - \alpha_2 p_1(x) - \beta_2 p_0(x)$$

$$= x \cdot x - \frac{\int_{-1}^{1} x \cdot x^2 dx}{\int_{-1}^{1} x^2 dx} x - \frac{\int_{-1}^{1} x \cdot x \cdot 1 dx}{\int_{-1}^{1} 1^2 dx} 1$$

$$= x^2 - 0 \cdot x - \frac{2/3}{2} \cdot 1$$

$$= x^2 - \frac{1}{3}$$

$(x_0 = -1/\sqrt{3}, x_1 = 1/\sqrt{3})$. The corresponding weights in the Gauss-Legendre rule are given by Eq. (5.29). So

$$w_0 = -\frac{(p_2, p_2)}{p_3(x_0)p'_2(x_0)}$$

$$= -\frac{\int_{-1}^{1} \left(x^2 - \frac{1}{3}\right)^2 dx}{p_3(-1/\sqrt{3})p'_2(-1/\sqrt{3})}$$

$$= -\frac{8/45}{-8/45}$$

$$= 1$$

(using $p_3(x) = x^3 - \frac{3}{5}x$). Then $w_1 = w_0$ because $p_2(x) = x^2 - \frac{1}{3}$ is symmetric with respect to the origin. Thus the weights are $w_0 = 1$, $w_1 = 1$.   ■

Unlike the simple examples we have seen so far, the weights in general are irrational numbers and so do not have simple forms. The nodes and weights may be explicitly entered in a program that computes with a fixed number of points $n + 1$, or may be generated by a numerical method (e.g., Newton's method to find the roots and a formula like Eq. (5.29) for the weights).

Gauss-   Another important class of Gaussian quadrature rules is based on the interval $[-1, 1]$
Chebyshev   and either the weight function
Rules

$$w(x) = \frac{1}{\sqrt{1 - x^2}},$$

which gives rise to the **Chebyshev**[6] **polynomials of the first kind** $T_n(x)$ and therefore the **Gauss-Chebyshev rule of the first kind,** or the weight function

$$w(x) = \sqrt{1 - x^2},$$

which gives rise to the **Chebyshev polynomials of the second kind** $U_n(x)$ and therefore the **Gauss-Chebyshev rule of the second kind.** These are called the **Gauss-Chebyshev rules.** The term *Gauss-Chebyshev rule* alone generally refers to the rule of the first kind, and in a similar way, the term Chebyshev polynomials refers to the polynomials of the first kind $T_n(x)$.

The first two Chebyshev polynomials are $T_0(x) = 1$ and $T_1(x) = x$. Others may be found from the three-term recurrence relation (Eq. (5.28)). A convenient representation is given by

$$T_n(x) = \frac{1}{2^{n-1}} \cos(n \arccos(x)) \tag{5.30}$$

$$= \frac{1}{2^{n-1}} \cos(n\theta)$$

($n \geq 1$) using the change of variables $\theta = \arccos(x)$. Clearly, $T_n(x)$ takes on values in $[-1, 1]$ (in fact, in $[-2^{-(n-1)}, 2^{-(n-1)}]$). It is not hard to show that

$$T_{n+1}(x) = x T_n(x) - \frac{1}{4} T_{n-1}(x) \tag{5.31}$$

for $n \geq 2$ (and $T_2(x) = x T_1(x) - \frac{1}{2} T_0(x)$), and that the roots of $T_n(x) = 0$ are given by

$$x_k = \cos\left(\frac{2k+1}{2n}\pi\right)$$

($n \geq 1$, $k = 0, 1, \ldots, n-1$), called the **Chebyshev nodes** (or **Chebyshev points**). A Gauss-Chebyshev rule based on $n + 1$ points would use the Chebyshev points that are the $n + 1$ roots of $T_{n+1}(x) = 0$ (see Fig. 5.8). Note that this formula does not give the points ordered as $x_0 < x_1 < \cdots < x_{n-1}$.

Note from the figure that the Chebyshev points tend to bunch up near the endpoints. This is entirely general, and becomes more pronounced as $n \to \infty$. In fact, the Chebyshev points are the points at which to interpolate a function defined on $[-1, 1]$ (or, with a linear change of variable, any finite interval) because of the following theorem.

Theorem 5.4.1

If $n \geq 1$ and $q(x)$ is a monic polynomial of degree n, then

$$\max_{x \in [-1,1]} (|T_n(x)|) < \max_{x \in [-1,1]} (|q(x)|)$$

unless $q(x) = T_n(x)$.

---

[6] You will see this name transliterated in different ways in different texts.

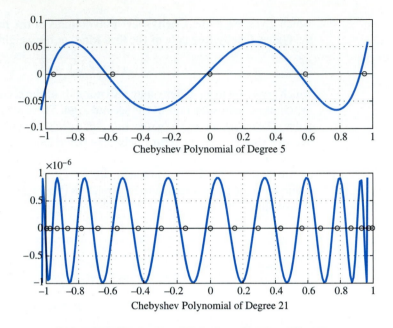

Figure 5.8 Chebyshev Points from $T_5(x)$ and $T_{21}(x)$.

Theorem 5.4.1 states that $T_n(x)$ is the polynomial of degree n that is "smallest" on $[-1, 1]$ in the sense that it has the least deviation from 0 (in the max norm; look at the vertical scales in Fig. 5.8). Recall Theorem 4.1.1 regarding polynomial interpolation: Let $a \leq x_0 < x_1 < \cdots < x_n \leq b$ and f in $C^{n+1}[a, b]$ be given. Then the polynomial interpolant $p(x)$ to f at $x_0, x_1, \ldots, x_n$ satisfies

$$f(x) - p(x) = \frac{f^{(n+1)}(\xi)}{(n + 1)!}(x - x_0)(x - x_1) \cdots (x - x_n) \tag{5.32}$$

(for any $x \in [a, b]$), for some $\xi = \xi(x)$ in (a, b). We cannot control $\xi(x)$, but in all likelihood $f^{(n+1)}(\xi(x))$ does not vary much over the interval. However, we can control the term

$$\varpi(x) = (x - x_0)(x - x_1) \cdots (x - x_n)$$

(see also Eq. (5.8)). By Theorem 5.4.1, this quantity is minimized over $[-1, 1]$ by choosing the nodes to be the $n + 1$ zeroes of $T_{n+1}(x)$, namely

$$x_k = \cos\left(\frac{2k + 1}{2n + 2}\pi\right) \tag{5.33}$$

($k = 0, 1, \ldots, n$). While this choice of nodes may not strictly minimize the RHS of Eq. (5.32), because of the presence of the unknown $\xi(x)$, it is very likely to be very close to the minimum, and is the best we can do with the available information. Hence, as a rule, interpolation at the Chebyshev points is to be preferred when we are not forced to use other points.

This also explains why Gauss-Chebyshev quadrature is the basis for a number of popular rules, as we discuss in the next section: All Gauss rules are interpolatory rules; they interpolate the function $f(x)$ in

$$\int_a^b w(x)f(x)dx$$

with a polynomial. The use of the Chebyshev points gives the polynomial interpolant of $f(x)$ that minimizes the maximum deviation $|f(x) - p(x)|$ over the interval of integration, which certainly should reduce the error. The error bound for Gauss-Chebyshev quadrature of the first kind is

$$E = \frac{\pi}{2^{2n+1}(2n+2)!} f^{(2n)}(\gamma_1)$$

for some $\gamma_1 \in (-1, 1)$. The error bound for Gauss-Chebyshev quadrature of the second kind is

$$E = \frac{\pi}{2^{2n+3}(2n+2)!} f^{(2n)}(\gamma_2)$$

for some $\gamma_2 \in (-1, 1)$. The bound for Gauss-Chebyshev quadrature of the second kind is smaller by a factor of 4 (assuming $f^{(2n)}(\gamma_1) \approx f^{(2n)}(\gamma_2)$), but the rule of the first kind is easier to apply because of the surprising fact that

$$w_i = \frac{\pi}{n+1}$$

$(i = 0, 1, \ldots, n)$ are the weights of the Gauss-Chebyshev rule of the first kind. Since w_i depends only on n, not i, we can save work in generating the weights and in computing the weighted average.

Example 5.4.2   Let's use Gauss-Chebyshev quadrature to approximate $\int_{-1}^{1} \cos(\pi x)dx$. We must first write this as

$$\int_{-1}^{1} \cos(\pi x)dx = \int_{-1}^{1} \left(\cos(\pi x)\sqrt{1-x^2}\right) \frac{1}{\sqrt{1-x^2}}dx$$

$$= \int_{-1}^{1} f(x)w(x)dx,$$

where $f(x) = \cos(\pi x)\sqrt{1 - x^2}$. Using $n + 1 = 5$ points gives

$$\int_{-1}^{1} \cos(\pi x)dx \approx \frac{\pi}{n+1} \sum_{i=0}^{n} f(x_i)$$

$$= \frac{\pi}{5} (f(x_0) + f(x_1) + f(x_2) + f(x_3) + f(x_4))$$

$$= \frac{\pi}{5} \left[f\left(\cos\left(\frac{\pi}{10}\right)\right) + f\left(\cos\left(\frac{3\pi}{10}\right)\right) + f\left(\cos\left(\frac{5\pi}{10}\right)\right) \right.$$

$$\left. + f\left(\cos\left(\frac{7\pi}{10}\right)\right) + f\left(\cos\left(\frac{9\pi}{10}\right)\right) \right]$$

$$\doteq -0.0323,$$

and the correct value is $\int_{-1}^{1} \cos(\pi x)dx = 0$. If we use instead $n + 1 = 21$ points we get -0.0019. These results are not very impressive, but we have traded a nice integrand like $\cos(\pi x)$ for $f(x) = \cos(\pi x)\sqrt{1 - x^2}$.

Let's try another example. We'll approximate $\int_{-1}^{1} \cos(\pi x)/\sqrt{1 - x^2}dx$. We have

$$\int_{-1}^{1} \frac{\cos(\pi x)}{\sqrt{1 - x^2}}dx \approx \frac{\pi}{n+1} \sum_{i=0}^{n} \cos(\pi x_i)$$

$$\doteq -0.9557,$$

whereas quad and quadl applied to $\cos(\pi x)/\sqrt{1 - x^2}$ both give -0.9558. This is excellent agreement for only 5 points.

If $f(x)$ is already an ugly function, then writing $\int_{-1}^{1} f(x)dx$ as $\int_{-1}^{1}(f(x)\sqrt{1 - x^2})/\sqrt{1 - x^2}dx$ and applying Gauss-Chebyshev quadrature to $g(x) = f(x)\sqrt{1 - x^2}$ is likely to at least do no harm; if $f(x)$ is very well-behaved, however, this may not be advisable. ∎

Chebyshev-type Rules

All weighted-average rules that have equal weights $w_0 = w_1 = \cdots = w_n$ for a given n, that is, all rules of the form

$$\int_{a}^{b} w(x)f(x)dx \approx c_{n+1} \sum_{i=0}^{n+1} f(x_i)$$

($w_i = c_{n+1}$ for all $i = 0, 1, \ldots, n$) are called **Chebyshev-type rules.** The use of equal weights reduces the effects of roundoff error, which can be especially useful for noisy functions, where f is known to fewer digits than we would like.

In light of Theorem 5.4.1 we might consider using an interpolatory rule for $\int_{-1}^{1} f(x)dx$ based on interpolating $f(x)$ at the Chebyshev nodes. That is, we might use the basic idea of the Newton-Cotes rule but without equally spaced nodes. (This differs from Gauss-Chebyshev quadrature because $w(x) = 1$.) Interpolating $f(x)$ at the Chebyshev nodes, mapped from $[-1, 1]$ to $[a, b]$, gives a rule known as the **classical Clenshaw-Curtis method** (or **Fejér formula**). Interpolating $f(x)$ at the Chebyshev *extrema*, mapped from $[-1, 1]$ to $[a, b]$, gives a rule known as the **practical Clenshaw-Curtis method.** The practical Clenshaw-Curtis formulas have certain computational advantages over, and similar performance to, the classical Clenshaw-Curtis formulas, which in turn are generally superior to Newton-Cotes formulas, though they have about the same degree of accuracy. Applying the Clenshaw-Curtis idea with a weight function other than $w(x) = 1$ gives a **modified Clenshaw-Curtis method.** A Clenshaw-Curtis method is the default numerical integrator in Maple, used unless a singularity is detected or a Newton-Cotes rule is explicitly requested (see `mhelp int[numerical]` in MATLAB if you have the MAPLE help).

PROBLEMS 5.4

1. a. Use the Gauss-Chebyshev rule based on $1, 2, 3, 4, 5$ points to approximate $\int_{-1}^{1} \sin(x)/\left(1 - x^2\right)^{1/2} dx$.

b. Repeat part (a) for $\int_{0}^{5} x \cos(3x) dx$. You will need to make a change of variables and then write the integrand as $f(x)/\left(1 - x^2\right)^{1/2}$ for some $f(x)$.

2. Use Eq. (5.29) to derive the weights for the Gauss-Legendre rule based on three points.

3. Of the rules that we have seen so far, which are Chebyshev-type rules?

4. The Chebyshev polynomials of the second kind $U_{n+1}(x)$ have zeroes $x_k = \cos((k + 1)\pi/(n + 2))$,

$k = 0, 1, \ldots, n$, and the Gauss-Chebyshev rule of the second kind has weights $w_k = (\pi/(n + 2)) \sin^2((k + 1)\pi/(n + 2))$, $k = 0, 1, \ldots, n$. Use the Gauss-Chebyshev rule of the second kind based on $1, 2, 3, 4, 5$ points to approximate $\int_{-1}^{1} \sin(x)\left(1 - x^2\right)^{1/2} dx$.

5. a. Find the first five Laguerre polynomials using Eq. (5.28), and then use Eq. (5.29) to derive as many Gauss-Laguerre rules as you can from these five polynomials. What are the degrees of accuracy of these rules?

b. Use your Gauss-Laguerre rules to approximate $\int_{0}^{\infty} \sin(x) \exp(-x) dx$.

MATLAB 5.4

Let's plot the first several Chebyshev polynomials of the first kind. We'll enter them explicitly rather than generate them by the recurrence relation. Enter:

```
» x=-1:.01:1;
» T0=ones(size(x));
» T1=x;
» T2=x.^2-.5;
» T3=x.^3-.75*x;
» T4=x.^4-x.^2+1/8;
» T5=x.^5-.8*x.^3+(5/16)*x;
» plot(x,[T0;T1;T2;T3;T4;T5]),grid
```

You can tell which polynomial is which by the number of roots (n for the degree n polynomial) or extrema ($n - 1$), and by the fact that the higher the degree the smaller the maximum deviation of the polynomial from 0. Let's check the orthogonality using the Symbolic Toolbox. Enter:

```
» syms x
» T3=x^3-.75*x;
» T5=x^5-.8*x^3+(5/16)*x;
» w=1/sqrt(1-x^2);
» int(w*T3*T5,x,-1,1)
```

Yes, this checks; $T_3(x)$ is orthogonal to $T_5(x)$ over $[-1, 1]$ with respect to the weight function $w(x) = (1 - x^2)^{-1/2}$.

Let's look at the interpolation properties of the Chebyshev points. The points are given by $x_k = \cos\left(\frac{2k+1}{2n+2}\pi\right)$ for $k = 0, 1, \ldots, n$. We'll use the Runge function (see Section 4.1), which we know is a difficult function for equally spaced points. Enter:

```
» clear all
» f=inline('1./(1+25*x.^2)')
» n=8;k=0:n;
» x=-1:.01:1;
» xc=cos(pi*(2*k+1)/(2*n+2))          %Chebyshev points.
» xl=-1:.25:1                         %Equally spaced points.
» xr=2*rand([1 9])-1                  %Randomly chosen points.
» xu=[-.95 -.8 -.6 -.3 0 .3 .6 .8 .95] %Unequally spaced points.
» pc=polyfit(xc,f(xc),8);
» pl=polyfit(xl,f(xl),8);
» pr=polyfit(xr,f(xr),8);
» pu=polyfit(xu,f(xu),8);
» yc=polyval(pc,x);
» yl=polyval(pl,x);
» yr=polyval(pr,x);
» yu=polyval(pu,x);
» plot(x,yc,'b',x,yl,'r',x,yr,'y',x,yu,'g',x,f(x),'k'), grid
```

If the yellow (random nodes) curve makes it difficult to see the differences between the other curves, close that figure and enter:

```
» plot(x,yc,'b',x,yl,'r',x,yu,'g',x,f(x),'k'),grid
```

The blue curve should be the best fit to the black curve. Enter:

```
» max(abs(yc-f(x)))
» max(abs(yl-f(x)))
» max(abs(yr-f(x)))
» max(abs(yu-f(x)))
```

The error is least for the Chebyshev nodes. Repeat this for a higher n (recall that interpolation by high-degree polynomials is usually a bad idea, especially with equally spaced nodes).

Of course, the Runge function is a particularly difficult function for interpolation; try this experiment again using $f(x) = \sin(x)$. Make a reasonable choice for xu (by eye). Try to beat the Chebyshev points by a smart choice of nodes for this particular function. You won't succeed in doing so.

ADDITIONAL PROBLEMS 5.4

6. Show that the Chebyshev polynomials are defined by Eq. (5.30) by proving directly that $\int_{-1}^{1} T_k(x)T_l(x)w(x)dx = 0$ if $k \neq l$ $(w(x) = (1 - x^2)^{-1/2})$, and then showing that $T_n(x)$ is monic.

7. a. Show that the nth Legendre polynomial contains only even powers of x and is an even function if n is even, and contains only odd powers of x and is an odd function if n is odd.

   b. Show that the nth Chebyshev polynomial of the first kind contains only even powers of x and is an even function if n is even and contains only odd powers of x and is an odd function if n is odd.

8. a. Prove that the three-term recurrence relation Eq. (5.28) is correct by first arguing that it is possible to write $p_{n+1}(x) = xp_n(x) - \alpha_{n+1}p_n(x) - \beta_{n+1}p_{n-1}(x) - \cdots - \gamma_{n+1}p_0(x)$ and then considering (p_{n+1}, p_n).

   b. Prove that Eq. (5.31) is correct.

9. Use the Gauss-Chebyshev rules of the first and second kind based on 5, 10, 15, 20 points to estimate the area under the Runge function. Do the same with the closed and open Newton-Cotes formulas based on 5, 10, 15, 20 points.

10. a. Prove that the Chebyshev nodes are given by Eq. (5.33).

   b. Prove that the extrema of $T_n(x)$ are given by $y_k = \cos(k\pi/n)$, $k = 0, 1, \ldots, n$. What is $T_n(y_k)$?

11. a. The Chebyshev polynomials of the second kind $U_n(x)$ satisfy $U_n(x) = \sin((n+1)\arccos(x))/\left(1 - x^2\right)^{1/2}$. What properties of $U_n(x)$ can you deduce from this relation?

   b. Verify the recurrence relations $U_{n+1}(x) - 2xU_n(x) + U_{n-1}(x) = 0$, $T_n(x) = U_n(x) - xU_{n-1}(x)$, $(1 - x^2)U_{n-1}(x) = xT_n(x) - T_{n+1}(x)$, and $T_n'(x) = nU_{n-1}(x)$.

12. Write a MATLAB program that accepts a function, a finite interval of integration, and a positive integer N and returns the integral of the function as approximated by the Gauss-Legendre rule based on N points. Test it on several functions.

13. a. Write a MATLAB program that accepts a function, a finite interval of integration, and a positive integer N and returns the integral of the function as approximated by the Gauss-Chebyshev rule of the first kind based on N points. Test it on several functions.

   b. Extend your program so that it accepts an additional positive integer m and performs N-point composite Gauss-Chebyshev quadrature on m panels. Test it on several functions.

14. Write a MATLAB program that accepts a function, an interval of integration of the form $(-\infty, b]$ or $[a, \infty)$, and a positive integer N and returns the integral of the function as approximated by the Gauss-Laguerre rule of the first kind based on N points.

15. The orthogonal polynomials generated by $w(x) = \exp(-x^2)$ and the interval $(-\infty, \infty)$ are the Hermite polynomials. Write a MATLAB program that accepts a function, an interval of integration of the form $(-\infty, \infty)$, and a positive integer N and returns the integral of the function as approximated by the Gauss-Hermite rule of the first kind based on N points. Test it on several functions.

5.5 Radau and Lobatto Quadrature

Suppose we perform approximate integration by a weighted-average rule and are unhappy with the error in our result. How can we refine it? The adaptive recursive method described in MATLAB 5.1 is one way. For Newton-Cotes rules we can simply add new points in the middle of each panel, allowing us to reuse the already computed values of $f(x_i)$ at the old nodes (as in quad). Unfortunately the Gauss nodes of a rule based on $n + 1$ points don't appear in any other Gauss rule in that family (with the possible exception of the origin), so if we double the number of points we must compute f-values at all nodes, not just half of them. This is inefficient, even leaving aside the difficulty of finding the nodes as roots of a polynomial of high degree.

Automatic Integration

We say that a method or program performs **automatic integration** if it accepts an integrand, interval and tolerance and then returns either the value of the integral to within that tolerance or an error message stating that the tolerance was not met (possibly because a limit such as the maximum recursion level or maximum number of function evaluations was exceeded). Every program you are likely to encounter for performing integration will be an automatic integrator.

If we want an automatic integrator based on increasing the number of points in the weighted average, we must have that

$$\sum_{i=0}^{n} w_i f(x_i) \rightarrow \int_{a}^{b} f(x) w(x) dx$$

as $n \rightarrow \infty$; that is, the rule must converge to the integral as n increases. If the interval of integration is finite, then every interpolatory rule that has nonnegative weights (for all n) converges for all Riemann integrable functions. (In particular, it converges for all continuous and piecewise continuous functions.) Hence, all Gauss rules converge. The simple Newton-Cotes rules can diverge.

Conditioning   There's another important advantage of Gauss rules. The condition number of a weighted-average rule is

$$K = \sum_{i=0}^{n} |w_i|,$$

(the Ω_n of Section 5.1), and so the larger this value is, the worse the results we expect. The condition number in this case bounds the effect of a perturbation $\tilde{f}$ of the integrand f as

$$E \leq K \max |\tilde{f} - f|, \tag{5.34}$$

where E is the absolute difference of the quadrature rule applied to the perturbed function $\tilde{f}$ and the quadrature rule applied to f itself. Small errors in evaluating f can be multiplied by a factor as large as the sum of the absolute values of the weights.

Which quadrature rules are well-conditioned? For the Newton-Cotes rules we know that

$$\sum_{i=0}^{n} |w_i| \rightarrow \infty$$

as $n \rightarrow \infty$, so they are ill-conditioned for large n. For the Gauss-Chebyshev rule, however,

$$\sum_{i=0}^{n} |w_i| = \sum_{i=0}^{n} \frac{\pi}{n+1}$$
$$= \pi,$$

so this method is well-conditioned for all n, as is the Gauss-Chebyshev rule of the second kind, which has a slightly smaller condition number. For the Gauss-Legendre rule,

$$\sum_{i=0}^{n} |w_i| = b - a,$$

so this rule is well-conditioned unless the interval of integration is very large. Gauss rules are generally well-conditioned.[7]

---

[7] Quadrature rules with nonnegative weights generally have better conditioning than those with weights of mixed sign.

Pre-Assigned Nodes

How can we build an automatic integrator based on a Gauss rule? Using it recursively or as a composite rule is possible, but there is another approach that is widely used and is the basis of several methods. The idea of this other approach stems from this question: Suppose we want to use an interpolatory rule based on $n + 1$ points, of which $m < n + 1$ have already been chosen (called the **pre-assigned nodes** or **pre-assigned abscissas**); how should we choose the remaining $n + 1 - m$ points so as to maximize the degree of accuracy of the resulting method? Gauss rules answer the question for $m = 0$, but now imagine the case where we have used a Gauss rule based on m points and wish to improve upon the approximation by using a rule based on $n + 1 > m$ points. We're going to give up the $2n + 1$ degree of accuracy we could obtain by using a Gauss rule in favor of the efficiency of being able to reuse the values

$$f(x_0), f(x_1), \ldots, f(x_{m-1}),$$

which are already computed, and are retained, from the previous rule. The degree of accuracy of the new rule is roughly the degree of accuracy of the old rule ($2m - 1$ for a Gauss rule based on m points) plus the number of points added ($n + 1 - m$).

Such techniques are not only useful for improving an estimate. How does an automatic integrator know if the tolerance has been met? Unlike our examples, the program won't know the true value of the integral. An automatic integrator generally monitors the error by computing the integral twice, at two different resolutions, and using these values to generate an estimate of the absolute error. This was hinted at in MATLAB 5.1 and is explored more fully in Section 5.6. This will be much more efficient if function values can be reused.

Suppose that we intend to use a Gauss rule recursively. For the sake of definiteness, let $[a, b] = [-1, 1]$. We might first apply the rule with $n + 1$ points over $[-1, 1]$ and then apply it with $2n + 1$ points over the same interval, allowing us to estimate the error. If the error is acceptable, we could stop and take as our result the estimate based on more points; if it isn't, we could apply both rules over $[-1, 0]$ and $[0, 1]$ and see which of these is the problematic interval (see Fig. 5.9). Since the interval over which we are applying the rule is smaller each time, the result should be better.

But if we use a Gauss rule on $[-1, 1]$, then none of the function evaluations will be usable for the application of that same rule on $[-1, 0]$! (Recall that all Gauss rules are open.) What if we use an "almost" Gauss rule that has pre-assigned abscissas $a = -1$, $b = 1$ and also use an odd number of points. Then when we apply the rule to the whole

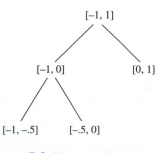

Figure 5.9 Recursive Integrator.

interval of integration $[-1, 1]$ we'd have to evaluate $f(-1)$, $f(0)$, and $f(1)$. We'd be able to use $f(-1)$ and $f(0)$ on the subinterval $[-1, 0]$, and $f(0)$ and $f(1)$ on the subinterval $[0, 1]$.

Lobatto Rule

The weighted-average rule based on $n + 1$ points for the interval $[-1, 1]$ that has the pre-assigned abscissas $x_0 = -1, x_n = 1$ and the maximum achievable degree of accuracy is called the **Lobatto quadrature rule** and is given by

$$\int_{-1}^{1} f(x)dx \approx \frac{2}{n(n+1)}(f(-1) + f(1)) + \sum_{i=1}^{n-1} w_i f(x_i),$$

where the nodes $x_1, \ldots, x_{n-1}$ are the $n - 1$ zeroes of $p_n'(x)$, the derivative of the Legendre polynomial of degree n, and the weights are given by

$$w_i = \frac{2}{n(n+1)k_n^2 p_n^2(x_i)} \tag{5.35}$$

$(i = 1, 2, \ldots, n - 1)$, where

$$k_n = \frac{(2n)!}{2^n (n!)^2}$$

is the leading coefficient of the nth Legendre polynomial when it is generated in a different way (and is not monic).[8] The zeroes of $p_n'(x)$ don't intersect those of $p_n(x)$, so this is well-defined. The error has the form

$$E = c_n f^{(2n)}(\gamma) \tag{5.36}$$

for some complicated c_n, and so the method has degree of accuracy $2n - 1$. This is 2 less than the maximum possible degree of accuracy $2n + 1$ (attained when we are free to choose the locations of all nodes) which makes intuitive sense; we have given up two degrees of freedom in insisting upon $x_0 = -1$ and $x_n = 1$.

Radau Rule

The weighted-average rule based on $n + 1$ points for the interval $[-1, 1]$ that has the pre-assigned abscissa $x_0 = -1$ and the maximum achievable degree of accuracy is called the **Radau quadrature rule** and is given by

$$\int_{-1}^{1} f(x)dx \approx \frac{2}{(n+1)^2} f(-1) + \sum_{i=1}^{n} w_i f(x_i),$$

where the nodes $x_1, \ldots, x_n$ are the n zeroes of

$$\frac{k_n p_n(x) + k_{n+1} p_{n+1}(x)}{x - 1}$$

(with $p_n(x)$ the monic Legendre polynomial of degree n) and the weights are given by

$$w_i = \frac{1 - x_i}{(n+1)^2 k_n^2 p_n^2(x_i)} \tag{5.37}$$

$(i = 1, 2, \ldots, n)$. The error has the form

$$E = d_n f^{(2n+1)}(\gamma)$$

---

[8] The recursion relation for the Legendre polynomials with leading coefficient k_n is $P_0(x) = 1$, $P_1(x) = x$, and $P_{n+1}(x) = \frac{2n+1}{n+1} x P_n(x) - \frac{n}{n+1} P_{n-1}(x)$. In this form $P_n(1) = 1$ for all n.

for some complicated d_n, and so the method has degree of accuracy $2n$. This is 1 less than the maximum possible degree of accuracy $2n + 1$ (attained when we are free to choose the locations of all nodes) which makes intuitive sense; we have given up one degree of freedom in insisting upon $x_0 = -1$. A Radau rule may also be defined with $x_n = 1$ pre-assigned and x_0 free (this is the **Radau right-hand formula; the Radau left-hand formula** was described above).

The Radau quadrature rule is useful in the numerical solution of ordinary differential equations. The Lobatto quadrature rule is used for automatic integration, for example, in the MATLAB `quadl` routine. Rules of this form, that have some pre-assigned abscissas with the remaining abscissas chosen so as to achieve the maximal degree of accuracy, are called **Gauss-type rules with pre-assigned abscissas.**

Clearly, having to find the nodes by solving for the zeroes numerically and then having to find the weights using Eq. (5.35) or Eq. (5.37) could be a time-consuming and error-prone undertaking, though Newton's method tends to work well for finding the nodes for moderate n. Typically a program does not perform Lobatto quadrature for an arbitrary n but rather performs automatic integration using the Lobatto rule for two fixed numbers of points, or uses a Lobatto rule followed by some other, more accurate, rule. The nodes and weights are listed numerically in the program.[9] Programs are available that perform Lobatto quadrature for arbitrary n, but they usually use a different approach for finding the weights; for example, one method is based on first forming a certain special matrix that has the nodes as its eigenvalues, and then finding the weights using its eigenvectors.

Example 5.5.1   Let's determine the Lobatto rule based on $n + 1 = 4$ points. Two of those points are $x_0 = -1$ and $x_3 = 1$. The remaining points x_1 and x_2 are the zeroes of

$$p_3'(x) = \left(x^3 - \frac{3}{5}x \right)'$$

$$= 3x^2 - \frac{3}{5},$$

so $x_1 = -1/\sqrt{5}$, $x_2 = 1/\sqrt{5}$. The weights are

$$w_1 = \frac{2}{12k_3^2 p_3^2(x_1)}$$

$$= \frac{1}{6 \left(\frac{6!}{8(3!)^2} \right)^2 \left(x_1^3 - \frac{3}{5}x_1 \right)^2}$$

$$= \frac{5}{6}$$

$$w_2 = \frac{2}{12k_3^2 p_3^2(x_2)}$$

$$= \frac{5}{6}$$

---

[9] The *Handbook of Mathematical Functions* edited by Abramowitz and Stegun lists the nodes and weights for Lobatto quadrature through 10 points, to 10 decimal places.

and $w_0 = w_3 = 2/12 = 1/6$. Thus the weights are

$$w \doteq (0.1667, 0.8333, 0.8333, 0.1667)^T$$

$$= \frac{1}{6}(1, 5, 5, 1)^T$$

(you can find the line defining these weights in `quadl`). Note once again that the endpoints are given lesser weight than the interior points. The nodes are always symmetric about the origin for Lobatto quadrature, and the weights of symmetric points are equal.

Let's use this rule on $\int_{-1}^{1} \frac{1}{e^x+1} dx = 1$. We already have the weights and the nodes, so we compute

$$\int_{-1}^{1} \frac{1}{e^x + 1} dx \approx \frac{1}{6} f(-1) + \frac{5}{6} f\left(-\frac{1}{\sqrt{5}}\right) + \frac{5}{6} f\left(\frac{1}{\sqrt{5}}\right) + \frac{1}{6} f(1)$$

$$\doteq 1$$

to the precision available, which is impressive for only 4 points. If we use the 4 point Lobatto rule on $\int_{-1}^{1} \sin(x) dx$, we have $\int_{-1}^{1} \sin(x) dx \approx 2.7756E - 17$, which is also an excellent approximation. ■

With the 4 point Lobatto quadrature algorithm we could approximate $\int_{-1}^{1} f(x) dx$ using $f(-1)$, $f(-1/\sqrt{5})$, $f(1/\sqrt{5})$, $f(1)$ and then refine our estimate by computing $\int_{-1}^{0} f(x) dx$ and $\int_{0}^{1} f(x) dx$ using the same rule. The Lobatto rule is such that we would need to compute only 2 new function values in $[-1, 0]$ and 2 new function values in $[0, 1]$ to get a new estimate of $\int_{-1}^{1} f(x) dx = \int_{-1}^{0} f(x) dx + \int_{0}^{1} f(x) dx$. This is the same cost in function evaluations as for the initial estimate. A true Gauss rule would require 6 new function evaluations if 0 was a node (odd number of points) and 8 new function evaluations otherwise (even number of points).

Error   A scheme like this, and any composite scheme, relies on the following theorem, which is complementary to the result on convergence as $n \to \infty$ given at the beginning of this section.

Theorem 5.5.1

A weighted-average rule for $\int_a^b w(x) f(x) dx$ that has degree of accuracy $d \geq 0$ satisfies

$$E = O(h^{d+2})$$

as $h = b - a \to 0$, for any function f that is at least $d + 1$ times continuously differentiable on $[a, b]$.

(This error estimate applies to the simple form of the quadrature rule; we expect $O(h^{d+1})$ behavior for the composite form.) Hence, if f is sufficiently differentiable and the rule integrates constants correctly, then the error in using the rule on a smaller and smaller subinterval goes to zero like h^{d+2}, which is at least h^2. For a rule like 4 point Lobatto quadrature which has degree of accuracy 7, this predicts that the error will decay like h^9. In other words, if the error in approximating $\int_{-1}^{1} f(x)dx$ is about ch^9, then the error in the approximation of $\int_{-1}^{0} f(x)dx$ or $\int_{0}^{1} f(x)dx$ is about $ch^9/2^9$ (neglecting roundoff error). The 4 point Lobatto rule is the basis of the MATLAB routine `quadl`, which, as you may recall, is recommended for smooth problems.

Example 5.5.2   Let's integrate $f(x) = \sin^2(x)$ over $[-1, 1]$. The correct value is 0.54535128658716. The 4 point Lobatto rule gives 0.54771978564889 for an absolute error of $\alpha_0 \doteq$ .00236849906173. Now we'll repeat over two subintervals, using Eq. (5.19)

$$\int_a^b g(t)dt = \frac{b-a}{2} \int_{-1}^1 g(t(x))dx,$$

where $t(x) = ((b-a)x + b + a)/2$. In our case this gives

$$\int_{-1}^0 \sin^2(t)dt = \frac{0-(-1)}{2} \int_{-1}^1 \sin^2(x)dx$$

$$= \frac{1}{2} \int_{-1}^1 \sin^2\left(\frac{(x-1)}{2}\right)dx.$$

(We could have mapped the nodes in $[-1, 1]$ to nodes in $[-1, 0]$ instead). The Lobatto rule now gives

$$\int_{-1}^0 \sin^2(x)dx \approx \frac{1}{2}\left(\frac{1}{6}f_{1,1}(-1) + \frac{5}{6}f_{1,1}\left(-\frac{1}{\sqrt{5}}\right) + \frac{5}{6}f_{1,1}\left(\frac{1}{\sqrt{5}}\right) + \frac{1}{6}f_{1,1}(1)\right)$$

$$\doteq 0.27268670270676$$

(where $f_{1,1}(x) = \sin^2((x-1)/2)$). Note that $f_{1,1}(-1) = f(-1) = \sin^2(-1)$ and $f_{1,1}(1) = f(0) = \sin^2(0)$, so we can reuse two function values here. Since $\int_{-1}^0 \sin^2(x)dx \doteq 0.27267564329358$, the absolute error is $\alpha_{1,1} \doteq 1.105941318502168E - 5$. Similarly,

$$\int_0^1 \sin^2(t)dt = \frac{1-0}{2} \int_{-1}^1 \sin^2\left(\frac{(x+1)}{2}\right)dx$$

$$\approx \frac{1}{2}\left(\frac{1}{6}f_{1,2}(-1) + \frac{5}{6}f_{1,2}\left(-\frac{1}{\sqrt{5}}\right) + \frac{5}{6}f_{1,2}\left(\frac{1}{\sqrt{5}}\right) + \frac{1}{6}f_{1,2}(1)\right)$$

$$\doteq 0.27268670270676$$

(where $f_{1,2}(x) = \sin^2((x+1)/2)$). Again note that $f_{1,2}(-1) = f(0)$ and $f_{1,2}(1) = f(1)$ have already been computed. We have

$$\alpha_{1,2} = \alpha_{1,1} \doteq 1.105941318502168E - 5$$

because $f(x)$ is an even function. Our new estimate of $\int_{-1}^{1} \sin^2(x)dx$ is $0.27268670270676 + 0.27268670270676 = 0.54537340541353$ with error

$$\alpha_1 \doteq 2.211882637004337E - 5.$$

Compared to the original error $\alpha_0 \doteq 2.368499061730000E - 3$, this is a considerable improvement.

From Theorem 5.5.1, if $\alpha_0 \doteq 2.368499061730000E - 3$ then we expect that $\alpha_{1,1} \approx \alpha_0/2^9 = 4.6260E - 6$. We didn't get results that good, but then we have taken only one step and h has only gone from $h = 2$ to $h = 1$. ■

Kronrod   More generally, we might apply a Gauss rule based on m points to an integral on
Extension $[-1, 1]$ and then wish to approximate the same integral with a Gauss rule based on $n + 1$ points, $n + 1 > m$. Because of efficiency concerns we would probably use a Gauss-type rule (based on $n + 1$ points) instead, with the first m abscissas pre-assigned so that we could reuse the corresponding function values. A special case of this is **Gauss-Kronrod quadrature** (or **Kronrod extension**), which uses $n = 2m$ and generates a Gauss-type rule based on $2m + 1$ points using the m pre-assigned abscissas. (The m previous weights must be discarded, however.) The new nodes interlace with the old nodes, and the resulting rule has degree of accuracy $3m + 1$ if m is even and $3m + 2$ if m is odd.

Kronrod extensions also exist for the Radau and Lobatto rules. If you look carefully at the MATLAB routine `quadl` you'll see the following lines:

```
% Four point Lobatto quadrature.
Q1 = (h/6)*[1 5 5 1]*y(1:2:7)';
% Seven point Kronrod refinement.
Q2 = (h/1470)*[77 432 625 672 625 432 77]*y';
```

The routine uses the same 4 point Lobatto rule we have been using, which uses four values of the previously computed vector y of function values (y_1, y_3, y_5, and y_7), followed by a Gauss-type rule that reuses those values and also uses the remaining three values of y (y_2, y_4, and y_6). This doesn't take a 4 point rule to a 9 point rule, because when this technique is applied to the Radau or Lobatto rules we don't consider the pre-assigned absicissas; that is, a Kronrod extension of a Lobatto rule based on m points gives a new rule based on $2(m - 2) + 1 + 2$ points (double the number $m - 2$ of points that were not pre-assigned in the original rule, add 1, and then add back in the 2 pre-assigned abscissas). For the 4 point Lobatto rule, $m - 2 = 2$ points are not pre-assigned, leading to a $2(m - 2) + 1 + 2 = 7$ point Kronrod extension.

The Radau and Lobatto rules can be generalized to give a weighted-average rule of the form

$$\int_{-1}^{1} w(x)f(x)dx \approx \sum_{i=0}^{n} w_i f(x_i)$$

with similar properties, where $w(x)$ is any admissable weight function. It is not possible to generalize the Gauss-Kronrod rules for every admissible weight function though it is possible in some cases.

PROBLEMS 5.5

1. Show that the 4 point Lobatto rule is exact for odd functions. What other rules is this true of?

2. Use the 4 point Lobatto rule to estimate $\int_{-1}^{1} \cos(x^2)dx$ and $\int_{-1}^{1} \sin^2(x)dx$.

3. Use the 4 point Lobatto rule recursively to estimate $\int_{-1}^{1} \exp(x)dx$ to within $1E-6$.

4. **a.** What are the nodes and weights in the 3 point Lobatto rule? Use the Legendre polynomial to determine the nodes and Eq. (5.35) to determine the weights. Use your result to explain the fact that Simpson's rule has a higher degree of accuracy than would normally be expected of a quadratic interpolatory rule.

   b. What are the nodes and weights in the 5 point Lobatto rule?

5. Find the first three Radau quadrature rules, and use them to estimate $\int_{-1}^{1} \exp(x)dx$.

MATLAB 5.5

The method of undetermined coefficients, also called the **method of moments** because the integrals $\int_{a}^{b} w(x)x^k dx$ are called **moments,** can be used to find the nodes and weights of Radau, Lobatto, and similar rules. Let's use this technique to find the 4 point Lobatto rule. The nodes $x_0 = -1$ and $x_3 = 1$ are pre-assigned, and we need to find x_1, x_2, w_0, w_1, w_2, and w_3. The rule with $n + 1 = 4$ points should have degree of accuracy 5. The equations are

$$w_0 \cdot 1 + w_1 \cdot 1 + w_2 \cdot 1 + w_3 \cdot 1 = \int_{-1}^{1} 1 dx$$
$$= 2$$

$$w_0 \cdot -1 + w_1 \cdot x_1 + w_2 \cdot x_2 + w_3 \cdot 1 = \int_{-1}^{1} x dx$$
$$= 0$$

$$w_0 \cdot 1 + w_1 \cdot x_1^2 + w_2 \cdot x_2^2 + w_3 \cdot 1 = \int_{-1}^{1} x^2 dx$$
$$= \frac{2}{3}$$

$$w_0 \cdot -1 + w_1 \cdot x_1^3 + w_2 \cdot x_2^3 + w_3 \cdot 1 = \int_{-1}^{1} x^3 dx$$
$$= 0$$

$$w_0 \cdot 1 + w_1 \cdot x_1^4 + w_2 \cdot x_2^4 + w_3 \cdot 1 = \int_{-1}^{1} x^4 dx$$
$$= \frac{2}{5}$$

$$w_0 \cdot -1 + w_1 \cdot x_1^5 + w_2 \cdot x_2^5 + w_3 \cdot 1 = \int_{-1}^{1} x^5 dx$$
$$= 0;$$

that is,

$$w_0 + w_1 + w_2 + w_3 = 2$$

$$-w_0 + w_1 x_1 + w_2 x_2 + w_3 = 0$$

$$w_0 + w_1 x_1^2 + w_2 x_2^2 + w_3 = \frac{2}{3}$$

$$-w_0 + w_1 x_1^3 + w_2 x_2^3 + w_3 = 0$$

$$w_0 + w_1 x_1^4 + w_2 x_2^4 + w_3 = \frac{2}{5}$$

$$-w_0 + w_1 x_1^5 + w_2 x_2^5 + w_3 = 0,$$

which is a nonlinear system of 6 equations in 6 unknowns. Let's see if Maple can solve this system using its `solve` command (from the Symbolic Toolbox). For information on this command, enter:

```
» help solve
```

(and `mhelp solve` for even more information). Enter:

```
» S=solve('w0+w1+w2+w3=2','-w0+w1*x1+w2*x2+w3=0', ...
    'w0+w1*x1^2+w2*x2^2+w3=2/3','-w0+w1*x1^3+w2*x2^3+w3=0', ...
    'w0+w1*x1^4+w2*x2^4+w3=2/5','-w0+w1*x1^5+w2*x2^5+w3=0')
```

and be patient. A symbolic answer is indicated. It is in the form of a structure (see `help struct` and MATLAB 6.4), so to get the individual components that we need we must access the proper fields. Enter:

```
» fieldnames(SS)
» S.w0
» S.w1
» S.w2
» S.w3
» S.x1
» S.x2
```

The first entries in each field correspond to one solution, and the second entries correspond to a second solution. This is because we did not indicate that $x_1 < x_2$. The solution is correct (note that `1/5*5^(1/2)` is equal to `1/sqrt(5)`).

If `solve` had failed we might have needed to find a numerical solution. The Maple floating point arithmetic system solver is `fsolve`. Enter:

```
» mhelp fsolve
» help maple
» s1='{w0+w1+w2+w3=2,-w0+w1*x1+w2*x2+w3=0,'
» s2='w0+w1*x1^2+w2*x2^2+w3=2/3,'
» s3='-w0+w1*x1^3+w2*x2^3+w3=0,'
» s4='w0+w1*x1^4+w2*x2^4+w3=2/5,'
» s5='-w0+w1*x1^5+w2*x2^5+w3=0}'
» s=[s1,s2,s3,s4,s5];
```

```
» t='{w0,w1,w2,w3,x1,x2}';
» maple('fsolve',s,t)
```

The answer is correct. If necessary, we could add search ranges. Enter:

```
» u1='{w0=0..1,w1=0..1,w2=0..1,w3=0..1';
» u=[u1,',x1=-1..0,x2=0..1}'];
» maple('fsolve',s,t,u)
```

The weights and nodes are found correctly again, as expected, but much more rapidly because the search range has been limited.

ADDITIONAL PROBLEMS 5.5

6. Compare the 4 point Radau and Lobatto rules experimentally. Comment.

7. Write a MATLAB program that accepts a function, an interval, and a tolerance and returns an estimate of the integral of the function over that interval. Your program should use the 4 point Lobatto rule followed by the 7 point Kronrod extension to get two estimates of the integral and terminate if the absolute difference between these two estimates is less than the tolerance; otherwise it should subdivide the interval into 6 new panels defined by the 7 points you've already computed and repeat this procedure. (This is the idea of `quadl`.) Make efficient use of previously computed function values.

8. The constant c_n in Eq. (5.36) is negative. Compare Eq. (5.36) based on $n + 1$ points to Eq. (5.27) based on n points; show that if $f^{(2n)}(x)$ is of one sign on the interval of integration, then the Gauss-Legendre rule based on n points and the Lobatto rule based on $n + 1$ points bracket the true value of the integral (neglecting round-off error). Since the constants in each of the error terms are comparable in magnitude, the weighted average of $(n + 1)/(2n + 1)$ times the Gauss-Legendre rule based on n points and $n/(2n + 1)$ times the Lobatto rule based on $n + 1$ points is typically a more accurate estimate of the integral than either rule alone. Demonstrate this experimentally.

9. **a.** Argue that it is reasonable to define the condition number of a numerical integration problem as the smallest value K that satisfies Eq. (5.34).

b. Note that K depends on both f and the quadrature rule, in general; show that the definition in part (a) implies that $K = \sum_{i=0}^{n} |w_i|$ by taking appropriate norms on both sides of Eq. (5.34).

10. Derive the 3 point Lobatto rule by fixing $x_0 = a$ and $x_2 = b$ and then using the method of undetermined coefficients.

11. Derive the 3 point Radau rule by fixing $x_0 = a$ and then using the method of undetermined coefficients.

12. Create a table of the condition numbers of all rules for which you have the explicit coefficients. Comment.

13. Write a MATLAB program that performs Radau quadrature for an arbitrary n. Use the formulas given in this section for the nodes (you may use the MATLAB `roots` command) and the weights.

14. **a.** Find the first three right-hand Radau formulas.

b. What are the first three right-hand Radau formulas transformed to an arbitrary finite interval $[a, b]$?

15. **a.** What are the first three Lobatto rules with respect to the first Chebyshev weight function $w(x) = 1/\sqrt{1 - x^2}$?

b. What are the first three Lobatto rules with respect to the second Chebyshev weight function $w(x) = \sqrt{1 - x^2}$?

5.6 Adaptivity and Automatic Integration

Riemann Sum Rules

We've skipped over some very simple quadrature rules. The composite midpoint rule may be modified to allow for unequally spaced points: Let $x_0, x_1, \ldots, x_n$ be ordered points in (a, b) and define $x_{-1} = a$, $x_{n+1} = b$. Let $h_i = x_{i+1} - x_i$. Then we can center a

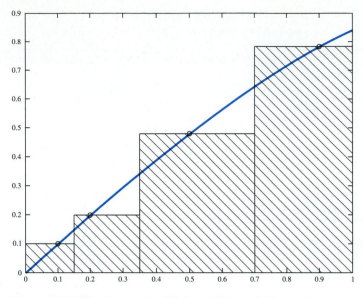

Figure 5.10 The Composite Midpoint Rule with Unequally Spaced Points.

rectangle at x_i with width

$$w_i = \frac{h_i}{2} + \frac{h_{i+1}}{2}$$

(see Fig. 5.10) and use the rule

$$\int_a^b f(x)dx \approx \sum_{i=0}^n w_i f(x_i)$$

to approximate the integral. (Note that the nodes are no longer truly midpoints of the interval; we could use the midpoints of the intervals defined by $x_0, x_1, \ldots, x_n$ if we have f but not if we have only a list of values $f(x_0), f(x_1), \ldots, f(x_n)$.) We could use a similar approach for the trapezoidal rule with unequally spaced nodes.

The midpoint rule is one of several rules that explicitly form a Riemann sum to approximate an integral and so are called **Riemann sum rules.** (Many other rules can be shown to be equivalent to a Riemann sum.) Other examples include the **left endpoint rule,** where we choose a number of panels and approximate the area under f over panel $[x_i, x_{i+1}]$ by the area of the rectangle with height $f(x_i)$ and width $h_i = x_{i+1} - x_i$; the **right endpoint rule,** where we approximate the area under f over panel $[x_i, x_{i+1}]$ by the area of the rectangle with height $f(x_{i+1})$ and width h_i; and Monte Carlo methods, where we generate a list of nodes $x_0, x_1, \ldots, x_n$ pseudorandomly and then apply any of these methods. All these rules are exact for constants, and so Theorem 5.5.1 applies; that is, the error goes to zero at least like h^2 on a single panel of width h, and hence it goes to zero like h for the sum of the contributions over all subintervals of the whole interval (as discussed in Section 5.1). Riemann sum rules are $O(h)$; the midpoint rule is an exception ($O(h^2)$).

A surprising amount can be said about rules that are exact for constants. Theorem 5.5.1, concerning, the order of the error as $h \to 0$, is just one such result. We also have the following theorem:

Theorem 5.6.1

A weighted-average rule for $\int_a^b f(x)dx$ with degree of accuracy $d \geq 0$ has absolute error E that satisfies

$$E \leq (b - a + K) \min \left(\max_{x \in [a,b]} (|p(x) - f(x)|) \right),$$

where the minimum is taken over all polynomials with degree at most d.

Proof.

It's convenient to write $Qf = \sum_{i=0}^n w_i f(x_i)$ and $\int f = \int_a^b f(x)dx$. The absolute error then satsifies

$$E = \left| Qf - \int f \right|$$

$$= \left| Qf + Qp - Qp + \int p - \int p - \int f \right|$$

$$= \left| Qf - Qp + \int p - \int f \right|$$

for any polynomial $p(x)$ of degree at most d because the rule is exact for such polynomials. So

$$E \leq |Qf - Qp| + \left| \int p - \int f \right|$$

$$= |Q(f - p)| + \left| \int (p - f) \right|$$

by the linearity of both the quadrature rule and integration. But

$$|Q(f - p)| = \left| \sum_{i=0}^n w_i (f(x_i) - p(x_i)) \right|$$

$$\leq \sum_{i=0}^n |w_i| \, |f(x_i) - p(x_i)|$$

$$\leq K \max_{x \in [a,b]} (|p(x) - f(x)|)$$

and

$$\left| \int (p - f) \right| = \left| \int_a^b (p - f) dx \right|$$

$$\leq \int_a^b |p - f| \, dx$$

$$\leq \int_a^b \max_{x \in [a,b]} (|p(x) - f(x)|) \, dx$$

$$= (b - a) \max_{x \in [a,b]} (|p(x) - f(x)|),$$

so

$$E \leq K \max_{x \in [a,b]} (|p(x) - f(x)|) + (b - a) \max_{x \in [a,b]} (|p(x) - f(x)|)$$

$$= (b - a + K) \max_{x \in [a,b]} (|p(x) - f(x)|)$$

for *every* polynomial $p(x)$ of degree at most d. In particular, this is true for the polynomial that minimizes

$$\max_{x \in [a,b]} (|p(x) - f(x)|).$$

This is the desired result.   ■

This theorem is easily modified to allow for a weight function in the integral. Clearly a higher degree of accuracy will mean a better result if K is bounded, as it is for the Gauss-Chebyshev rules and the Gauss-Legendre rule, since

$$\min \left(\max_{x \in [a,b]} (|p(x) - f(x)|) \right) = \min_{x \in P_d} \left(\| p(x) - f(x) \|_\infty \right)$$

can only decrease as d increases, because the space of all polynomials of degree at most d, P_d, is a subset of the space of all polynomials of degree at most m, P_m, if $m > d$.

We now have theoretical justification for improving the accuracy of our approximate integrations by increasing the degree of accuracy of our method (say, by using the Gauss-Legendre family of rules based on an increasing number of points), due to Theorem 5.6.1, or by using a fixed method in a composite manner and relying on the $O(h^{d+1})$ behavior promised by Theorem 5.5.1 for sufficiently differentiable functions. The latter approach is usually more efficient—do we really want to have to find the 101 nodes for a Gauss rule based on $n + 1 = 101$ points by repeated application of Newton's method? Furthermore, if time constraints limit us to about 101 function evaluations, wouldn't we be better off choosing them adaptively, that is, putting more where the function is changing more rapidly and fewer where it is changing more slowly, as a recursively called composite rule could do?

We've discussed some special-purpose routines for special situations. When you have to write your own code (which is generally not advisable if a professionally produced routine, such as the free codes at Netlib, will serve your purposes), and you know that you will be handling certain types of integrals with certain properties, you'll want to choose a rule that fits your needs. This may mean recognizing that a weight function appears naturally in your integrand, or that your problems always involve unbounded intervals or singular integrands; or, it may involve utilizing the availability of advanced computer architectures, or making speed versus accuracy trade-offs. Fortunately there are many rules from which to choose.

Rules for Automatic Integration

But how do we choose a rule for a general-purpose automatic integrator where f may or may not be well-behaved? To put it another way, why did the makers of MATLAB choose Simpson's rule and Lobatto quadrature, implemented recursively, as their integration routines? Why did the makers of Maple choose a Clenshaw-Curtis method as their general-purpose routine, with an option for a Newton-Cotes rule? What qualities should we be looking for in an automatic integrator that attempts to use adaptive methods to achieve a desired error tolerance as efficiently as possible? And exactly how does it determine whether the error is as small as desired?

A low-order Newton-Cotes rule such as Simpson's rule has the advantages of being simple and requiring less smoothness of the function. Simpson's rule has an error term involving $f^{(4)}(x)$, and so it expects a function with at least 4 continuous derivatives. The Gauss rules based on the same number of points have error terms involving $f^{(6)}(x)$, and so they expect a function with at least 6 continuous derivatives. This difference becomes more pronounced as n increases; a Gauss rule requires about twice the number of continuous derivatives of a Newton-Cotes rule. Therefore Newton-Cotes rules may make sense for less smooth functions, and Gauss rules may make sense for very smooth functions. This is reflected in the MATLAB routines `quad`, based on Simpson's rule, recommended for low accuracies and nonsmooth functions, and `quadl`, based on the Gauss-type Lobatto rule extended by Gauss-Kronrod quadrature, recommended for higher accuracies and smooth functions. (Similarly, the Maple numerical integrator uses a default Clenshaw-Curtis method, based on the Chebyshev nodes, and also provides a Newton-Cotes rule and a special method for singular integrals.) The Gauss and Gauss-type rules give better accuracy but require additional differentiability.

Estimating the Error

Let's discuss how we can estimate the error for the purposes of automatic integration. There are different approaches for different methods; we focus on composite Newton-Cotes formulas, but it should be clear how the methods generalize. Consider the trapezoidal rule

$$\int_\alpha^\beta f(x)dx = T_h f - \frac{(\beta - \alpha)h^2}{12} f''(\gamma_h),$$

where $T_h f$ is the result of applying the trapezoidal rule with spacing h. Let's assume that f is indeed twice continuously differentiable so that this error estimate is valid. Then the error for a spacing of $h/2$ is

$$\int_\alpha^\beta f(x)dx = T_{h/2}f - \frac{(\beta - \alpha)(h/2)^2}{12} f''(\gamma_{h/2})$$

$$= T_{h/2}f - \frac{(\beta - \alpha)h^2}{48} f''(\gamma_{h/2}).$$

That is,

$$T_h f - \frac{(b-a)h^2}{12} f''(\gamma_h) = T_{h/2} f - \frac{(\beta-\alpha)h^2}{48} f''(\gamma_{h/2})$$

$$T_h f - T_{h/2} f = \frac{(\beta-\alpha)h^2}{12} f''(\gamma_h) - \frac{(\beta-\alpha)h^2}{48} f''(\gamma_{h/2})$$

$$= \frac{(\beta-\alpha)h^2}{48}(4f''(\gamma_h) - f''(\gamma_{h/2}))$$

(notice that this is an equality, not an approximate equality). Now suppose that the interval $[\alpha, \beta]$ is not very large, presumably because we are applying the trapezoidal rule recursively and this is just one subinterval of a larger interval in which we're interested. Then we expect that

$$f''(\gamma_h) \approx f''(\gamma_{h/2}), \qquad (5.38)$$

and so

$$T_h f - T_{h/2} f \approx 3\frac{(\beta-\alpha)h^2}{48} f''(\gamma)$$

$$= -3E_{h/2},$$

where $E_{h/2}$ is the error in the approximation $T_{h/2} f$. Hence by computing with two rules with known error formulas we can approximate the error. If the absolute value of

$$E_{h/2} \approx -\frac{1}{3}\left(T_h f - T_{h/2} f\right) \qquad (5.39)$$

is sufficiently small, then we accept $T_{h/2} f$ as our approximation (or possibly use $T_{h/2} f$ and $T_h f$ to extrapolate to an even better solution; see the next section). Otherwise we subdivide the interval $[\alpha, \beta]$ and use the rule at two different resolutions again.

Example 5.6.1 Let $f(x) = \exp(x)$, $[\alpha, \beta] = [0, 0.1]$. Then with $h = 0.1$ we have

$$\int_0^{.1} \exp(x)dx \approx T_{.1} f$$

$$\doteq 0.10525854590378$$

and with $h = 0.05$ we have

$$\int_0^{.1} f(x)dx \approx T_{.05} f$$

$$\doteq 0.10519282777069$$

(note that we could have reused function values from the computation of $T_{.1} f$ here). Hence Eq. (5.39) gives

$$-\frac{1}{3}(T_{.1} f - T_{.05} f) \doteq \frac{1}{-3} \cdot 6.5718E - 5$$

$$= -2.19060E - 5$$

as the estimate of $E_{.05}$. In fact,

$$\int_0^{.1} \exp(x)dx - T_{.05}f \doteq 0.10517091807565 - 0.10519282777069$$

$$\doteq -2.19097E - 5$$

so that $-2.19060E - 5$ is a very good estimate of the true error $-2.19097E - 5$. The approximation $T_{.05}f$ may be used with some confidence that the error is within a tolerance of about $2.2E - 5$; we might also try to improve the estimate by adding back in the (signed) error estimate, that is,

$$T = T_{.05}f - \frac{1}{3}(T_{.1}f - T_{.05}f)$$

should cancel out most of the error (compare the idea behind the method of iterative refinement from Section 3.3). Indeed, the error in T has magnitude about $3.65E - 9$, a considerable improvement. However, note that we do not have an error estimate for T if we use this approach. We only have the estimate for $T_{h/2}f$, and this will likely be an overly conservative error estimate for T. ∎

We could do the same with Simpson's rule or any other rule for which the error E has a tractable form and for which we can make the statement that E_h is approximately equal to a fixed and known multiple of $E_{h/k}$ for some $k > 1$. This is true of a great many rules.

For any particular choice of h it could certainly happen that $T_h f$ is a better estimate of the integral than is $T_{h/2}f$. There are heuristics for checking whether a function or its derivatives are sufficiently smooth in some region so that this is unlikely to happen, but if h is small these checks are usually not necessary. After all, if we use the trapezoidal rule, then $T_{h/2}f$ should have error one-fourth of the error of $T_h f$, but the error tolerance is only halved on each subinterval. Sooner or later the trapezoidal method should win this race.

Adaptivity and Recursiveness

There are other error estimation techniques, some of which are specific to certain methods. If we can estimate the error, however, we can build an adaptive numerical integrator. We accept a function f, an interval $[a, b]$, and a tolerance τ, and attempt to return

$$\int_a^b f(x)dx$$

to within the tolerance. Let Q_h be a quadrature rule based on a spacing of h (possibly $Q_h = T_h$) and k an integer greater than 1. We proceed as follows: Evaluate $Q_{b-a}f$ and $Q_{(b-a)/k}f$. Estimate the error; if it is less than τ, return $Q_{(b-a)/k}f$. Otherwise, divide $[a, b]$ into k equal subintervals, and repeat the above process on each subinterval with tolerance τ/k. When the integral on each subinterval has been successfully approximated, sum up the contributions and return that result.

This is an adaptive recursive algorithm. It is adaptive because it chooses which intervals to focus on based on how difficult it finds the integrand to be, and recursive because it calls itself on these problematic regions, and then calls itself again on the problematic subregions of these problematic regions, continually parceling out proportional amounts of the tolerance τ, until convergence is achieved or some maximum number of function evaluations or recursive calls is reached. See Figure 5.11.

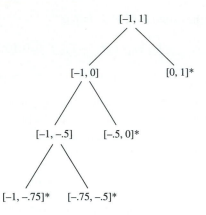

Figure 5.11 Possible Path of a Recursive Integrator. (∗ = Convergence Achieved on That Subinterval)

This approach uses the same error tolerance τ/λ on every subinterval of $[a, b]$ of length λ. This is inefficient. If we know in advance that the function has rough areas and smooth areas and we know where they are, then we might divide the tolerance τ unequally, allowing more error where the function is poorly behaved and less error where it is well-behaved. For a program intended as an automatic integrator, of course, we cannot make any such assumptions about the function to be integrated.

PROBLEMS 5.6

1. Write a MATLAB program for performing the composite midpoint rule with unequally spaced points. Compare this method with the standard composite midpoint rule.

2. **a.** Use the adaptive recursive trapezoidal rule to estimate $\int_0^1 (x + \sin(x^2))dx$ with an error tolerance of .01.
   b. Use the adaptive recursive trapezoidal rule to estimate $\int_0^1 \exp(-x)dx$ with an error tolerance of .001.

3. **a.** What is the error estimate corresponding to Eq. (5.39) for Simpson's rule?
   b. Write a detailed algorithm (pseudocode) for an adaptive recursive automatic integrator based on

Simpson's rule. The method should make efficient use of previously computed values.

4. **a.** Write a MATLAB program for performing adaptive recursive automatic integration based on the trapezoidal rule. Test your program.
   b. Modify your program to add back in the estimated error. Test your program.

5. Would it be feasible to build an adaptive recursive method based on Gauss-Legendre quadrature? What about Lobatto quadrature?

MATLAB 5.6

Let's check the error estimate $E_{h/2} \approx -\frac{1}{3} \left(T_h f - T_{h/2} f \right)$ from Eq. (5.39). We'll use a function with a known integral of course. Enter:

```
» f=inline('6*x.^5')
» h=.1;
» x=0:h:1;
```

```
» T1=trapz(x,f(x))
» x=0:h/2:1;
» T2=trapz(x,f(x))
» format long
» E_est=-(T1-T2)/3              %Estimated error.
» E=1-T2                        %Actual error.
» abs(E_est-E)
```

The error is on the order of 10^{-3}, and we have an estimate of it that's good to about 10^{-5}. That's pretty good. Let's try with a much smaller h; enter:

```
» h=.0001;
» x=0:h:1;
» T1=trapz(x,f(x))
» x=0:h/2:1;
» T2=trapz(x,f(x))
» E_est=-(T1-T2)/3              %Estimated error.
» E=1-T2                        %Actual error.
» abs(E_est-E)
```

The error is on the order of 10^{-9}, and we have an estimate of it that's good to about 10^{-15}. That's very good; the error estimate becomes better as h decreases. Enter:

```
» T2_c=T2+E_est              %Correct T2 using estimated error.
» abs(T2_c-1)
» format short
```

If we try to "correct" the estimate $T_{h/2}$ by adding to it the error estimate from Eq. (5.39), then we get an answer that, while not exact, is very good. This is also an efficent way to improve the accuracy. Enter:

```
» 1/h+1/(h/2)          %Number of function evals. used to
                            find T2_c.
» xx=linspace(0,1,30000);
» T3=trapz(xx,f(xx))
» abs(1-T3)
```

The error is on the order of 10^{-9}, as it was for T2; using Eq. (5.39) with spacings h and $h/2$ is more effective than using the same total number of function evaluations in a trapezoidal rule with a smaller h. This is a good example of working smarter, not harder. Unfortunately we do not have an error estimate for the "corrected" T2. Still, the formula $T_c = T_2 f - \frac{1}{3}(T_1 f - T_2 f)$ seems useful. If we use it, we typically report the error estimate for T_2 even though it is likely to be a gross overestimate of the true error. Enter:

```
» more on
» type quad
```

and look for the lines

```
% One step of Romberg extrapolation.
» Q = Q2 + (Q2 - Q1)/15;
```

This is the formula corresponding to $T_c = T_2 f - \frac{1}{3}(T_1 f - T_2 f)$ for Simpson's rule, which is the rule used in `quad`. You should now be able to understand everything done in the professionally written code `quad`. Study this code briefly.

We expand on this refinement technique in the next section, but for now, let's look at another Riemann sum rule. Monte Carlo methods make use of pseudorandom numbers such as those generated by `rand` (uniformly distributed) and `randn` (normally distributed); see also Section 7.4. A simple Monte Carlo quadrature method would be the composite midpoint rule or left or right endpoint rule with randomly selected nodes. Enter:

```
» more off
» f=inline('sin(x)')
» x=pi*rand([1 100]);          %100 randomly selected pts. in [0,pi].
» x=sort(x);                    %Get ordered nodes.
» h=diff(x);                    %Panel widths.
» A=dot(h,f(x(1:end-1)))       %Left endpoint rule.
```

(The correct answer is 2.) As a rule, the convergence of these methods is $O(1/\sqrt{n})$ if n pseudorandomly chosen points are used, independent of the degree of smoothness of the integrand. This order of convergence isn't very impressive, though the convergence of the corresponding Monte Carlo methods for multiple integrals is also $O(1/\sqrt{n})$, no matter the number of variables with respect to which we are integrating. So, there can be advantages in higher dimensions.

We might also use a quasi-Monte Carlo method that uses a quasirandom sequence of points. A quasirandom sequence doesn't appear as random as a pseudorandom sequence because it has certain desirable properties built into it, such as sampling every subregion of the integration region of a given size equally often. See Section 7.4.

ADDITIONAL PROBLEMS 5.6

6. a. What is the error estimate corresponding to Eq. (5.39) for Simpson's 3/8 rule?
   b. Write a MATLAB program for performing adaptive recursive automatic integration based on Simpson's 3/8 rule. Test your program.

7. Prove that all Riemann sum rules based on N points are at least $O(1/N)$.

8. Write a MATLAB program for performing the composite trapezoidal rule with unequally spaced points. Compare this method with the standard composite trapezoidal rule.

9. a. Use the adaptive recursive trapezoidal rule to estimate $\int_{.01}^{1} \sin(x^{-2})dx$. Create a diagram similar to Figure 5.11 showing how the interval of integration was subdivided.
   b. Use the adaptive recursive Simpson's rule to estimate $\int_{.01}^{1} \sin(x^{-2})dx$. Create a diagram similar to Figure 5.11 showing how the interval of integration was subdivided.

10. Verify Theorem 5.6.1 for a particular integral $\int_a^b f(x)dx$ and method and a variety of polynomials $p(x)$.

11. Choose a variety of functions and test whether Eq. (5.38) is a reasonable approximation.

12. Modify Theorem 5.6.1 to allow for a weight function in the integral.

13. Find several functions and corresponding values of h for which the error estimate Eq. (5.39) gives misleading results because $T_h f$ is a better estimate than $T_{h/2} f$.

14. a. What is the error estimate corresponding to Eq. (5.39) for Boole's rule?
   b. Write a MATLAB program for performing adaptive recursive automatic integration based on Boole's rule. Test your program.

15. Write a MATLAB program for performing Monte Carlo integration. Test your program.

5.7 Romberg Integration

In the last section we discussed a technique for estimating the error in a weighted-average rule for which we had an appropriate expression for the truncated error. For example, using the formula

$$\int_\alpha^\beta f(x)dx = T_h f - \frac{(\beta - \alpha)h^2}{12} f''(\gamma)$$

for the trapezoidal rule with spacing h, T_h, we derived the estimate

$$E_{h/2} \approx -\frac{1}{3} \left(T_h f - T_{h/2} f \right)$$

(Eq. (5.39)). This led to the idea of adding this (signed) error back into our estimate of the error to get an improved or "corrected" estimate

$$T_c = T_{h/2} f - \frac{1}{3} \left(T_h f - T_{h/2} f \right) \tag{5.40}$$

of the integral. This idea is used in the MATLAB quad routine, which uses the version of Eq. (5.40) that is appropriate for Simpson's rule.

Note that Eq. (5.40) can be viewed either as a way of getting increased accuracy out of the trapezoidal method or as a method in and of itself. We could substitute in the expression for the trapezoidal rule, rearrange it so that we do not compute any function values more than once, and consider Eq. (5.40) a quadrature method in its own right.

Acceleration   But what if the error still isn't small enough? What if we want to correct the correction? We might imagine generating a sequence of approximations like

$$T_h, T_{h/2}, T_{h/4}, T_{h/8}, \ldots$$

that converges to the correct value in the limit. We might look for an acceleration technique like Aitken's Δ^2 process (see Section 1.4) that turns the sequence $T_h, T_{h/2}, T_{h/4}, T_{h/8}, \ldots$ into a more rapidly convergeing sequence. But Aitken's Δ^2 process applies only to linearly convergent methods. Let's look at another technique. Recall from Section 5.2 that the simple Simpson's rule has the form

$$\int_a^b f(x)dx = \frac{h}{3} \left(f(a) + 4f(\frac{a+b}{2}) + f(b) \right)$$

$$-\frac{1}{90} f^{(4)}(x_0) h^5 + c_6 f^{(5)}(x_0) h^6 + c_7 f^{(6)}(x_0) h^7 \ldots$$

for some constants $\kappa_6, \kappa_7, \ldots$ (see Eq. (5.17)). That is, the truncation error E has the form

$$E = c_5 h^5 + c_6 h^6 + c_7 h^7 + \cdots \tag{5.41}$$

for some constants $c_5, c_6, c_7, \ldots$, depending on the values of the derivatives of f at the *known* point x_0. For a fixed application of the method, the c_i are fixed, and in principle they could be found. In practice we don't need to know their values.

Most of the methods we see have a truncation error that can be expanded in a form similar to Eq. (5.41). Suppose we're looking at a quadrature rule of the form

$$A = Q_h + E_h,$$

where A is the area, Q_h is the result of applying the numerical method with spacing h to the integrand, and

$$E_h = c_1 h + c_2 h^2 + c_3 h^3 + c_4 h^4 + \cdots \tag{5.42}$$

is the error, where the constants c_i ($i = 1, 2, 3, \ldots$) do not depend on h. Then

$$A = Q_{h/2} + E_{h/2},$$

where

$$E_{h/2} = c_1 \frac{h}{2} + c_2 \frac{h^2}{4} + c_3 \frac{h^3}{8} + c_4 \frac{h^4}{16} + \cdots$$

is the truncation error, which is $O(h)$ if $c_1 \neq 0$. But since the c_i are constants, we can eliminate terms in the truncation error! We take a weighted average of Q_h and $Q_{h/2}$ that still sums to A but with a superior error term. Let's try to eliminate the $O(h)$ term. We have

$$A = Q_h + E_h$$
$$= Q_{h/2} + E_{h/2}$$

so

$$A = 2A - A$$
$$= 2(Q_{h/2} + E_{h/2}) - (Q_h + E_h)$$
$$= 2Q_{h/2} - Q_h + 2E_{h/2} - E_h$$
$$= 2Q_{h/2} - Q_h + c_1 h + c_2 \frac{h^2}{2} + c_3 \frac{h^3}{4} + c_4 \frac{h^4}{8} + \cdots \tag{5.43}$$
$$- (c_1 h + c_2 h^2 + c_3 h^3 + c_4 h^4 + \cdots)$$
$$= 2Q_{h/2} - Q_h + \widetilde{c}_2 h^2 + \widetilde{c}_3 h^3 + \widetilde{c}_4 h^4 + \cdots$$
$$= Q_h^{(2)} + E_h^{(2)},$$

where $Q_h^{(2)} = 2Q_{h/2} - Q_h$ is a new quadrature rule that has an error term $E_h^{(2)}$ that is $O(h^2)$ rather than $O(h)$. We have used an $O(h)$ rule, evaluated at two different spacings, to generate an $O(h^2)$ rule.

We never used the fact that Q_h was a quadrature rule, so this technique works on any numerical method Q_h that approximates a quantity A with an error term as in Eq. (5.42).

Furthermore, the method can be iterated. Let's call the basic method $Q_h = Q_h^{(1)}$ so the $O(h^2)$ method is $Q_h^{(2)} = 2Q_{h/2}^{(1)} - Q_h^{(1)}$. From Eq. (5.43)

$$A = Q_h^{(2)} - \tilde{c}_2 h^2 + \tilde{c}_3 h^3 + \tilde{c}_4 h^4 + \cdots$$

$$A = Q_{h/2}^{(2)} - \tilde{c}_2 \frac{h^2}{4} + \tilde{c}_3 \frac{h^3}{8} + \tilde{c}_4 \frac{h^4}{16} + \cdots,$$

so we can knock out the $O(h^2)$ term—that is, the leading term in the error—using a linear combination of $Q_{h/2}^{(2)}$ and $Q_h^{(2)}$:

$$A = \frac{(4A - A)}{3}$$

$$= \frac{4}{3}(Q_{h/2}^{(2)} + \tilde{c}_2 \frac{h^2}{4} + \tilde{c}_3 \frac{h^3}{8} + \tilde{c}_4 \frac{h^4}{16} + \cdots) - \frac{1}{3}(Q_h^{(2)} + \tilde{c}_2 h^2 + \tilde{c}_3 h^3 + \tilde{c}_4 h^4 + \cdots)$$

$$= \frac{1}{3}(4Q_{h/2}^{(2)} - Q_h^{(2)}) + \frac{1}{3}(\tilde{c}_2 h^2 + \tilde{c}_3 \frac{h^3}{2} + \tilde{c}_4 \frac{h^4}{4} + \cdots) - \frac{1}{3}(\tilde{c}_2 h^2 + \tilde{c}_3 h^3 + \tilde{c}_4 h^4 + \cdots)$$

$$= Q_h^{(3)} + \hat{c}_3 h^3 + \hat{c}_4 h^4 + \cdots, \tag{5.44}$$

where

$$Q_h^{(3)} = \frac{(4Q_{h/2}^{(2)} - Q_h^{(2)})}{3}$$

$$= Q_{h/2}^{(2)} + \frac{Q_{h/2}^{(2)} - Q_h^{(2)}}{3}$$

$$= Q_{h/2}^{(2)} + \frac{Q_{h/2}^{(2)} - Q_h^{(2)}}{2^2 - 1}$$

Richardson Extrapolation

is a new $O(h^3)$ method (or possibly higher, if it should happen that $\hat{c}_3 = 0$). We can continue this process indefinitely; in general, if $Q_h^{(1)}$ is the $O(h)$ method, then $Q_h^{(i)}$ is an $O(h^i)$ method, where $Q_h^{(i)}$ is defined recursively by

$$Q_h^{(i)} = Q_{h/2}^{(i-1)} + \frac{Q_{h/2}^{(i-1)} - Q_h^{(i-1)}}{2^{i-1} - 1} \tag{5.45}$$

($i = 2, 3, \ldots$). This process is known as **Richardson extrapolation.** Performing it based on Q_h and $Q_{h/2}$ is common but not essential; we could use, say, Q_h and $Q_{h/3}$ and use the appropriate linear combination to eliminate the first term in the error expansion.

Example 5.7.1   Let's use the Richardson extrapolation technique with the left endpoint quadrature rule from Section 5.6,

$$\int_a^b f(x)dx = \sum_{i=0}^{n-1} f(a + ih)h + E_h$$

($h = 1/n$). It can be shown that E_h is of the proper form for Richardson extrapolation (Eq. (5.42)). We'll look for an $O(h^3)$ approximation. Let's use $h = 0.1$ and integrate

$f(x) = 4x^3$ from 0 to 1; the true value is 1. We have

$$Q_h^{(1)} = \sum_{i=0}^{n-1} f(a + ih)h$$

$$\doteq 0.8100$$

$$Q_{h/2}^{(1)} = \sum_{i=0}^{2n-1} f(a + ih/2)\frac{h}{2}$$

$$\doteq 0.9025$$

$$Q_h^{(2)} = Q_{h/2} + (Q_{h/2} - Q_h)$$

$$\doteq 0.9950$$

(note that $Q_h^{(2)}$ is a significantly improved approximation for negligible additional computation). Now we need $Q_{h/2}^{(2)}$ so we can form $Q_h^{(3)}$. We have

$$Q_{h/4}^{(1)} = \sum_{i=0}^{4n-1} f(a + ih)h$$

$$\doteq 0.9506$$

$$Q_{h/2}^{(2)} = Q_{h/4} + (Q_{h/4} - Q_{h/2})$$

$$\doteq 0.9988$$

$$Q_h^{(3)} = Q_{h/2}^{(2)} + \frac{Q_{h/2}^{(2)} - Q_h^{(1)}}{3}$$

$$\doteq 1,$$

and in fact $Q_h^{(3)} = 1$ to the number of digits displayed. It's customary to arrange these quantities in a table

$Q_h^{(1)}$		
0.8100		
$Q_{h/2}^{(1)}$	$Q_h^{(2)}$	
0.9025	0.9950	
$Q_{h/4}^{(1)}$	$Q_{h/2}^{(2)}$	$Q_h^{(3)}$
0.9506	0.9988	1.0000,

which is sometimes called an **extrapolation table.** The errors are

$Q_h^{(1)}$		
$E \doteq .1900$		
$Q_{h/2}^{(1)}$	$Q_h^{(2)}$	
$E \doteq .0975$	$E \doteq .0050$	
$Q_{h/4}^{(1)}$	$Q_{h/2}^{(2)}$	$Q_h^{(3)}$
$E \doteq .0494$	$E \doteq .0013$	$E \doteq .0000,$

and the errors for $Q_h^{(1)}$ are indeed $O(h)$ while those for $Q_h^{(2)}$ are about $O(h^2)$. The size of the error in $Q_h^{(3)}$ is better than expected. ∎

Trapezoidal Rule

Richardson extrapolation may be applied whenever we have a numerical method Q_h for approximating a quantity A that satisfies

$$A = Q_h + c_1 h^{m_1} + c_1 h^{m_2} + \cdots + c_1 h^{m_N} + O(h^{m_{N+1}}),$$

where

$$m_1 < m_2 < \cdots < m_N < m_{N+1}$$

are positive integers. We choose linear combinations to knock out the terms in h^{m_1}, $h^{m_2}, \ldots, h^{m_N}$ successively. It is not uncommon for a numerical method to have an error term that involves only even or only odd powers of h. In fact the trapezoidal rule is one such method; if f is infinitely differentiable, then the trapezoidal rule has the form

$$\int_a^b f(x)dx = T_h f + c_2 h^2 + c_4 h^4 + c_6 h^6 + \cdots,$$

where each c_i $(i = 2, 4, 6, \ldots)$ is in general nonzero. If f is at least $2k + 1$ times differentiable, then the trapezoidal rule has the form

$$\int_a^b f(x)dx = T_h f + c_2 h^2 + c_4 h^4 + c_6 h^6 + \cdots + c_{2k} h^{2k} + O(h^{2k+1}) \qquad (5.46)$$

(with the same c_i, $i = 2, 4, 6, \ldots, 2k$). Hence if f is sufficiently differentiable, then we may apply Richardson extrapolation to the trapezoidal rule as follows: Set $T_h^{(1)} = T_h$. Then define

$$T_h^{(2)} = \frac{4T_{h/2}^{(1)} - T_h^{(1)}}{3}$$

Romberg Integration

to eliminate the $O(h^2)$ terms (as in Eq. (5.44)). In general, the sequence of methods

$$T_h^{(i)} = \frac{4^i T_{h/2}^{(i-1)} - T_h^{(i-1)}}{4^i - 1} \qquad (5.47)$$

is the result of applying Richardson extrapolation to the trapezoidal rule, and Eq. (5.47) defines a method known as **Romberg integration** (or the **Romberg algorithm**). The resulting extrapolation table is called the **T-table** because of its lower triangular structure.

Each $T_h^{(i)}$ $(i \geq 2)$, when viewed as a method in its own right as opposed to one component of Romberg integration, is called a **Romberg formula**. Romberg formulas are not interpolatory rules (except the first few); in fact the degree of accuracy of $T_h^{(i)}$ is only $2i - 1$. They are, however, Riemann sum rules. (Recall that many quadrature methods can be viewed as Riemann sum rules.) The Romberg algorithm is an efficient way to generate highly accurate answers from the trapezoidal rule if the integrand f is sufficiently differentiable, but it can be very inefficient if the differentiability assumption is violated. A class of algorithms known as **cautious Romberg methods** uses the known degree of accuracy of $T_h^{(i)}$ to check for violations of the differentiability assumption and take corrective action if it is not met.

Although the term *Romberg algorithm* refers to Richardson extrapolation performed on the trapezoidal rule, the idea itself is widely applicable. We have seen it applied in the MATLAB quad command, which uses a single step of Richardson extrapolation to improve upon the Simpson's rule estimate. The idea is that it is so easy to do a single step of the extrapolation, and there is so much accuracy to be gained by doing so, that it is almost senseless to not do it. An exception would be when we are carefully controlling the error estimates, as we do not generate an estimate for the extrapolated value.

Example 5.7.2 Let's try Romberg integration on $f(x) = \exp(x)$ from 0 to 1. The true value is 1.7183 (to four decimal places). Although we can start with any h, we often start with $h = b - a$ in hopes of achieving convergence quickly with relatively few function evaluations. If we are storing previously computed values, then this is efficient because, for example, $T_{h/2}^{(1)}$ reuses all the values used in computing $T_h^{(1)}$. We have

$$T_h^{(1)} = \frac{h}{2}(f(0) + f(1))$$

$$\doteq 1.8591$$

$$T_{h/2}^{(1)} = \frac{h}{4}(f(0) + 2f(0.5) + f(1))$$

$$\doteq 1.7539$$

$$T_h^{(2)} = \frac{4T_{h/2}^{(1)} - T_h^{(1)}}{4 - 1}$$

$$\doteq \frac{4 \cdot 1.7539 - 1.8591}{3}$$

$$\doteq 1.7189$$

(note that the computation of $T_h^{(2)}$ requires no new function evaluations). The table is

$$T_h^{(1)}$$
$$1.8591$$
$$T_{h/2}^{(1)} \qquad T_h^{(2)}$$
$$1.7539 \qquad 1.7189$$

so far. If we want to get a better approximation, we need a new entry in the first column. This should let us get a slightly better estimate in the second column but a much better one in the third column. We have

$$T_{h/4}^{(1)} = \frac{h}{8}(f(0) + 2f(0.25) + 2f(0.5) + 2f(0.75) + f(1))$$

$$\doteq 1.7272$$

$$T_{h/2}^{(2)} = \frac{4T_{h/4}^{(1)} - T_{h/2}^{(1)}}{3}$$

$$\doteq 1.7183$$

$$T_h^{(3)} = \frac{4^2 T_{h/2}^{(2)} - T_h^{(2)}}{4^2 - 1}$$

$$\doteq \frac{8 \cdot 1.7183 - 1.7272}{7}$$

$$\doteq 1.7182$$

(note that we are still using $h = b - a$, not adjusting it for each application of the composite trapezoidal rule). The new table is

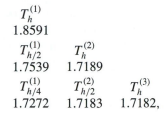

and $T_{h/2}^{(2)}$ is slightly more accurate ($E \doteq 3.7E - 5$) than $T_h^{(3)}$ ($E \doteq 4E - 5$). This happens because we are not yet into the limiting behavior, where the last entries in successive columns should be an order of h better estimates—at least, until we get to the point where roundoff error is significant. ■

The convergence criterion used is usually that the most accurate entry in the last column and the most accurate entry in the next-to-last column of the extrapolation table agree to within a given tolerance. However, before you use this convergence criterion with Romberg integration, be warned: During the first several stages of refinement (representing the first several columns of the extrapolation table), it is possible that two entries at the bottoms of their columns will agree to within the tolerance by chance, not because they are accurate. Because of this, we typically insist that the entries in the last three columns of the table must all agree to within some tolerance before we consider that convergence has been met. If not, we generate a new column.

It's worth repeating that extrapolation is a very general technique that may be applied to many different numerical methods. In trying to understand what method a piece of software is using, you will often discover that an extrapolation/acceleration technique has been woven into a standard method in a clever and efficient way that is difficult to "reverse engineer" from the code. It's important to document such modifications in the comments so that later users can understand the method being used by the program.

PROBLEMS 5.7

1. Show that Eq. (5.47) is the result of applying Richardson extrapolation to the trapezoidal rule using Eq. (5.46).

2. What happens if you apply Richardson extrapolation to the trapezoidal rule in the form of Eq. (5.45) (that is, as if the error term were of the form of Eq. (5.42))?

3. a. Use Eq. (5.46) to determine how many times f must be continuously differentiable for $T_h^{(i)}$ to be well-defined.

b. Use the Romberg algorithm on $f(x) = x^{1/2}$, $x^{3/2}$, $x^{5/2}$, $x^{7/2}$, and $x^{9/2}$ on [0, 1]. In each case generate

4 columns in the extrapolation table. Discuss your results.

4. a. Use Romberg integration to approximate $\int_0^1 \exp(x)dx$ to within 10^{-6}.

  b. Use Romberg integration to approximate $\int_0^1 \sin(\pi x)dx$ to within 10^{-6}.

5. Show that the line Q = Q2 + (Q2 - Q1)/15. in the MATLAB quad command represents a single step of Richardson extrapolation applied to Simpson's rule.

MATLAB 5.7

We've mentioned singular integrals before. By a *singular integral* we mean an improper integral that exists but is improper because of a singularity of the integrand either at one or both of the endpoints or somewhere in the interior of the interval of integration. In the MATLAB code for quad (enter type quad) you'll see:

```
if ~isfinite(y(1))
  y(1) = feval(f,a+eps*(b-a),varargin{:});
  fcnt = fcnt+1;
end
if ~isfinite(y(7))
  y(7) = feval(f,b-eps*(b-a),varargin{:});
  fcnt = fcnt+1;
end
```

The MATLAB code for quadl is similar. (Note that using ~isfinite detects both NaN and Inf values, whereas isinf would detect only Inf values.) As we discussed briefly in MATLAB 5.2, this is known as "avoiding the singularity" because we simply recognize its presence and stay away from it. Technically, this makes the rule open, but we imagine that we are simply adjusting the rule to avoid getting an infinite result. Note that the quad and quadl routines also check for an infinite or NaN region, assume if one is found, that it was the result of a singularity leading to an infinite function evaluation, and signal an error.

Another simple method of handling singularities is "ignoring the singularity," that is, doing nothing about it. We used this technique with the function $f(x) = 3x^2 + \ln((\pi - x)^2)/\pi^4 + 1$ in MATLAB 5.2.

Let's look at another example. Consider the function $f(x) = 1/\sqrt{|x|}$ on $[-1, 1]$. If we use a rule that attempts to evaluate $f(0)$ then we'll encounter a problem. We use Simpson's 3/8 rule $\int_a^b f(x)dx \approx \frac{3h}{8}(f(a) + 3f(a + h) + 3f(a + 2h) + f(b))$ because it avoids the singularity; Simpson's rule would land on the singularity immediately. (Since Simpson's 3/8 rule and Simpson's rule have the same order of error, it would probably be more efficient to use Simpson's rule and fudge the endpoints like quad and quadl do.) Enter:

```
» f=inline('1./sqrt(abs(x))');
» h=2/3;
» w=(3/8)*[1 3 3 1];
» x=[-1 -1/3 1/3 1];
» T11=dot(h*w,f(x))
```

The correct answer is 4. We can't just subdivide by dividing h in half because we would land on the singularity. Instead we'll use Simpson's 3/8 rule on each of the three panels, shifting the nodes x as needed. Enter:

```
» h=h/3;
» T12_1=dot(h*w,f((1/3)*(x-2)))        %Leftmost panel.
» T12_2=dot(h*w,f((1/3)*x))            %Middle panel.
» T12_3=dot(h*w,f((1/3)*(x+2)))        %Rightmost panel.
» T12=T12_1+T12_2+T12_3
```

This is an improved estimate, but it still isn't very good. Richardson extrapolation isn't justified because f is not differentiable, and so the error estimate $E = c_4 h^4 + c_5 h^5 + \cdots$ of Simpson's 3/8 rule isn't valid. Let's try it anyway. Since we are going from h to $h/3$ (not $h/2$), the term $c_4 h^4$ in E_h becomes $c_4 h^4/3^4$ in $E_{h/3}$, so we have $80A \approx 81 Q_{h/3} - Q_h$ i.e. $A \approx Q_{h/3} + (Q_{h/3} - Q_h)/80$ as the Richardson step. Enter:

```
» T2 = T12 + (T12 - T11)/80     %Richardson extrapolation.
```

This is a very slight improvement. For this nondifferentiable function we should probably be using a lower-order method than Simpson's 3/8 rule. Still, if we continue long enough we would see convergence. Let's try it with the adaptive recursive Simpson's rule. Enter:

```
» quad(f,-1,1)
```

The program checks for singularities at the end and avoids them but lands on the singularity at zero. Let's avoid the singularity by using the fact that quad will check for singularities at the endpoints and move slightly away from them. Enter:

```
» A1=quad(f,-1,0)+quad(f,0,1)
» abs(A1-4)
```

The default tolerance is $1E-6$ so we see that the method is having difficulty. It thinks it is making its tolerance, but in fact it is off by an order of magnitude. Enter:

```
» A2=quad(f,-1,0,1E-5)+quad(f,0,1,1E-5)
» abs(A2-4)
```

The tolerance of $1E-5$ is also not met. However, this isn't bad performance for a singular integrand. Enter:

```
» A3=quadl(f,-1,0,1E-5)+quadl(f,0,1,1E-5)
» abs(A3-4)
» A4=quadl(f,-1,0)+quadl(f,0,1)
» abs(A4-4)
```

In the second case the tolerance is met; in the former case it is just barely missed. (As always, you may see slightly different results.) There are special methods for singular integrals.

ADDITIONAL PROBLEMS 5.7

6. a. Show that the Romberg formula $T_h^{(2)}$ is Simpson's rule.

  b. Write out the Romberg formula $T_h^{(3)}$ explicitly.

  c. Write out the Romberg formula $T_h^{(4)}$ explicitly.

7. The midpoint rule also has an error expansion of the form in Eq. (5.46). Derive a method analogous to Romberg integration for the midpoint rule. (The resulting table is called the **M-table.**) Compare your method to Romberg integration.

8. Write a MATLAB program that accepts a function, interval, and tolerance and performs Romberg integration. Test your program.

9. Write a MATLAB program that accepts a sequence and applies Richardson extrapolation to it. Test it on several appropriate sequences, corresponding to the first column of an extrapolation table, and some inappropriate sequences (not corresponding to spacings of h, $h/2$, $h/4, \ldots$, for example, or not having an appropriate error expansion).

10. Write an analysis (in essay form, not pseudocode) of the `quad` and `quadl` programs. Explain the goals of automatic integration and how these programs attempt to meet them. Discuss the choices that were made in the implementation of these methods and what some alternatives were.

11. One way to structure the computation of the first column of the T-table efficiently is as follows: Take $h = b - a$ and define $T_i^{(1)} = T_{h/2^{i-1}}^{(1)}$ (that is, $T_i^{(1)}$ uses 2^{i-1} panels in the trapezoidal rule). Then $T_i^{(1)} = \frac{1}{2}\left(T_{i-1}^{(1)} + \frac{h}{2^{k-2}}\sum_{k=1}^{2^{i-2}} f\left(a + (2k-1)\frac{h}{2^{k-1}}\right)\right)$. Prove that this formula is correct and comment on its efficiency.

12. Perform a numerical experiment to verify that the trapezoidal rule satisfies $\int_a^b f(x)dx = T_h f + c_2 h^2 + c_4 h^4 + c_6 h^6 + \cdots$ if f is infinitely differentiable.

13. In MATLAB 1.5 we experimented with the finite difference Newton's method approximation $s = \frac{f(x+h)-f(x)}{h}$ of the slope of the function f at x. In particular, we took $f(x) = \ln(x)$, $x = 1$, and $h = 0.1$, and then reduced h and investigated the error in this approximation of $f'(x)$. Assuming that $f'(x) = \frac{f(x_k+h)-f(x_k)}{h} + c_1 h + c_2 h^2 + \cdots$, use Richardson extrapolation to produce more accurate estimates of $f'(x)$. Recall that this approximation was sensitive to roundoff error.

14. a. Describe a method for performing adaptive Romberg integration.

  b. Write a MATLAB program that implements your method. Test your program.

15. a. A **modified Romberg algorithm** is one that does not cut h in half at each step but instead uses some other progression. Typically such a method adds fewer new points than the Romberg algorithm would add so as to be more efficient and avoid the roundoff error that will eventually be problematic if we are using $h/2^k$ as our step size in the T-table. One such method starts with a single panel and then adds one panel at each step. What would be the formula corresponding to Eq. (5.47) for this modified Romberg algorithm?

  b. One modified Romberg algorithm that is particularly efficient is **Oliver's modified Romberg algorithm,** based on the number of panels $1, 2, 3, 4, 6, 8, 12, \ldots$, where this sequence is defined by the requirement that it include all numbers of the form 2^k and $3 \cdot 2^k$. What is the significance of this choice of panels? What would be the formula corresponding to Eq. (5.47) for Oliver's modified Romberg algorithm?

6 Differential Equations

6.1 Numerical Differentiation

ONE OF THE MOST IMPORTANT areas of numerical analysis is the numerical solution of differential equations. In this chapter we discuss the numerical solution (also called numerical quadrature) of *ordinary differential equations* (ODEs).

The numerical solution of *partial differential equations* (PDEs) is very important in practice. Most methods for solving these problems lead to a large linear system that must be solved by the direct methods of Chapter 2 or, more commonly, iterative methods such as those in Chapter 3. However, discussing numerical methods for solving PDEs would require more knowledge of the analytical theory of PDEs than we are assuming.

In this chapter we focus on the simple first-order ODE initial value problem $y' = f(x, y)$, $y(x_0) = y_0$ and assume that $f(x, y)$ is a well-behaved function. As we progress through the chapter, you will see many similarities to and applications of numerical integration.

Numerical Differentiation

Before we delve into the numerical quadrature of ODEs, though, we should discuss numerical differentiation. Suppose we have a differentiable function $f(x)$ or a list of data $y_0, y_1, \ldots, y_n$ representing observations of a differentiable function (either experimental data or the output of a program that implements the function) and we wish to approximate the derivative of the function using only function values. The obvious technique is to use

$$f'(x) = \lim_{h \to 0} \frac{f(x + h) - f(x)}{h}$$

and write

$$f'(x) \approx \frac{f(x + h) - f(x)}{h}$$

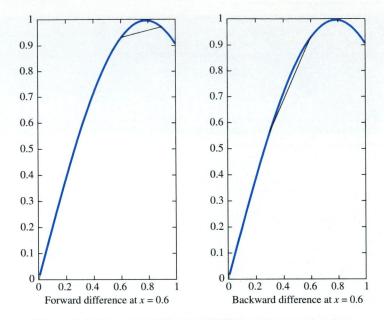

Forward difference at $x = 0.6$ Backward difference at $x = 0.6$

Figure 6.1 Forward and Backward Difference Approximations.

for some h that is small in absolute value. This is called the **forward difference** approximation; it uses a finite difference of f-values (as opposed to the infinitesimal difference $f(x + h) - f(x)$ as $h \to 0$). Similarly,

$$f'(x) \approx \frac{f(x) - f(x - h)}{h}$$

is called the **backward difference** approximation to the first derivative of f at x. In each case, h may be either positive or negative, though $h > 0$ is more common. When h is positive, we can interpret these approximations as secant approximations (see Fig. 6.1). The slope of f at x is approximated by the slope of the secant line.

Example 6.1.1   Let $f(x) = \cos(x)$. Then we may approximate $f'(0) = 0$ with finite differences using the forward difference approximation

$$f'(0) \approx \frac{f(0 + h) - f(0)}{h}$$

$$= \frac{\cos(h) - 1}{h}$$

or the backward difference approximation

$$f'(0) \approx \frac{f(0) - f(0 - h)}{h}$$

$$= \frac{1 - \cos(h)}{h}$$

and note that

$$\frac{1 - \cos(h)}{h} = \frac{1 - \left(1 - \frac{1}{3!}h^2 + \frac{1}{5!}h^4 - \cdots\right)}{h}$$

$$= \frac{1}{3!}h - \frac{1}{5!}h^3 + \cdots,$$

so this is an $O(h)$ estimate of the true value of the derivative. ∎

In general, the forward and backward difference approximations are not the negatives of one another. However, both these approximations *are* always $O(h)$. To see this, consider the Taylor series with remainder

$$f(x) = f(x_0) + hf'(x_0) + \frac{h^2}{2}f''(\xi)$$

for some ξ between x and x_0, assuming f is twice continuously differentiable. Since $x = x_0 + h$, this becomes

$$f(x_0 + h) = f(x_0) + hf'(x_0) + \frac{h^2}{2}f''(\xi)$$

$$f(x_0 + h) - f(x_0) = hf'(x_0) + \frac{h^2}{2}f''(\xi)$$

$$f'(x_0) = \frac{f(x_0 + h) - f(x_0)}{h} - \frac{h}{2}f''(\xi),$$

which shows that the forward difference approximation is $O(h)$. If we write $x = x_0 - h$ instead, then we have

$$f(x_0 - h) = f(x_0) - hf'(x_0) + \frac{h^2}{2}f''(\xi)$$

$$f(x_0 - h) - f(x_0) = -hf'(x_0) + \frac{h^2}{2}f''(\xi)$$

$$f'(x_0) = \frac{f(x_0) - f(x_0 - h)}{h} - \frac{h}{2}f''(\xi)$$

Central Differencing

so that the backward difference approximation is also $O(h)$. Consider again Figure 6.1; it seems sensible to average the two estimates, or equivalently to take the expansions

$$f(x_0 + h) = f(x_0) + hf'(x_0) + \frac{h^2}{2}f''(\xi_1) \tag{6.1}$$

$$f(x_0 - h) = f(x_0) - hf'(x_0) + \frac{h^2}{2}f''(\xi_2) \tag{6.2}$$

and subtract one-half times Eq. (6.2) from one-half times Eq. (6.1), giving

$$\frac{1}{2}(f(x_0 + h) - f(x_0 - h)) = \frac{1}{2}\left(f(x_0) + hf'(x_0) + \frac{h^2}{2}f''(\xi_1)\right)$$

$$-\frac{1}{2}\left(f(x_0) - hf'(x_0) + \frac{h^2}{2}f''(\xi_2)\right)$$

$$\frac{f(x_0 + h) - f(x_0 - h)}{2} = hf'(x_0) + \frac{1}{2}\left(\frac{h^2}{2}f''(\xi_1) - \frac{h^2}{2}f''(\xi_2)\right)$$

$$f'(x_0) = \frac{f(x_0 + h) - f(x_0 - h)}{2h} - \frac{1}{4}h(f''(\xi_1) - f''(\xi_2)),$$

which should be a better approximation of the derivative since we expect that $f''(\xi_1) \approx f''(\xi_2)$ if h is small. In fact, if we assume additional differentiability of f in Eq. (6.1) and Eq. (6.2), we can get a better error term. For,

$$f(x_0 + h) = f(x_0) + hf'(x_0) + \frac{h^2}{2}f''(x_0) + \frac{h^3}{6}f'''(\gamma_1)$$

$$f(x_0 - h) = f(x_0) - hf'(x_0) + \frac{h^2}{2}f''(x_0) - \frac{h^3}{6}f'''(\gamma_2)$$

giving

$$\frac{1}{2}(f(x_0 + h) - f(x_0 - h)) = \frac{1}{2}\left(f(x_0) + hf'(x_0) + \frac{h^2}{2}f''(x_0) + \frac{h^3}{6}f'''(\gamma_1)\right)$$

$$-\frac{1}{2}\left(f(x_0) - hf'(x_0) + \frac{h^2}{2}f''(x_0) - \frac{h^3}{6}f'''(\gamma_2)\right)$$

$$\frac{f(x_0 + h) - f(x_0 - h)}{2} = hf'(x_0) + \frac{1}{2}\left(\frac{h^3}{6}f'''(\gamma_1) + \frac{h^3}{6}f'''(\gamma_2)\right)$$

$$f'(x_0) = \frac{f(x_0 + h) - f(x_0 - h)}{2h} - \frac{1}{6}h^2\left(\frac{f'''(\gamma_1) + f'''(\gamma_2)}{2}\right)$$

$$= \frac{f(x_0 + h) - f(x_0 - h)}{2h} - \frac{1}{6}h^2 f'''(\gamma)$$

for some $\gamma \in [\gamma_1, \gamma_2]$, as by the Intermediate Value Theorem, the average

$$\frac{f'''(\gamma_1) + f'''(\gamma_2)}{2}$$

is achieved by $f'''(x)$ for some $x \in [\gamma_1, \gamma_2]$. Hence the approximation

$$f'(x) \approx \frac{f(x + h) - f(x - h)}{2h}$$

(see Fig. 6.2), called the **centered difference** (or **central difference**) approximation to $f'(x)$, is $O(h^2)$. This method is generally superior to forward difference and backward

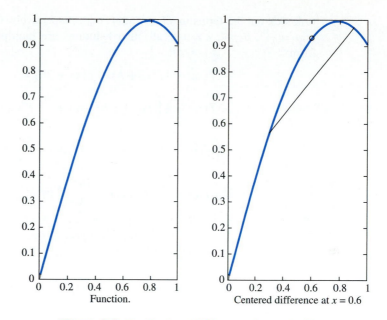

Figure 6.2 The Centered Difference Approximation.

difference approximations, but there are times when we need the other methods. For example, if x_0 is the first point, we cannot use a centered difference approximation because there is no point to the left of x_0.

A Special Method for the Endpoints

It's sometimes useful to have an $O(h^2)$ method for approximating f' at the endpoints. Can we get an $O(h^2)$ method for approximating $f'(x_0)$ using only $f(x_0)$, $f(x_1)$, and $f(x_2)$? We could use an approach analogous to the method of undetermined coefficients, asking that low-order polynomials be differentiated exactly. We could also interpolate f at x_0, x_1, and x_2 and use the derivative of the interpolant. A third approach is to expand

$$f(x_0) = f(x_0)$$

$$f(x_0 + h) = f(x_0) + hf'(x_0) + \frac{h^2}{2} f''(x_0) + \frac{h^3}{6} f'''(\gamma_1)$$

$$f(x_0 + 2h) = f(x_0) + 2hf'(x_0) + 2h^2 f''(x_0) + \frac{4h^3}{3} f'''(\gamma_2)$$

(assuming equal spacing) and attempt to knock out as many unwanted terms as we can. It's not immediately clear how many terms we need to retain in the Taylor series. We'd like to form a linear combination of the form

$$f'(x_0) \approx af(x_0) + bf(x_0 + h) + cf(x_0 + 2h) + O(h^2)$$

so we need

$$a + b + c = 0$$

$$\frac{b}{2} + 2c = 0$$

to knock out the terms in $f(x_0)$ and $f''(x_0)$, respectively. One solution of this system is $a = -3$, $b = 4$, $c = -1$; all other solutions are multiples of this solution. So we form

$$-3f(x_0) + 4f(x_0 + h) - f(x_0 + 2h) =$$

$$-3f(x_0) + 4\left(f(x_0) + hf'(x_0) + \frac{h^2}{2}f''(x_0) + \frac{h^3}{6}f'''(\gamma_1)\right)$$

$$-\left(f(x_0) + 2hf'(x_0) + 2h^2 f''(x_0) + \frac{4h^3}{3}f'''(\gamma_2)\right)$$

$$= 2hf'(x_0) + \frac{2h^3}{3}f'''(\gamma_1) - \frac{4h^3}{3}f'''(\gamma_2)$$

so

$$f'(x_0) = \frac{-3f(x_0) + 4f(x_0 + h) - f(x_0 + 2h)}{2h} \tag{6.3}$$

$$-h^2\left(\frac{1}{3}f'''(\gamma_1) - \frac{2}{3}f'''(\gamma_2)\right),$$

which is indeed an $O(h^2)$ estimate. The error term is

$$E = -h^2\left(\frac{1}{3}f'''(\gamma_1) - \frac{2}{3}f'''(\gamma_2)\right)$$

$$= -h^2\left(\frac{1}{3}(f'''(\gamma_1) - f'''(\gamma_2)) - \frac{1}{3}f'''(\gamma_2)\right)$$

$$\approx \frac{h^2}{3}f'''(\gamma_2)$$

if $f'''(\gamma_1) \approx f'''(\gamma_2)$, and indeed a different analysis shows that the error may be written in the form $E = h^2 f'''(\gamma)/3$ for some $\gamma \in [\gamma_1, \gamma_2]$. A similar formula holds for $f(x_n)$ in terms of x_{n-2}, x_{n-1}, and x_n.

The Second Derivative   A formula for $f''(x)$ may be found by differencing the forward and backward difference formulas for $f'(x)$ over an interval of length $2h$. The formula is

$$f''(x) \approx \frac{\frac{f(x+h)-f(x)}{h} - \frac{f(x)-f(x-h)}{h}}{2h}$$

$$= \frac{f(x + h) - f(x) - (f(x) - f(x - h))}{2h^2}$$

$$= \frac{f(x + h) - 2f(x) + f(x - h)}{2h^2},$$

and it is called the centered difference approximation to $f''(x)$. This approximation is $O(h^2)$. Similar formulas may be found for higher-order derivatives, and there are sources that list formulas for various derivative orders based on different numbers of points. (We talk of n-point formulas for approximating the derivative.) The more points used, the more attractive the error term can be made.

Stability   As we saw in MATLAB 1.5, numerical differentiation is unstable. This is hardly surprising when we look at, say, the forward difference approximation

$$f'(x) \approx \frac{f(x+h) - f(x)}{h},$$

which for small h involves both the subtraction of nearly equal numbers (in the numerator), and division by a small number. It's as though we were looking to design a difficult quantity to compute!

In fact, suppose that we can compute $f(x)$ to within some error ϵ (which likely will be rather larger than the machine epsilon). If we assume that all other computations are done without error, then when we attempt to approximate $f'(x)$ we actually have

$$f'(x) = \frac{f(x+h) - f(x)}{h} - \frac{h}{2}f''(\xi),$$

and the total (absolute) error is the sum of the truncation error $h|f''(\xi)|/2$ and the roundoff error

$$\left| \frac{f(x+h) - f(x)}{h} - \frac{fl(f(x+h)) - fl(f(x))}{h} \right|$$

$$= \left| \frac{(f(x+h) - fl(f(x+h))) + (fl(f(x)) - f(x))}{h} \right|$$

$$\leq \frac{\epsilon + \epsilon}{h}$$

$$= \frac{2\epsilon}{h}$$

in computing the approximation. That is, the total error is

$$E_T \leq \frac{h}{2}|f''(\xi)| + \frac{2\epsilon}{h}$$

$$\leq \alpha h + \beta \frac{1}{h} \qquad (6.4)$$

for some $\alpha > 0$, $\beta > 0$. The shape of this error curve is as in Figure 6.3. As $h \to 0$, the error grows (instability); as h increases, the total error eventually increases also, due to the truncation error.

There is a point at which the error bound is a minimum. Of course, because this is an upper bound it may or may not correspond to the true minimum of the error; but it is instructive to find this point. From Eq. (6.4) the error bound is

$$\alpha h + \beta \frac{1}{h}$$

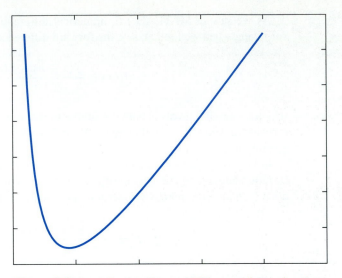

Figure 6.3 Total Error in Forward Difference Approximation.

$(h > 0)$, and differentiating this with respect to h and setting it to zero gives

$$\alpha - \beta \frac{1}{h^2} = 0$$

$$h^2 = \frac{\beta}{\alpha}$$

$$= \frac{2\epsilon}{|f''(\xi)|/2}$$

$$= \frac{4\epsilon}{|f''(\xi)|}.$$

That is, the optimal h for the error bound is

$$h = 2\sqrt{\frac{\epsilon}{M}}, \tag{6.5}$$

where M is $\max(|f''(\xi)|)$ over $[x, x + h]$. Assuming that M is on the order of unity, this means that if the errors ϵ in computing f are on the order of machine epsilon, say $\epsilon \approx 10^{-16}$, then h should not be chosen to be smaller than about 10^{-8}.

Example 6.1.2   Let $f(x) = \exp(x)$. Then $f'(0) = 1$. With $h = 10^{-k}$, the forward difference approximation to $f'(0)$ is

$$f'(0) \approx \frac{\exp(10^{-k}) - 1}{10^{-k}}$$

and a log-log plot of the absolute error in this approximation for $k = 1, 2, \ldots, 20$, as computed in MATLAB, is shown in Figure 6.4. The error drops by about an order of

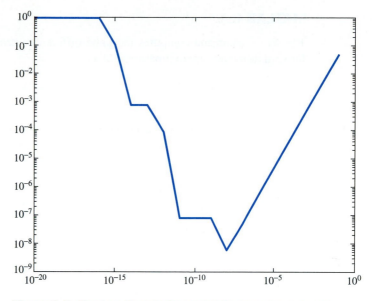

Figure 6.4 Absolute Error in Forward Difference Approximation; Log-Log Plot.

magnitude for each increase in k until the minimum is achieved at 10^{-8} (where the error is about $6E - 9$), and then it increases at the same rate until, starting at $k = 16$, the error is 1 because the numerator of the finite difference is evaluated as zero. ■

Reducing h too far is counterproductive. This is also the case when performing numerical integration, but because quadrature is stable, the eventual build-up of roundoff error is slow, and so roundoff error is unlikely to have disastrous consequences. In numerical differentiation, roundoff error can easily swamp our calculations. Think about it: We're working in double precision, but we can take h only about as small as the machine epsilon for single precision, and even that assumes that f is being computed to double precision accuracy. If the f-values are noisy, possibly because they're being computed by some other program that has a tolerance of, say, $1E - 6$, then we will have to use an even larger h.

PROBLEMS 6.1

1. Use the forward, backward, and centered difference approximations for the first derivative to approximate the derivative of $\ln(x)$ at $x = 1, 1.1, 1.2, \ldots, 2$. Compare your results to the true values. Then repeat at $x = 1, 1.05, 1.1, 1.1.5, \ldots, 2$.

2. Find the rule corresponding to Eq. (6.5) for the centered difference approximation for the first derivative.

3. For what order polynomials are the forward, backward, and centered difference approximations for the first

derivative exact? How about the centered difference approximation for the second derivative?

4. Use Taylor series to show that the centered difference approximation for the second derivative has error $E = -h^2 f''(\gamma)/12$.

5. Show that the centered difference approximation for the first derivative is the average of the forward and backward difference formulas.

MATLAB 6.1

The `diff` command computes the finite differences needed for the numerator of the forward difference approximation. Enter:

```
» z=[1 2 4 10]
» diff(z)
```

If the x values are equally spaced with spacing $h > 0$, the approximate derivatives are `diff(z)/h`. Enter:

```
» h =.001; x =0:h:pi;
» y=diff(sin(x))/h;
» plot(x,cos(x),'b',x(1:end-1),y,'r')
```

The agreement is excellent. Enter:

```
» format long
» max(cos(x(1:end-1))-y)
```

The worst-case error is not quite $5E - 4$. Since h is 10^{-3} and the method is $O(h)$, this is as expected. In fact, the absolute error for the forward difference approximation is $h|f''(\xi)|/2$, and for this f we have $\max(|f''(\xi)|) = 1$, so the error bound gives exactly $5E - 4$.

The command `diff(y,n)` may be used to difference the differences n times, as in the derivation of the centered difference approximation for the second derivative as the difference of two other approximations. Enter:

```
» format short
» z
» diff(diff(z))
» diff(z,2)
```

These are the numerators for the centered difference approximation for the second derivative. Enter:

```
» yy=diff(sin(x),2)/h^2;
» plot(x,-sin(x),'b',x(1:end-2),yy,'r')
```

Once again we have very good agreement between the analytical and the computed second derivative of $f(x)$.

If you have the Symbolic Toolbox, you can use `diff` to perform symbolic (ordinary or partial) differentiation. Enter:

```
» diff('x^2')
» diff('sin(x*y)','y')
» diff(sin(x*y),y)             %This gives an error.
» syms x y
» diff(sin(x*y),y)
```

If the variables are defined to be symbolic via `syms` then the single quotation marks aren't needed. If you don't have the Symbolic Toolbox, then `'x^2'` will simply be treated as a character string.

You may also have available the command to compute Taylor series symbolically. Enter:

```
» syms z
» taylor(sin(z))          %Taylor series about z=0.
» taylor(sin(z),8)        %More terms.
» taylor(sin(z),8,1)      %Centered about x=1.
```

The command `taylortool` gives an interactive graphical user interface (GUI) tool for computing and plotting Taylor series.

The commands `polyder` and `polyint` differentiate and integrate, respectively, polynomials given in terms of their coefficients (in the standard MATLAB format). If you have the Symbolic Toolbox, see also `help poly2sym` and `help sym2poly`.

ADDITIONAL PROBLEMS 6.1

6. Derive the centered difference approximation for the first derivative using polynomial interpolation as explained in the text. Verify that $E = h^2 f'''(\gamma)/3$.

7. Derive the analogue of Eq. (6.3) for the right endpoint of a set of data.

8. Use Taylor series to derive an $O(h^4)$ five-point formula for $f'(x)$ based on the values of f at the points $x - 2h$, $x - h, x, x + h, x + 2h$.

9. Use Taylor series to derive a formula for $f'(x)$ based on the values of f at the unequally spaced points $x - h$, $x, x + 2h$. Such formulas are needed when some data is missing.

10. a. Choose five different infinitely differentiable functions, and construct a plot like Figure 6.4 for each of them. (See `help loglog` for the plot.) Do you always get minimum error at $h = 10^{-8}$?

b. Choose five different once differentiable functions that are not twice differentiable, and construct a plot like the one in Figure 6.4 for each of them, approximating the derivative at a point where the function is only once differentiable. Do you always get minimum error at $h = 10^{-8}$?

11. How could you use the left endpoint quadrature rule (see Section 6.6) to approximately solve the ODE IVP $y' = f(x, y)$, $y(x_0) = y_0$? Demonstrate on $y' = \exp(2x)$, $y(0) = 1$, for $x = 0.1, 0.2, 0.3, \dots 2$. Compare your answers to the true solution. Cut the step size in half and repeat.

12. Draw the graphs of several functions for which the forward, backward, and centered difference approximations for the first derivative will give poor results at the resolution indicated. Discuss your graphs.

13. a. Show that the centered difference approximation for the first derivative has an error expansion that involves only even powers of h.

b. Use one step of Richardson extrapolation (see Section 5.7) to find an $O(h^4)$ approximation for the first derivative.

c. Apply Richardson extrapolation to form higher-order approximations to the first derivative of $f(x) = \exp(x)$ at $x = 0$ starting with $h = 0.5$. Continue until roundoff error destroys the accuracy of your results.

14. Write a MATLAB program that accepts a set of x and y values and uses `trapz` to approximate the integral of the underlying function $y = f(x)$. Approximate $f''(x)$ at every interior point x using the centered difference approximation, and use it to bound the absolute error $|(b - a)h^2 f''(\gamma)/12|$ in the composite trapezoidal rule.

15. Write a MATLAB program that accepts a set of x and y values and computes the clamped spline of the data using derivatives approximated by Eq. (6.3) and the corresponding formula for the right endpoint. You may use the `spline` command.

6.2 Euler's Method

Initial Value Problems

Now that we have discussed finite differences, we're ready to discuss the quadrature of the first-order ODE IVP $y' = f(x, y)$, $y(x_0) = y_0$. We know that analytical solutions are available in some special cases (e.g., first-order linear, separable, exact) but that in many cases no closed form solution can be found. Nonetheless $y(x)$ is a well-defined function (under appropriate assumptions on f) that we might attempt to find by approximate methods. One such method would be to look for a series solution and use its partial sums, though this requires that $y(x)$ be analytic at x_0. We'll focus on numerical methods, where we seek to approximate the solution $y(x)$ on a grid

$$x_0, x_0 + h, x_0 + 2h, \ldots, x_0 + nh$$

(we'll write $x_i = x_0 + ih$). If we had approximate values of $y(x_0)$, $y(x_1)$, $y(x_2), \ldots, y(x_n)$, then we could plot an approximate solution curve, for example.

Quadrature Rules

If $f(x, y)$ happens to be a function of x alone, that is, if the problem is of the form $y' = f(x)$, $y(x_0) = y_0$, then we may simply use a numerical quadrature rule. If we wish to solve, say,

$$y' = \sin(x^2)$$
$$y(0) = 0,$$

then the trapezoidal rule applied to compute

$$y(x) = y(0) + \int_0^x \sin(t^2)dt$$

with $h = 0.1$ gives

$$y_0 = 0$$

$$y_1 = y_0 + \frac{h}{2}(f(x_0) + f(x_1))$$

$$= \frac{0.1}{2}(f(0) + f(0.1))$$

$$\doteq 4.9999E - 4$$

$$y_2 = y_1 + \frac{h}{2}(f(x_1) + f(x_2))$$

$$= y_1 + \frac{0.1}{2}(f(0.1) + f(0.2))$$

$$\doteq 0.0030,$$

where y_i is the numerical approximation to $y(x_i)$. The MATLAB `quadl` command indicates that $y(0.1) \doteq 3.3333E - 4$ and $y(0.2) \doteq 0.0027$.

We could use the `cumtrapz` command to generate an approximate solution in this way, or we could use a more accurate method. But in general we will be working with the problem

$$y' = f(x, y) \tag{6.6}$$

$$y(x_0) = y_0, \tag{6.7}$$

where $f(x, y)$ depends on both x and y. In that case we cannot use the trapezoidal method, for in attempting to evaluate

$$y_1 = y_0 + \frac{h}{2}(f(x_0, y_0) + f(x_1, y_1))$$

$$= y_0 + h\frac{f(x_0, y_0) + f(x_1, y_1)}{2} \tag{6.8}$$

we know f, x_0, $x_1 = x_0 + h$, and y_0, but we do not know y_1; it is, after all, what we're trying to estimate. We could treat this equation as implicitly defining y_1 and use a root-finding method such as Newton's method on

$$y_1 - y_0 - \frac{h}{2}(f(x_0, y_0) + f(x_1, y_1)) = 0$$

and repeat this process to find $y_2, y_3, \ldots, y_n$. This is called the **trapezoidal scheme.** Implicit methods like this are used for certain special cases (see Section 6.6), but there are more efficient approaches for most problems.

Consider again the ODE Eq. (6.6) with the initial condition Eq. (6.7). There is an integration rule we can apply to it, namely, the left endpoint rule from Section 5.6. This is the Riemann sum rule that uses the approximation

$$\int_a^b \phi(x)dx \approx (b - a)\phi(a)$$

(see Fig. 6.5); that is, we approximate the area under the curve $y = \phi(x)$ by a rectangle

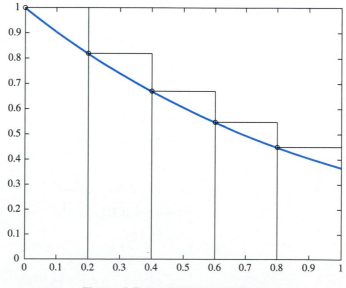

Figure 6.5 The Left Endpoint Rule.

with height equal to the value of the function at the left endpoint $x = a$. The solution of the ODE IVP is

$$y(x) = y_0 + \int_{x_0}^{x} f(t, y(t))dt,$$

so the left endpoint rule gives

$$y(x_1) = y_0 + \int_{x_0}^{x_1} f(t, y(t))dt$$

$$\approx y_0 + (x_1 - x_0)f(x_0, y(x_0))$$

$$y_1 = y_0 + hf(x_0, y_0)$$

Euler's Method   (where y_1 is the approximation to $y(x_1)$). We can iterate this:

$$y_1 = y_0 + hf(x_0, y_0)$$

$$y_2 = y_1 + hf(x_1, y_1)$$

$$\vdots$$

$$y_n = y_{n-1} + hf(x_{n-1}, y_{n-1})$$

The resulting method is known as **Euler's method.** Since the simple left endpoint rule is $O(h^2)$ for a single step, Euler's method is $O(h^2)$ in going from y_i to y_{i+1}; since the composite left endpoint rule is $O(h)$, Euler's method is $O(h)$ in going from y_0 to y_i ($i \geq 2$). As with numerical integration rules, it is the latter error estimate that concerns us. Euler's method is $O(h)$.

Example 6.2.1   Let's apply Euler's method to the ODE IVP $y' = 1 + y^2$, $y(0) = 1$. The true solution is $y(x) = \tan(x + \pi/4)$. We'll use $h = 0.5$ and solve over $[0, 2]$. We have

$$y_0 = 1$$

$$y_1 = y_0 + hf(x_0, y_0)$$

$$= 1 + 0.5(1 + 1^2)$$

$$= 2 \qquad (\approx y(0.5))$$

$$y_2 = y_1 + hf(x_1, y_1)$$

$$= 2 + 0.5(1 + 2^2)$$

$$= 4.5 \qquad (\approx y(1))$$

$$y_3 = y_2 + hf(x_2, y_2)$$

$$= 4.5 + 0.5(1 + 4.5^2)$$

$$= 15.125 \qquad (\approx y(1.5))$$

$$y_4 = y_3 + hf(x_3, y_3)$$

$$= 15.125 + 0.5(1 + 15.125^2)$$

$$\doteq 130.0078 \qquad (\approx y(2))$$

from Euler's method. How good are these results? We have the following:

Euler	Actual	Error
2	3.4082	1.4082
4.5	−4.5880	9.0880
15.125	−1.1527	16.2777
130.0078	−0.3721	130.3799

and so the results are very poor for this h. We see why this is so in MATLAB 6.2. ■

Euler's Method by Taylor Series   It's instructive to derive Euler's method in three other ways. One method is to simply expand $y(x)$, the unknown solution of the ODE IVP, in a Taylor series

$$y(x_0 + h) = y(x_0) + hy'(x_0) + \frac{h^2}{2}y''(\gamma)$$

$$\approx y(x_0) + hy'(x_0)$$

$$= y_0 + hf(x_0, y(x_0))$$

$$y_1 = y_0 + hf(x_0, y_0)$$

giving Euler's method. This derivation clearly requires that y'' exist and shows the $O(h^2)$ truncation error for a single step.

Euler's Method by Tangent Line Approximation   Another way to derive Euler's method is to note that the ODE IVP gives us knowledge of both one point on the solution $y(x)$, the point (x_0, y_0), and a way to compute the slope of the solution $y(x)$ there, $y'(x_0) = f(x_0, y_0)$. Hence we could use a tangent line approximation at (x_0, y_0) and linearly extrapolate to a value of y at $x_1 = x + h$, and then repeat from (x_1, y_1), and so on; see Figure 6.6. We omit the algebra and simply assert that this approach leads to Euler's method once again. Note that Euler's method approximates the slope of the function over $[x_i, x_{i+1}]$ using its value at the left endpoint, whereas the trapezoidal scheme (Eq. (6.8)) uses the average value of the slope over the interval (see Fig. 6.7). As would be expected, the trapezoidal scheme is more accurate $(O(h^2))$.

Euler's Method by Finite Differences   Finally, we can derive Euler's method using finite differences. We substitute the forward difference approximation for y' in Eq. (6.6), giving

$$y' = f(x, y)$$

$$\frac{y(x + h) - y(x)}{h} \approx f(x, y)$$

$$y(x + h) \approx y(x) + hf(x, y)$$

so we define

$$y_{i+1} = y_i + hf(x_i, y_i)$$

to be the approximate method. Euler's method may be viewed as a **finite difference**

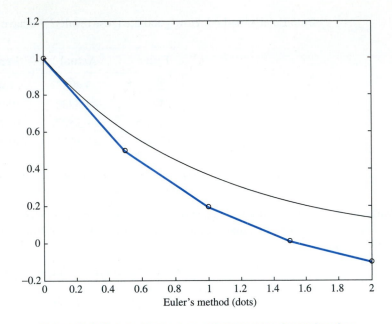

Figure 6.6 Euler's Method as a Tangent Line Approximation.

method, that is, a method found by replacing exact derivatives with finite difference approximations and neglecting the truncation errors introduced by this process.

Truncation Error and Stability

Given the relationship between Euler's method and the (unstable) forward difference approximation, we might wonder whether growth of roundoff error is an issue in Euler's method. Note that the truncation error is worse than it might at first appear: An ODE IVP

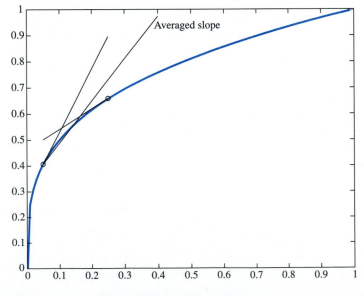

Figure 6.7 Trapezoidal Scheme.

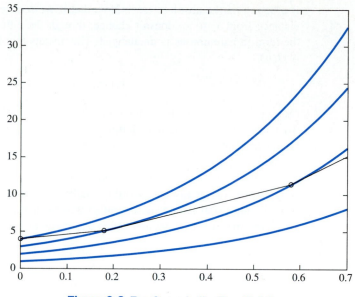

Figure 6.8 Top Curve is the True Solution.

like Eq. (6.6) with Eq. (6.7) represents one solution picked from the infinite one-parameter family of solutions defined by the ODE alone. Euler's method, viewed as a tangent line approximation, starts on the true solution (neglecting representation error in x_0 and y_0) but immediately steps off onto a second, "parallel" curve. The next iterate lands on yet another curve, which in general is even farther from the desired curve; the error builds and builds (see Fig. 6.8). If the curves aren't getting closer to one another as x increases, we'll eventually have a large error. This emphasizes the fact that Euler's method is $O(h)$ *at any fixed point* x^*; that is, if we consider the error only at some particular point x^*, then the error decreases as $O(h)$. The error grows, in general, with increasing x but decreases with decreasing step size h. The following theorem, which is proved in Section 6.4, provides a bound on this truncation error effect.

Theorem 6.2.1.

Let $y(x)$ be the solution of $y' = f(x, y)$, $y(x_0) = y_0$. If $f(x, y)$ is continuously differentiable with respect to both its independent variables in some open region R containing (x_0, y_0) and $|y''(x)|$ is bounded for x within R, then there is an $A > 0$, $B > 0$ for which the iterates $y_0, y_1, \ldots, y_n$ generated by Euler's method satisfy

$$|y(x_i) - y_i| \le hA(e^{Bih} - 1),$$

provided the iterates and the solution $y(x)$ remain in R.

The assumptions of this theorem can be weakened and A and B can be identified in terms of y and f, but the key point is that at a particular point $x_i = x_0 + ih$,

$$|y(x_i) - y_i| \le hA \left(e^{B(x_i - x_0)} - 1 \right)$$

is a bound on the absolute error. Note that if we reduce h for additional accuracy the distance from x_i to x_0 doesn't change, though the i that identifies it does. Therefore the term in parentheses is unchanged. This means that the error at any fixed point x^* is $O(h)$,

$$|y(x^*) - y^*| \leq hAM$$

($M = (e^{B(x_i - x_0)} - 1)$). But Theorem 6.2.1 also says that if instead of focusing on a particular point x^* we imagine letting $i \to \infty$ for a fixed step size h then we are looking at an exponentially growing error bound. Euler's method is $O(h)$ when we focus on *a particular point*.

In practice the actual error is almost never as bad as this worst-case estimate might suggest and is typically considerably smaller. In Figure 6.8, for example, if the curves were getting closer to one another rather than farther apart, then the error might actually be decreasing. If every member of the one-parameter family of solutions satisfies

$$y(x) \to 0$$

as $x \to \infty$, then even if we step onto the wrong curve we will eventually end up in the right place (a steady state at zero).

Theorem 6.2.1 addresses only truncation error, but roundoff error is also an issue. If an error of absolute value at most ϵ is made in evaluating each y_i (including the representation error in y_0) then, in place of Theorem 6.2.1, we will have

$$|y(x_i) - y_i| \leq \left(hA + \frac{\epsilon}{Bh} \right) \left(e^{B(x_i - x_0)} - 1 \right) + \epsilon e^{B(x_i - x_0)}$$

for the same A, B. The important thing to notice is that once again we have the error behavior

$$\alpha h + \frac{\beta}{h}$$

that we saw for the forward difference method. We have problems with the truncation error as h increases (the αh part) and problems with the roundoff error as h decreases (the β / h part), and so we must be wary of making h too small.

The methods we will be discussing in this chapter are for ODE IVPs. We'll see how to use them for higher-order IVPs such as

$$ay'' + by' + cy = f(x)$$
$$y(0) = y_0$$
$$y'(0) = v_0,$$

and for systems of ODE IVPs.

Euler's method can be an acceptable choice for ODE IVPs on small intervals with appropriately chosen step sizes. In such cases the simplicity of Euler's method may make it attractive. More importantly, though, the more common methods take its basic idea and modify it, as we'll soon see.

PROBLEMS 6.2

1. Use Euler's method with $h = 0.05$ to approximate the solution of $y' = y^2$, $y(0) = 1$ over $[0, 1]$. Compare your answer with the true solution.

2. Show that Euler's method is the result of using linear extrapolation starting from the known point (x_0, y_0) and with the known slope $y'(x_0) = f(x_0, y_0)$.

3. Use Euler's method with $h = 0.4$, $h = 0.2$, $h = 0.1$, and $h = 0.05$ to approximate the solution of $y' = -y$, $y(0) = 1$ over $[0, 4]$. Compare your answers with the true solution.

4. **a.** Use the trapezoidal scheme with $h = 0.05$ to approximate the solution of $y' = x + y + 1$, $y(1) = 1$ over $[1, 3]$.

    b. Use the trapezoidal scheme with $h = 0.05$ to approximate the solution of $y' = \sin(xy) + 1$, $y(1) = 1$ over $[1, 2]$.

5. Write a MATLAB program for performing Euler's method on a given function, initial condition, and interval, with a given step size. Test your program.

MATLAB 6.2

There are a number of commands for solving ODEs in MATLAB. If you are using MATLAB6, type `help ode` and hit the Tab key twice to see a list. Enter:

```
» odeexamples
```

and run the examples listed. Then select *Boundary Value Problems* from the drop-down menu and run those examples. These are ODE BVPs as opposed to ODE IVPs.

Let's look at an example. We'll use `ode23`, which is a low-order method (comparable to `quad`, as opposed to `quadl`). We'll use the ODE IVP $y' = x + y$, $y(0) = 1$. Enter:

```
» f=inline('x+y')
» ode23(f,[0 1],1)
```

A plot of the solution is produced. The inline function is $f(x, y)$, the vector `[0 1]` gives the initial and final values of x (or t), and the last argument is the initial condition $y(0)$. Enter:

```
» close all
» [x,y]=ode23(f,[0 1],1);
» plot(x,y)
```

The values of the nodes that were used, x, and the y-values found at those nodes, y, are returned. The method is adaptive (see Section 6.6) so the returned nodes will not always be equally spaced.

Let's compare the computed solution with the analytical solution of this first-order linear ODE. If you have the Symbolic Toolbox, enter:

```
» dsolve('Dy=t+y')              %General solution.
» dsolve('Dy=t+y','y(0)=1')     %Particular solution.
```

(It's simplest to use t for the independent variable.) The true solution is $y(t) = -t - 1 + 2\exp(t)$. Let's plot the two solutions together. Enter:

```
» hold on
» plot(x,-x-1+2*exp(x),'r')
```

The visual fit is excellent. Let's go further. Close the figure and then enter:

```
» close all
» [x,y]=ode23(f,[0 20],1);
» plot(x,y)
» hold on
» plot(x,-x-1+2*exp(x),'r')
```

This still looks pretty good, though note the vertical scale. Enter:

```
» norm(y-(-x-1+2*exp(x)))        %Absolute error.
» ans/norm(y)                    %Relative error.
```

The absolute error is considerable, but the relative error is about 1.5%. These errors are measured over the entire sequence. Let's look at them point by point. Enter:

```
» max(abs((y-(-x-1+2*exp(x)))))
» max(abs((y-(-x-1+2*exp(x)))))./abs(y))
```

This is the l_∞ measure of the error in the iterates (i.e., the max norm of the sequence generated by ode23).

Look again at Example 6.2.1. What goes so wrong there? We use a fairly large step size, of course ($h = .5$). Let's look at the true solution and the approximate solution. Enter:

```
» f=inline('1+y^2')
» y0=1;h=.5;
» y1=y0+h*f(y0)              %Approx. solution at x1=.5.
» y2=y1+h*f(y1)              %Approx. solution at x2=1.
» y3=y2+h*f(y2)              %Approx. solution at x3=1.5.
» y4=y3+h*f(y3)              %Approx. solution at x4=2.
» plot(0:.5:2,[y0 y1 y2 y3 y4],'b'),hold on
» plot(0:.5:2,[y0 y1 y2 y3 y4],'go'),
```

Now let's overlay the true solution $y(x) = \tan(x + \pi/4)$. Enter:

```
» xx=0:01:2;
» plot(xx,tan(xx+pi/4),'r')
» axis([0 2 -140 140])
» grid
```

Look carefully at this plot. The true solution is in red. Euler's method uses the slope at $x = 0$ to get an approximate value at $x = .5$. It then uses the slope at $x = .5$ to get an approximate value at $x = 1$. But, the solution has a discontinuity at $\pi/4 \doteq .79$, and Euler's method steps across this singularity without ever seeing it. From then on the y-value is so far off that it's simply luck whether we end up near the true solution again.

The point $(x_1, y_1) = (.5, 2)$ does not lie on the desired solution curve, but it does lie on some solution curve corresponding to some initial condition. If you have the Symbolic Toolbox, enter:

```
» dsolve('Dy=1+y^2')
```

to see that the general solution of the ODE $y' = 1 + y^2$ is $y(x) = \tan(x + c)$. Because of the discontinuity this solution may not continue from the origin to $x = 1$, but it is valid at $x_1 = .5$. Let's solve $y_1 = \tan(x_1 + c)$ for c. Enter:

```
» c=atan(2)-1/2
» tan(c)                  %Initial condition for this curve.
» plot(xx,tan(xx+c),'c')
```

The cyan curve should go through the point $(x_1, y_1) = (.5, 2)$. To see this more clearly, enter:

```
» axis([.4 .6 -10 10])
```

There is a similar curve for every point generated by Euler's method, unless it should happen to land on a point of discontinuity.

Let's try to see the $O(h)$ behavior of Euler's method. We'll use the ODE IVP $y' = y$, $y(0) = 1$. The true solution is $y(x) = \exp(x)$. Enter:

```
» f=inline('y')
» h=.5;
» yo=1;
» y1=y0+h*f(y0)           %Approx. solution at x1=.5.
» y2=y1+h*f(y1)           %Approx. solution at x2=1.
» E=abs(exp(1)-y2)
```

Even with two steps over [0, 1], the exponential function is growing so rapidly that linear approximations aren't very good. But we know that if we take h sufficiently small, then we can get an arbitrarily good approximation of $\exp(x)$ over any $[x, x + h]$. Enter:

```
» h=h/2,y=y0;
» for i=1:(1/h);y=y+h*f(y);end,y
» E=[E,abs(exp(1)-y)]
» h=h/2,y=y0;
» for i=1:(1/h);y=y+h*f(y);end,y
» E=[E,abs(exp(1)-y)]
```

The vector E now has three components, and the last two show about a 50% reduction in the error at $x = 1$. Repeat this process until E has 14 components; note the 50% reduction in error at each step. Note also that it is taking longer and longer as you go on. Enter:

```
» 1/h
```

This is $2^{14} = 16384$; that's how many steps we are now taking to reach $x = 1$. If we reduce h to 10^{-7}, then after a considerable time we get an error of about $1.3591E - 7$ as we would expect from an $O(h)$ method.

What if we wanted to solve this ODE IVP using ode23? Since ode23 expects the function to accept two arguments, enter:

```
» f=inline('0*x+y')
» [x,y]=ode23(f,[0 1],1);
» y(end)
» abs(y(end)-exp(1))              %Error.
» plot(x,y)
```

(If we were using an M-file instead, as is likely in practice, we could simply not use one of the input arguments to the program.) The value of $y(1)$ is approximated to about 4 decimal places.

There is also a solver ode45 that is similar to ode23 but uses a higher-order method (compare quad and quadl). It is usually advisable to try ode45 first and then switch to another method if the performance of ode45 is unacceptable.

ADDITIONAL PROBLEMS 6.2

6. a. Use Euler's method with $h = 0.05$ to approximate the solution of $y' = 1 + y^2$, $y(0) = 1$ over $[0, 0.5]$. Compare your answer with the true solution (see Example 6.2.1). Plot the approximate and analytical solution together. Then use a spline on the numerical solution and plot it together with the analytical solution. How accurate is the spline at x-values between the nodes?

  b. Attempt to extend your numerical solution to the interval $[0, 1]$ using ode23.

7. Write a MATLAB program for performing the trapezoidal scheme. Test your program.

8. What method, if any, results from using the backward difference approximation in Eq. (6.6)? How about the centered difference approximation?

9. The constant A in Theorem 6.2.1 is equal to $K/2B$, where K is max($|y''(x)|$) over the interval of interest and B is a Lipschitz constant for f with respect to y. Use Euler's method with $h = 0.05$ to approximate the solution of $y' = y + 1$, $y(0) = 1$ over $[0, 1]$. Compare your answer with the true solution and with the error bound from Theorem 6.2.1.

10. Show that the trapezoidal scheme is $O(h^3)$ for a single step and $O(h^2)$ in general.

11. a. Use Euler's method with $h = 0.4$, $h = 0.2$, $h = 0.1$, and $h = 0.05$ to approximate the solution of $y' = -8y$, $y(0) = 1$, and of $y' = -12y$, $y(0) = 1$ over $[0, 2]$. Compare your answers with the true solutions.

  b. Use Richardson extrapolation to improve your results.

12. Develop a method for solving ODE IVPs based on the right endpoint rule.

13. Euler's method may also be applied to a system of ODEs. If $y' = F(x, y)$, $y(x^{(0)}) = y^{(0)}$, where x and y are vectors, then Euler's method is $y^{(i+1)} = y^{(i)} + hF(x^{(i)}, y^{(i)})$. Use this method to approximate the solution of $y_1' = y_1 + 2y_2^2$, $y_2' = 2y_1^2 + 2y_2$, with the initial conditions $y_1(0) = y_2(0) = 1$.

14. Use Euler's method to approximate the solution of $y' = x + y^2$, $y(0) = 1$ over $[0, 2]$ for several values of h. Plot the absolute error at $x = 1.5$ as a function of h. Comment.

15. The constant A in Theorem 6.2.1 is equal to $K/2B$, where K is max($|y''(x)|$) over the interval of interest and B is a Lipschitz constant for f with respect to y. Compare the predictions of this error bound to the actual error for a variety of ODEs. Comment.

6.3   Improved Euler's Method

Euler's method is only $O(h)$. The reason is not hard to see: It uses a value of $f(x, y)$ at one endpoint of the subinterval $[x_i, x_{i+1}]$ to estimate the slope of the line it uses to extrapolate a value of $y(x_{i+1})$. But the slope is changing over that interval, possibly rapidly. The trapezoidal scheme

$$y_{i+1} = y_i + h\frac{f(x_i, y_i) + f(x_{i+1}, y_{i+1})}{2} \tag{6.9}$$

uses two values to get an average slope and is $O(h^2)$. Unfortunately it's an implicit method; that is, it defines the value y_{i+1} implicitly, forcing us to find it with a root-finding method.

Midpoint Scheme

Euler's method can be viewed as an application of the left endpoint quadrature rule. The trapezoidal scheme results from using the trapezoidal quadrature rule to integrate the ODE. The **midpoint scheme**[1]

$$y_{i+1} = f(x_i, y_i)$$
$$= y_i + hf(x_{i+1/2}, y_{i+1/2}),$$

(6.10)

where $x_{i+1/2} = x_i + h/2$ and $y_{i+1/2}$ is an approximation of $y(x_{i+1/2})$, results from applying the midpoint quadrature rule. Of course, although we can compute $x_{i+1/2} = x_i + h/2$, we do not have an estimate of $y(x_{i+1/2})$.

Improved Euler's Method

One simple idea turns the trapezoidal and midpoint schemes into explicit methods: Estimate the unknown values in these schemes using Euler's method, which is explicit. Thus the trapezoidal scheme of Eq. (6.9) is turned into the method

$$y_{i+1} = y_i + h\frac{f(x_i, y_i) + f(x_{i+1}, y_i + hf(x_i, y_i))}{2}$$

in which we are using the approximation

$$y_{i+1} = y_i + hf(x_i, y_i)$$

from Euler's method. This method is called the **improved Euler's method** (or **modified Euler's method**). The midpoint scheme becomes

$$y_{i+1} = y_i + hf\left(x_{i+1/2}, y_i + \frac{h}{2}f(x_i, y_i)\right)$$

(using Euler's method with step size $h/2$ in Eq. (6.10)). This is called the **midpoint method.** Note that the improved Euler's method and midpoint method are both explicit.

Example 6.3.1　Let's use the improved Euler's method on the ODE IVP $y' = x + y^2$, $y(0) = 1$. With $h = 0.1$ we have

$$y_1 = y_0 + h\frac{f(x_0, y_0) + f(x_1, y_0 + hf(x_0, y_0))}{2}$$
$$= 1 + \frac{0.1}{2}\left((0 + 1^2) + \left(0.1 + \widehat{y_1^2}\right)\right),$$

where

$$\widehat{y_1} = y_0 + hf(x_0, y_0)$$
$$= 1 + 0.1(0 + 1^2)$$
$$= 1.1$$

---

[1] The names of many of these methods are not standardized and so may vary from text to text.

is the estimate from Euler's method. So

$$y_1 = 1 + 0.05(1 + (0.1 + 1.1^2))$$

$$= 1.1155$$

is the improved Euler's method estimate. (The MATLAB command `ode23` gives 1.1165.) Then

$$y_2 = y_1 + h \frac{f(x_1, y_1) + f(x_2, y_1 + hf(x_1, y_1))}{2}$$

$$= 1.1155 + \frac{0.1}{2} \left((0.1 + 1.1155^2) + (0.2 + \widehat{y_2^2}) \right),$$

where

$$\widehat{y_2} = y_1 + hf(x_1, y_1)$$

$$= 1.1155 + 0.1(0.1 + 1.1155^2)$$

$$\doteq 1.2499$$

is the Euler's method estimate starting from (x_1, y_1). (Note that this is not the value we would get by applying Euler's method starting from $(x_1, \widehat{y_1}) = (0.1, 1.1)$.) So

$$y_2 = 1.1155 + 0.05((0.1 + 1.1155^2) + (0.2 + 1.2499^2))$$

$$\doteq 1.2708$$

is the improved Euler's method estimate. The MATLAB command `ode23` gives 1.2736. ■

Prediction and Correction

Methods for solving differential equations that turn an implicit method (such as the trapezoidal scheme) into an explicit method (such as the improved Euler's method) by using an explicit method (such as Euler's method) on the RHS of

$$y_{i+1} = f(y_{i+1}, p_1, \ldots, p_n)$$

are called **predictor-corrector methods.** (Here $p_1, \ldots, p_n$ are any other parameters such as x_i, y_i, etc.) We say that the explicit method makes a prediction and that the implicit methods corrects it, that is, improves it. In the improved Euler's method the predictor is Euler's method and the corrector is the trapezoidal scheme. There are many predictor-corrector methods.[2]

There is no reason that we must stop after a single correction. We can use the corrected value as a new prediction and correct it, continuing until the difference between successive corrections is acceptably small before moving on to the next point.

---

[2] We might also think of a predictor-corrector method as a way of solving an implicit method by fixed point iteration, using an explicit method to generate the initial guess.

Example 6.3.2   Consider the ODE IVP $y' = x - y$, $y(1) = 1$. Let's use the midpoint method $y_{i+1} = y_i + hf(x_{i+1/2}, y_i + \frac{h}{2} f(x_i, y_i))$ with $h = 0.1$. We have:

$$y_0 = 1$$

$$\widehat{y}_1 = y_0 + \frac{h}{2} f(x_0, y_0) \qquad \text{(predictor)}$$

$$= 1 + 0.05(1 - 1)$$

$$= 0$$

$$y_1 = y_0 + hf(x_{i+1/2}, \widehat{y}_1) \qquad \text{(corrector)}$$

$$= 1 + 0.1(1.05 - 0)$$

$$= 1.105$$

The true solution is $y(x) = x - 1 + \exp(1 - x)$, so $y(1.1) \doteq 1.0048$. Let's correct again:

$$y_1^{(2)} = y_0 + hf(x_{i+1/2}, y_1) \qquad \text{(corrector)}$$

$$= 1 + 0.1(1.05 - 1.105)$$

$$\doteq 0.9945$$

$$y_1^{(3)} = y_0 + hf\left(x_{i+1/2}, y_1^{(2)}\right) \qquad \text{(corrector)}$$

$$= 1 + 0.1(1.05 - 0.9945)$$

$$\doteq 1.0055$$

$$y_1^{(4)} = y_0 + hf\left(x_{i+1/2}, y_1^{(3)}\right) \qquad \text{(corrector)}$$

$$= 1 + 0.1(1.05 - 1.0055)$$

$$\doteq 1.0044$$

$$y_1^{(5)} = y_0 + hf\left(x_{i+1/2}, y_1^{(4)}\right) \qquad \text{(corrector)}$$

$$= 1 + 0.1(1.05 - 1.0044)$$

$$\doteq 1.0046$$

$$y_1^{(6)} = y_0 + hf\left(x_{i+1/2}, y_1^{(5)}\right) \qquad \text{(corrector)}$$

$$= 1 + 0.1(1.05 - 1.0046)$$

$$\doteq 1.0045$$

and further iterations do not change this value to the number of figures displayed, resulting in an error of about $3E - 4$. ■

We have seen three ways to reduce the error in our results: Using a higher-order method, using a smaller h, and repeatedly correcting. Higher-order methods are more difficult to program and require additional differentiability; smaller step sizes take more time to reach a desired point and can lead to the growth of roundoff error; and repeated correction takes more time. Repeated correction solves the predictor-corrector equation exactly, in the limit of repeated correction, since it is just fixed point iteration on that equation; but the numerical method being corrected is not the same as the ODE because of truncation error. Hence, repeated correction converges to the exact solution of a discrete approximation of the ODE, whereas reducing h leads to the correct solution of the ODE, in the absence of roundoff error. There's no one right approach, and this is reflected in the variety of methods for solving ODEs available in MATLAB and similar packages or software libraries.

Step Sizes   Note that the second-order methods we've been looking at use two function evaluations to take a step of length h. Euler's method uses a single function evaluation to take a step of length h, and hence Euler's method could take two steps each of length $h/2$ for the same cost. For h small the $O(h^2)$ error of a second-order method will certainly be considerably smaller than the $O(h/2)$ error of Euler's method with h halved. We generally like to take step sizes as large as we can, consistent with an error tolerance, to speed the computation.

Heun's Method   Another predictor-corrector method that is in common use and is similar to the improved Euler's method is **Heun's method**

$$y_{i+1} = y_i + \frac{h}{4}\left[f(x_i, y_i) + 3f\left(x_{i+2/3}, y_i + \frac{2h}{3}f(x_i, y_i)\right)\right],$$

where $x_{i+2/3} = x_i + 2h/3$. Heun's method uses a weighted average of the slope at the left endpoint, weighted 1/4, and the slope 2/3 of the way into the interval, weighted 3/4 (see Fig. 6.9).

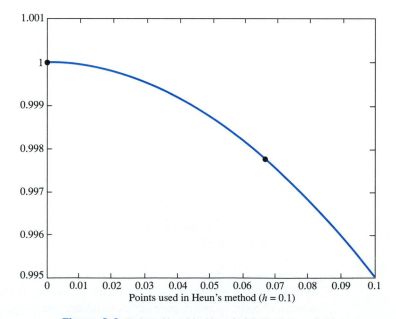

Points used in Heun's method ($h = 0.1$)

Figure 6.9 Points Used in Heun's Method ($h = 0.1$).

Theta Methods   Many methods of interest are special cases of the **theta method,** which is given, for any choice of $\theta \in [0, 1]$, by

$$y_{i+1} = y_i + h\left(\theta f(x_i, y_i) + (1 - \theta)f(x_{i+1}, y_{i+1})\right),$$

i.e., a weighted average of the values at the endpoints. Examples include Euler's method ($\theta = 1$), the trapezoidal scheme ($\theta = 1/2$), and for $\theta = 0$ the **backward Euler's method** (or **implicit Euler's method**)

$$y_{i+1} = y_i + hf(x_{i+1}, y_{i+1}).$$

The implicit Euler's method is useful in certain special cases that we discuss later. This method can also be thought of as arising from using the backward difference approximation

$$\frac{y_{i+1} - y_i}{h} \approx f(x_{i+1}, y_{i+1})$$

in the original ODE. Euler's method is sometimes called the **forward Euler's method** to differentiate it from this method.

How accurate are these methods? We show in the next section how to determine the order of methods such as these. For now we assert that the (implicit) midpoint scheme and the improved Euler's, midpoint, and Heun's methods are all $O(h^2)$. All theta methods are $O(h)$ except the trapezoidal scheme, which is $O(h^2)$.

PROBLEMS 6.3

1. a. Use the improved Euler's method with $h = 0.05$ to approximate the solution of $y' = y^2$, $y(0) = 1$ over $[0, 1]$. Compare your answers with the true solution and with your answers for Problem 1 in Section 6.2.

b. Repeat using the improved Euler's method with one extra correction step.

c. Repeat using the midpoint and Heun's methods.

2. Write a MATLAB program for performing the improved Euler's method.

3. Use the improved Euler's method with $h = 0.4$, $h = 0.2$, $h = 0.1$, and $h = 0.05$ to approximate the solution of $y' = -y$, $y(0) = 1$ over $[0, 4]$. Compare your answers with the true solution and with your answers for Problem 3 in Section 6.2.

4. a. Use the improved Euler's method with $h = 0.05$ to approximate the solution of $y' = x + y + 1$, $y(1) = 1$ over $[1, 3]$. Compare your answers with your answers for Problem 4a in Section 6.2.

b. Use the improved Euler's method with $h = 0.05$ to approximate the solution of $y' = \sin(xy) + 1$, $y(1) = 1$ over $[1, 2]$. Compare your answers with your answers for Problem 4b in Section 6.2 and with the results generated by `ode23`.

5. a. What is the predictor-corrector method found by using the forward Euler's method in the backward Euler's method?

b. What is the predictor-corrector method found by using the improved Euler's method in the backward Euler's method? Compare this method to the explicit method in part (a).

MATLAB 6.3

Several MATLAB commands allow for a vector of options to be passed to them, for example, `fzero`, the optimization commands `fminbnd` and `fminsearch` (discussed in Chapter 7), and the ODE commands. Enter:

```
» more on
» help ode23
```

and read about the OPTIONS variable, which is of a special type called a structure (see Section 6.4). Enter:

```
» help odeset
```

and read the help information. Enter:

```
» more off
» f=inline('x+y')
» [x,y]=ode23(f,[0 1],1);
» options=odeset('Stats','on')   %Display computational statistics.
» [x,y]=ode23(f,[0 1],1,options);
» options=odeset('S','off')
```

It isn't necessary to type the entire name of the option property being set, just enough of the name to distinguish it from other option properties.

The MATLAB ODE solvers use both an absolute error tolerance and a relative error tolerance, and choose whichever one is met first. That is, they try to make the absolute error α_i at each node x_i at most $\max(\alpha, \rho|y_i|)$, where α is the absolute tolerance AbsTol, which defaults to $1E-6$, and ρ is the relative tolerance RelTol, which defaults to $1E-3$. Enter:

```
» A=-t-1+2*exp(t);   %True solution at x=1.
» y(end)             %Approx. solution.
» abs(y(end)-A)      %Error.
```

The absolute error tolerance is not met, but the relative error tolerance is. Enter:

```
» options=odeset('A',1E-8,'Rel',1E-8)    %Alpha=1E-8, rho=1E-8.
» [x,y]=ode23(f,[0 1],1,options);
» abs(y(end)-A)                          %Error.
```

Once again the absolute error tolerance is not met, but the relative error tolerance is. The values of AbsTol and RelTol are required to be positive. This is advisable in any event.

The ODE routines are adaptive: The more rapidly the slope of the function is changing, the more points that will be placed in that region, analogous to the case for quadrature in Chapter 5. Enter:

```
» g=inline('log(x+y)');
» [x,y]=ode23(g,[1 20],1);
» plot(x,y,'o-')
```

Note that the circles, representing the nodes x_i, are more tightly clustered near the left side; the slope of the log function changes more rapidly for small arguments than for large arguments. The last two points are closely spaced because ode23 always computes a node at the final point.

The ode45 command uses a higher-order method than the ode23 command that we have been using. Enter:

```
» options=odeset('Stats','on')    %Tolerances are reset to defaults.
» [x23,y23]=ode23(f,[0 1],1,options);
» abs(y23(end)-A)
» [x45,y45]=ode45(f,[0 1],1,options);
» abs(y45(end)-A)
```

The higher-order method uses significantly more function evaluations but also gives an answer that is much better than requested. This may or may not be a good thing! If the selected error tolerances accurately reflect the precision that is meaningful for this problem and f is expensive to compute, then getting 8 decimal place accuracy slowly may be less attractive than getting 4 decimal place accuracy rapidly.

The default behavior of the ode45 routine is different from the default behavior of ode23 in one respect. Enter:

```
» more on
» help ode23
```

and read the information about the 'Refine' option. For ode45, but not for ode23, MATLAB automatically uses interpolation to generate additional points within each panel to provide for a smoother plot. Enter:

```
» more off
» length(x23),length(x45)
» options=odeset('Stats','on','Refine',1)
» [x45,y45]=ode45(f,[0 1],1,options);
» length(x45)
```

to see what happens when the 'Refine' option is set to the same value as the one it defaults to in ode23. The ode45 routine is the one you should try first on a problem unless you have reason to believe that another method will be better.

We discuss the mathematical ideas behind ode23, ode45, and the other ODE routines, in a later section. But for now, let's look at some other functionalities of the routines in the ODEs suite. We might want to display the one-parameter family of solutions. Enter:

```
» [x,y]=ode45(f,[0 1],0:.1:1,options);
» size(y)
```

The y vector contains solutions for all eleven initial conditions in 0:.1:1. Note that the same number of function evaluations are used as before, making it much more efficient to solve all eleven of the ODE IVPs simultaneously. This is a useful feature. Enter:

```
» plot(x,y)
```

Let's look at a more interesting ODE. Enter:

```
» f=inline('0*x+y.*(y-1)')
» [x,y]=ode45(f,[0 .4],0:.1:2,options);
» plot(x,y),hold on
» [x,y]=ode45(f,[0 5],0:.1:1,options);
» plot(x,y)
```

On one side of the equilibrium solution $y = 1$, the solutions diverge, while on the other side they tend to zero as $x \to \infty$.

The ODE may be solved at a pre-selected set of nodes by entering them in place of a time span. For example, enter:

```
» xx=sort(rand([1 6]))
» [x,y]=ode45(f,xx,1);
» x
```

The nodes x returned by ode45 are exactly the nodes xx that were given to it. However, to achieve the error tolerance, the routine may be computing function values at additional points.

The ODE routines can handle systems as well. As a very simple case we'll use a constant-coefficient linear 2×2 system with unit initial conditions, solved over $[0, 1]$. Enter:

```
» clear all
» f(x,y)=inline('0*x+[1 1;1 -1]*y')
» [x,y]=ode23(f,[0 1],[1 1]);
» whos
```

The y vector is actually a matrix; its first column is the first component y_1 of the solution of $y' = Ay$, and the second column is the second component y_2. To get a simple phase plane plot, enter:

```
» plot(y(:,1),y(:,2))
» eig([1 1;1 -1])
```

The origin is a saddle point, so this plot is consistent with the theoretical behavior of the system, starting from $y_1(0) = 1$, $y_2(0) = 1$. Another way to get such a plot is through odeset; enter:

```
» options=odeset('OutputFcn','odephas2')
» [x,y]=ode23(f,[0 1],[1 1],options);
```

A simple phase plot is produced. See help ode45, help ode45, help odeset, and help odeget for more capabilities of the ODE routines, including the 'Events' option, which may be used to detect zero-crossings of the solution. We mention again that although we have been using inline functions for the purposes of demonstration, the ODEs would more commonly be defined by an M-file.

ADDITIONAL PROBLEMS 6.3

6. a. Use the improved Euler's method with $h = 0.05$ to approximate the solution of $y' = 1 + y^2$, $y(0) = 1$ over $[0, .5]$. Compare your answer with your answers for Problem 6 of Section 6.2.

   b. Repeat using Heun's method.

7. Write a MATLAB program for performing the improved Euler's method with repeated correction. Correct until two successive iterates differ by no more than a user-supplied tolerance.

8. Conduct an experiment to compare the improved Euler's, Heun's, and midpoint methods. Does one tend to perform better than the others?

9. Use `ode23` to plot the one-parameter family of solutions of $y' = y(y - 1)(y + 1)$. Make sure that your plot captures all the interesting behavior of this family.

10. Plot the phase portrait of the system $x' = \sin(x)$, $y' = \cos(x)$ by first solving each ODE separately using `ode45`.

11. a. Use the improved Euler's method with $h = 0.4$, $h = 0.2$, $h = 0.1$, and $h = 0.05$ to approximate the solution of $y' = -8y$, $y(0) = 1$, and of $y' = -12y$, $y(0) = 1$ over $[0, 2]$. Compare your answers with your answers from Problem 11 of Section 6.2 and with the true solution.

   b. Repeat using the improved Euler's method with one extra correction step.

c. Repeat using the backward Euler's method.

d. Repeat using the **implicit midpoint rule** $y_{i+1} = y_i + hf(x_{i+1/2}, (y_i + y_{i+1})/2)$. Note that this method uses the midpoint idea but is not derived from the midpoint quadrature rule as the midpoint scheme and methods are. Also repeat using the explicit rule corresponding to this method with prediction by Euler's method.

e. Use Richardson extrapolation to improve your results for part (a).

12. Use the improved Euler's, Heun's, and midpoint methods to solve $y' = -30y$, $y(0) = 1$ over $[0, 10]$. Comment.

13. Use the Euler's, improved Euler's, Heun's, and midpoint methods to solve $y' = y(y - \pi)$, $y(0) = c$ over $[0, 10]$ for various values of $c > 0$. Note that if your initial condition is not equal to π (e.g., if you use $y0=pi$ to approximate $y(0) = \pi$), then your answer should tend either to 0 or to ∞, and that if $y(0) > 0$, then $y(t) > 0$ for all $t > 0$.

14. Use the improved Euler's method to approximate the solution of $y' = x + y^2$, $y(0) = 1$ over $[0, 2]$ for several values of h. Plot the absolute error at $x = 1.5$ as a function of h. Comment.

15. a. Show that the midpoint scheme is $O(h^2)$.

   b. Show that the midpoint method is $O(h^2)$.

6.4   Analysis of Explicit One-Step Methods

Classification of Methods

All the predictor-corrector methods we have seen so far, as well as Euler's method, are of a form known as **explicit one-step methods,** meaning methods of the form

$$y_{i+1} = y_i + h\Phi_f(x_i, y_i, h),$$

where Φ_f is called the **increment function.** In making Φ dependent on f, we mean that Φ may depend on the function f and possibly its derivatives. The method is explicit because it defines y_{i+1} explicitly in terms of known quantities and is one-step because it computes y_{i+1} in terms of y_i. The backwards Euler's method is an **implicit one-step method,**

$$y_{i+1} = y(x_i, x_{i+1}, y_i, y_{i+1})$$

and in fact the theta method with $\theta \in [0, 1)$ is always an implicit one-step method.

     An **explicit multi-step method,** also called an **explicit k-step method,** is of the form

$$y_{i+1} = \sum_{j=0}^{j=k-1} \alpha_j y_{i-j} + h\Phi_f(x_i, y_i, y_{i-1}, \ldots, y_{i-k+1}, f, h)$$

($k \geq 2$). (Note that $x_{i-1} = x_i - h$, and so on, so we need not list the other nodes as additional arguments.) The **implicit multi-step methods** or **implicit k-step methods** are methods of the form

$$y_{i+1} = \sum_{j=0}^{j=k-1} \alpha_j y_{i-j} + h\Phi_f(x_i, y_{i+1}, y_i, y_{i-1}, \ldots, y_{i-k+1}, f, h)$$

($k \geq 2$). We could generate an implicit two-step method for the ODE IVP $y' = f(x, y)$, $y(x_0) = y_0$ by integrating $y' = f(x, y(x))$ using Simpson's rule over an interval of width $2h$:

$$y' = f(x, y(x))$$

$$y(x_2) = y_0 + \int_{x_0}^{x_2} f(t, y(t))\, dt$$

$$y(x_2) \approx y_0 + \frac{h}{3}\left(f(x_0, y(x_0)) + 4f(x_1, y(x_1)) + f(x_2, y(x_2))\right) \tag{6.11}$$

$$y_2 = y_0 + \frac{h}{3}\left(f(x_0, y_0) + 4f(x_1, y_1) + f(x_2, y_2)\right)$$

where the last line defines the numerical method and $h = (x - x_0)/2$. This is an implicit two-step method; not only is it implicit in y_2, but we need a starter method, preferably of the same order, to get a value for y_1. Then the formula

$$y_3 = y_1 + \frac{h}{3}\left(f(x_1, y_1) + 4f(x_2, y_2) + f(x_3, y_3)\right)$$

for y_3 (and higher y_i) is still implicit but does not need to have additional values calculated by another method.

One-Step Methods

We return to multi-step methods in Section 6.7, but for now, let's discuss the analysis of explicit one-step methods. Consider the explicit one-step method

$$y_{i+1} = y_i + h\Phi(x_i, y_i, h), \tag{6.12}$$

Consistency

where it is understood that $\Phi = \Phi_f$. We say that the explicit one-step method is **consistent** with the ODE IVP $y' = f(x, y)$, $y(x_0) = y_0$ if

$$\Phi(x, y, 0) = f(x, y)$$

and $\Phi(x, y, h)$ is continuous at $h = 0$ (that is, $\lim_{h\to 0} \Phi(x, y, h) = \Phi(x, y, 0)$). *Consistency* means that as $h \to 0$, the difference equation $y_{i+1} = y_i + h\Phi(x_i, y_i, h)$ approximates the true equation $y' = f(x, y)$ more and more accurately.

LTE

We define the **local truncation error** (**LTE**) of an explicit one-step method at a point x_i to be the extent to which the true solution $y(x)$ of the ODE IVP fails to satisfy the numerical method Eq. (6.12). That is, the LTE is the difference

$$LTE_{i+1} = y(x_{i+1}) - [y(x_i) + h\Phi(x_i, y(x_i), h)] \tag{6.13}$$

Global Error

between $y(x_{i+1})$ and the value we would get for y_{i+1} *if we had used the exact value* $y_i = y(x_i)$ to make the step.[3] Note that this is a function of h. The **global error** is the

---

[3] Many texts write $LTE_i = h\tau_i$ and call τ_i the local truncation error.

difference

$$GE_{i+1} = y(x_{i+1}) - y_{i+1} \tag{6.14}$$

between the true value and the computed value. The global error is the quantity of interest to us but it is most convenient to analyze the global error using the local truncation error.

Convergence   Let $n = 1/h$. We say that a method is **convergent** if the global error tends to zero as h tends to zero, that is, if for a fixed interval $[a, b]$ (with $x_0 = a$, $x_n = b$) we have

$$\lim_{h \to 0} \max_{i=1}^{n} (|y(x_{i+1}) - y_{i+1}|) = 0$$

for all valid initial conditions $y(x_0) = y_0$. What we want out of a numerical scheme for solving $y' = f(x, y)$, $y(x_0) = y_0$ is that it is convergent, has error that goes to zero *Stability* sufficiently rapidly, and is stable with respect to roundoff error. We say that a method is **stable** if for all sufficiently small h and all $\epsilon > 0$ there is a $K > 0$ such that the numerical solution of $y' = f(x, y)$, $y(x_0) = y_0 + \epsilon$, using Eq. (6.12), differs from the numerical solution of $y' = f(x, y)$, $y(x_0) = y_0$, using Eq. (6.12), by at most $K\epsilon$ at the final node. In other words, *stability* means that if $\{y_i\}_{i=1}^{n}$ is the numerical solution of the unperturbed problem $y' = f(x, y)$, $y(x_0) = y_0$ and $\{w_i\}_{i=1}^{n}$ is the numerical solution of the perturbed problem $y' = f(x, y)$, $y(x_0) = y_0 + \epsilon$, then

$$|w_n - y_n| \le K\epsilon$$

for all h less than some h_0, where K is independent of ϵ and h. We could have defined stability to mean that

$$|w_i - y_i| \le K\epsilon$$

for $i = 1, \ldots, n$ but if it is stable for any endpoint x_n then it is stable for any point x_i because we could always consider x_i the endpoint of a subproblem.

Analysis of   That's a lot of definitions. Let's apply them to Euler's method $y_{i+1} = y_i + hf(x_i, y_i)$ *Euler's Method* and see what we get. Is Euler's method consistent? Yes; the increment function is $\Phi_f(x, y, h) = f(x, y)$, so trivially $\lim_{h \to 0} \Phi_f(x, y, h) = f(x, y)$. What is the local truncation error of Euler's method? From Eq. (6.13) we have

$$
\begin{aligned}
LTE_{i+1} &= y(x_{i+1}) - \left[y(x_i) + h\Phi_f(x_i, y(x_i), h) \right] \\
&= y(x_{i+1}) - y(x_i) - hf(x_i, y(x_i)) \\
&= \left[y(x_i) + hy'(x_i) + \frac{h^2}{2} y''(\xi_i) \right] - y(x_i) - hf(x_i, y(x_i)) \\
&= \left[y(x_i) + hf(x_i, y(x_i)) + \frac{h^2}{2} y''(\xi_i) \right] - y(x_i) - hf(x_i, y(x_i)) \\
&= \frac{h^2}{2} y''(\xi_i) \tag{6.15}
\end{aligned}
$$

and in particular the LTE at the point x_{i+1} is $O(h^2)$ (if the solution y is at least twice continuously differentiable). What about the global error? Fix an interval of integration $[a, b] = [x_0, x_n]$ and assume that y is at least twice continuously differentiable. From

Eq. (6.13) we have

$$y(x_{i+1}) = y(x_i) + h\Phi(x_i, y(x_i), h) + LTE_{i+1}$$

$$y(x_{i+1}) - y_{i+1} = y(x_i) + h\Phi(x_i, y(x_i), h) + LTE_{i+1} - y_{i+1}$$

$$= y(x_i) + h\Phi(x_i, y(x_i), h) + LTE_{i+1} - (y_i + hf(x_i, y_i))$$

$$GE_{i+1} = GE_i + h\left(f(x_i, y(x_i)) - f(x_i, y_i)\right) + LTE_{i+1}$$

$$= GE_i + h\left(f(x_i, y(x_i)) - f(x_i, y(x_i) - GE_i)\right) + LTE_{i+1}$$

using Eq. (6.14). Let $e_{i+1} = |GE_{i+1}|$. Then, by the triangle inequality, we have

$$e_{i+1} \le e_i + h\,|f(x_i, y(x_i)) - f(x_i, y_i)| + M,$$

where $M > 0$ is a bound on the absolute local truncation error $|LTE_i|$ over $x_0, \ldots, x_n$. Let L be a Lipschitz constant for f with respect to y. Then

$$|f(x_i, y(x_i)) - f(x_i, y(x_i) - GE_i)| \le L\,|GE_i|$$

$$= Le_i,$$

so

$$e_{i+1} \le e_i + hLe_i + M$$

$$= (1 + hL)e_i + M$$

$(i = 0, 1, \ldots, n - 1)$. It is easy to verify inductively that $e_{i+1} \le (1 + hL)e_i + M$ implies that

$$e_i \le \frac{(1 + hL)^i - 1}{hL} M + (1 + hL)^i e_0 \tag{6.16}$$

(compare the analysis of stationary iterative methods in Section 3.1). Using the inequality $1 + x \le \exp(x)$, we can write

$$(1 + hL)^i \le (\exp(hL))^i$$

$$= \exp(ihL),$$

so

$$e_i \le \frac{\exp(ihL) - 1}{hL} M + \exp(ihL)e_0 \tag{6.17}$$

is a bound on the global error. (Compare Theorem 6.2.1, where e_0 is zero because the arithmetic is assumed to be exact—we are analyzing the algorithm, not its implementation on a machine.) Note that

$$\frac{\exp(ihL) - 1}{hL} = O(h)$$

$$\exp(ihL) = O(1),$$

as $h \to 0$, so Eq. (6.17) means that

$$e_i \le O(h) + O(1)e_0,$$

and because $e_0 = 0$, the global error is $O(h)$. Again, the global error is the error in which we are interested. Euler's method is $O(h)$.

Convergent and Stable Methods

We have considered consistency, local truncation error, and global truncation error. What we really need of a numerical method, however, is convergence—that the global error tends to zero as $h \to 0$ so that refinement of the step size leads to improved accuracy—and stability with respect to roundoff error so that we may actually implement the method on a computer.[4]

Theorem 6.4.1

An explicit one-step method $y_{i+1} = y_i + h\Phi_f(x_i, y_i, h)$ with an increment function $\Phi_f(x_i, y_i, h)$ that is continuous with respect to x, y, and h for all $h < h_0$ for some $h_0 > 0$, and that is Lipschitz with respect to y, is stable. Furthermore, it is convergent if and only if it is consistent.

Therefore, Euler's method is convergent and stable. This theorem is of great practical importance. Look back at the demonstration that Euler's method is consistent, which was relatively easy, and the derivation of Eq. (6.17) followed by the demonstration that the global error tends to zero as $h \to 0$ (convergence), which was rather more work. We generally show that an explicit one-step method is convergent and stable by showing that it is consistent and appealing to this theorem. This is why we needed so many definitions: One set for what we care about (convergence, meaning that the solution of the difference equation tends to the solution of the differential equation as $h \to 0$) and the other for what we can easily show (consistency, meaning that the difference equation tends to the differential equation as $h \to 0$).

For a convergent explicit one-step method, if the local truncation error is $O(h^{m+1})$, then the global error is $O(h^m)$. This is convenient because the LTE is easier to estimate. In this case we define m to be the **order** of the method; Euler's method is of order one because of Eq. (6.15).

We emphasize that Theorem 6.4.1 applies only to explicit one-step methods. There are similar theorems for other types of methods. Typically these theorems require us to show consistency and *one* of stability and convergence; we get the remaining property for free. Since consistency is usually easy to show, this is still an improvement over having to show both stability and convergence.

Example 6.4.1　Let's look at the midpoint method. Recall that the midpoint method is the explicit one-step method

$$y_{i+1} = y_i + hf\left(x_{i+1/2}, y_i + \frac{h}{2}f(x_i, y_i)\right)$$

---

[4] Note that stability of the algorithm means protection not only from the effects of roundoff error but also from the effects of inaccuracies in the data, such as imprecise knowledge of y_0.

$(\Phi_f(x_i, y_i, h) = f(x_{i+1/2}, y_i + \frac{h}{2} f(x_i, y_i)))$. If f is continuous, then as $h \to 0$ with x, y fixed,

$$f\left(x_{i+1/2}, y_i + \frac{h}{2} f(x_i, y_i)\right) = f\left(x + \frac{h}{2}, y + \frac{h}{2} f(x, y)\right)$$

tends to $f(x, y)$, so the method is consistent. In addition $\Phi_f(x, y, h) = f(x + \frac{h}{2}, y + \frac{h}{2} f(x, y))$ is continuous, and if f is continuously differentiable with respect to y, then $\Phi_f(x, y, h)$ is differentiable with respect to y and is therefore Lipschitz with respect to y. Hence if f is continuous and continuously differentiable in y, then, by Theorem 6.4.1, the midpoint method is stable and convergent. ∎

We've defined global error, convergence, and stability for a general method but not consistency and local truncation error. *Consistency* is always defined to mean that as h shrinks the discrete equation tends to the ODE; *LTE* is always the extent to which the solution of the ODE fails to solve the difference equation, that is, it is the quantity that remains if we replace y_k with $y(x_k)$ in the numerical method.

Summary   Does all this analysis matter? Well, this type of thing *is* the "analysis" in "numerical analysis," and it certainly improves our confidence in a program if we know the method it is intended to implement is convergent and stable. Then, if something goes wrong, we know it must be either a programming error or a violation of assumptions such as continuity of the function.[5] Given the complicated devices and structures designed with the aid of a computer, such analysis seems worthwhile for a method that will be implemented as part of a scientific or engineering package. In addition, there is no analytical formula for the solution of most ODEs, so we cannot test our programs on "hard" cases and compare the answers to what they should be. A proof of convergence and stability is therefore important for building our confidence in the programs that perform these computations.

PROBLEMS 6.4

1. Use Theorem 6.4.1 to show that the improved Euler's method is convergent and stable. Find an expression for the LTE.

2. Show that Eq. (6.17) agrees with Theorem 6.2.1 by taking $e_0 = 0$ and expanding $\exp(ihL) - 1)/hL$ in a Maclaurin series.

3. Prove that Eq. (6.16) is correct.

4. Use Theorem 6.4.1 to show that Heun's method is convergent and stable. Find an expression for the LTE.

5. a. Use Eq. (6.11) with $h = 0.05$ to approximate the solution of $y' = x + y + 1$, $y(1) = 1$ over $[1, 3]$. Use Heun's method as a starter method. (This method is $O(h^3)$.) Compare your answer with the true solution.

b. Use this method with $h = 0.05$ to approximate the solution of $y' = y^2$, $y(0) = 1$ over $[0, 1]$. Compare your answer with the true solution.

MATLAB 6.4

We have already seen that the options for the ODE routines are data types called structures; the same is true of the optimization command `fminbnd` in Chapter 7. Let's take

---

[5] Or, extremely infrequently, a hardware problem.

a bit of a detour to learn a bit more about structures. Enter:

```
» help struct
```

and read the help text. Enter:

```
» more on
» help datatypes
```

to see information on the different types of variables available in MATLAB as well as commands for manipulating and converting between them.

A structure may be thought of as an array of arrays, where the element arrays may be of different sizes. The element arrays are also labeled by names. For example, enter:

```
» student(1).lastname='Adams'
» student(1).firstname='John'
» student(1).id=23571
» student(1).exams=[81 85 83]
» student(1).hw=[10 9 10 10 8 7 9 10 10]
» student(1).lastname='Benson'
» student(2).firstname='Mary'
» student(2).id=45731
» student(2).exams=[88 80 91]
» student(2).hw=[10 9 9 9 9 10 9 10 8 10]
» student
» student(1)
» student(2)
```

When we enter the name of the structure variable, we get a description, not a value. However when we ask for an indexed entry, we get all the data for that entry. We can think of each student(i) as a virtual index card with the data on the ith student. Each item on it (lastname, firstname, etc.) is called a *field*. Enter:

```
» student(2).lastname
» student(1).id
» student.id
```

The first two lines return regular string (see help strings) and numeric variables that we can operate on in the usual way. Enter:

```
» fieldnames(student)
» isfield(student,'id')
» isfield(student,'ego')
» student(1).ego
```

The isfield command checks for valid field names. The fieldnames command provides all field names as a cell array (more on this later).

We can access the contents of a field using the getfield command rather than the structure.fieldname form. Enter:

```
» getfield(student,'firstname')
» getfield(student(1),'firstname')
» getfield(student(2),'firstname')
```

We can set field values using the `setfield` command. Enter:

```
» setfield(student(1),'firstname','Jack')
» student(1)                %No change!
» student(1)=setfield(student(1),'firstname','Jack')
» student(1)                %Changed.
```

Fields can be removed using the `rmfield` command. Fields can be added to an existing structure; enter:

```
» student(1).grade='B+'
» student(1)
» student(2)
» student(2).grade
» student(2).grade='A'
» student(2)
```

Note that adding the field to one entry adds it to all entries. Notice also that entries in a given field need not be the same size in every entry, as with the grades and the homework scores.

Structures may also be created using the `struct` command. To create a structure similar to `student`, enter:

```
» S=struct('lastname',{'Adams','Benson'},'firstname', {'John','Mary'})
» S(1)
» S(2)
```

Note that the field names could be given as string variables, so this form of the command is fairly flexible. Structures can also be multiply indexed, for example, `S(i,j)`.

Structures are the type of variable used to pass information on options to the minimization and ODE routines. Enter:

```
» type odeset
```

and see if you can understand how `odeset` forms the structure variable that it creates for the ODE routines. A structure array is convenient in this case because some of the options have numeric values and some have string values; some can even be functions.

Let's look at cell arrays. Cell arrays are similar to structures in that they may hold other arrays of varying sizes, but they may be indexed in the usual way. Cell arrays may be created using curly braces, as was done in the use of the `struct` command above. Enter:

```
» classlist{1,1}='Adams'
» classlist{2,1}='John'
» classlist{3,1}=23571
» classlist{1,2}='Benson'
```

```
» classlist{2,2}='Mary'
» classlist{3,2}=45731
» classlist
» classlist(1)
» classlist(5)
» classlist{2,2}
```

The last form, classlist{i,j}, is the usual way to access elements of a cell array. Notice that a cell array is similar to a structure array; we sacrifice the convenience of field names but gain some flexibility in indexing. Enter:

```
» classlist{1,:}
» classlist{1:2,1:2}
» celldisp(classlist)
» cellplot(classlist)
```

The cellplot command displays the contents of a cell array graphically. The cell command may be used to create a cell array of a given size, initially empty, to be filled by indexing. Cells may be indexed more than twice; that is, C{2,4,6,2} can be valid if C is set up appropriately. This is also true of structures.

ADDITIONAL PROBLEMS 6.4

6. Show that Heun's method is convergent and stable directly, without using Theorem 6.4.1.

7. a. The **inverse Euler's method** is the scheme $y_{i+1} = y_i + hy_i f(x_i, y_i)/(y_i - hf(x_i, y_i))$. (We choose h to avoid division by a small number.) Show that the inverse Euler's method is of order one.
  b. Show that the inverse Euler's method is convergent.

8. Find an expression for the LTE of the backward Euler's method.

9. Derive Heun's method as a Radau quadrature rule.

10. Show that the trapezoidal scheme is convergent. Theorem 6.4.1 does not apply; use a direct approach.

11. Show that the backward Euler's method is convergent. Theorem 6.4.1 does not apply; use a direct approach.

12. a. Find the order of the theta methods.
  b. Show that the theta methods are convergent. Theorem 6.4.1 does not apply; use a direct approach.

13. Develop a numerical method for $y' = f(x, y)$, $y(x_0) = y_0$ using the centered difference approximation to the first derivative and a starter method. Test your method.

14. Test Euler's method and the improved Euler's method on a number of functions that are not Lipschitz. Compare how the error decreases with decreasing h to what happens for Lipschitz functions.

15. a. Show that if $f(x, y)$ is Lipschitz then so is the increment function for the improved Euler's method.
  b. Show that if $f(x, y)$ is Lipschitz then so is the increment function for Heun's method.

6.5 Taylor and Runge-Kutta Methods

We have been liberal in assuming that the ODE IVP $y' = f(x, y)$, $y(x_0) = y_0$ we wish to solve has certain desirable properties. We're going to be even more so now. If a solution $y(x)$ of the ODE IVP exists, then it is differentiable since $y'(x) = f(x, y(x))$. If it is twice differentiable then

$$\frac{d^2}{dx^2} y(x) = \frac{d}{dx} y'(x)$$

$$= \frac{d}{dx} f(x, y(x))$$

$$= \frac{\partial f}{\partial x} \frac{\partial x}{\partial x} + \frac{\partial f}{\partial y} \frac{\partial y}{\partial x}$$

$$= \frac{\partial f}{\partial x} \cdot 1 + \frac{\partial f}{\partial y} \frac{dy}{dx}$$

$$= \frac{\partial f}{\partial x} + \frac{\partial f}{\partial y} f(x, y),$$

where $\partial f / \partial x$ is the partial derivative of f with respect to its first variable, holding its second variable constant. Since f is always known, we can certainly compute its partial derivatives. Recall that one way we derived Euler's method in Section 6.2 was by neglecting the final term in

$$y(x_0 + h) = y(x_0) + hy'(x_0) + \frac{h^2}{2} y''(\gamma).$$

Taylor Methods   If we now write

$$y(x_0 + h) = y(x_0) + hy'(x_0) + \frac{h^2}{2} y''(x_0) + \frac{h^3}{6} y'''(x_0), \qquad (6.18)$$

we have the method

$$y(x_0 + h) \approx y(x_0) + hy'(x_0) + \frac{h^2}{2} y''(x_0)$$

$$y_1 = y_0 + hf(x_0, y_0) + \frac{h^2}{2} f'(x_0, y_0) \qquad (6.19)$$

$$= y_0 + hf(x_0, y_0) + \frac{h^2}{2} (f_x(x_0, y_0) + f_y(x_0, y_0) f(x_0, y_0))$$

and so on for $y_2, y_3, \ldots$. We could, if $y(x)$ is sufficiently differentiable, continue in this way and create higher and higher-order methods by taking a longer and longer Taylor series in Eq. (6.18) and using the chain rule to find the necessary derivatives of $f(x, y(x))$. The resulting methods are called the **Taylor methods of order k** if the neglected term is of the form

$$\frac{h^{k+1}}{k!} y^{(k+1)}(x_0) = \frac{h^{k+1}}{k!} f^{(k)}(x_0, y_0)$$

($k \geq 1$). Euler's method is the Taylor method of order one. Of course, we know from Theorem 6.2.1 that it suffices that f be continuously differentiable in Euler's method whereas viewing the method as a Taylor method requires that f be twice continuously differentiable.

Example 6.5.1   Let's use the Taylor method of order two on the ODE IVP $y' = x^2 y$, $y(0) = 1$. The solution is $y(x) = \exp(x^3/3)$. We have

$$f(x, y) = x^2 y$$
$$f_x(x, y) = 2xy$$
$$f_y(x, y) = x^2,$$

so the method is

$$y_{i+1} = y_i + hf(x_i, y_i) + \frac{h^2}{2}(f_x(x_i, y_i) + f_y(x_i, y_i)f(x_i, y_i))$$

$$= y_i + hx_i^2 y_i + \frac{h^2}{2}\left(2x_i y_i + \left(x_i^2\right)\left(x_i^2 y_i\right)\right)$$

$$= y_i + hx_i^2 y_i + \frac{h^2}{2}x_i y_i\left(2 + x_i^3\right)$$

$$= y_i + hx_i y_i\left(x_i + \frac{h}{2}\left(2 + x_i^3\right)\right)$$

(from Eq. (6.19)). Hence, using $h = 0.05$,

$$y_0 = 1$$

$$y_1 = y_0 + hx_0 y_0\left(x_0 + \frac{h}{2}\left(2 + x_0^3\right)\right)$$

$$= 1 + 0$$

$$= 1$$

$$y_2 = y_1 + hx_1 y_1\left(x_1 + \frac{h}{2}\left(2 + x_1^3\right)\right)$$

$$= 1 + (0.05)(0.05)(1)(0.05 + 0.025(2 + 0.05^3))$$

$$\doteq 1.0003$$

$$y_3 = y_2 + hx_2 y_2\left(x_2 + \frac{h}{2}(2 + x_2^3)\right)$$

$$= 1.0003 + (0.05)(0.1)(1.0003)(0.1 + 0.025(2 + 0.1^3))$$

$$\doteq 1.0011,$$

and the errors are

$$\alpha_1 = \left|y_1 - \exp\left(x_1^3/3\right)\right|$$

$$\doteq 4.2E - 5$$

$$\alpha_2 = \left| y_2 - \exp\left(x_2^3 / 3 \right) \right|$$
$$\doteq 3.3E - 5$$
$$\alpha_3 = \left| y_3 - \exp\left(x_3^3 / 3 \right) \right|$$
$$\doteq 2.6E - 5,$$

so our results are accurate to the number of places shown. We shouldn't be too worried about the fact that $y_0 = y_1$; the solution is changing slowly near x_0 ($y'(x_0) = 0$). ∎

Taylor methods are rarely used because of the obvious difficulty of differentiating f automatically. The Taylor method of order two uses three function evaluations (f, f_x, and f_y) and has local truncation error of order three, meaning its global error is of order two. The improved Euler's method uses two function evaluations, requires no automatic differentiation, and is also of order two, so the Taylor method is hardly competitive.

Making Taylor Methods Practical

What if we want methods of order higher than two but don't want to have to differentiate f? There are many approaches, but the one we are about to describe leads to one of the most widely used classes of numerical methods for ODEs. The idea is simple: The Taylor method of order two is

$$y_{i+1} = y_i + hf(x_i, y_i) + \frac{h^2}{2}(f_x(x_i, y_i) + f_y(x_i, y_i)f(x_i, y_i))$$
$$= y_i + h\left(f(x_i, y_i) + \frac{h}{2}(f_x(x_i, y_i) + f_y(x_i, y_i)f(x_i, y_i)) \right). \tag{6.20}$$

The fact that it is of order two means that the RHS is correct to $O(h^3)$, the LTE, if y_i is exact. What if we were to approximate the term

$$f(x_i, y_i) + f'(x, y(x))\big|_{(x_i, y_i)} = f_x(x_i, y_i) + f_y(x_i, y_i)f(x_i, y_i)$$

to $O(h^3)$? If we were to do this, using only values of f and not of its derivatives, the resulting method would also have $O(h^3)$ LTE and hence $O(h^2)$ global error. We would have a method of the same order that would use only function values. **Explicit Runge-Kutta methods** (or **ERK methods**) achieve this with the one-step formula

Runge-Kutta Methods

$$y_i = y_{i-1} + h(k_1 g_1 + k_2 g_2 + \cdots + k_N g_N),$$

where the g_i represent function evaluations and are defined by

$$g_1 = f(x_{i-1} + c_1 h, y_{i-1})$$
$$g_2 = f(x_{i-1} + c_2 h, y_{i-1} + a_{2,1} h g_1)$$
$$g_3 = f(x_{i-1} + c_3 h, y_{i-1} + a_{3,1} h g_1 + a_{3,2} h g_2) \tag{6.21}$$
$$\vdots$$
$$g_N = f(x_{i-1} + c_N h, y_{i-1} + a_{N,1} h g_1 + \cdots + a_{N,N-1} h g_{N-1})$$

and are called the **RK stages.** Hence, an ERK method is similar to Euler's method but uses a weighted average

$$k_1 g_1 + k_2 g_2 + \cdots + k_N g_N$$

at a variety of points in the interval instead of a single function value. Compare this to the idea of Heun's method and other methods from Section 6.3. The values of the k_i, c_i, and $a_{i,j}$ are chosen to give a method as accurate and as efficient (in terms of function evaluations) as the Taylor method that uses the same number of function evaluations.

Specifying RK Methods

The $\{c_i\}_{i=1}^N$ are called the **RK nodes** (typically $c_1 = 0$ and often $c_N = 1$), and the $\{k_i\}_{i=1}^N$ are called the **RK weights;** the lower triangular matrix $A = (a_{i,j})$ is called the **RK matrix** of the method. The choice of nodes, weights, and the RK matrix defines the ERK method. They are typically displayed in an **RK tableau**

$$k|c|A,$$

where k is the column vector of RK weights and c is the column vector of nodes.[6] Elements of A that are not in the strict lower triangle and hence must be null are simply left empty in the tableau. For example,

$$
\begin{array}{c|cccc}
\frac{1}{6} & 0 \\
\frac{1}{3} & \frac{1}{2} & \frac{1}{2} \\
\frac{1}{3} & \frac{1}{2} & 0 & \frac{1}{2} \\
\frac{1}{6} & 1 & 0 & 0 & 1
\end{array}
$$

defines an ERK method

$$y_i = y_{i-1} + h\left(\frac{1}{6}g_1 + \frac{1}{3}g_2 + \frac{1}{3}g_3 + \frac{1}{6}g_4\right)$$

$$g_1 = f\left(x_{i-1}, y_{i-1}\right)$$

$$g_2 = f\left(x_{i-1} + \frac{1}{2}h, y_{i-1} + \frac{1}{2}hg_1\right)$$

$$g_3 = f\left(x_{i-1} + \frac{1}{2}h, y_{i-1} + \frac{1}{2}hg_2\right) \tag{6.22}$$

$$g_4 = f\left(x_{i-1} + h, y_{i-1} + hg_3\right)$$

known as the **classical fourth-order Runge-Kutta method.** This is the most commonly employed ERK method except possibly for certain methods of order two (as we'll soon see).

Implicit RK Methods

The **implicit Runge-Kutta methods** (or **IRK methods**) are similar except that the matrix A need not be lower triangular; that is, each of the g_i is given by

$$g_k = f(x_{i-1} + c_k h, y_{i-1} + a_{k,1}hg_1 + \cdots + a_{k,N}hg_N)$$

($k = 1, \ldots, N$). We must solve a nonlinear system at each step, but the previous solution provides a good initial guess. Nontrivial examples of these methods are rarely seen in practice, despite their generally superior stability properties, so from now on when we say Runge-Kutta method or RK method we mean an ERK method.

Remember, our goal in using an RK method is to get an "approximate" Taylor method by approximating the terms involving derivatives of f to the same order as the truncation

---

[6] An alternative tableau notation writes the weights as a row vector beneath A.

error of the Taylor method. Let's try doing this for the Taylor method of order two

$$y_{i+1} = y_i + h\left(f(x_i, y_i) + \frac{h}{2}(f_x(x_i, y_i) + f_y(x_i, y_i)f(x_i, y_i))\right) \tag{6.23}$$

(from Eq. (6.20)). It's not immediately clear how many stages we need; on the one hand, there are three separate function evaluations (f, f_x, and f_y), so perhaps we'll need a three-stage method. On the other hand, there are methods of order two that use two function evaluations—the midpoint method, the improved Euler's method, Heun's method—so maybe we can get away with only two stages. Let's try a two-stage RK method

$$y_i = y_{i-1} + h(k_1 g_1 + k_2 g_2)$$
$$g_1 = f(x_{i-1}, y_{i-1})$$
$$g_2 = f(x_{i-1} + ch, y_{i-1} + ahg_1)$$

where we have taken $c_1 = 0$ (ensuring that we use the left endpoint of the interval). We need to find the weights k_1 and k_2 which will be attached to the two estimates g_1 and g_2 of the slopes, and c and a, which determine g_2. Write

$$\begin{aligned} g_2(x_i, y_i) &= f(x_{i-1} + ch, y_{i-1} + ahg_1) \\ &= f(x_{i-1}, y_{i-1}) + chf_x(x_{i-1}, y_{i-1}) + ahf(x_{i-1}, y_{i-1})f_y(x_{i-1}, y_{i-1}) \\ &\quad + O(h^2) \end{aligned}$$

using the Taylor series for a function $g_2(x, y)$ of two variables. Hence the RK method is

$$\begin{aligned} y_i &= y_{i-1} + h(k_1 g_1 + k_2 g_2) \\ &= y_{i-1} + h(k_1 f(x_{i-1}, y_{i-1}) + k_2(f(x_{i-1}, y_{i-1}) + chf_x(x_{i-1}, y_{i-1}) \\ &\quad + ahf(x_{i-1}, y_{i-1})f_y(x_{i-1}, y_{i-1})) + O(h^2)) \\ &= y_{i-1} + h(k_1 + k_2)f(x_{i-1}, y_{i-1}) + k_2 h^2(cf_x(x_{i-1}, y_{i-1}) \\ &\quad + af(x_{i-1}, y_{i-1})f_y(x_{i-1}, y_{i-1})) + O(h^3), \end{aligned}$$

which must match the Taylor method of order two

$$\begin{aligned} y_i &= y_{i-1} + h\left(f(x_{i-1}, y_{i-1}) + \frac{h}{2}(f_x(x_{i-1}, y_{i-1}) + f_y(x_{i-1}, y_{i-1})f(x_{i-1}, y_{i-1}))\right) \\ &= y_{i-1} + hf(x_{i-1}, y_{i-1}) + \frac{h^2}{2}(f_x(x_{i-1}, y_{i-1}) + f_y(x_{i-1}, y_{i-1})f(x_{i-1}, y_{i-1})) \end{aligned}$$

(Eq. (6.23)) to within $O(h^3)$, the same as its truncation error. But this is easy! We need only require that

$$k_1 + k_2 = 1$$
$$ck_2 = \frac{1}{2} \tag{6.24}$$
$$ak_2 = \frac{1}{2}$$

and the two methods agree to within $O(h^3)$, and therefore both have $O(h^2)$ global error. The system of Eq. (6.24) represents three *nonlinear* equations in four unknowns and has a meaningful solution for every $k_2 \in (0, 1)$. The standard RK methods of order two are (in tableau form)

$$
\begin{array}{c|cc}
0 & 0 & \\
\frac{1}{2} & 1 & \frac{1}{2}
\end{array},
$$

that is

$$
y_i = y_{i-1} + hf\left(x_{i-1/2},\, y_{i-1} + \frac{h}{2}f(x_{i-1},\, y_{i-1})\right),
$$

which we recognize as the midpoint method,

$$
\begin{array}{c|cc}
0 & \frac{1}{2} & \\
1 & \frac{1}{2} & 1
\end{array},
$$

the improved Euler's method, and

$$
\begin{array}{c|cc}
0 & \frac{1}{4} & \\
\frac{2}{3} & \frac{3}{4} & \frac{2}{3}
\end{array},
$$

Heun's method. Euler's method is the Taylor method of order one, and the midpoint method, the improved Euler's method, and Heun's method are the three most popular Runge-Kutta methods of order two.

Conditions on RK Methods
There are other ways to derive RK methods. Many IRK methods are equivalent to interpolatory quadrature rules. Some necessary conditions, such as that the sum of the entries in the ith row of A must equal c_i for an RK method to be at least $O(h)$, are known. Graph-theoretical methods are generally used for deriving high-order RK methods.

The most important RK method, other than the second-order ones we have already encountered in Section 6.3, is the classical fourth-order RK method of Eq. (6.22). This approximation of the Taylor method of order four is indeed $O(h^4)$ and is widely used.

Global Error
The global error of an RK method is $O(h^N)$, where N is the number of stages (and hence of function evaluations), *only* for $N \le 4$. We need six stages to get an $O(h^5)$ method, seven stages to get an $O(h^6)$ method, and nine stages to get an $O(h^7)$ method. This explains the popularity of the classical fourth-order RK method; fourth-order methods are the last ones where the order of the global error equals the number of function evaluations. In addition the A matrix for the classical method is as sparse as it can be, resulting in fewer arithmetic operations. (Of course, in most cases of interest these arithmetic operations cost very little in comparison to function evaluations.)

Example 6.5.2
Let's use the classical fourth-order RK method on the ODE IVP $y' = x^2 y$, $y(0) = 1$ from Example 6.5.1. We have, with $h = 0.05$,

$$
\begin{aligned}
g_1 &= f(x_0, y_0) \\
&= x_0^2 y_0 \\
&= 0
\end{aligned}
$$

$$g_2 = f\left(x_0 + \frac{1}{2}h, y_0 + \frac{1}{2}hg_1\right)$$
$$= f(0.025, 1)$$
$$= (0.025)^2 1$$
$$= 6.25E - 4$$

$$g_3 = f\left(x_0 + \frac{1}{2}h, y_0 + \frac{1}{2}hg_2\right)$$
$$= f(0.025, 1 + (0.025)(6.25E - 4))$$
$$\doteq 6.2501E - 4$$

$$g_4 = f(x_0 + h, y_0 + hg_3)$$
$$= f(0.05, 1 + (0.025)(6.2501E - 4))$$
$$\doteq 0.0025$$

$$y_1 = y_0 + h\left(\frac{1}{6}g_1 + \frac{1}{3}g_2 + \frac{1}{3}g_3 + \frac{1}{6}g_4\right)$$
$$\doteq 1.00004166715495$$

$$y(x_1) \doteq 1.00004166753473$$

$$\alpha_1 = |y(x_1) - y_1|$$
$$\doteq 3.8E - 10$$

(note that $g_2 \neq g_3$). Compare this with the corresponding result for the second-order method in Example 6.5.1. ∎

Adaptivity   The classical fourth-order RK method is not the fourth-order method in the MATLAB routine ode45, but ode45 does use a pair of fourth-order and fifth-order ERK methods in order to be able to estimate and hence control the error (by adjusting the step size h adaptively). The command ode23 works similarly; it uses a pair of second-order and third-order ERK methods.

PROBLEMS 6.5

1. a. Write out the RK tableau $k|c|A$, where $k = (1/4, 3/8, 3/8)^T$, $c = (0, 2/3, 2/3)^T$, and $a_{2,1} = 2/3$, $a_{3,2} = 2/3$, and $a_{i,j} = 0$ otherwise. Then write out the method in the form of Eq. (6.21). This method, called the **Nystrom scheme**, is a third-order method.

b. Use the Nystrom scheme with $h = 0.5$ to approximate the solution of $y' = y^2$, $y(0) = 1$ over $[0, 1]$. Compare your answers with the true solution and with your answers for Problem 1 of Section 6.2 and Problem 1 of Section 6.3, where $h = 0.05$ is used.

c. Repeat part (b) using the classical fourth-order RK method.

2. a. Continue Example 6.5.1 for three more steps. Find the absolute errors.

b. Continue Example 6.5.2 for five more steps. Find the absolute errors and compare them to the errors from the Taylor method of order two in part (a).

3. a. Repeat Example 6.5.2 with the improved Euler's method using $h = 0.025$ to get an approximation of

$y(x_1)$. This uses four function evaluations, as does the classical fourth-order RK method in Example 6.5.2. Which method is better?

b. Repeat part (a) using the midpoint and Heun's methods.

4. Write a MATLAB program that accepts vectors k and c and a matrix A and prints out the tableau of the corresponding ERK or IRK method. Your program should label the tableau, giving the number of stages and stating whether the method is explicit or implicit.

5. Write a MATLAB program that implements the classical fourth-order RK method.

MATLAB 6.5

Most of the methods we have seen so far generalize readily to methods for systems of ODEs. Runge-Kutta methods for systems are the same as Runge-Kutta methods for scalar equations if the order of the RK method is at most four. Let's use Euler's method $\vec{y}_i = \vec{y}_{i-1} + hf(x_{i-1}, \vec{y}_{i-1})$ to approximate the solution of the system of ODEs $R' = (a - bF)R$, $F' = (-c + dR)F$ ($R = R(t)$, $F = F(t)$) where a, b, c, and d are positive (this is called the **predator-prey equation**). We'll take $a = 2$, $b = .05$, $c = 1$, $d = .02$, $R(0) = 100$, $F(0) = 20$, and $h = .1$. Enter:

```
» h=.1;
» y0=[100 20]';
» f1=inline('(2-.05*F)*R');          %R'=f1(F,R).
» f2=inline('(-1+.02*R)*F');         %F'=f2(F,R).
» y1=y0+h*[f1(y0(2),y0(1));f2(y0(2),y0(1))]
» y2=y1+h*[f1(y1(2),y1(1));f2(y1(2),y1(1))]
» y3=y2+h*[f1(y2(2),y2(1));f2(y2(2),y2(1))]
» x=[0 .1 .2 .3]; y=[y0 y1 y2 y3];
» plot(x,y),legend('Rabbits','Foxes')
```

The predator-prey equations model the interaction of populations of prey $R(t)$, which we might imagine as rabbits, and predators $F(t)$, which we might imagine as foxes, starting from some initial population level $\vec{y}_0$. Repeat this with the improved Euler's method.

Let's try to get a better look at this solution. First let's write a single inline function for f that returns a vector. Enter:

```
» f=inline('0*t+[(2-.05*x(2))*x(1);(-1+.02*x(1))*x(2)]','t','x')
» [xx,yy]=ode45(f,[0 30],y0);
» plot(xx,yy),legend('Rabbits','Foxes'),grid
```

The population levels of the rabbits and foxes appear to be oscillating. This behavior is common and can be seen in the wild. Let's look at a phase plane plot. Enter:

```
» plot(yy(:,1),yy(:,2))
```

The plot is as expected for a periodic solution. Enter:

```
» options=odeset('outputfcn','odephas2')
» [xx,yy]=ode45(f,[0 20],y0,options);
```

to have MATLAB generate the phase plane plot. Make a phase portrait for this system with six different trajectories by using `hold`.

ADDITIONAL PROBLEMS 6.5

6. Show that the theta methods are Runge-Kutta methods.

7. **a.** Verify that all of the RK methods we have seen satisfy the necessary condition that the sum of the entries in the ith row of A equals c_i.

   b. Show that if the sum of the entries in the ith row of A does not equal c_i, then the corresponding RK method cannot be of order at least one as it does not integrate, say, $y' = 1$ to this accuracy.

8. **a.** Write out the RK tableau $k|c|A$, where $k = (1/6, 2/3, 1/6)^T$, $c = (0, 1/2, 1)^T$, and $a_{2,1} = 1/2$, $a_{3,1} = -1$, $a_{3,2} = 2$, and $a_{i,j} = 0$ otherwise. Then write out the method in the form of Eq. (6.21). This method is called the **classical third-order RK method** and is indeed third-order.

   b. Use the classical third-order RK method with $h = 0.5$ to approximate the solution of $y' = y^2$, $y(0) = 1$ over $[0, 1]$. Compare your answers with the true solution and with your answers for Problem 1 of Section 6.2, Problem 1 of Section 6.3, and Problem 1 of this section.

   c. Prove that this method is $O(h^3)$.

   d. Repeat parts (a)–(c) using **Ralston's method,** which has the RK tableau $k|c|A$, where $k = (2/9, 1/3, 4/9)^T$, $c = (0, 1/2, 3/4)^T$, and $a_{2,1} = 1/2$, $a_{3,2} = 3/4$, and $a_{i,j} = 0$ otherwise.

9. Show that if $f(x, y) = f(x)$, then an RK method is a quadrature rule. What is the relationship between the order of the RK method and the degree of accuracy of the quadrature rule?

10. Show that the implicit midpoint rule $y_{i+1} = y_i + hf(x_{i+1/2}, (y_i + y_{i+1})/2)$ is an IRK method. What is its tableau?

11. Show that the solution of $y' = \alpha y$ ($\alpha \in \mathbb{R}$) by an RK method with N stages is $y_i = y_0(\sum_{j=0}^{N}(h\alpha)^j/j!)^i$, $i = 0, 1, \ldots$. Comment.

12. The IRK method with tableau $k|c|A$, where $k = (1/2, 1/2)^T$, $c = (1/2 - \sqrt{3}/6, 1/2 + \sqrt{3}/6)^T$, and $a_{1,1} = 1/4$, $a_{1,2} = 1/4 - \sqrt{3}/6$, $a_{2,1} = 1/2 + \sqrt{3}/6$, $a_{2,2} = 1/4$ is fourth-order. Write a MATLAB program that implements this method. You will need to solve a nonlinear system at each step; what is the natural choice for an initial guess for the nonlinear system solver? Test your program.

13. Conduct an experiment to verify that the classical fourth-order RK method is indeed of order four.

14. Solve the predator-prey equation as given in the MATLAB subsection using the classical fourth-order Runge-Kutta method. Produce a times series plot and a phase plot.

15. Show that the requirements of Eq. (6.24) are unchanged if we start with a system of two ODEs and expand both components of g_2 in Taylor series to find an RK method.

6.6   Adaptivity and Stiffness

The numerical methods we have seen so far form the basis for programs that attempt to solve ODEs automatically, but there are many more issues to consider as we look at the efficient implementation of them in a useful and robust program. Users typically wish to simply submit an ODE and have the program return a list of nodes x and corresponding approximate function values y that can be plotted, splined, numerically integrated or differentiated, and so on. To make this a reality, we need ways of estimating the error so that the nodes may be chosen adaptively.[7]

Systems and Higher-Order Equations

Most programs insist that the ODE be given as a first-order system $y' = f(x, y)$, $y(x_0) = y_0$, where y may be a vector-valued quantity. Many programs insist that a higher-order ODE IVP such as

$$y'' + by' + cy = f(x)$$

$$y(x_0) = y_0 \qquad\qquad (6.25)$$

$$y'(x_0) = v_0$$

---

[7] This isn't all we need, but it's what we focus on in this section.

be converted into a first-order system by the user before attempting to solve it (if the program itself doesn't convert it automatically). To convert Eq. (6.25) to an equivalent first-order system, we let $v(x) = y'(x)$, giving

$$v' + bv + cy = f(x)$$
$$y(x_0) = y_0$$
$$v(x_0) = v_0,$$

that is

$$y' = v$$
$$v' = -cy - bv + f(x)$$
$$y(x_0) = y_0$$
$$v(x_0) = v_0$$

which is indeed a first-order system in the unknown functions $y(x)$ and $v(x)$. This system may now be handled by the methods of MATLAB 6.5. In this case the system is linear so we might also use an eigenvalue/eigenvector routine on the matrix of the system.

Adaptivity   How shall we choose the nodes adaptively? We'll look only at the scalar case $y' = f(x, y)$, $y(x_0) = y_0$. We want to use a numerical method to generate an estimate y_1 of the value of y at x_1. We'll approximate $y(x_1)$ twice, using two different methods, and use them to approximate the error. If the error is too large, we'll reduce h by half and approximate $y(x_{1/2})$. Then, when it's accurately approximated, we'll go from there to get an estimate for $y(x_1)$. If we have to reduce h several times to get an accurate estimate of $y(x_{1/2})$ first, so be it. We continually reduce h by one-half and take more steps if the error is too large.

If the error is much smaller than the tolerance, however, then we are using a step that is inefficiently small (for the given error tolerance). In such a case we would double h and take longer, and therefore more efficient, steps. Typically we would have minimum and maximum allowable step sizes.

Example 6.6.1   Let's see how this works if we have a way to find the exact local truncation error. Suppose we are solving $y' = f(x, y)$, $y(0) = 1$ with an initial $h = 0.2$ and an error tolerance $\epsilon = 10^{-6}$ for the LTE. We estimate $y_1 \approx y(0.2)$ using two different methods and find that the LTE is about 10^{-4}, so we reduce h to $h = 0.1$ and estimate $y(0.1)$. We find that the LTE is about 10^{-5}, so we reduce h again to $h = 0.05$ and estimate $y(0.05)$. The error is estimated as 10^{-6}, so we have a successful step. We then estimate $y(0.1)$. The error is estimated as 10^{-6}, so we have a successful step. We estimate $y(0.15)$ and find that the error is estimated as 10^{-8}; we have a *very* successful step so we assume that the region $[0, 0.1]$ was the difficult region and try to take larger steps. We double h to $h = 0.1$ and estimate $y(0.25)$. The error is estimated as 10^{-6}, so we have a successful step and we move on to estimating $y(0.35)$. Note that we never do find an estimate for $y(0.2)$, but we could always use interpolation to find such an estimate. ■

Error Control   Although we are controlling the local truncation error, the global error can be shown to be at most $(x_n - x_0)\epsilon$ if the local truncation error is kept to at most $h\epsilon$. Keeping the LTE to at most $h\epsilon$ is called **error control per unit step,** as opposed to **error control**

per step which is keeping the LTE to at most ϵ (as is done in Example 6.6.1). Error control per unit step is generally preferred; the smaller h is, the more steps we are taking, and hence the greater the accumulation of the global error. So when we are taking many small steps, we should use a tighter restriction than when we are taking fewer large steps.

Paired Methods   We need a pair of methods that can be used to estimate the error. Ideally they would use the same, or nearly the same, nodes, since controlling the error is only one goal and efficiency is the other. It's rather inefficient to double our computational effort in the hope that we can double our step size.

Such **paired methods** may be found. For RK methods they are called **embedded RK pairs.** One example is the **Runge-Kutta-Fehlberg method,**[8] which uses the following pair of fourth-order and fifth-order methods that together require only six function evaluations (rather than the ten that would be necessary for unpaired methods):

$$
\begin{array}{c|cccccc}
\frac{25}{216} & 0 \\
0 & \frac{1}{4} & \frac{1}{4} \\
\frac{1408}{2565} & \frac{3}{8} & \frac{3}{32} & \frac{9}{32} \\
\frac{2197}{4104} & \frac{12}{13} & \frac{1932}{2197} & \frac{-7200}{2197} & \frac{7296}{2197} \\
\frac{-1}{5} & 1 & \frac{439}{216} & -8 & \frac{3680}{516} & \frac{-845}{4104}
\end{array}
\tag{6.26}
$$

(order four) and

$$
\begin{array}{c|cccccc}
\frac{16}{135} & 0 \\
0 & \frac{1}{4} & \frac{1}{4} \\
\frac{6656}{12825} & \frac{3}{8} & \frac{3}{32} & \frac{9}{32} \\
\frac{28561}{56430} & \frac{12}{13} & \frac{1932}{2197} & \frac{-7200}{2197} & \frac{7296}{2197} \\
\frac{-9}{50} & 1 & \frac{439}{216} & -8 & \frac{3680}{516}{}_{5|3} & \frac{-845}{4104} \\
\frac{2}{55} & \frac{1}{2} & \frac{-8}{27} & 2 & \frac{-3544}{2565} & \frac{1859}{4104} & \frac{-11}{40}
\end{array}
\tag{6.27}
$$

(order five). Since all the k_i are likely to be nearly equal for small h, the negative values in the A matrix are unfortunate but we will accept them. Notice how many entries are the same in the tableaus in Eq. (6.26) and Eq. (6.27). For this reason an embedded RK pair like this one is sometimes written as a single tableau $k4|k5|c|A$, where $k4$ is the vector of weights for the fourth-order method, $k5$ is the vector of weights for the fifth-order method, c is the vector of nodes from Eq. (6.27), and A is the RK matrix from Eq. (6.27). We use the weights $k4$ and ignore the last row of the tableau for the fourth-order method, and the weights $k5$ and all of c and A for the fifth-order method.

Look again at the tableaus in Eq. (6.26) and Eq. (6.27). Except for the last row, they use the same A matrix and the same nodes, and therefore they use exactly the same function evaluations. The fourth-order method uses 5 function evaluations, and the fifth-order

---

[8] The term *Runge-Kutta-Fehlberg method* is used more and more often to describe any pair of ERK methods that differ in order by one and use nearly the minimum number of function evaluations required for the higher-order method.

method uses those same function evaluations plus one additional function evaluation. Since 6 function evaluations are needed to get a fifth-order ERK method anyway, this can't be improved upon if we want a pair with orders 4 and 5. This is very desirable—we get the fourth-order method for free.

How exactly do we make use of this pair of methods? The LTE of Eq. (6.26) is $O(h^4)$. Call the approximations generated by this method y_i because it is the main method, that is, the one whose error we are controlling with the higher-order method. Call the approximations generated by Eq. (6.27) v_i; the LTE is $O(h^5)$. Now RK methods are one-step methods, so the LTE of the lower-order method is

$$
\begin{aligned}
LTE4_{i+1} &= y(x_{i+1}) - [y(x_i) + h\Phi(x_i, y(x_i), h)] \\
&= y(x_{i+1}) - y(x_i) - h\Phi(x_i, y(x_i), h) \\
&\approx y(x_{i+1}) - y_i - h\Phi(x_i, y_i, h) \\
&= y(x_{i+1}) - (y_i + h\Phi(x_i, y_i, h)) \\
&= y(x_{i+1}) - y_{i+1}
\end{aligned}
$$

as $y(x_i) = y_i + O(h^4)$, and the LTE of the higher-order method is

$$
\begin{aligned}
LTE5_{i+1} &= y(x_{i+1}) - [y(x_i) + h\Phi(x_i, y(x_i), h)] \\
&= y(x_{i+1}) - y(x_i) - h\Phi(x_i, y(x_i), h) \\
&\approx y(x_{i+1}) - v_i - h\Phi(x_i, v_i, h) \\
&= y(x_{i+1}) - (v_i + h\Phi(x_i, v_i, h)) \\
&= y(x_{i+1}) - v_{i+1}
\end{aligned}
$$

as $y(x_i) = v_i + O(h^5)$. Therefore

$$
\begin{aligned}
LTE4_{i+1} &\approx y(x_{i+1}) - y_{i+1} \\
&= y(x_{i+1}) - v_{i+1} + v_{i+1} - y_{i+1} \\
&\approx LTE5_{i+1} + (v_{i+1} - y_{i+1}) \\
&\approx v_{i+1} - y_{i+1}
\end{aligned}
$$

if $LTE5_{i+1}$ is small compared to $LTE4_{i+1}$. Hence we may estimate the local truncation error of the main method as

$$
LTE4_{i+1} \approx v_{i+1} - y_{i+1}
$$

and compare this to our tolerance ϵ or, more commonly, to $h\epsilon$ (error control per unit step). This estimate is the missing piece we need to use adaptivity in our numerical ODEs routine.

Beyond Doubling and Halving   Although the doubling and halving approach is common, a more sophisticated step-size control than simply doubling or halving the step may be employed. Because the LTE of the lower-order method is $O(h^4)$, if h is sufficiently small, then

$$
LTE4(h)_{i+1} \approx Ch^4
$$

for some constant C. Hence the LTE for step size h/m is approximately

$$
LTE4(h/m)_{i+1} \approx C \left(\frac{h}{m} \right)^4
$$

$$
= \frac{LTE4(h)_{i+1}}{m^4},
$$

and so if the local truncation error is too large or too small, then we may use this formula to compute a new step size h/m, $m > 0$, such that the LTE is likely to be acceptable.

Returned Values   Although it is the LTE of the fourth-order method that is being controlled, most programs report the global error, estimated as ϵ times the length of the interval over which we have integrated the ODE. We would also have the program return the approximations from the higher-order method, even though the error estimate would be for the lower-order method, as was done for numerical integration (see Section 5.6); in this context this is referred to as **local extrapolation.** If the higher-order estimates aren't the more accurate estimates our entire premise was flawed anyway.

There are other minor implementation issues left, such as how to choose the initial step size. Hopefully you see that programming issues such as these often require mathematical understanding, intuition, and analysis!

There is another important topic we must now discuss that is related to the issue of choosing a step size. Consider Figure 6.10 below, in which we have solved the

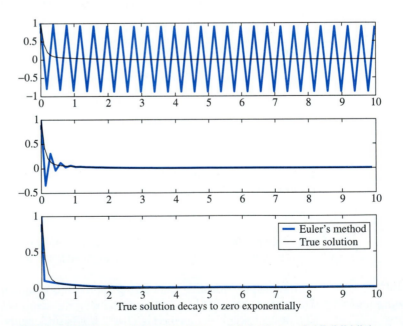

True solution decays to zero exponentially

Figure 6.10 Euler's Method Using $h = 0.2$ (top), $h = 0.15$ (Middle), and $h = 0.1$ (Bottom).

linear system

$$x' = -10x + y \qquad (6.28)$$

$$y' = -y$$

Step Size
Problems

$(x(0) = 1, y(0) = 1)$ using Euler's method with three different step sizes and have plotted the first component x of the numerical solution along with the first component of the true solution.

Is this instability? Yes, but the complete answer is a bit more involved than that. For $h = 0.2$ (top graph) we have spurious oscillations that persist. For $h = 0.15$ (middle graph) the numerical method seems to "think about" oscillating before settling in to the correct long-term behavior; if all we need is the steady-state solution, not the transient, this is acceptable. For $h = 0.1$ (bottom graph) all seems well. For sufficiently small h, we get the correct behavior, as we expect of a stable, convergent method.

But why is the behavior so far off, qualitatively as well as quantitatively, for $h = 0.2$? Euler's method for this linear system of ODEs is a linear difference equation in two variables

$$\vec{y}_{i+1} = \vec{y}_i + hA\vec{y}_i,$$

and it can be solved to give

$$\vec{y}_i = (1 - 10h)^i v_1 + (1 - h)^i v_2 \qquad (6.29)$$

for some vectors v_1, v_2. (Perhaps surprisingly, these vectors are the eigenvectors of A, just as in the analytical solution of the system of ODEs itself.) That means that if we are to have the *numerical* solution display the correct asymptotic behavior, tending to zero, then we need both of the following conditions to be satisfied:

$$|1 - 10h| \leq 1$$

$$|1 - h| \leq 1,$$

and the more restrictive condition is

$$|1 - 10h| \leq 1$$

$$h \leq \frac{1}{5}$$

(since $h > 0$). Indeed, $h = 0.2$ is a border case. We don't get convergence but instead get period two behavior asymptotically because the term

$$(1 - 10h)^i$$

alternates between 1 and -1; that is, we don't get convergence, but we don't get divergence to infinity either. Compare Figure 6.11 (note carefully the vertical scales). The system is the same as the system in Figure 6.10, but now h exceeds 0.2.

Stiffness

The system of Eq. (6.28) has a requirement that $h < 0.2$ for satisfactory answers. But what if we don't want to take such a small h? What if we need to approximate the answer for very large x and want to take large steps to save computing time? We can't. Systems such as this are referred to as *stiff* systems. There's no strict mathematical definition of a stiff system; they are systems that contain widely varying rates (as -10 and -1

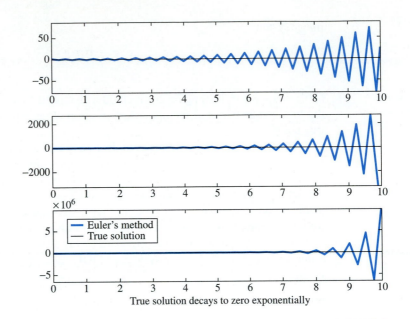

Figure 6.11 Euler's Method Using $h = 0.21$ (Top), $h = 0.22$ (Middle), and $h = 0.25$ (Bottom).

here) and that therefore force us to choose a smaller than desired h based on stability considerations. Note that if the matrix of the linear system were

$$\begin{pmatrix} -1000 & 1 \\ 0 & -1 \end{pmatrix} \qquad (6.30)$$

instead, then we'd need $h < 0.002$ for stability. We'd ideally like to choose our h based only on considerations of accuracy and computational time, but a stiff system forces us to use a small h, and therefore spend a lot of time computing, to avoid instability. And this is a *linear* system! What about a large, nonlinear system with rates varying over many orders of magnitude? Such systems occur all the time in practice—the name *Stiff System* comes from an early application involving mechanical springs of differing degrees of stiffness—and would wreak havoc with the doubling and halving system we discussed earlier. We might have to keep halving and halving and halving the step size until we reached whatever minimum step size we had set, at which point we still might not have a sufficiently small step size. Stiff systems can be very frustrating.

What can we do? Well, we have not mentioned an important point: Stiffness is a property of systems, not numerical methods, and not every numerical method is affected by it in the way that Euler's method is. The backward Euler's method

$$y_{i+1} = y_i + hf(x_{i+1}, y_{i+1}) \qquad (6.31)$$

and trapezoidal scheme, for instance, correctly reproduce the asymptotic behavior of Eq. (6.28) for any step size. We can devise special methods for stiff systems and use them to create special routines called *stiff solvers* for such systems. Backward differentiation and implicitness often figure into stiff solvers. (Implicit methods may be made adaptive, as we discussed earlier in this section.) Another method appropriate for stiff systems is

$$y_{i+2} - \frac{4}{3}y_{i+1} + \frac{1}{3}y_i = \frac{2}{3}hf(x_{i+2}, y_{i+2}), \tag{6.32}$$

BDF Methods   which again is implicit and can be viewed as the result of backward differencing.[9] In fact, Eq. (6.31) and Eq. (6.32) are the first- and second-order **backward differentiation formulas (BDF),** a class of methods that use successively higher-order backward finite difference approximations to y' to generate implicit methods. The methods in Eq. (6.31) and Eq. (6.32) are sometimes designated the **BDF1** and **BDF2** methods, respectively.

So we see an important reason why implicit methods are needed: Explicit methods frequently require very small step sizes for stiff systems, whereas implicit methods may allow us to take step sizes as large as we wish, compatible with our accuracy needs and other considerations. Of course, we pay a price in that we must solve a nonlinear system at each step.

Adaptivity is essential for the accurate and timely solution of stiff systems. It's also useful for nonstiff systems, and every professionally written ODE solver is adaptive. Writing such programs requires teams of people with expertise in a number of areas—mathematics, hardware, software, and often the area of scientific inquiry to which the program is to be applied—and for this reason it is advisable whenever possible to use professionally produced, team-written, time-tested code and avoid the temptation to write your own programs for scientific computation.

PROBLEMS 6.6

1. Consider Eq. (6.28). Attempt to solve it with Euler's method and error control per step, keeping the error to at most .01. (Use the true solution to find the error; see `help dsolve`.) Start with $h = 0.25$ and double or halve h as appropriate. Discuss what happens.

2. Consider Eq. (6.28). Attempt to solve it with the improved Euler's method and error control per step, keeping the error to at most .01. (Use the true solution to find the error; see `help dsolve`.) Start with $h = 0.25$ and double or halve h as appropriate. Discuss what happens. Repeat with the trapezoidal scheme.

3. Prove that Eq. (6.29) is correct. Find v_1 and v_2.

4. Use the backward Euler's method with $h = 0.1$ to solve $y' = x^2y$, $y(1) = 1$ over $[1, 3]$. Compare your answers to those generated by Euler's method, which is also a first-order method.

5. Write a detailed algorithm (pseudocode) for performing the Runge-Kutta-Fehlberg method with error control per unit step.

MATLAB 6.6

Let's look at the MATLAB stiff solvers: `ode15s`, `ode23s`, `ode23t` (for moderately stiff problems), and `ode23tb`. Enter:

```
» helpwin
```

to launch the Help window and select the `funfun` directory. Scroll down to the ODE solvers. Select each of the four solvers listed above and read the help for each.

After having read the help, select Contents on the left-hand side and select *MATLAB*→ *Using MATLAB*→ *Mathematics*→ *Differential Equations*→ *Initial Value*

---

[9] See Eq. (6.3) and Additional Problem 7 of that section.

Problems for ODEs and DAEs→Initial Value Problem Solvers. Read this section. Note carefully the advice to try `ode45` first and then, if the method is performing poorly, to try the stiff solver `ode15s`. Of course, if you know in advance that the system is stiff, you should go directly to a stiff solver.

The `ode23t` routine uses the trapezoidal scheme paired with a third-order method for error control. The `ode23s` routine uses a variant of IRK methods developed by Rosenbrock and is based on a pair of methods of order two and three. It does not use local extrapolation. The `ode23tb` routine uses the trapezoidal scheme for part of its steps and a variant of BDF2 for the remainder and is an IRK method. The `ode15s` routine uses formulas of orders one through five based on backward differentiation.

To see what a difference stiffness can make, let's compare the MATLAB routines `ode23` (for nonstiff problems) and `ode23s` (for stiff problems). Enter:

```
» more on
» help ode23s
```

and read the help. Let's use the stiff system suggested in the help text, known as the **Van der Pol system** $v' = w$, $w' = 1000w(1 - v^2) - v$. Enter:

```
» tic;[t,y]=ode23s(@vdp1000,[0 3000],[2 0]);toc
» plot(t,y(:,1));
```

Now let's try again using a nonstiff solver; enter:

```
» tic;[t,y]=ode23(@vdp1000,[0 3000],[2 0]);toc
» plot(t,y(:,1));
```

In all likelihood you'll want to use $\boxed{\text{CTRL}} + \boxed{\text{C}}$ to interrupt the computation. The nonstiff solver must take excruciatingly small steps to meet the error tolerance, but the stiff solver has no problem meeting it. This is the advantage of an implicit method over an explicit method, and perhaps finally shows why we bother to use implicit methods at all.

Try again with the higher-order explicit method `ode45` and with the recommended basic stiff solver `ode15s` (which uses a variable-order method, from one to five, as well as a variable step size); enter:

```
» tic;[t,y]=ode15s(@vdp1000,[0 3000],[2 0]);toc
» tic;[t,y]=ode45(@vdp1000,[0 3000],[2 0]);toc
```

Plot the results in each case. The stiff solver is considerably more efficient–again, the explicit method may well fail to finish in a reasonable time in this example. If so, experiment until you find a tolerance large enough that the explicit method does converge.

ADDITIONAL PROBLEMS 6.6

6. Repeat Problem 4 using the BDF2 method Eq. (6.32), started with the improved Euler's method. Compare your answers to those generated by the improved Euler's method, which is also a second-order method.

7. a. Use the backward Euler's method with various values of h to solve Eq. (6.28). Compare your answers to those generated by Euler's method, which is also a first-order method.

b. Repeat part (a) using the BDF2 method, started with the improved Euler's method. Compare your answers to those generated by the improved Euler's method, which is also a second-order method.

8. Write a MATLAB program for performing the Runge-Kutta-Fehlberg method with error control per step or error control per unit step at the user's discretion. Test your program.

9. Solve $y'' + 2y' + 2y = \sin(x)$, $y(0) = 1$, $y'(0) = -1$ using the improved Euler's method.

10. **a.** Repeat Problem 1, but change the A matrix to Eq. (6.30).

    b. Repeat Problem 2, but change the A matrix to Eq. (6.30).

11. **a.** Use the Runge-Kutta-Fehlberg method to solve $y' = 1 + (x - y)^2$, $y(0) = 1$ over $[0, 1]$. Use $\epsilon = 10^{-6}$ and error control per unit step. Compare your answers to the true solution.

    b. Repeat part (a) over $[1.5, 3]$ using the initial condition $y(1.5) = 1$.

12. Repeat Problem 11 using error control per step. Comment.

13. Compare and contrast the approaches taken in the design of the various MATLAB ODE solvers, and discuss which solvers are appropriate for which types of problems.

14. **a.** Derive the BDF2 method using a backward difference formula.

    b. Derive a third-order BDF formula by first deriving a method for backward differencing that is third-order (see Section 6.1) and then using it in $y' = f(x, y)$.

15. Show that the ERK methods in the Runge-Kutta-Fehlberg scheme have the orders claimed.

6.7 Multi-Step Methods

Multi-Step Methods

We have been focusing on one-step methods, but there is another important class of methods that we have seen several examples of already: multi-step methods. These were defined in Section 6.4 as methods of the form

$$y_{i+1} = \sum_{j=0}^{j=k-1} \alpha_j y_{i-j} + h \Phi_f(x_i, y_i, y_{i-1}, \ldots, y_{i-k+1}, f, h) \qquad (6.33)$$

(explicit multi-step or explicit k-step methods) or

$$y_{i+1} = \sum_{j=0}^{j=k-1} \alpha_j y_{i-j} + h \Phi_f(x_i, y_{i+1}, y_i, y_{i-1}, \ldots, y_{i-k+1}, f, h) \qquad (6.34)$$

(implicit multi-step or implicit k-step methods). The BDF2 formula

$$y_{i+2} - \frac{4}{3}y_{i+1} + \frac{1}{3}y_i = \frac{2}{3}f(x_{i+2}, y_{i+2})$$

$$y_{i+2} = \frac{4}{3}y_{i+1} - \frac{1}{3}y_i + \frac{2}{3}f(x_{i+2}, y_{i+2})$$

from the previous section is an implicit multi-step method with $k = 2$ steps. All multi-step methods in common use have an increment function of the form

$$\Phi_f(x_i, y_i, y_{i-1}, \ldots, y_{i-k+1}, f, h) = \sum_{j=0}^{j=k-1} \beta_j f(x_{i-j}, y_{i-j}) \qquad (6.35)$$

(explicit) or

$$\Phi_f(x_i, y_i, y_{i-1}, \ldots, y_{i-k+1}, f, h) = \sum_{j=0}^{j=k} \beta_j f(x_{i+1-j}, y_{i+1-j}) \qquad (6.36)$$

(implicit), where $x_{i-j} = x_i - jh$ as usual. We consider multi-step methods only of the form in Eq. (6.33) with Φ_f as in Eq. (6.35), or of the form in Eq. (6.34) with Φ_f as in Eq. (6.36). We also insist that α_j, β_j depend only on j. Any such method is called a **linear multi-step method (or LMM)**.

The lure of methods with memory is easy to see: We have already found $y_0, y_1, \ldots, y_i$ when we come to the task of finding y_{i+1}. Why not use some or all of the previous values to help extrapolate the next value? The previous values represent additional information that could be used to find a trend in the solution. From this point of view, one-step methods seem restrictive. After all, we are likely to be storing all these values anyway.[10]

How shall we determine α_j and β_j $(j = 0, \ldots, k-1$, plus β_k if the method is implicit)? As is so often the case, interpolation is the obvious approach, though it is not the only one. (Another natural approach, leading to the same methods, is to replace y' in $y' = f(x, y)$ with an approximation that is based on several points, such as that of Eq. (6.3).) Let's look at the explicit case first. We write

$$y(x_{i+1}) = y(x_i) + \int_{x_i}^{x_{i+1}} f(x, y(x)) \, dx \tag{6.37}$$

and approximate the integrand with an interpolating polynomial at the k nodes $x_{i-k+1}, \ldots, x_i$,

$$
\begin{aligned}
f(x, y(x)) &\approx \sum_{j=0}^{k-1} f(x_{i-j}, y(x_{i-j})) L_j(x) \\
&\approx \sum_{j=0}^{k-1} f(x_{i-j}, y_{i-j}) L_j(x),
\end{aligned}
\tag{6.38}
$$

in terms of the Lagrange interpolating polynomials (see Section 4.1), where we are using the fact that $y_m \approx y(x_m)$. Not all of the nodes fall within the interval of integration in Eq. (6.37), but that's fine; the interpolant is defined over this interval of integration, and its behavior is influenced by the nodes outside this interval (compare the semi-Simp quadrature rule). This gives a numerical method

$$
\begin{aligned}
y_{i+1} &= y_i + \int_{x_i}^{x_{i+1}} \sum_{j=0}^{k-1} f(x_{i-j}, y_{i-j}) L_j(x) \, dx \\
&= y_i + \sum_{j=0}^{k-1} f(x_{i-j}, y_{i-j}) \int_{x_i}^{x_{i+1}} L_j(x) \, dx \\
&= y_i + h \sum_{j=0}^{k-1} \beta_j f(x_{i-j}, y_{i-j}),
\end{aligned}
$$

---

[10] This isn't always the case. It's not uncommon to need only the steady-state solution. But large nonlinear systems, for which it is costly to store many vectors, are rare, and large linear systems of ODEs can be handled by eigenvalue/eigenvector routines.

where

$$\beta_j = \frac{1}{h} \int_{x_i}^{x_{i+1}} L_j(x)\,dx \tag{6.39}$$

Adams-Bashford Methods

$(j = 0, 1, \ldots, k - 1)$ are the coefficients. This method is of the desired form (Eq. (6.33) with increment function given by Eq. (6.35)) and is called the **Adams-Bashforth method of order** k (or the k-**step Adams-Bashforth method,** or simply **AB**k), and is indeed of order k for sufficiently smooth f. For $k = 1$ **AB**k reduces to Euler's method (a one-step method). For $k = 2$ we have

$$y_{i+1} = y_i + h\left(\frac{3}{2}f(x_i, y_i) - \frac{1}{2}f(x_{i-1}, y_{i-1})\right),$$

for $k = 3$ we have

$$y_{i+1} = y_i + h\left(\frac{23}{12}f(x_i, y_i) - \frac{4}{3}f(x_{i-1}, y_{i-1}) + \frac{5}{12}f(x_{i-2}, y_{i-2})\right),$$

and for $k = 4$ we have

$$y_{i+1} = y_i + h\left(\frac{55}{24}f(x_i, y_i) - \frac{59}{24}f(x_{i-1}, y_{i-1})\right.$$

$$\left. + \frac{37}{24}f(x_{i-2}, y_{i-2}) - \frac{3}{8}f(x_{i-3}, y_{i-3})\right).$$

Higher-order methods may be found using Eq. (6.39). We emphasize that the Adams-Bashforth methods are not the only explicit k-step methods; selecting the form Eq. (6.35) and then finding the coefficients β_j by interpolation is a choice, not a necessity.

The Adams-Bashforth methods are explicit. We also say that they are **open,** because the formula for approximating the integral

$$\int_{x_i}^{x_{i+1}} f(x, y(x))\,dx$$

does not use x_{i+1} as a node. (It does use x_i so *half-open* would probably be a more accurate description.) The corresponding implicit, or **closed,** methods are derived in the same way except that Eq. (6.38) becomes

$$f(x, y(x)) \approx \sum_{j=0}^{k} f(x_{i+1-j}, y_{i+1-j})L_j(x).$$

We then proceed as before:

$$y_{i+1} = y_i + \int_{x_i}^{x_{i+1}} \sum_{j=0}^{k} f(x_{i+1-j}, y_{i+1-j})L_j(x)\,dx$$

$$= y_i + \sum_{j=0}^{k} f(x_{i+1-j}, y_{i+1-j}) \int_{x_i}^{x_{i+1}} L_j(x)\,dx$$

$$= y_i + h\sum_{j=0}^{k} \beta_j f(x_{i+1-j}, y_{i+1-j}),$$

where

$$\beta_j = \frac{1}{h} \int_{x_i}^{x_{i+1}} L_j(x)\,dx \tag{6.40}$$

Adams-Moulton Methods

$(j = 0, 1, \ldots, k)$ are the coefficients. This method is of the desired form (Eq. (6.34) with increment function given by Eq. (6.36)) and is called the **Adams-Moulton method of order k** (or the **k-step Adams-Moulton method,** or **AMk**), and is indeed of order k for sufficiently smooth f. For $k = 1$ this reduces to the backward Euler's method (a one-step method). For $k = 2$ we have the Adams-Moulton method of order two,

$$y_{i+1} = y_i + h\left(\frac{5}{12} f(x_{i+1}, y_{i+1}) + \frac{2}{3} f(x_i, y_i) - \frac{1}{12} f(x_{i-1}, y_{i-1})\right),$$

while for $k = 3$ we have

$$y_{i+1} = y_i + h\left(\frac{9}{24} f(x_{i+1}, y_{i+1}) + \frac{19}{24} f(x_i, y_i) - \frac{5}{24} f(x_{i-1}, y_{i-1})\right.$$

$$\left. + \frac{1}{24} f(x_{i-2}, y_{i-2})\right)$$

and for $k = 4$ we have

$$y_{i+1} = y_i + h\left(\frac{251}{720} f(x_{i+1}, y_{i+1}) + \frac{323}{360} f(x_i, y_i) - \frac{11}{30} f(x_{i-1}, y_{i-1})\right.$$

$$\left. + \frac{53}{360} f(x_{i-2}, y_{i-2}) - \frac{19}{720} f(x_{i-3}, y_{i-3})\right).$$

Higher-order methods may be found using Eq. (6.40). Adams-Bashforth methods and Adams-Moulton methods are collectively called **Adams methods.**

An Adams-Moulton method of order k generally gives better results than the corresponding Adams-Bashforth method but at greater computational cost: At each step, a nonlinear system must be solved, usually by functional iteration or possibly by Newton's method. More commonly one uses the Adams-Bashforth method as a predictor and the Adams-Moulton method as a corrector, avoiding the work of solving the nonlinear system. If we do this with, say, the fourth-order methods, then the predictor is

Prediction and Correction

$$\widehat{y}_{i+1} = y_i + h\left(\frac{55}{24} f(x_i, y_i) - \frac{59}{24} f(x_{i-1}, y_{i-1})\right.$$

$$\left. + \frac{37}{24} f(x_{i-2}, y_{i-2}) - \frac{3}{8} f(x_{i-3}, y_{i-3})\right)$$

and the corrector is

$$y_{i+1} = y_i + h\left(\frac{251}{720} f(x_{i+1}, \widehat{y}_{i+1}) + \frac{323}{360} f(x_i, y_i) - \frac{11}{30} f(x_{i-1}, y_{i-1})\right.$$

$$\left. + \frac{53}{360} f(x_{i-2}, y_{i-2}) - \frac{19}{720} f(x_{i-3}, y_{i-3})\right),$$

and we could repeatedly correct until a certain tolerance was met if desired. (This is functional iteration.) Using the predictor-corrector method, rather than either the

Adams-Moulton or Adams-Bashforth method alone, requires only one additional function evaluation. Notice that at each step we generate two approximations $\widehat{y}_{i+1}$, y_{i+1} of $y(x_i)$; we might be able to base an error control scheme on these two approximations. Indeed, we can do this. To make this work we use a corrector that is one order lower than the predictor. As always in numerical analysis, if we go to the trouble of computing something, we want to milk all the information we possibly can out of it—this is the very motivation behind using multi-step methods—so it is natural to think about using these two estimates of the solution to estimate the error.

Starting Adams
Methods

The obvious issue that remains is that of generating the first several steps. For example, to use the Adams-Moulton method of order two

$$y_{i+1} = y_i + h\left(\frac{5}{12}f(x_{i+1}, y_{i+1}) + \frac{2}{3}f(x_i, y_i) - \frac{1}{12}f(x_{i-1}, y_{i-1})\right)$$

given only the ODE IVP $y' = f(x, y)$, $y(x_0) = y_0$, we must first choose a step size h. But then the method is defined only for $i = 1$ and higher,

$$y_2 = y_1 + h\left(\frac{5}{12}f(x_2, y_2) + \frac{2}{3}f(x_1, y_1) - \frac{1}{12}f(x_0, y_0)\right)$$

so we must generate y_1 by some other method. Then

$$y_3 = y_2 + h\left(\frac{5}{12}f(x_3, y_3) + \frac{2}{3}f(x_2, y_2) - \frac{1}{12}f(x_1, y_1)\right)$$

and y_4, y_5, ... will have available all the values that are needed for their computation. For higher-order methods we'll need to generate even more starting values before we can begin using the Adams (or other multi-step) method.

How can we do this? It should seem intuitive by now that using the first-order Euler's method to start, say, a fourth-order scheme, could affect the performance of the latter scheme. This is certainly so. It is a fact that a multi-step method of order k may be started with values generated by a method of order $k - 1$ without affecting the order of the multi-step method, although starting with a method of order k gives better results.[11]

Adaptivity

For this reason it has been traditional to start multi-step methods by using an ERK scheme of the same order. However, while this is fine for a nonadaptive method, it is very inefficient if the program is to be adaptive. If we find that we have to reduce the step size at the first step of the multi-step method, then we must generate new starting values using the fairly expensive ERK method. Realistically all programs should be adaptive, so we must address this issue. In the context of adaptivity, the significance of higher-order methods is that they allow us to take larger step sizes; an $O(h^4)$ method with step size $h = 0.2$ has much smaller error than an $O(h)$ method with $h = 0.01$ (compare $0.2^4 = 0.0016$), assuming the asymptotic error constants are comparable. So the classical fourth-order RK method, which uses 4 function evaluations to cover a step of length $h = 0.2$, can be much more efficient *and accurate* than Euler's method with $h = 0.01$, which requires 20 function evaluations to cover an interval of length 0.2.

But, we are free to change the order of methods as well as the step size so long as we continue to enforce the error control. Adams methods are usually implemented

---

[11] Results, in fact, that do not differ appreciably from the results we would have expected had we had exact starting values.

with a variable order: at any given step the order is selected to balance the needs for accuracy and efficiency as well as possible. With this in mind, we may reasonably start an Adams-Bashforth method of order k (ABk) by using the one-step method AB1 to get y_1 from y_0, and then using AB2 to get y_2 from y_0 and y_1, and so on until we reach the maximal order ABk (or drop back to a lower-order method because of error control considerations). Proceeding in this way is common.

The Adams methods and the other major class of linear multi-step methods, the BDF methods (which are important for stiff problems), allow previously computed information to be used in a natural way. This is always desirable in numerical analysis.

PROBLEMS 6.7

1. Show that Euler's method is an Adams-Bashforth method and that the backward Euler's method is an Adams-Moulton method.

2. a. Use AB1 to solve $y' = x + y$, $y(0) = 1$ over $[0, 1]$ with $h = 0.1$.
  b. Use AB2 to solve $y' = x + y$, $y(0) = 1$ over $[0, 1]$ with $h = 0.1$. Use AB1 to find y_1.
  c. Use AB3 to solve $y' = x + y$, $y(0) = 1$ over $[0, 1]$ with $h = 0.1$. Use AB1 to find y_1 and AB2 to find y_2.
  d. Compare your answers to the true solution. Plot the errors. Does ABk seem to be an order k method?

3. a. Use AM1 to solve $y' = x + y$, $y(0) = 1$ over $[0, 1]$ with $h = 0.1$.
  b. Use AM2 to solve $y' = x + y$, $y(0) = 1$ over $[0, 1]$ with $h = 0.1$. Use AM1 to find y_1.

c. Use AM3 to solve $y' = x + y$, $y(0) = 1$ over $[0, 1]$ with $h = 0.1$. Use AM1 to find y_1 and AM2 to find y_2.
  d. Compare your answers to the true solution. Plot the errors. Does AMk seem to be an order k method?

4. a. The multi-step methods in this section have coefficients that are of mixed sign. Is this desirable?
  b. What is the sum of the coefficients of the methods in this section? How does this compare to what we have seen in numerical differentiation and numerical integration formulas?

5. Write a MATLAB program that performs ABk. Start it off by using AB1 to get y_1 from y_0, and then use AB2 to get y_2 from y_0 and y_1, and so on until the maximal order ABk is reached.

MATLAB 6.7

Let's try using AB3 as a predictor and AM3 as a corrector for the ODE IVP $y' = x + y$, $y(0) = 1$. We'll take a constant step size $h = .1$. We have $y_0 = 1$, and we'll use AB1 (Euler's method) to find y_1; enter:

```
» y0=1;h=.1;f=inline('x+y');
» y1=y0+h*f(0,y0)
```

(We could correct using AM2, but we will not do so.) Now we'll use AB2, $y_{i+1} = y_i + h\left(\frac{3}{2}f(x_i, y_i) - \frac{1}{2}f(x_{i-1}, y_{i-1})\right)$, to find y_2; enter:

```
» y2=y1+h*(1.5*f(.1,y1)-.5*f(0,y0))
```

We can now use AB3, $y_{i+1} = y_i + h\left(\frac{23}{12}f(x_i, y_i) - \frac{4}{3}f(x_{i-1}, y_{i-1}) + \frac{5}{12}f(x_{i-2}, y_{i-2})\right)$, to find y_3; enter:

```
» y3=y2+h*(23*f(.2,y2)/12-4*f(.1,y1)/3+5*f(0,y0)/12)
```

The result is 1.38575. The solution of the ODE IVP is $y(x) = 2e^x - x - 1$, and at $x_3 = .3$ this gives $y(x_3) \doteq 1.39971761515201$ for an absolute error of about $1.4E - 2$ (check this). Let's correct. Enter:

```
» y3c=y2+h*(9*f(.3,y3)/24+19*f(.2,y2)/24-5*f(.1,y1)/24+f(0,y0)/24)
```

(this is AM3, $y_{i+1} = y_i + h(\frac{9}{24}f(x_{i+1}, y_{i+1}) + \frac{19}{24}f(x_i, y_i) - \frac{5}{24}f(x_{i-1}, y_{i-1}) + \frac{1}{24}f(x_{i-2}, y_{i-2}))$, used as a corrector rather than as an implicit equation to be solved for y_{i+1}). The result is 1.385590625 with an absolute error of about $1.4E - 2$ (check this); in fact, the absolute error is slightly worse for the corrected version! Let's correct again. Enter:

```
» y3c=y2+h*(9*f(.3,y3c)/24+19*f(.2,y2)/24-5*f(.1,y1)/24+f(0,y0)/24)
```

The values are not changing much. Let's move on to y_4; enter:

```
» y4=y3+h*(23*f(.3,y3)/12-4*f(.2,y2)/3+5*f(.1,y1)/12)
```

We use the corrected value because in general this is a good policy, but in this case it doesn't work out as well as we might have hoped at x_3. Now we can correct; enter:

```
» y4c=y3c+h*(9*f(.4,y4)/24+19*f(.3,y3)/24-5*f(.2,y2)/24+f(.1,y1)/24)
```

Check the absolute errors. Correct a few more times. Then continue until you reach $x_{10} = 1$. Is the correction of more value farther from the initial point? (Note that we are not controlling for error, and more accurate results would have been achieved with a smaller step size.)

Let's discuss a few MATLAB search capabilities. The MATLAB environment provides a number of useful utilities for locating MATLAB-provided functions. To see if MATLAB has a Horner's method program, for example, enter:

```
» lookfor horner
HORNER Horner polynomial representation.
```

Depending on what version of MATLAB you have and what MATLAB toolboxes are on your machine, you may find more, or no, results. The `lookfor` command looks for its argument in the first comment line (called the H1 line) of all M-files on the path. Type `help horner`; depending on your version of MATLAB the `horner` program may or may not do exactly what we discussed for Horner's method in MATLAB 4.1, but it does something equivalent to that in any event. Does MATLAB have a Newton's method program? Enter:

```
» lookfor newton
```

From `help newton` it appears that this is a very specialized subroutine. (Again, you may not find this particular M-file on your machine.) There is no general-purpose non-linear system solver in MATLAB (though there is in the Optimization Toolbox, as well as `solve` in the Symbolic Toolbox). To look for the word Newton in the entire first block of consecutive comment lines, enter:

```
» lookfor newton -all
```

The search is not case sensitive.

Both of these functions can be found by typing `help` and the name, but the name isn't always obvious. For example, to find a numerical integration routine, enter:

```
» lookfor integra
```

This finds several irrelevant routines because it matches the terms *integral*, *integrate* and *integration* but does locate the main numerical integration routines `quad` and `quad8`. You are unlikely to look for an integration routine under *q* unless you know that such routines are also called *q*uadrature routines.

If you are using MATLAB6, then in addition to the help available from drop-down menus, there is Tab completion. Type `h` and then strike the Tab key twice; that is, type:

```
» h
```

followed by Tab, Tab rather than Return. All commands beginning with the letter *h* are listed. Note that only one command begins with *hy*. Type *hy* and strike Tab once (not twice). The command is completed because there is only one possible choice, `hypergeom`; enter:

```
» hypergeom(1,2,3)
```

Then enter `help hy`, strike Tab once, and enter that line to see the help for the `hypergeom` function.

Additionally, MATLAB has a number of commands that relate to the operating system of your computer. Type `help which`, `help what`, and `help dir` to see how to locate the full path for a function, list the MATLAB files in the current directory, and list all files in the current directory, respectively. The `which` command is useful if two M-files happen to share the same name. (Of course, you should avoid this, but it happens sometimes when you put someone else's MATLAB programs on your machine.) Type `help path` and then enter:

```
» path
```

to see your current path. If two M-files share a name, the first one on the path is the one that will be executed. The help for `path` suggests ways in which the path may be manipulated; see `help startup` for a way to automate this each time you log on. You may also wish to add `format compact` to your startup file.

The `help` command works on directories as well. When you enter `help` the entries in the left-hand column are directory names. Enter:

```
» help matlab\polyfun
```

to see the functions available in the `polyfun` directory, all of which are interpolation or polynomial functions. Enter `type help.m` to see information on how you can integrate your functions into the help systems smoothly. It's probably advisable to have your own directory or directories for your M-files. You may wish to add M-files for common abbreviations like `ln.m` to compute the natural logarithm (which is `log.m` in MATLAB), `avg.m` for `mean.m`, or a `sqr.m` that squares its argument element by element. All of these additions would be for convenience only, but if you keep typing `ln` and getting an error, you can fix it!

The command `pwd` lists the current directory, and the command `cd` may be used to change it. These commands work on Windows machines and on Unix machines.

If you enter the exclamation point (`!`), then any text that follows it is interpreted as a command to the underlying operating system; see `help punct`. For example, in a Unix environment, the command:

```
» !ls -la
```

lists files. (Try `!dir` in a PC environment, and see also `help dos` and `help unix`.) There are many MATLAB commands that duplicate operating system functions, such as the `dir` command previously mentioned, `delete` for deleting files, and others.

In addition to `help`, the `doc` command may be used to view help documentation. It launches a browser for viewing HTML help files. Enter:

```
» doc
```

and try it. You may specify a particular topic by providing an argument to `doc`. It may be easier to search for information using the HTML help, or using the online help at http://www.mathworks.com (the MathWorks' web site), where you will also find many special-purpose and freely available M-files. If you have access to the Maple kernel, then the command `mhelp` will be available. This prints the Maple help for a command.

Use `lookfor` to search for MATLAB functions that implement some of the methods we have discussed or that will perform computations you need to perform in other classes. Use `help` and `type` to verify that they perform the expected computations.

ADDITIONAL PROBLEMS 6.7

6. a. Repeat the predictor-corrector experiment from MATLAB 6.7 using $h = 0.5$.
  b. Repeat the predictor-corrector experiment from MATLAB 6.7 using $h = 0.25$.

7. a. Repeat the predictor-corrector experiment from MATLAB 6.7 using the ODE IVP $y' = x^2 + y$, $y(0) = 1$.
  b. Repeat part (a) using $h = 0.05$.
  c. Repeat the predictor-corrector experiment from MATLAB 6.7 using the ODE IVP $y' = x^2y + y^2e^x$, $y(0) = 1$. Use one of the MATLAB ODE solvers to get accurate estimates of the true solution to compute the absolute error.
  d. Repeat part (a) using $h = 0.05$.

8. Replace y' in $y' = f(x, y)$ with the numerical differentiation scheme of Eq. (6.3). What method for solving ODEs does this give?

9. a. Verify that the formula given for AB1 is correct using Eq. (6.39).

  b. Verify that the formulas given for AB2, AB3, and AB4 are correct using Eq. (6.39).

10. Verify that the formulas given for AM1 through AM4 are correct using Eq. (6.40).

11. How could you use an Adams scheme to perform numerical integration? Discuss both ABk and AMk.

12. a. Find the AB5 formula.
  b. Find the AB6 formula.

13. a. Find the AM5 formula.
  b. Find the AM6 formula.

14. Compare the strengths and weaknesses of all the numerical methods for ODEs that we've studied so far.

15. Write a MATLAB program that solves ODEs by accepting a value k and the ODE, initial condition, final time, and step size, and by using ABk and AMk as a predictor-corrector pair. Correct at least three times for each prediction.

7 Nonlinear Optimization

7.1 One-Dimensional Searches

ROOT-FINDING, including the very special case $Ax = b$, and optimization are the most common problems in numerical computing. They frequently occur as sub-problems of other problems, as when we need to solve a linear system to fit a spline to given data.

Optimization Problems

Optimization problems are those in which we need to find the value of the argument x that makes some function $F(x)$ take on a value that is either a local minimum or a local maximum. If $F : \mathbb{R}^n \to \mathbb{R}$, then we write

$$\min_{x \in D} F(x) \tag{7.1}$$

to denote the problem of finding some value $x^* \in D \subseteq \mathbb{R}^n$ such that F has a local minimum at x^*; we also write $x^* = \min_{x \in D} F(x)$. (Recall that x^* is a local minimum of F in D if there is a neighborhood $N(x^*)$ in D such that if $x \in N(x^*)$, then $F(x) \geq F(x^*)$. The minimum is isolated, or strict, if in addition $F(x) > F(x^*)$ for $x \neq x^*$. We assume that the maxima and minima of the functions we consider are isolated.) Note that, like the language we use for zeroes of a function, when we speak of a minimization problem we are looking for the value of x that is the location of the minimum, not the value of the function at that minimum. We say that x^* is a local minimum of F, but when we wish to emphasize that it is an x-value, we say that x^* is the (local) minimizer.

We write $\max_{x \in D} F(x)$ to denote the problem of finding some value $x^* \in D \subseteq \mathbb{R}^n$ such that F has a local maximum at x^*; we also write $x^* = \max_{x \in D} F(x)$. We say that x^* is a local maximum of the function or, for emphasis, that it is a (local) maximizer.

The function F is usually called the **objective function.** We assume throughout this text that it is continuous. If the set D is in fact equal to $\mathbb{R}^n$, then we say that the problem is **unconstrained;** if D is a proper subset of $\mathbb{R}^n$, we say that the problem (or solution) is **constrained.** Optimization problems occur in many circumstances: finding the combination of prices and manufacturing that gives maximum profit; finding the point or configuration at which the energy is a minimum; finding the best-fit curve for a set of data points, that is, the curve that minimizes the error; and so on.

A case of great interest, where the objective function F is a linear function $F(x) = c^T x$ for some vector c and the problem is linearly constrained, is called a **linear programming (LP) problem.** (There are specialized methods for LP problems that we do not discuss; they are more commonly covered in an Operations Research course). When F is nonlinear we call it a **nonlinear optimization** or **nonlinear programming (NLP) problem.** We consider the nonlinear optimization problem in detail, and we assume sufficient differentiability of F as needed.

Since the minima of F are precisely the maxima of $-F$, we focus only on the minimization problem of Eq. (7.1). If F is differentiable, we might consider differentiating it and setting that derivative to zero, and then applying a root-finding method. Sometimes this can be done, but for problems of interest, we find the same difficulties that we found with Newton's method in the previous chapter—the function may be given as a program and hence not be differentiable; symbolic or automatic differentiation may not be available; the derivative may be too expensive to compute (recall that if $F : \mathbb{R}^n \to \mathbb{R}$, then $F(x)$ returns a single value, but the derivative of F is its Jacobian, with n^2 entries); and so on. In addition, some zeroes of F may be saddle points that are neither maxima nor minima. In any event if we find a zero of F, we must then determine whether it corresponds to a minimum or to a maximum of F. If we must solve the problem numerically anyway, we might as well leave it in the form given and solve it in that form if methods for doing so are available and equally efficient.

Line Searches Let's start with the case of one-dimensional minimization. Methods for finding minima of a function are also called **search methods,** and if $f : \mathbb{R} \to \mathbb{R}$, they are called **one-dimensional searches** or **line searches.** In analogy with root-finding we might start by seeking a bisection-like method. But two points do not suffice to bracket a minimum of a function, as Figure 7.1 and Figure 7.2 show.

However, looking at the graphs suggests that three points might suffice to bracket a minimum (or maximum). Indeed, if $a < b < c$ and f is continuous on $[a, c]$, then we

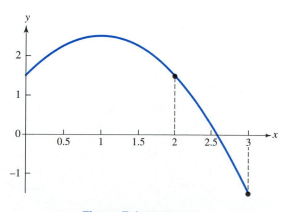

Figure 7.1 No Bracket.

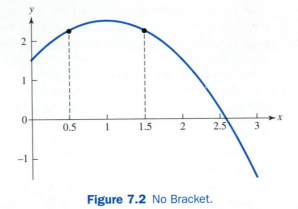

Figure 7.2 No Bracket.

know from the calculus that f achieves both its maximum and its minimum value over $[a, c]$. If $f(b) < f(a)$ and $f(b) < f(c)$, then the maximum may be achieved at one of the endpoints, but the minimum cannot be. There must be a local minimum in the interior of the interval (see Fig. 7.3). We have bracketed a minimum of the function. This is the basis of an **exhaustive search method for minimization** (see Section 1.1): Take small steps in a given direction until a bracket is found, and then repeat with a finer step size over that bracket.

Exhaustive
Search

Suppose we generate a new point d in some manner (using exhaustive search or the midpoint of the interval if the midpoint is not equal to b). If $a < b < d < c$, then either $f(d) < f(b)$, in which case $[b, d, c]$ is a new, smaller bracket (recall that $f(b) < f(c)$), or $f(d) > f(b)$, in which case $[a, b, d]$ is a new, smaller bracket. (We neglect for now the highly unlikely possibility that $f(d) = f(b)$.) Clearly, this method will converge to a local minimum of the function lying in $[a, c]$.

In the case of root-finding, the method of bisection always gives a 50% reduction in the width of the bracket; other methods typically converge faster but do not necessarily improve by a significant amount at every iteration. For root-finding, bisection gives the best *guaranteed* reduction at each iteration.

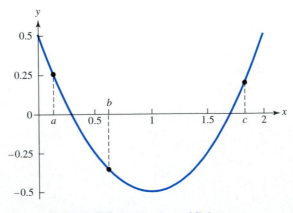

Figure 7.3 Bracketing a Minimum.

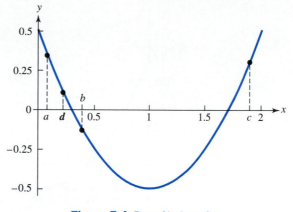

Figure 7.4 Poor Choice of d.

A Bisection-Like Method

In the case of minimization, however, where we have a three-point bracket, it's far from clear how to choose the next point to give the best *guaranteed* reduction in bracket width at each step. Suppose we have a bracket $[a, b, c]$. How should we choose $d \in (a, c)$? It seems clear that d should lie in the larger of the subintervals (a, b) and (b, c) because if, say, (a, b) is very small, then choosing some point d in that interval may give us very little reduction in bracket width (see Fig. 7.4).

Let's suppose that (b, c) is the larger subinterval. Let L be the length of the current bracket:

$$L = c - a$$
$$= (c - b) + (b - a).$$

Because d will lie in (b, c), the new bracket will be either $[a, b, d]$ or $[b, d, c]$. If $\Delta = d - b$, then the length of the new bracket is either

$$L_1 = d - a$$
$$= \Delta + (b - a)$$

if the bracket is $[a, b, d]$, or

$$L_2 = c - b$$

if the bracket is $[b, d, c]$. Since we cannot predict which length interval will result, our safest bet, giving the best guaranteed reduction in interval length at each step, is to choose d so that

$$L_1 = L_2.$$

This will give a guaranteed reduction from an interval of length L to one of length $L_1 = L_2$ every time. We have:

$$L_1 = L_2$$
$$\Delta + (b - a) = (c - b)$$
$$\Delta = (c - b) - (b - a)$$
$$= L - 2(b - a)$$

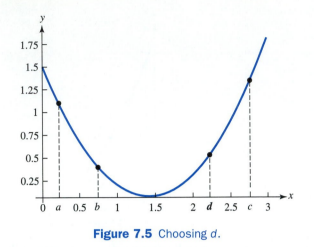

Figure 7.5 Choosing d.

so that in effect we divide the interval (a, c) into three subintervals of lengths $(b - a)$, Δ, and $(b - a)$, respectively (see Fig. 7.5). The length of the new bracket, which must include the center section, is necessarily $\Delta + (b - a)$. This gives

$$d = \Delta + b$$
$$= (c - b) - (b - a) + b$$
$$= c + a - b,$$

and any other choice of d allows for the possibility of both a smaller bracket, and at the same time of a larger one.

Suppose we iterate this approach. Note that d is found by taking a step of length Δ into the larger subinterval. If b were selected in the same manner as d, as would be the case if we are iterating, then it should come from taking a step of the same proportion from a into (a, c), the interval in which it would be chosen. That is,

$$\frac{\Delta}{c - b} = \frac{b - a}{c - a}$$

if previous points were selected in the same way that d was. If we set $\lambda = b - a$, then we can write this as

$$\frac{L - 2\lambda}{L - \lambda} = \frac{\lambda}{L}$$

or

$$\frac{1 - 2r}{1 - r} = r$$

in terms of the dimensionless quantity $r = \lambda/L$. Solving for r gives

$$1 - 2r = r(1 - r)$$
$$r^2 - 3r + 1 = 0$$
$$r_{1,2} = \frac{3 \pm \sqrt{5}}{2},$$

and because r is clearly less than 1, we reject the root $(3 + \sqrt{5})/2$ and take

$$r = \frac{(3 - \sqrt{5})}{2} \approx 0.3820. \tag{7.2}$$

From Eq. (7.2) we see that b is (or should be) found by stepping approximately 38% of the way from a into (a, c), and d is found by stepping approximately 38% of the way from b into (b, c).

Golden Section   The resulting algorithm is known as **golden section search:** Beginning with an initial
Search   bracket $[a, b, c]$ for a local minimum of a continuous function f, choose a new point d
by moving from b about 38.2% of the way into the larger of the two subintervals (a, b)
and (b, c). Compute $f(d)$ and choose a new, smaller bracket that includes d. The new
bracket will always be about 61.8% of the length $c - a$ of the previous bracket.

Example 7.1.1   Suppose we wish to find the first positive minimum of $f(t) = t^6 - 6t^4 - 3t + 1$. (By
a positive minimum we mean that the minimizer x^* is positive.) Taking the derivative
and setting it to zero would give a quintic equation that would still have to be solved
numerically. Since we can't avoid using a numerical method, let's use a minimization
method directly on f. Plotting the function suggests that the minimum is near $x = 2$ and
that $[1.5, 2, 2.5]$ would be a bracket. (Recall that we do not need a sign change as we
did for bisection.) Indeed,

$$f(1.5) \doteq -22.4844$$

$$f(2) = -37$$

$$f(2.5) \doteq 3.2656,$$

so this is a bracket ($f(2) < f(1.5)$ and $f(2) < f(2.5)$). The choice of $b = 2$ is not
optimal however; that would be $b = 1.5 + 0.382(2.5 - 1.5) \doteq 1.88$, for which we have
$f(1.88) \doteq -35.4402$. Since $[1.5, 1.88, 2.5]$ is a bracket, let's use it. We choose as the
next trial point $d = 1.88 + 0.382(2.5 - 1.88) \doteq 2.1168$. Since $f(2.1168) \doteq -35.8510$,
which is less than $f(1.88)$ and $f(2.5)$, the new bracket is $[1.88, 2.1168, 2.5]$. As expected,
the width $2.5 - 1.88 = 0.62$ is about 61.8% of 1.

Let's do another iteration. The right-hand subinterval $[2.1168, 2.5]$ is the larger
one, so we choose as the next trial point $d = 2.1168 + 0.382(2.5 - 2.1168) \doteq 2.2632$.
Since $f(2.2632) \doteq -28.8239$ and $f(2.1168)$ is less than $f(1.88)$ and $f(2.2632)$,
the new bracket is $[1.88, 2.1168, 2.2632]$. The width is $2.2632 - 1.88 = 0.3832$ and
$(0.618)(0.62) = 0.3832$, so this meets our expectations. The minimum lies somewhere
in $[1.88, 2.2632]$.   ∎

In fact even if we were to use the bracket $[1.5, 2, 2.5]$ instead and the same rule
(step 38.2% of the way into the larger subinterval each time), it would not be long
before the bracket achieves the form that it has in Example 7.1.1, with guaranteed
reduction to 61.8% of the length of the previous interval each time. The method is linear
with asymptotic error constant .618, comparable to bisection (though that has a slightly
lower asymptotic error constant of .5). Of course, in Example 7.1.1 we would achieve
more rapid convergence by applying Newton's method to $f'(t)$, since that method is

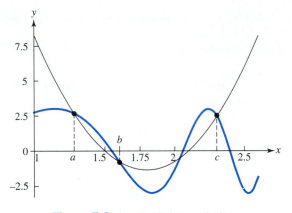

Figure 7.6 Quadratic Interpolation.

quadratically convergent. We will develop comparably fast methods for minimization (see Section 7.3).

The method is called golden section search because of its relation to the golden number $\Phi = (1 + \sqrt{5})/2 \doteq 1.618$, which occurs in many other areas of mathematics. In fact, recall that this is the order of convergence of the secant method.

Quadratic
Interpolation

Golden section search is the slow but steady method for minimization. Since we have a three-point bracket anyway, the obvious way to speed things up is to use quadratic interpolation (often called **Powell's method** in this context). We can interpolate a quadratic to the three points, use the location of the minimum of the quadratic as our estimate of the location of the minimum of the objective function, and update the bracket. If the objective function is sufficiently differentiable and $f''(x^*) \neq 0$, then the minimum will be nearly parabolic on a sufficiently small scale (by Taylor series), and so this is a reasonable approach. If we drop the requirement of a bracket and simply use the last three points, we have an analogue of Müller's method.

Quadratic interpolation for minima, as for roots, may make slow progress. Hence there is a **Brent's method for minimization** as well, which mixes quadratic interpolation and golden section search. The details are somewhat tedious, but the idea of Brent's method for minimization is the same as that in Section 1.6.

PROBLEMS 7.1

1. Perform ten iterations of golden section search on the objective function of Example 7.1.1 starting from the initial bracket [1.5, 2, 2.5] to estimate the location of the local minimum in that bracket. Show that the last bracket is divided into 38%/62% sections as predicted, even though the initial interval is not.

2. Use golden section search to estimate the location of any minimum of $f(x) = x^9 - 2x^7 + 5x^4 - 2x + 2$ to at least four decimal places.

3. Write a detailed algorithm (pseudocode) for performing minimization by quadratic interpolation, maintaining a bracket. Assume that a valid initial bracket will be given.

4. a. Perform four iterations of quadratic interpolation on the objective function of Example 7.1.1 starting from the initial bracket [1.5, 2, 2.5] to estimate the location of the local minimum in that bracket.

b. Perform four iterations of root-finding by quadratic interpolation on the derivative of the objective function of Example 7.1.1 starting from the initial point 1.5 to estimate the location of the local minimum in that bracket.

5. **a.** Use golden section search on $f^2(x)$ to approximate a zero of $f(x) = 1/x^3 - 10$ to three decimal places.

b. Use the quadratic interpolation minimization method on $f^2(x)$ to approximate a zero of $f(x) = 1/x^3 - 10$ to three decimal places.

MATLAB 7.1

The MATLAB one-dimensional minimization function is called `fminbnd` (in earlier versions, `fmin`). It requires a function name or inline function and a bracket. For example, enter:

```
» f=inline('(x-1)^2');
» fminbnd(f,-10,10)
```

to find the minimum at $x = 1$. Enter:

```
» fminbnd(f,-10,10,optimset('display','iter'))
```

(If you are using `fmin` then type `fmin(f,-10,10,1)` instead.) This displays the intermediate steps and shows that a version of Brent's method is being used by `fminbnd`, switching between golden section search and quadratic (that is, parabolic) interpolation. Experiment using `fminbnd` on several other functions.

If you enter `type fminbnd` you will see a comment line that states that "f must not be evaluated too close to" certain other points, and checks to see if this is so. Let's explore one reason that such a check might be used. (Another reason is simply to prevent the method from stagnating by taking very small steps.) Recall from Section 1.7 that, since there are only finitely many machine numbers, the distance from the machine number 1 to the next largest machine number is a positive number called the machine epsilon ϵ_M. Although smaller values than this can be represented and manipulated, when added to numbers as large as 1, they have no effect; enter:

```
» %Note the double equal sign, '==' not '='.
» 1+eps==1
ans =
     0
» 1+eps/2==1
ans =
     1
```

Adding $\epsilon/2$ to 1 has no effect. If we are working with numbers on the order of unity or larger, asking for a bracket of a root or minimum smaller than $[x^* - \epsilon, x^* + \epsilon]$ isn't feasible. Many programs for root-finding and minimization incorporate a check that compares the tolerance selected by the user to one based on the machine epsilon and uses the latter tolerance if the user's choice is unrealistically small.

For minimization problems, it can be argued that $\sqrt{\epsilon}|x^*|$ should be a rough lower bound on the tolerance. (Recall that the spacing between numbers grows as the size of the numbers grow; the spacing is equal to ϵ only near unity.) Since $f'(x^*) = 0$ at a parabolic minimum, the function is locally flat and changes very slowly near the minimum, and so values of x that are close will give very close function values. For example, if $f(x) = x^3 - 3x^2 - x + 3$, then there is a minimum between $x = 1$ and $x = 3$ (plot f to see this). Let's use the rough estimate $x^* \approx 2$; enter:

```
» tol=2*eps
tol =
      4.440892098500626e-016
```

on this machine. (Depending on your machine and version of MATLAB your results may vary. But because of the IEEE standard, they probably won't.) Enter:

```
» x=2
» f0=x^3-3*x^2-x+3
» x1=x+tol
» x1==2                          %Is x1 equal to 2?
» f1=x1^3-3*x1^2-x1+3
» x2=x-tol
» x2==2                          %Is x2 equal to 2?
» f2=x2^3-3*x2^2-x2+3
» f1==f0                         %Is f1 equal to f0?
» f2==f0                         %Is f2 equal to f0?
» f1==f2                         %Is f1 equal to f2?
```

Although x1 and x2 display as if they have the same value (even under `format long`) the equality tests show that they are different from 2; however, their function values come out precisely the same, as the tests for equality show. Think about this: The computer simply cannot see differences in function values over a range this small near the minimum because of the zero derivative. If you try this, say, near a point where $f'(x) = 1$, the f-values will differ, as you would expect.

The value $\sqrt{\epsilon}|x^*|$ is only an estimate, but it is sensible in general to check any user-supplied tolerances for reasonableness (and also to limit the maximum number of function evaluations). Not only is it wasteful to evaluate f in this range, but roundoff error could cause an incorrect decision to be made with respect to which points are kept for a bracket, which might destroy the bracket.

ADDITIONAL PROBLEMS 7.1

6. **a.** How many iterations of golden section search are required to reduce an initial bracket of width 2 to a bracket of width not more than 10^{-4}?

   b. If the bracket of width 2 is $[1, 3]$ and $\epsilon = 10^{-16}$, what is smallest final width we should ask for from golden section search?

   c. If the bracket of width 2 is $[1500, 1502]$ and $\epsilon = 10^{-16}$, what is smallest final width we should ask for from golden section search?

7. **a.** Repeat both parts of Problem 5, but use $|f(x)|$ instead of $f^2(x)$ as the objective function. Comment.

   b. Use MATLAB's fminbnd function on $f^2(x)$ and then on $|f(x)|$ to approximate a zero of $f(x) = 1/x^3 - 10$.

8. Suppose that $f(x)$ is a smooth function and that it has a parabolic minimum x^* at which $f(x^*) = m$ for some given real value m. Would it be reasonable to attempt to find x^* by using a root-finding method on $g(x) = f(x^*) - m$?

9. **a.** Show by drawing a sketch that the points $a < b < c$ need not bracket a minimum of a continuous function if $f(b) > f(a)$ or if $f(b) > f(c)$; also

show that $[a, b, c]$ *may* bracket a minimum in these cases.

b. If $a < b < c$ and $f(b) \leq f(a)$, $f(b) \leq f(c)$, must $[a, b, c]$ bracket a minimum of the continuous function f?

10. Write a detailed algorithm (pseudocode) for performing minimization by a version of Brent's method (mixing quadratic interpolation and golden section search). Assume that a valid initial bracket will be given.

11. Suppose that x^* is a parabolic minimum ($f''(x^*) \neq 0$) of a function. Expand $f(x)$ in a Taylor series about x^* and use it to justify the claim that the tolerance for a minimization method should not be smaller than about $\sqrt{\epsilon}|x^*|$.

12. Write a MATLAB program to determine the machine epsilon (without using the `eps` function). Compare your results with the value from MATLAB's `eps` function.

13. a. One version of Powell's method is as follows: Suppose that the objective function f has a parabolic minimum and that x_0 is an initial guess of its location. In addition, suppose that a step size $h > 0$ is given that is on the same scale as the distance x_0 is likely to be from the true minimum. (This is a measure of how rapidly the function changes.) Compute $f(x_0)$ and $f(x_0 + h)$; if $f(x_0) < f(x_0 + h)$ then compute $f(x_0 - h)$ else compute $f(x_0 + 2h)$. This gives a triple of points. Perform one iteration of quadratic interpolation, giving a fourth point. If the difference between the two lowest functions values is less than some tolerance, terminate; else choose the three points with the lowest function values and return to the quadratic interpolation step, *unless* choosing the point with the largest function value allows us to find a bracket. In that case, choose the bracketing triple and return to the quadratic interpolation step. Write a detailed algorithm

(pseudocode) for performing minimization by Powell's method.

b. Use Powell's method to approximate a minimum of $f(x) = x^6 - 5.5x + 3$.

14. Write a MATLAB program that performs golden section search on a given inline function. Include appropriate error checking. Test your program on several objective functions including `-humps(x)` (humps is a built-in function with two local maxima).

15. a. Golden section search is optimal for a single step. Suppose however that we plan to sample the function exactly twice. We might ask, are two golden section steps optimal? Consider the function $f(x) = -x^4 + 6x^3 - 6.25x^2 - 8.25x + 5$, which has a single local minimum bracketed by $[0, 1, 3]$. Compare two iterations of golden section search to evaluating the function at $x = 2$ and then at $x = 1.05$ and using these values to find a smaller bracket.

b. The choice of points in part (a) is based on the Fibonacci series $F_n = F_{n-1} + F_{n-2}$ with $F_0 = F_1 = 1$. The Fibonacci series occurs in the minimization method known as **Fibonacci search,** which gives the best possible reduction of bracket width for a fixed (in advance) number of iterations. Derive the method of Fibonacci search by assuming that the function will be evaluated precisely N times. *Hint:* Think again about part (a), where the initial bracket $[0, F_3]$ was divided into intervals of length F_1 and F_2; since $F_0 = F_1$ the last point is chosen to be very close to the next-to-last point. Develop a recursion relation for the interval lengths.

c. It is a fact that $\lim_{n \to \infty} F_n/F_{n-1} = (1 + \sqrt{5})/2 \doteq 1.618$. Use this fact to derive the method of golden section search from the method of Fibonacci search.

d. Why is golden section search used frequently in practice while Fibonacci search is used only rarely?

7.2 The Method of Steepest Descent

Davidon's Method

Golden section search is a linear method; the quadratic interpolation methods are superlinear. (The order is about 1.3 without brackets.) If we assume that derivative information is available, we should be able to do better. One such method for a differentiable function $f : \mathbb{R} \to \mathbb{R}$ is **Davidon's method,** which takes two points a, b and fits a cubic $y(x) = \alpha(x - a)^3 + \beta(x - a)^2 + \gamma(x - a) + \delta$ to the function by requiring not only that the cubic interpolate the objective function f at $x = a$ and $x = b$, but also that the derivatives of the cubic match those of f at those points; that is, we require that

$$y(a) = f(a)$$
$$y'(a) = f'(a)$$
$$y(b) = f(b)$$
$$y'(b) = f'(b),$$

where $f(a)$, $f(b)$, $f'(a)$, $f'(b)$ are assumed to be known (see Section 4.2). This gives

$$\delta = f(a)$$
$$\gamma = f'(a)$$
$$\alpha(b - a)^3 + \beta(b - a)^2 + \gamma(b - a) + \delta = f(b)$$
$$3\alpha(b - a)^2 + 2\beta(b - a) + \gamma(b - a) = f'(b)$$

and $\alpha, \beta, \gamma, \delta$ are easily found. Setting $y'(x) = 0$ gives a quadratic, one root of which corresponds to a minimum of y; the other corresponds to a maximum. We can use the second derivative test to determine which is the minimum, and that is our new estimate of the minimum of the function. We keep the two most recent points. Convergence is quadratic (under appropriate assumptions on f); since only two points are being maintained, a safeguarded method will typically bisect the interval when the method gets bogged down. As with root-finding in Chapter 1 and quadrature in Chapter 5, we see once again that higher-order interpolants may be used to derive more rapidly convergent methods with more complicated formulas.

Descent
Direction
    The idea of Davidon's method can be extended to a function $F : \mathbb{R}^n \to \mathbb{R}$. We take a different approach in this section, however, looking ahead to Newton's method for minimization in the next section. Suppose that $f : \mathbb{R} \to \mathbb{R}$. If we have no idea where a minimum of f might be, we might sample f at some point x_0 and also compute $f'(x_0)$. If $f'(x_0) < 0$, then the function is decreasing with increasing x, and so it makes sense to look for the minimum by taking our next point to the right of x_0 (see Fig. 7.7); if $f'(x_0) > 0$, then it makes sense to look to the left of x_0.

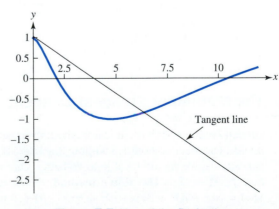

Figure 7.7 Use of the Derivative.

We could use this reasoning as part of a routine to search for an initial bracket for a minimum. Of course, we do not know how far we should step in the direction in which f is decreasing; we only know which way to go.

It's most appropriate to follow this reasoning further in a more general setting than functions on the real line. Suppose $F : \mathbb{R}^n \to \mathbb{R}$ is a smooth function; we write F as $F(x_1, \ldots, x_n)$ or as $F(x)$ where it is understood that x is a vector in $\mathbb{R}^n$. The natural notion of a derivative for such a function is its gradient

$$\nabla F(x) = \begin{pmatrix} \frac{\partial F}{\partial x_1} \\ \frac{\partial F}{\partial x_2} \\ \vdots \\ \frac{\partial F}{\partial x_n} \end{pmatrix}, \tag{7.3}$$

which is a vector-valued function on $\mathbb{R}^n$. For example, if $F(x, y, z) = x^2 y^2 z^2$, then Eq. (7.3) gives

$$\nabla F(x) = \begin{pmatrix} \frac{\partial F}{\partial x_1} \\ \frac{\partial F}{\partial x_2} \\ \frac{\partial F}{\partial x_3} \end{pmatrix}$$

$$= \begin{pmatrix} 2xy^2z^2 \\ 2x^2yz^2 \\ 2x^2y^2z \end{pmatrix}$$

is its gradient. Like the derivative, the gradient is zero at a minimum (that is, it is equal to the zero vector at a minimum).

The gradient is a vector, and at any point $(x_1, \ldots, x_n)$ the gradient vector $\nabla F(x_1, \ldots, x_n)$ points in the direction in which F is increasing most rapidly, called the direction of **steepest ascent;** it follows that $-\nabla F(x_1, \ldots, x_n)$ points in the direction in which F is decreasing most rapidly, called the direction of **steepest descent.** If we are looking for a minimum of F (we imagine F as a bowl-shaped region in space, and we are seeking the bottom of the bowl) starting from some given point x_0, it seems sensible to look in the direction of steepest descent.

Of course, it is highly unlikely that moving from x_0 in the direction of $-\nabla F(x_0)$ will take us directly to the local minimum (if in fact there is one); we will need to iterate. If x_0 is the initial guess, we take

$$x_1 = x_0 - \alpha \nabla F(x_0)$$

as the next point, for some $\alpha > 0$ that represents how far we step out in the direction of steepest descent. How shall we choose α? Because we want x_1 as close to the minimum as possible, we choose that value of $\alpha > 0$ that makes

$$F(x_1) = F(x_0 - \alpha \nabla F(x_0))$$

Method of Steepest Descent

as small as possible. Since x_0 is known, $F(x_0 - \alpha \nabla F(x_0))$ is a function of the single variable α, and so finding α involves only a (constrained) one-dimensional search no matter how large n may be. We then iterate in the form

$$x_{k+1} = x_k - \alpha_k \nabla F(x_k), \tag{7.4}$$

where α_k is chosen to minimize $F(x_k - \alpha_k \nabla F(x_k))$ at each step. (Ideally this will be the first minimum of $F(x_k - \alpha_k \nabla F(x_k))$ as we step away from x_k.) This is known as **(Cauchy's) method of steepest descent.** We may use $\|x_{k+1} - x_k\|$ (or $F(x_k) - F(x_{k+1})$) less than some tolerance as a convergence criterion, but typically we use the size of the residual $\|\nabla F(x_k)\|$, which will of course be zero at the minimum, as the principal convergence criterion.

Example 7.2.1   Let's apply the method of steepest descent to the function $F(x, y) = \sin(x^2 y^2 - 1)$. The gradient is $\nabla F(x, y) = (2xy^2 \cos(x^2 y^2 - 1), 2x^2 y \cos(x^2 y^2 - 1))^T$. Take $(x_0, y_0) = (1, 1)$. The direction of steepest descent is $\nabla F(1, 1) = (2 \cos(0), 2 \cos(0))^T = (2, 2)^T$. We need to find an α_0 that satisfies

$$\begin{aligned}
\alpha_0 &= \min_{\alpha > 0}\{F((x_0, y_0)^T - \alpha \nabla F(x_0, y_0))\} \\
&= \min_{\alpha > 0}\{F((1, 1)^T - \alpha(2, 2)^T)\} \\
&= \min_{\alpha > 0}\{F(1 - 2\alpha, 1 - 2\alpha)\} \\
&= \min_{\alpha > 0}\{\sin((1 - 2\alpha)^2(1 - 2\alpha)^2 - 1)\} \\
&= \min_{\alpha > 0}\{\sin((1 - 2\alpha)^4 - 1)\}.
\end{aligned}$$

The first minimum of the sine function occurs at $3\pi/2$, so

$$(1 - 2\alpha)^4 - 1 = \frac{3\pi}{2}$$

$$(1 - 2\alpha)^4 = \frac{3\pi}{2} + 1$$

$$\alpha = \frac{1}{2}\left(1 \pm \sqrt[4]{\frac{3\pi}{2} + 1}\right)$$

$$\doteq 1.2730, -0.2730$$

so $\alpha_0 \doteq 1.2133$. This gives

$$\begin{aligned}
\begin{pmatrix} x_1 \\ y_1 \end{pmatrix} &= \begin{pmatrix} x_0 \\ y_0 \end{pmatrix} - \alpha_0 \nabla F(x_0, y_0) \\
&= \begin{pmatrix} 1 \\ 1 \end{pmatrix} - 1.2730 \begin{pmatrix} 2 \\ 2 \end{pmatrix} \\
&= \begin{pmatrix} -1.5460 \\ -1.5460 \end{pmatrix}
\end{aligned}$$

and note that $F(x_0, y_0) = F(1, 1) = 0$, $F(x_1, y_1) = F(-1.5460, -1.5460) \doteq -1$. The gradient at this point is $\nabla F(-1.5460, -1.5460) \doteq (7E - 16, 7E - 16)^T$ with norm

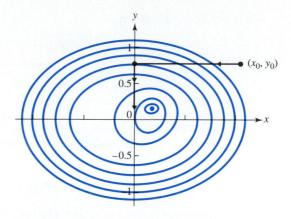

Figure 7.8 The Method of Steepest Descent.

$\|\nabla F(-1.5460, -1.5460)\| \doteq 10E - 16$, and clearly F cannot take on a smaller value than -1, so we have found a minimum.   ■

Rapid convergence of the method, as above, is *not* typical. In addition, the use of a line search algorithm will generally be necessary to find α, unlike the artificial case of Example 7.2.1. The dependence of the method of steepest descent on a one-dimensional search algorithm that is used at every iteration of steepest descent highlights the need for robust, reliable, and automated numerical methods. If we write a program to perform the method of steepest descent, we certainly don't want it to stop at each iteration and prompt the user for a bracket for the line search. (This issue is considered further in Problems 7.2.) One approach might be to use Davidon's method with some heuristic means of choosing the second point that is needed to fit the cubic interpolant.

Consider again Eq. (7.4). The method of steepest descent proceeds by selecting a search direction $(-\nabla F(x_k))$, stepping along it until it finds a local minimum in that direction (at which point it will be tangent to a contour of F), and then repeating this procedure from that point. It may take many seemingly unnecessary turns (see Fig. 7.8) and can stagnate in a region where $\|\nabla F(x)\|$ is small but nonzero, but it is very robust. Under mild conditions the method of steepest descent converges to a stationary point of F (that is, a point where $\nabla F(x) = 0$). Convergence to a stationary point that is neither a minimum nor a maximum is uncommon, although the method may make very slow progress while it is near such a point.

Steepest Descent as a Starter Method   However, the method of steepest descent is only linearly convergent, despite its use of derivative information. In the next section we look at a more rapidly convergent method, but for now we mention that the method of steepest descent is often used as a "starter" method for other algorithms. Because it converges for most initial guesses, several iterations of steepest descent may be used to improve an initial guess that is then handed to another, faster (but less robust) algorithm. This is done not only for minimization algorithms but also for root-finding algorithms such as Newton's method for systems. If we attempt to solve

$$F(x) = 0$$

where $F : \mathbb{R}^n \to \mathbb{R}^n$, that is,

$$F(x) = \begin{pmatrix} f_1(x_1, \ldots, x_n) \\ f_2(x_1, \ldots, x_n) \\ \vdots \\ f_n(x_1, \ldots, x_n) \end{pmatrix},$$

by Newton's method for systems (or some other root-finding method) with some initial guess x_0 and find that the method fails to converge, then we can use the method of steepest descent on the function

$$\|F(x)\|^2 = f_1^2(x) + \cdots + f_n^2(x)$$

(which is nonnegative and has minima precisely where F has zeroes) starting from this x_0. After several iterations of steepest descent, we return to Newton's method with what we hope is an improved initial guess. While this approach is not guaranteed to work, it is often successful in practice, and it is another example of the benefits of mixing methods that have different strengths.

Example 7.2.2   Suppose we are trying to solve the system

$$\ln(|x|) = 0$$

$$\ln(|y|) = 0$$

using Newton's method with the initial guess $(x_0, y_0) = (3.6, 3.6)$. For this very simple example, Newton's method for systems is just Newton's method applied separately to each component:

$$x_{k+1} = x_k - \frac{f_1(x_k)}{f_1'(x_k)}$$

$$y_{k+1} = y_k - \frac{f_1(y_k)}{f_2'(y_k)},$$

which is

$$x_{k+1} = x_k - x_k \ln(x_k)$$

$$y_{k+1} = y_k - y_k \ln(y_k)$$

for positive x, y, and

$$x_{k+1} = x_k + x_k \ln(-x_k)$$

$$y_{k+1} = y_k + y_k \ln(-y_k)$$

for negative x, y. With the given initial conditions, $x_k \to \infty$ and $y_k \to \infty$ (check this). Let's use the method of steepest descent on

$$g(x, y) = f_1^2(x, y) + f_2^2(x, y)$$

$$= [\ln(|x|)]^2 + [\ln(|y|)]^2$$

with the initial conditions $(x_0, y_0) = (3.6, 3.6)$. The gradient is

$$\nabla g(x, y) = \begin{pmatrix} \dfrac{2 \ln (x)}{x} \\ \dfrac{2 \ln (y)}{y} \end{pmatrix}$$

for x, y positive, and so $-\nabla g(3.6, 3.6) = (-0.7116, -0.7116)^T$ is the direction of steepest descent. We need to find an α_0 that satisfies

$$\alpha_0 = \min_{\alpha > 0}\{g((x_0, y_0)^T - \alpha \nabla g(x_0, y_0))\}$$

$$= \min_{\alpha > 0}\{g((3.6, 3.6)^T - \alpha(0.7116, 0.7116)^T)\}$$

$$= \min_{\alpha > 0}\{g(3.6 - 0.7116\alpha, 3.6 - 0.7116\alpha)^T\}$$

$$= \min_{\alpha > 0}\{[\ln (3.6 - 0.7116\alpha)]^2 + [\ln (3.6 - 0.7116\alpha)]^2\}$$

$$= \min_{\alpha > 0}\{2[\ln (3.6 - 0.7116\alpha)]^2\}.$$

The minimum occurs where $\ln (3.6 - 0.7116\alpha) = 0$, that is, where

$$3.6 - 0.7116\alpha = 1$$

$$\alpha = \frac{(3.6 - 1)}{0.7116}$$

$$\doteq 3.1759.$$

So, from the method of steepest descent,

$$\begin{pmatrix} x_1 \\ y_1 \end{pmatrix} = \begin{pmatrix} x_0 \\ y_0 \end{pmatrix} - \alpha_0 \begin{pmatrix} \dfrac{2 \ln (x_0)}{x_0} \\ \dfrac{2 \ln (y_0)}{y_0} \end{pmatrix}$$

$$= \begin{pmatrix} 3.6 \\ 3.6 \end{pmatrix} - 3.1759 \begin{pmatrix} 0.7116 \\ 0.7116 \end{pmatrix}$$

$$\doteq \begin{pmatrix} 1.3399 \\ 1.3399 \end{pmatrix}$$

is the next guess. At this point we could do a few more iterations of the (slow) method of steepest descent in hopes of further improving the guess, or return to Newton's method and try this guess. Let's do the latter: Using the new initial guess $(x_0, y_0) = (1.3399, 1.3399)$ in Newton's method gives

$$x_1 = x_0 - x_0 \ln (x_0) \doteq 0.9478$$

$$y_1 = y_0 - y_0 \ln (y_0) \doteq 0.9478$$

$$x_2 = x_1 - x_1 \ln (x_1) \doteq 0.9986$$

$$y_2 = y_1 - y_1 \ln (y_1) \doteq 0.9986$$

$$x_3 = x_2 - x_2 \ln (x_2) \doteq 1.0000$$

$$y_3 = y_2 - y_2 \ln (y_2) \doteq 1.0000,$$

and the method has converged to the solution $(1, 1)$. The method of steepest descent has salvaged this computation.   ∎

For a truly uncooperative root-finding problem, we might decide to use only the minimization strategy, that is, we might try to find the root by minimizing $\|F(x)\|^2$. Similarly, for certain minimization problems we might switch to root-finding on $f'(x)$ or $\nabla F(x)$. As a rule however it is advisable to solve the problem in the form in which it is posed.

Inexact Line Searches
Because the method of steepest descent is so well-behaved, the line search $\alpha_k = \min_{\alpha > 0}(F(x_k - \alpha \nabla F(x_k)))$ used to find α_k need not be performed exactly. It may be better to generate an approximate α_k quickly and take a step to a new search region than to spend a great deal of time getting a very precise value of α_k. Methods that find such a step size α_k are sometimes called **inexact line search** or **practical line search** methods; a common rule of thumb is that it suffices to get within about 10% of a minimum. A similar line of reasoning is sometimes used with Newton's method for solving nonlinear systems

$$x_{k+1} = x_k - [J(x_k)]^{-1} F(x_k)$$

in that we might solve

$$J(x_k)(x_{k+1} - x_k) = -F(x_k)$$

quickly but approximately for the step $x_{k+1} - x_k$. We reason once again that it's better to take quick large steps in the general direction of the solution than to take slow large steps in the true direction of the solution. (Near the minimum we may need to take more precise steps of course.) Such methods are called **inexact Newton's methods.**

PROBLEMS 7.2

1. a. Use the method of steepest descent to locate a minimum of $f(x, y, z) = 2x^2 - 2x + y^2 - 4y + z^2 - 6z + 13$. (Use calculus for the line search.)

b. Show that f has only one local minimum. What is the value of f at this minimizer?

2. What happens if the method of steepest descent is applied to a smooth function $f : \mathbb{R} \to \mathbb{R}$?

3. a. Show by example that the method of steepest descent can converge to a stationary point that is neither a local minimum nor a local maximum.

b. We say that a method is a **(general) descent method** for minimizing $F : \mathbb{R}^n \to \mathbb{R}$ if it has the form $x_{k+1} = x_k + \alpha_k s_k$ for some vector s_k and some positive constant α_k and, in addition, $F(x_{k+1}) \le F(x_k)$ at each step. We say that s_k is a **descent direction** for a differentiable function F if $s_k \cdot \nabla F(x_k) < 0$. Show

that the method of steepest descent is a general descent method that uses a descent direction (unless $\nabla F(x_k) = 0$ for some k).

c. Suggest another choice of s_k that might be used.

4. a. Repeat Example 7.2.1 using an inexact line search (e.g., take $\alpha = 1.15$ on the first step).

b. Repeat Problem 1 using an inexact line search and the same number of steepest descent iterations that you used in Problem 1. Comment on the efficiency of the two approaches.

5. In using the method of steepest descent to improve an initial guess for performing root-finding on $F(x) = 0$, it was suggested that the function $\|F(x)\|^2 = f_1^2(x) + \cdots + f_n^2(x)$ be minimized. Why is this preferable to minimizing $\|F(x)\|$?

MATLAB 7.2

The MATLAB multivariate minimization method is `fminsearch`. If `f` is an inline function (or the name of an appropriate M-file), then `fminsearch(f,x0)` attempts to find a local minimum of `f` near `x0`. Practical problems are generally sufficiently complicated that they require an M-file, but the inline functions are handy for experimentation. The algorithm used is the Nelder-Mead method (discussed in Section 7.6). This method does not use derivative information and hence may be applied to fairly general functions. But because of this, it is too slow for many purposes.

There are a number of MATLAB commands for handling functions of several variables. Enter:

```
» help gradient
```

This function computes numerical (approximate) gradients. Copy and paste the four lines under "`Examples:`" near the end of the help text and then hit the enter key. You'll see a contour plot of $z = xe^{(-x^2-y^2)}$ (that is, curves corresponding to those values of (x, y) on which $z = c$ for various choices of $c \in \mathbb{R}$). The arrows (supplied by the `quiver` command) point in the direction of the gradient at each point, and the lengths of the arrows are proportional to $\|\nabla z(x, y)\|$. Evidently there is a local minimum on the left (at the center of the concentric contours on the left-hand side) and a local maximum on the right.

To make a simple contour plot of a function $z = f(x, y)$ of two variables, for example, $f(x, y) = x^2 + y^2$, we must form a matrix of z-values. The command `meshgrid` can be used to create a matrix of x- and y-values that form a grid. For example, enter:

```
» [x,y]=meshgrid(-4:.1:4,-4:.1:4)
```

to generate a grid of (x, y) values that cover $-4 \leq x \leq 4$, $-4 \leq y \leq 4$ with a spacing of .1 in each direction. (Compare `linspace`.) Then the command:

```
» z=x.^2+y.^2;
```

computes the corresponding z-values. (Once again the use of the period (`.`) forces the operations to be performed element by element on the `x` and `y` matrices.) Note that `z` is a matrix of the same size as `x` and `y`. Enter:

```
» contour(z)
```

to see the contour plot. (The scales on the x- and y-axes are incorrect because the `z` matrix does not contain information concerning at which x- and y-values the function was evaluated, only what the heights z were at those points.) To approximate the gradient, enter:

```
» [dx,dy]=gradient(z,.1,.1);
```

which uses finite differences to approximate the components `dx` and `dy` of $\nabla z(x, y)$ (the second and third argument tell the `gradient` command what spacing was used between the z-values; enter `type gradient` to see the details). Then enter:

```
» hold on;quiver(dx,dy)
```

to display the gradient values over the contours. The arrow at every point (x, y) points in the direction of steepest ascent from that point.

You may be able to compute the gradient symbolically if your installation of MATLAB includes the Symbolic Toolbox. For example:

```
» diff('x^2+y^2','x')
» diff('x^2+y^2','y')
```

gives the first component and second component of the gradient of $f(x, y) = x^2 + y^2$, which may then be evaluated as inline functions. (If you get another answer, the Symbolic Toolbox is not available to you.) For example:

```
» g=inline('x^2*y^2*z^2');
» gx=diff(g,'x');gy=diff(g,'y');gz=diff(g,'z');
» gp=[feval(gx,1,-1,1),feval(gy,1,-1,1),feval(gz,1,-1,1)];
```

computes the components g_x, g_y, g_z of ∇g and then evaluates $\nabla g(1, -1, 1)$ (that is, $\nabla g(x, y, z)$ evaluated at the point $(x, y, z) = (1, -1, 1)$). At the risk of being repetitive, we say again: Symbolic methods like this are of more use for textbook problems than practical ones.

Let's discuss an aspect of the MATLAB environment that can be useful when you are writing programs. There are several debugging features. Enter:

```
» help debug
```

to see a list of debugging commands. Type `help dbstop`. The `dbstop` command places a debugging stop point (or breakpoint) at a given line in a program. When the breakpoint is reached, the program stops executing and displays a special prompt (K»); at this time we can inspect and modify variables. For example, enter the command:

```
» dbstop in fminsearch at 161
```

to set a breakpoint at line 161 of `fminsearch` (recall that `fminsearch` is just an M-file). Then enter:

```
» fminsearch('cos',3)
```

Execution should stop at the line `func_evals=func_evals+1` in the M-file (which apparently counts how often the objective function has been evaluated). (You might get something different if you are using a different version, especially if you are using `fmins` in Version 4 of MATLAB.) Debugging mode has been entered, as symbolized by the prompt:

```
K»
```

and the MATLAB editor has been launched with `fminsearch.m`. (This M-file implements the Nelder-Mead method of Section 7.6.) We can now inspect the values of various variables being used by the program. For example, it looks as if `xbar` contains the centroid of the simplex and `xr` is the reflected point. To see their values, enter:

```
K» xbar
K» xr
```

We can change them if desired:

```
K» xr=3.6
K» dbcont
```

The dbcont command continues execution of the program, using the new value of xr. (We should have changed fxr too.) Because the breakpoint lies in a loop, the program is halted again. Enter:

```
K» xr
K» dbclear all
K» dbcont
```

to see the current value of xr, clear all breakpoints in the M-file, and continue. The breakpoints are cleared and the program does not stop again until it ends successfully.

More than one breakpoint may be set, and breakpoints may be set to stop on errors or other conditions (not just at certain line numbers); see help dbstop. The dbstatus command lists all breakpoints that are currently set (for a given M-file). The dbquit command exits the debugger and also terminates execution of the program.

See help debug for other debugging commands. Using echo on can sometimes help in debugging a script. In addition, the keyboard command may be placed in an M-file at any point; this gives much the same functionality as dbstop but requires that the program be edited. When you are writing a program and find that you are having difficulty tracking down the source of an error, you can use dbstop to stop on an error or try placing the keyboard command near the location of the error and examining the variables when prompted (K»). As with dbstop, any MATLAB command may be entered at this point. Enter the command return to return to execution of the M-file. (The return command may also be used within an M-file to return to the M-file that called it or to the MATLAB prompt, as appropriate.) The keyboard command may also be used to input needed variables that were not given as calling arguments of the M-file; another way to do this is to use the input command. The command:

```
» z=input('What''s the next value of z? ')
What's the next value of z? 7
z =
    7
```

produces the indicated output. (A repeated single quote (' ') is used to enter a single quote character into a string; see help punct and help strings for more information.) You may give a MATLAB command (e.g., 3+4), which will be evaluated before being assigned to z. Enter:

```
» z=input('What''s the next value of z? ','s')
```

and again give the value 7 when prompted. Then:

```
» z
```

displays a 7, but:

```
» z==7
» z=='7'
```

shows that the effect of including the `'s'` is to force the input to be interpreted as a string variable. For example, enter:

```
» z=input('What''s the next value of z? ','s')
What's the next value of z? 3+4
z =
    3+4
```

As a rule, values should be passed to programs as arguments and not via the `keyboard` or `input` commands (or the GUI `questdlg` command).

The `load` command may be used within a program to load variables from a file. See `fread` and related commands (suggested at the end of the `fread` help text) for reading data from files.

ADDITIONAL PROBLEMS 7.2

6. a. Use the method of steepest descent to find a minimum of $f(x, y) = x^2(y^4 + \sin^2(xy))$ starting from the initial guess $(100, 100)$. Use `fminbnd` (finding the brackets by trial and error) or any other reasonable approach for the line search.

b. Are the minima of this function isolated?

c. Use two different initial guesses (on the same scale) to find two different minima of f.

7. a. For Problem 1, sketch the contours of $f(x, y)$ (use MATLAB if you wish), and then locate $(x_0, y_0), (x_1, y_1), \ldots$ on the plot. Sketch the vectors that indicate the steps taken from (x_0, y_0) to (x_1, y_1) and so on towards the solution.

b. The method of steepest descent $x_{k+1} = x_k - \alpha_k \nabla F(x_k)$ may be rewritten as $x_{k+1} - x_k = -\alpha_k \nabla F(x_k)$. Because α_k is a scalar, this equation indicates that the vector $x_{k+1} - x_k$ from x_k to x_{k+1} is proportional to $-\nabla F(x_k)$, and because α_k is positive, it is in the same direction as $-\nabla F(x_k)$, that is, in the direction opposite $\nabla F(x_k)$. Demonstrate this on your graph by sketching in $\nabla F(x_k)$ for several points (you may need to draw additional contours).

8. a. Consider a general descent method $x_{k+1} = x_k + \alpha_k s_k$ for some choice of the vectors s_k (see Problem 3). Show that if s_k is a descent direction, then there is always a choice of $\alpha_k > 0$ that ensures that $F(x_{k+1}) \le F(x_k)$.

b. Show by example that if s_k is not a descent direction, then there need not be an $\alpha_k > 0$ that ensures that $F(x_{k+1}) \le F(x_k)$.

9. Write a detailed algorithm (pseudocode) for performing the method of steepest descent. Assume that both the function and the gradient will be supplied, and that the norm of the gradient at the solution should be printed and the minimizer returned. Assume that an appropriate subroutine exists for the line search.

10. a. Write a detailed algorithm (pseudocode) for performing Davidon's method.

b. Use Davidon's method to estimate the locations of any two minima of $f(x) = x^9 - 2x^7 + 5x^4 - 2x + 2$ to at least four decimal places. Compare your results to those in Problem 2 of Section 2.1.

11. a. Use the method of steepest descent to find the minimum of $z = x^2 + y^2$. Use MATLAB's `fminbnd` function for the line search.

b. Repeat part (a) with an inexact line search.

12. a. Construct a function of two variables that has a small but nonzero gradient in some region, and for which the method of steepest descent stagnates (makes very slow progress) in that region.

b. Show by example that the method of steepest descent can be slow even if the function is quadratic (e.g., $f(x, y) = 2x^2 + 2xy + y^2 + 2$).

13. a. Using the objective function $f(x, y, z) = x^2 y^2 z^2 + 2x^2 + 3y^2 + 4z^2 + \cos(xy + z) - 1$, compare the method of steepest descent using line search by 15, 10, 5, and 3 iterations of golden section search, respectively. (Find the bracket by trial and error.) How many function evaluations are required in each case to achieve four decimal place accuracy? (Do not count any function evaluations used only to find a bracket.) Comment on the use of inexact line searches.

b. Use MATLAB's `fminsearch` command to find a local minimum of this f.

14. a. The method of steepest descent requires that a one-dimensional search be performed at each iteration. We will not be able to automate the method of steepest descent with a bracketing method used for the line search unless we have an automatic means of generating the bracket. Without an automatic means of generating the bracket the user must be prompted for a bracket at every step, which is clearly undesirable. Write a MATLAB program that accepts as input a function of a single variable and a single initial guess as to the location of a minimum and attempts to return a bracket for the minimum by some form of intelligent trial and error. Explain the method you develop in detail.

b. Modify your method and program to accept a scale parameter that measures how rapidly the function changes, as well as an initial guess. Use the scale parameter to decide how far you should step away from the current point when looking for a new point.

15. a. A general descent method may not descend rapidly enough to be of use. The **Armijo rule** requires that α satisfy $F(x_k - \alpha_k s_k) - F(x_k) < -\rho \alpha_k \nabla F(x_k) \cdot s_k$, where $\rho \in (0, 1)$ is a parameter ($\rho = 10^{-4}$ is a typical choice). We say that such an α_k gives **sufficient decrease** in the function value (rather than **simple decrease** $F(x_{k+1}) < F(x_k)$, which corresponds to the choice $\rho = 0$, or the nonincrease requirement $F(x_{k+1}) \leq F(x_k)$ of a general descent method). Prove that if ∇F is continuous and $\{F(x_k)\}_{k=0}^{k=\infty}$ is bounded from below, then the method of steepest descent using the Armijo rule produces a sequence $\{x_k\}_{k=0}^{k=\infty}$ that converges to a stationary point of F.

b. One method for finding an α_k that gives sufficient decrease is the method of **backtracking**, wherein we choose $\alpha_k = \delta^m$ for some $\delta \in (0, 1)$ and for the smallest integer $m \geq 0$ for which sufficient decrease is achieved. We start with $m = 0$ ($\alpha_k = 1$), and if it is not acceptable, we try $\alpha_k = \delta$, $\alpha_k = \delta^2$, $\alpha_k = \delta^3$, and so on, until the criterion is satisfied. (Note that we do not need to find an initial bracket with this approach.) Write a MATLAB program that implements the method of steepest descent with the Armijo rule for sufficient decrease, with α_k selected by backtracking. Test your program on several objective functions.

7.3 Newton Methods for Nonlinear Optimization

The method of steepest descent is too slow to use by itself. It is used to start other methods, such as Newton's method, and to add robustness to other minimization algorithms that switch to steepest descent when they encounter difficulties. In developing a faster method we will pay the usual price: It will require more assumptions and information (in this case, second derivatives) and it will be less robust with respect to the initial guess.

Newton's Method (Root-Finding)
As indicated previously, we can get a quadratically convergent method by using Newton's method to perform root-finding on $f'(x)$ (or Newton's method for systems on $\nabla F(x)$). If $f : \mathbb{R} \to \mathbb{R}$, then Newton's method applied to $f'(x)$ takes the form

$$x_{k+1} = x_k - \frac{f'(x_k)}{f''(x_k)}$$

if f is twice continuously differentiable. (Since we are dealing with f', our convergence theory requires that f be four times continuously differentiable so that f' is thrice continuously differentiable; see Section 1.3 and Section 1.4.) Although this suffers from all the potential problems cited in the beginning of Section 7.1, if we assume that x_0

is sufficiently close to a minimum x^* of f and that $f''(x^*)$ is nonzero, then we expect quadratic convergence of the method to x^*. Of course, if x_0 is not sufficiently close to a minimum, then we might converge to a maximum of f instead. Note all the assumptions that we must make: that the function is several times differentiable, that we can compute f' and f'', that the minimum is parabolic ($f''(x^*) \neq 0$, and in fact $f''(x^*) > 0$, since x^* is a minimum), and that x_0 is sufficiently close to the minimum.

Newton's Method for Nonlinear Optimization

If we are prepared to make all these assumptions, however, we *do* get a method that is quadratically convergent, and having such a method is certainly desirable. We might also derive this method as follows: If x_0 is an approximation of the location of the minimum, then near x_0 we have

$$f(x) \approx f(x_0) + f'(x_0)(x - x_0) + \frac{1}{2}f''(x_0)(x - x_0)^2. \qquad (7.5)$$

That is, near x_0, $f(x)$ is approximated by the quadratic model

$$q(x) = f(x_0) + f'(x_0)(x - x_0) + \frac{1}{2}f''(x_0)(x - x_0)^2.$$

The minimum of this quadratic occurs where $q'(x) = 0$. Differentiating Eq. (7.5) with respect to x and setting $f'(x)$ to zero gives

$$0 \approx 0 + f'(x_0) \cdot 1 + f''(x_0)(x - x_0)$$

(note that $f'(x_0)$ and $f''(x_0)$ are constants because we are differentiating with respect to x), and leads to the method

$$x_{new} = x_0 - \frac{f'(x_0)}{f''(x_0)}.$$

Hence if x_0 is an approximation of the location of the minimum x^*, then x_{new} should be a better approximation of x^*. From this point of view Newton's method for minimization

$$x_{k+1} = x_k - \frac{f'(x_k)}{f''(x_k)}$$

is truly an optimization method and not merely an application of Newton's method for root-finding. This is an important point, and viewing Newton's method as an optimization method rather than a root-finding method is generally preferable in optimization problems. However, we must remember that the method may converge to any point such that $f'(x) = 0$ (e.g., a local maximum) if x_0 is not sufficiently near a local minimum.

Example 7.3.1   Let's use Newton's method to find a minimum of $f(x) = (x - 10)(x - 20)(x - 50) = x^3 - 80x^2 + 1700x - 10000$. Clearly the only local minimum of this cubic lies between

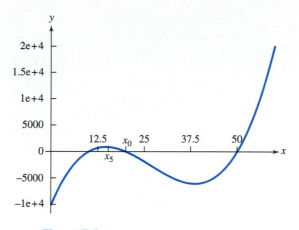

Figure 7.9 $y = (x - 10)(x - 20)(x - 50)$

$x = 20$ and $x = 50$. Let's use $x_0 = 20$; we have

$$x_1 = x_0 - \frac{f'(x_0)}{f''(x_0)}$$

$$= x_0 - \frac{(3x_0^2 - 160x_0 + 1700)}{(6x_0 - 160)}$$

$$= 12.5$$

$$x_2 = x_1 - \frac{f'(x_1)}{f''(x_1)}$$

$$\doteq 14.4853$$

$$x_3 \doteq 14.6471$$

$$x_4 \doteq 14.6482$$

$$x_5 \doteq 14.6482.$$

The method has converged, but to a local maximum (see Fig. 7.9). Perhaps this is not so surprising because $f''(20) = 6 \times 20 - 160 = -40$, so that at $x_0 = 20$ f has the concavity that corresponds to a maximum, not to a minimum ($f''(x^*) > 0$).

Let's try again with $x_0 = 30$, where $f''(30) = 6 \times 30 - 160 = 20$. We have:

$$x_1 = x_0 - \frac{f'(x_0)}{f''(x_0)}$$

$$= x_0 - \frac{(3x_0^2 - 160x_0 + 1700)}{(6x_0 - 160)}$$

$$= 50$$

$$x_2 = x_1 - \frac{f'(x_1)}{f''(x_1)}$$

$$\doteq 41.4286$$

$$x_3 \doteq 38.9401$$

$$x_4 \doteq 38.6878$$

$$x_5 \doteq 38.6852$$

$$x_6 \doteq 38.6852$$

and $f'(38.6852) \doteq -9.0949E - 013$, $f''(38.6852) \doteq 72.1110 > 0$, which is a good indication that we have found a local minimum. ■

Unlike other methods we have seen for one-dimensional minimization, this approach requires only a single initial guess. Despite this, Newton's method is rarely employed for one-dimensional minimization; however, it and its variants are very commonly used for multi-dimensional minimization.

Systems   The multi-dimensional form may be derived by applying Newton's method for systems (see Section 1.7) to find a stationary point of $F : \mathbb{R}^n \to \mathbb{R}$ by solving the nonlinear system of equations $\nabla F(x) = 0$, or by using Taylor series for a function of several variables to get the multi-dimensional analogue of Eq. (7.5). Taking the latter approach gives

$$F(x) = F(x_0) + \nabla F(x_0)^T (x - x_0) + \frac{1}{2}(x - x_0)^T H(x_0)(x - x_0) + \cdots, \qquad (7.6)$$

where $H(x)$ (also denoted $\nabla^2 F(x)$) is a matrix, called the **Hessian matrix**

$$H(x) = \begin{bmatrix} \dfrac{\partial^2 F}{\partial x_1^2} & \dfrac{\partial^2 F}{\partial x_1 \partial x_2} & \cdots & \dfrac{\partial^2 F}{\partial x_1 \partial x_n} \\[2mm] \dfrac{\partial^2 F}{\partial x_2 \partial x_1} & \dfrac{\partial^2 F}{\partial x_2^2} & \cdots & \dfrac{\partial^2 F}{\partial x_2 \partial x_n} \\[2mm] \vdots & \vdots & \ddots & \vdots \\[2mm] \dfrac{\partial^2 F}{\partial x_n \partial x_1} & \dfrac{\partial^2 F}{\partial x_n \partial x_2} & \cdots & \dfrac{\partial^2 F}{\partial x_n^2} \end{bmatrix}$$

(or simply the **Hessian**) of $F(x)$. The Hessian matrix is symmetric if F is twice continuously differentiable.

Consider Eq. (7.6) and assume that the higher-order terms are negligible. If we take x_0 to be x^*, we have

$$F(x) = F(x^*) + \nabla F(x^*)^T (x - x^*) + \frac{1}{2}(x - x^*)^T H(x)(x - x^*) + \cdots$$

$$= F(x^*) + \frac{1}{2}(x - x^*)^T H(x^*)(x - x^*) + \cdots$$

since $\nabla F(x^*)$ is zero. Since $F(x^*)$ is the locally minimum value of F, it must be that

$$(x - x^*)^T H(x^*)(x - x^*) \geq 0$$

at least for x near x^*; if the minimum is a strict local minimum, then we must have

$$(x - x^*)^T H(x^*)(x - x^*) > 0$$

($x \neq x^*$). The quantity $x - x^*$ is just a vector; call it y. Any symmetric matrix A with the property that $y^T A y \geq 0$ for all y is said to be a positive semi-definite matrix, and any symmetric matrix A with the property that $y^T A y > 0$ for all $y \neq 0$ is said to be a positive definite matrix (see Section 2.4). It can be shown that a symmetric matrix is positive semi-definite exactly when all its eigenvalues are nonnegative and that a symmetric matrix is positive definite exactly when all its eigenvalues are positive. For a sufficiently differentiable function, a local minimum must have a positive semi-definite Hessian matrix, and a parabolic local minimum must have a positive definite Hessian matrix.

Hence by using vector calculus either on Newton's method for finding roots applied to $\nabla F(x) = 0$, or on Eq. (7.6) to find its minimum (assuming in either case that $H(x^*)$ is positive definite), we arrive at Newton's method for minimization:

$$x_{k+1} = x_k - H^{-1}(x_k)\nabla F(x_k).$$

(If $H(x^*)$ is positive definite, then it is necessarily nonsingular, and so $H^{-1}(x)$ exists at the minimum $x = x^*$.) Of course, in practice we would actually write this as

$$H(x_k)(x_{k+1} - x_k) = -\nabla F(x_k), \tag{7.7}$$

solve for the step $d_k = x_{k+1} - x_k$, and then compute x_{k+1} from $x_{k+1} = x_k + d_k$.

Let's focus on the case of a sufficiently differentiable function of two variables $F : \mathbb{R}^2 \to \mathbb{R}$. For such a function $F(x, y)$ the gradient is

$$\nabla F(x, y) = \begin{pmatrix} \dfrac{\partial F}{\partial x} \\ \dfrac{\partial F}{\partial y} \end{pmatrix}$$

and the Hessian is

$$H(x, y) = \begin{bmatrix} \dfrac{\partial^2 F}{\partial x^2} & \dfrac{\partial^2 F}{\partial x \partial y} \\ \dfrac{\partial^2 F}{\partial y \partial x} & \dfrac{\partial^2 F}{\partial y^2} \end{bmatrix}.$$

The Hessian is positive definite wherever its eigenvalues are both positive; for a 2×2 symmetric matrix it can be shown that this occurs precisely when the determinant is positive and the $(1, 1)$ component of the matrix is positive. (The case of an $n \times n$ matrix is slightly more complicated.) Newton's method then takes the form

$$\begin{pmatrix} x_{k+1} \\ y_{k+1} \end{pmatrix} = \begin{pmatrix} x_k \\ y_k \end{pmatrix} - \begin{bmatrix} \dfrac{\partial^2 F}{\partial x^2} & \dfrac{\partial^2 F}{\partial x \partial y} \\ \dfrac{\partial^2 F}{\partial y \partial x} & \dfrac{\partial^2 F}{\partial y^2} \end{bmatrix}^{-1} \begin{pmatrix} \dfrac{\partial F}{\partial x} \\ \dfrac{\partial F}{\partial y} \end{pmatrix},$$

where the Hessian and gradient on the right-hand side are evaluated at $(x, y) = (x_k, y_k)$.

Example 7.3.2   Let's apply Newton's method to find a local minimum of the function $F(x, y) = xe^{(-x^2 - y^2)}$ (considered in MATLAB 7.2). We have

$$\frac{\partial F}{\partial x} = e^{-x^2 - y^2} - 2x^2 e^{-x^2 - y^2}, \quad \frac{\partial F}{\partial y} = -2xye^{-x^2 - y^2},$$

so $\nabla F(x, y) = (e^{-x^2 - y^2}(1 - 2x^2), -2xye^{-x^2 - y^2})^T$. Also

$$\frac{\partial^2 F}{\partial x^2} = -6xe^{-x^2 - y^2} + 4x^3 e^{-x^2 - y^2}$$

$$\frac{\partial^2 F}{\partial x \partial y} = \frac{\partial^2 F}{\partial y \partial x} = -2ye^{-x^2 - y^2} + 4x^2 ye^{-x^2 - y^2}$$

$$\frac{\partial^2 F}{\partial y^2} = -2xe^{-x^2 - y^2} + 4xy^2 e^{-x^2 - y^2}$$

so

$$H(x, y) = \begin{bmatrix} -6xe^{-x^2 - y^2} + 4x^3 e^{-x^2 - y^2} & -2ye^{-x^2 - y^2} + 4x^2 ye^{-x^2 - y^2} \\ -2ye^{-x^2 - y^2} + 4x^2 ye^{-x^2 - y^2} & -2xe^{-x^2 - y^2} + 4xy^2 e^{-x^2 - y^2} \end{bmatrix}.$$

Hence Newton's method for this function is

$$\begin{pmatrix} x_{k+1} \\ y_{k+1} \end{pmatrix} = \begin{pmatrix} x_k \\ y_k \end{pmatrix}$$

$$- \begin{bmatrix} -6xe^{-r^2} + 4x^3 e^{-r^2} & -2ye^{-r^2} + 4x^2 ye^{-r^2} \\ -2ye^{-r^2} + 4x^2 ye^{-r^2} & -2xe^{-r^2} + 4xy^2 e^{-r^2} \end{bmatrix}^{-1} \begin{pmatrix} e^{-r^2}(1 - 2x^2) \\ -2xye^{-r^2} \end{pmatrix},$$

where we have written $r^2 = x^2 + y^2$ for typographical convenience. Let's take $(x_0, y_0) = (-1, -1)$ as the initial condition. (Note that $(x_0, y_0) = (0, 0)$ would not work because $H(0, 0)$ is the zero matrix and hence singular.) We have

$$\begin{pmatrix} x_1 \\ y_1 \end{pmatrix} = \begin{pmatrix} -1 \\ -1 \end{pmatrix} - \begin{bmatrix} 6e^{-2} + -4e^{-2} & 2e^{-2} + -4e^{-2} \\ 2e^{-2} + -4e^{-2} & 2e^{-2} + -4e^{-2} \end{bmatrix}^{-1} \begin{pmatrix} -e^{-2} \\ -2e^{-2} \end{pmatrix}$$

$$= \begin{pmatrix} -1 \\ -1 \end{pmatrix} - \begin{bmatrix} 2e^{-2} & -2e^{-2} \\ -2e^{-2} & -2e^{-2} \end{bmatrix}^{-1} \begin{pmatrix} -1 \\ -2 \end{pmatrix} e^{-2}$$

$$= \begin{pmatrix} -1 \\ -1 \end{pmatrix} - \frac{e^2}{2} \begin{bmatrix} 1 & -1 \\ -1 & -1 \end{bmatrix}^{-1} \begin{pmatrix} -1 \\ -2 \end{pmatrix} e^{-2}$$

$$= \begin{pmatrix} -1 \\ -1 \end{pmatrix} - \frac{1}{2} \left(\frac{1}{-1 - 1} \right) \begin{bmatrix} -1 & 1 \\ 1 & 1 \end{bmatrix} \begin{pmatrix} -1 \\ -2 \end{pmatrix}$$

$$= \begin{pmatrix} -1 \\ -1 \end{pmatrix} + \frac{1}{4} \begin{pmatrix} -1 \\ -3 \end{pmatrix}$$

$$= \begin{pmatrix} -1.25 \\ -1.75 \end{pmatrix}$$

$$\begin{pmatrix} x_2 \\ y_2 \end{pmatrix} \doteq \begin{pmatrix} -1.3535 \\ -2.0314 \end{pmatrix}$$

$$\begin{pmatrix} x_3 \\ y_3 \end{pmatrix} \doteq \begin{pmatrix} -1.4416 \\ -2.2629 \end{pmatrix}$$

$$\begin{pmatrix} x_4 \\ y_4 \end{pmatrix} \doteq \begin{pmatrix} -1.5206 \\ -2.4654 \end{pmatrix}$$

$$\begin{pmatrix} x_5 \\ y_5 \end{pmatrix} \doteq \begin{pmatrix} -1.5933 \\ -2.6481 \end{pmatrix}$$

$$\begin{pmatrix} x_6 \\ y_6 \end{pmatrix} \doteq \begin{pmatrix} -1.6611 \\ -2.8161 \end{pmatrix}$$

$$\begin{pmatrix} x_7 \\ y_7 \end{pmatrix} \doteq \begin{pmatrix} -1.7251 \\ -2.9727 \end{pmatrix}.$$

At this point the gradient is $(-1.0291E - 4, -2.1308E - 4)$; we seem to be making very slow progress. Let's find the minimum analytically by setting the gradient equal to zero:

$$\begin{pmatrix} e^{-x^2-y^2}(1 - 2x^2) \\ -2xye^{-x^2-y^2} \end{pmatrix} = \begin{pmatrix} 0 \\ 0 \end{pmatrix}$$

$$\begin{pmatrix} (1 - 2x^2) \\ -2xy \end{pmatrix} = \begin{pmatrix} 0 \\ 0 \end{pmatrix}$$

$$x^2 = \frac{1}{2}, -2xy = 0$$

so $x = \pm 1/\sqrt{2}$, and so $y = 0$. The extrema are at $(1/\sqrt{2}, 0)$ and $(-1/\sqrt{2}, 0)$. We have $H(1/\sqrt{2}, 0) = [-1.7155 \, 0; 0 \, -0.8578]$ (in MATLAB notation), which is negative definite (maximum), and $H(-1/\sqrt{2}, 0) = [1.7155 \, 0; 0 \, 0.8578]$, which is positive definite (minimum). There is a parabolic minimum, but the method seems to be slowly diverging from it.

Let's try again with a closer initial condition, say $(x_0, y_0) = (-0.8, -0.1)$. We have

$$\begin{pmatrix} x_1 \\ y_1 \end{pmatrix} \doteq \begin{pmatrix} -0.6961 \\ 0.0058 \end{pmatrix}$$

$$\begin{pmatrix} x_2 \\ y_2 \end{pmatrix} \doteq \begin{pmatrix} -0.7070 \\ 0.0000 \end{pmatrix}$$

$$\begin{pmatrix} x_3 \\ y_3 \end{pmatrix} \doteq \begin{pmatrix} -0.7071 \\ 0.0000 \end{pmatrix},$$

and we have clearly converged to the minimum. (In fact, x_3 agrees with $x^* = 1/\sqrt{2}$ to 7 decimal places, and $y_3 \doteq 8E - 14$ is in excellent agreement with $y^* = 0$; $\|\nabla F(x_3, y_3)\| \doteq 8E - 9$.) As promised, convergence was rapid once we were sufficiently close (which in this case appears to mean very close). ∎

Convergence criteria typically include a consideration of the size of $\|\nabla F(x_k)\|$ and possibly the approximate relative and/or absolute errors. It's also wise to monitor the Hessian for positive definiteness. A simple approach is to test a few vectors to see whether $y^T H y < 0$ appears to hold. A better approach uses the Cholesky decomposition (see Section 2.4), stopping when the computation of this decomposition fails due to the need to take a square root of a negative number. The computation of the Cholesky decomposition can be modified to efficiently check for positive definiteness.

If the method fails for a given x_0, then it's worth trying a few iterations of steepest descent in the hope of moving the initial guess into a better region. Remember, steepest descent *is* capable of distinguishing a minimum from a maximum, although it may still get hung up on a saddle point or, in cases of incredibly bad luck, a maximum (if it should happen to land on one–this almost certainly won't happen in practice). A hybrid method like this is very commonly employed: Start with a few iterations of steepest descent, switch to Newton's method, and switch back if the going gets rough.

Finite difference approximations of the gradient and Hessian, constant or infrequently updated Hessians, damping, and other variants (see Section 1.5) are all used in conjunction with the idea of Newton's method. Because approximating the Hessian accurately is difficult when only F is known analytically, quasi-Newton methods are commonly employed. (In this context, they are frequently called variable metric methods; see Section 1.9.) The intention is to approximate $H^{-1}(x_k)$ with a sequence of matrices A_k that hopefully converge to $H^{-1}(x^*)$. Since A_k is typically not equal to $H^{-1}(x_k)$, it is common to incorporate various heuristics into any program implementing such a method. Such heuristics include periodically "restarting" the method by taking a step in a descent direction to ensure that progress toward a minimum is indeed being made, and by checking whether the Hessian or its approximation is staying positive definite.

In fact, Newton's method and its variants are usually implemented with a step-length parameter ϖ_k in the form

$$x_{k+1} = x_k - \varpi_k H^{-1}(x_k)\nabla F(x_k)$$

(and typically with some approximation A_k replacing $H^{-1}(x_k)$). The step length parameter will not necessarily represent damping (recall that $0 < \varpi_k \leq 1$ for the damped Newton's method). The parameter serves in part to ensure that we achieve sufficient decrease in the function value to keep the method progressing in regions where, for example, $\|\nabla F(x_k)\|$ is small but nonzero. A line search may be used to find ϖ_k.

PROBLEMS 7.3

1. a. Repeat Example 7.3.2 using the original initial guess $(x_0, y_0) = (-1, -1)$, but use the method of steepest descent instead of Newton's method.

 b. Repeat Example 7.3.2 using the original initial guess $(x_0, y_0) = (-1, -1)$, but perform several iterations of the method of steepest descent first to improve this guess before using Newton's method. Your final answer should be accurate to the last digit.

2. a. Use Newton's method to find a minimum of $F(x, y) = x^4 - 2xy + (x - 1)^2(y - 1)^2 e^{-xy}$.

 b. Use Newton's method to find a minimum of $F(x, y) = x^4 - 2xy + (x - 1)^2(y - 1)^2 e^{-xy}$, but update the Hessian matrix only every 3 iterations (that is, use $H(x_0)$ in finding x_1, x_2, and x_3, and then use $H(x_3)$ and to find x_4, x_5, and x_6, and so on).

3. Explain the divergence of Newton's method seen in Example 7.3.2 for the initial guess $(x_0, y_0) = (-1, -1)$ in terms of the shape of the objective function. (It may be helpful to plot its contours again; see MATLAB 7.2.)

4. Carefully state a convergence theorem for Newton's method for minimization in the special case of a function $f : \mathbb{R} \to \mathbb{R}$. (Use the results in Section 1.3 and Section 1.4.) Under what conditions is the convergence quadratic?

5. a. Prove that a symmetric 2×2 matrix $A = [a\ b; c\ d]$ is positive definite if and only if $a > 0$ and $ad - bc > 0$.

   b. Show by example that a symmetric 3×3 matrix A with $a_{11} > 0$ and $\det(A) > 0$ need not be positive definite.

MATLAB 7.3

In trying to visualize how Newton's method works, it is convenient to be able to plot functions of two variables. To see a demonstration of MATLAB's 3-D plotting capabilities (among other demos), type:

```
» demo
```

Select *Visualization*, then *3-D Plots*, then *Run*. (The specific menu path may differ slightly depending on your version of MATLAB.) The clc command is used in the demos to clear the command window and return the cursor to its "home" position.

The two main 3-D plotting commands in MATLAB are mesh and surf; mesh plots a simple mesh (wireframe) surface; surf plots a shaded surface graph. For example, enter:

```
» clc
» [x,y]=meshgrid(-2:.2:2,-2:.2:2);
» z=x.^2+y.^2;
» mesh(z)
» figure
» surf(z)
```

(The figure command makes a new figure window for the surf command; otherwise it would have replaced the mesh plot. Entering figure(i) makes Figure *i* the active window, if there is such a figure, or makes a new window otherwise. Try using the figure command to make different figures become the active window.) The surf command has shaded the surface between points, but otherwise the plot is similar to the mesh plot.

To make an even finer grid, edit the line that used meshgrid to define x and y and then recompute z and enter:

```
» close all
```

to close all the figures. Then repeat the mesh and surface plots in the form:

```
» mesh(x,y,z);figure;surf(x,y,z)
```

which gives the correct axis labeling. See the help for the commands xlabel, title, and text for more labeling options.

There are `fplot` and `ezplot` commands to go with `plot`; there is an `ezsurf` command to go with `surf` (and also an `ezmesh` to go with `mesh`). Enter:

```
» f=inline('x^2+y^2')
» ezsurf(f)
» ezsurfc(f)
» ezsurf('r*cos(t)','r*sin(t)','t')
```

and see the examples listed under `help ezsurf`. These commands give you considerable plotting power without demanding much expertise.

If you do develop the expertise, however, you will find that there are many MATLAB commands for manipulating the appearance of plots; MATLAB is frequently used to make plots for publication in professional journals. If you wish, use the `help` command to find out more about plotting and graphics. In particular, the `subplot` command may be used to put more than one plot into the same figure window; see also the `plot3` command.

ADDITIONAL PROBLEMS 7.3

6. a. Use Newton's method to find a local minimum of $f(x, y) = 4x^2 - 12xy + 9y^2 + x^3 - 6x^2y + 12xy^2 - 8y^3$.

  b. Find the extrema analytically by solving $\nabla f(x, y) = 0$. Classify the extrema.

7. Use Newton's method to find a local minimum of $f(x, y) = x^4 + 5x^2y^4 - 40x^2y^3 + 120x^2y^2 - 160x^2y + 80x^2 + \sin xy$.

8. What is the most general function $f(x_1, \ldots, x_n)$ that has a constant Hessian matrix?

9. Make a surface plot of the function $F(x, y) = xe^{(-x^2-y^2)}$ of Example 7.3.2 near its minimum that clearly shows that it is a local minimum.

10. Show that if $F : \mathbb{R}^2 \to \mathbb{R}$, then Eq. (7.6) corresponds to the usual tangent surface (tangent plane) approximation of $F(x, y)$ at (x_0, y_0) if we neglect the term involving the Hessian, and is a quadratic (in x and y) approximation of $F(x, y)$ at (x_0, y_0) if we include the term involving the Hessian.

11. Make a surface plot of the function $f(x, y) = 4\sin(xy) + 1 + x^2 + 3y^2$ for (x, y) in the first quadrant. Use it to find an initial guess for Newton's method to find a local minimum of $f(x, y)$. The minimum should also lie in the first quadrant. Find the minimum.

12. a. Find an initial guess such that Newton's method for the objective function of Example 7.3.2 diverges.

  b. The damped Newton's method is $x_{k+1} = x_k - \mu_k H^{-1}(x_k)\nabla F(x_k)$ for some damping sequence $\{\mu_k\}_{k=0}^{k=\infty}$, $0 < \mu_k \le 1$, and $\mu_k \to 1$ as $k \to \infty$. (Refer to Section 1.5.) Find a damping sequence that gives convergence for your initial guess from part (a).

13. a. Show that if $H^{-1}(x_k)$ is positive definite, then $s_k = H^{-1}(x_k)\nabla F(x_k)$ is a descent direction (unless $\nabla F(x_k) = 0$).

  b. Show that Newton's method is not always a general descent method.

  c. A **modified Newton's method** substitutes a descent direction s_k for $H^{-1}(x_k)\nabla F(x_k)$ when the latter does not appear to be a descent direction (e.g., when $H^{-1}(x_k)$ is not positive definite). One possible way to enforce descent is to use $x_{k+1} = x_k - \varpi_k M_k \nabla F(x_k)$ for some matrix M_k. Show that Newton's method and the method of steepest descent are both of this form for some sequence ϖ_k and some M_k.

  d. Write a detailed algorithm (pseudocode) for a modified Newton's method that switches to the method of steepest descent when $H^{-1}(x_k)$ is not positive definite. Assume that a test for positive definiteness is available.

14. Prove that a symmetric matrix A is positive definite if and only if A^{-1} is positive definite.

15. a. If A is symmetric, then the function $F(x) = x^T A x$ is called a **quadratic form** in x; its gradient is $2Ax$ and its Hessian is $2A$. If A is positive definite, what happens when Newton's method is applied to $F(x)$?

  b. Show by example that the method of steepest descent can be slow for a quadratic form with A positive definite. Must it converge nonetheless?

7.4 Multiple Random Start Methods

So far in this chapter, we have been focusing on finding local minima in the unconstrained case, that is, on the problem of finding any local minimum of $F : \mathbb{R}^n \to \mathbb{R}$, anywhere in $\mathbb{R}^n$.

Constrained
Problems

Among the problems that we do not explore is the constrained nonlinear optimization problem, where we add the condition that the minimum must lie in some proper subset D of $\mathbb{R}^n$. In many such cases, the region D (called the **constraint region** or **feasible region**) is defined in such a way that it can be difficult even to find an initial guess $x_0 \in D$ (called a **feasible point**) to start off an iterative method. Nonetheless there are algorithms for this type of problem (which is certainly an important type of problem in practice).

Least Squares
Problems

There are also certain situations that arise commonly and for which specialized methods have been developed. One of the most important such cases occurs when the objective function $F(x)$ is known to be a sum of squares of other functions

$$F(x) = \sum_{k=1}^{n} F_k^2(x)$$

(for example, if we are fitting a curve by nonlinear least squares). When F is known to have this form, we should consider employing a method developed for handling this type of problem. One such method is the **Levenberg-Marquardt method,** which attempts to switch intelligently between the method of steepest descent (far from the minimum) and the finite difference Newton's method (near the minimum). This method is discussed in Section 8.1. It is important that you be aware that such specialized algorithms exist.

Global
Minimization

In this section we consider the **global minimization** problem, that is, the problem of finding the global minimum x^* of F. This is the (not necessarily unique) point x^* such that $F(x) \geq F(x^*)$ for all $x \in \mathbb{R}^n$. As usual, our development assumes well-behaved parabolic global minima.

It may happen that there is only one local minimum of the function, but this need not be the global minimum. If $F(x) \to -\infty$ as $\|x\| \to \infty$, for example, then the global minimum may be undefined (see Fig. 7.10). If the function is **unimodal** (strictly increasing to either side of the minimum, like $y = x^2$, or in the case of a maximum strictly

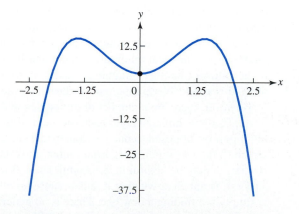

Figure 7.10 Local but not Global Minimum.

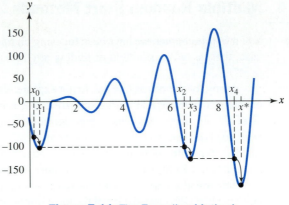

Figure 7.11 The Tunneling Method.

decreasing to either side of the maximum, like $y = -x^2$), then the local minimum must be the global minimum. The development of many minimization algorithms assumes that the function is unimodal in the region of interest (e.g., Davidon's method in Section 7.3). Clearly, no special global minimization method is needed for a unimodal function.

Tunneling Method

Any minimization algorithm might find the global minimum by chance; we want a method that does so by design. This is difficult. One approach is the **tunneling method:** Pick any initial guess x_0 and perform a local minimization starting from that point (using any local minimization method; for simplicity, let's say it's the method of steepest descent). Call the location of this point x_1, and let m_1 be the value $F(x_1)$ of F at this local minimum. We would like to find another, lower local minimum. Solve

$$F(x) = m_1 \tag{7.8}$$

(i.e., find a root of $F(x) - m_1 = 0$) for a point x_2 that is different from x_1, and perform a new local minimization starting from x_2 (see Fig. 7.11). This gives a new point x_3 with function value $m_3 = F(x_3)$. We solve

$$F(x) = m_3$$

for a point x_4 that is different from x_3, and start again with a new local minimization. Continue until $F(x) = m_k$ does not have a solution other than x_k.

If the global minimum is unique, this method should find it (in principle). The method tunnels from one local minimum, under other local minima, to a point that we hope lies in the valley of another minimum. The figure shows a function of one variable, but the method is applicable to functions of several variables.

However, there are a number of difficulties with this method. Even if the local minimization algorithm converges each time and furthermore converges each time to a new minimum (as opposed to one previously located, which is possible if it is not a descent method), the root-finding algorithm often finds the current minimum, not a new point. (Deflation may be helpful here.) Additionally, if the root-finding algorithm fails to find a root, it is not clear whether it fails because no other root exists or because the method is simply not finding a new one. There is no general fix for this problem.

MRS Method   Let's look at a different approach. Pick an initial guess x_0 and perform a local minimization starting from that point. (Once again, for simplicity, let's say that the method of steepest descent is used.) Call the location of this point x_{min}, and let $m = F(x_{min})$ be the value of F at this local minimum. Pick another x_0 at random and perform a local minimization starting from that point. If the value of F at this minimizer is lower than the current lowest known value m of F, make this minimizer the new x_{min}, and let m be the value $F(x_{min})$ of F at this new, lower local minimum. Repeat with a new x_0 chosen again at random; stop when some maximum allowable number of function values (or initial guesses) is exceeded.

If the starting points x_0 are in fact chosen at random (uniformly over the region of interest), then this method is known as the **multiple random start (MRS)** method, also called the **multistart** or **pure random search** method. Any local minimizer may be employed in this method.

Example 7.4.1   Let's use the MRS method on the function $F(x) = \sin^2(100\|x\|^2) + \|x\|^2$ (which clearly has a unique global minimum at the origin) for $x \in \mathbb{R}^2$. We'll confine our search to the region $-10 \le x, y \le 10$; we may view this as a constrained minimization problem where x and y must both be between -10 and 10 for the solution to make sense, or we may view the restriction $-10 \le x, y \le 10$ as a practical concession which must be made. The MATLAB function rand returns a value between 0 and 1, so:

```
» x0=20*(rand-.5),y0=20*(rand-.5)
```

gives an x_0 and a y_0 in the desired range (reason it out). Suppose the values returned are $x_0 = 9.0026$, $y_0 = -5.3772$. MATLAB's local optimization routine fminsearch may be employed:

```
» F=inline('sin(norm(x)^2)^2+norm(x)^2');
» x1=fminsearch(F,[x0 y0])
```

The result is a local minimum at $(-0.1594, 0.3628)$, where $F(x_1) \doteq 0.1571$ (use feval(F,x1)). Choose a new x_0 and y_0 by entering:

```
» x=20*(rand(1 2])-.5)
```

which generates a random 1×2 matrix (that is, a row vector with 2 randomly selected entries) and rescales them to the desired range. Let's say the values are $x_0 = 2.1369$, $y_0 = -0.2804$. Then:

```
» x2=fminsearch(F,x)
```

searches for a minimum near the vector x. The result is a local minimum at $(2.0301, -0.2974)$, where $F(x_2) \doteq 4.2097$ (from feval(F,x2)). Our best current estimate of the location of the global minimum is $x_1 = (-0.1594, 0.3628)$. Let's try once more:

```
» x=20*(rand(1 2])-.5)
» x3=fminsearch(F,x)
» feval(F,x3)
```

giving, say, $x_0 = 7.8260$, $y_0 = 5.2419$, and a local minimum at $(0.3061, -0.0228)$, where $F(x_3) \doteq 0.0942$. This is smaller than our previous best estimate 0.1571, so $(0.3061, -0.0228)$ is our new best estimate of the location of the global minimizer. ∎

In Example 7.4.1, (x, y) pairs closer to the global minimizer have function values closer to that of the global minimum, but in general this need not be true. In Example 7.4.1, we never find the same local minimum twice, but in general we would not be at all surprised if that were to happen.

Monte Carlo Methods   The n components of $x = (x_1, \ldots, x_n)$ are chosen uniformly over some domain that is typically of the form $l_i \leq x_i \leq u_i$ $(i = 1, \ldots, n)$, possibly a constraint region, by using the **pseudo-random number generator (PRNG)** provided by the computing environment. The numbers are called pseudo-random because they are generated by a deterministic algorithm that is designed to make the resulting sequences appear random though they are not truly random. Difficulties can arise because of this, but for now we do not consider them. Methods such as this, which use (pseudo-) random numbers, are called **Monte Carlo methods** (or **simulation methods**), and arise in several areas of numerical analysis.

What are the advantages of using a Monte Carlo approach? By choosing the initial guesses x_0 at random, we can give probabilistic estimates of the likelihood of finding the global minimum under various assumptions. Each new run of the program gives a new selection of initial guesses, so that if the method fails to find the minimum one time, it has a chance the next time. By not covering the region evenly, the method has a chance of finding small regions that would slip between the spacing of the grid, or of clustering several initial guesses in one region where there may be several closely spaced minima. If we have some specialized knowledge about our function—say, that there are only N local minima in the region of interest and each has a large parabolic valley—then we might use a different approach. But if we know (or assume) nothing about F, then we might look at a method based on pseudo-random numbers.

Quasi-Random Methods   In practice Monte Carlo methods are often an excellent choice for the global minimization of functions $F : \mathbb{R}^n \to \mathbb{R}$ with many local minima, especially if n is moderate and the global minimum has a reasonably sized parabolic valley; some initial guess is likely to land in it sooner or later. (As is the case with root-finding, missing a small blip—a very narrow valley—is always possible.) We might also consider a **quasi-Monte Carlo method** based on a **quasi-random number generator** that generates numbers that are quasi-random, meaning "just random enough for our purposes." Quasi-random number generators generate deterministic sequences that cover a region with a non-uniform grid. For each initial condition they generate different sequences, but these sequences do not pass nearly as many tests of randomness as a PRNG would; typically the quasi-random number generators ensure that every sub-region is sampled (that is, an x_0 lands in it) a certain number of times. For a PRNG this is highly likely but not guaranteed. Methods based on a PRNG are more common, partly because the PRNG is generally provided as a built-in function of the language; the error estimates are typically considerably better for quasi-Monte Carlo methods, called **quasi-random searches** in this context. The tools at our disposal (hardware and software) always affect which algorithms we choose (and what values of n we consider to be "moderate").

MMRS Method   The **modified multiple random start (MMRS)** method is similar to the MRS method with one modification: Every time a new x_0 is generated, we check to see whether $F(x_0)$ is less than the current lowest known value m; if it is, we proceed as before, and if it is not, we reject it and choose another x_0 until we find one such that $F(x_0) < m$. In practice the methods give similar results.

Example 7.4.2   Consider again the objective function $F(x) = \sin^2(100\|x\|^2) + \|x\|^2$ of Example 7.4.1, but now let us use the MMRS method instead. For the first iteration we find $x_0 = 9.0026$, $y_0 = -5.3772$, giving a local minimum at $(-0.1594, 0.3628)$ with function value $F(x_1) \doteq 0.1571$. For the second iteration we find $x_0 = 2.1369$, $y_0 = -0.2804$; for the MMRS method we do not immediately perform a minimization but instead compute $F(2.1369, -0.2804) \doteq 4.8414$. This is greater than 0.1571, so we reject this choice. For the third iteration we find $x_0 = 7.8260$, $y_0 = 5.2419$; $F(7.8260, 5.2419) \doteq 88.9773$ and once again we reject this choice.

If this seems inefficient, note that rejecting these two initial guesses costs us only two function evaluations, plus the cost of using `rand` to generate them; the use of `fminsearch` with the initial condition $x_0 = 7.8260$, $y_0 = 5.2419$ requires 121 function evaluations. If function evaluations are by far the most expensive part of our computations—and typically they are—then using MMRS represents a considerable savings of function evaluations that may be spent elsewhere. ∎

There are entire books of test problems for local and global minimization problems. These test problems are used to benchmark new software and algorithms. Some examples are the **three-hump camelback function**

$$f(x, y) = 12x^2 - 6.3x^4 + x^6 - 6xy + 6y^2, \tag{7.9}$$

which has three local minima including the global minimum at the origin (some authors use $f(x, y)/6$ for this function), and the **six-hump camelback function**

$$f(x, y) = 4x^2 - 2.1x^4 + \frac{1}{3}x^6 + xy - 4y^2 + 4y^4, \tag{7.10}$$

which has six local minima including two global minima at $(\pm 0.08984, \mp 0.71266)$. The **Levy No. 5** test problem is

$$f(x, y) = \sum_{i=1}^{5} i \cos((i-1)x + i) \sum_{j=1}^{5} j \cos((j+1)y + j) \tag{7.11}$$

$$+ (x + 1.42513)^2 + (y + 0.80032)^2, \tag{7.12}$$

and it has 760 local minima in $-10 \leq x, y \leq 10$, only one of which is the global minimum. Dropping off the last two terms gives the **Levy No. 3** test problem

$$f(x, y) = \sum_{i=1}^{5} i \cos((i-1)x + i) \sum_{j=1}^{5} j \cos((j+1)y + j), \tag{7.13}$$

which has 760 local minima in $-10 \leq x, y \leq 10$, but has 18 locations that are global minimizers.

There are many other global minimization algorithms besides the three we have discussed here. For a general function $F : \mathbb{R}^n \to \mathbb{R}$, finding a global minimizer can be a difficult problem, and so many approaches are available.

PROBLEMS 7.4

1. a. Use ten additional initial guesses and the MRS method to attempt to find the global minimum of the objective function in Example 7.4.1. You may use any local optimization algorithm you wish.

b. Which of the ten additional initial guesses you found in part (a) would be used as the starting point for a local optimization if you were using the MMRS method instead? Compare the MMRS estimate of the location of the global minimum to that of the MRS method.

2. a. Write a MATLAB program that performs the MRS method on a given inline function. You may use `fminsearch` or any other local optimizer. The user should supply a maximum number of allowable initial guesses.

b. Test your program on the objective function of Example 7.4.1. How often does it find the global minimum if it is allowed $N = 20$ initial guesses? (Run your program several times and compute an average; see `help mean`.) How often does it find the global minimum if it is allowed $N = 100$ initial guesses?

3. a. Write a MATLAB program that performs the MMRS method on a given inline function. You may use `fminsearch` or any other local optimizer. The user should supply a maximum number of allowable initial guesses. In addition to returning the minimizer, the program should display the number of local searches actually performed. (One way to do this is to initialize a variable `count=0` at the beginning of the program and then increment it with

`count=count+1` each time you accept an initial guess; use the command `disp(['Searches performed= ',num2str(count)])` to display the number.)

b. How many initial guesses does your program need to reliably find the global minimizer of the objective function in Example 7.4.1? How many local searches does it actually perform?

4. a. Under what circumstances would you expect MMRS to outperform MRS? Under what circumstances would you expect MRS to outperform MMRS?

b. How many initial guesses, on average, do you think would need to be generated in [0, 10] for each method to find the global minimum of the function in Figure 7.11?

c. If each local optimization of the function in Figure 7.11 uses 12 function evaluations (on average), which method is more efficient for it: MRS or MMRS?

5. a. If $D \subseteq \mathbb{R}^n$, a continuous function $F : D \to \mathbb{R}$ is said to be **convex** if for every $x, y \in D$ and every $\lambda \in [0, 1]$, $F(\lambda x + (1 - \lambda)y) \le \lambda F(x) + (1 - \lambda)F(y)$ (and strictly convex if the inequality is strict). The study of nonlinear optimization is often split into algorithms for optimizing convex functions (the **convex programming problem**) and nonconvex functions (the **nonconvex programming problem**). Show that if a function F is strictly convex, then it is unimodal.

b. Give an example of a convex function that is not unimodal. Could a convex function have two or more isolated local minima?

MATLAB 7.4

Let's explore a few of the MATLAB commands that are used in the reading and Problems. The command `fminsearch` uses the Nelder-Mead method, to be discussed in Section 7.6, to perform a local optimization for a scalar-valued function of a vector. To display the number of function evaluations used, enter:

```
» options=optimset('display','iter');
» fminsearch(F,x,options)
```

for an appropriate `F` (which may also be an M-file) and `x`. See `help optimset` and `help optimget` for more details. The `options` variable is a structure (see `help struct`), not a vector.

Recall that the `rand` function returns a pseudo-random matrix of the requested size; for example, `rand([M N])` is a pseudo-random $M \times N$ matrix. The PRNG depends on a seed—an initial condition—that is always set to the same value when MATLAB is started. (If you worked through Example 7.4.1 and found the same "random" numbers in the text, this is why.) To reset the PRNG to its initial state, enter `rand('state',0)`. This can be useful when debugging a program. See `help rand` for more information, and `help randn` for normally distributed pseudo-random numbers.

The `mean` command finds the average of a vector. For matrices, it averages down each column. For example:

```
» x=rand([1 1000]);
» mean(x)
```

should be very close to 1/2. Enter `type mean` to see that `mean` is just a simple M-file that uses the `size` and `sum` commands; `sum(x)` implements $\sum_{k=1}^{k=n} x_k$ for a vector of length n. The sequence of commands:

```
» x=[80 95 70 91 83 77 89 91];
» mean(x),median(x)
» sort(x)
```

averages and computes the mean and median of this data, then sorts the data into ascending order. There is a Statistics Toolbox for more sophisticated statistical functions.

The line `disp(['Searches performed= ',num2str(count)])` uses the `disp` command to display the character (as opposed to numeric) vector found by combining (concatenating) the two character vectors `'Searches performed= '` and `num2str(count)`. The `num2str` command converts a number such as 6 to a character `'6'`. To get a feel for this, try:

```
» disp(['Searches performed= ',num2str(6)])
» disp(['Searches performed=',num2str(6)])
» disp('Searches performed= ',num2str(6))
» disp(['Searches performed= ',6])
» disp('Searches performed= ',6)
» disp('Searches performed= ','6')
» disp('Searches performed= '),disp('6')
» disp('Searches performed= '),disp(6)
```

(some of which will give errors). The last version above is acceptable, but the formatting of the first version is preferable. See `help str2num` and `help str2double` for converting strings to numeric values.

Now let's discuss another MATLAB feature that may be of value in doing the problems. In addition to MATLAB programs, an M-file may be a *script*, that is, a list of MATLAB commands. Use the `edit` command to create a file named `lsearch.m` and enter the following lines (only):

```
x0=rand([1 N]);
x1=fminsearch(F,x0);
f1=feval(F,x1);
disp('lsearch ended successfully')
```

Save these four lines in `lsearch.m`. Enter:

```
» lsearch
```

Note that MATLAB uses the value of `N` and `F` defined in the workspace and performs these steps. For example, try:

```
» N=2;
» rand('state',0);
» F=inline('sin(norm(x)^2)^2+norm(x)^2');
» lsearch
```

This should duplicate the first search performed in Example 7.4.1. Check that `x0`, `x1`, and `f1` are returned to the workspace (that is, the variables are not local to the script as they would be in a function). Enter:

```
» lsearch
```

and ask again for the values of `x0`, `x1`, and `f1`; they have been updated. With such a script we can define an objective function `F` in the workspace and manage the overall logic of the MRS or MMRS method there, while calling a script to perform certain repetitive sequences of commands. As a rule, functions are preferred because they return values that may be used by other functions, as in the following; enter:

```
» cos(fminsearch(F,x0));
```

but there are situations in which scripts are convenient. The commands `pause` (pause execution of the script or function and wait until a key is pressed) and `echo` (turn the display of script commands on and off) can be useful when you are writing scripts.

ADDITIONAL PROBLEMS 7.4

6. a. Use MATLAB to make a contour plot and a surface plot of the three-hump camelback function (Eq. (7.9)).

 b. Use the MRS method to find the global minimum of the three-hump camelback function. Use your plots in part (a) to determine an appropriate range in which to generate the random points ($\alpha \leq x \leq \beta$, $\gamma \leq y \leq \delta$) and a reasonable number of initial guesses to use.

7. a. Use MATLAB to make a contour plot and a surface plot of the six-hump camelback function (Eq. (7.10)).

 b. Use the MMRS method to find a global minimum of the six-hump camelback function. Use your plots in part (a) to determine an appropriate range in which to generate the random points ($\alpha \leq x \leq \beta$, $\gamma \leq y \leq \delta$) and a reasonable number of initial guesses to use.

8. a. Use the MRS method to find the global minimum of the Levy No. 5 test problem (Eq. (7.11)). Repeat

with the MMRS method. Comment on the efficiencies of the two methods.

 b. Use the MRS method to find the global minimum of the Levy No. 5 test problem, limiting the method to 100 initial guesses. Do this a total of 20 times. What is the probability of finding the global minimum for this number of initial guesses?

 c. Repeat part (a) using the Levy No. 3 test problem (Eq. (7.13)).

 d. Repeat part (b) using the Levy No. 3 test problem.

9. a. Use the MRS method to find a global minimum of the **Powell function** $F(x) = (x_1 + 10x_2)^2 + 5(x_3 - x_4)^2 + (x_2 - 2x_3)^2 + 10(x_1 - x_4)^2$.

 b. Find all global minima of the Powell function analytically.

 c. Show that the Hessian of $F(x)$ is positive semi-definite but not positive definite at the origin.

10. Write a detailed algorithm (pseudocode) for performing the tunneling method. Assume that an appropriate local minimization routine is available. You will need to specify a criterion for termination based on the nonexistence of a root of Eq. (7.8).

11. a. Apply the tunneling method to the objective function of Example 7.4.1.

  b. Apply the tunneling method to the six-hump camelback function (Eq. (7.10)).

  c. Under what circumstances would you expect the tunneling method to outperform MRS and MMRS?

12. a. Apply the tunneling method to the Levy No. 3 problem (Eq. (7.13)).

  b. Apply the tunneling method to the Levy No. 5 problem (Eq. (7.11)).

13. a. Let $F : \mathbb{R}^n \rightarrow \mathbb{R}$ be a continuous function with finitely many local minima in a box $l_i \leq x_i \leq u_i$ $(i = 1, \ldots, n)$. Suppose that the local minimization routine always converges to the nearest local minimum within the box. Prove that the MRS and MMRS methods yield a sequence of function values that converge with probability 1 to the value of the function at its global minimum if the initial guesses are chosen uniformly at random over the box. (*Note:* We have assumed more than is actually needed to establish this result.)

  b. Must this result hold if pseudo-random numbers are used? Why or why not?

14. a. Show that if $f : \mathbb{R} \rightarrow \mathbb{R}$, then f is strictly convex exactly when the graph of f between any two points on f lies strictly below the line connecting those two points (see Problem 5).

  b. Show that if $f : \mathbb{R} \rightarrow \mathbb{R}$ is twice continuously differentiable, then f is strictly convex exactly when $f''(x) > 0$. What happens if there are points such that $f''(x) = 0$?

15. Show that if $F : \mathbb{R}^n \rightarrow \mathbb{R}$ is twice continuously differentiable, then f is strictly convex exactly when the Hessian of F is positive definite (see Problem 5). What happens if the Hessian is positive semi-definite?

7.5 Direct Search Methods

Let's leave global optimization and return to local optimization. For functions of one variable, we started off with bracketing methods that did not require derivatives (we say that they are *derivative-free methods*), namely golden section search and quadratic interpolation. Dropping the requirement of a bracket and fitting a quadratic to any three points gave us another derivative-free method.

Assuming the availability of the first derivative of f gave Davidon's cubic interpolation method for functions of one variable and the method of steepest descent for functions of several variables. Assuming a second derivative gave Newton's method for minimization. Minimization methods based on Newton's method are far and away the ones most common in practice: They are fast and reliable (for a sufficiently close initial guess), and if managed properly—restarted periodically, preceded by several steepest descent iterations, monitored for positive definiteness of the Hessian and progress towards the minimum, and various other computational heuristics—they work quite well.

But we cannot always assume that the function is differentiable or, even if it is, that we will be able to approximate the derivative(s) adequately. If $F : \mathbb{R}^n \rightarrow \mathbb{R}$ is continuous but not necessarily differentiable, we say that we have a **nonsmooth minimization problem** (or **nonsmooth programming problem**). For such a problem we need a minimization algorithm that uses only function values, similar to golden section search. If the function may not be differentiable, fitting a quadratic to it (Powell's method) is a questionable strategy. If the function is twice continuously differentiable but the derivatives are not available, then this method may be a reasonable approach because it uses only function values. The methods that we derive in this section are applicable to smooth functions as well as well as to nonsmooth functions, but when derivative information is available, it should almost always be used. That's worth repeating: If the derivatives are known or can be approximated accurately, it generally is worthwhile to make use of them.

Direct Search
Methods

If $F : \mathbb{R}^n \to \mathbb{R}$, then methods that assume only continuity and use only values of the objective function F are called **direct search methods** (or **function comparison methods**). One might argue that approximating derivatives with finite differences or by other approaches uses function values only, but these methods depend on an assumption of smoothness to be effective.

There is more than one way to proceed with a direct search method. Some methods sample the function at a number of points and use the values of F at these points to construct a simpler (and smoother) model of the function; often the algorithm uses a convex model function. We will not investigate this approach.

Unless significant additional assumptions are made concerning the objective function, bracketing is not feasible. The most common direct search methods either use some strategy for selecting new search directions and then explore in those directions, or else maintain a list of points defining a region that (it is hoped) contains the minimum. We give examples of the former type of algorithm in this section and the latter type in the next section. The developments generally assume that the function is unimodal in the region of interest, but this is not a requirement for their application.

Alternating
Variable Search

The simplest direct search method is **alternating variable search.** Let $F : \mathbb{R}^n \to \mathbb{R}$ be continuous, and write $x = (x_1, \ldots, x_n)$. Choose a point $P \in \mathbb{R}^n$ and fix $(x_2, \ldots, x_n) = (p_2, \ldots, p_n)$; this gives a function

$$g_1(x_1) = F(x_1, p_2, \ldots, p_n) \tag{7.14}$$

of a single variable x_1, and we may perform a univariate (that is, one-dimensional) search on $g_1(x_1)$, starting from p_1 and using any convenient line search algorithm. In effect, we are performing a one-dimensional search on $F(x_1, \ldots, x_n)$ parallel to the x_1-axis. If the result of the one-dimensional search is $q_1 = \min\{g_1(x_1)\}$, then we fix $(x_1, x_3, \ldots, x_n) = (q_1, p_3, \ldots, p_n)$ to get the function

$$g_2(x_2) = F(q_1, x_2, p_3, \ldots, p_n) \tag{7.15}$$

and perform a line search on it to find $q_2 = \min\{g_2(x_2)\}$. We repeat this process searching only on $x_3, x_4, \ldots, x_n$ until we arrive at the point $Q = (q_1, q_2, \ldots, q_n)$. This completes one iteration of the alternating variable search method; we now start over again, searching in x_1 starting from q_1 with $(x_2, \ldots, x_n) = (q_2, \ldots, q_n)$ held constant.

Example 7.5.1
Consider the function $f(x, y) = x^2 + 4xy + 4y^2$. Let's choose $P = (x_0, y_0) = (2, 2)$. From Eq. (7.14), $g_1(x) = f(x, 2) = x^2 + 8x + 16$. We wish to find the minimum of this function nearest $x_0 = 2$. Because g_1 is quadratic in x, the unique minimum is at $x^* = -8/2 = -4$. Call this q_1. This completes the search along x. From Eq. (7.15), $g_2(y) = f(-4, y) = 4y^2 - 16y + 16$. The minimum is at $y^* = -(-16)/8 = 2$. Call this q_2. This completes the search along y. Our new point is $Q = (-4, 2)$. Let's try another iteration. From Eq. (7.14), $g_1(x) = f(x, 2) = x^2 + 8x + 16$, so again $x^* = -8/2 = -4$. From Eq. (7.15), $g_2(y) = f(-4, y) = 4y^2 - 16y + 16$. The unique minimum is at $x^* = -(-16)/8 = 2$. The point $(-4, 2)$ is a fixed point of this method. Is it a solution? Let's check. We have $\nabla f(x, y) = (2x + 4y, 4x + 8y)^T$, so $\nabla f(-4, 2) = (0, 0)^T$; $(-4, 2)$ is a stationary point. The Hessian is $H = [2 \ 4; 4 \ 8]$, which is constant. Its

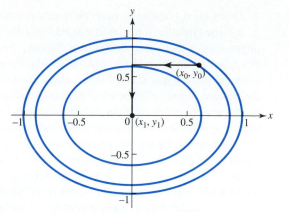

Figure 7.12 Alternating Variable Search (Fast Case).

eigenvalues can be found by the command:

```
» eig([2 4;4 8])
ans =
     0
    10
```

So, H is positive semi-definite. (Of course, we should be somewhat suspicious of any computed quantity that is *exactly* zero.) We have found a nonparabolic minimum. In fact, $f(x, y) = (x + 2y)^2$, so every point on the line $y = -\frac{1}{2}x$ is a global minimizer. ■

The alternating variable search method is very inefficient unless the objective function exhibits a great deal of symmetry with respect to the variables $(x_1, \ldots, x_n)$ (see Fig. 7.12 and Fig. 7.13). There is no guarantee that the univariate minimization steps will locate a local minimum: The current point may already be at the lowest point along that direction (even if F decreases in other directions), or the function may slope off to $-\infty$. These cases must be considered in a program realizing alternating variable search.

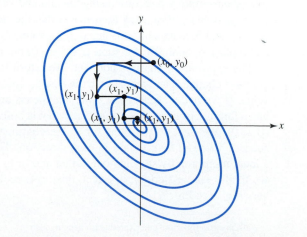

Figure 7.13 Alternating Variable Search (Slow Case).

Hill-Climbing

There are a number of possible improvements to this method, even if we continue to assume that the function is not necessarily differentiable. The motivation for the improvement that we consider is as follows: Experience shows that with methods of this type, if the method succeeds it is often because the method finds the bottom of a valley relatively quickly and then spends most of its time traveling along the crease at the bottom of the valley toward the solution. Furthermore, points on the crease tend to fall on a more or less straight path. (In fact this line of reasoning was originally applied to maximization problems, which are often viewed as "hill-climbing" problems: The method tends to locate a ridge, climb up to some point on it, and then spend most of its time following that ridge, and the ridge tends to be more-or-less in a straight line. Such physical and intuitive reasoning appears frequently as the motivation for a nonlinear optimization algorithm. In other cases, as in Newton's method or the method of steepest descent, calculus-based theory guides us.) If we can locate this crease (ridge) and follow it, then we should get faster convergence. See Problem 1 for an example of a function with this sort of valley.

Rosenbrock Search

Now, alternating variable search starts from a point P and produces a new point Q after we have searched along each of the n coordinate directions. But if we are on the crease (ridge)—where, we expect, the method stays for most of its iterations—then the vector $Q - P$ from P to Q should point along the crease (roughly). Why not try to follow it? This is the basic idea behind **Rosenbrock's method** (or **Rosenbrock search**), which also handles the line searches in a modified manner. For simplicity, we describe the method only in the case of a function $F : \mathbb{R}^2 \to \mathbb{R}$.

Let $F : \mathbb{R}^2 \to \mathbb{R}$ be continuous. Rosenbrock's method for finding a local minimum of $F(x, y)$, given an initial guess (x_0, y_0), begins with an *exploration phase;* we start by searching along a direction parallel to the x-axis, that is, by doing a one-dimensional search on $F(x, y_0)$. We take a step of size $\delta_x > 0$ from x_0 in the positive x direction. If $F(x_0 + \delta_x, y_0) \leq F(x_0, y_0)$, then we say that the step was a *success* and replace x_0 with $x_0 + \delta_x$ and δ_x with $\alpha\delta_x$ for some $\alpha > 1$ (increase the step size); if not, then we say that the step was a *failure* and replace δ_x with $\beta\delta_x$ for some $\beta \in (-1, 0)$ (reverse the direction and decrease the step size). In the case of a failure, we do not change x_0. In either case, we now turn to y and do the same: We take a step of size $\delta_y > 0$ from y_0 in the positive y direction (using the updated value of x_0 if its step was a success). If $F(x_0, y_0 + \delta_y) \leq F(x_0, y_0)$, then we say that the step was a success and replace y_0 with $y_0 + \delta_y$ and δ_y with $\alpha\delta_y$ for some $\alpha > 1$; if not, then we say that the step was a failure and replace δ_y with $\beta\delta_y$ for some $\beta \in (-1, 0)$ but do not change y_0.

The exploration phase is not over. We return to the x variable (which may or may not have changed) and repeat with the new δ_x, looking for a decrease from the previous value. If we had a success last time, this means an even larger step out ($\alpha > 1$); if we had a failure last time, this means a step that is both shorter and in the opposite direction ($\beta < 0$). We then do the same for y. We continue this process until we have found a success *followed by a failure* in each direction. The effect of this procedure is to find a local minimum by stepping out farther and farther along a direction of decrease until we finally take a step up; in effect, this brackets a minimum with respect to that one variable[1] (see Fig. 7.14).

---

[1] Well, not *exactly*, if the other variable is changing also.

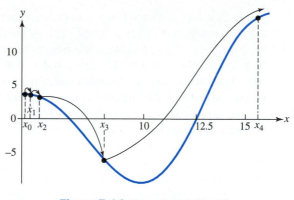

Figure 7.14 Rosenbrock Search.

In Figure 7.14, the method has taken three successful steps, each one larger than the previous one, and then has experienced a failure (x_4); a minimum (in that variable) has now been found, and the next step will be of length $\beta\delta$. Since $\beta \in (-1, 0)$, this next step will be both shorter and in the opposite direction, heading back toward the minimum if the last success has crossed it; if the last success was on the same side of the minimum as the others (as in Fig. 7.14), then we except a failure next time, after which we will turn around and head back towards the minimum. (Note also that this suggests a method for finding an initial bracket for golden section search or other bracketing methods in the one-dimensional search case, which is one of the reasons we present Rosenbrock's method.) Standard values are $\alpha = 3$, $\beta = -1/2$.

After the exploration phase is completed—we have a success followed by a failure in each direction—we perform the *search phase*. We set x_1 and y_1 to be the points at which a failure was obtained in the exploration phase. We then define the new search direction vectors p_1 and p_2 as follows: The vector p_1 is a unit vector in the direction of $(x_1, y_1)^T - (x_0, y_0)^T$ (the direction along the presumed crease, and we hope an approximate steepest descent direction), and the vector p_2 is a unit vector orthogonal to p_1. This completes the first iteration (or **stage**) of the method.

For the next iteration we proceed in exactly the same way, except that instead of searching in the directions of the axes, we perform our first search in the direction p_1 (starting from (x_1, y_1)), and then in the direction p_2, and repeat until we have a success followed by a failure in each of these directions. If the method is working as intended, then we should make good progress along p_1, which will bring the search along p_2 into a better region, and we will avoid some of the see-sawing of alternating variable search (as in Fig. 7.13). At each succeeding stage (iteration) we define a new p_1 as the vector from the old point to the new point (normalized), and a new unit vector p_2 perpendicular to it, and then explore along these directions.

Example 7.5.2 Let's apply the method of Rosenbrock search to the standard test function $f(x, y) = 100(y - x^2)^2 + (1 - x)^2$, which is known as **Rosenbrock's function.** (There is a unique local minimum at $(1, 1)$, which is therefore the global minimum.) We'll start from the initial guess $(2, -1)$ and take $\alpha = 3$, $\beta = -1/2$, and $\delta_x = \delta_y = 1$. First, we compute $f(2, -1) = 100(-1 - 2^2)^2 + (1 - 2)^2 = 2501$. Let's start the exploration phase: $f(x, -1) = 100(-1 - x^2)^2 + (1 - x)^2$ and at $x = 2 + \delta_x = 3$, this is $f(3, -1) = 100(-1 - 3^2)^2 + (1 - 3)^2 = 10004$. This is greater than 2501, so it is a failure, and we set $\delta_x = (-0.5)(1) = -0.5$. We turn to the y-direction and consider the function $f(2, y) = 100(y - 2^2)^2 + (1 - 2)^2 = 100(y - 4)^2 + 1$ at $y = -1 + \delta_y = 0$. This gives $f(2, 0) = 100(0 - 4)^2 + 1 = 1601$, which is a success (it is less than 2501). From here on we use $y = 0$ as the current value of y and set $\delta_y = (3)(1) = 3$.

The next round of exploration gives $f(2 + -0.5, 0) = f(1.5, 0) = 506.5$ (a success since it is less than 1601; from here on we use $x = 1.5$ and set $\delta_x = (3)(-0.5) = -1.5$), and then $f(1.5, 0 + 3) = f(1.5, 3) = 56.5$ (a success since it is less than 506.5; from here on we use $y = 3$ and set $\delta_y = (3)(3) = 9$). We have a success in each direction and are now looking for a failure in each direction.

The next round gives $f(1.5 + -1.5, 3) = f(0, 3) = 901$ (a failure since it is greater than 56.5; we set $\delta_x = (-0.5)(-1.5) = 0.75$) and $f(1.5, 3 + 9) = f(1.5, 12) = 9506.5$ (a failure since it is greater than 56.5; we set $\delta_y = (-0.5)(9) = -4.5$). We now have a success followed by a failure in each direction. In the next stage we will be searching backwards from the last success. The method is adjusting the scale parameters δ_x and δ_y to fit the function.

The exploration phase is over, and we must compute the new directions. The vector from $(x_0, y_0) = (2, -1)$ to $(x_1, y_1) = (1.5, 3)$ is $(1.5, 3)^T - (2, -1)^T = (-0.5, 4)^T$, so $p_1 = (-0.5, 4)^T / \|(-0.5, 4)^T\| \doteq (-0.1240, 0.9923)^T$. A perpendicular unit vector is $p_2 = (0.9923, 0.1240)^T$. This completes a single stage of the method.

For the second stage we begin by taking a step of length $\delta_x = 0.75$ along p_1 starting from $(x_1, y_1) = (1.5, 3)$. (Remember that in the long run we expect the direction of p_1 to roughly stabilize and so reusing the old δ_x from the previous stage would be quite reasonable.) We compute $f((x_1, y_1) + \delta_x p_1) = f(1.4070, 3.7442) \doteq 311.5385$ (a failure since it is greater than 56.5; we set $\delta_x = (-0.5)(0.75) = -0.375$) and then turn to p_2. We take a step of length $\delta_y = -4.5$ along p_2, giving $f((x_1, y_1) + \delta_y p_2) = f(-2.9654, 2.4420) \doteq 4049.63$ (a failure since it is greater than 56.5; we set $\delta_y = (-0.5)(-4.5) = 2.25$). We continue exploring, returning to p_1 with the new δ_x. ■

If $n > 2$ the method is unchanged, except that after we find the direction p_1 of the crease, we must define $n - 1$ directions $(p_2, \ldots, p_n)$ perpendicular to it. This can be accomplished using the Gram-Schmidt process from Chapter 2. Convergence criteria may include the number of function evaluations and a comparison of the distance traveled along p_1 to the total distance traveled along the other directions in each exploratory phase.

There are many other methods based on the basic idea of alternating variable search. Rosenbrock's method is one of the older variants. Two newer variants are discussed in Additional Problem 11.

PROBLEMS 7.5

1. a. Rosenbrock's function (see Example 7.5.2) is also called *Rosenbrock's valley* or the *banana function*. Make a contour plot of this function and use it to explain why these characterizations are accurate.

  b. Does the new search direction p_1 in Example 7.5.2 point roughly along the crease at the base of the valley?

2. Perform two iterations of alternating variable search on Rosenbrock's function, starting from $(x_0, y_0) = (10, 12)$.

3. a. Write a MATLAB program that inputs an inline function of a single variable, an initial guess, and a scale parameter (δ_x) and uses them to attempt to bracket a minimum of the function using Rosenbrock's method in one dimension.

b. Use Rosenbrock's method to find a minimum of $f(x) = x^9 - 2x^7 + 5x^4 - 2x + 2$.

4. Perform two complete stages of Rosenbrock's method on the objective function $f(x, y) = x^2 + 4xy + 4y^2$ of Example 7.5.1, starting from $(x_0, y_0) = (2, 2)$.

5. Perform three complete stages of Rosenbrock's method on the objective function $f(x, y) = |(\sin(xy)| + |2\cos(x)|$ starting from $(x_0, y_0) = (1, 1)$.

MATLAB 7.5

It's convenient to be able to save specific variables from one MATLAB session to the next. For instance, if you work through Example 7.5.1 by defining an inline function:

```
» f=inline('x^2+4*x*y+4*y^2');
```

then you may wish to access f and any other variables in another session (say, when working the Problems). To save f to a file named ch7sec5.mat, use the save command:

```
» save ch7sec5 f
```

Enter clear all and then who to verify that f has been cleared. Then enter:

```
» load ch7sec5
» who
```

to see that the load command has restored f to the workspace. You may enter:

```
» save temp1
```

to store all current variables in temp1.mat (omitting the filename causes MATLAB to use the default filename matlab.mat).

You may also use what is called the functional form of save; if you need to save a variable from a MATLAB program, where the name of the MAT-file is supplied by the user, say in the character variable s, you may use the save command as follows:

```
» s='matfile1';
» A=[2 1;1 2];
» save(s,'A')
```

This saves the matrix A in the file matfile1.mat. There is a similar functional form of load, and you may specify file names (see the help).

To remove a MAT-file from within MATLAB, you may use the operating system or the delete command. For example:

```
» delete matfile1.mat
» delete ch7sec5.mat
» delete('temp1.mat')
```

should remove the files we saved earlier. You may also use the exclamation point (!) to issue a command directly to the operating system and use its delete feature (e.g., !rm matfile.mat on a UNIX system). All the usual path-related issues apply. Enter:

```
» T=[1 3 5 7 9];
» save temp2 T
» which temp2.mat
```

to locate `temp2.mat`. Recall that the `path` command allows you to display and set the search path. An easier way to change the path for most needs is the `addpath` command; to add a directory to the path, enter (for Windows):

» `addpath c:\temp`

or for UNIX:

» `addpath /users/yourname/numerical`

(use a valid path). Creating a directory for your own M-files and appending it to the path can be useful. On a UNIX machine you may use the `cd` command (from MATLAB) to verify that you are in your home directory, and then enter:

» `!mkdir mfiles`
» `addpath /users/yourname/mfiles -end`

to create such a directory and add it to your path. The `-end` makes this the last directory on the path (and hence the last one checked).

You do not need to add the directory to the path each time. The file `startup.m` is executed each time you start MATLAB. If you wish to have a directory such as this on your path every time you use MATLAB, make an M-file `startup.m` with the line:

`addpath /users/yourname/mfiles -end`

in it. You may add any other commands you would like issued on startup, such as a preferred default like `format long` and/or `format compact`. Save the file in any directory on MATLAB's default path (on a UNIX system you should usually save it in your home directory). See `help matlabrc` for more information. There is also a file `finish.m` that is executed when you exit MATLAB; see `help quit`.

If you are not sure whether or not the file `startup.m` already exists, you may check for it from MATLAB. Enter:

» `exist('startup.m')`

If you get 0, there is no such file on the path; if you get 2, as you will for:

» `exist('matlabrc.m')`

then there is such a file. The `exist` command can provide information on other objects as well. If `f` is a variable (including an inline function) in the workspace, for example, then `exist('f')` will return 1.

ADDITIONAL PROBLEMS 7.5

6. Write a detailed algorithm (pseudocode) for performing alternating variable search.

7. Write a detailed algorithm (pseudocode) for performing Rosenbrock search on a function of two variables.

8. Apply two iterations of alternating variable search to the function $f(x, y) = x^2 + y^2$ starting from an arbitrary point (a, a) $(a \neq 0)$. Comment.

9. Apply two iterations of alternating variable search to the function $F(x, y) = x^4 - 2xy + (x - 1)^2(y - 1)^2 e^{-xy}$ starting from the point $(5, 5)$. Make a sketch similar to Figure 7.13 showing the steps taken. Does the method seem to be working?

10. a. Apply three iterations of Rosenbrock search to the function $f(x, y) = x^2 + y^2$ starting from the point $(2, 2)$. Use $\alpha = 3$, $\beta = -1/2$, and $\delta_x = \delta_y = 0.5$.

b. Apply four iterations of Rosenbrock search to the function $F(x, y) = x^4 - 2xy + (x - 1)^2(y - 1)^2 e^{-xy}$ starting from the point $(2, 2)$. Use $\alpha = 3$, $\beta = -1/2$, and $\delta_x = \delta_y = 0.5$.

11. a. The **Hooke and Jeeves pattern search** method starts with a point P and takes a single exploratory step in each coordinate direction, retaining the value of the coordinate if the step is a success and taking a similar step with the opposite sign if it is not. After all n directions have been searched in this manner, we have a new point Q. (Possibly $P = Q$ since we search at most twice in each coordinate direction.) Rather than simply moving from P to Q, we assume that $Q - P$ is a good direction and take an extended step to $Q + (Q - P)$ (called the *pattern move*), and then begin again. Draw several pictures indicating typical searches using this method in $\mathbb{R}^2$.

b. Repeat Additional Problem 10 using this method. Search one-half unit in each direction.

c. The **Davies, Swann, and Campey method** (or **D.S.C. method**) explores each direction in a manner similar to that of Rosenbrock search until it brackets a minimum in that direction. It then uses single-variable quadratic interpolation to better locate the minimum in that direction. The rest of the algorithm is similar to Rosenbrock search. Repeat Additional Problem 10 using this method.

12. a. Write a MATLAB program that implements alternating variable search.

b. Test your program on the Rosenbrock function.

13. a. Write a MATLAB program that implements Rosenbrock search for a function of two variables.

b. Test your program on the Rosenbrock function.

14. It is easier to provide convergence theorems for bracketing methods, the method of steepest descent, and Newton's method than for direct search methods such as alternating variable search and Rosenbrock search. Why?

15. Write a detailed algorithm (pseudocode) for performing Rosenbrock search on a function of n-variables. You will need to include the Gram-Schmidt orthonormalization procedure (see Section 2.8).

7.6 The Nelder-Mead Method

Rosenbrock's method illustrates the basic ideas of the direct search methods. It is most useful when the minimizer of the multivariate objective function is known to lie in a long, narrow valley, and it is widely used in one-dimensional line searches as a means of obtaining an initial bracket. The idea behind Rosenbrock's method is also used to find initial brackets for one-dimensional root-finding methods like Brent's method, beginning from a single initial guess. However, derivative-free minimization programs for general functions are more often based on a different approach, which we now describe.

Polytopes and Simplices
    A **regular simplex** in $\mathbb{R}^n$ is a set of $n + 1$ mutually equidistant points; in $\mathbb{R}^2$, for example, the regular simplex defines an equilateral triangle. A **simplex** (or **polytope**) in $\mathbb{R}^n$ is a set of $n + 1$ distinct points. (In fact we also use the term *simplex* or *polytope* to describe the region in $\mathbb{R}^n$ defined by these points; in $\mathbb{R}^2$ every simplex is a triangle.) **Simplex methods**[2] (or **polytope methods**) maintain a simplex at each iteration, which, we hope, encloses the location of the minimizer. In the $\mathbb{R}^2$ case this means maintaining and evolving a triangular region in the xy-plane that, if all goes well, will locate and then contract around the minimizer (x^*, y^*).

---

[2] Not to be confused with the well-known *simplex method* for linear functions. The method we are discussing is due to Spendley, Hext, and Himsworth.

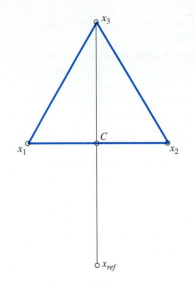

Figure 7.15 Polytope Method.

Polytope Method

The prototypical polytope method is as follows: Generate a regular simplex (also called a **design**) and order the points $x_1, \ldots, x_{n+1}$ so that $F(x_1) \le F(x_2) \le \ldots \le F(x_{n+1})$. Find the center of mass (centroid)

$$c = \frac{1}{n} \sum_{k=1}^{k=n} x_k$$

of the best n points of the simplex. (That is, we omit x_{n+1} from this average because it corresponds to the largest value.) Our goal is to replace the worst point x_{n+1} with a new point x_{ref} that has a lower function value. Since x_{n+1} is the highest point, we reflect it about the centroid, that is, we seek x_{ref} such that

$$x_{ref} - c = c - x_{n+1}$$

$$x_{ref} = 2c - x_{n+1}$$

(see Fig. 7.15). We then replace x_{n+1} with x_{ref}, reorder the points according to their function values, and start again with the new highest point; it is a fact that the new set of points will also form a regular simplex. We continue evolving the simplex in this manner.

Example 7.6.1 Let's try to find a minimum of the function $f(x, y) = (x + 1)^2 + 2(y + 1)^2$ starting from the regular simplex $\{(0, 0), (1/2, \sqrt{3}/2), (1, 0)\}$. (Verify that each point is exactly one unit away from each of the others.) The function values at these vertices are $3, 9.2141$, and 6, respectively, so $x_1 = (0, 0)^T$, $x_2 = (1, 0)^T$, and $x_3 = (1/2, \sqrt{3}/2)^T$. The centroid of the lowest points is $c = \frac{1}{2}((0, 0)^T + (1, 0)^T) = (1/2, 0)^T$ (note that this is just the midpoint of the line connecting x_1 and x_2), so $x_{ref} = 2c - x_3 = 2(1/2, 0)^T - (1/2, \sqrt{3}/2)^T = (1/2, -\sqrt{3}/2)^T$. These points are pictured in Figure 7.15. The new simplex is $\{(0, 0), (1, 0), (1/2, -\sqrt{3}/2)\}$ (again, verify that each point is the same distance from every other point). Since $f(1/2, -\sqrt{3}/2) \doteq 2.2859$, the reordered list of points is $x_1 = (1/2, -\sqrt{3}/2)^T$, $x_2 = (0, 0)^T$, and $x_3 = (1, 0)^T$.

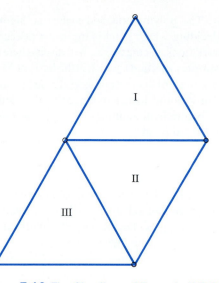

Figure 7.16 The Simplices of Example 7.6.1.

Let's do another iteration. The new centroid is $c = \frac{1}{2}((1/2, -\sqrt{3}/2)^T + (0, 0)^T) = (1/4, -\sqrt{3}/4)^T$, so $x_{ref} = 2c - x_3 = 2(1/4, -\sqrt{3}/4^T - (1, 0)^T = (-1/2, -\sqrt{3}/2)$. The new simplex is $\{(1/2, -\sqrt{3}/2), (0, 0), (-1/2, -\sqrt{3}/2)\}$ (again, verify that each point is the same distance from every other point). Since $f(-1/2, -\sqrt{3}/2) \doteq 0.2859$, the reordered list of points is $x_1 = (-1/2, -\sqrt{3})^T$, $x_2 = (1/2, -\sqrt{3}/2)^T$, and $x_3 = (0, 0)^T$. These three simplices are located in the plane in Figure 7.16. (Recall that the surface $z = f(x, y)$ is above this plane.) The sole local minimum is at $(-1, -1)$. ∎

When one vertex of the simplex lies near the minimum, it may be that it does not get replaced for a long time; the simplex turns about this point. For this reason the age (in number of iterations) of each point is monitored, and when any point is too old the entire simplex is shrunk towards it, that is, we replace each x_i by

$$x_i = x_{old} + \frac{1}{2}(x_i - x_{old})$$

$$= \frac{1}{2}(x_{old} + x_i),$$

where x_{old} is the oldest vertex of the design. We may now use the size of the simplex as a convergence criterion.

Given a point in $\mathbb{R}^n$, there are simple formulas for generating a regular simplex surrounding it (or for which it is one of the vertices), so the method can be used starting with a single initial guess and an edge length for the simplex. The principal complication that may occur in using the method is that if the reflected point x_{ref} is the new worst point, then reflecting *it* will find the old x_{n+1} that was used to generate x_{ref}, and the method will cycle (see Fig. 7.15 again and consider reflecting x_{ref} across c); this is easily handled by using the next-to-worst point in such a case.

Nelder-Mead
Method

The polytope method makes no significant use of the values of F other than for deciding which point is the worst at each iteration; we can do better. There are many variations, but the one we will discuss here is the **Nelder-Mead method** (or **Nelder-Mead simplex method**), which is the basis of MATLAB's fminsearch command. We begin with a set of distinct points $x_1, \ldots, x_{n+1}$ ordered so that $F(x_1) \leq F(x_2) \leq \ldots \leq F(x_{n+1})$. These points form a (not necessarily regular) simplex in $\mathbb{R}^n$. We compute the centroid c as before (still omitting x_{n+1} from the sum) and perform a *reflection step* by finding the reflected point

$$x_{ref} = c + \alpha(c - x_{n+1}), \tag{7.16}$$

where $\alpha > 0$ is called the *reflection coefficient;* $\alpha = 1$ corresponds to the x_{ref} in the basic polytope method, and $\alpha > 1$ corresponds to taking a larger step away from the highest point x_{n+1}. So far the only change from the basic polytope method is that we are not requiring the simplex to be regular.

We now compute $F(x_{ref})$. If $F(x_1) \leq F(x_{ref}) \leq F(x_n)$, then x_{ref} will be neither the new best point nor the new worst point, so we replace x_{n+1} by x_{ref}, reorder the points, and begin a new iteration by computing the centroid and reflecting.

If, however, either $F(x_{ref}) < F(x_1)$ or $F(x_n) < F(x_{ref})$, then x_{ref} is going to be either the new best point or the new worst point. If it's going to be the new best point, then the direction $c - x_{n+1}$ in which we stepped from c (Eq. (7.16)) seems to be a descent direction (particularly if the objective function is unimodal) and perhaps we should move farther in that direction. If x_{ref} is going to be the new worst point, then the direction $c - x_{n+1}$ in which we stepped from c seems to be the wrong direction or at least we have stepped too far along it so perhaps we should reconsider this step. (Note that the basic polytope method would simply accept a new worst point, no matter how large the function value there.) Looked at another way, if x_{ref} is going to be the new worst point, then perhaps the polytope is too large and we should shrink it in hopes of getting to the scale at which F is unimodal in this region.

So, if $F(x_n) < F(x_{ref})$ (x_{ref} will be the new worst point, though it may or may not be worse than the old worst point x_{n+1}), we perform a *contraction step*. We set

$$x_{con} = \begin{cases} c + \gamma(x_n - c) & \text{if} \quad F(x_{ref}) \geq F(x_{n+1}) \\ c + \gamma(x_{ref} - c) & \text{if} \quad F(x_{ref}) < F(x_{n+1}) \end{cases}, \tag{7.17}$$

where $\gamma \in (0, 1)$ is the *contraction coefficient*. We then compute $F(x_{con})$; if it is less than both $F(x_{ref})$ and $F(x_n)$, then we accept it as the new point, reorder the points, and begin a new iteration. If not (the contraction step fails), we *shrink* the polytope towards the best point in exactly the same way as in the basic polytope algorithm:

$$x_i = x_1 + \frac{1}{2}(x_i - x_1)$$
$$= \frac{1}{2}(x_1 + x_i)$$

$(i = 2, \ldots, n + 1)$. We then reorder the points and begin a new iteration.

What if x_{ref} would be the new best point? In that case stepping away from x_{n+1} has been very beneficial, and perhaps we should explore farther in this direction. We perform an *expansion step* by computing a new point

$$x_{exp} = c + \varepsilon(x_{ref} - c),$$

where $\varepsilon > 1$ is called the *expansion coefficient;* this is a point even farther along the line from x_{n+1} to c. If $F(x_{exp}) < F(x_{ref})$, the expansion is successful and we replace x_{n+1} with x_{exp}; otherwise (if the expansion fails) we replace x_{n+1} with x_{ref}. (We use the criterion $F(x_{exp}) < F(x_{ref})$ rather than $F(x_{exp}) \leq F(x_{ref})$ to keep the simplex small.) In either case we then reorder the points and begin a new iteration.

This completes the description of the Nelder-Mead method. Typical values of the parameters are $\alpha = 1$, $\gamma = 1/2$, and $\varepsilon = 2$. We stop when $F(x_{n+1}) - F(x_1)$ (or the standard deviation of $F(x_1), F(x_2), \ldots, F(x_{n+1})$, particularly if we view F as a "noisy" function) is sufficiently small, or when some maximum number of function evaluations is reached.

Example 7.6.2   Let's go back to the function $f(x, y) = (x + 1)^2 + 2(y + 1)^2$ and initial simplex $\{(0, 0), (1/2, \sqrt{3}/2), (1, 0)\}$ of Example 7.6.1. Just as in Example 7.6.1, the function values are $3, 9.2141$, and 6, respectively, so $x_1 = (0, 0)^T$, $x_2 = (1, 0)^T$, and $x_3 = (1/2, \sqrt{3}/2)^T$, and the centroid of the lowest points is $c = \frac{1}{2}((0, 0)^T + (1, 0)^T) = (1/2, 0)^T$. Once again $x_{ref} = 2c - x_3 = 2(1/2, 0)^T - (1/2, \sqrt{3}/2)^T = (1/2, -\sqrt{3}/2)^T$. In the polytope method we accepted this point and moved on to the next iteration; now we check $f(1/2, -\sqrt{3}/2) \doteq 2.2859$ and see that this will be the new best point. So an expansion $x_{exp} = c + \varepsilon(x_{ref} - c) = (1/2, 0)^T + 2((1/2, -\sqrt{3}/2)^T - (1/2, 0)^T) = (1/2, -\sqrt{3})^T$ is in order. We find that $f(1/2, -\sqrt{3}) \doteq 3.3218$, so the expansion step fails and we accept x_{ref}. The new reordered list of points is $x_1 = (1/2, -\sqrt{3}/2)^T$, $x_2 = (0, 0)^T$, and $x_3 = (1, 0)^T$, just as it was in Example 7.6.1.

Let's do another stage. The new centroid is $c = \frac{1}{2}((1/2, -\sqrt{3}/2)^T + (0, 0)^T) = (1/4, -\sqrt{3}/4)^T$, so $x_{ref} = 2c - x_3 = 2(1/4, -\sqrt{3}/4)^T - (1, 0)^T = (-1/2, -\sqrt{3}/2)$. Since $f(-1/2, -\sqrt{3}/2) \doteq 0.2859$, this will be a new best point. So we try an expansion, $x_{exp} = c + \varepsilon(x_{ref} - c) = (1/4, -\sqrt{3}/4)^T + 2((-1/2, -\sqrt{3}/2)^T - (1/4, -\sqrt{3}/4)^T) = (-5/4, -3\sqrt{3}/4)^T$. We find that $f(-5/4, -3\sqrt{3}/4) \doteq 0.2413$, so the expansion succeeds and x_{exp} is the new point. The reordered list of points is $x_1 = (-5/4, -3\sqrt{3}/4)^T$, $x_2 = (1/2, -\sqrt{3}/2)^T$, and $x_3 = (0, 0)^T$, and they no longer form a *regular* simplex. ∎

It is wise to periodically restart any polytope method. If the method fails it is typically because it is stagnating in some region, that is, it is making little progress, possibly as measured by a lack of sufficient decrease in the average value of the function

$$\frac{1}{n+1} \sum_{k=0}^{k=n} F(x_i) \tag{7.18}$$

over the simplex. Choosing a slightly different polytope that covers essentially the same region (but that defines new directions because of the new points) can be a useful heuristic. Nelder-Mead is usually restarted by retaining the best point and defining a regular simplex that includes that best point as a vertex; however, the fact that the Nelder-Mead polytopes can adjust their shape to the lay of the function around them is a useful facet of the method as well.

PROBLEMS 7.6

1. a. In Eq. (7.17) the first case is called an *inside contraction* and the other case is called an *outside contraction*. Draw a polytope in $\mathbb{R}^2$ and its centroid (see Fig 7.15). Mark the location of the reflected point and the points and polytopes that would result from a successful inside contraction step and a successful outside contraction step. What is the reason for having the two different types of contractions?

b. Draw a polytope in $\mathbb{R}^2$ and its centroid; mark the location of a reflected point and the points and polytopes that would result from a successful expansion step or from a shrinking of the polytope.

c. One variant of the Nelder-Mead method replaces the centroid c in Eq. (7.17) with the best point x_1 during a contraction step. Why might this be beneficial?

2. Write a detailed algorithm (pseudocode) for the basic polytope method (do not include restarting).

3. a. Apply four iterations of the basic polytope method to the function $F(x, y) = |2x^4 - 5xy + 1| + e^{-xy}$ starting from the polytope $\{(0, 0), (1/\sqrt{2}, 1/\sqrt{2}), (1, 0)\}$.

b. Sketch the successive polytopes on a single graph.

4. Write a detailed algorithm (pseudocode) for the Nelder-Mead method (do not include restarting).

5. a. Apply four iterations of the Nelder-Mead method to the function $F(x, y) = |2x^4 - 5xy + 1| + e^{-xy}$ starting from the polytope $\{(0, 0), (1/\sqrt{2}, 1/\sqrt{2}), (1, 0)\}$.

b. Sketch the successive polytopes on a single graph.

c. Use MATLAB's fminsearch command with the initial guess $(0, 0)$ to find a minimum of $F(x, y) = |2x^4 - 5xy + 1| + e^{-xy}$.

MATLAB 7.6

As we have seen, a benefit of working in MATLAB is that no loops are needed to use a formula such as Eq. (7.16); vector addition is built-in. Of course, all vectors must be the same size. Enter:

```
» x=ones([1 10]),y=zeros([1 10])
» size(x)==size(y)
```

The result is [1 1], so x and y conform for addition. Enter:

```
» sum(size(x)==size(y))==2
```

This is equal to 1 if the matrices conform for addition and 0 otherwise; there are many other ways to test this.

The average value of the function (as in Eq. (7.18)) is easy to compute using the mean command. If we wish to use the (sample) standard deviation as the convergence criterion, then we may use the std command; for example, enter:

```
» F=inline('abs(2*x.^4-5*x.*y+1)+exp(-x.*y)');
» P=rand([2 3])        %Simulate three points in R2.
» x=P(1,:)             %x-values are in row 1 of P.
» y=P(2,:)             %y-values are in row 2 of P.
» FP=feval(F,x,y)      %Evaluate F at the points P on the polytope.
» std(FP)              %Sample s.d.
```

Entering rand([2 3]) creates a 2×3 pseudo-random matrix, and we view each of the three columns as a vector (point) in $\mathbb{R}^2$. Hence x contains the x-coordinates of the three points and y contains the y-coordinates of the three points. We evaluate F at these points and then use the `std` command to compute their standard deviation.

To compute the centroid we need to order the points by their function values. With P and FP as above, enter:

```
» [FPS,IND]=sort(FP)
```

The vector FPS is the same as FP but sorted into ascending order, as desired. Recall that the vector IND is an index vector, which is a permutation of the integers 1 to `length(FP)`, and may be used to sort the P vector; enter:

```
» PS=P(:,IND)
```

This has the effect of sorting the columns of P in precisely the same way as FP. Now that we have sorted P as PS, we may compute the centroid. Recall that PS is a matrix. Type `help sum`. Evidently the centroid of all but the last point may be found as follows:

```
» N=size(PS,2)-1; %size(A,2)is the number of columns of A.
» c=sum(PS(:,1:N))
```

(Look at PS and verify that this is correct.) We could also use a single command; enter:

```
» c=sum(PS(:,1:end-1))
```

(see `help end` and note also that `1:end-1` is the same as `1:(end-1)`); using a variable such as N is generally clearer, however.

When using `fminsearch` recall that you may use `optimset` to set an `options` variable to change various defaults.

The Nelder-Mead method is distrusted by many numerical analysts because it lacks a complete convergence theory. However, heuristic methods must be employed at times, and there is *some* theoretical justification for expecting the method to converge in certain cases. Experiment with this method; does it seem useful?

ADDITIONAL PROBLEMS 7.6

6. a. Write a MATLAB program for performing the basic polytope method. Your method should input an initial regular simplex. Spendley, Hext, and Himsworth suggest that a point is "too old" when it has persisted for more than $1.65n + n^2/20$ iterations (when the points forming the polytope are points in $\mathbb{R}^n$). Use the size of the polytope as your convergence criterion. Do not include a restarting feature.

b. Test your program on the function $F(x, y) = |2x^4 - 5xy + 1| + e^{-xy}$ starting from the polytope $\{(0, 0), (1/\sqrt{2}, 1/\sqrt{2}), (1, 0)\}$.

7. A regular simplex containing a given point $x_0 \in \mathbb{R}^n$ as a vertex can be formed by setting $x_i = x_0 + \delta_1(J - e_i) + \delta_2 e_i$ $(i = 1, \ldots n)$. Here J is `ones([n 1])` (in MATLAB notation), e_i is the n-vector (which is equal

to zero everywhere except for the ith entry, which is equal to one), and $\delta_1 = ((n + 1)^{1/2} + n - 1)/n\sqrt{2}$, $\delta_2 = ((n + 1)^{1/2} - 1)/n\sqrt{2}$. Write a MATLAB program that inputs an initial point (use `size` or `length` to determine n) and returns a regular simplex containing it as a vertex.

8. Apply four iterations of the Nelder-Mead method to Rosenbrock's function $f(x, y) = 100(y - x^2)^2 + (1 - x)^2$ starting from the initial polytope $\{(15, 13), (14, -16), (-16, 17)\}$.

9. a. Write a MATLAB program for performing the Nelder-Mead method on a function of two variables. Your program should accept an inline function (or the name of an M-file) and a single initial guess and generate an initial polytope. Use $F(x_{n+1}) - F(x_1)$

for the convergence criterion. Do not include a restarting feature.

b. Test your program on the function $F(x, y) = |2x^4 - 5xy + 1| + e^{-xy}$ starting from the point $(0, 0)$.

c. Test your program on Rosenbrock's function $f(x, y) = 100(y - x^2)^2 + (1 - x)^2$ starting from the initial point $(4, 6)$.

10. Suggest a method for detecting stagnation in the Nelder-Mead method and then restarting it. Write a detailed algorithm (pseudocode) for implementing your method. (You may wish to refer to Additional Problem 6.)

11. Compare the performance of Newton's method and the Nelder-Mead method for Rosenbrock's function $f(x, y) = 100(y - x^2)^2 + (1 - x)^2$ starting from the initial points $(2, 2)$, $(10, -12)$, and $(100, 100)$. You may use fminsearch for the Nelder-Mead method or your own version.

12. a. What happens if you use the basic polytope method on a function of a single variable?

b. What happens if you use the Nelder-Mead method on a function of a single variable?

c. Use fminsearch to find any minimum of $f(x) = x^9 - 2x^7 + 5x^4 - 2x + 2$ to at least four decimal places.

13. Create a direct search method based on the idea of evolving a polytope. Explain your reasoning, and then give an algorithm for performing your method.

14. a. One test for true convergence, which is sometimes used with direct search methods based on polytopes, is to restart the method from a new regular simplex around the solution found by the first run of the method; if this second use of the method converges to the same point, we declare it the solution. Write a MATLAB program that implements this by calling fminsearch (or your version of the Nelder-Mead method) and, if it appears to converge, calls it again with a new starting simplex.

b. Test your program on Rosenbrock's function $f(x, y) = 100(y - x^2)^2 + (1 - x)^2$ starting from various initial points.

15. Referring to MATLAB 7.1, what is the smallest reasonable tolerance for the size of a polytope that might be used as a convergence criterion?

7.7 Conjugate Direction Methods

Quadratic Programming

In the study of nonlinear optimization, much attention is given to the special case of a quadratic objective function

$$F(x) = c - b^T x + \frac{1}{2} x^T A x \tag{7.19}$$

($c \in \mathbb{R}$, $b \in \mathbb{R}^n$, A an $n \times n$ matrix). One reason is obvious: A sufficiently differentiable function is well-approximated by a quadratic function near a parabolic minimum. Another reason is the connection of such functions to linear systems. If the constraints on the problem are linear, we call this a **quadratic programming (QP) problem.** We consider only the unconstrained case here.

Let's take $c = 0$ for convenience and suppose that A is positive definite. (Recall that such a matrix is symmetric and nonsingular.) Then if F is given by Eq. (7.19), its gradient is

$$\nabla F(x) = -b + Ax.$$

But the unique minimum of F occurs where $\nabla F(x) = 0$, that is, where $Ax = b$. (This is why we chose the sign of b as we did in Eq. (7.19).) For a positive definite matrix A, a method that solves Eq. (7.19) solves the linear system $Ax = b$, and a method that solves $Ax = b$ locates a minimum of $F(x)$ in Eq. (7.19). Hence, in this section *we are discussing both an optimization method and a method for solving positive definite linear systems.*

If the function is not truly quadratic, the A matrix we need is the Hessian $H(x)$ of F evaluated at the unknown minimizer x^*, and even then Eq. (7.19) is only an approximation

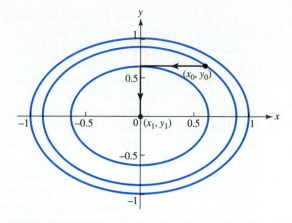

Figure 7.17 Alternating Variable Search (Fast Case).

of F near x^*. If the function is truly quadratic, however, the Hessian is a constant matrix and $A = H(x^*)$ will be given.

A-Orthogonality   The class of methods we are about to describe were developed for the purpose of solving $Ax = b$ when A is positive definite (and large); they are also used for minimizing $F(x) = -b^T x + \frac{1}{2} x^T A x$. Given a positive definite matrix A, we say that two vectors u, v are **conjugate with respect to A** (or **A-conjugate** or **A-orthogonal**) if

$$u^T A v = 0,$$

which is an inner product (u, v) defined by the matrix A. This inner product in turn induces a vector norm $\|u\|_A = (u^T A u)^{1/2}$, called the **$A$-norm** or, in many physical contexts, the **energy norm.**

It is a fact that if the vectors $d_1, \ldots, d_n$ are nonzero and pairwise A-conjugate, then they are linearly independent, and hence they form a basis for $\mathbb{R}^n$. We say that $\{d_1, \ldots, d_n\}$ is a set of **conjugate directions** (with respect to A).

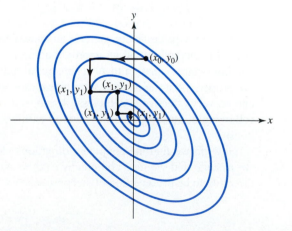

Figure 7.18 Alternating Variable Search (Slow Case).

Look at Figure 7.17 and Figure 7.18, which are reproductions of Figure 7.12 and Figure 7.13, respectively. When the function's contours line up just so with respect to the search directions (Fig. 7.17, which is in fact a quadratic), alternating variable search (which minimizes in each coordinate direction, one after the other) finds the location of the minimum *exactly* in a finite number of steps. When the contours don't line up just so (Fig. 7.18, which is also a quadratic), it does not. *Conjugate directions are the directions that are needed to make the case of Figure 7.18 behave like the case of Figure 7.17.* These directions depend on the matrix A, which defines the quadratic objective function, and determine just the right set of directions in which to search to find the location of the minimum after searching once along each direction. If we have a set of A-conjugate directions, then we will find the true minimum of $F(x) = -b^T x + \frac{1}{2} x^T A x$ in at most n steps *starting from any initial guess* by sequential minimization along these directions. (We say that the method exhibits **quadratic termination;** obviously, this assumes exact arithmetic.) The resulting algorithm is called the **conjugate direction method.**

Conjugate Direction Method

Example 7.7.1   Let's consider the function $F(x) = -b^T x + \frac{1}{2} x^T A x$ with $A = [2 \ -1; -1 \ 2]$ and $b = (2, 2)^T$. (Verify that A is positive definite.) Note that $(1, -1)A(1, 1)^T = 0$, so $d_1 = (1, 1)^T, d_2 = (1, -1)^T$ are A-conjugate. Let's start from the initial point $(x_0, y_0) = (3, 4)$. We have to find the minimum of F along d_1; that is, we must find the value α_0 that minimizes $g_1(\alpha_0) = F((x_0, y_0)^T + \alpha_0 d_1)$. (Note that since F is quadratic, this value of α_0 is unique.) Let's find this function of α_0: $g_1(\alpha_0) = F((3, 4)^T + \alpha_0(1, 1)^T) = F(3 + \alpha_0, 4 + \alpha_0)$ and, after some simplification, we find that $g_1(\alpha_0) = \alpha_0^2 + 3\alpha_0 - 1$, and so $\alpha_0 = -3/2$ is the minimizer. The new point is $(x_1, y_1)^T = (x_0, y_0)^T + \alpha_0 d_1 = (3, 4)^T + (-3/2)(1, 1)^T = (3/2, 5/2)^T$.

Now we must find the value α_1 that minimizes $g_2(\alpha_1) = F((x_1, y_1)^T + \alpha_1 d_2) = F(3/2 + \alpha_1, 5/2 - \alpha_1)$. After some simplification, we find that $g_2(\alpha_1) = 3\alpha_1^2 - 3\alpha_1 - \frac{13}{4}$, and so $\alpha_1 = 3/6 = 1/2$ is the minimizer. The solution, therefore, is at $(x_2, y_2)^T = (x_1, y_1)^T + \alpha_1 d_2 = (3/2, 5/2)^T + (1/2)(1, -1)^T = (2, 2)^T$.

Let's check this: The gradient is $\nabla F(x) = Ax - b$, and at the solution $A(2, 2)^T - b = (0, 0)^T$ as expected. Since the Hessian A is positive definite, this is the minimizer. ∎

Conjugate Gradient Method

If F is not quadratic but we have an approximation of the form of Eq. (7.19), we may apply the method to find an approximate minimizer of F. We then form an improved quadratic approximation to F at this point and repeat the process. We no longer have the property that the method terminates after finitely many iterations, but this method can be very effective nonetheless. Again, if F is truly quadratic, as we assume in the following discussion, then the method exhibits quadratic termination from any initial guess.

How do we find the conjugate directions? We describe only one approach, where we assume that we may compute $\nabla F(x) = Ax - b$ at any point. We choose the first direction to be the direction of steepest descent

$$d_0 = -\nabla F(x_0)$$
$$= b - Ax_0$$

starting from the given initial guess x_0, and choose α_0 to minimize $F(x_0 + \alpha_0 d_0)$ ($\alpha_0 \geq 0$ since d_0 is a descent direction). We then have

$$x_1 = x_0 + \alpha_0 d_0$$

as our new estimate of the minimizer. The method proceeds as follows: At each iteration, the new direction d_k is found from

$$d_k = r_k + \beta_k d_{k-1}$$

(where, as usual, $r_k = b - A x_k$ is the residual), with

$$\beta_k = \frac{\|r_k\|^2}{\|r_{k-1}\|^2}.$$

The directions $\{d_k\}_{k=0}^{n-1}$ can be shown to be A-conjugate. We minimize $F(x_{k-1} + \alpha_{k-1} d_{k-1})$ along this new direction to find α_{k-1} and then set $x_k = x_{k-1} + \alpha_{k-1} d_{k-1}$. When we have gone through all n directions we will be at the minimum (or possibly even sooner if we happen to land on a point with zero gradient first), excepting the effects of roundoff error. This is called the **conjugate gradient method.** Somewhat surprisingly, perhaps, a formula can be given for the α_k:

$$\alpha_k = \frac{\|r_k\|^2}{d_k^T A d_k} \tag{7.20}$$

($k = 0, \ldots, n - 1$). Hence we need not actually perform the line search, which enhances the efficiency of this method. We have the following algorithm for the conjugate gradient method:

Conjugate Gradient Method

1. Set $r_0 = b - A x_0$, $d_0 = r_0$.
2. Begin loop ($k = 1$ to n).
3. Set $\alpha_{k-1} = \|r_{k-1}\|^2 / d_{k-1}^T A d_{k-1}$.
4. Set $x_k = x_{k-1} + \alpha_{k-1} d_{k-1}$.
5. Set $r_k = r_{k-1} - \alpha_{k-1} A d_{k-1}$. If convergence criterion is met, exit.
6. Set $\beta_k = \|r_k\|^2 / \|r_{k-1}\|^2$.
7. Set $d_k = r_k + \beta_k d_{k-1}$.
8. End loop.

The algorithm uses the fact that the residual may be computed as $r_k = r_{k-1} - \alpha_{k-1} A d_{k-1}$. Since we must compute $A d_{k-1}$ anyway for use in computing α_k, storing that result and reusing it is more efficient than computing $A x_k$ then $r_k = b - A x_k$, if A is large. An efficient implementation of this algorithm would also maintain a variable for $s_k = \|r_k\|^2$ as needed.

We may use any of our usual termination criteria with this algorithm. One criterion that is often used requires that the relative residual $\|r_k\| / \|b\|$ be less than some specified tolerance. Since

$$r_k = b - Ax_k$$

is the residual error for the linear system $Ax = b$, this amounts to thinking of our problem as one of solving the linear system more than one of minimizing a quadratic objective function.

In the formulas for α_k and β_k notice that the Hessian matrix A is only ever needed to compute a matrix-vector product (the product Ad_{k-1}). The same is true of the computation of d_0 (requiring Ax_0) and of F itself (requiring Ax). This fact can be useful when A is so large that storing it and working with it directly are impractical, whether for a minimization problem or for solving $Ax = b$. We may write a special program that computes Ax from (a formula for) the entries of A without ever creating a copy of A; that is, the method is matrix-free (see Section 3.5).

The Nonquadratic Case

Because it is a particular instance of the conjugate direction method, the conjugate gradient method exhibits quadratic termination. However, it may be applied to other objective functions as well by forming a quadratic approximant of the objective function.

But forming a quadratic approximant is not how the method is generally applied to nonquadratic functions. Instead, we assume that $F(x)$ and $\nabla F(x)$ may be computed at any point and perform the line search $F(x_{k-1} + \alpha_{k-1}d_{k-1})$ by a univariate minimization method (as we have done in other algorithms) rather than using Eq. (7.20), which assumes a quadratic objective function. In addition we replace the formula for β_k (which requires the Hessian A) with a formula that does not require us to find the Hessian. Two of the most popular formulas are the **Fletcher-Reeves formula**

$$\beta_k = \frac{\nabla F(x_k)^T \nabla F(x_k)}{\nabla F(x_{k-1})^T \nabla F(x_{k-1})}$$

(giving the **Fletcher-Reeves method**) and the **Polak-Ribiere formula**

$$\beta_k = \frac{\nabla F(x_k)^T (\nabla F(x_k) - \nabla F(x_{k-1}))}{\nabla F(x_{k-1})^T \nabla F(x_{k-1})}$$

(giving the **Polak-Ribiere method**). Note that in each case the denominator is $\|\nabla F(x_{k-1})\|^2$. These formulas are used to produce conjugate directions starting from $d_0 = -\nabla F(x_0)$ using the formula

$$d_k = -\nabla F(x_k) + \beta_k d_{k-1}.$$

Both of these methods can be shown to produce Hessian-conjugate directions, even though they don't depend explicitly on the Hessian.

To maintain the conjugacy we must perform the line searches accurately (unlike other methods we have seen, which actually perform better with inexact line searches, which enable them to make bigger steps sooner). Nonetheless the method should be restarted periodically with the current steepest descent direction.

There are methods for generating conjugate directions that do not use the gradient (that is, which are derivative-free). The Gram-Schmidt process may be applied, although it is typically computationally expensive. Other approaches are more efficient.

PROBLEMS 7.7

1. a. Repeat Example 7.7.1, but use the conjugate directions in the opposite order ($d_1 = (1, -1)^T$, $d_2 = (1, 1)^T$) and use the initial guess (1003, 2005).

b. Perform two iterations of alternating variable search on the objective function of Example 7.7.1 using the initial guess $(x_0, y_0) = (3, 4)$.

2. a. Use the conjugate direction method to find the minimum of the function $F(x) = -b^T x + \frac{1}{2} x^T A x$ with $A = [3 \ -1; -1 \ 3]$ and $b = (4, -2)^T$. Use the conjugate directions $d_1 = (1, 1)^T$, $d_2 = (1, -1)^T$ (verify that A is positive definite and the directions are A-conjugate).

b. Repeat part (a) with the conjugate gradient method.

c. What is the solution of $Ax = b$?

3. a. Write a detailed algorithm (pseudocode) for the conjugate direction method. Assume that the conjugate directions will be supplied.

b. Show that if A is positive definite and diagonal, then alternating variable search is in fact a conjugate direction method for A and hence exhibits quadratic termination.

4. Write a detailed algorithm (pseudocode) for the conjugate gradient method. Select a reasonable convergence criterion and include a restarting provision.

5. Write a detailed algorithm (pseudocode) for the Fletcher-Reeves method.

MATLAB 7.7

Let's apply the conjugate gradient method to a moderately large sparse system. We'll use a matrix that appears in applications involving partial differential equations. To view a small example, enter:

```
» full(gallery('poisson',3))
```

Note that the matrix is sparse, banded, and weakly diagonally dominant; clearly there is other structure in it as well. Enter:

```
» A=gallery('poisson',50);
» size(A), nnz(A)/prod(size(A))
```

to create a larger example matrix. Enter:

```
» x=rand([2500 1])-.5;b=A*x;
» xlu=A\b;
» norm(x-xlu)
```

The solution found by the LU decomposition is certainly acceptable. Let's try using a few iterations of conjugate gradients. Enter:

```
» x0=ones(size(x));
» r0=b-A*x0;d0=r0;
» norm(r0)
» a0=(norm(r0)^2)/(d0'*A*d0)
» x1=x0+a0*d0;
» r1= r0-a0*A*d0;        %Should be reusing A*d0 from above.
» norm(r1),norm(b-A*x1)  %Check.
» b1=(norm(r1)/norm(r0))^2
» d1=r1+b1*d0;
```

We have completed one iteration of the conjugate gradients method, and have reduced the residual. Let's check the absolute error; enter:

```
» norm(x-x0),norm(x-x1)
```

Let's do another iteration. Enter:

```
» a1=(norm(r1)^2)/(d1'*A*d1)
» x2=x1+a1*d1;
» r2=r1-a1*A*d1;           %Should be reusing A*d0 from above.
» norm(r2),norm(b-A*x2) %Check.
» b1=(norm(r2)/norm(r1))^2
» d2=r2+b2*d1;
```

An efficient implementation would of course overwrite some of these quantities, but as usual we are not concerned about that at this point; right now we're just experimenting. Note that once again the norm of the residual has been reduced; we might wonder whether that is a general property of this method, as it is for GMRES in Section 3.5.

The MATLAB command `pcg` uses the preconditioned conjugate gradient method to solve a positive definite linear system and hence the corresponding optimization problem. See `help pcg` for more information.

ADDITIONAL PROBLEMS 7.7

6. a. Write a MATLAB program that implements the conjugate gradient method for a given quadratic function as in Eq. (7.19). Assume that A and b will be given, and argue that the value of c is irrelevant.
  b. Test your program on the problem of Example 7.7.1.

7. Use the conjugate gradient method to minimize $F(x) = \frac{1}{2}x^T Ax - b^T x$, where $A = [5\ 2; 2\ 3]$ and $b = (3, 2)^T$. (Verify that A is positive definite.)

8. Use the conjugate gradient method to minimize $F(x) = \frac{1}{2}x^T Ax - b^T x$, where $A = [5\ 2\ 1; 2\ 3\ 1; 1\ 1\ 1]$ and $b = (-4, 2, 1)^T$. (Verify that A is positive definite.)

9. a. Verify that the conjugate gradient method produces directions that are in fact conjugate.
  b. Verify that the residual satisfies $r_k = r_{k-1} - \alpha_k A d_k$ in the conjugate gradient method.

10. Verify experimentally that Eq. (7.20) produces the unique values α_k that minimize $F(x_{k-1} + \alpha_{k-1} d_{k-1})$ for the conjugate gradient method. Does the formula appear to work for the more general conjugate direction method?

11. a. Write a MATLAB program that implements the Fletcher-Reeves method for a nonlinear function $F(x)$.

  b. Test your program on the Rosenbrock function $f(x, y) = 100(y - x^2)^2 + (1 - x)^2$.

12. a. Let A be a matrix for which each entry on the main diagonal is 4, each entry on the first super- and subdiagonals is 0, each entry on the second super- and subdiagonals is -1, and all other entries are 0. Use MATLAB to verify that this matrix is positive definite for $n = 2, \ldots, 10$.

  b. To use conjugate gradients as a matrix-free algorithm, we must be able to compute Ax without forming A. Write a MATLAB program that accepts as input an order n and a vector x of length n and returns Ax for this A.

  c. Write a MATLAB program that implements the conjugate gradient method for a given quadratic function of the form in Eq. (7.19) and that calls a program such as your program from part (b) to compute Ax whenever needed. Your program should have access to A only via this routine.

13. Since A is assumed to be positive definite in Eq. (7.19), we could find the minimizer by solving $Ax = b$ using the Cholesky factorization of A. If A is large and sparse then the conjugate gradient method is usually superior, but if A is moderate in size and dense then Cholesky factorization might be superior. Show by example that the conjugate gradient method can be better for large sparse matrices and the Cholesky factorization might be better for smaller matrices.

14. a. The positive definite matrix A defines the inner product $(u, v) = u^T A v$ and hence the vector norm $\|u\|_A = (u^T A u)^{1/2}$. Verify that $\|\cdot\|_A$ is a valid vector norm. This norm is called the **A-norm** or, in many physical contexts, the **energy norm.**

b. For $A = [2\ 1; 1\ 2]$, compute $\|x\|_A$ for $x = (1, 1)^T$, $x = (1, -1)^T$, and $x = (-2, 1)^T$. Repeat for $A = [2\ -1; -1\ 2]$.

c. Is the standard inner product $(u, v) = u^T v$ of the form $(u, v) = u^T A v$ for some positive definite matrix A?

15. If x^* is the minimizer of Eq. (7.19), then under reasonable conditions the conjugate gradient method without restarting produces iterates that satisfy $\|x_k - x^*\|_A \le 2 \|x_0 - x^*\|_A \, [(\sqrt{\kappa(A)} - 1)/(\sqrt{\kappa(A)} + 1)]^k$,   where $\|x\|_A = (x^T A x)^{1/2}$. Comment on the speed of convergence this suggests for the conjugate gradient method.

8 Approximation Methods

8.1 Linear and Nonlinear Least Squares

Approximation

NUMERICAL ANALYSIS IS A MAJOR AREA OF APPLIED MATHEMATICS. Traditionally it has been considered a subcategory of *approximation theory*. Approximation theory considers ways to approximate functions (finite series, interpolants, and so on), whereas representation theory considers equivalent ways to represent functions (infinite series, Laplace transform, and so on). Apart from linear systems, much of what we've studied amounts to using low-degree polynomials to approximate functions and then working with those polynomials to solve the problem at hand. In this chapter we investigate approximation in more detail.

Least Squares

In Section 2.6 we discussed the method of approximation by least squares. Given a set of paired data $\{x_i, y_i\}_{i=0}^n$ we can fit a polynomial of degree m

$$y(x) = a_m x^m + a_{m-1} x^{m-1} + \cdots + a_1 x + a_0 \tag{8.1}$$

to the data in exactly one way if $m = n$ (so that there are as many data points as unknown coefficients in the polynomial), and no two x_i are equal. If $m < n$, however, the system is overdetermined and in general there is no solution, but we define the least squares solution to be the solution of the linear system

$$M^T M z = M^T b,$$

where the matrix M depends on the x_i, the vector b depends on the y_i, and z is the vector of the desired coefficients a_i $(i = 0, 1, \ldots n)$. This is the solution that minimizes the residual

$$r = \|b - Mz\|.$$

That is, it is the solution that minimizes the sum of squares of the differences between the observed y-values y_i and the y-values predicted by the model from Eq. (8.1),

$$r^2 = \sum_{i=0}^{n} (y_i - y(x_i))^2$$

$$= \sum_{i=0}^{n} \left(y_i - \left(a_m x_i^m + a_{m-1} x_i^{m-1} + \cdots + a_1 x_i + a_0 \right) \right)^2$$

and hence its name, the method of least squares. You may wish to review the first half of Section 2.6 at this point if you do not recall the details of least squares curve-fitting.

The method works because, although the polynomial $y(x)$ in Eq. (8.1) is nonlinear in x (for $m > 1$), it is *linear* in the unknowns $a_0, a_1, \ldots, a_m$. Because of this, the same method applies to any model of the form

$$y(x) = a_m g_m(x) + a_{m-1} g_{m-1}(x) + \cdots + a_1 g_1(x) + a_0 g_0(x) \tag{8.2}$$

because this is still linear in the unknowns $a_0, a_1, \ldots, a_m$. If we wish to minimize

$$r^2 = \sum_{i=0}^{n} (y_i - y(x_i))^2$$

$$= \sum_{i=0}^{n} (y_i - (a_m g_m(x_i) + a_{m-1} g_{m-1}(x_i) + \cdots + a_1 g_1(x_i) + a_0 g_0(x_i)))^2$$

then we simply form $Mz = b$ in the same way as before and solve the resulting system using whatever numerical linear algebra technique is appropriate and available.

Example 8.1.1   Consider the data $\{(0, 0), (1, 1), (2, 1), (3, 0)\}$. Suppose we wish to use the following nonlinear model:

$$y(x) = a_0 + a_1 \sin(x) + a_2 \cos(x)$$

(i.e., $g_1(x) = 1$, $g_2(x) = \sin(x)$, $g_3(x) = \cos(x)$). We want to fit the model to the data in the least squares sense. We have

$$a_0 + a_1 \sin(0) + a_2 \cos(0) = 0$$
$$a_0 + a_1 \sin(1) + a_2 \cos(1) = 1$$
$$a_0 + a_1 \sin(2) + a_2 \cos(2) = 1$$
$$a_0 + a_1 \sin(3) + a_2 \cos(3) = 0$$

that is,

$$a_0 + a_2 = 0$$
$$a_0 + a_1 \sin(1) + a_2 \cos(1) = 1$$
$$a_0 + a_1 \sin(2) + a_2 \cos(2) = 1$$
$$a_0 + a_1 \sin(3) + a_2 \cos(3) = 0$$

$$\begin{pmatrix} 1 & 0 & 1 \\ 1 & \sin(1) & \cos(1) \\ 1 & \sin(2) & \cos(2) \\ 1 & \sin(3) & \cos(3) \end{pmatrix} \begin{pmatrix} a_0 \\ a_1 \\ a_2 \end{pmatrix} = \begin{pmatrix} 0 \\ 1 \\ 1 \\ 0 \end{pmatrix},$$

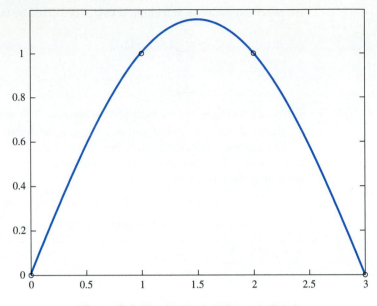

Figure 8.1 The Method of Example 8.1.1.

and using the LU decomposition applied to the cross-product matrix gives

$$a_0 \doteq -0.0877, \quad a_1 \doteq 1.2363, \quad a_2 \doteq 0.0877$$

so that

$$y(x) = -0.0877 + 1.2363 \sin(x) + 0.0877 \cos(x)$$

is the approximant. See Figure 8.1 for a graph of the least squares approximation and the data points; although the curve appears to go through the data points, it doesn't quite, apart from the origin. ∎

For a model of the form of Eq. (8.2) it is not clear that having all x_i distinct will suffice to ensure that the resulting linear system $Mz = b$ leads to a full-rank cross-product matrix $M^T M$. Hence it is not clear that the system $M^T Mz = M^T b$ has a unique solution (after all, what happens if all g_i are identically zero in Eq. (8.2)?).

This technique allows us to use linear least squares in many situations. Ordinarily we should use a model that represents the underlying physics if the data is observed data—in such a case the coefficients may have physical meaning. For example, in the case where voltage and current are measured many times for a given object and we use Ohm's Law $V{=}IR$ as our model and least squares to determine the coefficient R, that coefficient has a clear physical meaning. Choosing a more complicated model might give us a better fit (that is, a smaller residual) but would probably give us less insight into the physical situation.

Note that least squares produces a function, defined at least over $[\min\{x_i\}, \max\{x_i\}]$, that we believe is the best fit to the data from all curves of the form of Eq. (8.1) or more generally of the form of Eq. (8.2); the model is fixed, and we wish to estimate the

*Nonlinear
Models*

parameters $a_0, a_1, \ldots, a_m$ in the model. There is a large statistical theory of least squares methods that applies when the data consists of observations of a random variable y at fixed values of t (or x), which is very commonly the case (or at the least it is very commonly the model used).

Some situations call for a nonlinear model. In chemistry, a model used for the τ_1 relaxation time of nuclear magnetic resonance data is

$$y(t) = a + be^{-ct}, \tag{8.3}$$

where the quantity $1/c$ is a parameter of physical interest. If the model were simply

$$y(t) = be^{-ct},$$

then we could rewrite it as

$$\ln y(t) = \ln(b) - ct,$$

which is now linear in the unknowns $\ln(b)$ and c; the data is now $\{t_i, \ln(y_i)\}$. For the full model Eq. (8.3), however, there is no such trick. We must minimize the nonlinear function

$$r^2 = \sum_{i=0}^{n} (y_i - y(t_i))^2$$

$$= \sum_{i=0}^{n} \left(y_i - (a + be^{-ct_i}) \right)^2$$

with respect to a, b, and c. We can use any of the nonlinear optimization routines we have seen, or algorithms specialized to least squares problems.

*Nonlinear
Regression*

Why is a nonlinear least squares problem, also called **nonlinear regression analysis** or simply **nonlinear regression,** amenable to a specialized algorithm? As always, the answer is "because of its structure," but the structure in a nonlinear problem is not easy to see. Note that if the nonlinear model is

$$y(x; a_0, a_1, \cdots, a_m),$$

meaning that $y = y(x)$ depends on the parameters $a_0, a_1, \ldots, a_m$, then the objective function for the minimization problem is

$$F(a_0, a_1, \cdots, a_m) = \sum_{i=0}^{n} (y_i - y(x_i; a_0, a_1, \cdots, a_m))^2,$$

which depends on the $m+1$ variables $a_0, a_1, \ldots, a_m$ (in fact, we say that $F(a_0, a_1, \ldots, a_m)$ defines an $(m+1)$-dimensional **regression surface** on which we seek the global minimizer or minimizers). The x-variable does not appear in the function to be minimized because the x_i are just known values. In fact, the objective function may be written in the form

$$F(a_0, a_1, \cdots, a_m) = \frac{1}{2} \sum_{i=0}^{n} f_i^2(a_0, a_1, \cdots, a_m), \tag{8.4}$$

where

$$f_i = \sqrt{2} \, (y_i - y(x_i; a_0, a_1, \cdots, a_m))$$

$i = 0, 1, \ldots, n$. (The factor of $1/2$ in Eq. (8.4) is a convention.) Now, there *is* something interesting about a function F of the form

$$F = \frac{1}{2} \sum_{i=0}^{n} f_i^2$$

$$= \frac{1}{2} \| f \|^2$$

($f = (f_0, f_1, \ldots, f_n)^T$) if it is sufficiently differentiable. For, in many cases of interest the Jacobian $J(a_0, a_1, \ldots, a_m)$ of the vector $f(a_0, a_1, \ldots, a_m)$ is relatively easy to compute, and so

$$\nabla F = J^T f, \tag{8.5}$$

the gradient of F, is easy to compute using the Jacobian. (It may or may not be more efficient to compute ∇F by another approach.) More important, however, the Hessian matrix of F is

$$H = J^T J + \sum_{i=0}^{n} f_i \nabla^2 f_i. \tag{8.6}$$

If the model is good, then $f_i \approx 0$ (because the observed y_i is approximately equal to the predicted $y(x_i; a_0, a_1, \ldots, a_m)$, so that the residuals $r_i = y_i - y(x_i; a_0, a_1, \ldots, a_m)$ are nearly zero); also if the model $y(x_i; a_0, a_1, \ldots, a_m)$ is roughly linear, then the second derivatives $\nabla^2 f_i$ are nearly zero. Hence in some cases it is reasonable to use the approximation

$$H \approx J^T J, \tag{8.7}$$

meaning that if J is not too difficult to compute, then we may get the Hessian of F for the price of a matrix-matrix multiplication. In fact we may not want to form H but rather leave it in the form $J^T J$.

Thus, *the special structure of a nonlinear least squares problem is that the Hessian of the resulting objective function is frequently easy to compute.* For some problems, including very large problems, this is not so—the Jacobian and Hessian will simply be too expensive to calculate. But very often we are able to use Eq. (8.7) to find $H(a_0, a_1, \ldots, a_m)$ approximately, which allows us to use Newton's method

$$z_{k+1} = z_k - H^{-1}(z_k)\nabla F(z_k).$$

(and variants) in the form

$$H(z_k)(z_{k+1} - z_k) = -\nabla F(z_k)$$

$$J^T(z_k)J(z_k)(z_{k+1} - z_k) \approx -\nabla F(z_k)$$

($z = (a_0, a_1, \ldots, a_m)^T$) to minimize $F(a_0, a_1, \ldots, a_m)$. See Section 7.3 for details on Newton's method for nonlinear minimization.

Gauss-Newton Method   There are two major methods for solving nonlinear least squares problems. We sketch them but do not consider them in great detail. The first method is the **Gauss-Newton method,** which modifies Newton's method precisely as indicated above: Rather than use

$$H(z_k)(z_{k+1} - z_k) = -\nabla F(z_k),$$

we use the equation

$$J^T(z_k)J(z_k)(z_{k+1} - z_k) = -J^T f$$

(using Eq. (8.5) on the RHS and the approximation from Eq. (8.7) on the LHS). We perform a line search in the direction $s_{k+1} = z_{k+1} - z_k$ to ensure sufficient decrease in the value of the objective function and that the function appears to have the correct curvature in the region.

Levenberg-Marquardt Method

The second and better known of the two major specialized algorithms for solving nonlinear least squares problems is the **Levenberg-Marquardt method,** which uses the equation

$$\left[J^T(z_k)J(z_k) + \lambda_k D_k^T D_k\right](z_{k+1} - z_k) = -J^T f, \tag{8.8}$$

where $\lambda_k \geq 0$ and D_k is a diagonal matrix (often taken to be the identity matrix for all k). When λ_k is near zero, this takes the form of the Gauss-Newton method, which is essentially Newton's method, and so s_{k+1} represents a Newton step (modified by the results of the line search). When λ_k is large, the matrix

$$J^T(z_k)J(z_k) + \lambda_k D_k^T D_k$$

on the LHS of Eq. (8.8) is diagonally dominant and Eq. (8.8) has the form

$$S_k(z_{k+1} - z_k) = -J^T f$$
$$S_k(z_{k+1} - z_k) = -\nabla F(z_k),$$

and so the search direction $s_{k+1} = z_{k+1} - z_k$ is essentially the steepest descent direction,

$$s_{k+1} = -S_k^{-1} \nabla F(z_k),$$

where S_k is diagonally dominant and hence approximates a diagonal matrix. If $D_k = I$, for example, then $S_k = J^T(z_k)J(z_k) + \lambda_k I$ and if λ_k is sufficiently large, then this is nearly the identity matrix. Then $s_{k+1} \approx -\nabla F(z_k)$, which corresponds to the method of steepest descent (see Section 7.2).

The Levenberg-Marquardt algorithm, then, alternates between a small λ_k for a Newton-like step when the method is doing well, and a large λ_k for a descent direction step when the method is doing poorly. This gives the good behavior of Newton's method when the residuals r_i become small and retains the robustness of the method of steepest descent when the residuals are relatively large (because we are far from the solution or because the model is simply a poor fit for the data; in either case a wholly different method may be appropriate in the large-residual case). Methods for choosing λ_k vary from a simple strategy of increasing or decreasing λ_k by a constant factor depending on whether the previous search direction gave an increase—in which case the step is not taken and we compute a new proposed step with the larger λ—or decrease in function value, respectively, to more sophisticated methods that attempt to define a region in which the regression surface has a well-behaved minimum and in which steps of an appropriate size may be taken.[1] The parameter λ is sometimes called a **regularization**

---

[1] These are called *trust-region methods* and are beyond the scope of this book.

parameter as it helps to "regularize" the problem by taking into account the need for a more robust method in a less desirable region of the search space. Regularization is a large topic in its own right that we do not study here.

An actual code for performing nonlinear regression may switch to Gauss-Newton or Levenberg-Marquardt near a solution but use a more general nonlinear minimization routine far from the minimum, where the approximate Hessian in Eq. (8.7) may be a poor approximation and we may need to simply compute or approximate the true Hessian. As we have frequently seen, mixing methods can be beneficial.

Global
Minimization

You may have noticed that although we are looking for a global minimizer of Eq. (8.4), we are using local minimization routines. This is standard. These problems are often difficult, and we must assume that the user can supply plausible initial guesses, based on physical intuition and past experience, to get the method into the right region of the regression surface. If this is not the case and it is essential to get the actual global minimizer, then global minimization methods may be employed, using the Gauss-Newton or Levenberg-Marquardt method for the local minimization subproblems. It is important to realize, however, that typically, *a nonlinear regression program performs only a local minimization.*

The value of F at the minimizer is called the **residual sum of squares (RSS)** and is used as a measure of the goodness of the fit in the statistical theory of regression. There are statistical techniques for choosing between models; for instance, if we use the linear model

$$y(x) = a_m g_m(x) + a_{m-1} g_{m-1}(x) + \cdots + a_1 g_1(x) + a_0 g_0(x)$$

of Eq. (8.2) and then modify it by adding a single new term

$$y(x) = a_{m+1} g_{m+1}(x) + a_m g_m(x) + a_{m-1} g_{m-1}(x) + \cdots + a_1 g_1(x) + a_0 g_0(x),$$

then the RSS of the second model can only be smaller than that of the first model. After all, we may take $a_{m+1} = 0$ in the second model and use the parameters found for the first model to get the first model's RSS with the second model. (In other words, the second model contains the first model as a special case.) Is the decrease in the RSS that we see in the second model, with a_{m+1} not necessarily zero, a sufficiently large decrease to justify our saying that the second model is better? This is a statistical question and a modeling question.

PROBLEMS 8.1

1. a. Fit a quadratic model to the data $\{(-2, 1), (-1, 0), (0, 1), (1, 0), (2, 3)\}$. Plot the data and the model on the same graph. What is the RSS?

  b. Repeat for a cubic model with the same data.

  c. Repeat for a quartic model with the same data. Comment.

2. a. Fit the model $y(x) = a_0 + a_1 \sin(x) + a_2 \cos(x)$ of Example 8.1.1 to the data $\{(0, 1), (1, 0), (2, 1), (3, 0)\}$. Plot the data and the model on the same graph. What is the RSS?

  b. Repeat with the data $\{(0, 1), (1, 3), (2, 10), (3, 18)\}$.

3. Discuss the Gauss-Newton search direction equation $J^T(z_k)J(z_k)s_{k+1} = -J^T f$. What is an effective way to solve it for $s_{k+1} = z_{k+1} - z_k$ for various sizes and condition numbers of $J(z_k)$?

4. Perform two steps of the Gauss-Newton method using Eq. (8.3) as the model and with the data $\{(0, 10), (1, 8), (2, 5), (3, 1)\}$.

5. Perform two steps of the Levenberg-Marquardt method using Eq. (8.3) as the model and with the data {(0, 10), (1, 8), (2, 5), (3, 1)}. Start with $\lambda = 0.001$ and increase or decrease λ by a factor of 10 according to whether the step is unsuccessful or successful, respectively, until you have taken two actual steps.

MATLAB 8.1

The MATLAB slash command can be used for most linear least squares problems; it will automatically choose an appropriate method. See also `lsqr`. For difficult problems you may need to choose another approach, possibly including a specialized method for solving Vandermonde systems.

The command `lsqnonneg` solves a least squares problem with the additional restriction that the solution be nonnegative, which occurs in a number of applied problems. See `help lsqnonneg` for more information. You may have additional MATLAB least squares and regression analysis tools on your machine.

Let's look at the special functions in MATLAB as we'll be discussing them later in this chapter. Special functions are functions that are interesting enough to be named (like sine, cosine, exponential, and logarithm), though we usually mean the less common special functions when we use this term. To see a list of these functions, enter:

```
» help specfun
```

(Others are available through the Symbolic Toolbox.) The "Specialized math functions" listed are the special functions. Enter:

```
» help gamma
```

to see the help for the **gamma function** $\Gamma(x) = \int_0^\infty t^{x-1} \exp(t)dt$, which generalizes the factorial function (since $\Gamma(n) = (n-1)!$ if n is a positive integer). This special function occurs frequently in physics and statistics. Enter:

```
» gamma(3)          %Should be 2!=2.
» gamma(4)          %Should be 3!=6.
» gamma(3.5)        %This defines 2.5!.
```

The **incomplete gamma function** is $\Gamma_a(x) = (\int_0^a t^{a-1} \exp(t)dt)/\Gamma(a)$ (some authors define it differently). The corresponding MATLAB command is `gammainc`; enter:

```
» gammainc(3,1)
» gammainc(3,10)
» gammainc(3,100)
```

The commands accept vector arguments. Enter:

```
» x=.05:.01:4;
» y1=gamma(x);
» y2=gammainc(x,1);
» plot(x,y1,'r'),hold on,plot(x,y2,'b'),grid
```

to plot $\Gamma(x)$ and $\Gamma_1(x)$ on the same graph. The plot starts at $x = .05$ because $\Gamma(0)$ is infinity. Enter:

```
» type gamma
```

You might have expected that $\Gamma(x)$, because it is defined as an integral, would be evaluated by a numerical quadrature routine, but it is often more accurate and more efficient to write special-purpose routines for computing special functions that occur frequently in applications. Such routines often involve approximating the function by another, simpler curve (or several curves for various argument and parameter ranges; see MATLAB 8.3). That is what has been done here.

The Bessel functions appear frequently in the analytical solution of partial differential equations in fluid dynamics and electromagnetism. Enter help bess followed by Tab Tab to see a list of corresponding MATLAB functions. Enter help erf followed by Tab Tab to see the functions associated with the error function (which is related to the area under the bell-shaped curve of probability and statistics). Enter:

```
» type erf
```

to see that the error function $\mathrm{erf}(x) = 2/\sqrt{\pi} \int_0^x \exp(-t^2)dt$ is evaluated by a subfunction erfcore. Enter:

```
» type erfcore
```

and study it to see that this program uses an approximation of the actual function $\mathrm{erf}(x)$ and *not* a quadrature of the integrand $\exp(-t^2)$ to compute values of the error function. Enter:

```
» x=-2:.01:2;plot(x,erf(x)),grid
```

to plot the function that is being approximated. Again, when it is feasible, approximating such a function is often better than quadrature of the integrand.

Through the Symbolic Toolbox you can access other special functions (that are implemented in Maple). To see a list of such special functions, enter:

```
» mfunlist
```

See help mfun for information on how to use these routines.

Sometimes we need guaranteed error bounds on the value of a function, or indeed on the result of some other computation, such as the solution of a linear system or of a root-finding problem. This can be done using *directed rounding*. In essence, we do a computation twice, first rounding in such a way that we get a guaranteed overestimate x_u of the true answer x^*, then rounding in such a way that we get a guaranteed underestimate x_l of the true answer. (With some care we can avoid actually computing twice and instead just round twice.) We conclude that x^* lies in the interval $[x_l, x_u]$. We call this *interval arithmetic* because the answer is returned as an interval guaranteed to contain the true answer, not as a single value. The corresponding numerical methods are called *interval methods*. There is software available that performs the desired computations; for example, the free MATLAB toolbox *IntLab* which you may easily find by web search.

ADDITIONAL PROBLEMS 8.1

6. a. Write a detailed algorithm (pseudocode) for performing the Gauss-Newton method.

b. Write a detailed algorithm (pseudocode) for performing the Levenberg-Marquardt method.

7. Fit a linear, quadratic, cubic, quartic, and quintic model to the data $\{(1, 0.5), (2, 4), (3, 13.5), (4, 32), (5, 62.5), (6, 108), (7, 171.5), (8, 256)\}$. Which model is the best fit? (When the best model of this type is selected by statistical methods, it is called **stepwise regression.**) Explain your answer.

8. Is it reasonable to use a local minimization routine for nonlinear regression despite the fact that a global minimum is desired? Explain your reasoning.

9. Write a detailed algorithm (pseudocode) for a general method for solving nonlinear least squares problems that uses a method such as Newton's method unless the residuals are small, in which case it switches to the Gauss-Newton method. (In practice a variable metric method similar to the one discussed in Section 1.9, modified for optimization, would be used for the large residual method.) Explain any heuristics used; for example, how will you decide when the residuals are large?

10. Write a MATLAB program that performs the Gauss-Newton method. Input the data and any other quantities you may need; you may input the model or assume it will be provided as an M-file. Use a sufficient decrease criterion (you may make up a simple heuristic criterion).

11. Derive Eq. (8.5) and Eq. (8.6).

12. Conduct a numerical experiment to compare the quality of the approximation in Eq. (8.7) to the true values as found from Eq. (8.6) (or from any other convenient formula for the Hessian).

13. How much work is saved by using Eq. (8.7) rather than Eq. (8.6)?

14. a. The usual sufficient decrease and sufficient curvature criteria used for the Gauss-Newton method (and for other methods) are called the **Wolfe conditions,** which require that a proposed step s_{k+1} satisfy
$F(z_k + \alpha_k s_{k+1}) \leq F(z_k) + \gamma_0 \alpha_k [\nabla F(z_k)]^T s_{k+1}$
and $\gamma_1 [\nabla F(z_k)]^T s_{k+1} \leq [\nabla F(z_k + \alpha_k s_{k+1})]^T s_{k+1}$,
where $0 < \gamma_0 < \gamma_1 < 1$. It can be shown that, under mild assumptions, there are always steps that satisfy these criteria. Discuss these criteria; how do they serve to force a sufficiently large decrease in the function and a sufficiently negative curvature?

b. The **strong Wolfe conditions** use the first Wolfe condition but replace the second one by $|\gamma_1 [\nabla F(z_k)]^T s_{k+1}| \leq |[\nabla F(z_k + \alpha_k s_{k+1})]^T s_{k+1}|$. Comment on the differences between a step that satisfies the Wolfe conditions and one that satisfies the strong Wolfe conditions.

15. Write a MATLAB program that performs the Levenberg-Marquardt method. Input the data and any other quantities you may need; you may input the model or assume it will be provided as an M-file. Use a heuristic method for changing the regularization parameter λ.

8.2 The Best Approximation Problem

Operators

In an abstract setting, much of what we do in numerical analysis amounts to approximating an infinite-dimensional operator by a finite-dimensional operator. What does this mean? We'll demonstrate with an example. Consider the operator *differentiation*

$$\frac{d}{dx}$$

on the set $C_A^\infty(I)$ of all functions with convergent Taylor series[2] on some open interval I. If $f \in C_A^\infty(I)$, then we can write

$$f(x) = f(x_0) + f'(x_0)(x - x_0) + \frac{1}{2} f''(x_0)(x - x_0)^2 + \cdots ,$$

---

[2] Not all infinitely differentiable functions have a convergent Taylor series at every point; the subscript A denotes those *analytic* functions that do have such a series representation.

and if I contains the origin, we can use the Maclaurin series

$$f(x) = f(0) + f'(0)x + \frac{1}{2}f''(0)x^2 + \cdots$$

$$= \sum_{n=0}^{\infty} \frac{f^n(0)}{n!}x^n$$

$$= \sum_{n=0}^{\infty} a_n x^n$$

where $a_n = \frac{f^n(0)}{n!}$. We view the set $C_A^{\infty}(I)$ as a linear space (meaning, informally, that it is closed under addition and scalar multiplication and that it obeys the normal rules of arithmetic) and differentiation as an operator

$$\frac{d}{dx} : C_A^{\infty}(I) \to C_A^{\infty}(I)$$

acting on it: If

$$f(x) = \sum_{n=0}^{\infty} a_n x^n$$

then

$$\frac{d}{dx} f(x) = \frac{d}{dx} \sum_{n=0}^{\infty} a_n x^n$$

$$= \sum_{n=0}^{\infty} a_n \frac{d}{dx} x^n$$

$$= \sum_{n=0}^{\infty} n a_n x^{n-1}$$

$$= \sum_{n=0}^{\infty} b_n x^n$$

(where $b_0 = 0$). The point is that the functions in $C_A^{\infty}(I)$ can be written as infinite linear combinations of the functions

$$1, x, x^2, x^3, \cdots,$$

and the effect of differentiation can be viewed as its effect on the coefficients of those linear combinations. We say that the space $C_A^{\infty}(I)$ is infinite-dimensional, and so we are viewing differentiation as an operator on an infinite-dimensional space or, loosely, as an infinite-dimensional operator.

Approximating the Operator   A computer can't differentiate like this, unless it does so symbolically. But what if we were to approximate every function in $C_A^{\infty}(I)$ by its truncated Maclaurin series

$$f(x) \approx \sum_{n=0}^{N} a_n x^n$$

for some nonnegative integer N? For example, we might take $N = 2$ and get the approximation

$$f(x) \approx f(0) + f'(0)x + \frac{1}{2} f''(0)x^2$$

and use

$$D_2 f(x) = \frac{d}{dx}(f(0) + f'(0)x + \frac{1}{2} f''(0)x^2)$$
$$= f'(0) + f''(0)x$$

as an approximation of $f'(x)$, meaning that we are using the operator D_2 as an approximation of d/dx: $D_2 \approx d/dx$. The approximate differentiation operator D_2 doesn't, in general, give us the true derivative of f, but does give us an approximation of it.

Let's look at the approximate differentiation operator D_2 from a slightly different perspective. The effect of D_2 is easily represented by a matrix. If

$$f(x) \approx a_0 + a_1 x + a_2 x^2,$$

then, with respect to the finite list of functions $1, x, x^2$ that we are using to represent functions in this simpler space P_2, the coefficients of the linear combination are

$$\begin{pmatrix} a_0 \\ a_1 \\ a_2 \end{pmatrix},$$

and the effect of D_2 may be written as a matrix,

$$\begin{pmatrix} 0 & 1 & 0 \\ 0 & 0 & 2 \end{pmatrix} \begin{pmatrix} a_0 \\ a_1 \\ a_2 \end{pmatrix} = \begin{pmatrix} a_1 \\ 2a_2 \end{pmatrix},$$

where the matrix

$$\begin{pmatrix} 0 & 1 & 0 \\ 0 & 0 & 2 \end{pmatrix}$$

represents the action of the approximate differentiation operator D_2. Clearly, D_2 is finite-dimensional; the differentiation operator d/dx may be viewed as the action of an infinite-dimensional matrix

$$\begin{pmatrix} 0 & 1 & 0 & \cdots \\ 0 & 0 & 2 & \cdots \\ 0 & 0 & 0 & \cdots \\ \vdots & \vdots & \vdots & \ddots \end{pmatrix} \begin{pmatrix} a_0 \\ a_1 \\ a_2 \\ \vdots \end{pmatrix} = \begin{pmatrix} a_1 \\ 2a_2 \\ 3a_3 \\ \vdots \end{pmatrix}$$

on the infinite-dimensional vector of coefficients of the functions $1, x, x^2, \ldots$ in the Maclaurin series representation. These issues are explored in much more detail and in full rigor in a course on linear algebra.

Many of the things we have done throughout this text may be viewed, abstractly, as analogous to finding a manageable D_2 to use in place of the unwieldy d/dx. Our numerical quadrature rules replace integration, which on $C_A^\infty(I)$ would require adjusting all infinitely many coefficients in the expansion, with a rule based on only finitely many points, for example, replacing $\int_a^b dx$ with the trapezoidal rule T_h on $[a, b]$ (see Section 6.6). The quadrature rule is a finite-dimensional operator used to approximate the infinite-dimensional operator so that we may ultimately find an approximation to $\int_a^b f(x)dx$, which is the result of applying the operator to a particular function f. The same is true for a numerical differentiation rule that is used to approximate df/dx, which is the result of applying the operator d/dx to a particular function f. The differentiation rules we have developed approximate the differentiation operator with a finite-dimensional operator, which we then apply to the function. Note carefully the logic: To approximate

$$Lf,$$

where L is an operator (such as differentiation or integration), we generally first approximate L by finding a simpler rule and then use that approximation to approximate the desired quantity Lf. This is sensible because we typically want to write a program that solves ODEs, say, rather than one that solves a *particular* ODE (though this happens too); we want to approximate the act of solving ODEs.

What is the best finite-dimensional operator for approximating a certain infinite-dimensional operator? How do we find it? Answering these questions thoroughly would require more analysis than we have available. However we can mention some of the issues involved. Below we discuss the notion of the best way of approximating a function by another, simpler function—which amounts to finding a projection operator that projects the function onto a simpler space—but bear in mind that this generalizes to the situation in which we find the best way to approximate an operator by a simpler operator.

Approximating Functions

What then is the best way to approximate a function f by a simpler function g? There is no one answer. First we must specify what we mean by a "simple" function—say, a function from P_2, the set of all polynomials of degree at most 2. But the term "best" begs the question, "*Best* in what sense?" Best might mean easiest to manipulate, easiest to calculate, or closest to the function, or some compromise between these desiderata, depending on the application.

Even something as seemingly simple as asking that the approximant g give the closest approximation to f of all functions in the set of simple functions from which g is drawn doesn't define "best" unambiguously. By closest do we mean minimizing

$$\max |f(x) - g(x)| \tag{8.9}$$

over all x in some range (called the L_∞ norm of the difference $f - g$), minimizing

$$\int_a^b |f(x) - g(x)| \, dx \tag{8.10}$$

over the interval of interest $[a, b]$ (called the L_1 norm of the difference $f - g$), or minimizing

$$\left(\int_a^b (f(x) - g(x))^2 dx \right)^{1/2} \tag{8.11}$$

over the interval of interest $[a, b]$ (called the L_2 norm of the difference $f - g$; compare the discrete versions of these norms, with summations in place of the integrals, in Section 2.5)?

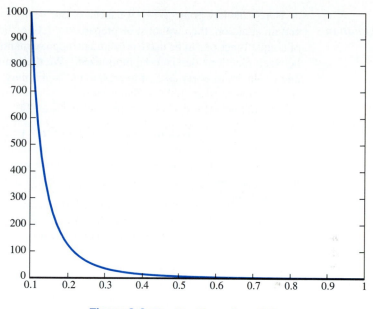

Figure 8.2 The Functions f_1 and f_2.

For example, consider the functions $f_1(x) = x^{-3}$ and $f_2(x) = 0$ on $[0.1, 1]$ (see Fig. 8.2). With respect to the L_∞ norm of Eq. (8.9), the functions are far apart, as over $[0.1, 1]$

$$\max |f_1(x) - f_2(x)| = 1000.$$

But with respect to the L_1 norm of Eq. (8.10), they are much closer,

$$\int_a^b |f_1(x) - f_2(x)| \, dx \doteq 49.5$$

(the area between the curves is only about 50 square units). If we hope to use f_2 to approximate the *values* of f_1, then we must expect errors on the order of 10^3. But if we hope to use f_2 to approximate *integrals* of f_1, then we should expect errors on the order of 10^1; f_2 is a much better approximant in the L_1 sense than in the L_∞ sense. If we were interested in root-mean-square (RMS) measurements, which are typically used to measure the difference between two waveforms, then we would consider L_2, which is in fact the most commonly employed norm.

We call the quantity $\max |f(x) - g(x)|$ the L_∞ distance between the functions f and g, and $\int_a^b |f(x) - g(x)| \, dx$ and $(\int_a^b (f(x) - g(x))^2 dx)^{1/2}$ the L_1 and L_2 distances, respectively, between f and g. (Compare the similar terminology for distances between vectors in Section 2.5. It's as though we're thinking of a function as a vector indexed by the uncountably many values in the interval on which the function is defined.) Of course, especially in the L_1 and L_2 cases, these do not correspond to "distances" as we usually think of them, but the concept is still useful. Note that the distance between f and g is just some norm of the function $h = f - g$.

Best
Approximation

Here's the key point: When we speak of our desire to find the best approximant in a certain situation, then we must be prepared to define "best" by specifying: (a) the class of simple functions to be used as candidate approximants, and (b) the notion of distance between functions that is to be minimized.[3] We then minimize the distance between f and g, which, in every case of interest to us, is given by

$$d(f, g) = \| f - g \|$$

for some norm. This is called a **best approximation problem.** For example, the problem that asks us to find the polynomial that best approximates $\sin(x)$ is insufficiently specific for us to proceed, but the problem that asks for the element of P_3 that minimizes the L_2 distance between it and $\sin(x)$ on the interval $[0, 1]$ is a problem that we understand to mean solving

$$\min_{g \in P_3} \left(\int_0^1 (\sin(x) - g(x))^2 dx \right)^{1/2},$$

that is, finding the values of a, b, c, and d that make

$$\int_0^1 (\sin(x) - (ax^3 + bx^2 + cx + d))^2 dx$$

as small as possible. This particular problem could be solved either analytically or by a numerical minimization routine.

Best
Approximation
in Various
Norms

The best approximation problem with the L_∞ norm is sometimes called **minimax approximation** because it minimizes the maximum distance between the two functions: that is, it finds the g that minimizes

$$\max |f(x) - g(x)|$$

over some interval, with g from some defined class of functions. Using the L_1 norm means minimizing the area between the curves (that is, the area of the function $h(x) = |f(x) - g(x)|$). Using the L_2 norm is called **least squares approximation** because it seeks to find the g that minimizes Eq. (8.11)

$$\left(\int_a^b (f(x) - g(x))^2 dx \right)^{1/2},$$

which is equivalent to minimizing

$$\int_a^b (f(x) - g(x))^2 dx,$$

which is, in essence, a sum (integral) of squares, similar to linear least squares in the sense of Section 2.6 and Section 8.1. (The L_2 norm is also called the **least squares** or **Euclidean norm.**) Least squares and minimax approximation are widely employed.

---

[3] We want the class of simple functions to be a subspace of a normed linear space that also includes f, and we use the distance induced by that norm.

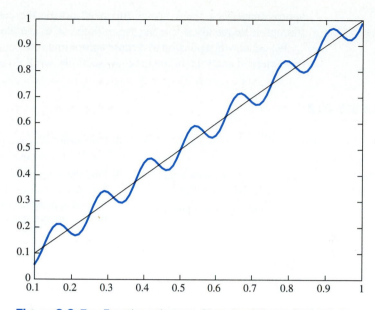

Figure 8.3 Two Functions that are Close but Whose Derivatives are not Close.

Another norm that is sometimes used is the **Sobolev r-norm,** which is defined (for sufficiently differentiable functions) by

$$\|f\|_{S,r} = \left(\int_a^b \left(f^2(x) + [f'(x)]^2 + [f''(x)]^2 + \cdots + [f^{(r-1)}(x)]^2 + [f^{(r)}(x)]^2 \right) dx \right)^{1/2}$$

for some integer $r \geq 1$. Note that two functions may be close in the L_∞ norm but far in the Sobolev r-norm if the functions remain close to one another but one wiggles, creating a large first derivative, while the other does not wiggle (see Fig. 8.3, where $|f'|$ is large for one function but not the other). If it is important not only that function values be close but also that the overall shape of the approximant be like that of the function being approximated, then it may be useful to consider using a Sobolev norm.

Note carefully that we are *approximating*, not *interpolating*. An approximant need never intersect the function it approximates (or, in a discrete case like linear or nonlinear least squares in the sense of Section 8.1, the data set it approximates); it need only be near the function, in the sense of some distance function.

The best approximation problem for a normed linear space $f \in V$ with approximants to be chosen from a subspace $W \subset V$ can be viewed as the problem of finding an **approximation operator** $P : V \to W$ such that if $f \in V$, then $Pf \in W$ is its best approximation (which we assume is unique). When working on the computer we may need to use an approximate approximation operator $\tilde{P}$.

Existence of Best Approximations   There is a theorem that states that, for reasonable choices of the class of "simple" functions and the norm defining the distance, a solution to the best approximation problem always exists. In the case of the L_2 norm the solution is also unique if the class of approximants is a linear space; this need not be the case for the L_1 and L_∞ norms (though it frequently is true in cases of interest, as we see in the next section).

We are now in a position to discuss approximation theory and apply it to the problems of numerical analysis. In the next few sections, we'll do just that.

PROBLEMS 8.2

1. Find the L_1, L_2, and L_∞ distances between $\sin(x)$ and $\cos(x)$ over $[0, \pi]$.

2. Find the L_1, L_2, and L_∞ distances between $\sin(x)$ and its Taylor series of orders 1, 3, and 5 over $[0, \pi]$.

3. Find the L_1, L_2, and L_∞ norms of $\exp(x)$ and x over $[0, 1]$.

4. Represent the approximate differentiation operators D_3 and D_4 (in the notation of this section) as matrices.

5. Find the element of P_3 that minimizes the L_2 distance between it and $\sin(x)$ on the interval $[0, 1]$ (that is, find the best approximation from P_3 for $\sin(x)$ on the interval $[0, 1]$ using the standard norm).

MATLAB 8.2

The MATLAB `norm` command finds the norms of vectors, not functions, so we must use the `int` or `quad` command to compute the L_1 and L_2 norms of functions. For example, enter:

```
» quad('abs(sin(x)-(x+x.^3))',0,pi)
```

to approximate the L_1 distance between $\sin(x)$ and $x + x^3$ over the interval $[0, \pi]$. Then enter:

```
» w=3;quad('abs(sin(x)-(x+x.^3/w))',0,pi)
» w=4;quad('abs(sin(x)-(x+x.^3/w))',0,pi)
» w=5;quad('abs(sin(x)-(x+x.^3/w))',0,pi)
» w=6;quad('abs(sin(x)-(x+x.^3/w))',0,pi)
```

The error is smallest when we use the Taylor polynomial $x + x^3/6$. This is not surprising, though it's far from clear that the Taylor polynomial is the polynomial that minimizes the L_1 norm. In general, it isn't.

Repeat the above command for several values of w (not necessarily an integer) and try to find the optimal value by trial and error. Plot $\sin(x)$, the Taylor polynomial $x + x^3/6$, and the best approximant you found by trial and error on a single graph. You could do even better by searching through the four-dimensional parameter space involving a, b, c, and d to find the best approximation of the form $ax^3 + bx^2 + cx + d$.

The best approximant of a function in one norm is not usually the best with respect to another norm. To see this, enter:

```
» sqrt(quad('(sin(x)-(x+x.^3/w)).^2',0,pi))
```

to find the L_2 distance between your best L_1 approximant of this form and the function. Then vary w until you find the best approximant with respect to the L_2 norm. Find its L_1 distance from the function.

ADDITIONAL PROBLEMS 8.2

6. Find the element of P_3 that minimizes the L_2 distance between it and $\sin(x)$ on the interval $[0, \pi]$ (that is, find the best approximation from P_3 for $\sin(x)$ on the interval $[0, 1]$ using the standard norm). Compare your answer for this problem with your answer for Problem 5.

7. Find the best approximation for $\exp(x)$ on $[0, 1]$ using linear combinations of 1, $\sin(x)$, and $\cos(x)$ and the L_2 norm.

8. Construct an example of two functions such that their difference over $[0, 1]$ has L_∞ norm less than a given $\epsilon > 0$ but Sobolev 1-norm greater than a given $\delta > 0$.

9. Compute the Sobolev 1-norm and the Sobolev 2-norm of the sine and cosine functions over $[0, \pi]$.

10. a. Find the best approximation for $\exp(x)$ on $[0, 1]$ from P_5 with respect to the L_2 norm. What is the distance of $\exp(x)$ from the approximant? What is the distance of $\exp(x)$ from its Taylor series of order 5?

    b. Repeat using the L_∞ norm.

    c. Repeat using the L_1 norm.

11. Show that the L_2 norm is a norm on the linear space $C[a, b]$ of all functions continuous on the finite interval $[a, b]$; that is, show that it satisfies the properties of positive definiteness, homogeneity ($\|\alpha f\| = |\alpha| \|f\|$ for all scalars α), and the triangle inequality (see Section 2.5).

12. Show that the L_1 norm is a norm on the linear space $C[a, b]$ of all functions continuous on the finite interval $[a, b]$.

13. Show that the L_∞ norm is a norm on the linear space $C[a, b]$ of all functions continuous on the finite interval $[a, b]$.

14. Show that the Sobolev r-norm is a norm on the linear space $C^r[a, b]$ of all functions r times continuously differentiable on the finite interval $[a, b]$.

15. Write a MATLAB program that uses `quad` to approximate the distance between two functions with respect to the L_1 or L_2 norms. Input the functions, the interval, and a flag variable indicating which norm is desired.

8.3 Best Uniform Approximation

We have treated least squares problems in Section 8.1, where we found a curve that in some sense approximates a data set, and again in Section 8.2, where we discussed finding a function that approximates another function in the least squares sense. These problems and the problem of approximating an operator in the least squares sense could be placed in one abstract setting for further mathematical study. The same could be done for approximation with respect to distances defined by other norms. This is useful for theoretical numerical analysis and approximation theory.

Minimax Approximation
    Let's look in more detail at minimax approximation, the best approximation problem with respect to the L_∞ norm. This is also called **best uniform approximation** when the space is (a subspace of) the space $C(I)$ of all continuous functions on some closed interval I. This is because the L_∞ norm

$$\|f\|_\infty = \max_{x \in I} |f(x)|$$

is also called the **uniform norm.** One reason that best uniform approximation is of interest is that a good L_∞ approximant is always a good L_1 and L_2 approximant, though the converse is not true in general. Let's prove this statement.

> **Theorem 8.3.1**
>
> Let f, g in $C(I)$ be given, where I is a closed interval of length L. Then
>
> $$\|f - g\|_1 \leq L^{1/2} \|f - g\|_2 \leq L \|f - g\|_\infty .$$

Proof.

Let $h = f - g$ and $I = [a, b]$. Then the Euclidean norm of h can be estimated by

$$\|h\|_2 = \left(\int_a^b h^2(\xi)d\xi \right)^{1/2}$$

$$\leq \left(\int_a^b \max_{x \in I}\{h^2(\xi)\}d\xi \right)^{1/2}$$

$$= \left(\int_a^b \left(\max_{x \in I}\{|h(\xi)|\} \right)^2 d\xi \right)^{1/2}$$

$$= \left(\int_a^b (\|h\|_\infty)^2 \, d\xi \right)^{1/2}$$

$$= \left(\|h\|_\infty^2 \int_a^b d\xi \right)^{1/2}$$

$$= \|h\|_\infty (b - a)^{1/2}$$

$$= L^{1/2} \|h\|_\infty$$

so that $L^{1/2} \|h\|_2 \leq L \|h\|_\infty$, which is the right-hand inequality. Let's look at the left-hand inequality. By definition,

$$\|h\|_1 = \int_a^b |h(\xi)| \, d\xi$$

$$= \int_a^b |h(\xi)| \cdot 1 d\xi$$

$$\leq \left(\int_a^b h^2(\xi) \, d\xi \right)^{1/2} \left(\int_a^b 1^2 d\xi \right)^{1/2}$$

where we have used the Cauchy-Schwarz Theorem. But this is just

$$\|h\|_1 \leq \|h\|_2 \|1\|_2$$

$$= (b - a)^{1/2} \|h\|_2$$

$$= L^{1/2} \|h\|_2$$

giving the desired result, $\|h\|_1 \leq L^{1/2} \|h\|_2 \leq L \|h\|_\infty$.   ■

Hence if the error $e_\infty = \| f - g \|_\infty$ in an approximation of f by g is small with respect to the uniform norm on a certain interval, then

$$e_1 \leq L e_\infty$$

$$e_2 \leq L^{1/2} e_\infty$$

so that the errors with respect to the L_1 and L_2 norms are at most a constant multiple of e_∞. As e_∞ is decreased, so are (the bounds on) e_1 and e_2, and hence as e_∞ goes to zero, so do e_1 and e_2. Perhaps surprisingly, it is not always the case that as $e_1 \to 0$ or $e_2 \to 0$, so does e_∞. This is one motivation for studying minimax approximation.

Recall that the least squares approximation problem always has a unique solution (if the class of approximants is a linear space). For the L_1 and L_∞ norms the best approximation problem always has a solution, but it need not be unique.[4]

Chebyshev Approximation

The best uniform approximation problem is also called the problem of **Chebyshev approximation** when the class of approximants is the space P_n of all polynomials of degree at most n. Typically when we perform best uniform approximation the approximants are either polynomials or rational functions. Splines and trigonometric polynomials are also used. Rational approximants generally give better results than polynomials, but for now we limit ourselves to polynomial approximants.

Let's consider then the problem of best approximation with respect to the uniform norm, using polynomials of degree at most n as our approximants. Why should we look at this problem? We will want to find polynomial approximations to special functions such as the error and gamma functions so that we can evaluate these approximations on a computer. The use of the uniform norm ensures that if we set an error tolerance—say, that evaluations of f must be accurate to within some given tolerance τ—then we can guarantee that the tolerance will be met by requiring that our approximation g satisfy

$$\max |f - g| \leq \tau$$

over the interval of interest. (This neglects the effects of roundoff error.) We know from Theorem 8.3.1 that if we have a good uniform approximation then we'll have a good L_1 and L_2 approximant as well.

Another use of best uniform approximation is to find a smooth approximation g to a discontinuous or nondifferentiable function f when we'd like to apply an algorithm to f that requires continuity or differentiability. If the approximation is good, we can use it in the algorithm in place of f. In this case we may also be concerned about how well g' approximates f' where f' exists (compare Hermite interpolation in Section 4.2).

Characterization of Chebyshev Approximation

Best uniform approximations have an interesting property: The existence of certain points at which the error is achieved with alternating signs. We state this as a theorem.

---

[4] In fact, if we use any Hölder p-norm with $1 < p < \infty$, then we will have a unique solution. Note that p need not be an integer.

> **Theorem 8.3.2 (Minimax Characterization Theorem)**
>
> If f is in $C[a, b]$ and p is a polynomial of degree n, then p is the unique best uniform approximation to f from polynomials of degree at most n if and only if there are distinct points $\xi_0, \xi_1, \ldots, \xi_{n+1}$ in $[a, b]$ such that the maximum error is achieved at each ξ_i, $i = 0, 1, \ldots, n + 1$ and the error alternates in sign at the ξ_i.

That is, if p is a Chebyshev approximation to f of degree n, then there are $n + 2$ points[5] ξ_i at which the worst-case error is actually achieved,

$$\|f - p\|_\infty = |f(\xi_i) - p(\xi_i)|, \tag{8.12}$$

and furthermore the errors

$$e_i = f(\xi_i) - p(\xi_i), \, e_{i+1} = f(\xi_{i+1}) - p(\xi_{i+1})$$

alternate in sign; that is,

$$f(\xi_i) - p(\xi_i) = -(f(\xi_{i+1}) - p(\xi_{i+1})) \tag{8.13}$$

(note that we allow the possibility of a zero error at some ξ_i). Furthermore, any polynomial of degree n that has $n + 2$ points satisfying Eq. (8.12) and Eq. (8.13) is necessarily a best uniform approximation to f. (We refer to Eq. (8.13) as the **alternating sign condition**.) The theorem also asserts that the Chebyshev approximation is unique.

Convergence of Chebyshev Approximation   How well do the Chebyshev approximations approximate the function for large n? Must they converge to the function being approximated in the limit? The answers are "very well (if f is sufficiently smooth)" and "Yes (if f is differentiable)." Again, we state this as a theorem.

> **Theorem 8.3.3 (Jackson's Theorem)[6]**
>
> If f is in $C^k[a, b]$ and p_n is the Chebyshev approximation of f of degree n, then
>
> $$\|f - p_n\|_\infty \leq \frac{c_k \| f^{(k)} \|_\infty}{n^k}$$
>
> for some constant c_k.

Note that c_k does not depend on the function f or on the degree n of the approximant, and so we have the result that $\|f - p_n\|_\infty$ is $O(n^{-k})$ as $n \to \infty$. In particular, the Chebyshev approximations converge to f as the degree n increases.

---

[5] Of course, if we attempt to approximate a linear function f by a polynomial of degree at most 10, then we'll get a degree 1 approximant with infinitely many points of intersection and hence zero error. We are focusing on the case where the polynomial approximant has maximal degree.

[6] This is only one of many closely related theorems that go by the name Jackson's Theorem.

Remes
Algorithm

We have some characterizations of best uniform approximations but not yet a way to find them. The best-known method for finding them is the **(second) Remes algorithm.** (*Remes* is sometimes spelled *Remez*.) The Remes algorithm is also known as the **exchange algorithm.**[7]

The Remes algorithm in outline is as follows. Let $f \in C[a, b]$ be the function to be approximated by approximants from P_n. (The elements of P_n are also called **test functions** or **trial functions** in this context.) Pick a set of $n + 2$ distinct points $\xi_0, \xi_1, \ldots, \xi_{n+1}$ such that

$$a \leq \xi_0 \leq \xi_1 \leq \cdots \leq \xi_{n+1} \leq b.$$

The set of points $\{\xi_i\}_{i=0}^{n+1}$ is called a **reference.** Next, find the element $p \in P_n$ that minimizes

$$\max_i\{|f(\xi_i) - p(\xi_i)|\} \tag{8.14}$$

and look at the error $e(x) = f(x) - p(x)$. If it's small, stop; otherwise, exchange points of the current reference with maxima of $e(x)$ to get a new reference, and repeat the process.

Remes Algorithm for Polynomial Approximation (Outline)

1. Pick an initial reference $\xi_0, \xi_1, \ldots, \xi_{n+1}$.

2. Find $p(x)$ that minimizes $\max_i\{|f(\xi_i) - p(\xi_i)|\}$.

3. If $\|f(x) - p(x)\|_\infty$ is small, stop.

4. Find one or more maxima of the error $e(x)$.

5. Exchange maxima with points of the reference to get a new reference.

6. Go to Step 2.

Typically we take $\xi_0 = a$ and $\xi_{n+1} = b$; if we can arrange for the initial reference to satisfy the alternating sign condition, so much the better. We need to fill in the details of Step 2 and Step 5. We'll also look at efficient ways to perform Step 3 and Step 4.

Let's start with Step 2, which calls for the minimization of Eq. (8.14) on the reference $\xi_0, \xi_1, \ldots, \xi_{n+1}$. It can be shown that $p(x)$ minimizes $\max_i\{|f(\xi_i) - p(\xi_i)|\}$, $i = 0, 1, \ldots, n + 1$ if and only if

$$f(\xi_i) - p(\xi_i) = -(f(\xi_{i+1}) - p(\xi_{i+1}))$$

for $i = 0, 1, \ldots, n$. (This is the alternating sign condition, Eq. (8.13).) Note that this p need not be the Chebyshev approximation of f since it minimizes the error at pre-selected points. A different reference might lead to a lower value of $\max_i\{|f(\xi_i) - p(\xi_i)|\}$; indeed, that is the very approach taken by the Remes algorithm: Keep changing the reference in hopes of lowering the value of $\max_i\{|f(\xi_i) - p(\xi_i)|\}$.

---

[7] This method is related to the exchange algorithm of linear programming.

It is convenient to set $h = f(\xi_0) - p(\xi_0)$. We call $\eta = |h|$ the **levelled reference error.** Then, using the standard basis for P_n, we have

$$p(x) = c_n x^n + \cdots + c_1 x + c_0,$$

and it follows from the alternating sign condition that

$$f(\xi_0) - (c_n \xi_0^n + \cdots + c_1 \xi_0 + c_0) = h$$
$$f(\xi_1) - (c_n \xi_1^n + \cdots + c_1 \xi_1 + c_0) = -h$$

$$\vdots$$

$$f(\xi_{n+1}) - (c_n \xi_{n+1}^n + \cdots + c_1 \xi_{n+1} + c_0) = (-1)^{n+1} h;$$

that is,

$$
\begin{aligned}
c_n \xi_0^n &+ \cdots + c_1 \xi_0 &+ c_0 &\quad\quad +h &= f(\xi_0) \\
c_n \xi_1^n &+ \cdots + c_1 \xi_1 &+ c_0 &\quad\quad -h &= f(\xi_1) \\
&\vdots \\
c_n \xi_{n+1}^n &+ \cdots + c_1 \xi_{n+1} &+ c_0 &\quad + (-1)^{n+1} h &= f(\xi_{n+1}),
\end{aligned}
\tag{8.15}
$$

giving $n + 2$ linear equations in the $n + 2$ unknowns $c_0, \ldots, c_n$ and h. This is essentially a Vandermonde system.

We now have a way to perform Step 2 by solving a linear system. It is a fact that the levelled reference error $\eta = |h|$ satisfies

$$\eta \leq \| f(x) - \pi(x) \|_\infty,$$

where $\pi(x)$ is the Chebyshev approximation of f that we are seeking, and that η is strictly increasing[8] as we proceed through the algorithm (though $\| f(x) - p(x) \|_\infty$ is not necessarily monotonically decreasing). Hence if

$$\big| \| f - p \|_\infty - \eta \big| \leq \tau, \tag{8.16}$$

then

$$\big| \| f - p \|_\infty - \| f(x) - \pi(x) \|_\infty \big| \leq \tau; \tag{8.17}$$

that is, the difference between the error in p as an approximation of f is within τ of the error in π as an approximation of f, and so we may accept p as our approximate Chebyshev approximation. This is a computable convergence criterion for Step 3 of the algorithm; we find a point x^* that maximizes

$$|e(x)| = |f(x) - p(x)| \tag{8.18}$$

and then $\| f - p \|_\infty$ is simply $|e(x^*)|$. We then test Eq. (8.16) against our tolerance τ.

How shall we find a maximum of $|e(x)|$ (Step 4)? Note that $e(x) = 0$ if x is a point in the reference. By continuity of f, there is at least one maximum or minimum of $e(x)$ between each pair of zeroes, and as p tends toward the Chebyshev approximation, these

---

[8] In fact, we could view the whole Remes algorithm as an attempt to maximize η in hope of making it as large as $\| f(x) - \pi(x) \|_\infty$.

maxima and minima should tend, by Theorem 8.3.1, to have the same absolute values, to be the only extrema between the adjacent zeroes, and to alternate between successive pairs of zeroes in the pattern minimum, maximum, minimum, etc. This gives us an easy way to find a bracket or to provide an initial guess to a minimization routine, and it implies that we expect well-behaved extrema if f is at least $C^2[a, b]$. If f is nondifferentiable, we will need an appropriate line search method. Overall Brent's method for minimization is a natural choice (see Section 7.1). This addresses Step 4 of the algorithm.

Standard Approach to Step 5

We still need a way to perform Step 5, the exchange. There are a number of ways to do this. The **standard version** of the Remes algorithm finds each of the n extrema of $e(x)$ by exhaustive search followed by a single quadratic interpolation to better localize the extrema (see Section 7.1). In doing this we are not finding the minima and maxima $x_1, \ldots, x_n$ of $e(x)$ to very great accuracy, because to do so would be very time-consuming. The replacement of points in the initial reference $\xi_0, \xi_1, \ldots, \xi_{n+1}$ by the extrema $\xi_1^{(1)}, \ldots, \xi_n^{(1)}$ of $e(x)$ gives a new reference

$$\xi_0, \xi_1^{(1)}, \cdots, \xi_n^{(1)}, \xi_{n+1}$$

for use in the next iteration. We arrange for the points in this new reference to be such that the alternating sign condition holds; this can be done because by Step 2 the approximant p satisfies a discrete version of a minimax approximation problem (over a discrete point set rather than the whole interval) and a discrete version of the Minimax Characterization Theorem states that there will be a set of points at which the maximum error is achieved and at which the alternating sign condition is satisfied (Eq. (8.12) and Eq. (8.13)). See Figure 8.4.

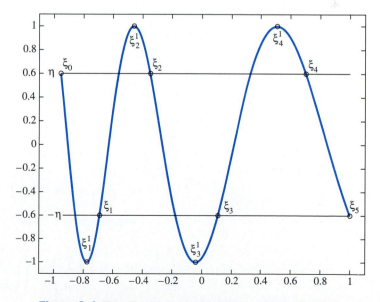

Figure 8.4 Error Function *e(x)* for Minimax Approximation.

We also arrange for the point x^* found for Eq. (8.18) to be one of the points $x_1, \ldots, x_n$. This ensures that the levelled reference error η will increase at the next iteration, as desired. If it were feasible to maximize $\eta(\xi_0, \xi_1, \ldots, \xi_{n+1})$ directly then we would do so; it is not, so we use this method. The point x^* that maximizes the error must be such that $e(x^*) > \eta$, but fortunately $e(x^*)$ typically exceeds y, as in Figure 8.4.

Alternate Approach to Step 5

Another approach to Step 5 is the **one-point exchange** version of the Remes algorithm, also known as the **one-point exchange algorithm.** This version exchanges a single point of the reference at each iteration of the algorithm. We take a single extremum of $e(x)$, say x^*, and exchange it with a point from the old reference, giving a new reference

$$\xi_0, \xi_1, \cdots, \xi_{i-1}, x^*, \xi_{i+1}, \cdots, \xi_{n+1} \tag{8.19}$$

for use in the next iteration. (Possibly x^* replaces ξ_0 or ξ_{n+1} in Eq. (8.19).) The goal is to arrange to have the alternating sign condition hold. Except possibly on the first iteration, if we choose a particular maximizer of $|e(x)|$, then there is only one way to exchange it with a point in the reference $\xi_0, \xi_1, \ldots, \xi_{n+1}$ so that the alternating sign condition holds. For example, if we choose $x^* = \xi_2^{(1)}$ in Figure 8.4, then we must exchange it with ξ_2 to maintain alternating signs of the error on the reference. The new reference would be

$$\xi_0, \xi_1, \xi_2^{(1)}, \xi_3, \xi_4, \xi_5$$

in this case. Any of the extrema of $e(x)$ may be used. Intuitively, it seems worthwhile to search for extrema in different areas of $[a, b]$ on different iterations so as to give each reference point a chance to be exchanged.

Example 8.3.1   Let's try to find the Chebyshev approximation of $f(x) = \ln(x)$ on $[1, 2]$ to within a tolerance of $5E - 4$, where the approximants are to be of the form $c_1 x + c_0$ (that is, the space of approximants is P_1). Since $n = 1$, we start with a reference consisting of $n + 2 = 3$ points. The obvious choice is $\xi_0 = 1, \xi_1 = 3/2, \xi_2 = 2$. (A better way to choose the initial reference is discussed in the next section.) We need to solve Eq. (8.15),

$$c_1 \xi_0 + c_0 + h = f(\xi_0)$$
$$c_1 \xi_1 + c_0 - h = f(\xi_1) \tag{8.20}$$
$$c_1 \xi_2 + c_0 + h = f(\xi_{n+1});$$

that is,

$$c_1 + c_0 + h = 0$$
$$c_1 \frac{3}{2} + c_0 - h = \ln\left(\frac{3}{2}\right)$$
$$2c_1 + c_0 + h = \ln(2)$$

$$\begin{pmatrix} 1 & 1 & 1 \\ 3/2 & 1 & -1 \\ 2 & 1 & 1 \end{pmatrix} \begin{pmatrix} c_0 \\ c_1 \\ h \end{pmatrix} = \begin{pmatrix} 0 \\ 0.4055 \\ 0.6931 \end{pmatrix} \tag{8.21}$$

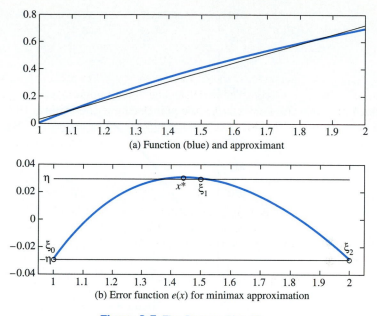

(a) Function (blue) and approximant

(b) Error function $e(x)$ for minimax approximation

Figure 8.5 The Remes Algorithm.

giving $c_1 \doteq 0.6931$, $c_0 \doteq -0.6637$, $h \doteq -0.0294$. The picture corresponding to Figure 8.4 for this case is Figure 8.5.

Note in the upper graph that the error is equal to the levelled reference error η at the reference points $\xi_0 = 1$, $\xi_1 = 1.5$, $\xi_2 = 2$, and that this fact is reflected in the lower graph as well. The maximum is at

$$e'(x) = 0$$

$$(\ln(x) - c_1 x + c_0)' = 0$$

$$\frac{1}{x} - c_1 = 0$$

$$x^* = \frac{1}{c_1}$$

$$\doteq 1.4427$$

(in practice we would use a numerical minimization method); see the detail in Figure 8.6. The convergence test of Eq. (8.16) gives

$$\mid \|f - p\|_\infty - \eta \mid = \mid e(x^*) - |h| \mid$$

$$\doteq .0303 - .0294$$

$$= 9E - 4.$$

This is larger than our desired tolerance $\tau = 5E - 4$, so we'll do the exchange and another iteration.

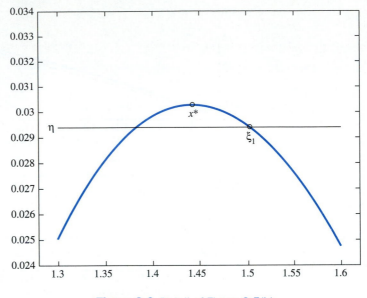

Figure 8.6 Detail of Figure 8.5(b).

The maximum error $e(x^*) \doteq .0303$ exceeds η, so we may use it to perform the exchange. The standard version and the one-point exchange versions are the same for this example; we have the new reference $\xi_0 = 1, \xi_1 = 1.4427, \xi_2 = 2$, and it is clear from the error plot in the lower graph of Figure 8.5 that the alternating sign condition is satisfied. We're now ready to start a new iteration of the algorithm.

For the second iteration, using the reference $\xi_0 = 1, \xi_1 = 1.4427, \xi_2 = 2$, Eq. (8.20) becomes

$$c_1 + c_0 + h = 0$$

$$1.4427c_1 + c_0 - h = \ln(1.4427) \qquad (8.22)$$

$$2c_1 + c_0 + h = \ln(2),$$

and note that only the middle row has changed. In performing the one-point exchange version of the algorithm, we would actually LU decompose the matrix in Eq. (8.21) and use an updating method to update the decomposition from iteration to iteration. (See the discussion of updating the QR decomposition in MATLAB 2.8.) The solution of Eq. (8.22) is $c_1 \doteq 0.6931, c_0 \doteq -0.6633, h \doteq -0.0298$. Note that, as expected, $\eta = 0.0298$ has increased. We have

$$x^* = \frac{1}{c_1}$$

$$\doteq 1.4427,$$

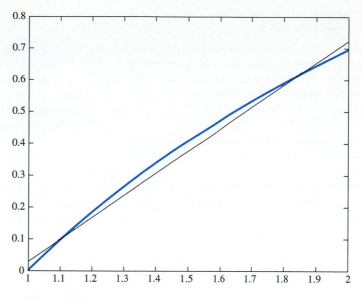

Figure 8.7 Function (blue) and Best Uniform Approximant.

and the convergence test gives

$$\big|\|f - p\|_\infty - \eta\big| = \big|e(x^*) - |h|\big|$$

$$\doteq .0303 - .0298$$

$$= 5E - 4,$$

which meets our convergence criterion. Hence,

$$p(x) = 0.6931x - 0.6633$$

is our (estimate of the) Chebyshev approximation. This is plotted in Figure 8.7. ■

Both versions of the Remes algorithm converge[9] for any choice of initial reference, though as always a good initial guess helps. The standard version converges quadratically, but we pay the price of having to find *all* the (well-separated and easily bracketed) extrema of a general function. For the one-point exchange version, if we consider every $n + 2$ iterations of the algorithm to be a mega-iteration, the convergence is quadratic with respect to those mega-iterations (and hence less than quadratic per actual iteration).

Rational Approximation   The Remes algorithm is actually an algorithm for finding the best uniform approximation to a function f from rational functions

$$R(x) = \frac{P(x)}{Q(x)},$$

where the degree of the numerator polynomials and of the denominator polynomial are fixed. The algorithm is essentially the same as given here, except that degenerate points can prevent convergence of the method.

---

[9] The convergence is with respect to the uniform norm, of course.

PROBLEMS 8.3

1. a. Use three iterations of the one-point exchange version of the Remes algorithm to approximate the best uniform approximant of $f(x) = \sin(x)$ on $[0, \pi]$ from P_1. Plot the function and the approximant on the same graph, and also plot the final error $e(x)$.

b. Repeat on $[0, \pi/2]$.

2. a. Use three iterations of the one-point exchange version of the Remes algorithm to approximate the best uniform approximant of $f(x) = \exp(x)$ on $[0, 1]$ from P_2. Plot the function and the approximant on the same graph, and also plot the final error $e(x)$.

b. Repeat on $[0, 2]$.

3. a. Show that Eq. (8.17) follows from Eq. (8.16).

b. Show that Eq. (8.17) may be rewritten as
$$\|f - p\|_\infty \le \|f(x) - \pi(x)\|_\infty + \tau.$$

4. a. Use three iterations of the standard version of the Remes algorithm to approximate the best uniform approximant of $f(x) = \sin(x)$ on $[0, \pi]$ from P_3. Plot the function and the approximant on the same graph, and also plot the final error $e(x)$.

b. Repeat on $[0, \pi/2]$.

5. Prove directly from the definition (that is, without using Theorem 8.3.2) that a Chebyshev approximation of a function in $C[a, b]$ from P_1 must have at least three points at which the error is maximal.

MATLAB 8.3

Methods for evaluating the standard special functions fall in several major categories, each of which has subcategories: Series expansions, approximation using rational functions, and special case formulas—things that just happen to work for that one function—are the most common. Numerical quadrature or numerical solution of an ODE and Monte Carlo simulation are methods of last resort for special functions.

In many cases we perform an argument reduction first: for example, to evaluate $\sin(x)$ we might relate it to a value of the sine function in $[0, \pi/2]$ and use a routine for evaluating sine in that interval. (This routine might be based on a best uniform approximation.) In a great many cases we use a transformation to simplify the problem or a relationship to another special function we have already approximated well.

As we have discussed previously, the gamma function $\Gamma(x)$ is implemented in MATLAB by the gamma command. Enter:

```
» doc gamma
```

and scroll down to the section labeled Algorithm. The gamma command uses one of several best uniform approximants depending on the argument ranges; the approximants are rational functions. These may be found by the more general form of the second Remes algorithm. Enter:

```
» more on
» type gamma
```

and look at the code for computing the gamma function.

It sometimes happens that a special routine is needed for a function related to a special function. Enter:

```
» help gammaln
```

This function computes $\ln(\Gamma(x))$ in a way that is often more accurate than using $\ln(\cdot)$

composed with $\Gamma(\cdot)$. Enter:

```
» exp(gammaln(50))-gamma(50)    %Should be equal.
» ans/gamma(50) %Relative error, if gamma(50) is accurate.
```

The absolute error is very large, though the relative error is small. Note that `gammaln` does not use `gamma`. Enter:

```
» type gammaln
```

to see the rational approximations used for approximating $g(x) = \ln(\Gamma(x))$ over various ranges of the argument. Enter:

```
» doc erf
```

and scroll down to the section labeled Algorithm. The error function and its variants are also computed by minimax or nearly minimax rational approximations; the inverse error function (`erfinv` in MATLAB) is found by a rational approximation, improved by a single step of a high-order root-finding algorithm (see Additional Problem 15 of Section 1.4). These functions are of great importance in statistics.[10]

Other cases that often require a special routine to get the desired accuracy are the functions $\exp(x) - 1$ and $\ln(x + 1)$, both for small x. Use of $\exp(\cdot)$ and $\ln(\cdot)$ may give poor results: for example, consider the severe cancellation of significant figures in computing $\exp(x) - 1$ for x very near zero. A rational approximation or series approximation may be used in each case.

ADDITIONAL PROBLEMS 8.3

6. a. Repeat Problem 1 part (a) using P_2.
   b. Repeat Problem 1 part (b) using P_2.

7. a. Repeat Problem 1 part (a) using P_3.
   b. Repeat Problem 1 part (b) using P_3.

8. a. Repeat Problem 2 part (a) using P_1 and then using P_3.
   b. Repeat Problem 2 part (b) using P_1 and then using P_3.

9. Repeat Problem 2 using the standard version of the Remes Algorithm for Polynomial Approximation.

10. Use the Remes Algorithm to find an approximation to $f(x) = \exp(x) - 1$ that is good to within a tolerance of 10^{-14} over $[-0.05, 0.05]$. Test your approximant, and plot it together with the function.

11. Use the Remes Algorithm for Polynomial Approximation to find an approximation to $f(x) = \Gamma(x)$ that is good to within a tolerance of 10^{-12} over $[1, 2]$. Test

your approximant, and plot it together with the function.

12. Write a MATLAB program that implements the one-point exchange version of the Remes Algorithm for Polynomial Approximation.

13. a. The **cyclic version** of the Remes algorithm is similar to the one-point exchange version but takes $\xi_0 = a$ and $\xi_{n+1} = b$ at every iteration, and on iteration 1 replaces ξ_1 with a nearby maximum of $|e(x)|$, then replaces ξ_2 with a nearby maximum on iteration 2, then replaces ξ_3 with a nearby maximum on iteration 3, and so on, cycling back to replacing ξ_1 every n iterations. This method converges for all initial references and further simplifies the maximization subproblem. Repeat Additional Problem 7 using this method, but cycle through all internal points of the reference at least three times.

---

[10] One of the most important early applications of computers was the creation of large, accurate tables of special functions for applications in statistics and engineering.

b. Repeat Additional Problem 8 using this method, but cycle through all internal points of the reference at least three times.

c. Write a MATLAB program that implements the cyclic version of the Remes Algorithm for Polynomial Approximation.

14. a. Write a MATLAB program that finds all extrema of the error $e(x)$ for Step 4 of the standard version of the Remes Algorithm for Polynomial Approximation. Make use of the known properties of $e(x)$.

b. Write a MATLAB program that implements the standard version of the Remes Algorithm for Polynomial Approximation.

15. Develop a version of the Remes algorithm that is appropriate for rational approximation.

8.4 Applications of the Chebyshev Polynomials

We shall address two principal questions in this section: How shall we choose an initial reference for the Remes Algorithm? Can we simplify the approximants found by that algorithm to make them more computationally efficient to use?

Chebyshev Polynomials

The answers to these questions (and many more) depend on the Chebyshev polynomials of the first kind $T_k(x)$. These were introduced in Section 5.4 where it is stated that in monic form they are

$$T_k(x) = \frac{1}{2^{k-1}} \cos(k \arccos(x))$$

$$= \frac{1}{2^{k-1}} \cos(k\theta) \tag{8.23}$$

(where $\theta = \arccos(x)$). Although it is not obvious, these are indeed polynomials in x; a recursion for computing them is given in Section 5.4. In this section we simply refer to the $T_k(x)$ as the *Chebyshev polynomials*[11] since the Chebyshev polynomials of the second kind don't figure into our discussion.

We begin by reviewing an issue discussed in Section 5.4 (and foreshadowed in MATLAB 4.1). The following theorem includes Theorem 5.4.1 and additional facts from that section.

Theorem 8.4.1

The Chebyshev polynomial of degree k, $T_k(x)$, satisfies

$$\max_{x \in [-1,1]} \{|T_k(x)|\} = \frac{1}{2^{k-1}}$$

and if $p_k(x)$ is any other monic polynomial of the same degree, then

$$\max_{x \in [-1,1]} \{|p_k(x)|\} > \max_{x \in [-1,1]} \{|T_k(x)|\};$$

that is, $T_k(x)$ has the strictly smallest L_∞ norm of all monic polynomials of degree k on $[-1, 1]$.

---

[11] The notation T_k derives from an alternative transliteration of *Chebyshev* as *Tschebyshev* (or variants of this).

What is the significance of this theorem? Consider again Theorem 4.1.1, which states that if $-1 \le x_0 < x_1 < \cdots < x_n \le 1$ are interpolation points for a function f in $C^{n+1}[-1, 1]$, then the polynomial interpolant $p(x)$ to f at these points satisfies

$$f(x) - p(x) = \frac{f^{(n+1)}(\xi(x))}{(n + 1)!} \varpi(x)$$

for any x, for some $\xi = \xi(x)$ in $(\min(x, -1), \max(x, 1))$. Here

$$\varpi(x) = (x - x_0)(x - x_1) \cdots (x - x_n). \tag{8.24}$$

What if we want our interpolant $p(x)$ to be the best possible interpolant? (Note that we have switched from the more general *approximation* to the more specific *interpolation* for now.) We cannot directly affect the factor

$$\frac{f^{(n+1)}(\xi)}{(n + 1)!}$$

in the error term; n is fixed and $\xi(x)$ is something we have no way of directly manipulating. But we *can* affect the size of the function in Eq. (8.24),

$$\varpi(x) = (x - x_0)(x - x_1) \cdots (x - x_n)$$
$$= x^{n+1} + \alpha_n x^n + \cdots + \alpha_1 x + \alpha_0,$$

by our choice of the nodes. Because this polynomial is monic, the L_∞ error bound is minimized by taking $\varpi(x) = T_{n+1}(x)$, giving

$$|f(x) - p(x)| = \left| \frac{f^{(n+1)}(\xi(x))}{(n + 1)!} \right| |T_{n+1}(x)|$$

or

$$|f(x) - p(x)|_\infty \le \frac{1}{2^n (n + 1)!} \left| f^{(n+1)}(\xi(x)) \right|_\infty \tag{8.25}$$

Chebyshev Nodes

(from Theorem 8.4.1). We get the best estimate of e_∞ for this interpolant by choosing our nodes to be the Chebyshev nodes (see Section 5.4 and MATLAB 4.1)

$$x_k = \cos\left(\frac{2k + 1}{2n + 2} \pi \right) \tag{8.26}$$

$(n \ge 1, k = 0, 1, \ldots, n)$ that are the zeroes of $T_{n+1}(x)$. This means that $\varpi(x)$ is $T_{n+1}(x)$, written in factored form (see Eq. (8.24)).

We emphasize that we have minimized the error *bound* here. Conceivably another set of points will give better results because it will happen to make $|f^{(n+1)}(\xi(x))|$ smaller. The variation of $|f^{(n+1)}(\xi(x))|$ is typically small, however, and as a rule, *if you decide to use polynomial interpolation and you may choose the nodes, you should choose them to be the Chebyshev nodes* (translated from $[-1, 1]$ to the interval of interest, as discussed in Section 5.3 for intervals of integration).

In previous sections we have frequently assumed that the nodes would be equally spaced because data is so often given in that form. Now we have a more complete explanation of why the Gaussian quadrature methods of Section 5.3 and Section 5.4 outperform the Newton-Cotes rules of Section 5.1 and Section 5.2: The Newton-Cotes

Uniform
Approximation

rules use equally spaced points for convenience, whereas the Gaussian rules use specially selected points (which in Section 5.4 are the Chebyshev nodes).

But that's interpolation; we want to discuss *approximation* in the uniform norm and in particular address the question of how to choose the initial reference for the Remes algorithm. Not surprisingly, the answer is that, unless we see an obviously good choice for the case at hand, we should probably use the Chebyshev nodes for the initial reference. It can be shown that if we use the Chebyshev nodes as the initial reference for Chebyshev approximation, where the space of approximants is P_n, and if the function to be approximated is in P_{n+1}, then convergence is obtained in a single step. Hence whenever f is well-approximated over the range of interest by a polynomial of degree at most $n + 1$, the Chebyshev nodes (Eq. (8.26)) make a good initial guess. A better initial guess would be the (approximate) location of the extrema of

$$e(x) = f(x) - \pi(x),$$

where $\pi(x)$ is the best uniform approximation of f from P_n, but in practice it is very unlikely that we would know what these are. Hence we typically use the Chebyshev nodes (mapped from $[-1, 1]$ to the interval of interest $[a, b]$) to start the Remes algorithm.

Now suppose that we have used the Remes algorithm to obtain a Chebyshev approximation of a function f over the interval $[-1, 1]$, say

$$p(x) = c_n x^n + \cdots + c_1 x + c_0. \tag{8.27}$$

Let $E = \|f - p\|_\infty$. Neglecting roundoff error, we can use $p(x)$ to evaluate $f(x)$ with a worst-case error of E, as MATLAB does for the gamma function, except that those approximants are actually rational, not polynomial. Rational approximations are generally more accurate, as we have mentioned previously, but they're harder to find and more expensive to compute.

Economization
of Power Series

Is there any way we can simplify or otherwise improve upon the approximation in Eq. (8.27)? Certainly we should evaluate it by Horner's method (see MATLAB 4.1) for reasons of efficiency and accuracy. But there is another possible simplification, using a technique known as **economization of power series.** Let's suppose that when we use Eq. (8.27) to approximate f that an error of no more than $\tau > E$ is desired. The current approximation obviously meets this criterion, with room to spare, since E is less than τ, and so it's natural to ask if a polynomial of lower degree, say

$$q(x) = \gamma_{n-1} x^{n-1} + \cdots + \gamma_1 x + \gamma_0,$$

might work. Even though it will have worst-case error $\|f - q\|_\infty \geq E$, it may still be that we can arrange to have $\|f - q\|_\infty \leq \tau$.

How shall we find q? We could apply the Remes algorithm again but now based on approximants from P_{n-1}. But Theorem 8.4.1 suggests another approach. Since $T_n(x)$ is the monic polynomial of degree n of least L_∞ norm, subtracting it from p should affect its norm relatively little; hence we consider the candidate $q(x)$ given by

$$q(x) = p(x) - c_n T_n(x) \tag{8.28}$$

and check its norm. If $\|f - q\|_\infty \leq \tau$, we can economize the power series from degree n to degree $n - 1$ and still meet our tolerance; otherwise the technique fails to produce an acceptable lower-degree approximant.

Nothing about the technique depends on the fact that the initial approximant was a best uniform approximant, so we may use it with any power series found by any method, such as Taylor series. However recall that a Taylor series is likely to be a good approximant only on a small interval about its center.

Example 8.4.1 Let's try to approximate $\sin(x)$ near $x = 0$ by its Maclaurin series to within a tolerance of $\tau = .005$. We'll take $[a, b] = [-1, 1]$ and use approximants from P_5. We have

$$\sin(x) \approx x - \frac{1}{6}x^3 + \frac{1}{120}x^5$$

and so we take the approximant to be

$$p(x) = x - \frac{1}{6}x^3 + \frac{1}{120}x^5.$$

Then

$$\|\sin(x) - p(x)\|_\infty = \max_{x \in [-.1,.1]} \left| \sin(x) - \left(x - \frac{1}{6}x^3 + \frac{1}{120}x^5 \right) \right|$$

which we may attempt to find by calculus or by a numerical method. Evaluating $f(x) - p(x)$ over a grid with spacing $h = 0.0001$ (see the MATLAB subsection) gives $E \approx 1.9568E - 4$. We'd like to eliminate the term in x^5 from $p(x)$. From MATLAB 5.4,

$$T_5(x) = x^5 - \frac{4}{5}x^3 + \frac{5}{16}x$$

($x \in [-1, 1]$), so from Eq. (8.28) we have

$$q(x) = p(x) - c_5 T_5(x)$$

$$= x - \frac{1}{6}x^3 + \frac{1}{120}x^5 - \frac{1}{120}\left(x^5 - \frac{4}{5}x^3 + \frac{5}{16}x \right)$$

$$= -\frac{4}{25}x^3 + \frac{383}{384}x$$

for which $\|\sin(x) - q(x)\|_\infty \approx .0041$. We may use $q(x)$ in place of $p(x)$; although the worst-case error for $p(x)$ is about 20 times smaller than that for $q(x)$, $q(x)$ still falls within our tolerance and saves us two additional multiplications by x (to compute x^5 from x^3), the multiplication by the coefficient $1/120$ of the x^5 term and the addition of the term $x^5/120$ into the sum. If we were using $p(x)$ or $q(x)$ to implement $\sin(x)$ on a computer or a calculator this savings might well be worthwhile since these functions are called so often and it is desirable to have them be fast as well as accurate. ∎

In Example 8.4.1 we actually reduced the degree by two since all functions were odd. In general if we successfully reduce $p(x)$ of degree n to $q(x)$ of degree $n - 1$, then we can try again, attempting to reduce $q(x)$ by a degree, and so on.

The question of how to approximate special functions such as sine, cosine, and the exponential to be able to compute them is a *design* issue faced by engineers and computer scientists who design computers, calculators, and compilers. Different machines and different languages require different approximants to meet their particular needs.

PROBLEMS 8.4

1. Find a linear formula for mapping the Chebyshev nodes to an arbitrary interval $[a, b]$.

2. **a.** Use economization of power series to reduce the degree of the polynomial $p(x) = \frac{1}{4}x^5 - \frac{1}{3}x^4 + \frac{1}{5}x^3 + \frac{1}{4}x^2 - \frac{1}{3}x + \frac{1}{6}$ by 1. Compare the norm of the polynomial before and after.

   b. Reduce the polynomial by 1 additional degree.

3. **a.** Use the Remes algorithm with the Chebyshev nodes for the initial reference to approximate the Chebyshev approximation of $\exp(x)$ over $[-1, 1]$ using P_5. What is the maximum error in this approximant?

   b. Use economization of power series to reduce the degree of this approximant by 1.

4. Use interpolation at 11 equally spaced nodes to interpolate the Runge function (see Section 4.1). Then repeat using Chebyshev nodes (the zeroes of $T_{11}(x)$). Compare your interpolants.

5. In the discussion of polynomial interpolation it is stated that $|f^{(n+1)}(\xi(x))|$ typically varies slowly. Perform a numerical experiment to see if this is so. Is there an analytical reason to believe this as well?

MATLAB 8.4

Chebyshev polynomials have many more applications in both theoretical and applied numerical analysis than we have indicated. We have seen them in polynomial interpolation (Section 4.1), Gaussian quadrature (Section 5.4), and now the Remes algorithm and economization of power series. They are a crucial tool in approximation theory.

Let's consider Example 8.4.1 in MATLAB. First, if you have the Symbolic Toolbox, enter:

```
» syms x;taylor(sin(x))
```

to compute the familiar Maclaurin series of order 5 for $\sin(x)$. (If you do not have the Symbolic Toolbox, enter the formula by hand.) To estimate $\|\sin(x) - p(x)\|_\infty$, enter:

```
» grd=-1:.0001:1;z=subs(ans,grd);E=max(abs(sin(grd)-z))
```

(See also the `sym2poly` command.) To estimate $\|\sin(x) - q(x)\|_\infty$, enter:

```
» w=((-4/25)*grd.^3+(383/384)*grd);
» E2=max(abs(sin(grd)-w))
```

Note that this is better than using the Maclaurin series of order 3; enter:

```
» syms x; taylor(sin(x),4)    %Four terms so third order.
» max(abs(sin(grd)-subs(ans,grd)))
```

The error here is twice that of the economized power series. Again, Taylor series generally make poor approximants.

Let's plot the function $\sin(x)$ and the two approximants we have found. Enter:

```
» plot(grd,[sin(grd);z;w])
```

The differences are hard to see. Enter:

```
» grd2=grd(1:1000);
» plot(grd2,sin(grd2),'b',grd2,z(1:1000),'r',grd2,
  w(1:1000),'y')
```

It's clear that the cubic approximant is worse than the quintic approximant in this range. Enter:

```
» grd3=grd(10001:11000);
» plot(grd3,sin(grd3),'b',grd3,z(1:1000),'r',grd3,
  w(1:1000),'y')
```

Now the yellow cubic curve is below the sine function, showing the alternating property of the (approximate) approximants.

Let's plot the first five Chebyshev polynomials (as we did in MATLAB 5.4). Enter:

```
» x=-1:.01:1;T0=ones(size(x));
» T1=x;
» T2=x.^2-.5;
» T3=x.^3-.75*x;
» T4=x.^4-x.^2+1/8;
» T5=x.^5-.8*x.^3+(5/16)*x;
» plot(x,[T0;T1;T2;T3;T4;T5]),grid
```

(Additional Chebyshev polynomials may be found using the recurrence relation $T_{k+1}(x) = xT_k(x) - \frac{1}{4}T_{k-1}(x)$; see Section 5.4.) Inspect the plot in light of Theorem 8.4.1. Experiment; try to make a monic polynomial of degree 5 with smaller maximum value. To do so, enter:

```
» plot(x,T5),grid,hold on
```

and plot any other monic quintic on the same plot. Of course, by Theorem 8.4.1 no other monic polynomial of degree 5 can have a maximum as small as that of T_5 on $[-1, 1]$.

ADDITIONAL PROBLEMS 8.4

6. Is it feasible to use a look-up table rather than an approximation to evaluate the sine function on a calculator or computer? Why or why not? Justify your answer.

7. a. Repeat Additional Problem 7 of Section 8.3 using the Chebyshev nodes as your initial reference.
   b. Repeat using P_5.

8. Write a MATLAB program that interpolates a given function at n points, where n is supplied by the user. The points should either be equally spaced or the Chebyshev nodes depending on a flag supplied by the user.

9. Plot the Chebyshev nodes for $k = 1, 2, 3, 4, 5$ on a single plot. (Use different colors for the different sets.)

What properties do these sets appear to possess? What can you say about the apparent relationship, if any, between the nodes for $T_k(x)$ and the nodes for $T_{k+1}(x)$?

10. a. Use the Remes algorithm with the Chebyshev nodes for the initial reference to approximate the Chebyshev approximation of $\sqrt{x}$ over $[1, 2]$ using P_{10}. What is the maximum error in this approximant?
   b. Use economization of power series to reduce the degree of this approximant while maintaining a worst-case error of 10^{-4}.

11. a. Find and classify the extrema of $T_k(x)$.

b. Repeat Additional Problem 10 using the extrema of an appropriate Chebyshev function. Discuss your results in the context of the practical Clenshaw-Curtis formulas discussed at the end of Section 5.4.

12. Show that $T_k(x)$ as defined in Eq. (8.23) is a monic polynomial of precise degree k and that its L_∞ norm is $2^{-(k-1)}$.

13. Perform a numerical experiment to compare polynomial interpolation with equally spaced nodes and with Chebyshev nodes. How helpful is it to use the Chebyshev nodes?

14. Use the triangle inequality to show that economization of power series will be successful if $|c_n| \leq \tau - E$ in the notation of this section. What will be the bound on $\|f - q\|$ in this case?

15. Write a pair of MATLAB programs: one that computes the Chebyshev approximation to a function using the one-point exchange version of the Remes algorithm with the Chebyshev nodes as initial guess, and another that uses the coefficients produced by the first program to compute values of the approximant. The user should supply the desired degree of the approximant. Test your programs.

Afterword

THE PURPOSE OF COMPUTING IS INSIGHT, NOT NUMBERS. R. W. Hamming[1]

I consider *numerical analysis* to be the side of the subject that uses (functional) analysis to do things like develop series representations that can be truncated to give a method (e.g., Newton's method), that uses the calculus to estimate the error in polynomial interpolation, that uses perturbation theory to perform a backwards error analysis, that uses the Fixed Point Theorem to estimate how rapidly a method converges, and so on. Numerical analysis is the set of formal mathematical techniques used to develop and analyze the methods, including roundoff error analysis.

I consider *scientific computation* to be the side of the subject that addresses how to choose the software and method, how to piece together a larger program from smaller available programs, how to make smart use of available hardware including advanced architectures, what the effects of the particular implementation of floating point arithmetic are, how best to code an algorithm for maximum efficiency, and how to guard against underflow, overflow, unrealistically small tolerances, and such. Scientific computation is also the art of choosing good initial guesses and good parameters, like the relaxation parameter ϖ in SOR or damping sequences in Newton's method. It's the side of the subject that "thinks computationally"[2] and makes the methods and software work in the difficult cases that occur so often. Master's degree programs in Computational Science are growing as people realize the need for professionals who know how to make effective use of the software that is already out there (like MATLAB, Netlib, and many specialized packages).

Throughout the text, we've seen lots of tricks and tips. At this point, given an equation to be used in a program, you should be looking for the presence of possible subtraction

---

[1] "Numerical Methods for Scientists and Engineers" (2nd ed.), Dover Pub., by Richard W. Hamming

[2] Paraphrasing W. Feller's comments about probability having two hands, one that knows about measure theory, convergence, and such, and one that "thinks probabilistically."

of nearly equal quantities or division by small numbers; for addition of small positive numbers first, to be added to larger ones later; for quantities of widely varying magnitudes; and for inefficiencies such as inverting a matrix when a solution of a linear system will suffice.

You should be looking for opportunities to reuse already computed quantities if they're at all expensive to compute the first time; for ways to rewrite the equation for improved memory usage; and for the possibility that a quantity might be approximated by some other, simpler method and give results just as good. You should be asking how the equation was derived and then checking to see whether a previous incarnation of the equation lends itself to more efficient or more accurate computation, possibly because another version was better-conditioned.

You should consider rewriting the equation to remove or at least separate out singularities, oscillatory terms, or other problems, and to center and rescale if appropriate. A change of variable or two can often make a numerical quadrature problem much easier to solve more accurately; splitting it into the sum of two integrals may allow you to choose a better method for each part than could possibly be selected for it as a single integral. One of those methods may well be symbolic rather than numerical. You should consider other forms of preprocessing the problem, such as preconditioning for linear systems, setting tiny quantities to zero or neglecting small terms, reordering terms or rows, adding automatic differentiation, and so on.

You should look for special properties of the problem. Is the matrix symmetric? Is the function being interpolated even or odd? This will help you choose the proper method and improve efficiency. In some truly special cases you may be able to find a symbolic answer. This may or may not be more efficient to use but is surely worth considering.

You should look for tolerances that have been set to unrealistically small values and other instances of overcomputing. A realistic tolerance should be set and the program should compute to that tolerance, not many orders of magnitude smaller (at much greater computational expense). Interval methods should be used if a guarantee is absolutely necessary but will generally be more expensive when it isn't needed–and usually it isn't.

You should be asking whether it's necessary to code a method yourself–which people often believe to be the case–or whether standard software will work. Using standard software is usually the better choice. If possible you should use standard, tested software and simply write a calling program for it. If you must code an algorithm yourself, always work through an example of the use of the algorithm *by hand* first. If you want to develop it rapidly or to test an idea (prototyping), a language like MATLAB is good; if you'll use the method every day, you should eventually recode it in Fortran or C++ or a similar language, making use of resources like Netlib.[3] Of course, often your employer or the need to interact with other programs will limit your software choices.

You should look for methods that are robust, either by the nature of the algorithm (e.g., Gaussian elimination with complete pivoting, or realistically Gaussian elimination with partial pivoting) or because they mix methods in an intelligent way (Newton's method for minimization mixed with the method of steepest descent) or attempt to correct for errors (reorthogonalization of the modified Gram-Schmidt orthogonalization algorithm). You should consider the underlying physics of the problem as you seek a good initial guess.

---

[3] If you work in C++, you should pretend you are working in C. Many object-oriented approaches are very slow for numerical work.

You should be asking how the answers will be used and what is *really* needed from the computation. Time and time again someone will ask for the inverse of a matrix when all that is needed is the solution of a linear system; for an interpolating polynomial when all that is needed is its values at some point; for the solution of an ODE at a sequence of points when all that is needed is the limiting, steady-state value. A common complaint is that least squares curve-fitting couldn't possibly work on *this* data set and so some more complicated method is needed; in almost all such cases, least squares curve-fitting will work just fine because it is so very robust.

This is an extremely important point in practice: If you are helping other people perform a computation, it will be necessary to quiz them at length to find out what they *really* need as opposed to what they *think* they need. In fact, once this has been done, the solution will often suggest itself—the type of method to be used will be obvious. For example, if someone has a linear system to solve that has a small to medium-sized matrix, in most cases there's little reason to consider anything other than Gaussian elimination with partial pivoting. If the matrix has special characteristics, such as being positive definite or tridiagonal, there may be a better, more specialized, approach. Once you've determined that the solution of $Ax = b$ is what's really needed and that the matrix is not too large and not too ill-conditioned, the method is obvious. In other areas, such as nonlinear optimization, there is a greater choice of plausible methods, but even then a proper understanding of the problem will help you narrow the choices down to a manageable number. Then choosing to use software that is already available will likely narrow your choices much further.

Experimentation is frequently needed. If one method doesn't work, try another! Vary the initial guesses. Plot the function or at least sample it pseudo-randomly. Mix methods, add damping, change parameters. Can you solve for the error, approximately, and subtract it out of your solution? Try your software on a simpler problem with a known solution.

If the method does appear to work, try to check your answers. Check residuals or other notions of error. Plot the answer and check it for plausibility. Once again, try your software on a simpler problem with a known solution.

For the most part, the software is already written. How you use it is up to you. You now have the tools to use it intelligently. Don't forget to apply those tools to the problem at hand!

What about Richard Hamming's famous quotation: "The purpose of computing is insight, not numbers." This is by far the most important thing that has ever been said about computing.[4] If we compute in the hope of generating numbers, our expectation will surely be met.

But that is not what we usually do. In most cases we want to *know* something. We want to know how the temperature of a metal plate at some point varies with its thermal conductivity when that parameter is not a constant over the plate. Often we don't want the numerical value of the temperature as much as we want an *understanding* of how it is affected by a change in the parameter—Does it increase quickly for a small change in the parameter, does it decrease slowly, or is it relatively insensitive to changes in the parameter, at least in some range?

---

[4] In second place is Edsger Dijkstra's comment on the perils of using a poor programming language: "The use of COBOL dulls the mind, and therefore its teaching should be banned as a criminal offense."

Even when we do something as simple as plot a function, what we want to know is often something qualitative, not quantitative: Does it appear to be continuous? Smooth? Slowly varying? Everywhere positive? We want *insight* into the function's nature and an ability to visualize it more than its numerical value at a particular point.

Much of the underlying analysis in numerical analysis relates to perturbation theory. Stability with respect to roundoff or representation errors can just as easily be considered stability with respect to other types of uncertainties. Numerical investigations of the stability of a response when the conditions are varied is of great interest in gaining insight and understanding.

When a computer model of an airplane is tested in a numerical wind tunnel, the big issue is how well it flies, not the value of the wind shear at a certain point. Those things matter too, but the big picture, how well the airplane performs, is the first issue–and its performance gives feedback to the engineers concerning the overall design. Later, specific numerical values will be compared to known tolerances—after insight, a physical "feel" for the design, has been gained.

When you're performing a computation, or better yet when you're *preparing* to perform a computation, consider what you want from that computation. Is it really just a numerical value? Or is it a more general sort of knowledge or intuition? Are you hoping to answer a crisp, quantitative question or to experiment to gain an understanding of something? Either way, be sure that the computation you are about to perform will give you what you need!

Good luck!

Answers

CHAPTER 1

Problems 1.1

1. For bisection, the brackets are $[.5, 1]$; $[.5, .75]$; $[.625, .75]$; $[.6875, .75]$; $[.71875, .75]$. The best estimate is the midpoint $.734375$ of the final bracket. For inverse linear interpolation, the brackets are (retaining only four decimal digits each time) $[.5, 1]$; $[.7255, 1]$; $[.7384, 1]$; $[.7391, 1]$; $[.7391, 1]$. The best estimate is $.7391$; $f(.7391) \doteq 2.8842E - 6$.

2. Note that $f(x) = 5x^7$ is monotonically increasing and takes on all real values and $g(x) = 1 - 2x$ is monotonically decreasing and takes on all real values so there is one and only one point of intersection.

4. The solution is 2.2361.

5. The solution is $.464$.

7. Bisection halves the width each time. To reduce the initial width of 2 to 10^{-4} means reducing it m times where $2/2^m = 10^{-4}$. Hence $m = 1 - \log_2(10^{-4}) \doteq 14.3$. We estimate 15 iterations.

8. We estimate 15 iterations (see the solution for Problem 7). For inverse linear interpolation, the brackets are, to four decimal digits, $[0, 2]$; $[0, 1.2963]$; $[.7562, 1.2963]$; $[.7562, .8194]$; $[.7562, .8078]$; and $.8078$ is correct to four decimal places. Only four iterations were actually needed.

11. c) The roots of $x^3 - 3x^2 + 3x - 1 = 0$ are 1, 1, 1.

13. There are countably many isolated zeroes in $(0, 1)$. The origin is not an isolated zero.

14. a) The solution is $v(t) = v_0/(1 + kv_0t)$.

    b) The solution is $x(t) = x_0 + \ln(1 + kv_0t)/k$.

    c) Solve $37 = 10 + \ln(1 + 30k)/k$, that is, $0 = -27 + \ln(1 + 30k)/k$, for k using bisection or false position.

Problems 1.2

1. The solution is .7391.
2. The solution is .4844.
4. The solution is 2.2361. For $f(x) = x^2$ the convergence to the root at the origin is very slow; in fact, it is not hard to show that $x_k = (1/2)^k x_0$.
5. The solution is .464.
9. Use $f(x) = \exp(-x)$ or $f(x) = 1/x$.
10. There is no root but Newton's method continues to search for one in the neighborhood of the minimum.
14. **a)** Write this as $dP/[P(M - P)] = k dt$, then $(1/M)(1/P + 1/(M - P)) dP = k dt$ using partial fractions, then integrate both sides to find $\ln(P/(M - P)) = kMt + C$ (using $0 \leq P(t) \leq M$ to simplify the absolute values in the logarithms).
    b) Solve $P(t) - M P_0/(P_0 + (M - P_0) \exp(-kMt)) = 0$ for M using Newton's method, with $t = 1$, $P(1) = 347$, $k = 2.1$, and $P_0 = 100$.

Problems 1.3

1. **a)** If $f(x) = x^2 - 2$ then $N_f(x) = x - (x^2 - 2)/2x = x - x/2 + 1/x = x/2 + 1/x = \frac{1}{2}(x + \frac{2}{x})$.
    b) The solution is 1.41421356.
2. The solution is 0.6412.
3. In the first case, the derivative exceeds unity (in absolute value) at the fixed point; in the second case it is less than unity (in absolute value).
4. **a)** If $x_0 \gg 1/a$ the method diverges.
6. **b)** The solution is .7391.
    c) The solution is .7391.
8. Although the method takes a long time to converge, it is rapid at the very end when it is sufficiently close to the root—which is all that is promised by the theorem.
13. **b)** For example, use a Taylor's series of $\sqrt{x}$ or a related function to get the initial guess.
14. **a)** Write $f(\gamma) = v^2 - [(\gamma - 3)^2 + 6]/[3(\gamma - 2)^2]$. Then $N_f(\gamma) = \gamma - f(\gamma)/f'(\gamma)$.
    b) For $v^2 = 2$, $\gamma = 3$ is a solution.
    c) Yes, write $v^2 = [(\gamma - 3)^2 + 6]/[3(\gamma - 2)^2]$ as $3(\gamma - 2)^2 v^2 = (\gamma - 3)^2 + 6$ then expand the factors in $\gamma - 2$ and $\gamma - 3$. Then use the cubic formula.

Problems 1.4

1. Hint: Write $p = 1 + \epsilon$ and write the limit as a product of two limits, one of which is the limit that must exist in the case of linear convergence.
2. For $p = 1$: .5000 .2500 .1250 .0625 .0313 .0156.
    For $p = 2$: .5000 .1250 .0078 .0000 .0000 .0000.
    For $p = 3$: .5000 .0625 .0001 .0000 .0000 .0000.
    The final entries are, respectively, .0156, $1.0842E - 19$, and $2.6612E - 110$. An order 3 method converges much more rapidly than an order 2 method.
7. Assume $p = 2$ and show directly that this limit must exist.
9. **a)** Use Taylor's series.
    b) Use the result of part a.
10. Consider $\lim_{k \to \infty} |1/(k + 1) - 0| / |1/k - 0|$.

12. **a)** Expand $\cos(x)$ in a Maclaurin series and use it with $x = 1/n$.
   b) The rate is $O(1/n^3)$ but the order is $p = 1$; in fact, since $M = 1$ there is no order, strictly speaking. (It is sublinear—see Problem 10.)
14. **a)** We have $(dy/dt)/(dx/dt) = dy/dx$ by the chain rule; but this also equals $-bx/ay$. Separation of variables gives the Lanchester square-law model.
   b) We have $y' = -bx$ so $y'' = -bx' = -b(-ay)$. Solve this second-order ODE for $y(t)$. Similarly for $x(t) = x_0 \cosh(\sqrt{abt}) - y_0\sqrt{a/b}\sinh(\sqrt{abt})$.
   c) Solve for the time $t > 0$ such that $x(t) - y(t) = 0$.

Problems 1.5

2. The secant method gains about 60% more digits of accuracy each iteration; Newton's method gains 100% more each iteration. To go from one digit of accuracy to sixteen digits takes about four iterations for Newton's method and about six iterations for the secant method. Hence it makes sense to switch to the secant method when function evaluations are so expensive that the two of them required for the finite difference Newton's method make four iterations of it take as long as six iterations of the secant method, which only uses one new function evaluation each time.

4. The value of c that gives superlinear convergence is $f'(x^*)$ where x^* is the root.

6. **a)** If $f(x) = 1/x - 10$ then $N_f(x) = x - (1/x - 10)/(-1/x^2) = 2x - 10x^2$. With $x_0 = 10$ we have $x_1 = -980$ and clearly $x_k \to -\infty$.

10. **a)** To get guarantees for Newton's method we still need to find a region with certain properties–similar to finding a bracket.
   b) Inverse linear interpolation, like Newton's method, can be misled, but bisection *always* gives a factor of two improvement.

12. The solution is 2.1544. Use the slope $f'(\sqrt[3]{10})$.

13. **a)** One solution is 1.446748.
   b) One solution is .464159.

Problems 1.6

3. **b)** The value is 1.8393.
5. To three decimal places, there is a zero at .464.
6. There is a root at .9579.
7. There is a root at .4516.
8. Note the severe cancellation in the expression for $g(x)$ due to the subtraction of nearly equal quantities.
9. **a)** Use the fact that $y_i = mx_i + b$ for some m, b in this case.
   b) Write the system as a system of two equations in two unknowns. Solve one equation for β in terms of α, and use it in the other equation to get an equation in α alone. Solve it for α, then find β.

Problems 1.7

1. **a)** Compute $x_4 = x_3 + x_2$ and $x_5 = x_4 + x_3$ by addition as indicated, and simplify.
2. **a)** We have $e \doteq 2.71828$, $\pi \doteq 3.14159$, and $e/\pi \doteq .865256$, $\pi/e \doteq 1.15573$.
3. The result is $1E - 5$ rather than zero. This is the smallest a number could differ from .66666 in this system and is not an unacceptable error.

4. It is advisable to compute sums of positive numbers by adding the smallest numbers first, else their contributions might be lost due to the size of the partial sums.

6. Take $r_2 = (-b - \sqrt{b^2 - 4ac})/2a$ and multiply by $(-b + \sqrt{b^2 - 4ac})/(-b + \sqrt{b^2 - 4ac})$ then simplify.

7. Since $|f(x) - f(y)| = f'(\theta)\,|x - y|$, if x is the true value at which we seek an f value and y is the nearby point at which f is actually evaluated then we expect a large absolute error $|f(x) - f(y)|$ where the derivative is large in absolute value and a small error where it is small in absolute value.

Problems 1.8

2. a) One solution is the origin.

3. We have $x_{k+1} = x_k - A^{-1}(Ax_k - b) = A^{-1}b$. This is correct but not necessarily helpful.

4. The Jacobian would have $20^2 = 400$ independent entries.

5. The appropriate notion of slope or secant is not clear in this context.

7. All that needs to be shown is that the Jacobian is the ordinary derivative in this case.

8. The derivatives will all be linear if the circles are represented in the form
$(x - a)^2 + (y - b)^2 = r^2$.

Problems 1.9

3. The solution is $x = 0$, $y = -1$.

5. Note that every row of uv^T is a multiple of v^T and so $\operatorname{rank}(uv^T) = 1$ unless $v = 0$ or $u = 0$.

6. A solution is $(9.0609, -4.2308)$.

10. One solution is the origin.

12. The method performs well even if the initial Jacobian is inaccurate.

13. One solution is $(0, 1, 1)$.

15. The formula is $(A + UV^T) = A^{-1} - A^{-1}U(1 + V^T A^{-1}U)^{-1}V^T A^{-1}$.

CHAPTER 2

Problems 2.1

1. a) The answer is $(-1, 1, 0)^T$.

   b) The answer is $(-10, 15, -6)^T$.

   c) Note that A is singular. The solution is $(-1 + \alpha, 1 - 2\alpha, \alpha)^T$ for any α.

4. a) The answer is $(0.00, 1.00)^T$.

   b) The answer is $(1.00, 1.00)^T$.

   c) After scaling, the answer is $(5.00, .995)^T$.

7. a) The answer is $(-1500, -14)^T$. Your answer may vary depending on your version of MATLAB.

   b) The absolute error is about $1E - 12$.

8. a) The answer is $(0.00, 1.00)^T$.

   b) The answer is $(1.00, 1.00)^T$.

9. b) The solution is $(.0263, -.1316, -.1228, .0088)^T$.

10. For $N = 10, 11, 12$ the condition numbers are on the order of $10^{13}, 10^{14}, 10^{16}$ respectively.

14. a) Solve $mr^2 + cr + k = 0$ with the given values to find $\alpha \doteq -2.5000E - 2$ and $\beta \doteq 6.3245$. Then set $x_0 = x(0)$ and $v_0 = x'(0)$ to get two equations in the two unknowns

A and B. For the second part, set $x(1)$ and $x'(1)$ from the formula for $x(t)$ equal to the given values.

b) Same as part a.

Problems 2.2

1. a) The determinant is 24.

   b) We have $|L| = 1$, $|U| = 24$.

6. a) We have $L = [1, .5, -.25; 0, 1, .25; 0, 0, 1]'$, $U = [4, 0, 0; 5, 1, 0; 6, -2, 4]'$.

   b) In MATLAB form, $[4, .5, -.25; 5, 1, .25; 6, -2, 4]'$.

   c) The solution is $(-1, 2, 1)^T$.

8. The matrix is $[1, 2, 1; -.2, .6, -.2; .4, .3, 1.4]$.

9. The matrix is $[5, -2.5, 1.5; -1, 2.5, .7; 3, -.5, 5.4]'$.

11. a) Use the determinant.

   b) Use the fact that the determinant of a triangular matrix is the product of its diagonal entries.

   c) Use the formula $(AB)^{-1} = B^{-1}A^{-1}$ if A and B are nonsingular.

   d) Use the formula $(AB)^T = B^T A^T$.

   e) Only if they are diagonal, which would make $L = I$.

12. a) The decomposition is $L = [1, 0, 0, 0; 1/2, 1, 0, 0; 0, 2/3, 1, 0; 0, 0, 3/4, 1]$, $U = [2, 1, 0, 0; 0, 3/2, 1, 0; 0, 0, 4/3, 1; 0, 0, 0, 5/4]$.

   b) The decomposition is $L = [1, 0, 0, 0; -1/2, 1, 0, 0; 0, -2/3, 1, 0; 0, 0, -3/4, 1]$, $U = [2, -1, 0, 0; 0, 3/2, -1, 0; 0, 0, 4/3, -1; 0, 0, 0, 5/4]$.

Problems 2.3

3. Apply the formula $c_{ij} = \sum_{k=1}^{n} a_{ik}b_{kj}$ for the product of two matrices A and B and note the location of the zeroes.

6. We have $L = [1, .5, .125; 0, 1, 1; 0, 0, 1]'$, $U = [8, 0, 0; 8, -1, 0; -3, 9.5, -11.125]'$, and $P = [0, 0, 1; 0, 1, 0; 1, 0, 0]$.

7. For the zero matrix, we can take $L = I_n$ and $U = 0_n$. The lower half of L may be filled in arbitrarily.

8. Note that some entries of L cannot affect the product LU.

9. Consider solving $ML = I_n$ for $M = L^{-1}$, column-by-column.

11. a) The decomposition is $L = [1, 0, 0; -1/2, 1, 0; 1/2, -1/3, 1]$, $U = [2, -1, 1; 0, 3/2, -1/2; 0, 0, 4/3]$.

   b) Compare D=diag(diag(U)); D\U to L.

   c) Show that $x^T LDL^T x = (L^T x)^T D(L^T x)$ is positive if x is nonzero.

   d) Use $A = LDL^T$ and write $D = D_1^2$ where the diagonal entries of D_1 are the square roots of those of D.

   e) Show that $x^T LL^T x = (L^T x)^T (L^T x) = \|y\|^2$ (where $y = L^T x$) is positive if x is nonzero.

14. a) The roots are 1, 2, 3, and 4.

   b) You're unlikely to find a useful way to do this.

Problems 2.4

1. a) The Cholesky factor is $R = [2 \ 1 \ .5; 0 \ 1.4142 \ .3536; 0 \ 0 \ 1.9039]$.

   b) The solution is $(1, -1, 1)^T$.

2. The Cholesky factor is $R = [2 \ .5 \ 0 \ .5; 0 \ 1.9365 \ 1.0328 \ -0.6455; 0 \ 0 \ 1.7127 \ -0.7785; 0 \ 0 \ 0 \ 1.6514]$.

5. **a)** We have $(EAE^T)^T = E^{TT}A^T E^T = EA^T E^T = EAE^T$, so EAE^T is symmetric.

6. **a)** The Cholesky factor is $R = [2 \ 1 \ .5; 0 \ 1 \ .5; 0 \ 0 \ 1.5811]$.
   b) The solution is $(0, -.2, .4)^T$.

9. **a)** If A is symmetric then $A = Q^T DQ$ with $Q^T = Q^{-1}$ so $x^T Ax = x^T Q^T DQx = (Qx)^T D(Qx) = y^T Dy$ where y is arbitrary by the nonsingularity of Q. Taking $y = e_i$ gives $y^T Dy = \lambda_i$ where λ_i is the ith eigenvalue of A. Hence we must have all eigenvalues of A positive for A to be positive definite, and all eigenvalues of A nonnegative for A to be positive semi-definite.

14. **a)** Use Gerschgorin's Theorem.

Problems 2.5

3. **a)** Note by submultiplicativity that $\|A^2\| \le \|A\|^2$.
   b) Consider for example the matrix $A = [0 \ 1; 0, \ 0]$.
   d) The natural norm is $\|I\|_M = \max_{\|x\|_v = 1}(\|Ix\|_v) = \max_{\|x\|_v = 1}(\|x\|_v) = 1$.

4. This follows from $\|M\|_s \le \|M\|_F$ for any matrix M.

6. **a)** Use the commands `A=hilb(8);b=[1 -1 1 -1 1 -1 1 -1]';x=A\b` in MATLAB.
   b) Use the `cond` and `invhilb` commands.

8. **a)** We have $\kappa(cA) = \|cA\| \ \|(cA)^{-1}\| = cc^{-1}\|A\|\|A^{-1}\| = \kappa(A)$.
   b) We have $\kappa(A) = \|A\| \ \|A^{-1}\| = \|A^{-1}\|\|A\| = \kappa(A^{-1})$.

11. No, the determinant is a poor measure of near-singularity for numerical purposes. For example, ϵI_n with ϵ small has determinant ϵ^n which is very small but (see Problem 8 part a, and Problem 3 part d). $\kappa(\epsilon I_n) = 1$ with respect to any natural norm.

Problems 2.6

4. **a)** The matrix is $A = [1/\sqrt{2} \ \sqrt{2}; 0 \ 3; -1/\sqrt{2} \ \sqrt{2}]$.
   c) The least squares solution is $(-2/3, 1/3)^T$.

7. **a)** In this case $Q = I$ and $R = A$ *except* that the signs of some entries on the main diagonal of Q may be negative if the corresponding r_{ii} was negative, and the corresponding row of R must have the signs changed on its entries.
   b) In this case $Q = A$, $R = I$.
   c) Simply change the signs in the appropriate columns of Q and rows of R.

8. **a)** Take determinants in the equation $Q^T Q = I$ and recall that $\det(Q^T) = \det(Q)$.
   b) Show that the equation $Q^T Q = I$ implies the equation $(-Q)^T(-Q) = I$.
   c) Recall that matrix-matrix multiplication may be viewed in terms of dot products of the rows of the first matrix with the columns of the second matrix.

9. Row 3 is the sum of rows 1 and 2; the same must be true of b.

14. This is done in Sec. 2.4.

Problems 2.7

1. **a)** Multiply them out to show that $H^T H = I, G^T G = I$.
   b) Let $M = [\alpha \ \beta; \gamma \ \delta]$ and set $M^T M = I$. Solve for the entries in M.

4. Check your answer with the command `[Q,R]=qr(reshape(1:16,4,4))`.

6. In this case $Q = [0 \ 0 \ -1; 0 \ 1 \ 0; -1 \ 0 \ 0]$ and $R = [-1 \ 0 \ 0; 0 \ 1 \ 0; 0 \ 0 \ -1]$.

8. a) Set $[-\cos(\theta)\ \sin(\theta); \sin(\theta)\ \cos(\theta)] = [\cos(\phi)\ -\sin(\phi); \sin(\phi)\ \cos(\phi)]$ and derive a contradiction (or note that $\det(H) = -1$, $\det(G) = 1$).

b) Perform the multiplication to show that $G^T G = I$.

12. b) Simplify $s\sqrt{(x_1/s)^2 + (x_2/s)^2}$.

c) See Sec. 1.7, Problem 12.

Problems 2.8

1. a) The o.n. basis is $(1/\sqrt{3}, 0, 1/\sqrt{3}, 0, 1/\sqrt{3})^T$, $\sqrt{3/26}(1/3, 2, -2/3, 2, 1/3)^T$, $\sqrt{3/26}(11/9, -4/3, 4/9, 14/9, -5/3)^T$.

6. a) Check your answer with the command $[Q,R]=qr(reshape(1:16,4,4))$.

b) Your answer should be the same as in part a. if you insisted on $r_{ii} > 0$.

7. a) Note that $|A| = |R|$.

8. a) The least squares solution is the solution of $A^T Ax = A^T b$. If A has full rank, $A^T A$ is nonsingular, so the solution is given by $x = (A^T A)^{-1} A^T b = A^+ b$.

b) We have $A^+ A = [(A^T A)^{-1} A^T]A = (A^T A)^{-1}(A^T A) = I$.

e) By this definition it doesn't exist since $_m 0_n$ is not of full rank. A more general definition of A^+ gives $0^+ = 0$.

9. a) We have $\|A\|_s = \|QR\|_s = \|R\|_s$ because Q is orthogonal.

b) We have $\|A\|_s = \|R\|_s$ so $\|A^{-1}\|_s = \|R^{-1}Q^{-1}\|_s = \|R^{-1}\|_s$ so $\kappa_s(A) = \|R\|_s\|R^{-1}\|_s$.

13. b) We have $A^+ A = A^T(AA^T)^{-1}A$ and if A is not square then this need not equal I; if A is square then $A^+ A = A^T(AA^T)^{-1}A = A^T(A^T)^{-1}A^{-1}A = I$ since A has full rank. But note that $AA^+ A = AA^T(AA^T)^{-1}A = (AA^T)(AA^T)^{-1}A = A$ as claimed.

Problems 2.9

1. One possibility is $I_4 = I_4 I_4 I_4^T$, but note for example that signs could be changed in U and V.

2. The singular values are 2, 1; the rank is 2.

4. Use the fact that the first rank(A) columns of U form a basis for Col(A).

5. Note that $A^T A = (U\Sigma V^T)^T U\Sigma V^T = V\Sigma^T \Sigma V^T = V\Sigma^2 V^T$ and that V has orthonormal columns.

6. The sizes of U, Σ, and V in its full SVD are 6x6, 6x4, and 4x4, respectively. The sizes of U_1, Σ_1, and V in its reduced SVD are 6x4, 4x4, and 4x4, respectively.

CHAPTER 3

Problems 3.1

2. a) For $A = [4\ 2\ 1; 1\ 3\ 1; 1\ 1\ 4]$, $-D^{-1}(U + L)$ has $\rho(M) \doteq .6404$. hence after five iterations the error should have decreased by a factor of roughly $.64^5 \doteq .1074$.

b) Here $-(D + L)^{-1}U$ has $\rho(M) \doteq .2041$.

3. a) Use the max norm and strict diagonal dominance.

b) Same as for part a.

5. a) Use the definition of a natural norm and pick x to be an eigenvector of A associated with an eigenvalue of maximum modulus.

b) Show that the eigenvalues of $I - M$ are all nonzero.

c) Note that U must be singular.

8. For example, you could use `ind=1:6;disp([.3.^ind;.5.^ind])`.
12. **a)** This insures that the spectral radius is at most unity in absolute value so $\rho(M)^k \to 0$.
    b) Use `A=rand(N);M=A'*A` to generate the positive definite matrices.

Problems 3.2

1. For the matrix $A = [1\ 0\ 1\ 0; -1\ 0\ 0\ 0; 0\ 5\ 0\ 0; 0\ 0\ 0\ -2]$ we have $r = (1, 1, 2, 3, 4)$, $c = (1, 3, 1, 2, 4)$, and $v = (1, 1, -1, 5, -2)$.
2. For this matrix $a_{32} = -5$ and $a_{61} = 0$. The size is at least 8x8.
5. Since each element of A requires three entries to store, A must have no more than one-third nonzero entries if the entries of r, c, and v require the same amount of storage as those of A.
7. Consider interchanging the first and last rows and/or columns of the matrix.
14. One example is a tridiagonal matrix where all entries in the main diagonal, first subdiagonal, and first superdiagonal are nonzero.

Problems 3.3

1. One step of Jacobi iteration starting from $x_0 = (1, 1)^T$ gives $x_1 = (-.250, -.500)^T$. The residual is $r = (1.50000, 1.25000)^T$ (to 6 digits). Then $e = A\backslash r$ gives $e = (.250, 1.00)^T$ and so $x_1 + e = (.000, .500)^T$ which is the true solution. In this case, the extended precision did not actually help us.
2. One step of Jacobi iteration starting from $x_0 = (1, 1)^T$ gives $x_1 = (-.025, 5.00)^T$. The residual is $r = (6.00000, 1.02500)^T$ (to 6 digits). Then $e = A\backslash r$ gives $e = (-.425, 14.5)^T$ and so $x_1 + e = (-.450, 9.50)^T$ which is the true solution. The extended precision does help here (try it with fixed precision).
5. You may use the Hilbert matrices. The process should give excellent accuracy except possibly after the condition number reaches about 10^{16} (depending on your machine and software).
7. Perform $r = b - Ax_0$; $e = A\backslash r$; $x_1 = x_0 + e$; and iterate. Starting at $m = 16$, x_1 becomes a very poor estimate, but an additional one or two steps of improvement works very well. Even for $m = 100$, 7 performing steps of iterative improvement leads to a good solution. The method leads to the correct solution until NaNs are encountered, though as m increases, more steps of iterative improvement are needed.
12. **c)** The ratio is $2n\epsilon\kappa_\infty(A)/\epsilon = 2n\kappa_\infty(A)$; since $\kappa_\infty(A) \geq 1$, the fixed precision technique is at least a factor of $2n$ worse. For the large matrices under discussion, this is significant.

Problems 3.4

1. **a)** For example, if $A = [5\ 1\ 1; 1\ 5\ 1; 1\ 1\ 3]$ then $\text{cond}(A) \doteq 2.6909$ but $\text{cond}(D^{-1}A) \doteq 2.0931$; also $\|A - I\| \doteq 5.5616$ and $\|D^{-1}A - I\| \doteq .5276$.
   b) If $A = [5\ 1\ 1; 1\ 5\ 1; 1\ 1\ 3]$ then $\text{cond}(A) \doteq 2.6909$ but $\text{cond}((D + L)^{-1}A) \doteq 1.3654$; also $\|A - I\| \doteq 5.5616$ and $\|(D + L)^{-1}A - I\| \doteq .3256$.
4. (Refer to MATLAB 3.1.) Similar to the approach used for Gauss-Seidel preconditioning, one could use $P^{-1} = (D + \varpi L)^{-1}$ for some ϖ.

9. If U is unitary then $\|UA\| = \|A\|$ so U could not be used to lower the condition number of A. Of course, it might be possible to use U to shift the eigenvalues of A if that is the goal of preconditioning.

10. Without preconditioning, the absolute error already exceeds unity (in the 2-norm) by $N = 8$. With Jacobi preconditioning, this doesn't happen until $N = 9$ (set N=4 then iterate a sequence of commands like N=N+1; b=ones([N 1]); H=hilb(N); D1=inv(diag(diag(H))); norm((D1*H)\(D1*b)-invhilb(N)*b)). With Gauss-Seidel preconditioning (use `tril(H,-1)`), the absolute error exceeds unity at $N = 9$ but is smaller than it was for Jacobi preconditioning at $N = 9$ (about 2.5 as opposed to about 4). Given the extra computational costs associated with the Gauss-Seidel approach, the Jacobi approach seems like a good choice here.

14. **a)** For 1000×1000 random matrices (produced by `rand(1000)`), `condest` returns answers that are the same to five digits but are produced in about 2/3 the time.

  b) For a random matrix, `normest1` often takes longer than `norm`. though it gives the same results. Note that `normest1` has many options that may be used to fine-tune it in special cases.

Problems 3.5

1. The true solution is $(1, 1, 1)^T$.

5. Take A to be upper triangular with all diagonal entries 1 and $A = [2\ 1\ 0\ 0; 1\ 2\ 0\ 0; 0\ 0\ 2\ 1; 0\ 0\ 1\ 2]$, respectively.

7. Use `gmres(A,b,4,[],4)` for the first case. Use `gmres(A,b,2,[],2)` for the second case. Use `gmres(A,b,4,[],4,P)` for the third and fourth cases, with P=diag(diag(A)) and P=diag(diag(A+tril(A,-1))), respectively.

12. An easy way to do this is to take A to be symmetric. For example, $A = [2\ 1\ 1; 1\ 2\ 1; 1\ 1\ 2]$ is normal, and two of its eigenvectors are $(1, -1, 0)^T$ and $(1, 1, 1)^T$. Hence we may take $b = (2, 0, 1)^T$ and expect convergence in 2 iterations. Use `gmres` to perform the computation and compare the result to the answer found by the backslash command.

13. For $k = 1$, the test polynomials must have the form $p(x) = cx + 1$. For $k = 2$, the test polynomials must have the form $p(x) = c_2 x^2 + c_1 x + 1$. Show that you can choose c, c_1, and c_2 so that $\|r_1\| = \|p(A)r_0\|$ and $\|r_2\| = \|p(A)r_1\|$. Verify experimentally that other choices of c, c_1, and c_2 give higher values of $\|p(A)r_0\|$ and $\|p(A)r_1\|$.

Problems 3.6

3. Pick $x_0 = (1, 0)^T$. Then $x_1 = A^{-1}x_0/\mu_1 = (2/3, -1/3)^T/(2/3) = (1, -.5)^T$; $x_2 = (1, -.8)$ ($\mu_2 \doteq .8333$); and $x_3 \doteq (1, -0.9286)^T$ ($\mu_3 \doteq .9333$). This seems to be approaching the eigenvector $(1, -1)^T$ associated with the eigenvalue $\lambda_1 = 1$. Our best estimate is $\mu_3 \doteq .9333$ but we could improve it using the Rayleigh quotient.

4. **a)** Because complex eigenvalues of real matrices occur in complex conjugate pairs. Each eigenvalue of the pair has the same absolute value as the other and so neither can be dominant.

  b) Consider again the equation $A^k v_0 = \alpha_1 \lambda_1^k x_1 + \cdots + \alpha_n \lambda_n^k x_n = \lambda_1^k (\alpha_1 x_1 + \alpha_2 \frac{\lambda_2^k}{\lambda_1^k} x_2 + \cdots + \alpha_n \frac{\lambda_n^k}{\lambda_1^k} x_n)$ but now use the fact that λ_2^k/λ_1^k is 1 (if the multiplicity is at least 2), and similarly for λ_3^k/λ_1^k if the multiplicity is at least 3, and so on. The eigenvalues still converge but the limiting vector may be some linear combination of the eigenvectors associated with λ_1. But this is still an eigenvector associated with λ_1, so the method works as before.

c) It's the corresponding eigenvalue.

7. Enter type `condeig`. The formula is in the form of a sum, given as a for loop.

9. The eigenvalues are $3, -3$ so there is no dominant eigenvalue.

14. Consider again the equation $A^k v_0 = \alpha_1 \lambda_1^k x_1 + \cdots + \alpha_n \lambda_n^k x_n = \lambda_1^k (\alpha_1 x_1 + \alpha_2 \frac{\lambda_2^k}{\lambda_1^k} x_2 + \cdots + \alpha_n \frac{\lambda_n^k}{\lambda_1^k} x_n)$ and note that if $\lambda_1 = \rho e^{i\theta}$ then $\lambda_2 = \rho e^{-i\theta}$ and so $A^k v_0 = \lambda_1^k (\alpha_1 x_1 + \alpha_2 e^{-i2\theta k} x_2 + \cdots + \alpha_n \frac{\lambda_n^k}{\lambda_1^k} x_n)$. In the limit the iteration eithersettles into a periodic cycle or wanders in a never-repeating sequence, depending on θ.

CHAPTER 4

Problems 4.1

1. The quadratic interpolant is $y = -x^2 + 2x + 1$.

5. a) The cubic interpolant is $y = 4x^3 - 11x^2 + 8x - 1$.

b) The Newton form is $y = a(x - 2)(x - 1)x + b(x - 1)x + cx + d$. Comparing coefficients gives the linear system $a = 4$, $b - 3a = -11$, $2a - b + c = 8$, and $d = -1$. The solution is $a = 4$, $b = 1$, $c = 1$, $d = -1$, so $y = 4x(x - 2)(x - 1) + x(x - 1) + x - 1$.

6. a) Use `N=10` and `x=-1:2/N:1; y=1./(1+25*x.^2); p=polyfit(x,y,N);` `plot(x,polyval(p,x))` to fit and plot the polynomial. Use `plot` and `polyval` to plot it. To approximate the maximum, use `z=-1:1/200:1; Y=polyval(p,z);` `W=1./(1+25*z.^2); max(abs(Y-W))`. This is approximately 1.9156.

b) Repeat with `N=15`. The maximum difference is about 2.1041.

c) Repeat with `N=20`. The maximum difference is about 59.8223.

d) Repeat with `N=50`. The maximum difference is about $4.7301E6$. No, the approximation does not seem to be improving.

e) The points `x=[-1 -.9 -.8 -.5 -.2 0 .2 .5 .8 .9 1]` give an interpolant that is oscillatory but closer than the interpolant based on equally spaced points.

11. With 1000 points, at $k = 15$, the maximum value of the function is .9880. At $k = 16$, the function evaluates to zero (precisely).

14. a) Yes, it exists, and yes, it is unique.

b) We must fit a polynomial of degree at most 7 to the data by requiring $p(x_i) = \sin(x_i)$ and $p'(x_i) = \cos(x_i)$ at the four data points. So, if $p(x) = ax^7 + bx^6 + cx^5 + dx^{42} + ex^3 + fx^2 + gx + h$, then $h = 0$ by interpolation at $x = 0$ and $g = 1$ by interpolation of the derivative values at $x = 0$. Solve for the remaining six coefficients by constructing a linear system using the two conditions at each of the remaining three nodes.

Problems 4.2

2. a) This means that we must have $Mh^2/8 \le .01$. Taking $M = 2$, this gives $h \le .2$.

b) Write a MATLAB program to do the testing.

3. a) Use the indicated MATLAB commands.

b) Use `x=linspace(-1,1,10)` instead.

c) This is a matter of opinion.

4. Apply the Cauchy Remainder Theorem for Polynomial Interpolation with $n = 1$ to get a bound for linear interpolation over a single interval. Then view that interval as a subinterval in a piecewise linear interpolation problem.

5. If $c_1(x) = ax^3 + bx^2 + cx + d$ then $0 = d$, $1 = a(\pi/2)^3 + b(\pi/2)^2 + c(\pi/2) + d$, $1 = c$, $0 = 3a(\pi/2)^2 + 2b(\pi/2) + c$. This gives $a = -0.1107$, $b = -0.0574$. Similarly for c_2.

6. Use the `title`, `xlabel`, `ylabel`, `legend`, and `text` or `gtext` commands.

Problems 4.3

4. Yes. Only one BC can be applied (not two).

5. We require that $S(x_i) = y_i$, $i = 0, \cdots n$; that $S'(x_i)$, $S''(x_i)$, $S'''(x_i)$, and $S^{(iv)}(x_i)$ exist, $i = 1, \ldots, n - 1$; and that $S''(x_0) = 0$, $S''(x_n) = 0$ (natural BCs). This gives $2(n + 1) + 4(n - 1) + 2 = 6n$ conditions on the $6n$ coefficients of the n quintics.

11. Let $p_0(x) = a_0 x^3 + b_0 x^2 + c_0 x + d_0$ and $p_1(x) = a_1 x^3 + b_1 x^2 + c_1 x + d_1$. Set $p_0'(x_1) = p_1'(x_1)$, $p_0''(x_1) = p_1''(x_1)$, and $p_0'''(x_1) = p_1'''(x_1)$. The last condition gives $6a_0 = 6a_1$ so $a_0 = a_1$. Then the next to last condition gives $b_0 = b_1$, and so on. Similarly for the right-hand side of the spline.

12. **a)** Use the matrix formulation from the text to find the coefficients, but use the `spline` command in MATLAB for the plot.
    b) Differentiate the spline's components and the function.
    c) Differentiate the spline's components and the function again.

15. The Hermite interpolant is unique, and the cubic interpolates itself and matches its own derivative values, so the cubic is its own Hermite interpolant. The clamped cubic spline is unique, and the cubic satisfies all the conditions on it, so the cubic is its own clamped cubic spline.

Problems 4.4

1. Perform the integration that gives the formula for $S'(x)$. Since the numerators will have the form $x^2/2 - xx_{i+1}$ and $x^2/2 - xx_i$, complete the square in each case and absorb the extra constant terms into τ_i. For example, $x^2/2 - xx_i = (x - x_i)^2/2 - x_i^2/2$, but $x_i^2/2$ is just a constant that can be put in the constant of integration τ_i. Then the integration that gives the formula for $S(x)$ is straight-forward.

3. Combine like terms in σ_{i-1}, σ_i, and σ_{i+1}, and identify the coefficients and right-hand side in terms of ϖ_i and r_i.

8. The matrix has the same basic structure as before. The condition that $p_0''(x_0) = p_{n-1}''(x_n)$ is a simple statement about the σ_i. For the condition $p_0'(x_0) = p_{n-1}'(x_n)$, compare what was done for the clamped spline.

12. Remove the nodes at x_1 and x_{n-1} and use a single cubic over $[x_0, x_2]$ and another over $[x_{n-2}, x_n]$, then add back in the two extra conditions that the spline interpolate at x_1 and x_{n-1}.

14. Pick a function and fit a clamped cubic spline to it. Refine the step size and verify that the error drops off like h^4.

CHAPTER 5

Problems 5.1

6. **a)** The solution is `erf(0:.1:3)` (in MATLAB).
    b) Use $(b - a)h^2 M/12 \leq 1E - 4$ with $a = 0$, $b = 3$, and M a bound on $f''(x)$ (use the Fundamental Theorem of Calculus to find $f'(x)$).

8. a) The degree of accuracy is 3 (see Eq. (5.18) in Section 5.3).

b) The rule in 8) a.) performs better than the trapezoidal rule, in general.

9. a) For Simpson's rule, the polynomial is $P(x) = \Lambda_0(x)f(x_0) + \Lambda_1(x)f(x_1) + \Lambda_2(x)f(x_2)$, where $\Lambda_0(x) = (x - x_1)(x - x_2)/(x_0 - x_1)(x_0 - x_2)$, $\Lambda_1(x) = (x - x_0)(x - x_2)/(x_1 - x_0)(x_1 - x_2)$, and $\Lambda_2(x) = (x - x_0)(x - x_1)/(x_2 - x_0)(x_2 - x_1)$. Compute $\int_{x_0}^{x_2} \Lambda_i(x)$, $i = 0, 1, 2$. Similarly for the Simpson's 3/8 rule, where the polynomial has degree 3.

b) The six-point rule is $\int_{x_0}^{x_5} f(x) \approx \frac{5}{288}h(19f_0 + 75f_1 + 50f_2 + 50f_3 + 75f_4 + 19f_5)$.

Weddle's rule is $\int_{x_0}^{x_6} f(x) \approx \frac{1}{140}h(41f_0 + 216f_1 + 27f_2 + 272f_3 + 27f_4 + 216f_5 + 41f_6)$. (Note, sometimes the name *Weddle's Rule* is used to mean the formula $\int_{x_0}^{x_6} f(x) \approx \frac{3}{10}h(f_0 + 5f_1 + f_2 + 6f_3 + f_4 + 5f_5 + f_6)$, which is similar to a closed Newton-Cotes formula but isn't one, strictly speaking.)

10. a) No. In Simpson's 3/8 rule, a cubic is interpolated to every four consecutive points; in a cubic spline, a cubic is interpolated to every two consecutive points, with additional conditions specified.

b) Clamped splines are generally superior to free and not-a-knot splines because they use additional information. To compare to polynomial interpolation rules, you might consider Theorem 4.1.1 and Theorem 4.4.1 to compare how well the curves approximate the functions in addition to numerical experimentation.

15. Use a function which is known to integrate to zero, e.g. $f(x) = \sin(x)$ over $[0, 2\pi]$. The absolute values of the numerical quadratures are then the absolute errors. Call these errors $E_1, E_2, E_3, \ldots$ corresponding to $h = h_1, h_2, h_3, \ldots$, and compute E_i/h_i^2 (trapezoidal rule). If this is roughly constant, then $E_i \approx ch_i^2$ for some c, so the error is $O(h^2)$. Do the same for the Simpson's rule but use h_i^4 instead.

Problems 5.2

1. Apply Cramer's rule $x_i = |A_i|/|A|$ for the solution of $Ax = b$ to the Vandermonde system above Eq. (5.14). (Here A_i is the matrix A with column i replaced by b.) Then use $b - a = 2h$ to get the form used in Section 5.1.

3. The half-simp rule is $\int_{x_0}^{x_1} f(x)dx \approx \frac{h}{12}(5f_0 + 8f_1 - f_2)$.

4. a) For $n = 0$, the degree of accuracy is 1; for $n = 1$, the degree of accuracy is 1; and for $n = 2$, the degree of accuracy is 3.

b) To show the degree of accuracy is not 4, it suffices to show that the rules are not exact for some particular quartic on some particular interval of integration. Try integrating x^4 over $[0, 1]$ exactly, and approximately. For Simpson's rule, for example, this gives $\int_0^1 x^4 dx \approx (1/6)(0) + (2/3)(1/2^4) + (1/6)(1) \doteq 0.2083 \neq 1/5$.

5. The reasoning is the same as in Section 5.1.

8. As you might have expected from comparing their error formulas, the closed rules generally perform slightly better. (E.g., the rules based on 2 points have error bounds that look like $h^3 M_c/12$ (closed) and $3h^3 M_o/4$ (open) where M_c and M_o are values of the second derivative, possibly different in each case. The open rule has an asymptotic error constant that is 9 times larger than that for the closed rule.) The open rules are useful for certain numerical ODEs problems, however.

15. a) The rule is $\int_a^b f(x)dx \approx \frac{5h}{24}[11f(x_0) + f(x_1) + f(x_2) + 11f(x_3)]$.

b) Proceed as was done for Simpson's rule in this section.

c) The rule is $\int_{x_0}^{x_6} f(x) \approx \frac{1}{140}h(41f_0 + 216f_1 + 27f_2 + 272f_3 + 27f_4 + 216f_5 + 41f_6)$.

Problems 5.3

1. Consider $\int_{-1}^{1} g(t(x))dx$. At $x = -1, t = a$; at $x = 1, t = b$. Also, $dt/dx = (b-a)/2$. Hence, by the method of substitution, $\int_{-1}^{1} g(t(x))dx = \frac{2}{b-a} \int_{-1}^{1} g(t(x))\frac{dx}{dt}dt = \frac{2}{b-a} \int_{a}^{b} g(t)dt$. In particular, $\int_{2}^{4} \sin(t^2)dt = \frac{4-2}{2} \int_{-1}^{1} \sin((((4-2)u + 4 + 2)/2)^2)du$ (taking $t = t(u)$ as the dummy variable of integration). This is $\int_{-1}^{1} \sin((u+3)^2)du \approx \sin((-1/\sqrt{3}+3)^2) + \sin((1/\sqrt{3}+3)^2) \doteq -0.1732$.

2. This follows immediately from approximating $f(x)$ by a polynomial interpolant in Lagrange form.

3. You may simply plug the given values of w_0, w_1 and x_0, x_1 into the system and verify that they are a solution.

4. For example, $\|x\|^2 = \int_{-1}^{1} 1 \cdot x \cdot x dx = (1^3 - (-1)^3)/3$ so $\|x\| = \sqrt{2/3}$.

9. The Gauss-Legendre rules perform considerably better, in general.

Problems 5.4

3. Two examples are the trapezoidal rule and the first Gauss-Legendre rule.

5. **a)** The first four Laguerre polynomials are $L_0(x) = 1$, $L_1(x) = -x + 1$, $L_2(x) = \frac{1}{2}x^2 - 2x + 1$, $L_3(x) = \frac{1}{6}(-x^3 + 9x^2 - 18x + 6)$.

6. Consider using the change of variables $x = \cos(\theta)$. To show that $T_n(x)$ is monic, use the recurrence relation.

7. **a)** Consider Example 5.4.1. and note that $\int_{-1}^{1} x^n dx$ is 0 if n is odd and nonzero if n is even. Use this to establish the result inductively.

   b) Proceed as in part a.

10. **a)** Note that you may simply substitute the forumula for the nodes into the formula $T_n(x) = \cos(n \arccos(x))$ and simplify.

    b) Differentiate $T_n(x) = \cos(n \arccos(x))$ with respect to x and set the result equal to zero to find the extrema. All extreme values of T_n are $\pm 2^{-(n-1)}$.

11. For example, all U_n are polynomials in x; for odd n, $U_n(x)$ contains only odd powers of x and so is odd, and for even n, $U_n(x)$ contains only even powers of x and so is even.

Problems 5.5

1. The rule is given in Example 5.5.1 and applies on $[-1, 1]$. If $f(x) = -f(-x)$ then the rule always gives zero, which is correct for an odd function over an interval that is symmetric about the origin. This explains why the value of $\int_{-1}^{1} \sin(x)dx$ is zero apart from round-off error in Example 5.5.1.

2. The rule is given in Example 5.5.1. We have $\int_{-1}^{1} \cos^2(x)dx \approx (1/6)\cos^2(-1) + (5/6)\cos^2(-1/\sqrt{5}) + (5/6)\cos^2(1/\sqrt{5}) + (1/6)\cos^2(-1) \doteq 1.4523$ and $\int_{-1}^{1} \sin^2(x)dx \approx (1/6)\sin^2(-1) + (5/6)\sin^2(-1/\sqrt{5}) + (5/6)\sin^2(1/\sqrt{5}) + (1/6)\sin^2(-1) \doteq 0.5477$.

3. The rule is given in Example 5.5.1. At the first level we have $\int_{-1}^{1} \exp(x)dx \approx (1/6)\exp(-1) + (5/6)\exp(-1/\sqrt{5}) + (5/6)\exp(1/\sqrt{5}) + (1/6)\exp(1) \doteq 2.3505$. The true value is 2.3504.

6. In general, the Radau rule outperforms the Lobatto rule.

10. For the interval $[-1, 1]$, the nodes are $\{-1, 0, 1\}$ and the corresponding weights are $\{1/3, 4/3, 1/3\}$.

11. For the interval $[-1, 1]$, the nodes are $\{-1, (1 - \sqrt{6})/5, (1 + \sqrt{6})/5\}$ and the corresponding weights are $\{2/9, (16 + \sqrt{6})/18, (16 - \sqrt{6})/18\}$.

Problems 5.6

3. a) For the composite Simpson's rule with step size h, S_h, the error is $E_h = -\frac{(b-a)h^4}{180} f^{(4)}(\gamma)$. That is, $\int_a^b f(x)dx$ is equal to $S_h f - \frac{(b-a)h^4}{180} f^{(4)}(\gamma_h)$ which is equal to $S_{h/2} f - \frac{(b-a)(h/2)^4}{180} f^{(4)}(\gamma_{h/2})$. Hence $S_h f + 16 E_{h/2} \approx S_{h/2} f + E_{h/2}$ (assuming $f^{(4)}(\gamma_h) \approx f^{(4)}(\gamma_{h/2})$), or $E_{h/2} \approx -\left(S_h f - S_{h/2} f\right)/15$.

b) See MATLAB 5.6 but use Simpson's rule and your estimate from part a instead.

5. These methods do not use the same points at the next level of recursion, which raises efficiency issues. See the discussion of Kronrod extensions in Section 5.5.

6. a) For the composite Simpson's 3/8 rule with step size h, Σ_h, the error is $E_h = c(b - a)h^4 f^{(4)}(\gamma)$ for some constant c. That is, $\int_a^b f(x)dx = \Sigma_h + c(b - a)h^4 f^{(4)}(\gamma_h) = \Sigma_{h/2} + c(b - a)(h/2)^4 f^{(4)}(\gamma_{h/2})$. Hence $\Sigma_h + 16 E_{h/2} \approx \Sigma_{h/2} + E_{h/2}$ (assuming $f^{(4)}(\gamma_h) \approx f^{(4)}(\gamma_{h/2})$), or $E_{h/2} \approx -\left(\Sigma_h - \Sigma_{h/2}\right)/15$. This is the same as for Simpson's rule because they both are governed by an h^4 error term. The value of c is not needed.

b) See MATLAB 5.6 but use Simpson's 3/8 rule and your estimate from part a instead.

7. Note, these rules interpolate a zero-degree polynomial to the function on each interval to get a piecewise constant approximation. Hence they have degree of accuracy at least zero. Now apply Theorem 5.5.1.

14. a) For the simple Boole's rule, the error varies as $h^7 f^{(6)}(\gamma)$ (in fact, $E_h = \frac{-8h^7}{945} f^{(6)}(\gamma)$). So for the composite Boole's rule with step size h, B_h, the error is $E_h = c(b - a)h^6 f^{(6)}(\gamma)$ for some constant c. That is, $\int_a^b f(x)dx = B_h + c(b - a)h^6 f^{(6)}(\gamma_h) = B_{h/2} + c(b - a)(h/2)^6 f^{(6)}(\gamma_{h/2})$. Hence $B_h + 64 E_{h/2} \approx B_{h/2} + E_{h/2}$ (assuming $f^{(6)}(\gamma_h) \approx f^{(6)}(\gamma_{h/2})$), or $E_{h/2} \approx -\left(B_h - B_{h/2}\right)/63$. The value of c is not needed.

b) See MATLAB 5.6 but use Boole's rule and your estimate from part a instead.

Problems 5.7

1. From $\int_a^b f(x)dx = T_h f + c_2 h^2 + c_4 h^4 + c_6 h^6 + \cdots + c_{2k} h^{2k} + O(h^{2k+1})$, form the quantity $A = (4A - A)/3$ as $A = (4(T_{h/2} f + c_2 \frac{h^2}{4} + c_4 \frac{h^4}{16} + c_6 \frac{h^6}{64} + \cdots + c_{2k} \frac{h^{2k}}{2^{2k}} + O(h^{2k+1})) - (T_h f + c_2 h^2 + c_4 h^4 + c_6 h^6 + \cdots + c_{2k} h^{2k} + O(h^{2k+1})))/3$. Write this as $A = \left(4 T_{h/2} f - T_h f\right)/3$ plus the terms in h^4 and higher. Set $T_h^{(2)} = \frac{4 T_{h/2} f - T_h f}{4 - 1}$ and write $T_h^{(1)} f$ for $T_h f$. Now, note that the error term for $T_h^{(2)}$ has the same form as that for $T_h f$ save that it begins with a $c_4 h^4/16$ term, so we can repeat the process but using $A = (4^2 A - A)/15$ instead.

2. The results will not be wrong, but they will be wasteful, as every other step we are knocking out a term that isn't actually present in the error expansion.

9. You should find that, as a rule, applying the extrapolation to inappropriate sequences is not helpful.

10. In addition to the general structure you could, for example, comment on how the initial subintervals are selected in quad and why they're unequal, what is meant by fudging the endpoints in quadl, what error checks are made and what warnings are returned, and so on.

12. There are several possible approaches. Pick a nonperiodic infinitely differentiable function (for reasons that are not addressed in the text, the trapezoidal rule works particularly well on periodic functions), with known integral. Compute $T_h f$ for several values of h. Estimate c_2 by dividing the errors by h^2. Then consider the error minus $c_2 h^2$ and divide it by h^4 to estimate c_4. If these values settle down quickly as h decreases, this provides evidence that the error term is as indicated. A more sophisticated approach might fit polynomials of the form $c_2 h^2 + c_4 h^4$ to the error and compare these fits to ones involving odd powers of h.

CHAPTER 6

Problems 6.1

3. Forward, backward: degree 1 (since the error depends on $f''(x)$). Centered for first derivative: degree 2 (since the error depends on $f'''(x)$). Centered for second derivative: degree 1 (see Problem 4).

4. Proceed as was done starting with Eq. (6.1) and Eq. (6.2) and leading to the centered difference formula for the first derivative. Since the error term involves $f''(\gamma)$, you may use the expansions in Eq. (6.1) and Eq. (6.2) without extending them to higher-order terms.

5. We have $\frac{1}{2}[\frac{f(x+h)-f(x)}{h}] + \frac{1}{2}[\frac{f(x)-f(x-h)}{h}] = \frac{f(x+h)-f(x)+f(x)-f(x-h)}{2h} = \frac{f(x+h)-f(x-h)}{2h}$.

8. The five-point formula is $f'(x_0) = \frac{1}{12h}(f(x_0 - 2h) - 8f(x_0 - h) + 8f(x_0 + h) - f(x_0 + 2h)) + \frac{h^4}{30} f^{(5)}(\gamma)$. Note that $f(x_0)$ is not actually used.

10. a) No, the minimum is not always at 10^{-8}, though it should be within a couple of orders of magnitude of this most of the time.

   b) Use functions like the integral of $|x|$ ($-x^2/2$ on the left, $x^2/2$ on the right) or the function that is zero for $x < 0$ and x^2 for $x \geq 0$, and approximate the derivative near the problematic point. The results are poor. No, the minimum is not always at 10^{-8}.

12. The forward and backward methods do poorly near an extreme point, where they may even get the wrong sign. The centered method, by the Mean Value Theorem (which is what this formula essentially is), must at least give the correct derivative for some point in the interval.

Problems 6.2

1. The approximate solutions through $x = .5$ are (in the form $[x_i, y_i]$ from Maple's dsolve command with classical[foreuler] option; see mhelp dsolve): $[.05, 1.05]$, $[.1, 1.105125]$, $[.15, 1.16619006328125]$, $[.2, 1.234190026466046]$, $[.25, 1.310351277537459]$, $[.3, 1.396202301064662]$, $[.35, 1.493671344339575]$, $[.4, 1.605224048584635]$, $[.45, 1.734061260892357]$, $[.5, 1.884409683718737]$. Your answers may vary depending on how many digits you kept between computations. The final estimate is $y_1 \approx 9.552668020989672$. The true solution is $y(x) = 1/(1 - x)$ which is infinite at $x = 1$. Using a smaller h would give a larger y_1.

2. Starting at (x_0, y_0) and using a slope of $f'(x_0, y_0)$, we get the linear approximation $y - y_0 = f'(x_0, y_0)(x - x_0)$. At $x = x_0 + h$, we have $y - y_0 = f'(x_0, y_0)((x_0 + h) - x_0)$ or $y = y_0 + hf'(x_0, y_0)$ which is Euler's method.

3. For $h = .05$, the approximate solutions through $x = .5$ are (in the form $[x_i, y_i]$): $[.05, .95]$, $[.1, .9025]$, $[.15, .857375]$, $[.2, .81450625]$, $[.25, .7737809375]$, $[.3, .735091890625]$, $[.35, .69833729609375]$, $[.4, .6634204312890625]$, $[.45, .6302494097246094]$, $[.5, .5987369392383789]$. Your answers may vary depending on how many digits you kept between computations. The true solution is $y = \exp(-x)$.

6. a) The approximate solutions are (in the form $[x_i, y_i]$): [.05, 1.10], [.1, 1.210500], [.15, 1.33376551250000], [.2, 1.472712034616719], [.25, 1.631156071461965], [.3, 1.814189577935327], [.35, 2.028753769169785], [.4, 2.284545861965816], [.45, 2.595503351737073], [.5, 2.982335234180992]. The true solution is $y = \tan(x + \pi/4)$.

    b) Use f=inline('1+y.^2','t','y'); ode23(f,[0 1],1).

12. This gives the implicit method $y_1 = y_0 + hf(x_1, y_1)$.

Problems 6.3

1. a) The approximate solutions through $x = .5$ are (in the form $[x_i, y_i]$ from Maple's dsolve command with classical[heunform] option; like a number of texts, Maple refers to what we have called the improved Euler's formula as Heun's method): [.05, 1.052562500000000], [.1, 1.110948907208062], [.15, 1.176182338797478], [.2, 1.249540037580860], [.25, 1.332637340578856], [.3, 1.427547224266731], [.35, 1.536974305022700], [.4, 1.664514529252157], [.45, 1.815054022913110], [.5, 1.995402284573740]. See also the solution for Problem 1 of Section 6.2.

    b) Correct by feeding the resulting slope back in to the improved Euler's formula and recomputing the approximate solution at each point.

    c) Use the midpoint method $y_{i+1} = y_i + hf(x_{i+1/2}, y_i + \frac{h}{2}f(x_i, y_i))$ and Heun's method $y_{i+1} = y_i + \frac{h}{4}[f(x_i, y_i) + 3f(x_{i+2/3}, y_i + \frac{2h}{3}f(x_i, y_i))]$.

3. For $h = .05$, the approximate solutions through $x = .5$ are (in the form $[x_i, y_i]$): [.05, .9512500000000000], [.1, .9048765625000000], [.15, .8607638300781250], [.2, .8188015933618164], [.25, .7788850156854279], [.3, .7409143711707633], [.35, .7047947955761886], [.4, .6704360492918494], [.45, .6377522918888718], [.5, .6066618676592893]. See also the solution for Problem 3 of Section 6.2.

6. a) The approximate solutions through $x = .5$ are (in the form $[x_i, y_i]$): [.05, 1.105250000000000], [.1, 1.222775837556521], [.15, 1.355551612262997], [.2, 1.507546853599451], [.25, 1.684185500810509], [.3, 1.893082815774667], [.35, 2.145277728362006], [.4, 2.457395882719499], [.45, 2.855674909921102], [.5, 3.384015504815370]. See also the solution for Problem 6 of Section 6.2.

    b) Use Heun's method $y_{i+1} = y_i + \frac{h}{4}\left[f(x_i, y_i) + 3f(x_{i+2/3}, y_i + \frac{2h}{3}f(x_i, y_i))\right]$.

8. The performance of the improved Euler's and Heun's methods is comparable, though Heun's method may show a slight advantage.

12. This equation is stiff (see Section 6.6) and none of these methods will perform well on it.

Problems 6.4

9. Use the two-point Radau left-hand formula with $x = x_0$ preassigned (see Section 5.5).

11. Mimic the corresponding proof given in the text for Euler's method.

12. a) All are $O(h)$, except for the trapezoidal scheme which is $O(h^2)$.

    b) Mimic the proof given in the text for Euler's method, treating $\theta = 1/2$ as a special case.

13. For example, you could use $(y_{i+1} - y_{i-1})/2h \approx f(x_i, y_i)$ to get the method $y_{i+1} = y_{i-1} + 2hf(x_i, y_i)$. You could use the improved Euler's method to start it.

14. The error does not decrease as $O(h)$ and $O(h^2)$, respectively, for non-Lipschitz functions.

Problems 6.5

6. Treat the theta methods as IRK methods (except for Euler's method $\theta = 1$) and identify the stages in terms of θ.

9. In this case we have the simple ODE $y' = f(x)$ which is merely a quadrature problem. To get the order of accuracy, recall that a RK method approximates a Taylor method, and that a polynomial is its own Maclaurin series.

10. The tableau is $1|\frac{1}{2}|\frac{1}{2}$.

13. Show that E_h/h^4 is roughly constant for your problem(s).

14. The times series plot should show alternating peaks and valleys for the two populations. The phase plot should look roughly like an oval in the first quadrant.

Problems 6.6

1. The true solution is $(x(t), y(t))^T = c_1(1, 0)^T e^{-10t} + c_2(1, 9)^T e^{-t}$ for $c_1 = 8/9$, $c_2 = 1/9$.

2. The true solution is $(x(t), y(t))^T = c_1(1, 0)^T e^{-10t} + c_2(1, 9)^T e^{-t}$ for $c_1 = 8/9$, $c_2 = 1/9$.

3. Substitute $\vec{y}_i = (1 - 10h)^i v_1 + (1 - h)^i v_2$ into $\vec{y}_{i+1} = \vec{y}_i + hA\vec{y}_i$, $A = [-10 \ 1; 0 \ -1]$ and use the fact that $v_1 = (1, 0)^T$ and $v_2 = (1, 9)^T$ are eigenvectors of A.

4. The true solution is $y = c \exp(x^3/3)$. Neither method performs well for a function that grows so extremely rapidly,

7. a) The implicit method outperforms the explicit method for this stiff system.

   b) The implicit method outperforms the explicit method for this stiff system.

9. Write it as the system $\left[(y, v)^T\right]' = A(y, v)^T + (0, \sin(x))^T = F(x, (y, v)^T)$, $A = [0 \ 1; -2 \ -2]$, with initial condition $(1, -1)^T$, and apply the improved Euler's method.

Problems 6.7

1. Euler's method is of the form $y_{i+1} = y_i + h \sum_{j=0}^{k-1} \beta_j f(x_{i-j}, y_{i-j})$ with $k = 1$ and $\beta_0 = 1$. The backward Euler's method is of the form $y_{i+1} = y_i + h \sum_{j=0}^{k-1} \beta_j f(x_{i+1-j}, y_{i+1-j})$ with $k = 1$ and $\beta_0 = 1$.

2. a) Note, AB1 is simply Euler's method.

   b) Use $y_{i+1} = y_i + h(\frac{3}{2} f(x_i, y_i) - \frac{1}{2} f(x_{i-1}, y_{i-1}))$, but find y_1 using Euler's method.

   c) Use $y_{i+1} = y_i + h(\frac{23}{12} f(x_i, y_i) - \frac{4}{3} f(x_{i-1}, y_{i-1}) + \frac{5}{12} f(x_{i-2}, y_{i-2}))$, but use $y_{i+1} = y_i + h(\frac{3}{2} f(x_i, y_i) - \frac{1}{2} f(x_{i-1}, y_{i-1}))$ to find y_2 after using Euler's method to find y_1.

4. a) No, because the values they multiply are apt to be nearly equal so we run the risk of subtraction of nearly equal numbers. Consider for example the subtraction $\frac{55}{24} f(x_i, y_i) - \frac{59}{24} f(x_{i-1}, y_{i-1})$ in AB 4.

   b) The sum of the coefficients is h.

6. a) Use the commands `y0=1;h=.5;f=inline('x+y'); y1=y0+h*f(0,y0);` `y2=y1+h*(1.5*f(h,y1)-.5*f(0,y0));` to set up the first few values, then use `y3=y2+h*(23*f(2*h,y2)/12-4*f(h,y1)/3+5*f(0,y0)/12)` to predict and `y3c=y2+h*(9*f(3*h,y3)/24+19*f(2*h,y2)/24-5*f(h,y1)/24+f(0,y0)/24)` to correct. This gives $y_1 \doteq 1.5000$, $y_2 \doteq 2.7500$, $y_3 \doteq 5.2188$, and $y_{3,c} \doteq 5.3066$ for the first few values. Using `y3c=y2+h*(9*f(3*h,y3c)/24+19*f(2*h,y2)/24-5*f(h,y1)/24+f(0,y0)/24)` to correct again gives $y_{3,c}^{(2)} \doteq 5.3231$.

   b) Changing h to $h = .25$ and using the same commands gives $y_1 \doteq 1.2500$, $y_2 \doteq 1.875$, $y_3 \doteq 2.3398$, and $y_{3,c} \doteq 2.3924$, $y_{3,c}^{(2)} \doteq 2.3426$.

12. a) The AB5 formula is $y_{i+1} = y_i + h(\frac{1901}{720} f(x_i, y_i) - \frac{2774}{720} f(x_{i-1}, y_{i-1}) + \frac{2616}{720} f(x_{i-2}, y_{i-2}) - \frac{1274}{720} f(x_{i-3}, y_{i-3}) + \frac{251}{720} f(x_{i-4}, y_{i-4}))$.

   b) The AB6 formula is $y_{i+1} = y_i + h(\frac{4277}{1440} f(x_i, y_i) - \frac{7923}{1440} f(x_{i-1}, y_{i-1}) + \frac{9982}{1440} f(x_{i-2}, y_{i-2}) - \frac{7298}{1440} f(x_{i-3}, y_{i-3}) + \frac{2877}{1440} f(x_{i-4}, y_{i-4}) - \frac{475}{1440} f(x_{i-5}, y_{i-5}))$.

13. a) The AM5 formula is $y_{i+1} = y_i + h(\frac{475}{1440} f(x_{i+1}, y_{i+1}) + \frac{1427}{1440} f(x_i, y_i) -$
$\frac{798}{1440} f(x_{i-1}, y_{i-1}) + \frac{482}{1440} f(x_{i-2}, y_{i-2}) - \frac{173}{1440} f(x_{i-3}, y_{i-3}) + \frac{27}{1440} f(x_{i-4}, y_{i-4}))$.

   b) The AM6 formula is $y_{i+1} = y_i + h(\frac{19087}{60480} f(x_{i+1}, y_{i+1}) + \frac{65112}{60480} f(x_i, y_i) -$
$\frac{46461}{60480} f(x_{i-1}, y_{i-1}) + \frac{37504}{60480} f(x_{i-2}, y_{i-2}) - \frac{20211}{60480} f(x_{i-3}, y_{i-3}) + \frac{6312}{60480} f(x_{i-4}, y_{i-4}) -$
$\frac{863}{60480} f(x_{i-4}, y_{i-4}))$.

CHAPTER 7

Problems 7.1

2. There is a minimum at 0.4745.

5. a) The answer is 0.464 (to three places).

   b) The answer is 0.464 (to three places).

7. a) The answer is 0.464 (to three places). Golden section search is not significantly affected by the change in objective function.

   b) Quadratic interpolation performs less well on $|f(x)|$ than on $f^2(x)$.

8. This is probably a bad idea unless we know that there are no other points at which $f(x) = m$ as otherwise the root-finding method may well find some of these solutions. But, if m is the unique global minimum value of $f(x)$, then $f(x) - m \geq 0$ so we cannot bracket the root, which leads to its own set of problems. Hence, this is generally a bad idea in every case.

9. a) For the counterexamples, a linear function suffices in each case ($y = x$ and $y = -x$ respectively). For the examples, use the counterexamples and draw a blip between any two points.

   b) Yes, by the Extreme Value Theorem: Since f achieves its minimum on $[a, c]$, there must be a minimum in that interval, and since $f(b)$ is not larger than the values at the endpoints, there is a minimum in (a, c) (possibly at b). Note, this allows the possibility that f is a constant function and that the minimum is therefore not isolated.

Problems 7.2

1. a) The minimum is at (0.5000, 2.0000, 3.0000).

   b) Complete the squares: The objective function is
$2x^2 - 2x + y^2 - 4y + z^2 - 6z + 13 = 2(x - \frac{1}{2})^2 + (y - 2)^2 + (z - 3)^2 - \frac{1}{2}$, so the minimizer is at $(1/2, 2, 3)$ where $f(1/2, 2, 3) = -1/2$.

3. a) Use $f(x) = x^3$ with a positive x_0, or a similar function of two or more variables.

   b) This follows immediately from the direction of steepest descent property of the gradient.

5. It preserves the differentiability of $F(x)$, where as $\|F(x)\|$ involves a square-root.

6. a) There is a minimum at the origin.

   b) No, there are minima wherever $x = 0$ or $y = 0$ for $x^2(y^4 + \sin^2(xy))$. Note that $f(x, y) \geq 0$.

   c) See part b.

11. a) The minimum is at the origin.

   b) The minimum is at the origin. For a function with circular contours like this, exact line search may pay off.

Problems 7.3

3. Compare Figure 1.2.6.

5. a) Write $A = [a\ b; b\ d]$ since A is symmetric. Then $x^T A x = ax_1^2 + 2bx_1x_2 + dx_2^2$. Fix x_2. If $a > 0$, $y = ax_1^2 + 2bx_1x_2 + dx_2^2$ is a parabola opening up in the x_1y-plane, unless x_1 is zero. It is always positive if its roots are complex, that is, if the discriminant satisfies $(2b)^2 - 4ad < 0$. But we are given that $ad - b^2 > 0$. If $x_1 = 0$, then $y = dx_2^2$ which can only be zero if x_2 is also zero. Note that $ad - b^2 > 0$ implies $d > 0$ since $b^2 \geq 0$. Hence, if $a > 0$ and $ad - b^2 > 0$, the matrix is positive definite. Similarly, if $x^T Ax = ax_1^2 + 2bx_1x_2 + dx_2^2$ is known to be positive unless x_1 and x_2 are both zero, we quickly deduce that $a > 0$ (else $x_1 = -1$, $x_2 = 0$ gives a zero or negative value), $d > 0$ (else $x_1 = 0$, $x_2 = -1$ gives a zero or negative value), and $(2b)^2 - 4ad < 0$ (else the quadratic can take on zero or negative values for nonzero x).

b) For example, take $A = [1\ 0\ 0; 0\ -1\ 0; 0\ 0\ -1]$ which has $|A| = 1$ but $e_2^T Ae_2 = -1$.

8. A function consisting of sums of terms of the form x_i, x_ix_j, and constants, that is, a polynomial of degree 2 in $x_1, \ldots, x_n$.

9. Use the `surf` or `ezsurf` command, e.g. `ezsurf('x*exp(-x^2-y^2)',[-1 1 -1 1])`.

11. Use a command like `ezsurf('4*x^3-x*y^2+log(x*y)+1',[0,5,0,5])` to visualize the function. From `ezsurf('4*x^3-x*y^2+log(x*y)+1',[0,1,0,1])`, a good guess seems to be $(.5, .5)^T$.

Problems 7.4

6. a) Use the `contour` and `surf` commands.
   b) The global minimum is at the origin.
7. a) Use the `contour` and `surf` commands.
   b) The global minima are at $(0.08984, -0.71266)$ and $(-0.08984, 0.71266)$.
11. a) The global minimum is at the origin.
   b) The global minima are at $(0.08984, -0.71266)$ and $(-0.08984, 0.71266)$.
   c) When there are relatively few local minima and the function is not so complicated that the root-finding phase of the tunneling method is difficult.
13. a) In each case, the fact that there are finitely many minima, say N, means that there are at most N regions to consider (because of our idealized local minimization routine), and each has nonzero hypervolume. With probability one, an initial guess will eventually fall in each such region.
   b) It depends on the quality of the pseudo-random number generator.
14. a) This is just a rephrasing of the strict convexity condition that for $\lambda \in [0, 1]$,
$$F(\lambda x + (1 - \lambda)y) < \lambda F(x) + (1 - \lambda)F(y)$$ (consider $\lambda x + (1 - \lambda)y$ the parametric form of a line segment, with parameter λ).
   b) This is a standard result of the calculus. Where $f''(x) = 0$ the concavity is changing.

Problems 7.5

1. a) The valley has banana-shaped contours.
   b) Overlay a vector parallel to p_1, which is in the direction $(-.5, 4)^T$, on the contour plot of the Rosenbrock function.
3. a) The program should search until it detects a decrease in function value followed by an increase in function value.
   b) The minimum is at 0.4745.
6. Note, you must specify or input an initial guess; choose an order to process the variables; specify a one-dimensional minimization method, and what to do if it fails; and specify a convergence criterion. You should consider limiting the maximum number of function evaluations.

8. The perfectly circular contours make alternating variable search converge immediately.

14. It's the same phenomenon seen when one studies discrete mathematics: One quickly comes to miss the calculus, which gives an algorithmic way to solve many problems ("take the derivative, according to these rules, set it equal to zero, and solve"), because discrete problems are so much harder to handle.

Problems 7.6

11. Newton's method works much faster for this problem.

12. **a)** The polytope is a pair of points. We can still compute $x_{ref} = 2c - x_{n+1}$.
    b) Again, $x_{ref} = c + \alpha(c - x_{n+1})$ can be computed.
    c) The minimum is at 0.4745.

13. Look at the Nelder-Mead method and think about some other types of reflections, contractions, or similar operations that you think would likely lead to a better estimate of the minimum.

14. **a)** Choose the next point pseudorandomly, but on the same general scale as x_0.
    b) The global minimum is at (1, 1).

15. The smallest reasonable width is $\sqrt{\epsilon}\, \|x^*\|$ where x^* is the true solution.

Problems 7.7

7. The minimum is at $A^{-1}b \doteq (0.4545, 0.3636)^T$. Note, A is positive definite as it is symmetric and its eigenvalues are 1.7639, 6.2361.

8. The minimum is at $A^{-1}b \doteq (-1.5714, 1.2857, 1.2857)^T$. Note, A is positive definite as it is symmetric and its eigenvalues are 0.5764, 1.8465, 6.5771.

12. **a)** Use the `eig` command to verify that the eigenvalues are all positive.
    b) Within the program, you may either form A and then Ax or, better, compute the dot product of $[-1\ 0\ 4\ 0\ -1]$ and the appropriate values from x.
    c) Use your program from part b.

13. It may be easiest to generate small-to-medium sized positive definite matrices by using the fact that if A is symmetric then $A = UDU^{-1}$ for some diagonal matrix D and some orthogonal matrix U. Such a matrix is positive definite if and only if all diagonal entries of D are strictly positive. Generate such a D (use `diag`) and then an orthogonal U (perhaps by using `orth(rand(N))`). For large sparse positive definite matrices, use `sprandsym` (note that you may specify the eigenvalues).

14. **a)** You must show that $\|x\|_A > 0$ unless x is the zero vector, in which case $\|x\|_A = 0$ (positive definiteness); $\|\alpha x\|_A = |\alpha|\|x\|_A$ for all scalars α (homogeneity); and $\|x + y\|_A \le \|x\|_A + \|y\|_A$ for vectors x, y (the triangle inequality). For positive definiteness, we have $\|x\|_A = \sqrt{x^T A x}$ which is positive (note that $x^T A x > 0$) unless $x = 0$, in which case it is zero. For homogeneity, $\|\alpha x\|_A = \sqrt{(\alpha x)^T A(\alpha x)}$ which is just $|\alpha|\sqrt{x^T A x} = |\alpha|\|x\|_A$. For the triangle inequality, $\|x + y\|_A^2 = (x + y)^T A(x + y) = (x^T + y^T)(Ax + Ay) = x^T A x + y^T A x + x^T A y + y^T A y$); but $y^T A x = (x^T A y)^T$ and $x^T A y$ is a scalar, so we have $\|x + y\|_A^2 = \|x\|_A^2 + 2x^T A y + \|y\|_A^2$. Write $A = H^2$ for the positive definite square root of A (see Section 2.4). Then $x^T A y = x^T H^2 y = (Hx)^T(Hy) \le \|Hx\|\|Hy\|$ by the Cauchy-Schwarz inequality. (Note, we have switched from the energy norm to the standard norm.) But $\|Hx\| = (Hx)^T(Hx) = x^T H^2 x = x^T A x = \|x\|_A$, and similarly for $\|Hy\| = \|y\|_A$, so $\|x + y\|_A^2 \le \|x\|_A^2 + 2\|Hx\|\|Hy\| + \|y\|_A^2 = \|x\|_A^2 + 2\|x\|_A\|y\|_A + \|y\|_A^2 = (\|x\|_A + \|y\|_A)^2$. Hence, $\|x + y\|_A^2 \le (\|x\|_A + \|y\|_A)^2$, or $\|x + y\|_A \le \|x\|_A + \|y\|_A$.

b) For $x = (1, 1)^T$, $\|x\|_A = [(1, 1)A(1, 1)^T]^{1/2} = \sqrt{6}$; for $x = (1, -1)^T$, $\|x\|_A = [(1, -1)A(1, -1)^T]^{1/2} = \sqrt{2}$; for $x = (-2, 1)^T$, $\|x\|_A = [(-2, 1)A(-2, 1)^T]^{1/2} = \sqrt{6}$.

c) Yes (take $A = I_n$).

CHAPTER 8

Problems 8.1

1. **a)** The coefficients are 0.4286, 0.4000, 0.1429.
   b) The coefficients are 0.1667, 0.4286, −0.1667, 0.1429.
   c) The coefficients are 0.4167, 0.1667, −1.4167, −0.1667, 1.0000.
3. If we are given H rather than $J^T J$ then we cannot expect to be able to remove the J^T factor on each side of the equation but otherwise we can. Note that $J^T J$ is a cross-product matrix so much of the discussion in Section 2.6 applies to working with it.
7. The data comes from the cubic $y = x^3/2$ so any polynomial of degree at least 3 works; by Occam's razor, the cubic is best.
8. This is commonly done, because global minimization is so difficult. If we have a good initial guess and there are not too many local minima this is not unreasonable.
12. Your results will depend very much on the type of functions you choose. The approximation is good for (nearly) linear functions and less so for nonlinear functions.

Problems 8.2

1. These are $\int_0^\pi |\sin(x) - \cos(x)| dx \doteq 2.8284$, $[\int_0^\pi (\sin(x) - \cos(x))^2 dx]^{1/2} = \sqrt{\pi}$, and $\max_{x \in [0,\pi]}(|\sin(x) - \cos(x)|) = 1$, respectively.
2. For order 1, these are $\int_0^\pi |\sin(x) - x| dx \doteq 2.9348$, $[\int_0^\pi (\sin(x) - x)^2 dx]^{1/2} \doteq 2.3713$, and $\max_{x \in [0,\pi]}(|\sin(x) - x|) = \pi$, respectively.
3. These are $\int_0^1 |\exp(x)| dx = e - 1$, $[\int_0^1 (\exp(x))^2 dx]^{1/2} = \sqrt{(e^2 - 1)/2}$, and $\max_{x \in [0,1]}(|\exp(x)|) = e$, respectively.
8. For example, you could use $f(x) = 0$ and $g(x) = \epsilon \sin(2(\delta/\epsilon)x)$.
9. The 1-norm for $\sin(x)$ is $(\int_0^\pi (\sin^2(x) + [\cos(x)]^2) dx)^{1/2} = (\int_0^\pi 1 dx)^{1/2} = \sqrt{\pi}$. The 1-norm for $\cos(x)$ is $(\int_0^\pi (\cos^2(x) + [-\sin(x)]^2) dx)^{1/2} = (\int_0^\pi 1 dx)^{1/2} = \sqrt{\pi}$.

Problems 8.3

3. **a)** Note that all quantities are nonnegative. In the second equation we are subtracting a larger quantity than in the first equation; in addition, $\|f - p\|_\infty$ exceeds $\|f - \pi\|_\infty$ as $\|f - \pi\|_\infty$ is the smallest possible value of $\|f - g\|_\infty$ from this class of functions.
   b) Use the triangle inequality $\|a\| - \|b\| \le \|a + b\| \le \|a\| + \|b\|$.
5. The approximant is of the form $y = \alpha x + \beta$. To show that $\max(|f(x) - y(x)|)$ is achieved at at least three points, note first that it is achieved at at least one point by the Extreme Value Theorem. Plot a few examples and ask what would happen if you varied the slope of the line by rotating it at the middle of the three points—one of the two outer points would see its error decrease, but at the other outer point the error would increase. Formalize this insight.
10. Your answer will depend on your initial reference
11. Your answer will depend on your initial reference. You may wish to use the gamma command in MATLAB.
15. See Section 8.5 (on the web).

Problems 8.4

1. If $x \in [-1, 1]$ is to be mapped to $y \in [a, b]$ linearly, use the linear map $y = c_1 x + c_2$ that maps $x = -1$ to $y = a$ and $x = 1$ to $y = b$. This is $y = ((b - a)/2)x + (b + a)/2$.

4. The interpolant that uses the Chebyshev nodes is much better.

5. Yes, for a wide variety of functions this is so. Since fairly arbitrary functions can be well-approximated by polynomials, one might expect that the derivatives eventually look constant. Of course, this isn't always so (e.g., $\sin(x)$), in part because the Weierstrass Approximation Theorem only asserts that function values are well-approximated, not derivative values.

6. No. There isn't enough memory to store $\sin(x)$ for every floating point number (see Section 1.7).

12. The L_∞ norm is immediate since $\max(|\cos(x)|) = 1$. To show that these are monic polynomials, it is easier to use the recurrence relation of Section 5.4 but you can use trigonometry to simplify the trigonometric expression given in this section.

13. Compare the L_1, L_2, and L_∞ norms of the errors in each case. Typically the use of the Chebyshev nodes gives noticeably superior results.

Bibliography

Most of these books influenced the present text; others are here for completeness. If you need more information on subjects in this text, these are good places to start. The books are listed, *very roughly,* in the order this author would send an advanced undergraduate to them for additional information on the topic at hand. Most of the books listed under General References include most of the other listed topics.

GENERAL REFERENCES

Press, William H., Brian P. Flannery, Saul A. Teukolsky, and William T. Vetterling. *Numerical Recipes: The Art of Scientific Computing.* Cambridge: Cambridge University Press, 1986.
[A reference with many algorithms, emphasizing applications.]

Stewart, G. W. *Afternotes on Numerical Analysis.* Philadelphia: SIAM, 1996.
[An informal introduction to basic numerical analysis.]

Stewart, G. W. *Afternotes Goes to Graduate School: Lecture Notes on Advanced Numerical Analysis.* Philadelphia: SIAM, 1998.
[An informal introduction to graduate-level numerical analysis.]

Burden, Richard L., and J. Douglas Faires. *Numerical Analysis.* 6th ed. Pacific Grove: Brooks/Cole, 1997.
[A popular introductory undergraduate-level textbook.]

Van Loan, Charles F. *Introduction to Scientific Computing: A Matrix-Vector Approach Using MATLAB.* 2nd ed. Upper Saddle River: Prentice-Hall, 2000.
[An introductory survey with an emphasis on computing in MATLAB.]

Allen, Myron B., III, and Eli L. Isaacson. *Numerical Analysis for Applied Science.* Hoboken: John Wiley, 1998.
[A graduate-level treatment of the subject.]

Ueberhuber, Christoph W. *Numerical Computation 1: Methods, Software, and Analysis.* New York: Springer-Verlag, 1997.

[A graduate-level treatment of the fundamentals of scientific computing, including hardware issues.]

———. *Numerical Computation 2: Methods, Software, and Analysis.* New York: Springer-Verlag, 1997.

[A graduate-level treatment of numerical methods.]

Ralston, Anthony, and Philip Rabinowitz. *A First Course in Numerical Analysis.* 2nd ed. Reprint, New York: Dover, 2001.

[An older, comprehensive advanced text on the subject, reprinted by Dover.]

Hamming, R. W. *Numerical Methods for Scientists and Engineers.* Reprint, New York: Dover, 1986.

[An older, comprehensive text on the subject, reprinted by Dover.]

CHAPTER 1, NONLINEAR EQUATIONS

Kelley, C. T. *Iterative Methods for Linear and Nonlinear Equations.* Philadelphia: SIAM, 1995.

[A modern treatment of Newton and quasi-Newton methods.]

Traub, J. F. *Iterative Methods for the Solution of Equations.* Upper Saddle River: Prentice-Hall, 1964.

[An older text on nonlinear equations and nonlinear systems.]

Brent, Richard P. *Algorithms for Minimization Without Derivatives.* Reprint, New York: Dover, 2002.

[Includes Brent's method for root-finding.]

Rheinboldt, Werner C. *Methods for Solving Systems of Nonlinear Equations.* Philadelphia: SIAM, 1974.

[An older monograph on nonlinear equations and nonlinear systems.]

Griewank, Andreas. *Evaluating Derivatives: Principles and Techniques of Algorithmic Differentiation.* Philadelphia: SIAM, 2000.

[A comprehensive introduction to automatic differentiation.]

CHAPTER 2, LINEAR SYSTEMS

Hager, William W. *Applied Numerical Linear Algebra.* Upper Saddle River: Prentice-Hall, 1998.

[An undergraduate-level introductory textbook.]

Trefethen, Lloyd N., and David Bau, III. *Numerical Linear Algebra.* Philadelphia: SIAM, 1997.

[An informal graduate-level applied introduction to numerical linear algebra.]

Stewart, G. W. *Matrix Algorithms.* Vol. I, *Basic Decompositions.* Philadelphia: SIAM, 1998.

[A detailed, modern book about matrix decompositions.]

Golub, Gene H., and Charles F. Van Loan. *Matrix Computations.* 3rd ed. Baltimore: Johns Hopkins University Press, 1996.

[The classic reference on the subject.]

Demmel, James W. *Applied Numerical Linear Algebra.* Philadelphia: SIAM, 1997.

[A comprehensive graduate-level text.]

Björck, Åke. *Numerical Methods for Least Squares Problems.* Philadelphia: SIAM, 1996.

[A detailed graduate-level reference.]

CHAPTER 3, ITERATIVE METHODS

Hager, William W. *Applied Numerical Linear Algebra.* Upper Saddle River: Prentice-Hall, 1988.
[An undergraduate-level introductory textbook.]
Trefethen, Lloyd N., and David Bau, III. *Numerical Linear Algebra.* Philadelphia: SIAM, 1997.
[An informal graduate-level applied introduction to numerical linear algebra.]
Greenbaum, Anne. *Iterative Methods for Solving Linear Systems.* Philadelphia: SIAM, 1997.
[A modern graduate-level survey of iterative methods.]
Duff, I. S., A. M. Erisman, and J. K. Reid. *Direct Methods for Sparse Matrices.* Oxford: Oxford University Press, 1986.
[Emphasizes the LU decomposition for sparse systems.]
Kelley, C. T. *Iterative Methods for Linear and Nonlinear Equations.* Philadelphia: SIAM, 1995.
[Emphasizes the conjugate gradient method and variants.]
Golub, Gene H., and Charles F. Van Loan. *Matrix Computations.* 3rd ed. Baltimore: Johns Hopkins University Press, 1996.
[The classic reference on the subject.]
Stewart, G. W. *Matrix Algorithms.* Vol. II, *Basic Eigensystems.* Philadelphia: SIAM, 2001.
[A detailed, modern book about the eigenvalue problem.]
Wilkinson, J. H. *The Algebraic Eigenvalue Problem.* Oxford: Oxford University Press, 1965.
[The classic reference on the eigenvalue problem.]
Demmel, James W. *Applied Numerical Linear Algebra.* Philadelphia: SIAM, 1997.
[A comprehensive graduate-level text.]
Parlett, Beresford N. *The Symmetric Eigenvalue Problem.* Philadelphia: SIAM, 1998.
[The classic reference for the symmetric case.]
Briggs, William L., Van Emden Henson, and Steve F. McCormick. *A Multigrid Tutorial.* 2nd ed. Philadelphia: SIAM, 2000.
[An introduction to multigrid methods.]

CHAPTER 4, POLYNOMIAL INTERPOLATION

de Boor, Carl. *A Practical Guide to Splines.* New York: Springer-Verlag, 1978.
[A classic text on splines.]
Chui, Charles K. *Multivariate Splines.* Philadelphia: SIAM, 1988.
[A graduate-level monograph on splines in several dimensions.]
Davis, Philip J. *Interpolation and Approximation.* New York: Dover, 1975.
[A classic text on interpolation and approximation in a general setting.]

CHAPTER 5, NUMERICAL INTEGRATION

Krommer, Arnold R., and Christoph W. Ueberhuber. *Computational Integration.* Philadelphia: SIAM, 1998.
[A modern, comprehensive treatment of the subject.]
Davis, Philip J., and Philip Rabinowitz. *Methods of Numerical Integration.* 2nd ed. New York: Academic Press, 1984.
[The classic reference on the subject.]

Stroud, A. H. *Numerical Quadrature and Solution of Ordinary Differential Equations*. New
York: Springer-Verlag, 1974.
[An older, detailed text.]

CHAPTER 6, DIFFERENTIAL EQUATIONS

Fatunla, Simeon Ola. *Numerical Methods for Initial Value Problems in Ordinary Differential
Equations*. San Diego: Academic Press, 1988.
[A concise but complete text.]
Iserles, Arieh. *A First Course in the Numerical Analysis of Differential Equations*. Cambridge:
Cambridge University Press, 1996.
[A modern introductory text with a mix of theory and application.]
Shampine, Lawrence F. *Numerical Solution of Ordinary Differential Equations*. New York:
Chapman and Hall, 1994.
[A detailed, modern text.]
Stroud, A. H. *Numerical Quadrature and Solution of Ordinary Differential Equations*. New
York: Springer-Verlag, 1974.
[An older, detailed text.]
Strikwerda, John C. *Finite Difference Schemes and Partial Differential Equations*. Wadsworth,
1989.
[A modern introduction to finite difference methods.]
Smith, G. D. *Numerical Solution of Partial Differential Equations: Finite Difference Methods*.
3rd ed. Oxford: Oxford University Press, 1985.
[An introduction to finite difference methods.]

CHAPTER 7, NONLINEAR OPTIMIZATION

Nocedal, Jorge, and Stephen J. Wright. *Numerical Optimization*. New York: Springer-Verlag,
1999.
[A comprehensive text.]
Gill, Philip E., Walter Murray, and Margaret H. Wright. *Practical Optimization*. New York:
Academic Press, 1981.
[A comprehensive reference.]
Kelley, C. T. *Iterative Methods for Optimization*. Philadelphia: SIAM, 1999.
[A modern, applied reference.]
Brent, Richard P. *Algorithms for Minimization Without Derivatives*. Reprint, New York: Dover,
2002.
[Includes Brent's method for root-finding and for optimization.]
Horst, Reiner, Panos M. Pardalos, and Nguyen V. Thoai. *Introduction to Global Optimization*.
Kluwer, 1995.
[A survey of global optimization methods.]
Ratschek, H., and J. Rokne. *Computer Methods for the Range of Functions*. Chichester: Ellis
Horwood, 1984.
[An introduction to interval methods, including Hansen's method.]
Floudas, Christodoulos A., Panos M. Pardalos, Claire Adjiman, William R. Esposito, Zeynep H.
Gümüs, Stephen T. Harding, John L. Klepeis, Clifford A. Meyer, and Carl A. Schweiger.
Handbook of Test Problems in Local and Global Optimization. New York: Kluwer, 1999.
[A collection of test problems.]

Niederreiter, Harald. *Random Number Generation and Quasi-Monte Carlo Methods.*
Philadelphia: SIAM, 1992.
[An introduction to quasi-Monte Carlo methods.]

CHAPTER 8, APPROXIMATION METHODS

Rivlin, Theodore J. *An Introduction to the Approximation of Functions.* New York: Dover, 1969.
[A classic introduction to approximation theory.]
Powell, M. J. D. *Approximation Theory and Methods.* Cambridge: Cambridge University Press,
1981.
[A modern, formal treatment of approximation theory.]
Ralston, Anthony, and Philip Rabinowitz. *A First Course in Numerical Analysis.* 2nd ed. Reprint,
New York: Dover, 2001.
[A good general reference that includes many approximation techniques.]

THEORY OF NUMERICAL ANALYSIS

Stoer, J., and R. Bulirsch. *Introduction to Numerical Analysis.* New York: Springer-Verlag, 1980.
[The classic reference work.]
Higham, Nicholas J. *Accuracy and Stability of Numerical Algorithms.* Philadelphia: SIAM, 1996.
[A modern treatment of error analysis.]
Wilkinson, J. H. *Rounding Errors in Algebraic Processes.* New York: Dover, 1994.
[The classic text on error analysis.]
Tyrtyshnikov, Eugene E. *A Brief Introduction to Numerical Analysis.* Boston: Birkhäuser, 1997.
[A concise, modern introduction to the theory of numerical analysis.]

SOFTWARE AND HARDWARE

Overton, Michael L. *Numerical Computing with IEEE Floating Point Arithmetic.* Philadelphia:
SIAM, 2001.
[An introduction to floating point arithmetic for scientific computation.]
Higham, Desmond J., and Nicholas J. Higham. *MATLAB Guide.* Philadelphia: SIAM, 2000.
[An informal guide to the capabilities of MATLAB, with examples.]
Anderson, E., Z. Bai, C. Bischof, S. Blackford, J. Demmel, J. Dongarra, J. Du Croz, A.
Greenbaum, S. Hammarling, A. McKenney, and D. Sorenson. *LAPACK Users' Guide.* 3rd ed.
Philadelphia: SIAM, 1999.
[The reference book for LAPACK, also available online at *http://www.netlib.org.*]

Index